S0-CPB-790

Rethinking Peace and Conflict Studies

Series Editor
Oliver P. Richmond
University of Manchester
Manchester, UK

This agenda-setting series of research monographs, now more than a decade old, provides an interdisciplinary forum aimed at advancing innovative new agendas for approaches to, and understandings of, peace and conflict studies and International Relations. Many of the critical volumes the series has so far hosted have contributed to new avenues of analysis directly or indirectly related to the search for positive, emancipatory, and hybrid forms of peace. New perspectives on peacemaking in practice and in theory, their implications for the international peace architecture, and different conflict-affected regions around the world, remain crucial. This series' contributions offers both theoretical and empirical insights into many of the world's most intractable conflicts and any subsequent attempts to build a new and more sustainable peace, responsive to the needs and norms of those who are its subjects.

More information about this series at
http://www.palgrave.com/gp/series/14500

Jolyon Mitchell · Giselle Vincett ·
Theodora Hawksley · Hal Culbertson
Editors

Peacebuilding and the Arts

Editors
Jolyon Mitchell
New College
University of Edinburgh
Edinburgh, UK

Theodora Hawksley
London, UK

Giselle Vincett
Burlington, ON, Canada

Hal Culbertson
University of Notre Dame
Notre Dame, IN, USA

Rethinking Peace and Conflict Studies
ISBN 978-3-030-17874-1 ISBN 978-3-030-17875-8 (eBook)
https://doi.org/10.1007/978-3-030-17875-8

This Palgrave Macmillan imprint is published by the registered company Springer Nature Switzerland AG
The registered company address is: Gewerbestrasse 11, 6330 Cham, Switzerland

To
Jo and Alison Elliot

Acknowledgements

This book brings together a wide range of peacebuilders, scholars and creative artists, with experience of working all over the world. It emerged out of a series of workshops hosted at the Universities of Edinburgh in Scotland and the University of Notre Dame in the United States. These interdisciplinary and intergenerational conversations were co-organized by the Peacebuilding through Media Arts Project at the University of Edinburgh and the University of Notre Dame's Kroc Institute for International Peace Studies, now part of the Keough School of Global Affairs. Most of the chapters originate from these workshops, others were brought in later as part of our ongoing conversations. Participants had experience of working with different peacebuilding projects, including in Jerusalem and Ramallah, Belfast and Derry/Londonderry, Kigali and Mindanao, Nepal and Tajikistan, Kenya and Northern Uganda, the Balkans and Colombia.

Without naming themselves as such, many who participated in the workshops also act as local builders of sustainable peace. The editors are thankful to their hosts and contributors in more ways than can be expressed here, except to say that this book has evolved with the assistance of many creative, insightful and hospitable peacebuilders. We are particularly grateful to many different people who have assisted and challenged through offering probing questions, insightful comments and inspiring presentations, including: Nick Adams, Tom Allbeson, Sara Afshari, Andrew Barr, Liz Barr, Linden Bicket, Roland Bleiker, David Brown, Stewart Jay Brown, Bernadette Burbridge, Cecelia Clegg,

Cynthia Cohen, Vanessa Contopulos, J. Martin Daughtry, David Fergusson, Michael Fryer, David Ford, Jim Harris, Susan Hayward, Asher Kaufman, Emmanuel Katongole, Jeremy Kidwell, Anna King, Pauline Kollontai, David Little, Patrick Madden, Mihaela Mihai, Peter Mitchell, Ebrahim Moosa, Michael Northcott, Atalia Omer, Ioana Popescu, Gerard Powers, Judith Stevenson, Milja Radovic, Leah Robinson, Bill Rolston, Jane Sapp, Ulrich Schmiedel, Megan Shore, Sarah Snyder, Suzie Snyder, Jason Springs, Steve Sutcliffe, James Thompson, Peter Wallensteen and to each of the contributors for all they have given to this volume. Listening to friends, colleagues and students has inspired us to think further about the complex role of the arts in creating peaceful environments.

We are indebted to our series editor Oliver P. Richmond for his many helpful encouragements, to our commissioning editor at Palgrave Macmillan, Sarah Roughley, the editorial assistant Oliver Foster and the project manager Meera Mithran. The insightful and encouraging comments by the anonymous readers were also invaluable. Heartfelt thanks to Catharine Beck, Iona Birchall, Linzy Brady, Kit and Janet Bowen, Karen Duncan, Jamie and Sandy Frost, Louisa Grotian, Peter Landau, Barbara Lockwood, Karoline McLean, Anne Riordan, Jean Reynolds, Cindy Swonger, who in different ways have helped make this project fly.

Scott Appleby has provided outstanding support and wise advice along the way. The discussions in Edinburgh were enriched by the presence and contributions of George Wilkes director of the *Religion and Ethics in the Making of War and Peace* project, generously funded by Porticus. We are also very grateful to the Carnegie Trust for their support. The *Peacebuilding Through Media Arts* project housed in the *Centre for Theology and Public Issues* (CTPI), was generously supported by the Binks Trust. They provided considerable financial support for our workshops, seminars and related research, enriching this publication. Without the support of Jo Elliot and Dr Alison Elliot this book would not have happened. This volume is dedicated to them in admiration and friendship.

Jolyon Mitchell is also particularly thankful to Clare, and our children, Sebastian, Jasmine and Xanthe, who all continue to demonstrate how building peace takes time and creativity. He is also indebted and deeply grateful to his co-editors Giselle, Hal and Theodora, without whom this book would not have seen the light of day.

Contents

Part II Music

Part III Literature

Part IV Film

Part V Theatre and Dance

Editors and Contributors

About the Editors

Jolyon Mitchell is a Professor who specializes in Religion, Violence and Peacebuilding, with particular reference to the arts, at the University of Edinburgh. Jolyon worked as a Producer and Journalist with BBC World service before moving to Edinburgh. He has served as President of TRS-UK (the national association for Theology and Religious Studies in the UK, 2012–2018) and is currently Director of CTPI (the Centre for Theology and Public Issues) at the University of Edinburgh. His publications include *Promoting Peace and Inciting Violence: The Role of Religion and Media* (Routledge, 2012); *Martyrdom: A Very Short Introduction* (OUP, 2012) and *Media Violence and Christian Ethics* (CUP, 2007).

Giselle Vincett is a sociologist of religion, having received her Ph.D. in sociology of religion from Lancaster University. Her work has concentrated primarily on everyday performances of belief and on everyday and spatial experiences of deprivation in the West. Her research and wide range of publications has been focused on individuals and groups who are marginalized and/or vulnerable. Most recently, she was a Mercator Fellow at Leipzig University on a project examining adult experiences of deprivation in several European countries.

Theodora Hawksley is a Roman Catholic theologian specializing in the area of peacebuilding and Catholic social teaching. Initial training in ecclesiology and ethnography has given her an abiding interest in interdisciplinary work, and she has undertaken ethnographic research for churches and for a bilingual education programme for indigenous Amerindian children in Guyana. She is a contributor to the *Wiley Blackwell Companion to Religion and Peace* and her book *What Makes for Peace: Peacebuilding and Catholic Social Teaching* is forthcoming with University of Notre Dame Press in 2020.

Hal Culbertson is Associate Dean for Operations at the University of Notre Dame's Keough School of Global Affairs. Previously, Culbertson worked at the Kroc Institute for International Peace Studies for 17 years, serving as Executive Director from 2007–2014. Culbertson holds a J.D. and M.A. in philosophy from the University of Illinois at Urbana-Champaign and an M.A. in international peace studies from Notre Dame. Hal teaches international NGO management, particularly focusing on project design and evaluation in the peacebuilding context. He is a co-author of *Reflective Peacebuilding: A Planning, Monitoring, and Learning Toolkit* (Notre Dame: Kroc Institute and CRS, 2007).

Contributors

Thania Acarón Rios is a lecturer, performer, choreographer and dance movement therapist from Puerto Rico, currently based in Wales. She obtained her Ph.D. on the role of dance in violence prevention at the University of Aberdeen and holds a master's degree in Dance Education from New York University. She is certified as a clinical supervisor and dance movement psychotherapist in the United Kingdom and United States. Thania currently works as a lecturer at the Dance Programme at the University of South Wales in Cardiff. She offers international workshops on movement and wellbeing and interdisciplinary practice.

Ketty Anyeko is a Vanier Scholar, pursuing a Ph.D. in Interdisciplinary Studies at University of British Columbia. She has a Psychology degree from Makerere University and a Peace Studies M.A. from the University of Notre Dame. She previously worked in non-profits and grant making agencies as a gender, peace and justice practitioner in Uganda for 12+ years. She has engaged with communities and policymakers in Cambodia, Philippines, Colombia, South Africa, Kenya, United States and Canada. Ketty did action research, documentation and policy advocacy at grassroots, national and international levels. Her current research focuses on justice and reparations for wartime sexual violence in Uganda.

R. Scott Appleby is the Marilyn Keough Dean of Notre Dame's Keough School of Global Affairs and a professor of history at the university. His research examines the various ways in which religious movements and organizations shape, and are shaped by, national, regional and global dynamics of governance, deadly conflict, international relations and economic development. He is the author or editor of 15 books, including *The Fundamentalism Project*, co-edited with Martin E. Marty (University of Chicago); and *The Ambivalence of the Sacred: Religion, Violence and Reconciliation* (Rowman & Littlefield, 1999). Most recently, Appleby co-edited (with Atalia Omer and David Little) *The Oxford Handbook on Religion, Conflict and Peacebuilding*.

Rachel Beckles Willson is Professor of Music at Royal Holloway, University of London, and also a performing musician and composer. Her research has examined music through the lens of international relations. She is author of *Ligeti, Kurtag and Hungarian Music During the Cold War* (Cambridge, 2008) and *Orientalism and Musical Mission: Palestine and the West* (Cambridge, 2013), and has recently focused on the travels of musical instruments in the context of globalization (www.oudmigrations.com). Currently she is based in eastern Sicily, developing strategies for music education among victims of forced displacement.

Lizelle Bisschoff is a researcher and curator of African film and the founder of the Africa in Motion (AiM) Film Festival, an annual African film festival taking place in Scotland since 2006. Lizelle holds a Ph.D. in African cinema from the University of Stirling in Scotland, in which she researched the role of women in African film. She has published widely on sub-Saharan African cinema and regularly attends African film festivals worldwide as speaker and jury member. She is currently a lecturer in Film and Television Studies at the University of Glasgow, where she teaches African cinema and continues her research on classic and contemporary African film.

Paul Burbridge is Artistic Director of Riding Lights Theatre Company, based at Friargate Theatre, York. He has a first-class degree in English Literature from Oxford and, since its foundation in 1977, has overseen the development of Riding Lights into one of the UK's most productive independent touring companies. He has directed many of the company's major productions, including classics such as *The Alchemist, Mistero Buffo* and *The Winter's Tale* or new plays like *African Snow, Balancing Act* and

Simeon's Watch. More recently, he co-directed the 2012 *York Mystery Plays* and created *Baked Alaska*, calling for urgent action on Climate Change.

Frances Clemson is Assistant Professor in Theology and Ministry at Durham University. She was previously a Research Associate at the University of Cambridge, working within the Cambridge Inter-faith Programme, which seeks to build connections between Jews, Christians and Muslims. She specializes in interdisciplinary work on modern Christian theology and the arts, with a particular interest in drama. She is the author of *Showing Forth God's Act in History: Theology and Drama in the Work of Dorothy L. Sayers*, forthcoming with Bloomsbury.

Adrienne Dengerink Chaplin is an independent scholar and Visiting Research Fellow at the Department of Theology and Religious Studies at King's College London. She gained her doctorate in philosophy from the VU University of Amsterdam and taught philosophical aesthetics at the Institute for Christian Studies in Toronto where she also served as president of the Canadian Society for Aesthetics. Currently living in Cambridge, UK, she is the founder and curator of the travelling exhibition 'Art, Conflict and Remembering: the murals of the Bogside Artists' and her forthcoming book on the philosophy of Susanne Langer will be published by Bloomsbury.

Sandra M. Gustafson is Professor of English and concurrent Professor of American Studies at the University of Notre Dame. Sandra has published extensively on American literature and culture. She became a faculty fellow at the Kroc Institute for International Peace Studies in 2010 and has taught numerous courses for the program. At present, she is working on a book about the American novel from James Fenimore Cooper to Leslie Marmon Silko that draws on peace studies methodologies. Her early work on the project was supported by funding from the Kroc Institute and a fellowship from the National Endowment for the Humanities.

Robert K. Johnston is Professor of Theology and Culture at Fuller Theological Seminary, Pasadena, California and Co-Director of Fuller's Reel Spirituality Institute. He served on the Ecumenical Jury at the Locarno Film Festival in 2017 and at the Cannes Film Festival in 2018. The author or editor of sixteen books, Johnston's works include the most widely used text in English on religion and film, *Reel Spirituality: Theology and Film in Dialogue* (2000, 2006). Other works include *God* *in the Movies* (2017, co-written with Catherine Barsotti), *God's Wider Presence* (2014), and *Deep Focus* (2019, co-written with Craig Detweiler and Kutter Callaway).

Kathryn Jourdan is a performer, teacher and researcher based in Edinburgh, Scotland. She freelances as a viola player with the Scottish Chamber Orchestra and teaches academic music, viola and chamber music in the specialist setting of St Mary's Music School. In 2015 she completed a Ph.D. in the field of the Philosophy of Music Education, in the Faculty of Education, Cambridge University. Kathryn is a member of the editorial boards of both the British and *International Journals of Music Education*, and continues to present and publish academic research. She is a board member of Sistema Scotland.

Joseph G. Kickasola is Professor of Film and Digital Media and Director of the Baylor in New York program, Baylor University. He is the author of the award-winning monograph *The Films of Krzysztof Kieślowski: The Liminal Image*, as well as essays in *Film Quarterly*, *The Quarterly Review of Film and Video*, and numerous film studies anthologies. He recently guest edited a special issue of *Religions*, dedicated to "Film and Lived Theology," and his film and video work has screened around the world. He lives in New York City with his wife and two children.

Sebastian Kim is Professor of Theology and Public Life and Executive Director of the Korean Studies Center at Fuller Theological Seminary. Kim's scholarship interests include public theology, world Christianity, Asian theologies, and theology and peacebuilding. He has authored four books: *A History of Korean Christianity* (CUP, 2015), *Theology in the Public Sphere* (SCM, 2011), *In Search of Identity: Debates on Religious Conversion in India* (OUP, 2005), and *Christianity as a World Religion* (2008 and 2016). Books he has edited include *A Companion to Public Theology* (Brill, 2017), *Cosmopolitanism, Religion, and the Public Sphere* (Routledge, 2014); and *Christian Theology in Asia* (CUP, 2008).

John Paul Lederach is Professor Emeritus at the University of Notre Dame and serves as Senior Fellow at Humanity United. Widely known for his pioneering work in conflict transformation, Lederach has engaged in conciliation work in Colombia, the Philippines, and Nepal, plus countries in East and West Africa. Lederach is the author of 26 books and manuals including *When Blood and Bones Cry Out: Journeys Through the Soundscape of Healing and Reconciliation*, (University of Queensland

Press, 2010), *The Moral Imagination: The Art and Soul of Building Peace* (Oxford University Press, 2005), and *Building Peace: Sustainable Reconciliation in Divided Societies* (USIP, 1997). Lederach holds a Ph.D. in sociology from the University of Colorado.

Olivier Morel a French and American scholar and filmmaker, is the director of several award-winning feature-length nonfiction films and author of essays including one graphic novel, *Walking Wounded* (NBM publishing, New York, 2015), with the artist and writer Maël. His academic work as well as his films highlight the importance of creation and the arts (music, literature, cinema, photography…) in the perception of historical events. He teaches in the Department of Film, Television and Theatre, and the Department of Romance Languages and Literatures at the University of Notre Dame (USA).

Juliane Okot Bitek is a poet and a Ph.D. candidate at the University of British Columbia, in Canada. Her *100 Days* (University of Alberta, 2016) was nominated for several writing prizes including the 2017 BC Book Prize, the Pat Lowther Award, the 2017 Alberta Book Awards and the 2017 Canadian Authors Award for Poetry, and won the 2017 IndieFab Book of the Year Award for poetry and the 2017 Glenna Lushei Prize for African Poetry. Juliane's poem "Migration: Salt Stories" was shortlisted for the 2018 National Magazine Awards for Poetry in Canada. Juliane is also the author of *Sublime: Lost Words* (The Elephants, 2018).

Lindsay McClain Opiyo is a Development and Partner Specialist at Generations For Peace in Uganda. Originally from Nashville in the United States, Lindsay has lived and worked in northern Uganda for much of the last nine years. Her main interests are the role of the arts in peacebuilding and victim-centered transitional justice. In 2010, she and two northern Ugandan musicians founded Music for Peace, a community-based organization that promotes the power of music for positive social change. Lindsay holds a B.A. from the University of Tennessee and a M.A. in Peace Studies from the Kroc Institute for International Peace Studies at the University of Notre Dame.

Alison Rice is Associate Professor of French and Francophone literature and film at the University of Notre Dame. Her first two books focus on autobiographical writings by authors from Algeria and Morocco. Titled *Francophone Metronomes: Worldwide Women Writers in Paris*, her current book project is an in-depth study of a variety of contemporary authors complemented by a series of filmed interviews. A faculty fellow of the Kroc Institute for International Peace Studies at Notre Dame, Alison has taught courses and published articles on Francophone peace studies. Her next book/film project is on "Francophone Women Writers and International Human Rights."

Sandra Milena Rios Oyola is a Colombian sociologist and received her Ph.D. in Sociology from the University of Aberdeen. Sandra is the author of the book *Religion and Social Memory Amid Conflict: The Massacre of Bojayá in Colombia* (Palgrave Macmillan, 2015) and the co-editor of *Time and Temporality in the Study of Transitional Societies* (Routledge, 2018). In 2018, Sandra obtained a FNRS postdoctoral grant; she is currently a researcher at the Université Catholique de Louvain, where she studies how transitional justice helps restore victims' human dignity, with a focus on the case of Colombia's Truth Commission, Historical Memory Commission and Reparations.

Tamara Shaya Hoffmann an Iraqi-American, has had a passion for peacebuilding from a young age. For over a decade, Tamara has worked in government and non-governmental roles that combined her passion for storytelling and international affairs. Tamara currently works at the U.S. Department of State. In her previous roles at the U.S. Agency for International Development (USAID), Tamara served as the Senior Desk Officer for the Lebanon Desk; a Peacebuilding Advisor; and a Communications Specialist for the Office of Gender Equality and Women's Empowerment. Prior to this, Tamara worked as a consultant to the ONE Campaign and as Director of Public Relations at a non-profit that fostered dialogue between Christians and Muslims. Tamara received her M.A. in Peace Studies from the University of Notre Dame and her B.A. in Media Communications from Taylor University.

Geoffrey Stevenson is a lecturer and writer who teaches Homiletics at the University of Edinburgh where he is an Honorary Fellow, and where he contributed to the Peacebuilding through Media Arts project. After an Oxford M.A. in Philosophy and Theology, he trained as an actor and mime artist, then toured his own theatre shows for 18 years, before returning to academic life. From 1996–2005 he was Director of the Centre for Christian Communication at St John's College, University of Durham. He has published five books on communications and the arts.

List of Figures

CHAPTER 1

Introduction

Theodora Hawksley and Jolyon Mitchell

This is the field where the battle did not happen,
  where the unknown soldier did not die.
  This is the field where grass joined hands,
  where no monument stands,
  and the only heroic thing is the sky.
  Birds fly here without any sound,
  unfolding their wings across the open.
  No people killed – or were killed – on this ground
  hollowed by the neglect of an air so tame
  that people celebrate it by forgetting its name.[1]
  William Stafford
  (1914–1993)

T. Hawksley (✉)
London, UK

J. Mitchell
New College, University of Edinburgh, Edinburgh, UK
e-mail: Jolyon.Mitchell@ed.ac.uk

J. Mitchell et al. (eds.), *Peacebuilding and the Arts*,
Rethinking Peace and Conflict Studies,
https://doi.org/10.1007/978-3-030-17875-8_1

The Horizon of Peace

This is a book about peacebuilding. Given that we will be considering throughout the possibility, processes and practices of peacebuilding, it is perhaps most appropriate to begin at the end, that is, with some consideration of the end of the peacebuilder's labours. How is peace to be understood?

Ask for a definition or image of violence, and a thousand images and examples may crowd the imagination. News footage can loop over and over again and again in the mind's eye: a plane flies into a building and people run through dust and debris, covering their mouths; a woman stands over the body of her son, wailing to heaven; a protester hurls a brick towards an advancing line of riot police. Beyond these iconic images of violent struggle and armed conflict, it is possible to call to mind less visible kinds of violence: criminal violence, violence in prisons, police institutions and detention centres, domestic violence and sexual harassment.[2] Thinking deeper still, it is possible to identify those kinds of structural violence which, though perhaps more subtle and harder to picture, nevertheless crush countless individuals and communities: poverty, racism, gender inequality, political disenfranchisement and repression.[3]

Violence and its effects can be comparatively simple to picture—but peace? Asked for a definition or image of peace, many falter. It is all too easy to reach for clichés—a soaring dove, children holding hands around a globe, sunset over a calm sea—or begin, like the poem with which this chapter opens, to think of peace as a sort of absence, a not-happening. Peace is the field where battle did not happen, where no monument stands, where nobody was killed or died. Peace is an unknown country beyond the frayed edge of a violent world that we find all too easy to imagine: peace is, as Stafford puts it, an empty field. In this volume, however, we have in view a different kind of peace, at once more utopian and more plausible. It will be helpful to make three points here.

The first point concerns the relationship between peace and conflict. The peaceful Eden of Stafford's poem may be thus because there are no human beings there to cause conflict, no-one to hear the bird in flight, to know the ground or name it. Conflict may well be inherently human, but it need not be understood as inherently negative. conflict is normal, and it occurs regularly in the ordinary negotiation and re-calibration of human relationships. It is, as John Paul Lederach puts it, the motor of change:

without conflict on an interpersonal level, our relationships would stagnate and remain superficial; without conflict on a structural level in human societies, social, economic and political institutions and processes would remain static.[4] Conflict is not just unavoidable, but necessary if communities and individuals desire change, development or growth. Conflict is like a crossroads, where one road may stretch towards death, and the other towards life. In situations where there are structural resources and processes in place for negotiating conflicting ideas, desires and needs in non-violent ways, conflict can present opportunities for increased justice and human flourishing; in situations where there are no such forums or processes, conflicts over political, social, economic, religious or ethnic grievances—to name only a few common flashpoints—can begin to work themselves out in violent ways.

So, peace is not an absence of conflict and, accordingly, the building of peace is not a matter of discouraging or squashing conflict. Rather, peacebuilding involves conflict transformation,[5] a deliberate movement away from violent modes of negotiating conflicting ideals, needs or desires, towards establishing or utilizing spaces, structures and processes through which conflict can be negotiated non-violently and constructively. Peace is not a space in which conflict does not happen, as in Stafford's empty field.[6] Peace is an ongoing, dynamic process, a journey that sets human relationships on the road to life.

The second point concerns the relationship between peace and justice. If peace does not imply the absence of conflict in interpersonal or societal relationships, then it is best to define it in terms of what should be positively *present* in those relationships: justice.[7] Without a commitment to transforming inhumane conditions on a societal level, such that people's fundamental human dignity is recognized and their basic rights met, and without a commitment to transforming inhumane power structures and establishing processes through which past wrongs and future conflict can be constructively engaged, any peace agreement negotiated in the short term will be unstable, and liable to collapse back into renewed violence. Peace implies the presence of justice, and peacebuilding requires that both communities and individuals seek it. This means that peacebuilding involves more than short-term, intense efforts to negotiate the cessation of deadly violence. Peacebuilding involves a long-term commitment to transforming the societal structures and relationships in which that deadly violence is rooted, and to which that violence does further damage.

This understanding of peace as *just* peace brings us to the third point. If the kind of peace we have in view in this volume is not just the absence of violent conflict, but a positive presence of justice, then the task of peacebuilding entails not just negotiating an end to direct violence, but a more comprehensive commitment to fostering human flourishing. This means that the task of peacebuilding does not begin with the first rumblings of war and end with the cessation of open hostilities. If it seeks human flourishing, then peacebuilding must involve positive efforts to promote just relationships at all stages of the conflict cycle, and it can take place before, during and after open violent conflict. Peacebuilding therefore includes a commitment to conflict prevention, conflict cessation and "the healing of broken humanity" well after violent conflict has subsided.[8] Reconstruction after violent conflict involves repairing infrastructure and the built environment, but must also involve rebuilding constructive relationships at all levels of society, and working to restore the capacity for trust and hope without which such relationships cannot exist or be sustained.

Much more needs to be said, but the essays that follow will take up the task of expanding and qualifying this understanding of peace. For now, it will be enough to note that "peace" as we understand it is not the end of the peacebuilder's labours at all, if by "end" we mean a finished product, or a steady state of affairs that can be safely left to endure until the next time violence breaks out. Peace is not the end point of the peacebuilder's labours,[9] but an ongoing, dynamic process which, through the building of constructive relationships at all levels of society, seeks the reduction of violence, the pursuit of justice, and the fostering of human flourishing.[10] This perspective resonates with a number of peacebuilding practices and traditions, including the Quakers who regularly underline not only that peacebuilding is an active process that even needs conflict to progress, but also is a personal and social responsibility, something that *must* be done at all levels by a wide range of individuals and communities.[11]

Insights from Adam Curle, the founding professor of Peace Studies at the University of Bradford,[12] are pertinent here. Curle was "as much concerned with the human condition in general as with specific conflicts, which often represent only the tip of a pyramid of violence and anguish". Highlighting "all the pain and confusion that impede our unfolding and fulfilment", he claimed that these "circumstances" often "force us to focus on extreme examples of unpeacefulness". Nevertheless, Curle argued that there was a danger of limiting "our attention to these" violent instances, "neglecting the soil out of which they grow and would continue to grow". For this reason he suggested that "the social worker, the teacher, the wise legislator, or the good neighbour is just as much a peacemaker as the woman or man unravelling some lethal international imbroglio".[13] One of the claims of this current book is that this can be extended and adapted to include the artist, the film-maker, the musician, the writer, the actor, the dramatist, and the "spect-actor".[14] Artists and creators can be among those who "train to wage peace"[15] and contribute to processes of education, communication and healing in the service of peace.

The Landscape of Conflict

This understanding of peace forms the horizon for our discussion of peacebuilding in what follows. While, like a horizon, it may seem a distant and unreachable goal, we are nevertheless convinced that progress towards it is possible. In order to make such progress, there is a need for a clear-eyed assessment of the different kinds of contexts in which such peacebuilding takes place. Clearly the individual essays in this volume range over different terrain in their particular journeys towards the same horizon, covering conflicts in different locations and settings, each of which brings its own challenges and demands its own response. Nonetheless, before we begin, it is worth sketching a preliminary map, detailing some of the global dynamics of violent conflict that shape aspects of the approaches that follow to the task of peacebuilding. So what are the key features of the landscape of contemporary global conflict, even as it continues to evolve? And how do these key features affect the way we cover the ground in what follows?

On December 17 2010, a twenty-six-year-old Tunisian street vendor called Mohamed Bouazizi set himself on fire outside the provincial headquarters in Sidi Bouzid. Unable to find other work, he had been selling fruit and vegetables from a roadside cart for seven years. On the morning of December 17, Bouazizi was harassed by the local police, who fined him, verbally abused him and confiscated his wares. An hour later, Bouazizi set himself alight in protest. His self-immolation sparked outrage across Tunisia, and protests quickly flared as Tunisians demonstrated against corruption, police brutality, the authoritarian government, unemployment and high living costs. On January 14, President Ben Ali was forced from power and fled to Saudi Arabia. The revolution in Tunisia acted as a catalyst for growing unrest across the Arab world; leaders were forced from power in Egypt, Yemen and Libya, and civil unrest erupted and continues in many more. The Arab Spring has become, for some, the Arab Winter, with a vicious civil war in Syria rapidly escalating after 2010 into an international proxy conflict,[16] a multi-faction civil war in Libya and the temporary expansion of ISIS (also known as ISIL or IS)[17] across swathes of Iraqi and Syrian territory.[18]

What do these violent movements reveal about the landscape of conflict at this moment in the twenty-first century? First, it is a good example of how conflicts are unfolding in an increasingly globalized and interdependent world. The Tunisian revolution was caused not just by factors internal to Tunisia itself, but also by global economic forces, as rising food prices and the high cost of living created a reservoir of frustration among the general populace. Across the Arab world, social media played a significant role in enabling and organizing protests, and communicating unfolding uprisings to an international audience; later, social media would also become an increasingly effective propaganda and recruitment tool for Islamist radical groups, destabilizing emerging democratic processes. Complex currents concerning the negotiation of religious and sociocultural identity, both within Islam and in relation to the secular West, are also obviously in play.[19] It is worth noting, too, that the same features we see in the Tunisian example—economic pressures, social media, religious and socio-cultural identity politics—are equally though differently visible in the subsequent rise of nationalist and right-wing ideologies across Europe. In our period, violent conflicts and attacks are increasingly caused and shaped by transnational factors: not only religious, but also economic, political, ethnic, technological and cultural.

Second, the Tunisian example reflects the fact that, since the end of the Cold War, the majority of violent conflicts worldwide have been intrastate.[20] It is no longer the case that the majority of wars are fought between nation states. Instead, most conflicts take place either between state authorities and non-state actors, such as rebel groups or various minorities demanding self-determination, or between non-state groups themselves. Many of these intra-state conflicts become internationalized through the movement of refugees and weapons, or through international involvement in the form of military intervention and the deployment of regional and international peacekeeping forces. Characteristic of many such intra-state conflicts is the proximity of the conflict to ordinary life: war is being waged not at a distance, at some remote border or in another state, but locally, and such conflicts very often involve local civilians as protagonists and victims. This makes intra-state conflicts, as is painfully evident in

Syria, both highly traumatic for the civilian population and highly destructive of civilian infrastructure. Many such conflicts fall outside the news frames of major media organizations, and therefore lack visibility on the international stage.[21]

The same factors that cause violent conflicts and influence their course also shape the kinds of peacebuilding activity undertaken to resolve them. It is no longer the case that states and governments are the only, or even the primary actors in efforts to negotiate the end of violent conflicts. In an increasingly globalized and interdependent world, the effects of violent conflicts cannot be contained within national boundaries, and so a wide range of official and unofficial actors engage with the challenges of negotiating an end to violence and rebuilding shattered communities and nations, including governments of other countries, regional alliances, international agencies and charitable organizations.

Strategic Peacebuilding

What do these features of the global landscape of conflict mean for the approach taken in what follows? In a context where violent conflicts are marked by complexity, globalization and a multiplicity of actors, peacebuilding needs to be *strategic*, acknowledging and engaging constructively with the kind of complexity just described. In light of the comprehensive understanding of peace we have set out above, four points are worth drawing out regarding our approach to the task of peacebuilding.

First, the changing shape of deadly conflicts over the past fifty years demands an approach to peacebuilding that engages multiple actors across multiple levels in affected communities. If the majority of violent conflicts are intra-state, and governments are no longer the only or primary actors in waging or resolving them, then it is no longer possible to approach the task of peacebuilding as straightforwardly one of high-level negotiations leading to ceasefires and peace accords. Track one diplomacy will be of continuing importance, but complex intra-state conflicts demand an approach to peacebuilding that engages "track two" actors—public figures, religious leaders, universities and other spaces of civic engagement—and "track three", grassroots work, including actors on the level of local communities and networks.[22] Strategic peacebuilding is committed to this kind of flexible engagement with multiple actors as a matter of principle. As well as being attentive to the multiple "horizontal" levels at which engagement is necessary, peacebuilders are beginning to attend more carefully to the "vertical" connections between these levels. Embracing the unique "hybrid nature of peace",[23] some peacebuilders are recognizing the importance of multi-level processes and the value of identifying, drawing upon and building up existing networks and connections between local, regional, national and global actors in order to create sustainable change.

Second, given the localized nature of contemporary intra-state conflict, attention to the local level and the human person is particularly important. Without seeking justice through addressing past wrongs and establishing structures for negotiating conflict non-violently in the future, and without efforts to heal and rebuild constructive relationships on a local level, peace agreements negotiated by political elites will have little traction in the long term. Building this kind of sustainable peace will only be possible if local actors and cultural resources are seen as part of the solution to deadly violence rather than part of the problem. Effective peacebuilding in the twenty-first century demands a positive commitment to subsidiarity.

Third, we have noted that contemporary conflicts take place in both an increasingly globalized and fragmented world. The many different local and global factors influencing the causes and shape of any given conflict also offer multiple frames for analysing and engaging with it: as a conflict rooted in climate change,[24] water and food security issues,[25] as a conflict rooted in the rise of religious fundamentalisms,[26] and so on. Often, these different ways of viewing a particular conflict are represented "on the ground" by the presence of various different organizations and agencies, each with its own particular focus for analysis and action. Strategic peacebuilding is not just aware of the globalized nature of contemporary conflict: it deliberately utilizes it as a potential resource for conflict transformation. Rather than arguing for a single-cause analysis or solution for any given conflict, strategic peacebuilding recognizes the value of multiple analyses and points of engagement, and looks to integrate available resources in order to tackle conflicts as a whole, in their various political, economic, environmental, religious and social aspects. Each of the essays in this book interacts with different creative arts as particular lenses through which violent conflicts can be viewed or engaged, but many of them also draw on other lenses of analysis and action.

Fourth, given that we have in view not just short-term reduction of deadly violence but long-term transformation of conflict, our approach to peacebuilding recognizes the value and importance of initiatives addressing all stages of the conflict cycle. This means that the essays in this volume engage the arts as resources for peacebuilding in its broadest sense: their concern is not limited to the shift from open violent conflict to the immediate post-violence period, but addresses the full range of activities needed for the long-term, sustainable transformation of conflict (e.g. Chapters 5, 9 and 13). Several contributors address in general terms the arts' ability to draw on and foster human capacities for empathy and compassion (e.g. Chapters 2, 12 and 14) pointing out different arts' potential role in building constructive relationships that remain resilient in the face of renewed conflict. Others focus on the role the arts can play in the healing of trauma during and after violent conflict (e.g. Chapters 7, 11 and 20), exploring their role in remembering well. In focussing on the role of the arts in protest and non-violent civil disobedience, several chapters (e.g. Chapters 3, 16 and 19) encourage us to think about the ways in which the arts can help societies to negotiate conflict in constructive, non-violent ways.

With our understanding of peace and basic approach to peacebuilding sketched out, it will now be helpful to comment on our particular focus in this volume: the creative arts. The artistic sediment laid down by the river of violence as it winds through history is also considerable. Whether as "high" art or popular culture, visual arts, music, literature, film and many other art forms have been implicated in legitimating unjust power, celebrating and promoting violence, and creating ethnic, religious and national identities that result in structural violence or deadly conflict. Much less immediately evident is the role that the arts have played, and continue to play, in the building and sustaining of peaceful and just societies.

Nevertheless, the conviction underpinning this volume is that the creative arts can and do play a unique and crucial role in the building of peaceful and just societies. More than that, our argument, made in various and overlapping ways in different essays, is that the insights brought by artistic actors and perspectives are indispensable for the task of peacebuilding, and often overlooked when efforts to resolve conflict draw exclusively on frameworks drawn from development studies, human security studies, or social science. These claims are bold, and the burden of demonstrating and critically exploring them falls largely on the essays that form the bulk of this book. Before launching into those particular arguments, however, it will be helpful to offer a more general account of the role of the arts in strategic peacebuilding as we understand and explore it in what follows.

The Arts

They speak of the art of war,
but the arts
draw their light from the soul's well,
and warfare
dries up the soul and draws its power
from a dark and burning wasteland.
When Leonardo
set his genius to devising
machines of destruction he was not
acting in the service of art,
he was suspending
the life of art
over an abyss,
as if one were to hold
a living child out of an airplane window
at thirty thousand feet.[27]
Denise Levertov
(1923–1997)

It is easy to speak about the arts of war, and to find myriad examples of various creative arts being enlisted in the inciting and waging of violent conflict. Think of the caricatured portrayals of Jews in the Nazi publication *Der Stürmer*, or the role of hate radio in inciting the genocide in Rwanda, and their respective roles in the attempted extermination of entire peoples (see Chapter 15).[28] Think of the political murals of Northern Ireland, and their historic role in expressing and reinforcing narratives about national, sectarian and religious identities (see Chapter 4). Think about the use of news or films in the "war on terror", on one side being used to glorify martyrdom or spectacular executions as a way of promoting violent, fundamentalist forms of Islam and, on the other, being used to dehumanize and demonize the enemy and justify military intervention and the use of torture.[29]

Similar examples could be drawn from any civilization or country, or any period in history, and they point to a single fact: that the arts are dangerous, and have the capacity to lead individuals and communities into a dark and burning wasteland of injustice and violence. But if the arts have the capacity to draw out the worst in human beings, they also have the ability to express and foster genuine goodness and beauty, justice and humanity. Think now of the quartets playing in the concentrations camps of the Second World War, or the theatre productions whose presence in those hellish places bore witness to human dignity and creativity in the face of destruction and hopelessness.[30] Think of the medals struck during the campaign for the abolition of slavery in the United Kingdom, the immediacy of the image of a slave and his claim: "Am I not a man and a brother?" or the later adaptation: "Am I not a woman and sister?"[31] Think of the music of the Civil Rights movement in the United States, its capacity to express hope and call for justice, and all the other ways in which the ways the arts have been used in creative, non-violent protest. Think of the ways in which new images can express a common vision for a different possible future, like the South African flag adopted at the general election of 1994. Like conflict itself, the arts can set human communities on the road to death, or the road to life. Their role is ambivalent.

These examples all evince the arts' tremendous power to express, to reflect and to contribute to the shaping of our personal, social, national, ethnic and religious identities, in ways that are deliberately intended, as well as in ways of which we are only inchoately aware, and in ways that can be profoundly destructive as well as salutary. The arts are not just ambivalent, but volatile. When we deliberately utilize the arts for one extraneous purpose or another, whether we intend it for good or ill, we find that their power does not lie entirely within our control. They are volatile partly because they are a social phenomenon, whose meaning and practice are shaped and reshaped by social forces the momentum of which we can scarcely understand, let alone foresee. But control over the arts and their effects elude us also because we are rather less in control of our *selves* than we like to think. The arts have the capacity to engage us on a visceral level, accessing, creating and reinforcing beliefs and prejudices, desires and repulsions. Their ability to tap into and awaken our deepest fears and desires in ways that can, for better or worse, bypass our normal and more reflective ways of thinking and acting, serves to illustrate the degree to which our image of ourselves as self-possessed and rational is only partially accurate. The potential of the arts, as well as their danger, lies in their ability to touch us, as Levertov puts it, at "the soul's well", at a depth of ourselves not entirely accessible to us.

Working alongside each other, and used creatively, different arts can help contribute to the cultivating of a more peaceful environment. Many scholars point to the role played by the high-level peace talks hosted by the lay Catholic Sant' Egidio Community in Rome during the late 1980s and early 1990s in bringing an end to the Mozambican civil war. In *A Different Kind of War Story*, the Anthropologist Carolyn Nordstrom qualifies this perspective, developing an explanation that sees beyond the peace talks by political élites. Drawing upon her own ethnographic research in Mozambique, she asserts that "average citizens unmade the possibility and the power of violence, and in doing so set the stage for peace". For Nordstrom, it was neither through the work of international news organizations nor through the efforts of United Nations troops, but through locally produced plays, prose, poetry and pictures that Mozambicans themselves "created the conditions for peace. They made war an impossibility". She goes on to argue that it was on such local, grassroots artistic work that "the peace accords were built".[32]

We noted earlier that some kinds of violence are less visible than others, or accorded less importance. This is often true of violence against women or against black and minority ethnic persons in majority white societies. In a similar way, certain kinds of art and artists can also easily go unnoticed or be ignored.[33] As in the Mozambican example above, various types of grassroots art, and their role in peacebuilding can easily be overlooked. This can be especially true of local forms of arts, which are often led and developed by women: peace tapestries and quilts,[34] or knitting for peace.[35] Like everyday practices of storytelling, folk-singing, wood carving or embroidery, such activities are sometimes viewed as mere "crafts", and thus left out of discussions of the role of the arts in peacebuilding. Though there is not sufficient room in this volume to cover every kind of artistic practice, we wish to recognize the importance of a variety of arts, and note that so-called "high" arts do not emerge out of an artistic vacuum, but out of rich local and grassroots traditions.

Our interest in this volume is in the ways that the arts offer a range of contributions to the processes and practices of peacebuilding as we have described them above. How can the creative arts contribute to the long-term process of transforming relationships, healing wounds, seeking justice and fostering human flourishing? Such questions are pertinent to both practitioners and theorists, seeking to understand and build peace.

Discussions About Peacebuilding and the Arts

Until recently the arts have been commonly overlooked or relegated to the periphery in discussions related to peacebuilding.[36] While a number of recent studies focus on the relationship between peacebuilding and communications media, the creative arts have received comparatively little attention.[37] This is beginning to change, however, as increasing numbers of theorists and practitioners have begun to recognize the potential of the creative arts for contributing to processes of peacebuilding and conflict transformation.

Evidence of the growing interest related to peacebuilding and the arts can be found in a number of recent publications, though the field is still comparatively under-explored. In *Mediating Peace* (2015) a range of authors briefly explore a wide range of examples of "reconciliation through Visual Art, Music and Film".[38] Reflecting diverse approaches, covering individual, communal, and religious peacebuilding, almost all the chapters in *Mediating Peace* emerged from a single international conference at the Hebrew University of Jerusalem in 2012. The range and diversity of authors and perspectives in this volume reflect both the diversity of that gathering, and the growing interest in this emerging field from a range of practitioners and theorists.

This growing interest can be discerned even more clearly in Le Baron and Welch's 2012 literature and resource review on *Arts, Creativity and Intercultural Conflict Resolution*.[39] Several recent books focus on the role of specific arts in building peace, including music (e.g. John Paul Lederach and Angela Jill Lederach's *When Blood and Bones Cry Out*),[40] theatre (e.g. Nilanjana Premaratna's *Theatre for Peacebuilding*, and Cohen et al's *Acting Together*),[41] dance (e.g. Le Baron et al's *The Choreography of Resolution*),[42] photography and art (e.g. Frank Möller's *Visual Peace: Images, Spectatorship and the Politics of Violence*).[43] Our volume contributes to these discussions, but does so in a distinctive, coherent and original fashion; it also fills a number of lacunae in the existing literature on peacebuilding and the arts.

There are several edited books which, in their general aims and scope, intersect with aspects of our book, but few specifically address peacebuilding and the arts as their central focus.[44] The recent collections that touch on this theme mainly draw upon North American scholarship, perhaps attending more exclusively to theorizing and case studies of war and conflict as well as peace processes; the arts are often left to the side or covered by only one or two chapters. The extensive collection on *Advances in Peacebuilding*, for example, includes only one chapter explicitly on "art and peacebuilding", exploring "how theatre transforms conflict in Sri Lanka" on personal, emotional and societal levels.[45]

A few other books offer more wide-ranging discussions of the role of the arts. In *The Glorious Art of Peace* John Gittings provides a range of historical examples, drawing upon Greek tragedies, Shakespeare's later plays, and Tolstoy's *War and Peace* (1867), to explore both how peace has been perceived from "ancient times to today" and to bring to life "a small portion" of "peace advocacy and imagery" in "philosophy and political argument, in literature and art".[46] Gittings provides a highly selective and rich discussion rather than a systematic or comprehensive account. There are also increasing numbers of scholarly articles exploring the relation between peacebuilding and the arts.[47] These texts provide further examples of an emerging area of research, teaching and conversation.

There are related discussions on the role of the arts in peacebuilding to be found in texts emerging out of politics and international relations. This can be clearly seen in several editions of the journal on *Arts and International Relations*[48] and the edited book entitled *Visual Global Politics*, where over fifty authors discuss different aspects of the complex role of visuality and visual artifects in a wide range of political contexts.[49] Many of the essays in *Visual Global Politics* add support to editor Roland Bleiker's claim that works of art "can lead us to see the world in a new light and rethink assumptions we have taken for granted". They can also "help us imagine the unimaginable".[50] How this process can enhance peacebuilding endeavours will be explored further in several of the chapters that follow.

Other scholars working on politics and international relations have recently dealt explicitly with questions relating to the ambiguous role of the arts in relation to conflict and/or peace.[51] This can be seen in Michael Shapiro's *Cinematic Geopolitics*,[52] Jenny Edkins's *Face Politics*,[53] and Holly Ryan's Political Street Art: Communication, Culture and Resistance in Latin America.[54] In *Shows of Force: Power, Politics and Ideology in Art Exhibitions* Timothy Luke discusses a number of art exhibitions, including one extensive display in the National Gallery of Art in Washington in 1988 about Daimyo Japan, from 1185–1886. He observes how the curators took special pains to balance equally the ways of the *bu* (arts of the sword) and *bun* (arts of peace) in the display. Samurai swords and battle armour were used as examples of *bu*, while painting, poetry and calligraphy, were used to illustrate *bun*. Numerous images of religious figures, such as Buddhas and Zen priests, highlighted the "ambiguous but powerful spirituality of Daimyo Japan".[55] Luke's discussion demonstrates the ambiguous role of the arts, where both the "arts of the sword" and the "arts of peace" can be embedded within particular objects of art and within an entire exhibition. This ambiguity is also highlighted in a number of publications (e.g. on *The Arts of Transitional Justice* and *The Art of Truth-Telling About Authoritarian Rule*), that consider the role of the arts in different aspects of transitional justice, and in response to violent atrocities, abuses of power and related traumas.[56]

There is still much work to do and in the light of these reflections upon the current literature in this evolving field, it is clear that this volume on *Peacebuilding and the Arts* breaks new ground. It aims to strengthen and to develop this developing field by exploring how various arts, including visuals arts, music, literature, film, theatre and dance can play a part in reducing violent conflict and creating peaceful and just communities, through healing trauma, fostering compassion, expanding empathy and building communication across cultural, ethnic, religious and social divides. The project from which this book emerged has already brought together artists, musicians, film-makers, theatre professionals, dancers with academics and peacebuilders through several seminars, conferences, exhibitions and a series of interdisciplinary workshops in both North America and the UK. The aim of these discussions and events was to share expertise, foster critical conversation around the theory and practice of peacebuilding through the arts, and explore the ways in which arts-based peacebuilding both supplements and challenges conventional diplomatic means of conflict transformation.

It is important to underline that we are not suggesting that through skilful and artistic packaging of messages audiences can be turned into more peaceful citizens. One aim of this book is rather to tease out the "ambivalence of the arts" in a number of different communicative and artistic contexts,[57] by providing critical insights upon those artistic practices which contribute to the development of sustainable and peaceable environments. In the midst of such dynamic practices and diverse settings, a further objective is to highlight the importance of location, cultural contexts and history for building postive, as opposed to negative, peace.[58]

Outline of Chapters

This book is structured around five parts, each containing four chapters: Visual Arts (1), Music (2), Literature (3), Film (4), Theatre and Dance (5). Each part follows a similar structure, beginning with an introductory essay, which is followed by two more in-depth case studies and a concluding reflective essay. These essays often resonate with each other, echoing themes through both indirect and direct conversation. The twenty-one chapters that follow are by no means an attempt to provide comprehensive coverage of peacebuilding and the arts. They offer instead a fresh framework and a set of rich and diverse examples for developing a sharper and more critically nuanced understanding of the role of the arts in building peace.

In the introductory chapter on **Visual Arts (Chapter 2)**, Jolyon Mitchell observes that "war and visual arts" has a far larger existing literature than the work on representing peace visually, an observation that holds true for the arts more broadly. Discussing a number of well-known pieces of art by the likes of Paul Nash and Otto Dix, Käthe Kollwitz and Pablo Picasso, as well as less well-known work, Mitchell analyses the ways in which artists can not only bear witness to the costs of violent conflict, but also through their creations extend the moral imagination, and thereby contribute to building peace. As he observes "no picture can wish away war", but it can raise questions about the wisdom and results of conflict, alongside depicting the long and often difficult journey towards a sustainable peace. This is complemented by a consideration of how art can be used to express powerful emotions such as grief and anger, as well as develop imaginaries of peace.

The two case studies that follow (Chapters 3 and 4) invite the reader to reflect on examples from Korea and Northern Ireland. In his essay on "Peacebuilding Through Minjung Art", Sebastian Kim demonstrates how visual art, especially woodcuts and murals, do not take place in a cultural, religious or artistic vacuum. Kim's analysis of the role of Minjung Art in peacebuilding is enriched by his discussion of related poetry and practical protests, highlighting the importance of promoting justice in order to bring peace. Mitchell (Chapter 2) and Kim (Chapter 3) discuss contrasting portrayals of a man and woman embracing: while Mitchell considers the twentieth century sculpture in Coventry originally entitled *Reunion* (renamed later as *Reconciliation*), Kim reflects on the mural (1983) and wood block (1987) *Dreaming of Reunification*. In different ways, both examples highlight how visual arts can imagine hoped for, though very different, forms of peace. By contrast, several of the murals considered in Adrienne Chaplin's essay on "Art, Protest and Peace: the Murals of the Bogside Artists" refer back to contested histories and painful memories (Chapter 4). Chaplin makes the case that these huge mural help locals and visitors alike to face the wounds of the past, in a way that has the potential to promote certain kinds of peace.

In the final essay in the Visual Arts part, Theodora Hawksley's chapter on "Proposing Peacebuilding through the Arts" (Chapter 5) steps back from the two earlier concrete case studies from Korea (Chapter 3) and Northern Ireland (Chapter 4) to reflect on the ways in which arts approaches to peacebuilding are proposed, arguing that the arts' capacities for engaging witness, empathy, memory and vision, should not be abstracted "from their place in the moral imaginations of particular artists or communities". She roots her theoretical proposal in a detailed discussion of the work of South African artist William Kentridge, showing how his powerful and haunting engagement with political and peacebuilding themes emerges from a deep fidelity to both his context and his craft.

Part II on **Music** provides a counterpoint to the first on **Visual Arts**. In the opening essay in this part John Paul Lederach argues that it is "astounding that so little attention has been paid to music in the formal literature of peacebuilding" (Chapter 6). Poetic insights about the qualities of music are matched by more theoretical reflections on music's potential to contribute to building peace in unexpected ways. Lederach's chapter resonates with and builds upon his earlier 2010 work, *When Blood and Bones Cry Out*, which was written with his daughter, musician Angela Jill Lederach.[59] This volume drew on their collective experience of peacebuilding to make a fresh proposal for the relevance of musical practices and metaphors for the task of peacebuilding. In his chapter in our present volume, Lederach explores how "music writ large evokes, provokes, and invokes". He suggests that when approaching music and peacebuilding, "we must enter through the doorway of soundscape", recognizing how music can evoke depth of meaning, provoke active responses and invoke engagements with and journeys through the past, present and future towards peace.

The case study based essays that follow invite the reader first to Uganda and then to the Middle East. In "Engaging the 'Other': Contemporary Music as Perspective-Shifting in Post-Conflict Northern Uganda" (Chapter 7), Lindsay McClain Opiyo explores the relationship between music and peacebuilding in developing constructive relationships in Northern Uganda, the site of over two decades of conflict between the Ugandan government and various rebel groups, particularly the Lord's Resistance Army (LRA). By focusing on three popular and poignant conflict-era songs, this essay suggests that there is significant potential for transformative peacebuilding when music strategically engages with groups labelled by society as the "other". Building on a discussion of the songs themselves, Opiyo makes a case for recognizing the value of music for nurturing perspective-shifting within groups and between groups polarized by protracted conflict. The longstanding conflict between Palestinians and Israelis provides part of the backdrop for Rachel Beckles Willson's critical reflection on "the Early Years of the Barenboim Said Foundation (2003–2009)"

(Chapter 8). Based upon extensive fieldwork, Willson explores the tension between what music can represent and what it embodies, with particular reference to the ostensibly bridge-building orchestra of Daniel Barenboim. By drawing out the tension between "representation and embodiment", she shows how widely publicized musical peacebuilding initiatives may have less value at the grass roots level than initially perceived, partly because "peacebuilders may well import their own reconciliation processes without acknowledging its dangers".

The final essay in this part on Music, Kathryn Jourdan's "the Role of Music-Making in Peacebuilding: a Levinasian Perspective" (Chapter 9), begins by contrasting these two case studies (Chapters 7 and 8), one which celebrates the transformative role of songs in peacebuilding in Northern Uganda and the other which highlights the problematic "importation of music-making in the Western classical tradition into the West Bank Palestinian territories". Jourdan argues that music-making, especially as "ethical encounter", has the potential to contribute to peacebuilding. Drawing on the work of the French Jewish philosopher Emmanuel Levinas she explores both the limitations and the extraordinary potential of music to create common worlds, face the "Other" and build non-violent relationships that can change societies.

Part III on **Literature** offers several discussions of the portrayal of both violent and non-violent relationships. In the introductory essay, Sandra Gustafson lays foundations for reflecting on the relationship between "Literature and Peace Studies" (Chapter 10). Observing the relative paucity of work on literature and peacebuilding, Gustafson initially draws on Stephen Pinker's work on the historical reduction of violence. In *The Better Angels of Our Nature*, Pinker argues that one of the causes of the humanitarian and rights revolutions, as well as the "long peace", was the development of the novel, which allowed readers to inhabit other people's worlds. Gustafson supports the claim that by contributing to greater empathy, the novel helped cultivate more peaceful environments.[60] Gustafson also draws upon Lederach's work on the moral imagination, especially the value of developing webs of relationships, using it as a foundation for "the peacebuilders hermeneutic". This in turn enriches her discussion of Marmon Silko's novel *Ceremony* (1977), and two Gulf War novels that interrogate different forms of militarism.

The following case study essay returns to Northern Uganda, this time reflecting on "Storytelling and Peacebuilding" (Chapter 11). Ketty Anyeko and Tamara Shaya argue that storytelling can be a powerful tool for peace-building, and explore in their chapter how storytelling has helped women traumatized by war in Northern Uganda to develop a sense of agency, to call for their rights, to pursue justice, and to make sense of their experiences. Anyeko and Shaya argue that the practice of storytelling gave these local women a space in which to express and process their traumatic memories of war, thus helping to alleviate their feelings of isolation, shame and guilt, and giving them the confidence and freedom to participate in their local communities. The essay that follows "What Choice between Nightmares?" engages with the same setting and project, but offers a very different approach (Chapter 12). Juliane Okot Bitek was asked to write the stories told by the women in Anyeko and Shaya's project. She describes how her own experience of writing up traumatic stories troubled her deeply. Nevertheless, she was determined to reflect upon and to express the unspeakable, so she created her own imaginative story, rooted in the troubling reality. The result is a merging of literary theory and creative practice, which illustrates the power of storytelling to engage with trauma, memory and healing.

These two complementary essays on the Ugandan women's project explore the ways in which violent conflict can be gendered, and draw attention to the significance of literary forms and spaces where women can speak and write about violence against women. Bitek uses the work of American author Toni Morrison, whose work strives to give voice to those doubly silenced women of American slavery (through silence about racial violence and silence about gendered violence), while also implicating the reader in that silence. Bitek also draws upon recent work with Indian women who have been victims of gendered violence and who have a particularly gendered response. Both case study chapters in the Literature part therefore also highlight how the arts can both shed light on gendered violence, and offer ways of engaging transformatively with it.

In "Literary Strains", Alison Rice draws upon examples of writing after the 1994 genocide in Rwanda, as well as the preceding essays, to explore literature's role in bearing witness (Chapter 13). For Rice, writing has the potential to "recreate the past, revive individual memory, contribute to collective and historical memory", while also participating in moves towards justice. Recognizing the "shortcomings of memory" especially after traumatic events, she goes on to claim that literature can bring about self-awareness, revealing prejudices, presuppositions and stereotypes. Different kinds of literature have the potential to nuance and complexify understandings of reality, encouraging readers and writers to look at the world differently and move beyond binary ways of perception. In this way, literature can contribute to laying further foundations for understanding between traumatized individuals and divided communities.

Film has the potential to do something similar, but in very different ways and in Part IV on Joseph Kickasola begins by reflecting on the embodied experience of cinema (Chapter 14). Kickasola begins his essay with a couple of surprising cinematic examples, one satirizing the yearning for "world peace", and the other highlighting how peaceful rhetoric can be used to promote violent ends. By contrast, in this essay he considers how film can play a role in re-humanizing conflict situations, in spite of its potential to do the opposite. He does this through a discussion of what "re-humanization" might mean, outlining some fundamental areas for what he describes as re-humanizing cinema. He does not attempt to outline a "recipe" for peace through cinema, but instead reflects on how the cinema can be a tool in multivalent peacebuilding efforts, by encouraging empathy, world-making, truth-telling and imagining alternative futures.

Cinema as a tool for peacebuilding can be seen in the two case studies that follow. In "Peacebuilding and Reconciliation in and through film" (Chapter 15), Robert Johnston examines how films can bear witness to what happened during and after the 1994 genocide in Rwanda. Discussing four films in some detail, he claims that film can transform the perspectives of both international and local audiences, as well as contribute to the development of a new film industry. Johnston mentions one of the pioneering figures in the rapidly evolving Rwandan film industry, Eric Kabera, the founder and president of the Rwanda Film Centre, director of films such as *Keepers of Memory* (2004), which focuses on those survivors who look after genocide memorials and more recently *Intore* (2014), which highlights the work of musicians and dancers in building peace for both the present and future of Rwanda. Kabera, like Johnston, has a strong belief in the power of film to act as both a mirror that bears witness to painful memories and difficult realities, and as a catalyst for building peace.

Kabera's work is worth a brief illustrative detour here. While *Keepers of Memory* focuses on those survivors who look after genocide memorials, *Intore* highlights the work of musicians and dancers in building peace for both the present and future of Rwanda. This documentary also shows how film can contribute to celebrating other arts' role in peacebuilding, *Intore* begins by focusing on the loss of culture, "like a tree whose roots have been cut", that took place during the 1994 genocide. Nevertheless, twenty years on, several different interviewees celebrate the role of music and musicians who they believe "are contributing to the peace of Rwanda". One local musician claims: "We are the ones to talk about peace because we know when there is not peace we know what happens". They are confident that the "power of music can help to heal the wounds of the past".[61] So *Intore* highlights the combined potential of different arts (film and music in this case) working together to help to build environments of peace.

In the second case study in the film part, "The Power of Film: Grassroots Activism in Ousmane Sembène's *Moolaadé*" (Chapter 16), Lizelle Bisschoff highlights another aspect of film's potential for contributing to building peace. Bisschoff analyses how Sembène's groundbreaking 2004 film *Moolaadé* reveals in a nuanced and narrative fashion (unlike some other films she discusses) the violence of female genital mutilation (FGM). Here is another form of gendered violence, often hidden from public view, that some peacebuilders are increasingly shedding light upon. For Bisschoff, this film has considerable educational power. Through memorable drama *Moolaadé* shows the agonizing effects of FGM, the contested nature of the practice, the tensions it provokes between generations and genders, as well as the ways in which grassroots activism can challenge violent and harmful practices, while also recognizing FGM's cultural weight and embededness. Read together, Johnston and Bisschoff's essays shed light on the potential of film to bear witness to violence, to tease out the deadly tensions that emerge within and between communities, and to imagine more hopeful futures.

A fresh perspective is offered by Olivier Morel in the concluding essay of the Film part, "Towards a Disarmed Cinema" (Chapter 17). Morel begins by considering those theorists who claim that cinema commonly makes violence visible and peace invisible. In spite of cinema's tendency to be a theatre for violence, he explores how far it is possible for film to move in a different direction from its dominant history and not "fall into the trap of being used as a war machine". Morel does this by considering the work of three different film-makers who have attempted to "disarm cinema" by producing powerful non-fiction films during the past decade.[62] The films that Morel considers contribute subtly to the peacebuilding enterprise, by revealing the frame, writing the history of victims and rehearsing the crimes of perpetrators. These examples show how film can change audience perceptions of overlooked "standard operating procedures" at the prison in Abu Ghraib, in the Khmer Rouge's genocide in Cambodia, and in a largely forgotten massacre in Indonesia. For Morel, these and other film-makers can disarm cinema, by making the invisible visible, by opening a space for reconciliation, and by envisaging a different kind of world from the one being presented.

Theatre also has the potential to transform ways of imagining conflicts. This can be seen in the fifth part, which covers **Theatre** and other performing arts, such as **Dance**. In the introductory essay on "Peacebuilding and the Performing Arts through the Collaborative Lens" (Chapter 18), Hal Culbertson explores the relationships between peacebuilding and performing arts organizations, showing how these relationships can take on a variety of distinct forms, each with its own strengths and weaknesses. By considering instrumental, interactional and transformational collaborations he demonstrates how the performing arts can serve as a tool for peacebuilding. For Culbertson, "Theatre can function as a mirror on society, as commentary, as an escape or diversion, as catharsis, as a reflective space, or in myriad other capacities". It is vital to recognize the potential of Theatre, and indeed other performing arts, for peacebuilding. This "requires peacebuilders who understand the inherent capacity of the performing arts", as well as "performing artists who engage the peacebuilding endeavor critically and creatively".

This dynamic two-way relationship is explored in more detail in the two case studies that follow. In "Peacebuilding and the Theatre Arts" (Chapter 19), experienced director and performer, Paul Burbridge and Geoffrey Stevenson, consider a single work of live theatre in the context of the present conflict in Israel/Palestine. They wrestle with the question of whether the experiences that "a member of an audience might have in the imagined world of theatre" can contribute to building peace in the real world. To answer this they focus upon a particular production, which sought to avoid using polemical, propagandist or "agit-prop" theatre and instead explored the Palestinian/Israeli conflict through portraying the microcosm of a series of tense familial and neighbour relations. Through their discussion, they highlight how theatre is commonly a highly collaborative endeavour, which can explore the ambiguity, the messiness and the unpredictablity of both staging a play and individual conflicts. By focusing upon collaborative practices they show how theatre can become a safe space where difficult memories and dangerous ideas can be creatively explored, and argue that it thereby has the potential to contribute to peacebuilding processes and conflict transformation.[63]

Performing arts can help to commemorate and even untangle painful histories. This can be seen in the second case study in this final part, which turns to consider dance in Colombia, focusing on "Peacebuilding and Dance in Afro-Colombian Funerary Ritual" (Chapter 20). Dance is often overlooked in the peacebuilding literature and this essay seeks to address this omission. Sandra Milena Rios and Thania Acarón suggest that dance can "mediate social transformation and can support peacebuilding processes in settings where atrocities have recently occurred and where threats of violence are still present". They focus upon specific dance performances, which form part of funerary rituals performed in the annual commemoration of the massacre of Bojayá, Colombia. As Rios and Acarón demonstrate, these dances have a striking impact on both performers and spectators. The rituals embody painful memories and ongoing grievances and, like the theatre discussed in the previous chapter, can be highly ambiguous practices. Nevertheless, they show how dance can both memoralize and protest, providing "a shield that allows people to speak about violence and injustice in a non-confrontational manner". In this way, the body itself can become a "vehicle of resistance, expression, and visibility of the potential" for different kinds of conflict and personal transformation.

In the final essay in this Part V on "Theatre and Dance", Frances Clemson builds on the three preceding chapters, addressing "Doing Justice to the Past: Time in Drama and Peacebuilding" (Chapter 21). Clemson's chapter explores these themes through a largely forgotten but rich play by Dorothy Sayers, produced soon after the end of the Second World War, *The Just Vengeance*. The play brings an airman from Lichfield, killed in the earlier conflict, into conversation with "generations of citizens from across the city's past, themselves perpetrators and victims of violence". Here again, "live" theatre brings the past back to life in unexpected ways, bearing witness to past suffering and heartbreak, while also envisaging more hopeful futures. In this way theatre, like the other arts, can also raise profound and poignant questions about the roles that history, belief and time can play in building peace.

Recurring Themes

The chapters that follow demonstrate the arts' contribution to peacebuilding in a far richer and more detailed way than any summary offered above, but it is nevertheless worth drawing out several broad areas of interest and exploration.

The first is communication. We are interested in exploring the ways in which various creative arts have been and can be employed in the negotiation of conflict in constructive, non-violent ways. How might things like protest songs, political murals and agit-prop theatre provide spaces for raising, debating and constructively addressing conflict over political and social injustice? How can they become safe spaces for raising dangerous memories and issues?[64] We have noted that the arts are often bound up in the creation of problematic senses of community identity, based on exclusion, superiority over and demonization of the other. Conversely, we are interested in the arts' capacity for building and expressing national, ethnic and religious identities that are simultaneously distinctive and capable of co-existing and flourishing alongside others in relationships of mutual interdependence. In all of these ways, the arts can contribute to the rebuilding or creation of patterns of communication that set communities on the road to life.

Our second area relates to bearing witness. The arts can bear witness to both past violence and future hopes for peace in creative and distinct ways. They can show histories, articulate memories and express hope for the future via sights and sounds, pictures and music, touch and textures. Visual arts, music, literature, film, theatre and dance all have the potential to bear witness to dangerous and painful memories as well as present complexities and future possibilities. The powerful character of this artistic witness is unpredictable, sometimes even messy and uncontrollable, but it can help to produce transformative moments of shift and human connection in situations of intractable conflict.

A third area of interest is empathy. When faced with conflict on an interpersonal or societal level, a common reaction is to throw up barriers between ourselves and the other party. We become defensive, denying or minimizing our own fault, and aggressive, pushing the other away by demonizing them. Communication breaks down and, with it, empathy. Our ability to imagine others' experience and to care about it shuts down. In violent conflicts this dissociation can be particularly acute: we can wish, even inflict, horrendous violence on others, and become hardened not just to their suffering, but also to the suffering that the ongoing conflict is causing to our own community. In these kinds of situations, we are interested in the arts' capacity to bear witness to the costs of conflict, to reconnect people to the force of their compassionate (or moral) imagination, and reawaken empathy—the ability to imagine the experience and suffering of others, and the ability to reach across the lines of conflict in order to engage with it. We are also interested in exploring the arts' ability to preserve and strengthen the moral imagination, connecting us to others in relationships of interdependence that remain resilient in the face of renewed violence.

Our fourth area of interest is healing. We are interested in the ways in which the arts can help to heal individuals and communities, enabling them to respond to and recover from trauma sustained in the course of violent conflict. This includes interest in the arts' potential to help perpetrators and victims to remember well, communicating and remembering stories of conflict in ways that are oriented towards truth-telling and bearing witness,[65] rather than fostering resentment and sowing further violence. We are interested too in the arts' potential to develop and articulate people's vision of a future beyond the violent conflict in which they are caught up, a vision that, on a practical level, strengthens their resolve for peace, and for the long and difficult journey towards it.

These four areas are by no means a comprehensive list of the themes and topics covered in the chapters that follow. Nevertheless, they highlight the distinctive and original nature of this volume and what it may contribute to discussions and practices related to creative peacebuilding. While we are interested in exploring examples of the arts "working" in the service of peacebuilding, the discussions that follow are not focussed on telling sequential stories, where the arts are deployed in a given situation of violent conflict, and peace is the result. Neither do we build our case for the value of arts approaches to peacebuilding on a narrowly empirical base, by assessing the impact of short-term arts-based interventions in situations of violent conflict. Instead, we are interested in exploring the role that the arts play in creating and sustaining systems of just peace at all stages, in settings ranging from societies suffering with protracted armed conflicts to societies that are, at least relatively speaking, peaceful. Our interest in the arts is pragmatic, but not instrumentalizing. In what follows, we want to engage not in a monologue about how the arts can be co-opted into the work of professional peacebuilders, but a dialogue, in which creative artistic practice sheds light on the art and practice of peacebuilding itself. We hope that the conversations begun in this volume will gather more participants, constructive perspectives and critical voices in the years to come.

Notes

1. William Stafford, "At the Un-National Monument along the Canadian Border", in Kim Stafford, editor, *Every War Has Two Losers: William Stafford on Peace and War* (Minneapolis, MN: Milkweed Editions, 2003), 87. See

also William Stafford, *The Way It Is: New and Selected Poems* (Minneapolis, MN: Graywolf Press, 1998).

2. These forms of violence are commonly hidden and in many countries still go largely unreported. The *#MeToo*, the *#Black Lives Matter* and *#NotOneMore* movements are recent examples of what has been called "Hashtag Activism" that seeks to bring various forms of violence into the public sphere, making it more visible.
3. On structural violence, see for example Johan Galtung, *Peace by Peaceful Means: Peace and Conflict, Development and Civilisation* (London, UK: Sage Publications, 1996).
4. John Paul Lederach, *The Little Book of Conflict Transformation* (Intercourse, PA: Good Books, 2003), 5.
5. "Conflict transformation" is now the term commonly preferred to "conflict resolution" by many scholars of peace. See, for example, John Paul Lederach, *Preparing for Peace: Conflict Transformation Across Cultures* (New York: Syracuse Press, 1995); Hugh Miall, editor, *Conflict Transformation: A Multi-dimensional Task* (Bergh of Research Center for Constructive Conflict Management, 2004). Conflict transformation seeks to go beyond simple resolutions of conflicts to engaging with the underlying and structural causes of violence by both seeking to repair human relationships and to confront injustices.
6. "Positive peace" is much more than simply absence of violence (this is often described as "negative peace"). Positive peace is commonly seen as the eradication of structural violence and the establishment of just societies. See D. Cortright, *Peace: A History of Movements and Ideas* (Cambridge, UK: Cambridge University Press, 2008), 6–7. See also Johan Galtung, "Twenty-Five Years of Peace Research: Ten Challenges and Some Responses". *Journal of Peace Research* 22(2) (1985): 141–158.
7. For a full treatment of this theme, see Daniel Philpott, *Just and Unjust Peace: An Ethic of Reconciliation* (Oxford, UK: Oxford University Press, 2012).
8. John Paul Lederach and R. Scott Appleby, "Strategic Peacebuilding: An Overview" in *Strategies of Peace: Transforming Conflict in a Violent World*, eds. Daniel Philpott and Gerard F. Powers (Oxford: Oxford University Press, 2010), 19–44 (28).
9. In the words of the unconventional Quaker Sydney Bailey (1916–1995): 'Peace is a process to engage in, not a goal to be reached'. Quoted in 'Our peace testimony' in *Quaker Faith and Practice* (Fifth Edition), 24.57. http://qfp.quaker.org.uk/chapter/24/ (accessed 28 May 2018).
10. For Quakers, peace is in the doing, and "the means become the ends". See "Our peace testimony" in *Quaker Faith and Practice* (Fifth Edition), Chapter 24.
11. Consider, for example, the claim that: "The peace testimony is about deeds not creeds; not a form of words but a way of living. It is the cumulative lived

witness of generations of Quakers… The peace testimony is not about being nice to people and living so that everyone likes us. It will remain a stumbling block and will itself cause conflict and disagreement. The peace testimony is a tough demand that we should not automatically accept the categories, definitions and priorities of the world". The London Yearly Meeting, 1993, in "Our peace testimony" in *Quaker Faith and Practice* (Fifth Edition), 24.11. http://qfp.quaker.org.uk/chapter/24/ (accessed 28 May 2018).

12. See also Tom Woodhouse, "Adam Curle: Radical Peacemaker and Pioneer of Peace Studies", *Journal of Conflictology*, [S.l.], volume 1, no. 1, July 2010. http://journal-of-conflictology.uoc.edu/joc/en/index.php/journal-of-conflictology/article/view/vol1iss1-woodhouse, (accessed 28 May 2018).
13. Quoted in 'Our peace testimony' in *Quaker Faith and Practice* (Fifth Edition), 24.35. http://qfp.quaker.org.uk/chapter/24/ (accessed 28 May 2018).
14. See Augusto Boal, *Games for Actors and Non-actors*, Second Edition, translated by Adrian Jackson (London and New York: Routledge, 1992), 15. On the basis of his observation that "all human beings are Actors (they act!) and Spectators (they observe!)", he developed the new term of "Spect-actors", highlighting how spectators can become involved in the performative process.
15. The London Yearly Meeting, 1993, in "Our peace testimony" in *Quaker Faith and Practice* (Fifth Edition), 24.11.
16. See Lyse Doucet, Correspondent, *Syria: The World's War*, BBC 2 (3rd and 4th May 2018).
17. See William McGants, *The Isis Apocalypse: The History, Strategy, and Doomsday Vision of the Islamic State* (New York, NY: St. Martin's Press, 2015).
18. ISIS, and other groups such as Al-Shabaab and Boko Haram, are commonly linked with Wahhabism/Salafism. As such many of the arts discussed in this book would be entirely rejected, or even destroyed. See, for example, James Noyes, *The Politics of Iconoclasm: Religion, Violence and the Culture of Image-Breaking in Christianity and Islam* (London and New York: IB Tauris, 2013), especially chapters 2 and 3.
19. The circulation and regular replaying of images of Muslims suffering in different parts of the world have been used to justify further violence. As Islamist parties begin to win considerable portions of the vote in newly democratic Arab nations, it is also evident that other factors are in play. The Terrorist attacks at the Bardo museum in Tunis (March 2015) and on the beach at Sousse, Tunisia (June 2015), are obviously very different from Mohamed Bouazizi's self-immolation some five years before, appearing partly to be violent expressions of radicalization within certain strands of Islam. These attacks, mostly claiming the lives of tourists, made headlines in the West, in a way that later even more deadly attacks did not.

20. See the Human Security Report's analysis of armed conflicts by type in the years 1946–2007. http://www.hsrgroup.org/our-work/security-stats/State-Based-Armed-Conflicts-By-Type.aspx. (accessed 17 February 2017).
21. See Jolyon Mitchell, *Media Violence and Christian Ethics* (Cambridge, UK: Cambridge University Press, 2007), especially chapters 1 and 2.
22. These can include many different kinds of creative artists and performers. Of course, in some settings certain art forms are frowned upon, prohibited and even destroyed. As will be demonstrated later in the book flexibility and cultural sensitivity is rightly seen by many practitioners vital for peacebuilding through the arts.
23. See Oliver P. Richmond and Audra Mitchell, editors, *Hybrid Forms of Peace: Everyday Agency to Post-Liberalism* (New York, NY: Palgrave Macmillan, 2016 [2012]). See also Roger Mac Ginty, *International Peacebuilding and Local Resistance: Hybrid Forms of Peace* (New York, NY: Palgrave Macmillan, 2016).
24. See James R. Lee, *Climate Change and Armed Conflict: Hot and Cold Wars* (Abingdon, Oxon and New York, NY: Routledge, 2009).
25. See Laura Parker, "What you need to know about the World's Water Wars" *National Geographic*, 14 July 2016. https://news.nationalgeographic.com/2016/07/world-aquifers-water-wars/ (accessed 30 May 2018).
26. See Karen Armstrong, *Fields of Blood: Religion and the History of Violence* (London: Vintage, 2015 [2014]), especially 334–370.
27. Denise Levertov, "Misnomer", in Denise Levertov and Peggy Rosenthal, *Making Peace* (New York, NY: New Directions Bibelot, 2006). For more on this American poet see: "Denise Levertov", https://www.poetryfoundation.org/poets/denise-levertov (accessed 28 May 2018).
28. See Jolyon Mitchell, *Promoting Peace, Inciting Violence: The Role of Religion and Media* (London, UK and New York, NY: Routledge, 2012), chapter 3 on "Cultivating Violence".
29. See Judith Butler, *Frames of War: When is Life Grievable?* (London: Verso, 2016).
30. See Curt Daniel, "Theatre in the Nazi Concentration Camp: Creativity and Resistance in Dachau and Buchenwald", https://www.myjewishlearning.com/article/theatre-in-the-nazi-concentration-camps/ (accessed 27 March 2018)
31. See Sojourner Truth's (1797–1883), later and likely deliberate use of this phrase in her famous speech later titled as "Ain't I a Woman?" (at the Women's Convention in Akron, Ohio, on May 29, 1851). Truth, a well known anti-slavery speaker, was born into slavery in New York State and gained her freedom at thirty in 1827.
32. Carolyn Nordstrom, *A Different Kind of War Story: The Ethnography of Political Violence* (Philadelphia: University of Pennsylvania Press, 1997), 220.

33. Evidence for this may be seen in the dearth of top-grossing female artists and how works by women artists are regularly valued lower than art by men. See http://www.bbc.co.uk/news/entertainment-arts-44216361 (accessed 29 May 2018).
34. See, for example, "Middle East Peace Quilt", http://www.middleeastpeacequilt.ca/theartist.php (accessed 29 May 2018).
35. See, for example, "Knit for Peace", http://www.knitforpeace.org.uk/about/ (accessed 29 May 2018).
36. This continues to be the case in many significant texts. See, for example, Wolfgang Dietrich et al, *Peace Studies: A Cultural Perspective* (New York, NY: Palgrave Macmillan, 2011). It is noteworthy how little the arts is discussed in this diverse, extensive, international volume exploring the many different cultural understandings of peace.
37. See, for example, Julia Hoffmann and Virgil Hawkins, editors, *Communication and Peace: Mapping an Emerging Field* (London and New York: Routledge, 2016); J. P. Singh, "Media and Peacebuilding" in Craig Zelizer, *Integrated Peacebuilding: Innovative Approaches to Transforming Conflict* (Boulder, CO: Westview Press, 2013), 225–247; and S. Gibson and S. Mollan, *Representations of Peace and Conflict* (Basingstoke, Hampshire and New York, NY: Palgrave Macmillan, 2012). See also, Jolyon Mitchell, *Promoting Peace, Inciting Violence: The Role of Religion and Media* (London, UK and New York, NY: Routledge, 2012).
38. Sebastian Kim, Pauline Kollontai and Sue Yore, *Mediating Peace: Reconciliation Through Visual Art, Music and Film* (Newcastle, UK: Cambridge Scholars, 2015).
39. M. Le Baron and D. Welch, *Arts, Creativity and Intercultural Conflict Resolution: Literature and Resources Review* (Vancouver: Conflict Resolution, Arts and Intercultural Experience Publishing, 2005). See also York St John University, *Bibliography of Academic Sources on Religion, Peace and Reconciliation* (York: Published Online, 2013) see especially the section on 'Peace and Reconciliation in the Arts', 35-38. https://www.yorksj.ac.uk/media/content-assets/schools/humanities-religion-philosophy/documents/Bibliography-on-Peace-and-Reconciliation-Dec-2013.pdf (accessed 1 July 2018).
40. John Paul Lederach and Angela Jill Lederach. *When Blood and Bones Cry Out: Journeys Through the Soundscape of Healing and Reconciliation* (Oxford, UK: Oxford University Press, 2010).
41. Nilanjana Premaratna, *Theatre for Peacebuilding* (Basingstoke, Hampshire and New York, NY: Palgrave Macmillan, 2013). See also Cynthia E Cohen, Roberto Gutierrez Varea, Polly O. Walker, eds. *Acting Together: Performance and the Creative Transformation of Conflict*. Volumes 1 and 2 (Oakland, CA: New Village Press, 2011). See also Yvette Hutchison, 'Women Playwrights in Post-Apartheid South Africa: Yael Farber, Lara Foot-Newton, and the

Call for *Ubuntu*', in *Contemporary Women Playwrights into the Twenty-First Century*, eds, Lesley Ferris and Penny Farfan (Basingstoke and New York: Palgrave Macmillan, 2013), 148–163.

42. Michelle LeBaron, Carrie MacLeod, and Andrew Floyer Acland, *The Choreography of Resolution: Conflict, Movement, and Neuroscience* (Chicago, IL: American Bar Association, Section of Dispute Resolution, 2013).
43. Frank Möller, *Visual Peace: Images, Spectatorship and the Politics of Violence* (Basingstoke, Hampshire and New York, NY: Palgrave Macmillan, 2013). A new edited volume on Peacbuilding and Photography is currently being produced by Tom Allbeson and Jolyon Mitchell. See also John Paul Lederach, *The Moral Imagination: The Art and Soul of Building Peace* (New York, NY and Oxford, UK: Oxford University Press, 2010 [2005]); John Peffer, *Art and the End of Apartheid* (Minneapolis, MN: University of Minnesota Press, 2009).
44. See, for example, Atalia Omer, R. Scott Appleby and David Little, *The Oxford Handbook of Religion, Conflict, and Peacebuilding* (Oxford: Oxford Univeristy Press, 2015). See, especially, Atalia Omer's chapter on: "The Exotic, the Good and the Theatrical", pp. 3–27.
45. See Nilajana Premaratana and Roland Bleiker, "Art and Peacebuilding: How Theatre Transforms Conflict in Sri Lanka," in *Palgrave Advances in Peacebuilding: Critical Developments and Approaches*, ed. Oliver P. Richmond (New York, NY: Palgrave Macmillan, 2010), 376–391.
46. John Gittings, *The Glorious Art of Peace: From the Illiad to Iraq* (Oxford: Oxford University Press, 2012), 8.
47. See, for example, Antony Adolf, "What Does Peace Literature Do? An Introduction to the Genre and Its Criticism." *The Canadian Journal of Peace and Conflict Studies* 42:1–2 (2010): 9–21; Babu Ayindo, "Arts Approaches to Peace: Playing Our Way to Transcendence?" In *Peacebuilding in Traumatized Societies*, edited by Barry Hart, 185–203. Lanham, MD: University Press of America, 2008; Michael Shank and Lisa Schirch. "Strategic Arts-Based Peacebuilding." *Peace and Change* 33:2 (2008), 217–242.
48. See, for example, Emilie Aussens, 'Reconciliation: Does Music Matter?', 33–38 and Frédéric Ramel and Michael Jung, 'The Barenboim Case: How to Link Music and Diplomacy Studies', in a Special Issue on 'International Relations are Acoustic. Let's Listen!' in *Arts and International Affairs*, 3: 2, Summer/Autumn (2018), 39–68.
49. Roland Bleiker, editor, *Visual Global Politics* (Abingdon, Oxon, and New York, NY: Routledge, 2018).
50. Ibid., pp. 3–28.
51. See, for example, Cerwyn Moore & Laura J. Shepherd, 'Aesthetics and International Relations: Towards a Global Politics', Global Society, 24:3 (2010), 299–309.

52. Michael Shapiro, *Cinematic Geopolitics (Abingdon, Oxon and New York, NY*: Routledge, 2008).
53. Jenny Edkins, *Face Politics (Abingdon, Oxon and New York, NY*: Routledge, 2015).
54. Holly Ryan, *Political Street Art: Communication, Culture and Resistance in Latin America (New York, NY and Abingdon, Oxon, 2018).*
55. Timothy W. Luke, *Shows of Force: Power, Politics and Ideology in Art Exhibitions* (Durham and London: Duke University Press, 1992).
56. See, for example, Lizelle Bisschoff and Stefanie Van de Peer, eds. *Art and Trauma in Africa* (London: Tauris, 2013); and Peter D. Rush and Olivera Simić, eds. *The Arts of Transitional Justice: Culture, Activism and Memory After Atrocity* (New York: Springer, 2014). See also Ksenija Bilbija, Jo Ellen Fair, Cynthia E. Milton, Leigh A. Payne, eds. *The Art of Truth-Telling about Authoritarian Rule*, (Madison: University of Wisconsin Press, 2005).
57. This is an adaptation of R. Scott Appleby's thesis in *The Ambivalence of the Sacred: Religion, Violence, and Reconciliation.* (Lanham, MD: Rowman and Littlefield Publishers, 2000).
58. See endnote 4 of this introduction and David Cortright, *Peace: A History of Movements and Ideas* (Cambridge, UK: Cambridge University Press, 2008), 6–7.
59. John Paul Lederach and Angela Jill Lederach, *When Blood and Bones Cry Out: Journeys Through the Soundscape of Healing and Reconciliation* (Oxford, UK: Oxford University Press, 2010).
60. See Steven Pinker, *The Better Angels of Our Nature: Why Violence Has Declined* (New York, NY: Viking, 2011), 211.
61. Eric Kabera, director, *Intore* (2014) is a seventy six minute documentary.
62. These films and discussions are very different from the sub-genre of 'anti-war' films that emerged after the First World War. See, for example, *Sites of Memory, Sites of Mourning: The Great War in European Cultural History* (Cambridge, UK: Cambridge University Press, 1995), 132–8.
63. This project resonates with the work of the Brazilian theatre practitioner and drama theorist Augusto Boal who asserted that: "Theatre is a form of knowledge; it should and can also be a means of transforming society. Theatre can help us build our future, rather than just waiting for it" Augusto Boal, *Games for Actors and Non-actors*, Second Edition, translated by Adrian Jackson (London and New York: Routledge, 1992), 16.
64. See, for example, Chapter 19 of this book in which Burbridge and Stevenson discuss this question in relation to theatre.
65. See Jolyon Mitchell, *Promoting Peace, Inciting Violence: The Role of Religion and Media* (London, UK and New York, NY: Routledge, 2012), Chapters 4 and 5 on "Bearing Witness" and "Searching for Truth and Reconciliation" through film.

PART I

Visual Arts

CHAPTER 2

Peacebuilding Through the Visual Arts

Jolyon Mitchell

Introduction

War has often proved to be an irresistible topic for artists. The Victorian art critic, John Ruskin (1819–1900), claimed 'there is no great art possible to a nation but that which is based on battle ... war is the foundation of all great art'. This controversial claim is from his lecture to soldiers at the Royal Military Academy in 1865, Ruskin continued 'you *must* have war to produce art'.[1] There are many examples to support Ruskin's assertion: ancient Greek vases depicting warriors fighting, Roman triumphal arches celebrating victorious campaigns and mosaics showing gladiators in hand-to-hand conflict. Descendants of this ancient family of conflict-based art include medieval tapestries narrating stories of Norman conquests, Renaissance paintings portraying battle scenes and chivalric jousting, and early modern drawings depicting bloody sieges in Central Europe. Huge canvasses illustrate retreats through snow blizzards in Russia, colourful renditions in oil show explosive sea-battles in the Atlantic and Japanese woodcuts capture scenes of sword-fighting in Chinese forests. A watercolour of

J. Mitchell (✉)
The University of Edinburgh, Edinburgh, Scotland, UK
e-mail: Jolyon.Mitchell@ed.ac.uk

J. Mitchell et al. (eds.), *Peacebuilding and the Arts*,
Rethinking Peace and Conflict Studies,
https://doi.org/10.1007/978-3-030-17875-8_2

war-elephants charging down their enemies in India, a china plate commemorating a victory in the Boer War and a more recent war-rug from Afghanistan may be less well-known than twentieth-century depictions of modern warfare, but taken together, they illustrate how a wide range of visual materials can be used to portray violent conflict. Through these and many other forms of visual arts, fighting figures are commonly glorified and victories celebrated.

Artists have long made a living by re-creating heroic scenes within conflicts.[2] Richard Caton Woodville (1856–1927), for example, was regularly commissioned by the *London Illustrated News* to depict Imperial battle scenes from both the Boer War and Afghanistan, including his famous *The Charge of the Light Brigade, 1854* (painted in 1894).[3] There is a much more extensive literature on visual arts and war, than there is on art that contributes to peace. In this chapter, I argue that artists have much to contribute to building peace. They do this through their craft as they bear witness, as they remember empathetically, provocatively, and wisely. Through their work artists can contribute to creating an environment in which the 'moral imagination' can be cultivated, and so contribute to building peace.[4]

Some earlier artists created war art with a decidedly critical attitude towards the conflict they depicted. Even though Sir Peter Paul Rubens (1577–1640) 'accepted commissions that celebrated war victories, such as the Spanish defeat of the Dutch fleet at Calloo', nevertheless, according to Margaret McKechnie-Glover, 'his vision of war remained deeply pessimistic'.[5] This can be seen in several of his paintings, such as *Minerva Protects Pax from Mars* (1629–1630) and *The Consequences of War* (1638–1639), which is commonly claimed to have informed Picasso's *Guernica* (1937) and his less well-known *Massacre in Korea* (1951).[6] So simply because war is a common topic for artists does not mean that representations of peace are entirely excluded. Embedded within these portrayals, it is also possible to identify interrogations of the use of violence. In this essay, I consider how far the visual arts can contribute to the complex processes involved in building sustainable and lasting peace.

One artist that both celebrates and critiques warfare is the American William Trego (1858–1909), who painted both idealistic and realistic portrayals to represent conflicts such as the American War of Independence (1775–1783) and the American Civil War (1861–1865). For example, in his *Color Guard* (1888) Trego depicts a heroic French Cavalry charge during the Franco-Prussian War (1870–1871). At the centre of the picture, among the riders on brown and black mounts, is a white horse with a helmeted and moustached lieutenant holding a flapping red, white and blue (tricolour) flag high above his head. Trego, whose hands and feet were severely damaged, probably because of polio during his infancy, painted his own face onto this horseman. Charging onwards, doing what he could never do in real life, he leads a company of French dragoons into the fray. One of their compatriots is thrown back in his saddle, an open hand and head facing up to the heavens, mortally wounded. Nearby another rider appears to have been shot, but there are no signs of fear on the faces of the charging cavalrymen. Through this painting, Trego reminds his French viewers, perhaps still smarting from defeat by the Prussians in 1871, of the gallantry and sacrifice of their own troops.

By contrast, Trego's Civil War battle scene, *Battery Forward* (1887), captures the moment one of the mounted artillery-men has been shot and another struggles to restrain his terrified horse.[7] Unlike *Color Guard*, this painting shows a body face-down in the grass, the wheels of the gun carriage narrowly avoiding this blue-uniformed body. Not as bleak or corpse filled as Timothy O'Sullivan's famous black and white photographs (e.g. *The Harvest of Death*) taken after the Battle of Gettysburg (1863), there is nonetheless a harsh reality to many of Trego's Civil War paintings. While *Color Guard* stands in a long tradition of pictures that primarily celebrate heroic and courageous exploits by soldiers,[8] *Battery Forward* represents an example of paintings created by artists who do not shy away from depicting the agonizing realities of war.

By bearing witness, by remembering grief and loss, as well as by showing how weapons of war can be transformed into implements of peace, paintings, sculptures and other forms of visual art all help to illustrate vividly the costs of violence and protest against it.

Bearing Witness

Art drawn from personal experience bears witness to the realities of the battlefield. While propaganda pictures from the First World War largely avoided revealing the agonies, sounds and smells of trench warfare, two artists, who had fought on opposite sides in the Great War, each chose to bear witness to the traumatic reality they had witnessed of ravaged landscapes and the shattered bodies of their comrades. They both stand in a number of related fragmented artistic movements that emerged partly in response to the First World War.[9]

One of the most notable German artists at this time was Otto Dix (1891–1969), who trained and then worked as a painter and printmaker. He began the war in 1914 as an eager volunteer hoping the war would be both cleansing and regenerative. He served as a machine gunner at the Battle of Somme (1915), then at the Eastern Front, and finally in Flanders, where he participated in the 1918 Spring Offensive and volunteered to train as a pilot. While at the Front he produced several hundred drawings, often using postcards and his diary as his canvas. He portrayed wide-eyed wounded soldiers, devastated and corpse-strewn fields. Describing these pictures as 'Reports from Hell', Dix used charcoal, crayon, soft black pencil and black chalk, creating a series of unsentimental, often grotesque portrayals of life and death at the battlefront. His ambivalent view of war as both 'horrible' and 'tremendous',[10] as well as his interactions with Futurism, Cubism and Dadaism, informed his artistic expression. Though even more significant was his own personal experience. Wounded repeatedly, including in his neck, and awarded the Iron Cross (Second Class), Dix's traumatic wartime experiences and post-war nightmares would profoundly shape his art. 'The rubble and debris was constantly in my dreams'.[11] Through his art produced after the war, he was not only exorcising the ghosts of his own memory, he was also bearing witness to the physical and psychological wounds of the war and its aftermath. In his post-war representations of maimed veterans, begging or selling matches (e.g. *The Match Seller*, 1920), Dix had travelled a long way from any celebration of heroic and noble warriors.

Defined as a 'verist', part of the post-expressionist *Neue Sachlichkeit* (the 'new objectivity' or 'new realism') movement,[12] Dix was determined to reproduce the 'reality' of what he had experienced. In Basel (1923), he studied Jacques Callot's eighteen prints that make up *The Miseries and Misfortunes of War* (1633) and Francisco Goya's eighty-two etchings revealing *The Disasters of War* (1810–1820).[13] He even practised painting the corpses and body parts that he saw at anatomy classes, and he scrutinized the shocking photographs of mutilated faces and bodies from Ernst Friedrich's anti-war *Krieg dem Kriege* (1924). He later claimed: 'We wanted to see things in a very naked, clear way, almost without any art'.[14]

Several years after the end of the war, in 1924, some fifty of Dix's new drawings were published, under the title of *Der Kreig* (the war). Through these etchings, he delved back into his own memories to re-present dark night-time scenes, glimpses of a wounded soldier, a nocturnal encounter with a madman, storm troopers advancing with gas masks looking like skeletal aliens—images that make for painful, haunting viewing. Dix's realistic art was controversial, described as ugly, sordid and shocking, and sometimes even destroyed. Dix's *Der Schützengraben* (The Trench, 1920–1923) places 'the viewer at a point deep in the trench. Amid death and rotting corpses, the viewer is forced to look up at the gruesome hill of the trench, on top of which hangs a soldier's body impaled on metal stakes'. As Ashley Mullin goes on to observe: 'Dix uses his typical hyper-realistic style in rendering every grotesque minute detail, such as the bloody bullet holes riddling the corpse's legs'.[15] *The Trench* provoked public controversy: initially it was displayed behind a grey curtain and ultimately it was rejected by the museum in Cologne. For a while, it was taken from city to city by activists in a group committed to 'No more war', and then reprinted in the 1925 anthology *Nie wieder Krieg* (No More War). In 1933, the Nazis seized the painting, displayed it as 'painted military sabotage' and probably burnt this piece of 'degenerate' art in or after 1940.[16]

His *War Cripples: 45% fit for service* (*Kriegskrüppel*, 1920) depicts four of the estimated 80,000 disfigured amputees back from the Front. Dix portrays them as uniformed veterans marching in a line along a street, faces disfigured, relying upon crutches, a wheelchair and prosthetic limbs to walk. It was later described by the Nazis as unpatriotic: 'an insult to the German heroes of the Great War' and included in the 1937 'Degenerate Art' exhibition in Munich.[17]

Dix's most powerful surviving response to spending several years in the trenches was created over a decade after the war in his *Triptych* (1929–1932).[18] The central panel portrays a shattered landscape, collapsed buildings, fragments of bodies, skeletons and a burnt-out tree stump. It is reminiscent of the now lost *The Trench*. A skeletal figure with wisps of white shroud-like-cloth dangles from a girder, dominates the painting, and at the same time half frames the devastation below. His arm is outstretched, and his finger points downwards towards a corpse head down, bullet-pocked legs pointing skyward, blood trickling out of its mouth. The dominant colours are white, grey and shades of ochre with traces of fiery red. X-rays reveal the use of many different layers, heavy brushstrokes alongside careful attention to details on the soldiers' uniforms. This is particularly clear on the left panel, where well-equipped soldiers march through ground level mist past a wooden wheel towards uncertain futures up on the Front with a foreboding red-black sky above. X-rays also reveal how Dix initially included tanks and aeroplanes, but removed these to concentrate upon the human forms and their many disfigurements. He even includes himself on the right-side panel. In ghostly white, he cradles a wounded comrade, and his face is half in shadow as he stares out unforgivingly at the viewer.

This painting was a recreation of the many drawings that Dix made while immersed in the conflict (1914–1918), his earlier post-war portrayals of trench warfare (1919–1924) such as *The Trench* (1920–1923), his own memories and famous paintings by the 'masters'. In particular, he appears to be quoting from Grünewald's Isenheim altarpiece (1512–1516). Dix was even described as the 'New Grünewald'.[19] Just as Christ's body was covered by sores, so the legs of the central corpse in Dix's *Triptych* were similarly scarred. Museum curator and art critic, Frédérique Goerig-Hergott, contrasts the pointing finger of John the Baptist in Grünewald's work, which points towards the sacrifice of Christ on the cross, with 'the finger of the dead, impaled man hovering above the sinister, smashed-up landscape in Dix's work', which points towards 'the sacrifice of soldiers at war and, more precisely, at the corpse riddled with bullets, crucified upside down … at the bottom left, the torn-off head of a soldier, surrounded by a crown of barbed wire, is also evocative of Christ'.[20]

During the war, the Isenheim altarpiece was moved to an art gallery in Munich where it became a site of pilgrimage, particularly popular with injured soldiers and grieving relatives.[21] Its return to French Alsace at the end of the war provoked grief, as well as reminding Germans of so many other losses in 1919. It is possible to interpret Dix's *Triptych* as a visual parody of an altarpiece, art which underlines the loss of belief. Another later interpretation, informed by German theologians such as Jürgen Moltmann,[22] is that Christ is not only *with* these fallen soldiers, but also actually there in the soldiers' suffering. From this perspective, the painting becomes an indictment of the whole German valorisation of Roman strength through military might and power: the left panel, with soldiers marching on the Way of the Cross up to a new Calvary, the middle mayhem as a new kind of crucifixion, and the right, with Dix's own form holding a bandaged body, returning from the war, as the deposition and lamentation over the body of Christ. With the *predella*, reminiscent of Holbein's 1521 *Christ in the Tomb*, offering a buried Christ adjacent to two sleeping guards.[23]

Some critics suggested Dix was unpatriotic and defeatist. In response he would claim he was not an anti-war artist or pacifist: 'It was my endeavour to present war objectively, without any desire to invoke pity, without any propagandistic intent'.[24] His desire was for a 'fanatical and impassioned naturalism', along with 'a fervent and unerring truthfulness'.[25] The Triptych was rejected by museums in both Cologne and Berlin. As historian Jay Winter suggests 'allegory was far more powerful than photographic realism' for capturing the apocalyptic and 'infernal character of the Great War'.[26] Dix's representations were too raw, too shocking and too threatening, especially to those who would promote a return to arms in the 1930s.

One of Britain's leading war artists, Paul Nash (1889–1946), also bears witness to what he saw and remembered of the Great War. Nash served near Ypres in 1917. While Dix poured considerable effort into sketching shattered human forms and faces, Nash would become famous for his portrayals of devastated landscapes. Nash was initially as 'excited as a schoolboy' to be at the Front, observing how 'beauty was more poignant'.[27] One night, absorbed in trying to see the results of a bombardment, he accidentally tumbled into a trench and dislocated a rib, which led to his repatriation in 1917. It is probable that this accident saved his life as most of the officers and the rest of his regiment were killed a few days later during the early days of the Battle of Passchendaele (at the Battle for Hill 60). Back in England, Nash worked from his sketches and memory, producing 20 pictures in chalk, ink and watercolours. In these paintings, the natural order has not yet been overwhelmed by war. There are few bodies, although the landscape is punctuated with broken trees. The titles and colours are revealing and include his green and pastoral *Chaos Decoratif* (1917), his predominantly dark brown *Broken Trees, Wytschaete (1917)*, the light brown ground and puddles of white in *The Field of Passchendaele* (1917) and his darkened landscape slightly brightened by a partly obscured sun in *Ruins of the church at Mont St Eloi* (1917).

Returning in November as an official war artist to the Ypres Salient, Nash saw the landscape very differently from how he remembered it from the Spring. His letters home reveal a smouldering rage at what he now saw, a recognition that 'no pen or drawing can convey' the reality of the battlefield, a belief that 'no glimmer of God's hand is seen anywhere'. In the same letter to his wife Margaret, written on 16 November 1917, he describes what he sees as 'unspeakable, godless, hopeless'. He says that his role now is to serve as a witness: 'I am no longer an artist interested and curious - I am a messenger who will bring back word from the men who are fighting to those who want the war to go on forever. Feeble, inarticulate, will be my message, but it will have a bitter truth, and may it burn their lousy souls'.[28]

Over a period of six weeks at the Front, he drew some 50 sketches mostly on brown paper, which would become the basis for his one-person show in May 1918 at the Leicester Galleries in London, entitled *Void of War*. One of his most thought-provoking pieces was displayed in this exhibition; ironically titled, *We are Making a New World* (1918) (Fig. 2.1).

This oil was to become one of the defining and best-known paintings emerging out of the war. Based upon his eye-witness pen and ink drawing *Sunrise, Inverness Copse* (1918) of a devastated landscape near Ypres in Belgium, *We are Making a New World* shows a pale sun illuminating decapitated trees, splintered and deformed, a few spindly branches dangling downwards. They are without leaves. Most are little more than stumps. A single uprooted tree lies dead, fallen across the earth. More like a lunarscape the earth is deformed semi-circular humps and dark patches reminiscent of

Fig. 2.1 Paul Nash, *We are Making a New World* (1918) (© Imperial War Museum [Art. IWM ART 1146])

craters. This sunrise sheds light upon a wasteland. Brown and grey dominate. Here are contours crafted by war. Gravestones made out of earth. There are no visible human forms: representing British soldiers' bodies was prohibited,[29] but the land itself has become a disfigured body with scarred flesh and burnt skin.[30] Unlike Henry Tonks' well-known depictions of soldiers' painfully disfigured faces, Nash used disfigured landscapes to be visual memorials of the costs of war.[31] Nash's childhood love for trees is transformed through this painting into a melancholic and poignant visual elegy for shattered nature. For some historians, paintings such as these bear witness to the end of a Romantic view of nature, and are visual 'elegies for the death of landscape'.[32] For others, this is an example of a 'metaphysical landscape', where the weapons of the machine and industrial age mute visions of pastoralism.[33] Art historian Herbert Read suggests that Nash successfully revealed the war's 'outrage on Nature – the Nature which had been so delicate and sensuous'.[34]

While the official censor, Colonel A. N. Lee, wondered if Nash was having a 'huge joke with the British public, and lovers of 'art' in particular', his exhibition, *Void of War*, met with critical acclaim in 1918. Arnold Bennett in his prefatory note to the exhibition catalogue celebrated Nash's ability to bear witness on the grounds that he has 'seen the Front' and found the 'essentials of it', which are 'disfigurement, danger, desolation, ruin, chaos' with 'little figures of men creeping devotedly and tragically over waste'.[35]

One of Nash's tutors at the Slade School of Art (Henry Tonks) had told him before the war that he couldn't paint the human figure, a criticism that stayed with him, and is perhaps one reason why the human form is rarely depicted by Nash, and when portrayed, they are small like 'human pawns of battle' furtively scurrying between dead trees and oily water in craters.[36] Unlike Christopher Nevinson's *Paths of Glory* (1917) or John Singer Sargent's *Gassed* (1919), in which the human form is at the centre of the painting what dominates Nash's work, according to Bennett, are the 'decapitated trees, the fangs of obdurate masonry, the weight of heavy skies, repeated again and again, monotonously, endlessly'.[37] The wastelands of the '*New World*' that Nash depicts, and other First World War artists portrayed', would be discussed and quoted by later artists.[38] Sophie Ristelhueber's *Iraq* (2001) captures on a photograph a desert forest of decapitated palm trees, puddle-filled shell holes and sand, devoid of humanity.[39]

Nash's experience would have its own psychological effects. After the war, wrestling with his own psychological demons and physical ailments, he experienced a nervous breakdown. His painting continued to provide some comfort, and during the Second World War, he returned to representing the breakages of war, offering a shattered landscape of wings and fuselage of German planes in *Totes Meer* (Dead Sea, 1940–1941). Some see this as propagandistic and triumphalist, but for others, it reveals the breaks in Nash's own psyche.

For both Dix and Nash there was a considerable emotional and psychological cost to bearing witness. Their artistic visions of the 'great seminal catastrophe'[40] of the twentieth century, over one hundred years after Dix and Nash painted *Triptych* and *We are Making a New World*, still stand as a vivid reminder of the horrors of war. There is, however, an emotional distance in both Dix and Nash's work which makes it hard to identify closely with the characters or landscapes depicted.

Remembering Grief, Suffering and Anger

By contrast to Dix and Nash, the works of non-combatant artists show how responding emotionally and by expressing deep personal feelings of grief and anger can be a way to protest against war. Closely connected to bearing witness, powerful emotional reactions to conflict can inspire a desire to work for peace. Some suffering is not easily translated. As with many of the war poets, the four years of conflict transformed the ways artists expressed themselves. In the shadows of the First World War, visual artists drew upon, combined and adapted a range of styles (including Expressionism, Cubism and Vorticism) and a variety of media (oil paintings, watercolours and sculptures), in a wide range of public and private spaces, to express what they had seen and felt. For example, Käthe Kollwitz's (1867–1945) *Grieving Parents* statues, at Vladslo cemetery in Belgium, offer a window onto grief (Fig. 2.2).

These statues are composed of two larger than life pale grey granite figures kneeling on granite blocks. It is possible to walk between them. Like two separate silent Egyptian statues or giant sombre Lewis chessmen, they put a question mark over art that recalls war as epitomized by heroic sacrifice. The female figure, based on Käthe herself, stares down towards the ground. She clutches one hand tight to her chest, just below her neck. The other hand is obscured by her large cloak that enfolds her body and her sadness. A few feet away a man (Karl, Käthe's doctor husband) also kneels stiffly, looking outwards towards one of the numerous flat memorials stones, each of which has twenty names inscribed on it. Karl appears to be

Fig. 2.2 Käthe Kollwitz, *Grieving Parents*, 1932 (© Photo Jean Mil—Belgium)

focusing on one that includes the name of their 18-year-old son Peter Kollwitz, who fell early in the war at Flanders in November 1914. He is one of 25,644 soldiers now buried at Vladslo cemetery in Belgium near Ypres.[41]

Käthe Kollwitz declared in the month following his death that she would create a memorial sculpture for her son Peter, 'There is in our lives a wound, a wound which will never heal. Nor should it'.[42] From reading Kollwitz's diaries and letters it is clear that in the years following she experimented with several different designs for Peter's memorial. At first, the figures were portrayed close together, but she separated them to highlight the distancing effect of grief. She struggled with deciding where to place and how to represent her son's body, especially in relation to his father Karl's and her own figures. Part of the reason for her wrestling with this task was her growing sense of unease with glorifying the cult that promoted 'heroic sacrifices'. Moreover, she increasingly felt guilt for her role in letting him go and thereby cutting the 'umbilical cord' a second time that would result in his premature death.[43] By October 1916 she would write of the 'frightful insanity' of 'the youth of Europe hurling themselves at one another', and that she could now 'only see insanity in the war'. This understanding leads her to wonder: 'Is it a breach of faith with you Peter, if I can only see madness in the war?' After the war she put this project to one side, producing a series of black and white wood engravings *Die Krieg* (The War, 1921–1923), which included one with parents not separated by, but clasped together in grief (*Die Eltern*, The Parents, 1921–1922). Several other posters drew attention to famines in Russia and Austria, as well as

Germany's Children Are Starving (1924). Her depiction of a woman shouting *Nie Wieder Krieg* (No More War, 1924) was widely reproduced,[44] and with her other prints influenced artists as far afield as China.[45]

It took Kollwitz eighteen years, about the same amount of time as Peter had lived, to produce the simple and poignant memorial, *Grieving Parents*. When she visited the cemetery where they were originally placed in July 1932 she 'stood before the woman, looked at her, my own face. I wept and touched her cheeks'. She did not notice her husband, Karl, just behind her, until he simply whispered: 'Yes. Yes'. These statues are more than simply an expression of grief. They are also perhaps a confession of guilt and a request for forgiveness for members of a generation who encouraged, or at least did not discourage, their sons from enlisting to fight. In this way, they offer a distinctive way of remembering those lost, those left behind and the conflagration that had caused their suffering and deaths.

On the twenty-third anniversary of Peter's death, Kollwitz wrote in her diary in 1937: 'I am working on a small sculpture which has developed out of my attempt to make a sculpture of an old person. It has become something like a Pietà. The mother is seated and has her dead son lying between her knees in her lap. There is no longer pain - only reflection'. Unlike her public *Grieving Parents*, where the body is absent, in her sculpted *Mother with Dead Son* the body nestles back into an all-encompassing, cloaked female form. Kollwitz appears to have developed her earlier drawings of a mother holding her dead child who was modelled upon Peter as a young child (Lithograph, *Woman with Dead Child*, 1903). Similarly, in the 1937 version, the mother is not offering her son as a sacrificial victim, like so many other Pietàs, rather she is in grief holding him close while also shielding him (Fig. 2.3).

Remembering wisely can be both a complicated and a contested practice. This can be seen in the reactions to the choice by Chancellor Helmut Kohl in 1993 to have this small bronze Pietà-like sculpture enlarged fivefold (by Harald Haacke) and then placed in the central wreath laying space in Berlin, at *Neue Wache* (the New Watch or Royal Guard house building), as a memorial: 'To victims of war and tyranny'.[46] Critics of Kohl's choice pointed out that Kollwitz had not intended her sculpture to be used as a national memorial, that when so many of the victims of tyranny had been Jewish, the *Pietà* form was too Christian a symbol, and that its referent points were too limited (a soldier's mother from the First World War). Such was the controversy, that a few weeks before it was to be unveiled in 1993, it was agreed that a separate memorial for Jewish victims would be

Fig. 2.3 Käthe Kollwitz, *Mother with her Dead Son* (original 1937, enlarged by Harald Haacke in 1993) (© Photo Jolyon Mitchell)

created. A bronze plaque and multi-lingual explanatory notices were also placed by the door of the *Neue Wache* detailing those who 'have suffered because of war'.[47] In this way, Kollwitz's artistic expression of her personal memories and private grief were universalized. Just as the mother failed to protect her son, so for many the German State, the *Vaterland*, failed to protect her peoples.

It is clear from the heated discussions around this memorial, remembering suffering through the visual arts can become a highly contested practice. Nevertheless, by provoking strong emotions and vivid memories, sculptures such as these highlight the human costs of conflict. Through her art, Kollwitz particularized and personalized the war. In the jumble of universalistic and patriotic discourses which promoted the war, she moves beyond those tropes, and offers memorable particularities. Such is its honesty that it is hard to 'look away from the pain' that she re-presents.[48] Like *The Grieving Parents*,[49] it continues to provoke strong responses, as can be heard in a 2018 BBC Radio 4 Documentary, *The World in 3D*. One respondent described how *Mother with Dead Son* works in a far more subtle way than the desensitizing deluge of images on the news of 'blood and death'. His observation moves from the particular to the universal. For him, this sculpture represents 'every war, and every child that was ever lost in the war, and the meaninglessness of that. It is just heart-breaking'.[50]

In 1937, the same year that Kollwitz had created her small and secular 'Pietà', one of Europe's best-known artists would produce perhaps Europe's best-known piece of anti-war art. Pablo Picasso, shocked by what he read in the newspapers and saw in magazines about a three-hour-long aerial bombing of a small town in the Basque Region, created *Guernica*.[51]

He transformed his 1937 Paris International Exposition commission into an artistic expression of grief, protest and rage.[52] In about forty days of extraordinary creative activity, he filled almost thirty square metres of canvas. Through this black, grey and white picture, Picasso not only bears witness to the horrors of the Spanish Civil War,[53] he also anticipates the impact of conflict upon civilian populations in the Second World War soon to follow. The viewer is offered a disjointed collection of disturbing and confusing shapes: open mouths and dilated eyes, clasping fingers and extended hands. Human and animal forms are muddled together. A screeching bird and an impaled horse are juxtaposed with flat human faces that speak of disbelief, shock and agony. Beneath a grotesque bull a female figure, head arched upwards, cradles a baby dangling lifeless like a rag-doll. Unlike Kollwitz's secular *Pietà*, the mother's form is not sheltering the child's corpse. The woman appears to be screaming against the heavens, her tongue shaped like an accusing dagger.[54] For some writers, this should be interpreted as 'a secular Madonna placed' in the centre of a deeply troubling news event,[55] where the horse's body is created out of fading newspaper. Some interpreters have challenged the claim that Picasso was creating an anti-war picture, but as John Gittings points out, 'even while at work on the picture' Picasso 'said that it expressed his "abhorrence of the military caste which has sunk Spain into an ocean of pain and death"'.[56]

It is striking to compare Picasso's *Guernica* with the *Hiroshima Panels* (Genbaku no Zu, 1950–1982) painted by a Japanese husband and wife (Iri and Toshi Maruki), who lost their uncle, nieces and many friends through the Atomic bombs dropped on Japan in August 1945.[57] Within a few days of the first attack, they were in Hiroshima helping the injured and cremating the dead. Three years later they began to 'paint what they had seen', employing a form of traditional Japanese art, using brush, black ink and white paper, which they sometimes mixed with red, to represent the atomic fire (see the second panel, *Fire*, 1950). Toshi Akamatsu Maruki (1912–2000) described why they decided to embark on this project that grew to a total of 15 large panels made up of 8 screens: 'We painted the bomb because we had seen Hiroshima, and we thought there had to be some records of what had happened'.[58]

These large, haunting portrayals are full of emotional power and poignancy. Viewers are forced into a troubling engagement with the victims: a sister hugs her sibling, a pile of children's bodies lie untended; mothers hold their dying or dead babies. The artists wrote vivid commentary to accompany aspects of each scene:

> Wounded mother and dead infant,
> the statue of despair.
> Let the mother and child be
> a symbol of hope as it has always been.
> It must be![59]

There is little obvious hope to be found in these panels, except perhaps the continued expressions of love, care and human affection through unimaginable suffering and horror. They later described how they had experienced and painted 'hell'. Their work has been the subject of several documentaries[60] and is sometimes now re-presented alongside music composed in response to the attacks.[61] The Panels were exhibited in over two hundred locations in Japan during the early 1950s. They would later be shown in America, Europe, Asia, Africa and Australia.

While the mushroom cloud itself became one of the icons of the twentieth century, the 'panels showed close up the horror of the effects on a civilian population', and some critics believed they brought together Eastern and Western styles of art, as they wanted 'to influence viewers to think about peace'.[62] Yukinori Okamura, the curator of the Maruki Gallery where the panels are normally housed, wrote:

> It is a seed that can grow into a new world view.

> The seed may be small, but it can be the beginning of everything.[63]

While these panels serve partly as a memorial, reminding us of the terrible effects of nuclear violence, they also serve as an incitement towards peace.

Picasso's portrayal of *Guernica* can also be interpreted as a memorial. Precisely how many women, children and men were killed in the attack on the village of Guernica on 26 April 1937 is still debated, possibly as many as 1000. However many died on that fateful market day in Gernika (Basque spelling), Picasso's painting has become not only a memorial, but also a warning of what happens when, what in the following century would be described as 'shock and awe' is dropped from the skies. The complete original picture itself is now housed in Madrid's Museo Reina Sofia, and it is widely available online. Known internationally as *Guernica* it has become part of popular culture, with its own biography.[64]

The tapestry copy of *Guernica*, housed at the United Nations in New York, was shrouded with blue curtains when Colin Powell attempted to justify the American case for the invasion of Iraq in February 2003. Afterwards, it was described by one commentator as an 'inconvenient masterpiece'.[65] Copies of the image of the woman cradling the dead child were later used in protests against the Iraq War. The huge picture has been reduced, copied and circulated digitally and on many different kinds of materials, including stamps, posters, and shirts. At the top of the painting is a bare light-bulb, like an iris and pupil, in the middle of an open eye. The word in Spanish for electric bulb, *bombia*, is reminiscent in English of what was dropped from the skies. This painting sheds light onto violent darkness, but near a severed arm clutching a broken sword there is one tiny glimpse of hope, hard to discern at first glance: a small flower.

Representing Peace-Building

In this third section, I consider the role that the arts can play in offering realistic visions of how to create peace. Some artists use portrayals of violence and the effects of conflict as a way of promoting peace, while some offer utopian perspectives, and a few have attempted to show concrete ways in which peace can be built.

So far I have concentrated on visual arts born out of the artists' close involvement with violence by actual participants or by close observers. The very existence of their art, often full of disturbing beauty, not only bears witness to heartbreak and reminds viewers of the cost of conflict but also represents a small seed of hope. Implied in their creation is the unstated assertion that the world should not be dominated by violence. Other kinds of art go beyond being simply against war. Some show how weapons of violence can be transformed.

Different projects have found ways of transforming arms into art.[66] Best known is the initiative that emerged in Mozambique, following the sixteen-year civil war (1976–1992). This example is worth recounting. Lengthy peace negotiations eventually brought a cessation to fighting, but several million weapons were kept hidden by people as insurance against a return to conflict. An Anglican Bishop, Denis Sengulane, was concerned that this was like keeping a snake at home which one day would awaken, only to bite the population again. He worked with Christian Aid to establish a scheme whereby Mozambicans were encouraged to hand over their weapons in 'exchange for items like ploughs, bicycles and sewing machines. One village gave up all its weapons in exchange for a tractor'.[67] Even children exchanged old bullets for pencils. Over half a million weapons were handed in and then decommissioned. Observing how often art has been used to glorify war, Bishop Sengulane approached local Mozambican artists and asked: 'What about using your skills to glorify peace? We have got these guns – could you see whether you could convey a message of peace by using the bits and pieces of these guns?'[68]

These local artists transformed many of the weapons into works of art, including metallic birds, crocodiles and even a pianist playing. Best-known are the *Tree of Life* and the *Throne of Weapons*, which can now be seen at the British Museum in London.[69] Both are made up of weapons originally produced outside Mozambique, but used during the Civil War. They not only act as memorials for the one million victims but they also embody more hopeful and peaceful imaginings. In 2005–2006 the *Throne* was taken around the UK, exhibited in ten museums, nine schools, and various other settings, each with their own local histories of violence such as the Ulster Museum in Belfast, Pentonville Prison in London and Coventry Cathedral on Remembrance Sunday. Over 100,000 people saw the *Throne* while it was on tour, many responded through poetry, prose or music.[70] Others participated in discussions, workshops and debates. Peripatetic art became a catalyst for discussions about building peace. As audiences interacted with it creatively or critically, the *Throne* took on new layers of meaning.[71] The practice of transforming arms into art has been replicated around the world, including in Cambodia, the USA and Iraq.[72]

This artistic vision is very different from the devastated worlds re-created by the likes of Dix, Nash and Picasso. In the light of their creations, one could add to Michael O'Neill's assertion that: 'nothing can mend a war, no words wish it away',[73] but while the transformation of weapons into art also cannot 'wish war away', it can contribute to a symbolic landscape that offers alternatives to the way of the gun. These creations, while not denying agonizing violent pasts, can nevertheless point towards more peaceful futures.

The sculpture by Josefina de Vasconcellos (1904–2005), originally a small bronze titled *Reunion* (1955), was inspired by her reading a newspaper account of a woman who had crossed Europe on foot to find her husband. The sculptress was so moved that she created what she then thought 'wasn't only about the reunion of two people but hopefully a reunion of nations which had been fighting'.[74] As a gift to the newly established Peace Studies department at the University of Bradford, it was renamed in 1977: *Reconciliation*.

Fifty years after the end of the Second World War the sculpture would be repaired (1994) and also recast in bronze (1995). New versions were placed in Coventry Cathedral's ruins, as well as in the peace garden in Hiroshima (fifty years after the dropping of the Atomic bomb), and later in the grounds of Belfast's Stormont castle. There is even hope that another version will one day be placed in Jerusalem. To mark the opening of Berlin's rebuilt *Reichstag* and the tenth anniversary of Wall's fall another cast was placed at the Berlin Wall memorial (1999, Fig. 2.4). This is located in the former 'death strip' close to the place where the Protestant Church of the Reconciliation had originally stood, but which was demolished in 1985. Some of the rubble from the original church was used to make up the plinth. Unlike other versions, upon the plinth lies a bible, cast by Vasconcellos from an open bible found in the ruins. It is placed between the two figures, and the bible itself is wrapped in barbed wire. For the artist, this was a way of representing the divisions that still need to be overcome in order for there to be real reconciliation.

Some artists create utopian worlds permeated with 'a plenitude of overflowing serenity'.[75] At first sight, the series of *The Peaceable Kingdom* series by the Quaker artist Edward Hicks (1780–1849) looks as if it is living up to its title. These paintings appear to portray a peaceful gathering, including at least one lion and leopard, with lamb and baby goat, along with a young child, all close together and in apparent harmony. However, study the evolution of his depictions over his 62 existing representations of *The Peaceable*

Fig. 2.4 Josefina de Vasconcellos, *Reconciliation* (1999, cast based upon a small 1955 bronze and 1977 sculpture) (© Photo Jolyon Mitchell)

Kingdom (painted between 1816–1849) and it is possible to discern how they are becoming less peaceable. The lion looks increasingly tired and the leopard even growls aggressively in one painting (1847). Some art historians interpret this as a sign of Hick's fatigue with his own divided Quaker denomination and his increased pessimism regarding hopes for reconciliation.[76]

Peace-making, peace-keeping and peace-building are long and complex processes. Representing these processes visually can be almost as complicated as creating conditions for actual sustainable peace. Peace-making, whether at the grass-roots, at mid-level or at elite levels, takes time and is not always successful. William Orpen's depiction of *the Signing of Peace in the Hall of Mirrors, Versailles, 28 June 1919*, reveals some 30 male faces, politicians, diplomats, soldiers and at least one journalist, who had all attended Versailles (Fig. 2.5).

Fig. 2.5 William Orpen, *The Signing of Peace in the Hall of Mirrors, Versailles, 28 June 1919.* (1919) (© Imperial War Museum [Art. IWM ART 2856])

They are dwarfed by Louis XIV's lavish room, especially by the mirrors behind and gold ornamentation above the arches. The imposed treaty conditions were received with disbelief in Germany. For many Germans, it was a 'disgraceful treaty' (as described by the newspaper *Deutsche Zeitung*, 28

June 1919), particularly the 'war guilt' Clause 231, that would sow the seeds for future conflict. While Orpen's painting does not anticipate the ultimate failure of the attempted peace-making, the distorted reflections of the mirrors hint at the limitations of what had been achieved, the difficulties of a top-down approach to peace-making and Orpen's own frustration with the participants' inability to recognize and to respect the sufferings of the soldiers. The disabled and disfigured French soldiers who were brought to the signing of the treaty are left out of the frame.

As part of his three painting commission, which earned him £3000 (10 times more than John Singer Sargent earned [only £300] for his considerably larger 1919 *Gassed*), Orpen created *To the Unknown British Soldier in France* (1921–1928). Simplified in the light of criticism, it became a single coffin draped with a union jack, lying in a lofty and ornate marble hall, beneath a chandelier, in front of an arch that leads into a dark corridor with a sliver of light in the distance. The role of peace-makers and peace-keepers is commonly less dramatic than that of soldiers in action and therefore less appealing to many artists.[77] Orpen's painting provides a stark reminder of the loss and suffering behind many attempts to make and to keep peace.

If peace-making and peace-keeping are not easy to represent visually, peace-building is like a complex tapestry and is even harder to depict. Creating environments where sustainable and lasting peace can be built goes far beyond the signing of peace treaties and the deployment of military monitors, to face underlying structural, cultural and societal issues. These include tackling powerful emotions and sensitivities, revisiting dangerous memories, and establishing legal constraints; as well as rebuilding infrastructure, utilities and education systems, demobilizing and disarming former fighters; alongside helping heal damaged bodies, souls, communities and environments.

A series of late medieval, early Renaissance, frescoes by Ambrogio Lorenzetti, that show the effects of both good and bad government (1338–1339),[78] bring to life the benefits and complexities of building peace, as well as the costs of resorting to war (Fig. 2.6). They were initially commissioned by the ruling council of the Nine to celebrate the power of Siena and the value of their own good governance[79] and are still displayed in Siena's Town Hall (*Palazzo Pubblico*) in the Salon of Nine (*Sala dei Nove*). They underline how both city and countryside will flourish in conditions of peace, or decay and die when overrun by violence and poor governance.

In the fresco on *The Effects of Good Government on the City and Country*, the city dominated by peace, shops are open, artisans are working, students

Fig. 2.6 Ambrogio Lorenzetti, *The Effects of Good Government on the City and Country* (1338–1339) (© Photo Sebastian Mitchell)

are being educated, as children play and adults relax (see Fig. 2.6a). Some chat or dance, while others calmly process on horseback in front of peaceful bystanders.[80] Other riders move down from the city into a world of activity in the Tuscan countryside.[81] Activities of different seasons are brought together into one picture, as the land is ploughed, the crops collected and the fruit of the land tended (see Fig. 2.6b). It is not surprising that many peace scholars discuss these murals in considerable detail.[82]

While not as horrific as Dix's trenches or as scarred as Nash's landscapes, the poorly governed city and the countryside dominated by war illustrate the costs of the failure to build peace. Even though the fresco is damaged and harder to make out, the murals reveal how in a city of bad governance order has broken down, buildings are damaged or in ruins,

Fig. 2.6a Ambrogio Lorenzetti, *The Effects of Good Government on the City* (1338–1339) (© Photo Sebastian Mitchell)

Fig. 2.6b Ambrogio Lorenzetti, *The Effects of Good Government on the Country* (1338–1339) (© Photo Sebastian Mitchell)

and fields untended as soldiers run riot, children are hungry. They have a long history of interpretation. They are clearly celebrating a certain kind of social control, that may use Justice, with the support of state-sanctioned violence, such as capital punishment to try and ensure peace is kept. One of the earliest uses of the entire series of frescoes to critique the effects of war and promote peace is to be found in a sermon preached in Sienna during Lent in 1425 by Bernardino da Siena (1380–1444), focusing on the 'destruction and waste of war':

> When I was outside of Siena, and preached about peace and war, I reflected on the beautiful inventiveness of the [Peace and War] frescoes that you painted. When I turn to Peace, I see commercial activity; I see dances, I see houses being repaired; I see vineyards and fields being cultivated and sown, I see people going to the baths, on horses, I see girls going to marry, I see flocks of the sheep… On the other hand, when I turn to the other I do not see commerce; I do not see dances, [I see] killing; no houses being repaired, [they are] damaged and burnt; the fields are not being cultivated; the vineyards are cut down; there is no sowing, the baths are not used nor [are there] other delights, I do not see anyone going out. Oh women! Oh men! The man is dead, the woman raped, the herds are prey [to predators]; men treacherously kill one another; Justice lies on the ground, her scales broken, she is bound, her hands and legs are bound. And everything is done with fear.[83]

War is portrayed here not as a civilizing force or something which establishes peace. It does the opposite. War is depicted in these frescoes, and is later interpreted by this Italian Franciscan preacher, as something which interrupts the natural cycles of the land, which is despoiled and diminished, and halts human flourishing. Bernardino also celebrates the violence of the man hanging from the scaffold of Justice, but otherwise, the effects of conflict are vividly critiqued. Why did Bernardino, in his sermon, focus more on war, rather than what many others have done in response to these frescoes and discuss in greater detail the images of peace? 'Bernardino was preaching during a period of political instability and civic strife in Siena', according to Nirit Debby, he therefore 'concentrated on the most urgent problem of the day, that of internal conflict'.[84] Even if this was not the original reason for their painting, it illustrates how striking depictions can be put to different uses. Put these allegorical pictures together and even the twenty-first-century viewer is still offered a vivid reminder of the dangers of war and the benefits of peace.

But what of the location of peace-promoting art? These frescoes, depicting the effects of war and peace, are housed inside the medieval town hall. Many of the other works discussed earlier are also to be found indoors, displayed in art galleries or museums. This may protect them from the elements, but it also excludes many people from seeing them. Certain forms of art are more exposed to being seen in public. There is a long tradition of art on public walls, some of which is used to promote peace. Contemporary murals in Northern Ireland have been used to portray not only sectarian identities and divides as well as bearing witness to past violence, but also the search for peace and justice. In Belfast and Derry (Londonderry), several local artists, from both nationalist and unionist traditions, have worked together to create 'peace' murals in proximity to historic sectarian images, as well as newly painted images of men with balaclavas and guns (see Chapter 4).[85] In London, 'peace' murals in Brixton and Broadwater have contributed to the rebuilding of communities divided by riots. Like all outdoor art, they compete with wind, rain and building projects. They are not always easy to see, such as the 'Nuclear Dawn' murals (c.1982) in Brixton which are only partly visible.

In Edinburgh, by contrast, some 170 murals painted over 30 years by 'Artists for Justice and Peace' annually on display during the Festival weeks on the outside of St John's Episcopal Church on Princes Street, are highly visible, and have provoked national debate. Their prominence is compounded by the numbers of passers-by during the festival season, which can increase to over half a million viewers in the space of a month. The location of visual art matters. Banksy's controversial graffiti murals on the dividing wall or 'separation barrier' on the West Bank or his guerrilla art emerging out of the rubble in Gaza offers visions of more peaceful spaces and playful characters than are usually observable in the divided local Palestinian community.[86] Their digital ubiquity allows his art to go beyond the walls that are used to separate.

Ashley Rawson's *Glasgow Kiss* (c.2003) depicts a man and woman, one in a blue Rangers football top and the other in a green and white striped Celtic jersey passionately kissing under a moonlit sky, an empty bottle of Buckfast tonic wine at their feet. Flying above them in front of a hazy full moon is a dove. The title *Glasgow Kiss* is playful, as a '*Glesga Kiss*' normally refers to an aggressive head butt. This image is now regularly sold as a print to passers-by in at least one central Glasgow shopping centre. Rawson hopes this image can assist in the 'fight against sectarianism', by emphasizing that 'love conquers all', and showing 'we don't have to choose to hate each other'.[87] The surprise here is that two Old Firm fans, supporters of the arch-rival football clubs of Rangers and Celtic who would more often be represented as bitter enemies, are instead depicted embracing (Fig. 2.7).

Ashley Rawson's *Glasgow Kiss* is very different artistically from Josefina de Vasconcellos's sculpture of a *Reunion/Reconciliation*, but their intended peaceful aims resonate with each other. An embrace, a kiss, a lion and a lamb, a group of politicians, all represent different kinds of symbols used in the building of peace. Oil, canvas and bronze seem like weak materials when compared to weighty weapons of war, and yet their very lack of obvious physical power may be part of their unexpected strength, as they can inspire imaginings of a world where weapons can be transformed into art and divided communities can communicate through walls.

Fig. 2.7 Ashley Rawson, *Glasgow Kiss* (c.2003) (© Photo Ashley Rawson)

Conclusion

Up to this point, we have seen how the visual arts can bear witness to the costs of violent conflict. Both realism and heightened realism are used to reflect back realities that we may overlook, be ignorant of, or would rather ignore. Visual representations can be a channel by which anger and grief are expressed. Whether it is paintings of disfigured bodies or shattered landscapes, granite statues of grieving parents or a vast canvas shedding light on a screaming mother, raw emotion has been translated into new forms. These translations are not ways to tame overwhelmingly powerful emotions of loss or rage, rather they are invitations to look hard at events we might prefer to forget. Many artists appear almost to force us to face up to the reality of suffering. In some cases, it may have been years since the event, but the picture can ensure that emotion is made raw again, as we stand again with grieving parents and traumatized communities. Each image is an invitation to become witnesses, to face the shattered land, the grieving parent, or the torn apart soldier.

The result of such visual creativity is hard to predict. Looking, seeing, even touching these creations may provoke strong emotions, but interacting with such art does not necessarily lead to the building of peace. Showing the picture of an embrace in conflict situations in order to encourage reconciliation may provoke anything but a desire for peace, especially when there are strong feelings of unresolved injustice. Seeing through art and then imagining a peaceful future, is not the same as inhabiting a peaceful environment. Audiences interact in many different ways with what they see, making meaning in new and unexpected ways with what they look at and hear.[88] Nevertheless, the visual arts can contribute to creating both imaginative and realistic environments that invite or encourage viewers to step into others worlds, to go beyond historic divides and to imagine why a peaceful future is worth working for.

In communicative environments where rapidly moving and ever-changing representations of spectacular violence often dominate consciousness, pictorial art can offer thought-provoking alternatives to contemporary news reports and painful historical memories. At first sight, these paintings and sculptures may be perceived as 'old fashioned' media, offering unexpected perspectives, especially to younger viewers. There is clearly a distinction between art that is shown in a gallery and art that is available in public space and digital spaces. Considering how architecture, video, digital and online art, can contribute to building peace is largely beyond the

Fig. 2.8 Maurice Harron, *Hands Across the Divide* (1992) (Photo Courtesy of CAIN [cain.ulster.ac.uk])

scope of this essay, but is worthy of further careful consideration.[89] With ever expanding new digital media, old art finds new venues. Just as street art, such as murals and graffiti, become accessible to far wider audiences. These dynamic, creative active processes have the potential to interrupt and interrogate both power and communities in conflict. Certain kinds of street art and digital art are more 'anti-war' in form than 'peace-building', but such creations can also be among the first steps towards building peace. The move from separated individuals or communities divided by grief, guilt and anger, to individuals or communities able to embrace over barbed wire, can take generations.

In Derry (Londonderry), Northern Ireland, there is a piece of art in which two figures are neither separate (as with Kollwitz's *Grieving Parents)*, nor embracing (as with Vasconcellos' *Reconciliation*), or kissing (as with Dawson's *Glasgow Kiss*): they reach out towards each other, arms outstretched, hands not quite touching. Maurice Harron's *Hands Across the Divide* (1992), unveiled twenty years after Bloody Sunday,[90] captures not only the ongoing divisions in Northern Ireland (even after the Good Friday agreement of 10 April 1998) but also the desire for peace.[91] Its power lies in its simplicity and its ambiguity, reflecting both the possibility and the difficulty of building links across divided communities (Fig. 2.8).

Significantly, using two simple human figures, it also shows how art can capture the hope for peace. A tree made out of weapons originally designed to kill, or a fresco offering visions of a peaceful cityscape, or a sculptured tentative embrace are all equally inspiring. They may be redolent of ambiguity and recalling heartbreak. They may provoke painful memorials, highlighting the long shadows caused by conflict. As the historian Margaret MacMillan suggests the arts are 'very good at showing the ambiguities of war'.[92] As has become clear through this chapter, they are also very good at highlighting the ambiguities and complexities of peace. Nevertheless, amid the countless historic and contemporary images of suffering and violence, such visual representations have the potential, at least, to become small, fragile flowers of hope emerging out of the rubble of broken swords and shattered bodies. Easily overshadowed by the devastation that is around them, they can nonetheless help viewers imagine and then work for a more peaceful world.

Notes

1. John Ruskin, *The Crown of Wild Olive* (London: George Allen, 1904), 116–120. While war can obviously be both a background to and a catalyst for the arts, the generalised nature of Ruskin's assertions are clearly open to critical questioning.
2. See, for example, paintings such as *Vive L'Empereur* (1891) [also known as *Charge of the 4th Hussars at the Battle of Friedland, 14 June 1807*] by the French military artist Jean-Baptiste Édouard Detaille (1848–1912), who some believe influenced Trego, discussed below in this essay.
3. Oil on Canvas, also known as: *Bringing Up the Battery*; *Artillery to the Front*; *Civil War Battle Scene*. James A. Michener Art Museum, Doylestown, PA.
4. See John Paul Lederach, *The Moral Imagination: The Art and Soul of Building Peace* (Oxford, UK: Oxford University Press, 2005). See also Jolyon Mitchell, *Promoting Peace, Inciting Violence: The Role of Religion and Media* (London, UK: Routledge, 2012), 7–8.
5. Margaret McKechnie-Glover, "Artists as Peace Activists", in *The Oxford International Encyclopedia of Peace*, ed. Nigel Young (Oxford, UK: Oxford University Press, 2010). See also Margaret Glover, *Images of Peace in Britain: From the Late Nineteenth Century to the Second World War* (Unpublished PhD Thesis: University of Reading, 2002). Volume 1: 378 and volume

2: 474. For an illustrated consideration of British Artists who were conscientious objectors during the First and Second World Wars see Gill Clarke, *Conflicting Views: Pacificist Artists* (Bristol: Sansom and Co, 2018).

6. See Jane Dillenberger and John Handley, *The Religious Art of Pablo Picasso* (Berkeley: University of California Press, 2014), 69–71.
7. Oil on canvas, also known as: *French Dragoons Charging; la garde du drapeau*, West Point Museum Art Collection, United States Military Academy, West Point, New York.
8. See, for example, Charles Fripp's 1885 portrayal of *The Battle of Isandlwana, 1879.* This painting shows a huddle of red-coated British soldiers, some dying or dead, being overwhelmed by a force of Zulu warriors. See Peter Harrington, *British Artists and War: The Face of Battle in Paintings and Prints, 1700–1914* (London, UK: Greenhill Books, 1993).
9. Several of these movements were explored through an exhibition at Tate Britain in 2018. See Emma Chambers, ed., *Aftermath: Art in the Wake of World War One* (London, UK: Tate Publishing, 2018).
10. Helen Gardner, *Gardner's Art Through the Ages* (New York: Harcourt, Brace & World, 1970), 1035.
11. Fritz Loffler, *Otto Dix: Life and Work*, trans. R.J. Hollingdale (New York: Holmes and Meier, 1982), 66. See also John Willet, "Dix: War", in Susan Brades and Roger Malbert (eds.), *Disasters of War: Callot, Goya and Dix* (Manchester: Cornerhouse Publications, 1998), 57–75.
12. Museum director Gustav Hartlaub coined the term *Neue Sachlichkeit* to describe a travelling exhibition he created, which included seven works by Dix. It is hard to translate precisely but is sometimes read as meaning a "matter of factness" or representing things as they actually are. See Nils Buttner, ed., *Otto Dix and the New Objectivity* (Stuttgart, Germany: Hatje Cantz, 2013).
13. See Loffler, *Otto Dix: Life and Work*, 70. Goya's (1746–1828) pictures were not published until 1863, 35 years after his death. See also Susan Sontag's discussion in *Regarding the Pain of Others* (London, UK: Penguin, 2004 [2003]); D.J.R Bruckner, Seymour Chwast, and Steven Heller, *Art Against War: 400 Years of Protest in Art* (New York, NY: Abbeville Press, 1984).
14. Buttner, *Otto Dix and the New Objectivity*, 11.
15. Ashley Mullen, "Otto Dix's *The Trench* and Anti-War Art in Post-World War 1 Germany", *Bowdoin Journal of Art* (2015): 9.
16. See "Lost Art: Otto Dix, *The Trench* 1920–1923", https://www.tate.org.uk/art/art-terms/n/neue-sachlichkeit/lost-art-otto-dix, accessed 1 May 2018.
17. Stephanie Barron, ed., "*Degenerate Art*": *The Fate of the Avant-Garde in Nazi Germany* (New York, NY: Harry N. Abrams, 1991), 54.
18. Otto Dix, *Triptychon Der Krieg (War Triptych)*, 1929–1932, tempera on wood, central panel 204 × 204 cm, side panels 204 × 102 cm

each, Gemäldegalerie Neue Meister, Dresden. See https://albertinum.skd.museum/en/exhibitions/archive/der-krieg/ and https://artsandculture.google.com/asset/the-war/CwHM2HdTO3l2vg?hl=en-GB, accessed 7 January 2019.

19. See Mullen, "Otto Dix's *The Trench* and Anti-War Art in Post-World War 1 Germany", 10.
20. Frédérique Goerig-Hergott, "Otto Dix: Painting to Exorcise War", at Arts & Societies Seminar Conjuring Away War, 3 March 2013, http://www.artsetsocietes.org/a/a-goerig.html Also cited by Philip McCouat, "The Isenheim Altarpiece Pt 2: Nationalism, Nazism and Degeneracy", *Journal of Art in Society*, www.artinsociety.com, accessed 17 August 2015.
21. See Ann Stieglitz, "The Reproduction of Agony: Toward a Reception-History of Grünewald's Isenheim Altar After the First World War", *Oxford Art Journal* 12:2 (1989): 87–103.
22. See Jürgen Moltmann, *The Crucified God*, Revised edition (London, UK: SCM, 2001).
23. Nils Buttner, "From the Trenches into New Objectivity", in *Otto Dix and the New Objectivity*, ed. Buttner 82.
24. Fritz Löffler and Otto Dix, *Otto Dix, Life and Work* (New York, NY: Holmes & Meier, 1982), 66.
25. Otto Dix, *War Journal*, from entry on 1 August 1918. Cited in *Otto Dix: 1891–1996*, *exh. Cat.* (London, UK: 1992), 106.
26. Jay Winter, *Sites of Memory, Sites of Mourning: The Great War in European Cultural History* (Cambridge, UK: Cambridge University Press, 1995), 159–164.
27. See Merrion and Susie Harries, *The War Artists* (London, UK: Michael Joseph, IWM and Tate, 1983), 56. Nash wrote to his wife Margaret on 7 March 1917: "I am happier in the trenches than anywhere out here. It sounds absurd, but life has a greater meaning out here and a new zest, and beauty is more poignant". Cited in Toby Thacker, *British Culture and the First World War: Experience, Representation and Memory* (London, UK: Bloomsbury, 2014), 164.
28. See Paul Nash, *Outline: An Autobiography and Other Writings* (London, UK: Faber & Faber, 1949), 1–271 and 211. See also Andrew Causey, *Paul Nash Landscape and the Life of Objects* (Farnham, UK: Ashgate, 2013) and Richard Cork, *A Bitter Truth—Avant Garde Art and the Great War* (New Haven, CT: Yale University Press and The Barbican Art Gallery, 1994).
29. For an exception see Christopher Nevinson's painting *Paths of Glory* (1917), which depicts two soldiers unburied face down amidst barbed wire. It was censored on the grounds that it would hinder the war effort but Nevinson displayed it at the Leicester Galleries (1918), with "Censored" written on brown paper obscuring the bodies.

30. See Andrew Graham Dixon, *Paul Nash: The Ghosts of War*, Episode 1 of series on *British Art at War: Bombert, Sickert and Nash* (BBC 4, 17 September 2014). Dixon develops this argument further, suggesting the disfigured faces he had seen were inscribed into his portrayals of scarred landscapes.
31. See Chambers, ed., *Aftermath: Art in the Wake of World War One*, 51.
32. Samuel Hynes, *A War Imagined: The First World War and English Culture*, New edition (London, UK: Pimlico, 1992). Hynes also suggests that "The Wordsworthian idea of natural benevolence had died".
33. Bryan Appleyard, *The Pleasures of Peace: Art and Imagination in Post-War Britain* (London, UK: Faber & Faber, 1989), 61.
34. Cited in David Boyd Haycock, *A Crisis of Brilliance: Five Young British Artists and the Great War* (London, UK: Old St Paul Publishing, 2009), 280.
35. Arnold Bennett, "Prefatory Note," to *"Void of War" An Exhibition of Pictures by Lieut. Paul Nash* (London, UK: Ernest Brown and Phillips, 1918), 4–5.
36. Paraphrase of script by Andrew Graham Dixon, in *Paul Nash: The Ghosts of War*, Episode 1 (BBC 4, 17 September 2014). See also, for examples, Nash's *The Mule Track* (1918) or the sixty square foot oil: *The Menin Road* (1919).
37. Bennett, "Prefatory Note", 5. See also Nash's watercolour with chalk and ink entitled: *Wire*, 1918–1919.
38. For example, the artist and sculptor, Alice Channer (b.1977) highlights the contemporary relevance of Nash's work in the face of aspects of ecocide: '*We Are Making a New World*' … 'looks exactly like contemporary aerial pictures of rainforest deforestation… Here we are, nearly a century later, looking out at identical and vast landscapes of industrial destruction … Nash's war landscapes give us some idea of how we got here'. See Mark Chaimowicz, et al., 'From the Surreal to the Decorative' *Tate Etc.* Issues 8 (Autumn 2016), 64–75. https://www.theartstory.org/artist-nash-paul-life-and-legacy.htm and http://alicechanner.com/files/AC_PRESS_160900_ConversationNashTateETC.pdf, accessed 7 January 2019
39. Kathleen Palmer, *Women War Artists* (London, UK: IWM, Tate Publishing, 2011), 24. See also https://sophie-ristelhueber.format.com/irak#0, accessed 7 January 2019.
40. George F. Kennan, *The Decline of Bismark's European Order: Franco-Russian Relations 1875–1890* (Princeton, NJ: Princeton University Press, 1981), 3.
41. Peter's body was originally buried at the Belgian cemetery of Roggevelde. The statues were initially placed there in 1932, but when his grave and remains were transported to the nearby German war cemetery Vladslo, the *Grieving Parents* statues were also moved.
42. Käthe Kollwitz, *The Diary and Letters of Kaethe Kollwitz* (Evanston, IL: Northwestern University Press, 1988 [1955]). "To give birth to a child, to raise him, and after eighteen precious years to see his talents developing, to

see what rich fruit the tree will bear – and then to have it cut short…!" See also, Leo Van Bergen, *Before My Helpless Sight: Suffering, Dying and Military Medicine on the Western Front, 1914–1918* (Farnham, UK: Ashgate, 2009), 496.

43. She had originally been "charmed" by Peter to persuade his father and her husband Karl to permit him to enlist. On 5 October 1914, she wrote a prophetic farewell letter about Peter: "As if the umbilical cord is cut again. The first time it was to give him life, now it is to give him to death." Seven days later she said goodbye to Peter for the very last time at a railway station.
44. See W.L. Guttsman, *Art for the Workers: Ideology and the Visual Arts in Weimar Germany* (Manchester, UK: Manchester University Press, 1997), 121.
45. See, for example, the work of Jiang Feng, Li Hua, and Gu Yuan, who developed a radical use of woodcuts to challenge oppressive militarism of the Chinese Nationalist regime in the 1920s.
46. Henry W. Pickford, *The Sense of Semblance: Philosophical Analyses of Holocaust Art* (New York, NY: Fordham University Press, 2003), 97–105.
47. These include: "persecuted", "innocent", "murdered Jews", "Roma", those who died because of their "religious or political convictions", resisted tyranny and died because they would not compromise their conscience.
48. Poet Ruth Padel in *Käthe Kollwitz: Suffering Witness* part of the BBC Radio 4 series on *Germany: Memories of a Nation* (29 October 2014).
49. Ruth Padel also reflected Kollwitz's memorial for her youngest son, Peter, in BBC Radio 3's *The Essay, Minds at War*. Series 1. Episode 10 of 10, https://www.bbc.co.uk/programmes/b047zvd0, accessed 7 January 2019).
50. Lucy Lunt, producer, *The World in 3D* on Kollwitz's *Mother with Dead Son* (London: BBC Radio 4, 1 March 2018). https://www.bbc.co.uk/programmes/b09sqk02, accessed 1 July 2018.
51. See Russell Martin, *The Destruction of Guernica, and the Masterpiece that Changed the World* (London, UK: Plume, Penguin Books, 2003). It is possible that Picasso was also influenced by seeing earlier news reports of bombings on other civilian targets.
52. Picasso was commissioned to create a mural for the Spanish Display at the 1937 Paris International Exposition. See https://www.pablopicasso.org/guernica.jsp, accessed 7 January 2019.
53. The Spanish Civil War lasted from July 1936 to April 1939. It was fought between the Republicans and the Nationalists, who were eventually led by General Franco. The Nationalist forces were ultimately successful, leading to Franco being in power for 36 years.
54. See also the tongues of the horse and bull. Jolyon P. Mitchell, "Journalism", in John C. Lyden and Eric Michael Mazur (eds.), *The Routledge Companion to Religion and Popular Culture* (London, UK: Routledge, 2015), 65–79.

55. See Gijs van Hensbergen, "Piecing Together Guernica", http://news.bbc.co.uk/1/hi/7986540.stm, accessed on 1 October 2018.
56. John Gittings, "Icons of War and Peace", in *The Oxford International Encyclopedia of Peace*, ed. Nigel Young (Oxford, UK: Oxford University Press, 2010).
57. See "The Hiroshima Panels and the Truth of War", http://www.aya.or.jp/~marukimsn/english/indexE.htm, accessed on 7 October 2018.
58. See John W. Dower and John Junkerman, (eds.), *The Hiroshima Murals: The Art of Iri Maruki and Toshi Maruki* (Tokyo, Japan: Kodansha International, 1985). More details about these haunting and harrowing ink paintings, created on rice paper, can be found at http://www.aya.or.jp/~marukimsn/english/indexE.htm, accessed 7 October 2018.
59. *The Hiroshima Panels* III "WATER", 1950, 1.8 m × 7.2 m, http://www.aya.or.jp/~marukimsn/gen/gen3e.html, accessed 7 December 2016.
60. *Hellfire: A Journey from Hiroshima*, Directed by John Junkerman (New York, NY: First Run Features, 1986), nominated for an Oscar for Best Documentary.
61. See, for example, *Hiroshima Murals I* - Ohki Symphony No. 5 "Hiroshima" (1953), https://www.youtube.com/watch?v=dIOTMiVQarM, accessed 7 December 2016.
62. See "The Hiroshima Panels Exhibition 2015", especially Yukinori Okamura, "Three Unique Aspects of the Hiroshima Panels", http://www.aya.or.jp/~marukimsn/english/2015ustour.html, accessed on 7 December 2016.
63. Okamura, "Three unique aspects of the Hiroshima Panels".
64. See Gijs van Hensbergen, *Guernica: The Biography of a Twentieth-Century Icon* (London, UK: Bloomsbury, 2004).
65. Alejandro Escalona, "75 years of Picasso's Guernica: An Inconvenient Masterpiece", *The Huffington Post*, 23 May 2012.
66. See Jolyon Mitchell, *Promoting Peace, Inciting Violence: The Role of Religion and Media* (London, UK: Routledge, 2012). This detailed discussion has led to a wide range of responses, highlighting other examples from around the world (e.g. in Cambodia, Iraq, Lebanon, the UK and the USA) of weapons being transformed into art.
67. See Mitchell, *Promoting Peace*. As demonstrated in this book and elsewhere there are clearly different ways of bearing witness, through practices such as film-making, photography and news reporting.
68. Neil MacGregor, *A History of the World in 100 Objects* (London, UK: Penguin, 2010), 644.
69. The *Tree of Life* was created by four Mozambican artists, Adelino Serafim Maté, Hilario Nhatugueja, Fiel dos Santos, and the creator of the *Throne of Weapons* was Cristóvão Canhavato (Kester).
70. For more on the tour, see https://www.britishmuseum.org/PDF/throne.pdf, accessed 1 July 2018.

71. Neil MacGregor, "Director's Foreword", in *Throne of Weapons: A British Museum Tour*, ed. J. Holden (London, UK: British Museum, 2006), 5.
72. Mitchell, *Promoting Peace*, 232–233. See also Wallis Kendal and Sandra Bromley, "The Gun Sculpture" made up of AK47's, landmines, rocket launchers and shells.
73. Michael O'Neil, "Memorial", in *The Arts of Peace: An Anthology of Poetry*, ed. Adrian Blamires and Peter Robinson (Reading, UK: Two Rivers Press, 2014), 43.
74. Allison Cullingford, *100 Objects Blog*, 25 April 2012, https://100objectsbradford.wordpress.com/2012/04/25/52-reunion-and-reconciliation-the-peace-sculpture-by-josefina-de-vasconcellos/, accessed 1 July 2018. See also 'Reunion and Reconciliation: the Peace Sculpture by Josefina de Vasconcellos'. Number 52 of '100 Objects from the Special collection from the University of Bradford'.
75. Patrick McCarthy, "Peace and The Arts", in Charles Webel and Johan Galtung (eds.), *Handbook of Peace and Conflict Studies* (London, UK: Routledge, 2007), 357.
76. See Carolyn J. Weekley, *The Kingdom of Edward Hicks* (New York, NY: The Colonial Williambsburg Foundation, 1999), especially 90–155.
77. Exceptions to this observation include Australian artists, Jon Cattapan who created a series of portrayals depicting the role of Australian soldiers in the peacekeeping force in East Timor (2008); and eX de Medici, who did the same in the Solomon Islands in 2009.
78. See Timothy Hyman, *Sienese Painting: The Art of a City Republic (1278–1477)* (London, UK: Thames & Hudson, 2003), 94–121.
79. Nirit Ben-Aryeh Debby, "War and Peace: The Description of Ambrogio Lorenzetti's Frescoes in Saint Bernardino's 1425 Siena Sermons", *Renaissance Studies* 15:3 (September 2001): 272–286. See 276, especially n.28.
80. See https://artsandculture.google.com/asset/WAFg-CSkcQJsMw, accessed 7 January 2019.
81. See https://artsandculture.google.com/asset/effects-of-good-government-in-the-countryside/1QEdJ3E935Z8-A, accessed 7 January 2019.
82. See, for example, John Gittings, *The Glorious Art of Peace: From Iliad to Iraq* (Oxford, UK: Oxford University Press, 2012), 84–88.
83. Debby, "War and Peace: The Description of Ambrogio Lorenzetti's Frescoes in Saint Bernardino's 1425 Siena Sermons", 276, note 7. Strikingly Bernardino also observes a 'man being hanged in order to maintain holy justice'. He claims that because of such severe justice 'everyone lives in holy peace and concord'.
84. Debby, "War and Peace", 282.
85. See Bill Rolston, *Drawing Support 4: Murals and Conflict Transformation in Northern Ireland* (Belfast, UK: Beyond the Pale Publications, 2013). See

also Stuart Borthwick, *The Writing on the Wall: A Visual History of Northern Ireland's Troubles* (Liverpool, UK: Bluecoat Press, 2015); Andrew Hill and Andrew White, "Painting Peace? Murals and the Northern Ireland Peace Process", *Irish Political Studies* 27:1 (2011): 71–88; and Neil Jarman, "The Ambiguities of Peace: Republican and Loyalist Ceasefire Murals", *Causeway* (Spring 1996): 23–27.
86. Raziye Akkoc, "Banksy in Gaza: Street Artist Goes Undercover in the Strip", *The Telegraph*, 26 February 2015. See also Hettie Bingham, *Banksy: Art Breaks the Rules* (London, UK: Wayland, 2016), 22–23.
87. "Love Conquers Old Firm Hate", *Daily Mirror*, 24 July 2003, https://www.thefreelibrary.com/LOVE+CONQUERS+OLD+FIRM+HATE.-a0105763090, accessed 7 December 2017.
88. See, for example, Stewart M. Hoover, *Religion in the Media Age* (New York and London: Routledge, 2006); Stewart M. Hoover and Lynn Schofield Clark, (eds.), *Practicing Religion in the Age of Media: Explorations in Media, Religion, and Culture* (New York: Columbia University Press, 2003); and Lynn Schofield Clark, *From Angels to Aliens: Teenagers, the Media and the Supernatural* (Oxford: Oxford University Press, 2003).
89. See, for example, Mihaela Mihai, "Architectural Transitional Justice? Political Renewal within the Scars of a Violent Past", *International Journal of Transitional Justice*, 12:3 (November 2018): 515–536.
90. Bloody Sunday is also sometimes known as the Bogside Massacre. It took place on 30 January 1972. See Chapter 4 of this volume.
91. These different drives were reflected by a local Derry youth theatre company, who used Maurice Harron's *Hands Across the Divide* as a stimulus for a production reflecting on local divisions and how they might be healed. An extract of the play was later used a catalyst at a workshop 'exploring related issues of stereotyping and prejudice' (2009). See David Oddie, *A Journey of Art and Conflict: Weaving Indra's Net* (Bristol and Chicago: Intellect and the University of Chicago Press, 2015), 151.
92. See Margaret MacMillan, *The Reith Lectures 2018 - The Mark of Cain*, especially Lecture 5: *War's Fatal Attraction*, 24 July 2018. BBC Radio 4. This was only heard at final proof stage of this book, but MacMillan's lecture provides complementary insights into how the arts can be cathartic, defiant, hopeful, triumphant, intimidating, commemorative, lamenting, showing both the beauty and the horror of war.

CHAPTER 3

Peacebuilding in Korea Through *Minjung* Art: Struggle for Justice and Peace

Sebastian Kim

Introduction

During the period of military-backed government (1961–1988), South Korea faced various political and economic challenges: poverty and inequality in society; human rights abuses by military governments; and confrontation with the communist North. To understand both some of the tensions within South Korea and the ambiguous role of religious groups in peacebuilding at this time, it is useful to reflect on the role of the local churches. Throughout this period, the South Korean churches were deeply divided theologically into conservative and liberal positions, which posed a struggle for those grappling with the political situation. Peace was defined more narrowly as something akin to political stability by the military-backed government, which tried to persuade the people to support its rule on the basis of security and prosperity. The government and *Jaebul*, family-run large companies, argued that in order to maintain security and see economic

S. Kim (✉)
Fuller Theological Seminary, Pasadena, CA, USA
e-mail: sebastiankim@fuller.edu

J. Mitchell et al. (eds.), *Peacebuilding and the Arts*,
Rethinking Peace and Conflict Studies,
https://doi.org/10.1007/978-3-030-17875-8_3

progress in peace and well-being, the citizens would have to sacrifice certain aspects of their rights, including workers' rights and civil liberties. The majority of religious leaders saw the importance of political and economic security, with many Christian leaders mainly focusing their attention on church growth and spiritual renewal. But a group of Christians, led by *minjung*[1] theologians, stood against the injustice brought by the capitalist market system and military-backed governments, and also brought the agenda of peace and reconciliation in the Korean peninsula.

While *minjung* theologians developed the theoretical framework for the democratization movement, *minjung* artists made a significant impact on the movement by providing a platform for expressing people's *han*[2] and aspirations. The artists were working alongside *minjung* theologians but were particularly effective among students and ordinary people who were campaigning against the military-backed government because of human rights abuses. In a sense, they were "doing theology in the public sphere"[3] or, as Volker Küster put it, they "devote[d] their creativity as means of communication into the service of the common goal".[4] The artists used woodcuts because they could be easily duplicated for flyers, leaflets, books and other printed media without great cost, thereby "democratizing" art. In addition to Chinese woodcut techniques, they adopted German expressionism and genre paintings of the Korean Yi dynasty.[5] Lee Chul-soo, Oh Jun and Hong Song-dam were among the most prominent artists in that era and, in addition, students produced banners and murals as they participated in demonstrations against the government. In this period, *minjung* artists were concerned with three issues: poverty and injustice among factory workers and farmers; political oppression and human rights abuses by the military-backed governments; and the peaceful unification of the two Koreas. As I discuss these in turn, in each case I have identified a historic event which became a focus for the concerns of the *minjung* artists: the Chun Tae-il incident (1970); the Gwangju uprising (1980); and the National Council of Churches of Korea (NCCK) Declaration (1988).

Struggle for Equality and Justice for Farmers and Factory Workers in the 1970s and the Death of Jeon Tae-il

In the 1970s, South Korean workers were exploited by multinationals, by Korean conglomerates and by medium and small businesses under pressure to supply the others. Light industry predominated and much of the workforce was fresh from the countryside and living in dormitories, slum housing or shanty towns. In the workplace, training was poor, and health and safety were grossly overlooked. Social security was virtually non-existent and management was rough and sometimes brutal. Although collective bargaining was practised, unions were generally organized or manipulated by employers rather than representing the interests of employees.[6] In addition to personal grievances, as the working class grew and observed that the rewards for their labour seemed to be disproportionately benefitting the Korean business elite, and that powerful Japanese and American business interests were increasingly dictating domestic policy, so industrial unrest grew and in 1968 resulted in the first large-scale strike.[7]

Christians sought to address the needs of industrial workers in several different ways. Christian owners employed industrial chaplains, who had mainly evangelistic and pastoral roles; other Christians did social work such as running night schools and early childhood care and education and some directly tried to improve conditions for the workers and challenged management.[8] Foremost among the latter category were Urban and Industrial Mission (UIM) and *Jeunesse Ouvrière Chrétienne* (JOC; [Young Christian Workers]). UIM was a project of the World Council of Churches (WCC), which built on the Protestant Social Gospel tradition and the theology of Reinhold Niebuhr, and was also inspired by the Catholic worker-priest movement. It had been active in Korea since 1958. UIM workers were mainly young university graduates who had disguised their identities and deliberately took factory work to discover what it was like and to make workers aware of their rights.[9] Although the most vocal supporters of UIM tended to be the theologically radical, mainstream churches and leaders in the NCCK also backed them. In addition, they received funds and personnel from foreign church agencies, such as the Australian Presbyterians who supported the work at Yeongdeungpo market in Seoul for factory workers from 1964. JOC was a Catholic Action movement founded in Belgium by Joseph Cardijn which received papal approbation in 1925 for its work for labour justice and the encouragement of Catholic trade unions. In 1967, JOC was involved in a successful action against the Ganghwa Island Simdo garment company. This resulted in a statement by the Bishops' Conference in February 1968 which declared "the Church has a right and responsibility to teach Christian social justice" and to uphold the dignity of workers.[10] In 1970, the Bishops' Conference formed a Korean Justice and Peace Committee and in November 1971 the bishops issued a pastoral letter saying economic and social development should go hand-in-hand.[11] JOC in Korea also had an agricultural wing that, in 1972, became the Korean Catholic Farmers' Movement.

Both UIM and JOC worked by forming small groups for leisure activities, problem-sharing, conscientization and bible study.[12] They played an important role in politicizing labour, linking the intellectual community with the workers and broadening the social background of participants in the labour movement.[13] Using media, street demonstrations and other protest methods, they drew attention to the cause. When industrial workers found their own struggle for labour justice suppressed, they tended to gravitate towards the Christian progressives because of their organizational structures and international connections, and also because they were less susceptible than intellectuals to accusations that they were Communist.

One single event—the self-immolation of Jeon Tae-il in November 1970—"marked the beginning of South Korea's working-class formation", "awakened the intellectual community to the dark side of the export-oriented industrialisation", and stirred Christian consciences into action.[14] Twenty-two-year-old Jeon worked as a tailor in sweatshop conditions in the Peace Market in Cheonggyecheon in Seoul, which was full of garment factories employing mainly young women workers. He was also a Sunday school teacher at Changhyeun Methodist Church, which was started among people displaced by slum clearance. Jeon documented how young women, 15–18 years old, were spending 15-hour days in exceedingly cramped conditions with no sunlight for very low payment, even by the standards of the time. In 1969 he started a workers' group and began to campaign for better pay and conditions for them. After letters to the relevant government ministry met no response, and peaceful protests were forcibly broken up, Jeon set himself on fire outside the market.[15] This incident shocked the nation and triggered the *minjung* movement among students, church members, factory workers, and ordinary people, which was largely Christian-led.

In the context of the labour movement, *minjung* artists were active in representing critical voices from the ordinary people. The forums for this included university campuses and small group meetings for conscientization. They employed music, poetry and drama as well as paintings and woodblock art. The best example is the "Gold-Crowned Jesus", a musical drama written by Kim Chi-ha, a Catholic dissident, with music by Kim Min-ki, a student composer, and sung by Yang Hee-eun, a Protestant student, most of whose songs were banned by the authorities. It was first performed in 1973 at a Catholic centre in Wonju. The plot involves beggars, lepers and prostitutes on the street; a nun who wants to help them; a company owner who exploits these vulnerable people; police, university students and a priest who ignore them; and the gold-crowned Jesus who was captured and held in a concrete prison. Jesus had given the gold crown to those on the street, but the priest, police and company owner took it and put it onto Jesus' head and hid him within concrete. The cynical attitude displayed in the play towards those who had power and authority was widely shared by people at the time; in particular the music, "Oh Lord, be here now" became an expression for seeking God's justice and also of defiance towards the injustice done to the poor and marginalized. The play included a vivid description of the "frozen sky" and "frozen field", a darkened sun, and "street of despair". It asks "Where are they from?" these "Thin-faced people", and "What are they looking for?" with "bone-dry hands". Those who are rejected inhabit a lonely, dark and poor street, are portrayed as perhaps hoping for a "green forest beyond death", while crying out to God to "Be with us here".[16] It is a haunting piece of drama and writing.

Oh Yoon was particularly interested in the poverty and exploitation of factory workers and produced a number of woodblocks. "Dawn for Labor" (1984)[17] is a portrayal of a labourer getting up in the early morning for work. It was used for Park No-hae's poetry book when it was first published in 1984.[18] The rugged back of the labourer expresses the hardship of work and the shape of the figure suggests tiredness from the long hours of work for most factory workers during the early period of industrial development. When government and company owners insisted that for the sake of economic prosperity and security in a competitive capitalist market, workers needed to make sacrifices, the *minjung* protagonists were arguing that justice for the workers needed to be achieved first and that prosperity and justice are not mutually exclusive. In the midst of the Yushin Constitution controversy (see below), there was a struggle for justice for factory workers and farmers in the context of exploitation by company owners. There were a number of artworks done by *minjung* artists, such as "Rice in Soup and Hope" (Oh Yoon),[19] "Night Work" and "Laborer's Family" (Hong Sung-dam) and "Dream of a Female Factory Worker" (Lee Chul-soo).[20] They express the poverty and hardship of factory workers in inhumane conditions, but also present some aspirations and hope in the midst of despair and injustice. In particular, "Rice is Heaven", a poem by Kim Chi-ha (written in 1975) and illustrated by Lee Chul-soo (1987)[21] drew much popular attention. It equated rice with "heaven" that has to be shared. This refrain is repeated several times.[22]

The idea of rice as heaven was a radical one for Korean Christians, who tended to see heaven in spiritual rather than material terms, and yet it was inspiring. Kim challenged people that the nature of heaven is sharing. We cannot monopolize it, and so it is imperative that we all share what we have. The artwork vividly portrays the imaginary heaven which contrasts starkly with the daily urban reality of factory workers. It is a typically Korean depiction of a pine tree surrounded by mountains, stars, moon and sun. They are all contained together in a rice bowl, signifying that both rice and heaven are integral to our spiritual aspirations as well as to our understanding of everyday reality. For many, this challenged the dichotomy of sacred and secular, suggesting that rice and heaven should be understood as integral parts of our life and that material and spiritual cannot be separated. It also linked views of heaven as a place of peaceful coexistence with current political and social injustices. It is likely that this conception influenced the Christians who led the nationwide "Rice of Love" campaign which was started in 1989 and "The South-North Sharing Campaign", founded in 1993, that gained widespread support from the Korean Protestant churches, from both conservative and progressive circles.[23]

Political Oppression by Military-Backed Governments and the Gwangju Uprising (or Democratization Movement) in May 1980

During the 1970s, the political atmosphere in South Korea became increasingly tense as the government became more aggressive towards opposition politicians, students and religious leaders. Eventually, President Park brought in the Yushin Constitution in 1972 justifying it on the basis of the threat from the North. The new Constitution gave Park unlimited tenure in office and powers to appoint the cabinet, prime minister and a third of the national assembly. He now ruled largely by emergency decree, each more restrictive than the last. This brought critical opposition from church groups who openly protested against the government on the basis of religious freedom and attendant human rights.

In 1973, a group of Christians declared "The Korean Christian Manifesto", which condemned the new Constitution. They believed they were commanded to obey God's word in the historical context, that Koreans were looking to Christians for action, and that they had a responsibility to carry out God's salvation through action. They saw this as a continuation of the liberation movement during Japanese rule. They criticized Park for ruling by "power and threat" instead of "law and dialogue". They accused the government of limiting freedom of expression and faith, distorting the facts and brainwashing the people. The government, declared the Manifesto, persecuted their political opponents, criticized intellectuals, intimidated innocent people and exploited the poor and the workers in the name of economic development. The Manifesto warned that no one is above the law and Christians are called to be involved in proclaiming truth and justice and fighting for the poor, marginalized and oppressed. The Manifesto made three calls for action: for rejection of the Yushin Constitution and unity for democratization, for renewal of the Church for the poor and oppressed, and for garnering support from the world Church.[24] The declaration was the beginning of a human rights movement among some Protestant churches, which was led by *minjung* theologians, but it also signalled the polarization of political positions among Christians, which continues to the present day.

The NCCK held a "consultation on human rights in Korea" in November (1973) and soon the NCCK and YMCA buildings and leading liberal churches in Seoul—Tonghap, Methodist and Kijang—became recognized centres of anti-government activity.[25] At this time, there were a number of high profile human rights abuses by the government including the arrest of Catholic bishop Chi Hak-soon, and other Christian ministers, and the People's Revolutionary Party's case (1974–1975) in which eight men were sentenced and executed the same day through a sham trial. Students, the NCCK and the National Catholic Priests Association for Justice were at the forefront of protests against the government, which united other denominations as well in opposition to it.

In 1976 a joint Catholic-Protestant service was held on the highly significant date of 1 March[26] in Myeongdong (Catholic) Cathedral, which was rapidly becoming the main centre of anti-government activity. It was attended by the Christian civil leaders who formed the core of the opposition: political leaders Kim Dae-jung and Yun Bo-seon, religious leaders including Ham Seok-heon, NCCK General Secretary Kim Kwan-seok, and *minjung* theologians Ahn Byung-mu and Suh Nam-dong. Twelve of them prepared the Declaration for the Democratic Salvation of the Nation, which was read out during the service by Lee U-jung, head of Korean Church

Women United. The 1976 Declaration used secular liberal democratic concepts of freedom and rights for broad appeal and posed a significant intellectual challenge to the rationale for the Yushin Constitution by pointing to the importance of dealing with the underlying economic context and North-South tension in order to release funds and resources to achieve democracy and social justice. Park was re-elected in 1978, but he was assassinated in the following year by the head of the Korean Central Intelligence Agency. Following the ensuing chaotic period, Major General Chun Doo-hwan seized power on 17 May 1980 and imposed martial law.

It was in this context that the brutal suppression of a student demonstration took place in the south-western city of Gwangju, which prompted the Gwangju Uprising. University students defied the curfew and continued to demonstrate. Chun responded by sending in troops to put down the rebellion. In the process of brutal treatment by the soldiers, civilians soon joined in and a major conflict arose between the people and the central government. This resulted in the deaths of about 600 students and civilians, although the exact number is still in dispute. The Gwangju Uprising or Democratization Movement was also a turning point for the opposition Christians. In particular, some Catholic priests in Gwangju actively participated in the struggle and made it known to the nation despite a media blackout.[27]

Hong Sung-dam, who was from Gwangju, and was profoundly affected by the uprising, created a number of artworks expressing the situation, fifty of which were collected and later published as *May Gwangju*.[28] The work called "Mother" (1982) is an expression of the hardship that young Koreans and their mothers faced during the time of turmoil. This Korean pietà is the "expression of the suffering … of all mothers in Korea" as she holds her dead son. Her ragged face and hand shows the hard life and agony she went through in her life to raise her son and now, as she is holding his dead body, she has lost all hope and has only the deep anguish of *han*, which no one can console. Yet, like the pietà of Mary, the suffering of *han* may bring justice and then peace in the troubled land (see Fig. 3.1 [1999]). Theologian Suh Nam-dong insisted that *han* is the key theme for theology in the Korean context and that if "one does not hear the signs of the *han* of the *minjung*, one cannot hear the voices of Christ". So the artwork not only portrays the despair and agony of the mother against the injustice done to her through the loss of her son, but also provides a glimpse of hope for the future when justice and peace will be restored.[29]

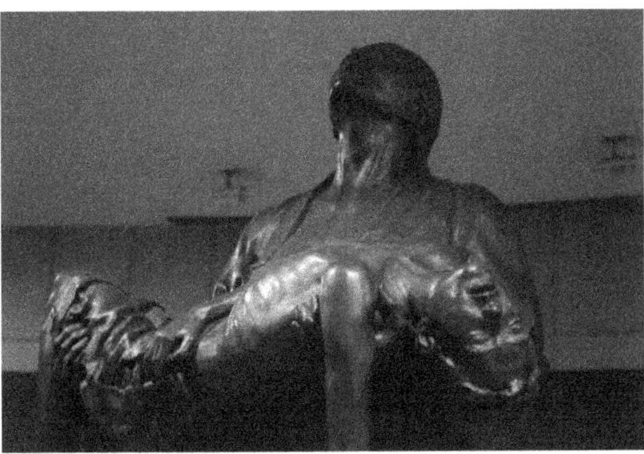

Fig. 3.1 "Mother Holding Her Son" (1999), Jae-Gil Woo, bronze statue in the Gwangju 5.18 Memorial Park (© Photo Sebastian Kim)

On the same issue of political struggle, the mural at Chonnam National University (1980; Fig. 3.2) portrays the Gwangju Uprising (Democratization Movement) as a movement of the *minjung*. In the front of the mural, a student holds a banner of "liberation of the people", and in the background there are students and armed civilians fighting against military forces. On the lower left part of the mural, there are women and children making soup to feed the resistance parties. In the upper part of the mural, there is a large figure of a student holding a rifle who, together with his colleagues in the background, encourages others to join the cause and to protest. The students and civilian army in Gwangju were portrayed by the military government as trouble-makers intent on harming national security, peace and stability and they were therefore brutally suppressed. The Gwangju Movement represented not only the deep resentment of the people in that region, who have been marginalized for centuries of Korean history, but also of all those who had suffered unjust treatment by the authorities and others who exercise power over the weak and the poor.

The political tensions continued and were reignited in 1987 when Park Jong-cheol, a student who had died in custody, was later discovered to have been tortured. There were large demonstrations and a commemorative Mass was held on 26 January at Myeongdong Cathedral at which Cardinal Kim Sou-hwan challenged the government with the words: "Are you not afraid of God? … God is now asking where is Park Jong-cheol

Fig. 3.2 Mural at Chonnam National University, *Liberation of the People* (1980) (© Photo Sebastian Kim)

– your son, your student, your citizen – just as he asked Cain who killed Abel".[30] Participation in the demonstrations expanded from a few university students, opposition politicians and some church leaders to the general public and even conservative Christians. In June, a nationwide demonstration started when protestors gathered at the Anglican Cathedral in the centre of Seoul and then at Myeongdong Cathedral from the following day. They continued to gather support from civilians in most major cities. *Minjung* demonstrators, artists and students refused to accept the argument of the government and large companies that security and prosperity would bring peace and eventually a just society, but argued instead that justice and peace have to go hand in hand and that there will not be peace without justice. They called for democracy and frequently demanded justice for the victims of Gwangju. Perceived US complicity with the suppression of the Gwangju Democratization Movement produced anti-American slogans as well. Nationwide demonstrations by people from all walks of life eventually brought the government to its knees and an end to dictatorship. President Chun was forced to promise a democratic election in the following year. However, due to a split between the opposition parties, President Noh, a former military general was elected in 1988 and South Korea had to wait another five years to see a full civilian and democratic government.

Numerous murals were painted during the time of the June demonstrations.[31] The murals in this period were produced by students calling for democratization, self-reliance and unification who were strongly supporting farmers and workers. They were also anti-American because they believed that the USA was supportive of the military-backed government due to their shared anti-communist policy and was imposing the various trade arrangements which they thought were destroying their livelihoods. The most well-known and also the most controversial mural was the one at Dong-A University in Busan entitled, "June Resistance Panorama" or "Self-reliance, Democracy and Unification" (1987; Fig. 3.3). It shows

Fig. 3.3 Mural at Dong-A University, *June Resistance Panorama* (1987) (© Photo Sebastian Kim)

Mount Baekdu, a symbol of Korean identity, with a dragon rising up from it, which indicates the strength and dynamic power of the movement. It is surrounded by people of the North and South dancing with the joy of liberation and in the middle a man tearing the chains and the American flag binding him and running across the sea of trouble, supported by farmers and company workers on the right-hand side of the mural. Another mural was at Kyunghee University. Entitled "Young Man", it is dominated by a strong figure with his fist raised. The figure is rising out of the crater lake in Mount Baekdu, and cheered on by farmers, company workers and fellow students (1988; Fig. 3.4). It reflects the nature of the June Protest and the desire for democratization and unification.

Fig. 3.4 Mural at Kyunghee University, *Young Man* (1988) (© Photo Sebastian Kim)

The main issue of concern in the early 1970s was the socio-economic problems of poor workers and farmers, but towards the end of the 1970s and 1980s, the concern became political and ideological tensions in relation to democracy. The first *minjung* theologians identified with and mobilized the "mass" of workers and farmers over against the employers and land owners. But the later *minjung* theologians and artists had only minority support because they rather uncritically adopted Marxist ideology. Particularly after the Gwangju massacre, *minjung* theologians and artists shifted their attention to ideological issues, taking a socialist-communist line, favouring North Korea, and confronting what they perceived as the illegitimate government of the South, which was in association with the United States. This created a gap between the *minjung*, who were not prepared to be on the side of the North, and those intellectuals who tried to integrate *minjung* theology into their ideological combat.[32]

Peace and Reconciliation in the Korean Peninsula—The NCCK Declaration, February 1988

The activists for democracy in South Korea came to see the division of the peninsula as the flip side of the suppression of civil and human rights since both were maintained on grounds of national security. So it was natural that, having ousted the military regime, they should turn their attention to unification. Perhaps the most important step in this direction was in February 1988, when the NCCK issued the "Declaration of the Churches of Korea on National Unification and Peace", which made a significant impact both within the church and on the whole nation.[33] The NCCK declaration was welcomed by many Christians, but also generated heated discussion. It brought to the fore within the churches the issue of peace and reconciliation and motivated even conservative Christians to participate in the debate. The declaration, while affirming the three principles expressed in the Joint North–South Declaration of 1972—self-determination, peace and grassroots unification of the Koreas—added the priority of humanitarian practice and the participation of the *minjung* (the general population), who are the victims of the divided Korea, in the unification discussions. The Declaration then proclaimed the year 1995 as a jubilee year for peace and unification when Koreans could celebrate the fiftieth anniversary of the liberation from Japan.

In the following year, Presbyterian minister and scholar Moon Ik-hwan went on his own initiative to North Korea to meet Kim Il-sung and was arrested by the South Korean government as he returned. From his position regarding reunification and democratization, he argued that peace and justice are inseparable and that, while North Korea should work for the freedom and human rights of its people, the South also needed to work towards more equality and just distribution of wealth.[34] Although he did not criticize human rights issues in North Korea—a major weakness of most *minjung* perspectives on the peace and justice between the two Koreas—he expressed the same view as most people who wished to make reconciliation with the North: that one could not talk about unification and peace in the Korean peninsula without dealing with democratization and justice at home. Later the same year, Im Su-gyeung a Catholic university student, attended the World Festival of Youth and Students in Pyongyang and received an overwhelming welcome from the people in the North as "the flower of unification".[35] She too was arrested by South Korean authorities after she crossed back over the border.

Minjung artists were very much encouraged by the development of a reconciling spirit between the two Koreas and the peace movement among *minjung* activists, particularly through the NCCK declaration and the visits of Moon Ik-hwan and Im Soo-kyeung to the North. There were a significant number of artworks created to reflect the desire for peace and reconciliation in the Korean peninsula including "Daybreak" (1987),[36] "Wish for the Reunification" (1988),[37] "Day is Breaking, Beat the Drum!" (1988),[38] and "Hope for the Unification" (1985).[39] The most well-known work on the topic is "Dreaming of Reunification" by Lee Chul-soo (1983 and 1987).[40] This was a mural at Dolsan Church done in 1983 and later reworked as a woodblock with colour added. Against a background of the mountains of Korea, a man and woman embrace each other, representing the shapes of North and South Korea respectively. They clutch one another as if they do not wish to be parted again. They may be crying or they may be whispering as they talk about the years of separation. This work reminds us of so many families separated by the border. Only a very few have had occasion to meet up for a few days by the arrangement between the two governments. The cloud-bridge in the foreground suggests the East Asian folk story of "The Weaver Girl and the Cowherd" ("Gyeonu and Jiknyeo") who were separated and only meet once a year in heaven. The artwork reflects the sad reality of a divided nation and yet the hope for reunification.

The approach of the South Korean government towards the North changed drastically in the late 1990s when President Kim Dae-jung announced the "Sunshine Policy", which had three principles: no armed provocation will be tolerated; the South will not attempt to absorb the North in any way; and there would be reconciliation and cooperation wherever possible. This policy had two important dimensions: first, affirming a partnership of the nations, rather than merging the North into the South along the lines of German reunification, and second, insisting that initiatives on the issue be taken by North and South Korea themselves, rather than by outside interference. As a result of this initiative from the South and a change of relationship between the North Korean and US governments, the first ever meeting of the heads of the two Koreas in Pyongyang in June 2000 was a landmark moment for divided Korea. The joint declaration at the end of the meeting was focused on acceptance of each other as partners in peaceful coexistence, dialogue rather than conquest, and attempting to find common solutions to unification step-by-step. This initiative was followed by economic cooperation between the two Koreas, both at governmental and civilian levels, as well as an increase of humanitarian support from the South to the North. The succeeding government in South Korea continued the policy of peaceful coexistence and the gradual reunification of the two Koreas but the talks between the two Koreas are like waves, sometimes raising high expectations but often disappointing people on both sides. Nevertheless, although the political relationship has often appeared tense and aggressive, the exchange of people and trade and the social and cultural cooperation have been steadily increasing, which is a positive sign that there is growing reconciliation between the two Koreas.

Contribution of *Minjung* Art to Peacebuilding

Although there were many causes of democratization, the church's contributions to justice were widely acknowledged by both church and secular historians.[41] In particular, the participation of *minjung* artists and theologians in this cause was significant. However, they were criticized by many conservative Christians who saw national security and stability as taking priority over justice and equality, arguing that justice would be achieved eventually as the South Korean economy and society continued to progress and stabilize.

Minjung theologians, who played an influential role in shaping *minjung* art, articulated a holistic understanding of peace that gave a central place to justice. The prominent *minjung* theologian Ahn Byeung-mu, in a talk on "Justice and Peace", criticized people who accept that peace can be achieved without discussing justice and insisted that it is impossible to achieve peace without justice.[42] He argued this on the basis of his own experience in the Korean peninsula in which the government justified human rights abuses due to the need for economic development and national security. He insisted that the basis of peace will be achieved when true justice in Korea can be achieved, that is when the *minjung* are liberated from exploitation, and democratization and human rights are restored. And furthermore, he claimed that justice and peace should be understood from a *minjung* perspective, which is learnt through understanding the historical Jesus who was on the side of the poor and oppressed. Second, Ahn insisted that when we discuss justice we have to talk about the sharing of material wealth on the basis of faith that everything is under God's sovereignty and authority. The first step for achieving justice and peace is to let go of private concepts of what we own. In other words, for Ahn, the concept of "public" is vital in the same way as in the poem "Rice is Heaven". As the early Christians shared their food with one another, so Christians today should share what they have with others. God's kingdom is closely related to the concept of a food-sharing community.

Like the theologians, the *minjung* artists critiqued the narrow, politically motivated understanding of peace as stability promulgated by the regime. They offered a visually striking portrayal of the violence and injustice that it entailed, while also suggesting a more holistic, but no less arduous, path to a more peaceful society. As the earlier discussion has indicated, *minjung* artists gave widely accessible visual expression to some of the concepts and ideas that were motivating social and political movements. This is seen not only in the methods they used, which allowed for easy reproduction and public viewing of their work, but also in the themes they explored, which frequently offered commentary on public issues and events that illustrated the regime's failings.

The *minjung* artists brought the unique capacities of the visual arts to these movements in ways which both expanded and challenged the overall movement for change. Visual images, such as the rice bowl containing heaven, gave concrete expression to injustice, and, in the case of the murals, sought to challenge official narratives by documenting events from the point of view of students or others who were being oppressed. For example, during the height of unrest, broadcast media was strictly controlled by the government, therefore people who were not directly affected by the protests or uprisings either had no information or only distorted information provided by government sources. *Minjung* arts not only provided information through visual arts (murals and banners) and other art forms (including music, drama and dance) at the time of the events, but also provided an alternative documentation for the future. In these ways, *minjung* art made a significant contribution to Korean cultural memory and contributed to the political will for peacebuilding and justice-seeking. The visual representations also challenged those who were part of the movement to reflect more deeply on its meaning and goals. The equation of rice with heaven challenged theologians and religious communities to consider more deeply how their faith tradition contributed to their understanding and involvement in current events.

Finally, the *minjung* artists creatively drew on religious and cultural understandings as sources for peacebuilding. The reference to a pietà in the woodcut "Mother" by Hong Sung-dam suggests possibilities for hope, even in the midst of great suffering and loss. The cloud-bridge in Lee Chul-Soo's "Dreaming of Reunification" draws on Korean folk stories to capture the sense of how fleeting the possibilities for reconciliation are between North and South Korea, but, at the same time, how cherished those possibilities for peace are to Koreans.

Conclusion

The Korean experience of the *minjung* struggle in the 1970s and 1980s demonstrates the key importance of justice for the poor and oppressed. Although the issues and concerns are different from context to context, I would argue that the fight for justice for the poor and oppressed is what has brought a sustainable peace in South Korea. For this, *minjung* artists made lasting contributions to the movement by providing creative imagination, challenging authority and sustaining the legitimacy for protest, and above all, persuading people that seeking justice should result in lasting peace. They not only touched people's hearts by expressing the struggle and *han* of the people but also by demonstrating hope and aspirations for the future. In a time of despair and confusion, the *minjung* artists took the risk and led their own protest through various art forms. They may not be the ones who initiated protest by presenting arguments, and they may not have directly confronted the authorities by being involved in street protest, but their work encouraged ordinary people to reflect upon and remember the injustice and exploitation and persuaded them to sustain their protest in the face of the threats and oppressive measures of the military-backed government. The works of the *minjung* artists remind us about their struggle to pursue justice in their search for lasting peace and democracy in South Korea, and also about wisdom, discernment, determination and engagement when we face a challenging situation. Pope Paul VI declared that "If you want peace, work for justice!"[43] Desmond Tutu, speaking on the situation of Arab-Israeli conflict, strongly asserted that "a true peace can ultimately be built only on justice" since he believed that "injustice and oppression will never prevail. Those who are powerful have to remember the litmus test that God gives to the powerful: 'how do you treat the poor, the hungry, and the voiceless?'".[44] Of course, justice and peace can be represented simultaneously as the text "justice and peace will kiss each other" (Psalm 85.10) implies, but if, and often this is the case, one has to prioritise between the two, in the light of the Korean case above, I would argue that justice-seeking has to take precedence. As the Minjung artists demonstrate: Peace without justice is not a peace worth pursuing.

Notes

1. The word *minjung*, which is a Sino-Korean term for ordinary people or masses (民衆; 민중). *Minjung* theology is associated with a particular history of popular uprising, including the *Donghak* Peasant Revolution in the late nineteenth century, was influenced by liberation theology and tended to hold ideologically to the left. Unlike black theology, feminist theology and *dalit* theology, *minjung* theologians have had difficulties equating this term with a concrete and tangible group. See Sebastian Kim, "Minjung Theology: Whose Voice for Whom?" in *Moving Forms of Theology: Faith Talk's Changing Contexts*, ed. Israel Selvanayagam (Delhi: ISPCK, 2003), 149–153.
2. A difficult to translate Korean concept akin to lament in the face of unavenged injustice. An anguish and deep despair like a mother who lost her child.
3. See Sebastian Kim, *Theology in the Public Sphere* (London: SCM Press, 2011), 3–26.
4. Volker Küster, "Minjung Theology and Minjung Art", *Mission Studies* XI:1 (1994): 108–129 at 115.
5. Küster, "Minjung Theology and Minjung Art", 116.
6. George E. Ogle, *Liberty to the Captives: The Struggle Against Oppression in South Korea* (Atlanta, GA: John Knox Press, 1977).
7. Bruce Cumings, *Korea's Place in the Sun: A Modern History*, 2nd edition (New York, NY: W. W. Norton, 2005), 372–374.
8. Ha-gen Koo, "Emerging Civil Society: The Role of the Labor Movement", in *Korean Society: Civil Society, Democracy and the State*, ed. Charles K.

Armstrong, 2nd edition (London, UK: Routledge, 2007), 73–94 at 76; Ogle, *Liberty to the Captives*, 67–68.

9. Ogle, *Liberty to the Captives*, 33–65.
10. Kim Sou-hwan, *The Story of Cardinal Kim Sou-hwan* (in Korean) (Seoul, Korea: Pyeonghwa Broadcasting, 2009), 199–202.
11. Eric O. Hanson, *Catholic Politics in China and Korea* (Maryknoll, NY: Orbis Books, 1980), 102.
12. Koo, "Emerging Civil Society", 75. The term "conscientization" (*conscientização* in Portuguese) is about developing critical awareness of one's social reality through action and reflection. It was initially developed by Paulo Freire. See Paulo Freire, *Pedagogy of the Oppressed*, trans. Myra Ramos (London, UK: Continuum, 2000 [1970]).
13. Hak-kyu Sohn, *Authoritarianism and Opposition in South Korea* (London, UK: Routledge, 1989), 180.
14. Koo, "Emerging Civil Society", 70–72.
15. See Tae-il Jeon, "Letter to the President", in *Creeds and Confessions of the Korean Church* (in Korean), ed. Rhie Deok-joo and Cho Yee-jei (Seoul, Korea: Han Deul, 1997), 307–309.
16. Chi Ha Kim, *The Gold-Crowned Jesus & Other Writings* (Maryknoll, NY: Orbis Books, 1978), 85–131.
17. Yoon Oh, *Collected Works II: Dokkaebi Who Holds the Sword* (Seoul, Korea: Hyunshil Books, 2010), 129.
18. No-hae Park, *Dawn of Labor* (Seoul: Neurin Geoleum, 2004), 93–95.
19. Oh Yoon, *Collected Works II*, 142.
20. Chul-soo Lee, *A Mind Carved in Wood: Selected Woodblock Prints, 1981–2011* (Seoul, Korea: Culture Books, 2011), 59.
21. Lee Chul-soo, *A Mind Carved in Wood*, 70.
22. Chi-ha Kim, *The Gold-Crowned Jesus & Other Writings* (Maryknoll, NY: Orbis Books, 1978), 30.
23. During the early stage of the campaign, Christians were encouraged to set a bowl of rice aside whenever they cooked and then bring the rice to their church for collection.
24. Rhie and Cho, eds., *Creeds and Confessions of Korean Church*, 271–276. See also Dong-sik Yoo, *The Mineral Vein of Korean Theology* (Seoul, Korea: Dasan Geulbang, 2000), 258–259.
25. Chung-shin Park, *Protestantism and Politics in Korea* (Seattle, WA: University of Washington Press, 2003), 194.
26. The first of March is a national holiday in both North and South Korea commemorating the Independence Movement in 1919 against Japanese colonial rule of Korea and the restriction of Korean citizens' rights and freedoms.
27. Jun-tae Kim, "Oh, Gwangju! The Cross of Our Nation!", trans. Chae-Pyong Song and Melanie Steyn, https://jaypsong.wordpress.com/2012/05/06/oh-gwangju-the-cross-of-our-nation-by-kim-jun-tae/, accessed 11 February 2017.

28. Sung-dam Hong, *May Gwangju* (Gwangju, Korea: Institute of the Study of Jeonnam Social Issues, 1989).
29. Nam-dong Suh, "Toward a Theology of Han", in *Minjung Theology: People as the Subjects of History*, ed. Kim Yong Bock (Maryknoll, NY: Orbis Books, 1983), 51–65.
30. Kim, *The Story of Cardinal Kim Sou-hwan*, 368.
31. Although there have been various traditions of murals and satires in response to the authorities, the murals dating from the 1980s in Korea seem to be most influenced by murals from Northern Ireland, Mexico and Paris. The main characteristics of these Korean murals are that they are generally done by visual art university students; that they include factory workers, farmers, Mount Baekdo (in North Korea and a symbol of the foundation of Korean and also unification of the two Koreas); and that they often contain anti-government and anti-American depictions. Most of the murals, however, have been destroyed due to government interference and the modernization of buildings.
32. Sun-jae Kim, "Yesterday, Today and Tomorrow of Minjung Theology", *Sinhak Sasang* (Spring 1998): 8–9.
33. "Declaration of the Churches of Korea on National Reunification and Peace", in *Peace and Reconciliation: In Search of Shared Identity*, ed. Sebastian Kim, Pauline Kollontai, and Greg Hoyland (Aldershot, UK: Ashgate, 2008), 185–195. See also Mahn-Yol Yi, *Korean Christianity and the National Unification Movement* (Seoul, Korea: Institute of the History of Christianity in Korea, 2001), 389–414.
34. Ik-hwan Moon, *How Can Unification Be Achieved?* (Seoul, Korea: Hakminsa, 1984), 36–44.
35. There is a mural at her university, Hankuk University of Foreign Studies, entitled, "The Flower of Unification".
36. Chul-soo Lee, *A Mind Carved in Wood*, 72–73.
37. Chul-soo Lee, *A Mind Carved in Wood*, 77
38. Chul-soo Lee, *A Mind Carved in Wood*, 81.
39. Yoon Oh, *Collected Works II*, 251.
40. Chul-soo Lee, *A Mind Carved in Wood*, 69.
41. See Korea Democracy Foundation, *A History of the Democracy Movement in Korea*, vols. 2 and 3 (Seoul, Korea: Dolbegae, 2009).
42. Byeung-mu Ahn, *Christ in the Midst of Minjung Event* (Seoul: Korea Theological Study Institute, 1989), 34–59.
43. Pope Paul VI, 'If you want peace, work for justice' (1 January 1972), http://www.vatican.va/holy_father/paul_vi/messages/peace/documents/hf_p-vi_mes_19711208_v-world-day-for-peace_en.html, accessed 1 June 2016.
44. Desmond Tutu, "Foreword", in *Speaking the Truth About Zionism and Israel*, ed. Michael Prior (London, UK: Melisende, 2004), 9–12.

CHAPTER 4

Art, Protest and Peace: The Murals of the Bogside Artists

Adrienne Dengerink Chaplin

> Reconciliation happens when my enemy tells me my story and I am able to say: "Yes, that is my story." (Stanley Hauerwas)

Introduction

How can images of rioters, soldiers and tanks serve as forces for peace, healing and reconciliation? And how can murals depicting the Troubles in Northern Ireland, as experienced by one community, be non-sectarian?

Between 1994 and 2006 three local artists, Tom Kelly, his brother William, and their friend Kevin Hasson, painted twelve large-scale murals on the gables of the blocks of flats in the Bogside area of Derry/Londonderry.[1] The Bogside, its name derived from the spillover of the nearby River Foyle that once flooded the land outside the city walls,

A. Dengerink Chaplin (✉)
King's College London, London, UK

J. Mitchell et al. (eds.), *Peacebuilding and the Arts*, Rethinking Peace and Conflict Studies,
https://doi.org/10.1007/978-3-030-17875-8_4

had been the center of the pivotal incidents that sparked what became known as "The Troubles"—a violent, thirty-year conflict that is generally considered to have begun on October 5, 1968 with a non-sectarian civil rights march in Derry and concluded with the Good Friday Agreement on April 10, 1998, in Belfast.[2] The murals depict key moments during that period as they affected the Bogside community. They serve as a memorial and talking point for people to process the past and seek hope for the future. The murals can be seen from Rossville Street, which runs through the center of the Bogside. The artists are known as the Bogside Artists. The murals' official name is *The People's Gallery*.[3]

The Importance of the Murals' Location: A Short History

In order to understand the significance of the murals in relation to their location, it is important to trace some of the history of the neighborhood. The Bogside lies at the bottom of what was once a wooded hill that provided Derry with its original name "Doire" or "Oak Grove." Early habitation of the region had begun as a monastic settlement on the side of the hill of the Bogside. It was founded by Saint Columba before he sailed on to the Island of Iona to establish a monastery and missionary school in 563. Saint Columba is still Derry's patron saint. For centuries, Derry and its surrounding region were sparsely populated with monks and migrating Gaelic Irish farmers who used the grasslands for their cattle. Following the Norman invasion of Ireland in the twelfth century, the country came under English rule culminating in the victory of Elizabeth I in 1603 after the Nine Years War.

Although the North of Ireland had always shown the strongest resistance to foreign occupation, when the last Gaelic chiefs were forced to flee the region in 1607 (known as "The flight of the Earls"), English rule put a definite end to all Irish autonomy. In order to consolidate its power and pre-empt further rebellions, King James I undertook a controlled colonization of the Northern region by English and Scottish Protestants. This "Plantation of Ulster" created the first division between the North and the South along the ethnic and religious differences that were to become a major source of tensions and conflicts in the future.

As part of the Plantation, the sea-port town Derry was given to a consortium of London merchants who developed the town into a center of English commerce and trade. They fortified the city's walls and, in 1613, changed its name by Royal Charter to Londonderry. While the Protestant English and Scots largely settled within the grand houses within the city walls, the native Irish Catholics were mostly relegated to the cramped and damp hovels in the boglands on the outside.

Drawing on the cheap labor of local women and children, the settlers built a thriving textile industry with worldwide exports of linen shirts. When the mid-nineteenth-century Great Famine in Ireland drove many Irish peasants across the border to seek work in Derry's docks and factories, conditions in the already overcrowded Bogside reached breaking point. Many decided to leave their country for good. Over a million Irish Catholics boarded boats in Derry to emigrate to America or Australia.

Growing resentment and rebellion against British rule, including the failed "Easter Rising" in Dublin in 1916, prompted the British Government to divide Ireland into two territories: an independent Republic governed by the Irish in the South and the six counties of Ulster, including their jewel in the crown, Londonderry, governed by Britain in the North.[4] There are contrasting interpretations both of the origins of the Troubles and of the more recent historical record, which also remains contested.[5] Nevertheless, there is considerable evidence that in order to keep Derry's majority population of Catholics under control, local government employed differing degrees of discrimination against Catholics in a number of spheres, including jobs, housing and voting.[6] Ongoing rigging of the electoral system meant that Catholics could never obtain a majority vote on the city council.[7] While the women continued to work as cheap labor in the British shirt factories, there was mass unemployment among men. According to Derry-born Nobel Peace Prize winner John Hume, Derry was the worst case of Protestant discrimination against Irish Catholics in the whole of Northern Ireland.[8]

Widespread discontent and frustration among Catholics led to frequent riots between the Catholics and the Royal Ulster Constabulary (RUC), the majority Protestant-dominated police force of Northern Ireland (1922–2001). These riots escalated during the marching season when "Orange Order" groups celebrated two major historic Protestant victories: the successful defense of the city walls by the Apprentice Boys during Catholic King James II's siege of the city in 1689, and King James' defeat by William of Orange during the Battle of Boyne the year after. Since the marches followed a route over the walls overlooking the Bogside, they were provocative assertions of Protestant superiority over the Bogside Catholics.[9]

In the late 1960s, Catholic protests took on another dimension. Inspired by Martin Luther King's civil rights movement in the USA, Catholics started to organize their own marches on the streets of Derry. Joined by Protestant socialists, the marches were part of a global protest movement fighting for democratic rights for people irrespective of race, religion or ethnicity. In 1967, Protestant Ivan Cooper and Catholic John Hume founded the Northern Ireland Civil Rights Association (NICRA) demanding an end to the Unionists' discriminatory policies against Catholics. The large gatherings and demonstrations created a sense of solidarity, excitement and hope for the future. Sadly, this was not to last for long.

Three Key Incidents

Three incidents, in particular, were to change this mood of hope and determine the future not only of the people of Derry but of the course of history of Northern Ireland as a whole.

The first event was the Civil Rights march organized by the Derry Housing Action Committee (DHAC) on October 5, 1968. The march was broken up by the RUC leading to widespread battles between them and the marchers. With footage of baton-charging police beating protestors broadcast around the world on the evening news, Northern Ireland's situation was now fully on the political map as it was to be for the next three decades. Three months after the incident, the Bogside declared itself the first "no go" area, displaying the defiant slogan "You are Now entering Free Derry" on its entry gable wall.[10]

The second event, subsequently referred to as the "Battle of the Bogside," consisted of a three-day riot in August 1969, following clashes between Catholics and Protestants during the annual Protestant Apprentice Boys parade. With the local RUC no longer in control, the government sent in the British Army to impose order. Although the soldiers were initially welcomed as protecting peacekeepers against the unbridled attacks of the RUC, this soon changed as round-the-clock surveillance, searches and arrests resulted in increasing tensions between local residents and the British military.

The third and most decisive incident took place on January 30, 1972, during a large protest march organized by NICRA.[11] Anticipating further riots and in order to keep what they called the "Young Derry Hooligans" (YDH) under control, the British Government had called on its elite 1st Parachute Regiment to re-enforce the British troops with the specific brief to target and arrest the YDH's ringleaders.[12] When, due to miscommunications about the route, the march turned into clashes with the police, the Regiment stepped in and fatally shot over a dozen unarmed protesters, six of them just seventeen years old. The killings took place within less than half an hour, in full daylight and in front of many witnesses. On the evening news that same day, the British General Commander defended his soldiers' actions by claiming that the Regiment had responded to shots being fired and that they had acted in self-defense. This account of the day was repeated in a report produced soon afterward by Lord Widgery, subsequently described as a "whitewash" and, by Father (later Bishop) Edward Daley, as "a second atrocity."[13] Notwithstanding the blatant falsity of the account, this version of the events remained the Government's official position until the publication of Lord Saville's Report in 2010. Following a twelve-year inquiry, the longest and most expensive in British history, Lord Saville concluded that there had been "a serious and widespread loss of fire discipline among the soldiers of Support Company," and that the "firing by soldiers of 1 PARA on Bloody Sunday caused the deaths of 13 people and injury to a similar number, none of whom was posing a threat of causing death or serious injury."[14]

The events of the day, and the way they had been reported by the British media, left the Bogside community in shock, disbelief and anger. Mourning the loss of their fathers, brothers and sons, they felt deeply betrayed. Not only were their protests suppressed and their campaigners classed as "hooligans," their civil rights campaign as a whole was recast as a primitive tribal warfare between ethnic and religious factions that needed to be kept under British control. As a result, NICRA membership dwindled and people flocked to the local division of the Provisional Irish Republican Army (PIRA), where a then twenty-two-year-old Martin McGuinness was Second-in-Command.[15] As Lord Saville puts it in the conclusion of his report:

> What happened on Bloody Sunday strengthened the Provisional IRA, increased nationalist resentment and hostility towards the Army and exacerbated the violent conflict of the years that followed. Bloody Sunday was a tragedy for the bereaved and the wounded, and a catastrophe for the people of Northern Ireland.[16]

The above three incidents are central to the story that is depicted on the murals on Rossville Street where most of the action took place. The murals honor civil rights leaders Bernadette Devlin, Ivan Cooper and John Hume, as well as ordinary residents, including women and children. Unlike standard sectarian murals, the murals were not designed as declarations of identity, political propaganda or territorial markers, but as ways of telling the stories of people as they had lived through the period. The artists believe that this telling and remembering are a necessary stage in the process of healing and a crucial step on the road to peace. In order to show how the murals differ from standard sectarian murals, it is worth providing a brief history of mural painting in Northern Ireland.

Murals in Northern Ireland

Throughout their history, murals in Northern Ireland have served a variety of purposes: consolidating ethnic, religious or national identity; commemorating historic events, heroes or martyrs; expressing political views and opinions; campaigning for causes; marking territory; celebrating local culture; and so on. Some murals are regularly and carefully maintained, others are transient and short-lived. Some are the result of community consultation, others are painted unilaterally or imposed under threat.[17]

The earliest mural painting in Northern Ireland took place in Protestant communities in the early twentieth century. Most popular among them was the image of Prince William of Orange, affectionately called "King Billy," crossing the river Boyne on his horse during the battle against Catholic King James II in 1690. The "Battle of the Boyne" marked the beginning of the "Protestant Ascendancy," the long period of Protestant political, economic and social domination of Ireland.

After the partition of Ireland in 1922, the commemoration of their victory over Catholics remained an important aspect of Protestant culture and identity, expressed in annual parades, bonfires, banners, flags and murals. Their need to remind themselves of their history can be partially explained by their Reformed fears of subordination to Rome, with the Vatican being seen not only as a religious center but also as a political power. The dominant anxiety was that Irish "Home Rule" implied "Rome Rule." This fear is also reflected in the defensive rhetoric of slogans such as "No Surrender," "Ulster says No," and "Still under Siege."

While prior to the Troubles Protestant murals consisted mainly of classically painted historical scenes, after their outbreak there was a sharp rise in aggressive and belligerent imagery—masked gunmen brandishing rifles, clenched fists, intimidating slogans and so on. Different Loyalist groupings, such as the Ulster Defence Association (UDA) and the Ulster Volunteer Force (UVF), started to adopt different emblems and insignia to mark their dominance in particular neighborhoods. The style of images changed too, no longer drawing its main inspiration from classical paintings but from contemporary graphic and poster art.

By contrast, Catholics Nationalists did not have a comparable tradition of mural painting. With public space controlled by Protestant Unionists, Catholics were more restricted in the public expression of their views. This changed however in the late 1970s when the gable ends of terraced houses in Catholic communities were beginning to be used by Republicans to express and promote their causes. Some of the earliest murals expressed support for the Republican hunger strikers in the Maze prison.[18] The portrait of Bobby Sands, who died in 1981, became one of the most popular images on Republican murals.[19] Other murals drew on Irish and Celtic history and mythology, including the Flight of the Earls, often executed in colorful Celtic designs with decorative borders of interlaced ribbons. More recent murals also show support for political struggles in other parts of the world, especially South Africa, Nicaragua and Palestine. Interestingly, many Republican muralists, such as Danny Devenny, first learned to paint in art classes taught at prison.

Re-imaging Civic Society

After the Good Friday Agreement in 1998, Stormont's new power-sharing Office of the First Minister and Deputy First Minister (OFMDFM) was eager to re-establish Northern Ireland as "a normal, civic society."[20] A central question then, as it continues to be today, was how to deal with the visible manifestations of sectarianism, in particular flags, parades and murals.[21] On the one hand, in order to reassure foreign investors and tourists, Stormont was eager to re-brand Northern Ireland as a safe, inclusive, post-sectarian society that was economically viable and forward-looking. On the other hand, they did not want to alienate its (mainly working class) Catholic and Protestant voters and communities by suppressing what was considered their legitimate cultural expression. From 2004 onwards the government began to offer generous grants to communities for the replacement of aggressive and belligerent murals with peaceful and conciliatory ones. By that time the most polemical murals were not those in Republican neighborhoods but in Loyalist communities who continued to feel themselves "under siege."

In 2006, with an initial budget of £3.3m, the Government launched the "Building Peace through the Arts — Re-Imaging Communities Programme." Administered by the Arts Council of Northern Ireland it was meant to encourage communities "to promote tolerance and understanding while using the arts to express who they are and what culture means to them."[22] To date, it has spent over £5m. Although arguably well intended, the program was fundamentally misguided. Traditionally grass roots, community-based practice and mural painting now became a government regulated, tender-based enterprise involving bureaucratic application procedures unsuited to local, mainly non-professional, artists. Decisions on content, too, proved controversial. In one case, an intimidating looking "Grim Reaper" was replaced by an image of William of Orange on his white horse, sword and all. While defended by the Arts Council as reflecting "the Orange culture of the community," this effectively meant the public funding of a polemic, triumphalist Loyalist symbol celebrating a Protestant victory over Catholics. Another problem with the program was the lack of detail in its guidelines. Since the most aggressive murals were mainly found in the most politicized neighborhoods, newly painted replacements could often be seen flanked by still remaining para-militaristic images, or even painted over as soon as the Arts Council's cheque had cleared.[23] Finally, since the main thrust of the re-imaging program was to de-politicize murals, there was a general tendency to approve rather bland and clichéd images—iconic sports people such as George Best, cheerful playgrounds or exotic landscapes—often at odds with the bleak reality of the mural's actual surroundings. Not being owned by the community, they were prone to being vandalized.[24]

To add to the complexity, since the Peace Agreement in 1998, Northern Ireland's sectarian murals had become a major tourist attraction. This, in turn, provided lucrative business for local cab drivers and tour guides—often ex-prisoners and ex-paramilitaries struggling to find employment elsewhere. Bringing in much-needed revenue for deprived working-class neighborhoods, the Northern Ireland Tourist Board even began to advertise the murals as a "must-see experience" alongside Northern Ireland's other cultural and coastal attractions. Glamorized by our culture's fascination with violence, this "dark tourism" was typically most interested in the most aggressive and most intimidating murals.

The People's Gallery

It is against this complex background of competing needs and interests that *The People's Gallery* needs to be viewed. Born and raised in the Bogside, the artists Tom Kelly (b. 1959), William Kelly (1948–2017) and Kevin Hasson (b. 1958) witnessed the conflict first hand. For over thirty years, they and their families lived with raids and riots, gas and petrol bombs, bullets and funerals. British tanks and soldiers patrolled their streets and surveillance towers overlooked their neighborhood day and night. All three lost relatives and friends, several of them commemorated on the murals. Young people lost out on regular education. The local rule of order was in the hands of the IRA.

The artists painted their first mural in 1994, while the conflict was still going on and four years before the Peace Agreement. Prior to painting it, the artists had collected over two thousand signatures from local residents for a petition to the Northern Ireland Housing Executive (NIHE), which owned the blocks of flats on which the murals were to be painted.[25] With the approval of the Housing Executive's Head Office in Belfast, the previously graffitied walls were cleaned and rendered with smooth cement at the Executive's expense in order to facilitate the painting of the murals. At that time the area was a derelict urban wasteland with broken up streets, debris rubble, burnt out cars and widespread graffiti—the result of decades of neglect and vandalism.[26] The RUC and the British Army were still heavy on the ground. Indeed, the first murals were painted under the watchful eyes of, and variously sneering or admiring remarks by, patrolling police and soldiers. That the murals have never been vandalized by local youth is a testimony not only to the power of their artistic impact but also to the affection in which they are held by the local community.

The first mural, the Petrol Bomber (1994), in monochrome black and white, was completed in 1994. Like several of their murals, the image is based on an historic photograph, thus highlighting the important role of the media at the time. Taken by Clive Limpkin the photograph shows a young boy, a cousin of Tom and William Kelly, wearing an old (and defunct) World War II gas mask and about to throw a handmade bomb (Fig. 4.1). It is a compelling and ambiguous image—on the one hand a vulnerable child wearing a protective mask, on the other hand a sinister looking active combatant holding a lethal missile. The mural was a resounding success in the community and this sparked the idea to paint all twelve gables on the

Fig. 4.1 "The Petrol Bomber" (1994), Photo credit Kevin Hasson

street. With the encouragement of the local residents and the full approval of the Housing Executive, this was the beginning of *The People's Gallery*.

Facing the *Petrol Bomber* is *Bernadette* (1997), showing the young MP Bernadette Devlin addressing the crowds on the streets during the Battle of the Bogside. In the background, one can see the gable with the words "Free Derry Corner."

Bloody Sunday (1997) was painted to commemorate the twenty-fifth anniversary of the fatal shootings and shows Father Edward Daly ahead of a group of men carrying the limp body of Jack Duddy, a young Bloody Sunday victim. The mural is painted in black and white and constructed from two famous news photos taken by Italian journalist Fulvio Grimaldi.[27] The only color on the mural is the red stain on the civil rights banner under the feet of the British soldier. The image of a small group of people carrying a wounded or lifeless body has become a familiar feature of our daily news streams, whether from Syria or elsewhere. This may explain the powerful resonance felt by many visitors.

In *Death of Innocence* (1999), we see the large image of a young girl in her school uniform (Fig. 4.2). The girl is fourteen-year-old Annette McGavigan, a cousin of Kevin, the first girl to be killed and the hundredth civilian victim of the Troubles. Caught in a crossfire between the rioters

Fig. 4.2 "Death of Innocence", Photo credit CAIN (www.cain.ulster.ac.uk)

and the military, she was shot in the back by a British Paratrooper while looking for colored stones for a school art project in 1971.[28] The mural also depicts a gun, a simple outline of a butterfly, and the shape of a cross in the midst of the rubble. When they finished the mural in 1999, the artists intentionally left the butterfly near Annette's head only in outline, and the rifle on the sidebar intact, thus indicating the still-fragile peace. When the mural was repainted in 2006, however, the butterfly was colored in and the rifle broken in half, a symbolic gesture that was marked with a neighborhood celebration. To the artists Annette represents all innocent children who are victims of the conflict, including those killed by IRA bombings. The mural can be clearly seen from the old city walls. Annette is looking straight at the viewer.

The mural *Hunger Strike* (2000) was repainted in 2015. Originally, it showed hunger striker Raymond McCartney, who survived the strike and had since become a Member of the Legislative Assembly (MLA). Growing dissatisfaction with Sinn Féin leadership, however, meant that it was frequently attacked with paint bombs by dissident Republicans. The new image represents two other Derry-born hunger strikers, Patsy O'Hara and Mickey Devine, who both died as a result of their strike, shown underneath the portraits of their mothers. The artists want to remind people of the suffering of the mothers of the strikers—the often forgotten victims of the conflict. One other additional new feature is the image of a lamb seen faintly above the women. This image hints at the view that some hunger strikers may have died as sacrificial lambs to further the electoral ambitions of their leaders.[29]

The *Civil Rights* mural (2004) is arguably the most important mural of the series in that it reminds people of the importance of the civil rights movement and the early non-violent struggle for equal democratic rights (Figs. 4.3 and 4.4). The image conveys the happy excitement that characterized the early marches. Several of the people depicted are family members of residents still living in the area. The fact that the Troubles were initially sparked by clashes between the British backed local police and the civil rights campaigners has been seriously underreported by the British media. Instead, they typically represented the civil unrest in Northern Ireland as a primitive religious, sectarian clash between Catholics and Protestants, thereby enforcing the public's belief in the need for ongoing British control in the region. That said, after Bloody Sunday, the civil rights movement was in effect hijacked by Republicans seeking to establish a united Ireland. In order to remind people of the early civil rights movement and to honor

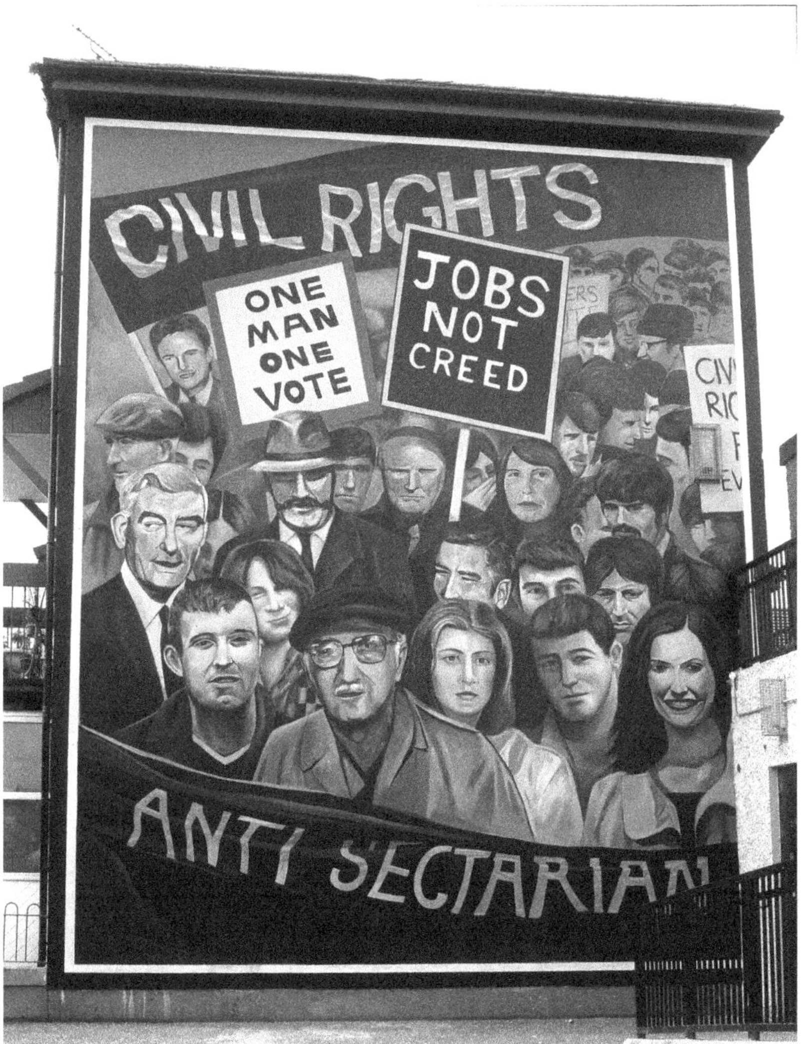

Fig. 4.3 "Civil Rights", Photo credit CAIN (www.cain.ulster.ac.uk)

its leaders, the artists made a point of including Ivan Cooper and John Hume as part of their renovated mural in 2015.[30]

Fig. 4.4 "William Kelly working on the Civil Rights mural", Photo credit Kevin Hasson

Three further monochrome murals refer to important events at the time: *Operation Motorman* (2001) shows a towering figure breaking down a door with a sledgehammer, representing the British Army's 1972 house raids to retake "no-go areas." Visitors from Palestine often comment on how this image reminds them of their situation at home. *The Runner* (2006) depicts a young boy in full flight from a cloud of the CS gas used by the British Army. The boy in the mural represents seventeen-year-old Brian Coyle, an IRA volunteer who was killed by a prematurely exploding home-made bomb meant for a British foot patrol. The incident happened in the backyard of Tom Kelly's home. The mural is both a commemorative lament and a critique of IRA paramilitaries who failed to protect children by radicalizing them for their violent warfare. The mural also shows the portraits of two other school friends of Tom who were killed. One of them was hit by shrapnel from an IRA-bomb while watching a Bloody Sunday commemoration in 1990. The other, a fifteen-year-old cousin of Tom called Manus Deery, was killed by a bullet fired from the city walls by a British sniper in 1972. Manus had just left a chip shop celebrating his first wage packet with friends. Brian's family was just offered £100 in compensation for their loss. After a forty-four-year fight by his sister for an inquiry, the coroner finally confirmed that Manus had been unarmed and an innocent victim of an unjustified shooting.[31]

The Rioter (2001), showing a lonely local youth in a stand-off with the British Army, evokes the photo of the "Tank-Man" student in front of the tanks on Tiananmen Square. When standing in front of *The Rioter*, one can simultaneously glimpse the colorful *Peace Mural* (2004) in the distant background (Fig. 4.5).

In sharp contrast to the monochrome grays of most of the other murals, this mural shows an explosion of brightly colored pattern of squares with a large dove painted over it. Based on ideas from local children, the dove is a symbol of peace as well as the city's patron Saint Columba emerging from an oak leaf—a reference to the city's original name (Fig. 4.6).

Finally, *Tribute to John Hume* (2008) depicts the co-founder and former leader of the Social Democratic and Labour Party, John Hume who played a major role in brokering the Peace Agreement. In 1998, alongside his Protestant counterpart David Trimble, he was awarded the Nobel Peace Prize. The mural shows Hume surrounded by other Nobel Peace Prize Laureates Martin Luther King, Mother Teresa and Nelson Mandela.

Difference from Sectarian Murals

How then are the murals of the People's Gallery different from sectarian murals? Significantly, unlike their sectarian counterparts, the murals by the Bogside Artists do not contain any political slogans or texts. They neither appeal to Irish history or Celtic mythology, nor do they show any emblems, flags or symbols that would associate them with a particular political party or paramilitary group. The main aim of the Bogside Murals is to remember and tell the story of ordinary residents, whose main worries until the Troubles had been how to house, feed and school their families, but who had their

Fig. 4.5 "The Rioter" and "The Peace Mural", Photo credit CAIN (www.cain.ulster.ac.uk)

lives turned upside down as they stood up for their rights and had to suffer the tragic consequences for doing so.

Importantly, the story told by the Bogside murals is told from the very stage where the events took place. Indeed, the *Bloody Sunday* mural still contains the bullet holes of the shots that were fired by the Parachute Regiment that day—art and life fusing together. The sheer size of the murals, as painted on the sides of three-story apartment blocks, enables a bolder design than that typically used in traditional sectarian murals done on the gable ends of small two-story terraced houses. This also means that they can be clearly seen from the city walls, the loaded symbols of past Protestant rule and power. The Annette mural, as mentioned, is looking straight at the viewer. As one television correspondent put it: "The message that emerges is that the desire to create art reflects the need to tell a story no

Fig. 4.6 "The Peace Mural" (2004), Photo credit Kevin Hasson

matter how difficult, painful or controversial that may be. Only in this case, the entire street is the artists' canvas."[32]

Unlike most political mural painters, the Bogside Artists do not see themselves as political activists who happen to paint—indeed, the three of them hold very different political views—but painters who capture a profound human experience that is inevitably also deeply political. They want *The People's Gallery* to be approached first and foremost as *a work of art*, not as a political statement or piece of propaganda. This is not meant as a comment on their or other murals' relative artistic quality or merit, but to emphasize that they are standing in their own right as independent expressions of affective lived human experience rather than message boards for particular political groups.

Truth and Reconciliation After the Peace Agreement

As the artists work on mainting and restoring their murals on their scaffolding, local residents often stop by for a chat or to offer refreshments. The artists are aware that many of them feel a deep need to share their own personal stories and recollections of the Troubles.[33] The murals offer a safe space to express their often mixed and complex feelings—grief, anger, hope, fear, hate, resentment, despair, regret and so on. The artists sometimes refer to their scaffolding as the neighborhood's "confession box."

This invitation to reflect and recollect is all the more important since, unlike South Africa and other countries, Northern Ireland never had—and never may have—a process of truth and reconciliation.[34] Although there is now a power-sharing government in Northern Ireland, the main political parties are still deeply divided about the causes that gave rise to the Troubles. As Lord Saville put it in his conclusions:

> The question whether or not the Troubles were primarily a republican struggle for a united Ireland or a socialist struggle for internal reforms and human rights is still a matter of debate, with different parties trying to (re-)write history to their own advantage.[35]

As a result, there is as yet no strongly shared political will to engage in a truth and reconciliation process.

In such a climate, it is often difficult for victims to share their own, uniquely individual stories and experiences of the Troubles, stories that do not fit the basic binary categories of the master narratives. Many victims suffered violence and intimidation from within their own communities. Any dealings with "the enemy," whether providing services or having close friendships, were potentially dangerous, risking punishment beatings or worse. The perpetrators of these crimes are rarely brought to justice. Moreover, part of the Peace Agreement was the controversial decision to release some five hundred Loyalist and Republican paramilitary prisoners, many of them previously convicted of serious crimes. As a result, victims were often told "to forget the past and move on." This has rendered many ordinary citizens not only without justice, but also without voice.

In this context, the murals provide a highly visible, public reminder of the harrowing events that have impacted their lives for good. The murals tell us *not* to forget. As a high profile memorial, they express, preserve and shape the public memory of a wounded community. They provide a natural talking point for non-directive, free-flowing conversation and recollections—an essential step in the process of healing.

Although the murals tell the story of a particular community at a particular time, they have a significance that extends beyond the people of the Bogside. Not long after the Good Friday Agreement, the first tourists started to arrive in Derry, drawn by the city's historic heritage and ancient walls but also, and increasingly so, by the Bogside murals. Kevin Hasson comments: "No-one expected an international influx of visitors. .... The only foreigners we had seen were wearing camouflage uniforms and TV cameras so the whole tourism aspect was never on our agenda."[36] As it turned out, the images strongly resonated with visitors from other parts of the world involved in similar struggles for basic civil rights. Many visitors share their responses with the artists on site. Sometimes, the artists feel that the murals are better understood by outsiders than people in their own city, especially the local council, many of whom remain locked into traditional sectarian thinking. For those outsiders, the murals are about the struggle for civil rights not only in their own country but in any country. This inclusive approach transcends the narrow binary definitions of Northern Ireland's history, identity, culture and politics. The murals invite the viewer to imaginatively enter and remember human suffering and oppression wherever or whenever it arises. Such a call is not intended to legitimate indulgence in past hurts or incitement to revenge, but rather as *an affective act of solidarity* with victims of violence both then and now and a plea for justice as a condition for lasting peace.[37]

The artists often quote Bishop Desmond Tutu saying: "A wound must be cleaned out and examined before it will heal. It is the unexamined wound that festers and finally poisons."[38] The artists see their murals as showing the wounds. They do not claim a monopoly on suffering. They recognize that, while the murals can inevitably only tell *their* story, many others have suffered as well. For the artists, the need to confront one's wounds always crosses ethnic and religious divides. They acknowledge that, during the years of conflict, both Catholics and Protestants suffered immensely as the result of the institutionalization of sectarianism.[39] While the Bogside is their story, their sympathies are with all of the people who have suffered in Northern Ireland whatever their class, creed, politics or belief systems. They deeply believe that only when both communities of Catholics and Protestants have confronted the wounds they have inflicted on each other, and on themselves, can there be the possibility of healing or forgiveness.

Such healing or forgiveness is more complex than a mere formal peace agreement or public reconciliation between two communities. Reflecting on the murals, one Australian viewer articulated his own reaction thus:

> The scale of the daily violence experienced by the people of the North of Ireland is not to be assessed just in terms of fatalities and the physical and emotional results of the violence. There is a deeper spiritual dimension that is communicated. I find myself responding most to the overpowering message of the murals: This is our story, where is yours?[40]

It has long been acknowledged by those working in the fields of peace and reconciliation that, in order to restore mutual trust and understanding, it is essential to both share and learn to listen to each other's stories. As theologian Stanley Hauerwas once put it: "Reconciliation happens when my enemy tells me my story and I am able to say: 'Yes, that is my story.'"

There are some signs that other communities are also beginning to write their stories. Until recently it has been very difficult for the Protestant community to share their own painful experiences. During the height of the Troubles, an estimated fifteen thousand people—almost ninety percent of all Protestant families—were forced to leave Derry's city center due to fear of Republican violence and intimidation. Unwilling or unable to return, they feel exiled and uprooted from their old social fabric and roots. A church in Derry has recently commissioned a playwright to write a series of short dramas—"The Exile"—addressing the effect of the Protestant exodus on the lives of the people involved.[41]

In the summer of 2016, the artists and I produced a traveling exhibition on the story of the murals and the Troubles. The exhibition consists of photographs of the murals juxtaposed with black and white historic photographs of Derry during the Troubles, many of which were taken by local amateur photographers. The idea of the exhibition emerged after we had conducted a day-long seminar on the murals in a community center in the heart of Derry in 2015. The day had been endorsed both by the Catholic and by the Anglican Bishop of Derry, as well as other church leaders.[42] Several local Protestants who attended the seminar confessed to never having given the murals any attention which, on the basis of their location, they had assumed were just Republican propaganda. Yet, after meeting and listening to the artists they commented that they had a much better and more sympathetic understanding not only of the murals, but also of the people and the history of the Bogside. When we showed the exhibition at Greenbelt Festival in 2016, a Christian Arts Festival in the UK, similar encounters of new mutual understanding occurred. Prompted by the image of the mural *Motorman*, one British ex-soldier shared how, age nineteen, he had been posted in Derry without knowing anything about the history and background and had been thoroughly confused.[43] He also shared his experience of the lack of support and aftercare for soldiers like him after their return from Northern Ireland, compared to those having served in other areas of conflict. This often added to their sense of confusion and trauma. As had been the case in Derry, this personal encounter and exchange, prompted by the images and conducted in the safe context of the exhibition, turned into a source of healing and mutual understanding between individuals previously considered wide apart. Similar encounters occurred when the exhibition was shown in other places, including Coventry Cathedral with its long-standing esteemed ministry of reconciliation.[44]

Talking about the evil of sectarianism the artists write:

> The institutionalisation of sectarian exclusivity is the very essence of the conflict. It is a crime against both Catholics and Protestants. Our fervent wish is that the peace process will give us time to put right what has been so drastically put wrong. To this end we devote our craft and our energy, our imagination, our story and our hope. [45]

At the time the artists wrote the above, the peace process was still at its very beginning. At the time of writing this chapter some twenty years later, there have been many positive developments. Yet there is still a long way to go. The murals make sure that the past is not forgotten and that important lessons can be learned.

Notes

1. The dual name of the city reflects a long-standing naming dispute between Nationalists and Unionists, the first preferring Derry, the latter Londonderry. The oldest name for the city was Doire which was later anglicised to Derry. In recognition of the settler merchants and investors from London during the Plantation of Ulster, this was changed by Royal Charter to Londonderry in 1613. In 1984, the city's local authority changed its name to "Derry City Council." After merging with nearby Strabane in 2015, this became "Derry and Strabane District Council." Since the name "Derry" is

widely used informally, and almost always locally, I will, for the remainder of this chapter, use that name to refer the city.

2. The combined number of deaths during this period—inflicted by both Republican and Loyalist paramilitaries as well as British security forces—exceeded 3600. In addition, over 50,000 people were physically maimed or injured, with countless others psychologically traumatised and damaged. For detailed information and statistics on the Troubles see CAIN (Conflict Archive on the INternet) based at the University of Ulster. www.cain.ulst.ac.uk, accessed 10 December 2018.
3. For an overview of the murals, see www.cain.ulst.ac.uk/bogsideartists/menu.htm, accessed 10 December 2018. For a book on the murals written by the Bogside Artists, see Anthony C. Joseph, *The People's Gallery* (Derry, NI: A joint production by The Bogside Artists, 2007).
4. (Mainly Catholic) Nationalists and Republicans seek a re-unification of Northern Ireland with Ireland while (mainly Protestant) Unionists and Loyalists want Ulster to remain part of Britain.
5. See John Whyte, *Interpreting Northern Ireland* (Oxford: Oxford University Press, 2003 [1990]).
6. There is a vast literature related to "the Troubles," including discussion of discrimination. See, for example, John Whyte, "How Much Discrimination Was There Under the Unionist Regime, 1921–1968", in *Contemporary Irish Studies*, ed. Tom Gallagher and James O'Connell (Manchester: Manchester University Press, 1983).

   For bibliographies and further resources see the website of CAIN (Conflict Archive on the Internet), which contains a wide range of useful primary source and secondary materials on 'the Troubles' and politics in Northern Ireland from 1968 to the present. http://cain.ulst.ac.uk/, accessed 22 December 2018.
7. In an interview, John Hume explains election rigging in Derry as follows: 'The Catholic population, who would have been known as Nationalist Irish, were 70% of the population. But they were all in one district and that one district elected eight councillors. The Unionists, the Protestant people, were in two districts. 30% of the population in two separate districts and each district elected six councillors. So they won every election 12-8 and they were in control of public housing. And when I was first elected one of my major things in my campaign was to fight to get housing taken out of the hands of local government and an independent housing authority set up. That was one of my first great achievements.' www.nobelprize.org/nobel_prizes/peace/laureates/1998/hume-interview-transcript.html, accessed 10 December 2018. Not long before his death, even Ian Paisley admitted that the voting conditions had been unfair: "It wasn't one man—one vote … it was not acceptable at all." Ian Paisley, Face to Face with Mallie' BBC interview January 2014.

8. www.nobelprize.org/nobel_prizes/peace/laureates/1998/hume-interview-transcript.html, accessed 10 December 2018.
9. This included the marchers throwing pennies down over the wall to deliberately provoke the local Catholics. See, for instance, the entry on the 1969 Battle of the Bogside in the history of parades on the CAIN Website: "The Apprentice Boys held their annual parade on the 12 August and as they paraded past the Bogside (a working-class Catholic part of Derry) they jeered and threw pennies at Catholics. Catholics responded with stones, and loyalist supporters and the Royal Ulster Constabulary (RUC) then became involved. By 7.15 that evening, a full scale riot was in progress, later referred to as the 'Battle of the Bogside'." http://cain.ulst.ac.uk/issues/parade/chronpa2.htm, accessed 2 January 2019. See also the memorandum submitted by the Bogside Residents' Group to the Select Committee of Northern Ireland Affairs, dated July 19, 2001: "Parades along the Walls were particularly controversial. Apprentice Boys would hurl missiles, including pennies onto the streets of the Bogside to demonstrate their contempt for people living there." www.publications.parliament.uk/pa/cm200001/cmselect/cmniaf/120/1020606.htm, accessed 2 January 2019; Ruth Weiss, *Peace in our Time: War and Peace in Ireland and Southern Africa* (London: I.B. Tauris, 2000), 45; Tim Pat Coogan, *The Troubles: Ireland's Ordeal 1966–1995 and the Search for Peace* (London: Arrow Books, 1996), 87–88.
10. Although the house on which the slogan was painted has since been destroyed, the wall itself was saved and moved to a traffic island in the middle of Rossville Street, where it now serves as a monument and gathering point for meetings and demonstrations. At one time John Hume's grandmother lived in the house.
11. The estimated number of marchers was over 20,000.
12. www.bbc.co.uk/news/10322583, accessed 10 December 2018. "In the secret memo to his superior, dated 7 January 1972, Sir Robert [the most senior general on the ground on Bloody Sunday] said he was 'coming to the conclusion that the minimum force necessary to achieve a restoration of law and order is to shoot selected ringleaders amongst the DYH (Derry Young Hooligans), after clear warnings have been issued." The memo is referred to in Lord Saville's *Report of the Bloody Sunday Inquiry*, see Lord Saville of Newdigate, William Hoyt, and John Toohey, *Report of the Bloody Sunday Inquiry*, vols. I–X (London: HMSO, 15 June 2010), available at www.gov.uk/government/publications/report-of-the-bloody-sunday-inquiry, accessed 10 December 2018. Clause 2.6: "The situation in Londonderry in January 1972 was serious. By this stage the nationalist community had largely turned against the soldiers, many believing that the Army, as well as the RUC, were agents of an oppressive regime. Parts of the city to the west of the Foyle lay in ruins, as the result of the activities

of the IRA and of rioting young men (some members of the IRA or its junior wing, the Fianna) known to soldiers and some others as the 'Derry Young Hooligans'. A large part of the nationalist area of the city was a 'no go' area, which was dominated by the IRA, where ordinary policing could not be conducted and where even the Army ventured only by using large numbers of soldiers." And Clause 2.13: "At the beginning of January 1972, Major General Robert Ford, then Commander of Land Forces in Northern Ireland, had visited Londonderry. He wrote a confidential memorandum to Lieutenant General Sir Harry Tuzo, his senior and the General Officer Commanding Northern Ireland, in which he expressed himself disturbed by the attitude of the officers commanding the resident troops and that of Chief Superintendent Lagan. He recorded that they had told him that the area of damage in the city was extending and that even the major shopping center would be destroyed in the coming months. He referred in particular to the 'Derry Young Hooligans' as a factor in the continued destruction of the city, and expressed the view that the Army was 'virtually incapable' of dealing with them. He also expressed the view that he was coming to the conclusion that the minimum force required to deal with the 'Derry Young Hooligans' was, after clear warnings, to shoot selected ringleaders."

13. Quoted in Susan McKay, *Bear in Mind These Dead* (London: Faber & Faber, 2008), 312.
14. Lord Saville of Newdigate, William Hoyt, and John Toohey, "Principal Conclusions and Overall Assessment of the Bloody Sunday Inquiry", in Saville et al., *Report of the Bloody Sunday Inquiry*.
15. The Irish Republican Army (IRA) was the paramilitary wing of Republicanism. From 1970 until 1972, when the Official IRA (OIRA) declared a ceasefire, it was called Provisional IRA (PIRA) also called the "Provisionals" or "Provos." During the Troubles, Sinn Féin was considered to be the political voice of the IRA. For a glossary of terms related to the conflict, see www.cain.ulst.ac.uk/othelem/glossary.htm, accessed 10 December 2018.
16. Lord Saville et al., "Principle Conclusions."
17. For a comprehensive history of murals in Northern Ireland, see Bill Rolston, "The War of the Walls: Political Murals in Northern Ireland", *Museum International* 56:3 (2004): 38–54 and his series: *Drawing Support*, vols. 1–4 (Belfast, NI: Beyond the Pale, 1992, 1995, 2003, 2013). Other publications include: Adrian Kerr, ed., *Murals of Derry* (Derry, NI: Guildhall Press, 2016) and Stuart Borthwick, *The Writing on the Wall: A Visual History of Northern Ireland's Troubles* (Liverpool, UK: Bluecoat Press, 2015).
18. Until 1976 paramilitary prisoners had been treated as political prisoners with Special Category Status and not as standard criminals. This meant that they did not have to wear prison uniforms or be employed for prison work. After 1976 newly convicted paramilitaries were no longer granted this privilege. In protest, the prisoners started a series of protests, including soiling their

cells and wearing blankets instead of uniforms, hence their honorary label of "blanket men." The protests culminated in two major hunger strikes, one in 1980 and one in 1981, during which in total twelve prisoners died.

19. Bobby Sands was the first hunger striker to die. Months before his death he had been elected as a Member of Parliament. Although the strike did not lead to any major concessions, Sands' election as a Member of Parliament significantly boosted Sinn Féin's standing as a credible nationalist political movement.
20. Stormont is the home of the Northern Ireland Assembly and the Office of the First Minister and Deputy First Minister. For two documents outlining the Government's proposed policies, see *A Shared Future: Policy and Strategic Framework for Good Relations in Northern Ireland* (Belfast, NI: Community Relations Unit and Office of the First Minister and Deputy First Minister, March 2005), available at www.niacro.co.uk/sites/default/files/publications/A%20Shared%20Future-%20OFMDFM-Mar%202005.pdf, accessed 10 December 2018 and The Executive Office for Northern Ireland, *Together: Building a United Community Strategy* (Belfast, NI: Executive Office for NI, 23 May 2013), available at www.executiveoffice-ni.gov.uk/articles/about-together-building-united-community-tbuc, accessed 10 December 2018.
21. See the section "Tackling the Visible Manifestations of Sectarianism and Racism" in "A Shared Future," 19. For a brief overview of the issues in recent discussions, see "NI Talks Issues Explained: Flags, Parades, the Past and Welfare Reform", *BBC Northern Ireland*, 12 December 2014, www.bbc.co.uk/news/uk-northern-ireland-25429676, accessed 10 December 2018.
22. For a description of the scheme, see http://artscouncil-ni.org/the-arts/visual-arts1/re-imaging-communities, accessed 10 December 2018.

    For a discussion of the program, see Bill Rolston, "Re-imaging: Mural Painting and the State in Northern Ireland", *International Journal of Cultural Studies* 15:5 (2012): 447–466.
23. For a critical assessment of the scheme see Allison Morris, "Public Should Not Pay—Whether Murals Go or Stay", *The Irish News*, 16 October 2014, www.irishnews.com/opinion/2014/10/16/news/public-should-not-pay---whether-murals-go-or-stay-105214, accessed 10 December 2018.
24. A similar scheme in early 1970s, sponsoring art students to "brighten up" deprived areas, had failed for the same reasons. See Julian Watson, "Brightening the Place Up?", *Circa* 8 (January–February 1983): 4–10.
25. The Northern Ireland Housing Executive (NIHE) was established in 1971 as an independent body to take decisions on housing allocation away from Unionist councils. See also footnote 4 on John Hume's role in the foundation of the NIHE.

26. Before working on *The People's Gallery*, Tom Kelly had led cross-community arts workshops for the Outreach Program of the Orchard Gallery, founded by Declan McGonagle.
27. Fulvio Grimaldi wrote a short book, *Blood in the Street*, about his experiences on Bloody Sunday shortly after the event which was re-issued by Guildhall Pressin 1998. In 2018, film makers Pietro Laino, Rocco Forte produced a film about Grimaldi and the Bogside Artists around the people and events depicted on the murals. www.lulifilm.net/bogside-story, accessed 10 December 2018.
28. For a brief commentary on the mural by Kevin Hasson, see www.youtube.com/watch?v=hT9VnXveQF0, accessed 10 December 2018.

    The soldier has never been identified or prosecuted and the family of the girl is still seeking justice. www.derryjournal.com/news/local-news/friday-september-8-sunday-families-support-search-for-truth-about-annette-mcgavigan-1-2109114, accessed 10 December 2018.
29. In his book *Blanketmen: An Untold Story of the H-Block Hunger Strike*, former prisoner and public relations officer Richard O'Rawe, for instance, claims that Gerry Adams prolonged the strike unnecessarily in order to gain support for another parliamentary seat for Sinn Féin. Richard O'Rawe, *Blanketmen: An Untold Story of the H-Block Hunger Strike* (Dublin, IE: New Island Books, 2016).
30. www.derryjournal.com/what-s-on/arts-culture/hume-and-cooper-honoured-in-bogside-artists-restored-mural-1-7019100, accessed 10 December 2018.
31. "Derry Teenager Manus Deery 'totally innocent', Says Coroner", *BBC*, 10 April 2017, www.bbc.co.uk/news/uk-northern-ireland-foyle-west-39551974, accessed 10 December 2018. For the full Coroner's Report, see Justice Adrian Colton, "In the Matter of an Inquest into the Death of Manus Deery", available at www.judiciary-ni.gov.uk/sites/judiciary-ni.gov.uk/files/decisions/In%20the%20matter%20of%20an%20inquest%20into%20the%20death%20of%20Manus%20Deery.pdf, accessed 10 December 2018.
32. UTV's North West Correspondent Mark McFadden, reporting from the Bogside, *Evening News*, 8 April 2015.
33. Joseph, *The People's Gallery.*
34. For a helpful discussion of truth recovery in Northern Ireland, see Kirk Simpson, *Truth Recovery in Northern Ireland: Critically Interpreting the Past* (Manchester, UK: Manchester University Press, 2009).
35. Lord Saville et al., *Report of the Bloody Sunday Inquiry.* For another angle on this question, see Peter Taylor, "Who Won the War? Revisiting Northern Ireland on 20th Anniversary of Ceasefires", *BBC News Online*, 26 September 2014, www.bbc.co.uk/news/uk-northern-ireland-29369805, accessed 10 December 2018.

36. Kevin Hasson quoted in "The Bogside Artists: 20 Years on and Still Standing Strong", *Derry Journal*, 7 September 2014, www.derryjournal.com/what-s-on/arts-culture/the-bogside-artists-20-years-on-and-still-standing-strong-1-6283526, accessed 10 December 2018.
37. For a theological discussion of the role of compassion and forgiveness in Northern Ireland, see Nigel Biggar, "Forgiving Enemies in Ireland", *Journal of Religious Ethics* 36:4 (2008): 559–579; Stephen N. Williams, "Forgiveness, Compassion, and Northern Ireland: A Response to Nigel Biggar", *Journal of Religious Ethics* 36:4 (2008): 581–593.
38. Joseph, *The People's Gallery.*
39. It is sobering to remember that of the total death toll of 3272, Republicans were responsible for 2058, Loyalists for 1026 and British Forces for 363. www.cain.ulst.ac.uk/sutton/book/#append, accessed 10 December 2018.
40. Peter Sheehan, Vice-Chancellor of the Australian Catholic University in Sydney, at one of the artists' exhibitions. Quoted at www.cain.ulst.ac.uk/bogsideartists/statement.htm, accessed 10 December 2018.
41. Jonathan Burges, "The Exile." The Church that commissioned the play is Christ Church (Church of Ireland) under Archdeacon Robert Miller. "Play Tackles Exile of Derry Protestants", 6 February 2013.
42. The event was recorded by the City Centre Garden of Reflection Lunchtime events on, www.youtube.com/watch?v=K-UKOF3itxk, Accessed 10 December 2018. The event was sponsored by Contemporary Christianity, The Irish Churches Project, the European Union Regional Development Fund, The European Union's Peace III Programme managed by the Special EU Programmes Body, and the Office of the First Minister and the Deputy First Minister (OFMDFM).
43. For an article in *The Church Times* featuring the exhibition, see: www.churchtimes.co.uk/articles/2015/17-july/features/features/where-their-art-is-housed, accessed 10 December 2018.
44. http://www.coventrycathedral.org.uk/wpsite/our-reconciliation-ministry/, accessed 10 December 2018. For photos of the exhibition and events at Coventry Cathedral, see www.bogsideartistsexhibition.org/photo-gallery, accessed 10 December 2018.
45. www.cain.ulst.ac.uk/bogsideartists/statement.htm, accessed 10 December 2018.

CHAPTER 5

Drawings for Projection: Proposing Peacebuilding Through the Arts

Theodora Hawksley

Introduction

Trey Parker's 2004 film *Team America: World Police* is not rich in subtlety.[1] The film's opening scenes depict the eponymous Team America, an elite cadre of counter-terrorist personnel, completely destroying the centre of Paris—helpfully subtitled for the viewer as Paris, France—as they pursue some bearded and be-turbaned terrorists across the capital. Idyllic French markets and fountains, the Louvre Museum and finally the Eiffel Tower itself collapse in flames. But as well as sending up, in spectacular puppet hyperbole, a certain brand of Western "peacebuilding" and the tactics it employs, the film also strikes a little closer to home. Opposing Team America's incendiary and culturally blundering approach to international affairs stands the Film Actors' Guild, under the irresistible leadership of Alec Baldwin. Having had enough of Team America's approach to peacebuilding, they decide to launch their own peace initiative, drawing on their cultural capital and artistic sensibilities. Kim Jong-Il, spying an opportunity,

T. Hawksley (✉)
London, UK

J. Mitchell et al. (eds.), *Peacebuilding and the Arts*,
Rethinking Peace and Conflict Studies,
https://doi.org/10.1007/978-3-030-17875-8_5

organizes a World Peace Festival and invites Alec Baldwin to address the gathered world leaders on behalf of the Film Actors' Guild, all the while, of course, plotting to blow them all up and take over the world. But the path of world peace never did run smooth, and the dénouement of the film sees the Film Actors' Guild brandishing firearms themselves as they seek to repel the efforts of Team America to stop the festival.

It is this irony—if puppets of Helen Hunt and Matt Damon firing automatic weapons from behind pot plants qualify as anything quite so subtle—that I want to pick up on at the start of this paper, because a less obvious version of it can easily creep into proposals for peacebuilding through the arts. The irony, simply put, is this: a "hard" proposal for a "soft" approach can end up missing, or undermining, the point of that "soft" approach in the first place.

Peacebuilders engaging with the arts often note as strengths of their approach the ways in it can supplement and correct some of the weak points of classic liberal peacebuilding, which has historically been dominated by social scientific modes of analysis and evaluation. Thus, arts approaches draw our attention to the human and personal level, encouraging us to pay attention to the cultural and the symbolic, to the spiritual and religious and to the healing of interpersonal relationships; they encourage non-linear thinking and resist a narrowly results-driven mentality or a quantitative account of "success". However, when advocates of arts-based peacebuilding come to formally *propose* their approaches, they often slip back into drawing upon the same "hard" modes of analysis and evaluation that, through the use of the arts, they are seeking to challenge. In seeking to justify and promote peacebuilding through the arts, they end up doing the things they are trying to resist: measuring, generalizing, quantifying and abstracting. The move towards proposal seems to involve, almost inexorably, a move towards generalization and the generating of transferable insights, and the elision of the personal and irreducibly particular.

John Paul Lederach notes this same tendency at the beginning of *The Moral Imagination*. The book is, in a sense, concerned with theory: Lederach is searching for the "simplicity on the other side of complexity" and spends much of the book reflecting back on decades of personal experience of the complexities of peacebuilding, trying to discern what he calls the BOIDS of peacebuilding—the fundamental attitudes or capacities which make possible the moral imagination, the transformation of relationships and the building of peace.[2] But at the same time as he searches for this simplicity beyond complexity, Lederach is careful never to let the personal slip from view—it is a temptation of which he is aware and which he actively resists:

> In the professional world of writing, we view with caution, even suspicion, the appearance of the personal, and lend a higher accent of legitimacy to models and skills, theory, well-documented case studies, and the technical application of theory that leads toward what we feel is the objectivity of conclusion and proposal.[3]

Yet in the process of arriving at the objectivity of conclusion and proposal, Lederach argues, we can end up doing

> ...a disservice to our professions, to the building of theory and practice, to the public, and ultimately to ourselves. The disservice is this: When we attempt to eliminate the personal, we lose sight of ourselves, our deeper intuition, and the source of our understandings – *who we are* and *how we are* in the world.... We believe in the knowledge we generate, but not in the inherently messy and personal process by which we acquired it.[4]

This instinct about the importance of preserving the personal, messy process, articulated at the outset of *The Moral Imagination*, is the reason Lederach's book defies easy classification by genre: the book is part theory, part autobiography, part peacebuilding and part spiritual reading. The commitment to preserving the personal is also, I think, the reason the book is so powerful.

In the chapters that comprise this current book, the personal is by no means absent. However, precisely because many contributors are seeking to project arts-based peacebuilding beyond our particular experience and advocate its wider practical use and theoretical study, the social scientific instinct to generalize and abstract is by no means absent either. There is a natural tendency to start from a success story and work backwards, by trying to isolate the characteristics or capacities of the arts that make them effective tools for peacebuilding, by trying to identify effective artistic techniques, processes or products and bring into focus how it is that these engage with and transform actors in conflict and ultimately the conflict itself. Though many of the chapters discuss particular case studies (at least two in each of the five sections), the insights they offer about peacebuilding and the arts are for export, as it were, for adaptation to and application in other situations. In this first section on the "Visual Arts", both Sebastian Kim's discussion of "Peacebuilding in Korea Through *Minjung* Art" (Chapter 3) and Adrienne Chaplin's consideration of "Murals of the Bogside Artists" (Chapter 4) provide a contrasting set of examples from Korea and Northern Ireland. These examples, alongside Jolyon Mitchell's opening discussion on "Peacebuilding Through the Visual Arts" (Chapter 2), highlight the ambiguities of the arts, especially in relation to building peace. These three chapters also provide rich concrete material for developing theories that can help to describe how the arts can contribute to peacebuilding. Now, this movement towards proposal and theory is valuable, as is the instinct for investigating *how* the arts are effective in peacebuilding—we are not interested in simply inundating the reader with repeated case studies that show *that* the arts are effective or simply multiplying uncritical testimonies to that end. So what is the danger here? The danger is that, in slipping back into "hard" modes of proposal for the effectiveness of "soft" forms of peacebuilding, we risk losing sight of the personal and hence losing sight of what lies, I suggest, at the heart of arts approaches to peacebuilding.

In what remains of this chapter, my argument is not going to focus on identifying how proposals for peacebuilding through the arts tend to drift towards generalization and the occlusion of the personal. Instead, this chapter is a positive argument for preserving the personal and takes shape as a study of a particular artist, William Kentridge. In surveying Kentridge's work, I will deliberately draw attention to four themes often cited as capacities of the arts more broadly, in connection with their role in the moral imagination and peacebuilding: witness, empathy, memory and vision. However, the argument that builds throughout the chapter and surfaces at the end is that, important as these characteristics are, a satisfactory account of the effectiveness of Kentridge's work cannot be given without attention to the personal, to his own character and sense of vocation. This is, ultimately, something I am proposing as a more general argument. If we want to discern the BOIDS, or *sine qua nons*, of arts approaches to peacebuilding, then we need not just generalizations about the arts' capacity to bear witness, awaken empathy, preserve memory or evoke vision, but also attention to three rather more elusive and personal qualities: vocation, process and obliquity.

William Kentridge

William Kentridge (b.1955) is a South African artist, of Lithuanian and German Jewish descent. Kentridge trained as an artist in a wide range of media, from early work in printmaking at the Johannesburg Art Foundation, to later training in theatre in Paris (1981–1982), followed by a few years working in filmmaking back in South Africa. His work over the past forty years has included etchings and silkscreen prints, sculpture and video installations, theatre work, and opera productions, but he is perhaps best known for his charcoal drawings and what he calls "stone age" animation—short films created by making, photographing, minimally adjusting and re-photographing large charcoal drawings, to create a sort of stop-motion animation.[5] In the discussion that follows, I will focus on the films in the *Drawings for Projection* series (1989–1998): *Johannesburg, 2nd Greatest City After Paris* (1989), *Monument* (1990), *Mine* (1991), *Sobriety, Obesity & Growing Old* (1991), *Felix in Exile* (1994), *History of the Main Complaint* (1996) and *Weighing...and Wanting* (1998).[6]

Kentridge's choice of medium, charcoal drawing, and the slow process of making the short films is significant. Early on in his development as an artist, he realized that working in paint and colour was not possible for him and that the context in South Africa demanded something different. He was aware of his geographical remoteness from Europe and its traditions, but, more than anything, it was the political situation of South Africa that demanded charcoal drawing.[7] Although Kentridge expresses appreciation for the "achieved paradise" painted by Impressionist and Post-Impressionist painters in spite of the human misery that surrounded them, he admits that "[t]his state of grace is inadmissible to me".

> There are some artists, from Matisse to the colour-abstract field, who have managed to maintain an innocence or blindness and continue working like this to this day without bad faith gnawing at their work. I would love to be able to work like this. But it is not possible...Perhaps, working away from here in some European or rural haven, I would be able to paint apples and colours, but I doubt it.[8]

In an interview for a television documentary from 2000, Kentridge describes how colour in paintings often seems to end up "at the service of colour", and artists can end up absorbed in the "abstract act of making a picture". Working in black and white, he reflects, is closer to writing, and images can become a kind of shorthand at the service of something other than themselves—ideas, themes and questions.[9] Drawing is also pragmatic: unlike the slow process of oil painting, images drawn in charcoal can be made and erased easily, "as quickly as you can think", which Kentridge suggests gives his work "a kind of immediacy".[10]

Drawing, however, is only part of Kentridge's process. To create the short films in the *Drawings for Projection* series, Kentridge worked with large charcoal drawings on heavy paper, which allowed multiple drawings, erasings and re-drawings on the same sheet. So, in order to draw the character Soho Eckstein depressing the plunger on a cafetière, Kentridge would draw the cafetière, photograph the drawing, erase the plunger and re-draw it shifted downwards a fraction, take a second photograph, and erase and re-draw again. Charcoal can be erased easily but not completely, and the shadows of moving objects, people and limbs are visible in the finished films. Initially, Kentridge worked hard to get rid of these shadows, regarding them as imperfections, but gradually realized that the shadows were integral to the work and indeed served one of his frequent themes: the relationship between memory and erasure and the persistence of the past in the present.[11] The process of drawing, walking to the camera, photographing and re-drawing also became an important part of Kentridge's artistic method. The films were not planned out in advance in storyboard form, but unfolded as new and unexpected themes and developments emerged during the process of walking back and forth. This, again, speaks to a deeper concern in Kentridge's work to which I will return: his oblique way of approaching broader societal themes through exploring their traces in the individual unconscious.

Animation allows Kentridge to portray not just static scenes, but transformation.[12] This is perhaps most evident in way he deals with the landscape, which is usually the mining-scarred and nondescript countryside around Johannesburg. Unlike the tradition of colonialist art, in which African landscapes were depicted as lush, pristine and depopulated, Kentridge depicts them marked by human activity and presence: mining, pylons, roads and screens, pools of water, columns of people marching or large crowds massing to the horizon.[13] The transformation of the landscape also becomes a way for Kentridge to reflect on "the terrain's hiding of its own history" and the societal and psychological equivalents of "disremembering".[14] *Felix in Exile* (1994) illustrates this most clearly. The film opens with the surveyor character, Nandi, making drawings of the landscape, before shifting to Felix Teitlebaum—one of the regular characters in the *Drawings for Projection* series—sitting alone in a hotel room, going through a suitcase full of images of dead and still bleeding bodies. Returning to Nandi, it becomes evident that she is surveying and recording these deaths: red chalk marks appear around the bodies, and stakes grow out of the ground around them.[15] Newspaper lying around the bodies flies up and covers them, and they sink back into the landscape. There are contradictory things going on here. On the one hand, through the character of Nandi and the process of film making, Kentridge is recording, witnessing and, through drawing, "giving burial to these anonymous figures in the photographs".[16] Goya's *3rd of May 1808* and his series *Desastres de la Guerra* (1810–1820) are in the background here and the idea of the artist as witness-bearer.[17] On the other hand, through the reabsorption of the bodies back into the landscape, leaving almost no trace, Kentridge explores the process of "disremembering" or forgetting:

> The difficulty we have in holding onto passions, impressions, ways of seeing things, the way that things that seem so indelibly imprinted on our memories still fade and become elusive, is mirrored in the way the terrain itself cannot hold onto the events played out upon it.[18]

By making the viewer of the film a witness, Kentridge raises questions of our relationship to the events depicted, including our complicity and responsibility.[19] Kentridge's work holds together these opposing forces of remembering and forgetting, marking and erasing, without trying to reconcile them. In doing so, he engages South Africa's own post-apartheid process of remembering and forgetting, amnesty and amnesia.[20]

As well as posing pointed questions to its own South African context, *Felix in Exile* prompts deeper reflection on the themes of witness and empathy. In the film, Nandi's sketches stack up in Felix's suitcase and cover the floor of the room. Felix runs a basin of water, which fogs up the mirror, and he clears it by splashing it with water. Nandi appears in the mirror, and Felix is able to share her vision by looking through her surveying equipment at the landscape and crowds of protestors; the sink overflows and fills the room. Water is a recurring theme for Kentridge, and its blue colour in earlier films is usually linked to love and the erotic relationship between Felix Teitlebaum and Mrs. Eckstein, which is contrasted with the arid wasteland of the landscape around Johannesburg and the concrete of Soho Eckstein's empire. As Felix looks at drawings of Nandi, the room floods, and drawings float around him. Are we looking at Felix learning to see through Nandi's eyes, as she documents the violence around her, learning to see beyond his love for Mrs. Eckstein, in which he was absorbed in the previous film *Sobriety, Obesity and Growing Old* (1991)? Or are we looking at Felix wallowing in empathy, drowning in images, and still shut up in his hotel room, viewing events from a distance? Kentridge does not pose the question in such simple terms, but this ambivalence about witnessing and empathy recalls comments he has made about the "disease of urbanity":

> Urbanity, the refusal to be moved by the abominations we are surrounded by and involved with, hangs over us all. This question of how passion can be so fleeting and memory so short-lived gnaws at me constantly. It is a deep-rooted question.[21]

The resilience that enables people to survive terrible structural and direct violence also inoculates them to it; the proliferation of images of violence that awaken people to situations of injustice also inure them to it.[22] Kentridge, as always, does not chalk this ambivalence up as an abstract paradox, but depicts it on a human scale.

Felix in Exile also provides an interesting vindication of Kentridge's claims about his artistic process. The images of the bodies in the film were taken from police photographs of murder victims. Having been told about the photographs by a friend, he had pictured the bodies lying out in the open veld. The photographs actually depicted the victims lying in enclosed spaces—rooms or corridors—but Kentridge situates them in the place where he first imagined them, in the open landscape. It was only after *Felix in Exile* was completed that Kentridge realized the connection to one of his earliest memories. William Kentridge's father, Sydney Kentridge, was a prominent anti-apartheid lawyer, defending Nelson Mandela during his trial for treason and representing the family of Steve Biko at the inquest into his death. As a child of about six, William had ventured into his father's study and opened a box that he thought contained chocolates. It contained $8 \times 10''$ glossy photographs of the victims of the Sharpeville massacre.[23] The experience seems to bear out Kentridge's hope that "without directly plunging a surgeon's knife, the arcane process of obsessively walking between the camera and the drawing board will pull to the surface, intimations of the interior".[24]

With its 1950s office paraphernalia, golden age jazz soundtracks and nods to Weimar-era artists, Kentridge's work can sometimes feel quaint, but his interest in memory and the unconscious is largely worked out not through engaging with the past, but through exploring metaphors of depth and interiority.[25] *Mine* (1991) explores many of these themes through the literal exploration of depth—the mine owned by property magnate Soho

Eckstein. An *Ife* head sculpture from Nigeria wears a miner's lamp, and a map of the mine recalls a map of a slave ship packed with human bodies, with no space unused. The miners' stacked bunks recall photographs of concentration camp inmates. Kentridge sketches lines of continuity between past and present violence and scores discontinuity between the black world of exploitation in the mine, in which land and people are exploited for the benefit of the world of white commerce and leisure above ground. In *History of the Main Complaint* (1996), the metaphor becomes medical.[26] Soho lies in a hospital bed, surrounded by doctors. X-rays reveal office objects in his internal anatomy, and an ultrasound scan becomes a car journey in which events of violence Soho has witnessed are replayed. Soho's eyes—which are also the eyes of Kentridge himself—look back at us from the mirror, watching us as we witness the same violence. Soho's car hits someone, who bounces off the windscreen, and he awakes with a start; the film closes with Soho back in his office, cigar and telephone in hand. Again, Kentridge has faced the viewer with questions of witness, with what it means to see violence and to "wake up", but not in any straightforward or moralistic sense.

History of the Main Complaint was made during the first hearings of the Truth and Reconciliation Commission, and Kentridge reflects in this connection on Soho's "awakening":

> I suppose that it is true that Soho can only be wakened from his coma by an acknowledgement of immediate responsibility (for the death of someone in a car accident!). A case in which there may not be blame but there is responsibility. But, of course, Soho is not killed by this responsibility – and can even accommodate it (condensed and displaced into the objects on his desk). [27]

This is a reflection not just on the TRC hearings, but on the kind of future for South Africa that will emerge through them, which brings us to our final theme in Kentridge's work: vision. Utopian visions of a new, transformed South Africa are not to be found in Kentridge's work, and he has expressed mild cynicism at the idea of the "Rainbow nation".[28] It is true that the transformation of South African society is at the heart of his work, but his relationship to this process is more one of questioning and exploration than unambiguous encouragement.[29] Kentridge's work clearly criticizes the injustices of the apartheid regime, but it does not propose or envision any particular alternative: the banners carried by the workers marching through the landscape and protesting in the streets are blank. What does Kentridge's work offer to the moral imagination, then? How does it touch on "the mystery of the unknown that lies beyond the far too familiar landscape of violence?"[30] The answer, at least in *Drawings for Projection*, lies in the way that Kentridge treats the possibility of transformation in his characters and particularly Soho Eckstein. As the film series unfolds—without planning, as we have already seen—it is suggested that Soho and Felix are two sides of the same, complex personality, reacting in different ways to the events unfolding around them.[31] Their resemblance to Kentridge himself invites this interpretation by the viewer and invites them to consider their own split personalities or complex emotions in the face of change. Commenting on the development of the Soho character in *Sobriety, Obesity & Growing Old*, Carolyn Christov-Bakargiev writes:

> If Soho represents white power in South Africa during apartheid, this transformation from the flat, stereotypical characterisation of the first few films, to a more rounded figure capable of emotions, metaphorically points to the progressive growth of awareness within the white community, along with the rise of activism and organised protest on the part of the black community. By implication, it underscores how these parallel kinds of awareness could contribute to toppling the system of segregation.[32]

Conclusion: Drawings for Projection?

While much of William Kentridge's work might be described as political, Kentridge does not understand himself as a peacebuilder, except in his joking comment that "I am a second child and hence a peace-maker; reconciling opposites has been a job for life".[33] And, while we have seen that his work engages themes of witness, empathy, memory and vision, we have also seen that it does not do so in any straightforward or uncritical way: Kentridge understands himself not as a political commentator, but as an artist, and one interested in "an art that raises as many ambiguities and contradictions as there are".[34] The effectiveness and power of Kentridge's work, and its ability to engage its viewers' moral imagination with the South African situation in all its complexity stem not from his deliberate effort, nor from the directness of his approach. Rather, I want to suggest that the power of his work stems from its instantiation of the three qualities I mentioned earlier on as the more elusive BOIDS of arts approaches to peacebuilding: integrity of vocation, patience with process and faith in obliquity.

Integrity of Vocation

The shape of Kentridge's work has been driven by his faithfulness to his sense of vocation as an artist, and he has resisted the temptation to subordinate his artistic process or work to extraneous concerns, however worthy, that might distort or blunt it by demanding that it make its themes too obvious or too clear. In spite of his acute political awareness, Kentridge has rarely approached political themes head-on in his work, and a brief stint working with an agitprop theatre group in the 1970s led him to distance himself from direct approaches to political art. He recalls:

> We would stage a play which showed domestic workers how badly they were being treated, implying that they should strike for equal rights...I remember standing at the back of the hall while a play was being performed. I had told the actors that if I couldn't hear them, I'd wave a shirt at the back as a cue for them to speak louder. I remember standing at the back waving the shirt frantically, hopelessly, while the play carried on regardless.[35]

Kentridge began to suspect that this work was about the actors' needs rather than its meaning for the audience.[36] Kentridge states that he does not produce work *for* an audience, with an audience's needs in mind, at all: his work is about "current issues for me" and draws upon his own memories and experience, even his own dreams, as its principal source.[37] This focus on self brings with it the possible charge of self-absorption or self-indulgence, but the effect for Kentridge's work is quite the opposite. Far from leaving him free to paint an "achieved paradise", which would be merely decorative at best, and at worst a kind of complicity in the violence surrounding him, this commitment to examining his own experience returns him to the same concerns—witness, empathy, memory and vision—but in a voice which is authentic and powerful precisely *because* it is so personal.[38] Rather than closing down Kentridge's work into a narrowly autobiographical or introspective project, the effect is to open it out: exploring the contradictions of life in South Africa on a human scale allows a more ready identification with that experience.

The question for arts approaches to peacebuilding is this: When we are arguing that the arts can play an important role in peacebuilding, are questions of person, vocation—even virtue—also sufficiently in view? Proposing peacebuilding through the arts requires that we investigate the arts' capacities for engaging witness, empathy, memory and vision, but it also demands that we do not abstract these capacities from their place in the moral imaginations of particular artists or communities and treat them as straightforwardly transferable products. A "hard" proposal for a "soft" approach risks losing sight of that approach's most valuable insights.

Patience with Process

I have already noted Kentridge's convictions about the importance of faithfulness to his process of walking backwards and forwards between camera and drawing paper, as a way of "pulling to the surface, intimations of the interior". Again, this faithfulness to his own artistic process is not a kind of inward-turned preciousness about "inspiration", nor blind faith that following a certain set of steps will produce a particular kind of result. When drawing landscapes, Kentridge has a habit of setting out with the intention of driving a precise number of miles; when selecting a view to draw, he avoids looking for the most scenic or best-composed vista, often finding the best view and then turning through 180° to draw the nondescript view behind it. Kentridge's artistic processes are geared towards subverting what might be thought of as normal artistic instincts, in order to attend to the real.

It is worth noting that two things are held in balance here. On the one hand, Kentridge displays patience with his own process, which he does not allow to be short-circuited by beginning with too clear an idea of what the finished product or the "message" of the finished piece will be. On the other hand, he does not elevate his process to the status of an end in itself or place it on an "artistic" plane, beyond criticism—there is no mystique here, and Kentridge's attitude is quite workmanlike. His patience with his process is ultimately a patience with himself, a faith that his personal concerns—witness, empathy, memory, vision, transformation, justice, forgetting and so on—*will* inevitably surface and, if allowed to do so in their own way, will be ultimately clearer and more real.

The question for arts approaches to peacebuilding is this: How can we make sure that arguing for the *effectiveness* of the arts does not result in a focus on reproducible results which short-circuits the messy and unpredictable process by which genuinely effective results are often attained? When we are trying to make the case that arts approaches to peacebuilding should be more widely used and taken seriously, there is an understandable inclination to reach for case studies that show clear messages and outcomes and an understandable desire to foreground stable artistic products and processes that can be transplanted and reproduced in different settings. This focus on successful results, however, must not undercut our attention to, and patience with, the messy and sometimes unpredictable processes by which these successes are produced.

Faith in Obliquity

Kentridge's approach to large-scale political and social themes is characteristically small-scale and personal. In the *Drawings for Projection* series, he approaches the theme of apartheid obliquely, through various characters whose stories, as Christov-Bakargiev points out, allow multiple points of engagement and analysis.[39] This reflects Kentridge's conviction that, in his own words, "The more general it becomes, the less it works".[40] What people recognize in his work is not emotion or the drama of conflict writ large and obvious, but the reality writ humanly small, as it is experienced. In the same lecture, Kentridge argued that

> Part of the dismal failure of some recent films about South Africa is the fact that the film's starting point is to show apartheid. The rock is faced head on. Squads of extras are dressed, and either police or comrades are marshalled, to take part in these exercises to scale the rock. The rock always wins. Certainly there are some PR victories along the way, some hearts and minds changed, some tears extracted. But overall, the impression left is feeble. Even when the group of climbers is limited and the story focuses on a few people rather than THE PEOPLE ON THE MOVE, the films are defeated by the fact that the people inhabiting the film are being used as a metaphor, as a way of revealing something other than themselves.[41]

In proposing arts approaches to peacebuilding, many of the authors in this volume and the field more widely are arguing the case for disciplinary, and indirectly financial, support for such approaches. "Hard" peacebuilders of the *Team America* school are unlikely to be won over by arguments that the arts can deliver ambivalence, ambiguity and complexity, and so those proposing arts approaches can be forgiven for being drawn to big themes and head-on approaches: the dove, the children holding hands, the rock and the people on the move. But what Kentridge's work shows is the importance not just of the right scale, but the right angle. By showing the small, personal, costly and compromising paths traced through the complexity of social conflict, it is possible to see more clearly the small acts of humanization, of resistance and of moral imagination that might transform it.

Notes

1. *Team America: World Police*. Directed by Trey Parker (Hollywood, CA: Paramount Pictures, 2004).
2. BOIDS is the name of a simple computer program developed in the 1980s by which researchers, by inputting a few simple rules, were able to create a visual that mimicked the appearance of flocking birds. Lederach uses the idea of BOIDS to explore the basic elements of peacebuilding. His reflections centre on "a small set of disciplines, or practices, out of which the complexity of peacebuilding emerges in all of its beauty. Put in a slightly different way, I asked myself about essence in this way: What disciplines, *if they were not present*, would make peacebuilding impossible? On exploration I discovered that when held together and practiced, these disciplines form the moral imagination that make peacebuilding possible. The essence is found in four disciplines, each of which requires imagination. They are relationship, paradoxical curiosity, creativity, and risk" See John Paul Lederach, *The Moral Imagination* (New York, NY and Oxford, UK: Oxford University Press, 2005), 33–34.
3. Lederach, *Moral Imagination*, viii.
4. Lederach, *Moral Imagination*, viii.
5. Carolyn Christov-Bakargiev, *William Kentridge* (Brussels, Belgium: Société des Expositions du Palais des Beaux-Arts de Bruxelles, 1998), 61.
6. William Kentridge, *Johannesburg, 2nd Greatest City After Paris*, 35mm, shown as video projection (1989) (London, UK: Tate Gallery); William Kentridge, *Monument*, 35mm, shown as video projection (1990) (London, UK: Tate Gallery); William Kentridge, *Mine*, 35m, shown as video projection (1991) (London, UK: Tate Gallery); William Kentridge, *Sobriety, Obesity and Growing Old*, 35mm, shown as video projection (1991) (London, UK: Tate Gallery); William Kentridge, *Felix in Exile,* 35mm, shown as video projection (1994) (London, UK: Tate Gallery); William Kentridge, *History of the Main Complaint*, 35mm, shown as video projection (1996) (London, UK: Tate Gallery); William Kentridge, *Weighing…and Wanting*, 35mm, shown as video projection (1998).
7. Christov-Bakargiev, *William Kentridge*, 11.

8. Christov-Bakargiev, *William Kentridge*, 55–56.
9. *Certain Doubts of William Kentridge*. Directed by Alex Gabassi (São Paulo, Brazil: Associação Cultural Videobrasil, 2000).
10. Christov-Bakargiev, *William Kentridge*, 14. His choice of the media of drawing and printmaking also places Kentridge within the tradition of South African resistance art. Unlike oil paintings or sculpture, slow to create, expensive to transport and difficult to reproduce, drawings on paper are inexpensive and prints are easily produced and circulated—all qualities that were important to political artists under apartheid. For helpful background on the visual arts in South Africa prior to and during the state of emergency, see the first two chapters of John Peffer, *Art and the End of Apartheid* (Minneapolis, MN: University of Minnesota Press, 2009).
11. Carolyn Christov-Bakargiev, "Interview with William Kentridge", in Dan Cameron et al., ed. *William Kentridge* (London, UK: Phaidon, 1999), 17.
12. *William Kentridge on His Process* (San Francisco, CA: San Francisco Museum of Modern Art, 2005).
13. In Kentridge's *Colonial Landscape* series (1995–1996), he draws lush African landscapes marked up with surveyor's marks in red chalk, drawing attention to colonial images as both projections onto the landscape and "sizing up" the depopulated land for exploitation. See Christov-Bakargiev, *William Kentridge*, 23.
14. Christov-Bakargiev, *William Kentridge*, 96–97.
15. Other surveying equipment also appears, notably a seismograph and an astrolabe.
16. Christov-Bakargiev, *William Kentridge*, 97.
17. See Christov-Bakargiev, *William Kentridge*, 28–29. For a reflection on the relevance of Goya's *Desastres de la Guerra* for humanitarian work, see Paul Bouvier, "'Yo Lo Vi.' Goya Witnessing the Disasters of War: An Appeal to the Sentiments of Humanity", *International Review of the Red Cross* 93:884 (2011): 1107–1133.
18. Christov-Bakargiev, *William Kentridge*, 96.
19. In a lecture at Northwestern University, Kentridge explained, "In the same way that there is a human act of disremembering the past, both immediate and further back, that has to be fought through writing, education, museums, songs and all the other processes we use to try to force us to retain the importance of events, there is a natural process in the terrain through erosion, growth, dilapidation that also seeks to blot out events. In South Africa, the process has other dimensions. The very term 'new South Africa' has within it the idea of a painting over the old, the natural process of disremembering, the naturalization of things new". See Christov-Bakargiev, *William Kentridge*, 97.
20. "Amnesty/Amnesia" is one of the near-anagrams or near-homonyms Kentridge plays with. See Christov-Bakargiev, *William Kentridge*, 93, 96.

21. Christov-Bakargiev, *William Kentridge*, 57. Elsewhere, he writes, "Urbanity by which I mean the ability to absorb everything, to make contradiction and compromise the basis of daily living seems characteristic of how people operate in South Africa". See Christov-Bakargiev, *William Kentridge*, 49.
22. This is not just a reflection on white guilt in South Africa. For Kentridge, the question of people's ability to endure violence goes further: "People far closer to the violence and misery [than the white community] still return out of the tear smoke and an hour later are cooking their dinners or watching 'The A-Team' on television". Christov-Bakargiev, *William Kentridge*, 57.
23. Christov-Bakargiev, *William Kentridge*, 28.
24. Christov-Bakargiev, *William Kentridge*, 112.
25. The "quaint" feel of Kentridge's work is rather more to do with his location on the cultural periphery: "Much of what was contemporary in Europe and America during the 1960s and 1970s seemed distant and incomprehensible to me…The art that seemed most immediate and local dated from the early twentieth century, when there still seemed to be hope for political struggle rather than a world exhausted by war and failure. I remember thinking that one had to look backwards – even if quaintness was the price one paid". See Dan Cameron, "Survey: A Procession of the Dispossessed", in Dan Cameron et al., ed. *William Kentridge* (London, UK: Phaidon, 1999), 10.
26. Kentridge writes, "While making the film I was also fascinated by the new ways of seeing the body using X-rays, CAT and MRI scans, sonar etc. What is hidden under the skin? And is our blindness to this similar to our blindness to the effects of our actions?" See Christov-Bakargiev, *William Kentridge*, 111.
27. Christov-Bakargiev, *William Kentridge*, 111. Dan Cameron suggests, "Perhaps this is Kentridge's underlying fear in making this film: will the citizens of South Africa use the TRC as a way of compartmentalizing their sense of responsibility for crimes perpetrated in the past, and will this affect the way they work together towards a better future?" See Dan Cameron, "Survey", 71.
28. *Certain Doubts of William Kentridge*, 2000.
29. With regard to his work's relationship to politics, Kentridge writes, "I'm essentially interested in an art that is political but which allows an ambiguous politics, an art that encompasses as many ambiguities and contradictions as there are". See Christov-Bakargiev, *William Kentridge*, 164.
30. Lederach, *The Moral Imagination*, 5.
31. Christov-Bakargiev, *William Kentridge*, 72.
32. Christov-Bakargiev, *William Kentridge*, 72–73.
33. Christov-Bakargiev, *William Kentridge*, 57.
34. Christov-Bakargiev, *William Kentridge*, 164.
35. Christov-Bakargiev, "Interview", 15.

36. "There was a false assumption about the public, in that we 'knew' what 'the people' needed, so I stopped my involvement with these groups". Christov-Bakargiev, "Interview", 15
37. *Certain Doubts of William Kentridge*, 2000.
38. Even the characters of Kentridge's films blend in and out of self-portraits: Felix Teitlebaum strongly resembles Kentridge physically, and his persona—the dreaming artist—interrogates his role and pretensions as an artist.
39. See Christov-Bakargiev, *William Kentridge*, 34.
40. Christov-Bakargiev, "Interview", 34.
41. Christov-Bakargiev, *William Kentridge*, 75–76. He adds, "...subjects that have an origin outside of a particular object may often be more illuminating in their oblique light than the full searchlights of the project that stares straight at this object. The difficulty I am trying to show is that this object [apartheid] is so large, our distance from it so small, that it is difficult to get any sort of obliqueness into our view" (76).

PART II

Music

CHAPTER 6

Music Writ Large: The Potential of Music in Peacebuilding

John Paul Lederach

Introduction

In the empirical and theoretical development of the field of peacebuilding and conflict transformation, music has rarely been present. The wider field of peace studies, if I may use a provocative metaphor, remains in the era of silent films. Yet, social change or the opposite, some form of protecting the status quo, cannot be imagined without *music writ large*. I use this phrase to broaden our reflection and exploration well beyond the narrow view of music as simply song and performance. Music writ large returns to the core of music as embodied and embedded within who we are as human beings, within the soundscape of human experience.

We have ignored this soundscape, the ever-present, surrounding and penetrating presence of vibration within human experience, through which the perceptual, emotional, and interpretive schemes that shape the human search for meaning emerge, adapt, and respond.[1] It is not possible to imagine that *in the beginning was the word*—in whatever particular origin myth

J. P. Lederach (✉)
University of Notre Dame, Notre Dame, IN, USA

J. Mitchell et al. (eds.), *Peacebuilding and the Arts*,
Rethinking Peace and Conflict Studies,
https://doi.org/10.1007/978-3-030-17875-8_6

or tradition we explore—without the environment of vibration and music. Most traditions believe that all we have been gifted and share on this extraordinary living and breathing earth began in sound. Research now suggests that music, the intentional and shared use of controlled vibration, pre-dated the formal use of language and created the tissue, the glue that made possible the notion of "social" relations. In the most profound sense, the human community paradoxically is held together, and pushed apart, by making sense of our soundscape. From this view, music writ large evokes, invokes, and provokes human consonance and dissonance.

In contemporary times we tend to relegate the word *music* to only refer to the formal creation of socially coordinated productions of entertainment, primarily in the form of song. However, the etymology of the term can be traced in both Latin (musica) and Greek (mousikos) to the "art of the muses," and refers to the disciplines which muses preside over, including rhythm and beat, lyric and melody, poetry and song, and the noted presence and use of silence. In Greek mythology the nine daughters of Zeus and Mnemosyne are the muses engaged in finding ways to remember and inspire, thus intimately connected to and embodiments of *memory and the creative arts.*

In his short set of essays on memory, forgiveness and reconciliation, Wole Soyinka chooses a *muse* to express his understanding of hope in the midst of unspeakable devastation.[2] As Soyinka weaves through the challenges of conflicts and abuses in Africa, deploring the deep frustrations provoked by these atrocities, he questions whether forgiveness in the wake of sustained dehumanization is even possible, much less a characteristic virtue of the peoples of Africa. Soyinka ends his book recounting a story about the mystical power of an aged African balafon—a kind of ancient, African xylophone—that ended a war. This poet of the people, who declares the need to carry the "burden of memory," speculates about the presiding presence of the *Muse* of forgiveness, mercy, and generosity. Like classical writers, Soyinka understands that the muses bring not only creative inspiration, but emotions and dispositions that are perhaps more easily engaged through the creative arts. Soyinka arrives at a place where he indicates a sensation of speechlessness. It is at this place, where words fail and fall silent, that soundscape re-emerges.

When we approach music and peacebuilding, we must enter through the doorway of soundscape and how music in this broadest sense inhabits our human experience. Three related but distinct affirmations and lenses set the stage for this chapter: music writ large evokes, provokes, and invokes.

Each of these merits a brief exploration, particularly observing how each resonates with the more common ways the field of peace and conflict is defined. I do not see these three terms as categories in a taxonomy. This would follow our more common scientific tendency to build knowledge by breaking things apart, failing in the process to more fully capture the essence and character of music writ large. Instead, I see these more as points of resonance—as places where the vibrations of music writ large hold and produce deep reverberations in human experience—precisely because this approach has greater consistency with the very empirical nature and metaphoric use of sound as touching, surrounding, penetrating, deepening, and circling. Music writ large cuts across the vast majority of heuristic categories we create to define and study within conflict and peace studies. To understand conflict and peace, we must find ways to account for the elements that go below and beyond the linear modalities of making sense of things. Rational thought cannot disembody itself from who we are as persons. I want to argue here that music writ large enables us to explore deep human experiences through a more holistic and paradoxical lens that at once has capacity to hold memory or dreaming; call to action or appeal for contemplation; incite confrontation or nurture healing; invoke anger or empathy; appeal to revenge or forgiveness. In the following pages I want to briefly explore each of these three portals of evoking, provoking and invoking.

To Evoke: The Penetrative and Embedded Nature of Sound

Song and music, based on sound and vibration, provide a very different kind of medium through which to explore the deep human experiences that arise from encounters with conflict and peace. It is important to note that the very root of the term sound, or *son* in the Latin, also forms the essence of our word *person,* most literally that we are "for sound." Similarly in Greek drama, the word for the mask through which one spoke was called the *prosopon,* literally a face, in that an actor's voice and persona performed through his mask. Both underscore how sound is integral to the performance of being human. We are in a very real sense made for and from sound. Indeed, our earliest experience of life, universally experienced, takes place within a womb where we are surrounded by steady rhythm and sound.

Evocare is formed from a combination of *ex-*, or "out of," with *vocare*, or "to name or to call." Music *evokes* precisely because it is embodied with our human *being-ness*. It evokes because it emerges from deep within and seeks to find its way back into a shared world where we as *beings* in our humanity attempt to make sense of what lies within and around us. Moreover, it is important to emphasize that to 'evoke' is an embodied experience, like the reaction we experience in hearing our own name called.

Based on vibration, we first *feel* music in our bodies emotionally and only subsequently attach rational explication to what we feel. Music touches deep into the human experience. It resides in an emotional memory that interacts sometimes in unexpected ways with cognitive memory. Neuroscientists tell us that the brain processes music and sound in reference to memory, perception, and the construction of meaning in quite different ways than other modalities of human interaction and speech.[3] The medical field, for example, has pursued studies of what people remember while under anesthesia. While anesthesia holds most of our facilities and senses temporarily in check, Gaynor cites Rodgers' research that the "auditory pathway, unlike all other sensory systems, has an extra relay. Auditory fibers are not affected by anesthetics, so they continue to transmit sound. Simply stated: We never stop hearing."[4] He further notes that sound and vibration interact in a holistic manner with the body: "If we accept that sound is vibration, and we know that vibration touches every part of our physical being, then we understand that sound is 'heard' not only through our ears but through every cell in our body."[5] When we approach music and sound, we inquire and look into a phenomenon that penetrates the human experience, sonically and physically.

Alan Watts once noted that understanding is most often achieved through repetition: "most students do not understand one's ideas unless they are repeated – under differing analogies or in varying forms and words, as a musician constructs variations on a theme. Besides, what I mean by understanding is not simply verbal comprehension--*it is feeling it in your bones*."[6] That is, this repetitive play of thought, writing and speech helps to create a deep, embodied understanding. Watts himself wrote in this repetitive way, as a way of constantly working toward new understandings. Further, Watts' phrase 'feeling it in your bones' refers to the vibration-based sense of sound and repetition that emerges from within the interior world and through interaction in the social world, and back again. The search for understanding and response is embedded, embodied, and holistically and instantly held in the soundscape of human experience. Here is where music resides and why it has evocative capacity and source.

We may understand music's evocative power best by way of our earliest experiences. Music as lullaby, for example, can provide a pathway back to a sense of being surrounded and held. Boyce-Tillman has noted the capacity of music to function "like a container." "Music," she writes, "is a way of holding." A lullaby holds a person though it "can be sung without physically touching the person"...yet the "song is a vehicle of transmission of love."[7] Music, sound and vibration, as stated earlier by Gaynor, touch every cell in the body. In essence, music evokes "feeling" things that are not always easily conveyed through the spoken word; the touching of a level of experience not held by explanatory conversation. Sound penetrates to and emerges from a deeper level. It resides at the primordial level, the source beneath voice by which the expressive elements of conflict and peace emerge. While music is well researched in the fields of wellness or healing, it is *astounding* that so little attention has been paid to music in the formal literature of peacebuilding.

The evocative capacity of music writ large has deep significance for "locating" music as related to conflict. Conflict disrupts, often creating a deeply felt dissonance. It stops our normal process of making sense through accepted and often unquestioned assumptions about what events, people, and issues mean. Conflict prompts us to inquire. We are faced with a challenge that we must now make sense of because our assumed understanding has been disrupted. In short, conflict requires us to (re)locate ourselves, (re)locate others, (re)locate events, and inevitably (re)locate meaning.

Music writ large evokes interpretation and response, and creates the environment that attends to humans' meaning making and how humans choose to respond to meaning. Like the soundtrack to a film, music writ large imbues depth and meaning into our experiences, in turn shaping our perceptions, interpretations, and responses. It is not possible, for example, to imagine the civil rights movement of Martin Luther King, Jr. without the soundscape of music writ large—the sound of King's voice or the intoning of We Shall Overcome at nearly every event and march throughout the core years of the movement. It is equally impossible to imagine the machinery of World War II without the soundscape of music writ large—the sound of Nazi rallies, the noise of bombing raids, propaganda and resistance songs. It is impossible to imagine the Truth and Reconciliation process of South Africa without music writ large—the voices of testifiers, the inclusion of the song 'Nkosi Sikele iAfrica' in the South African anthem. Why should this be so? Music writ large *evokes* the *embodied soundscape* held individually and collectively, underpinning the dissonances and consonances that shape the overall context. But more than this, music writ large evokes the voices and construction of meaning emergent in those settings.

Provoke: The Challenge of Response

Music provokes response. Again, if we look at the derivation of the word, *pro* references purposeful advancement of an idea or a goal and when combined with *vocare* creates call to response and engaged action. When we affirm that music writ large has capacity to provoke we recognize the power to mobilize human action emergent from meaning.

To explore the provocative nature of music within conflict and peace studies, as part of my teaching I have on some occasions played two contemporary songs, *The Gulf War Song* written and released by Moxy Fruvous (1993), and *Courtesy of the Red, White, and Blue* by Toby Keith (2002). Written a decade apart and engaging primarily North American audiences, both songs challenge, appeal, and justify responses to the events surrounding the first Iraq war and the events of 9/11 a decade later. But they provoke very different responses. *The Gulf War Song* critiques and incites a response that questions the military-media-industrial call for war. It makes an appeal to reject and resist the official justification of war and violence. Conversely, *Courtesy of Red, White, and Blue* calls for and justifies a nation rallying around the patriotic call to war against enemies in response to 9/11. Side by side, they represent what we find nearly universally true about music writ large: It *evokes* a depth of meaning that *provokes* action, which may subsequently mobilize toward violence and revenge, or equally may mobilize toward nonviolence and reconciliation.

Examples abound of this extraordinary capacity of music to provoke. Martin Luther King Jr. consistently requested Mahalia Jackson to sing *Precious Lord*, a gospel tune, to inspire, to prepare, and to mobilize the crowds during civil demonstrations. It is in fact the last song he requested from the porch of the Lorraine Motel prior to his assassination. The combination of melody and lyrics, appealing for strength *to stand* even though we are *weak and worn,* provided a soundscape of nonviolent discipline in the face of direct violence. On the other hand, in the early 1990s in Somalia, song and poetry could easily mobilize sub-clans to revenge killings or could in turn appeal for an end to violence and reconciliation.[8]

The chapters in this section delineate numerous ways that the provocative capacity of music engages with action in peacebuilding. Of particular interest here is a fluid bridge that emerges between the evocative and the provocative found in music writ large. What Gayner called the "whole cell" intake of music in human experience, describes a deep nexus between perception, interpretation, and action that in turn forms a point of resonance within the soundscape that holds deep significance for how human communities mobilize meaning and respond to conflict. We must be careful not to fall prey to the linearity of project reductionism that asks primarily instrumentalist questions of whether music somehow represents a tool of inputs producing projected outcomes. Music writ large creates and evolves the context of how both meaning and action emerge, adapt, and are shaped.

Invoke: The Healing Mystery of Music

In the following chapters of this section on Music, perhaps the least developed discussion pertains to the mystery of music and the human spirit. Violence inflicts deep harm, its ultimate outcome remains death, the silencing of voice by way of ending embodied vibration. For those who survive, violence numbs the soul and voice of people well beyond the physical damage. People seek meaning and explanation for a phenomenon that defies rational explanation. In a recent book, *When Blood and Bones Cry Out*, I noted with Angela Lederach that in the everyday language of survivors, the basic capacity to "feel" again, and to recuperate a sense of agency, is often expressed as touching or re-gaining "voice," which correlates with sensing vibration and connection, both within the deepest inner self and out into relationships.[9] The journey to explain the inexplicable creates a most extraordinary challenge precisely because we humans know and experience things for which we do not have words that adequately convey or explain meaning. Music writ large, by its very nature attends to this inner landscape and opens us toward the mysterious ways in which peace-as-healing cannot merely be understood with reference to the material world, but instead requires us to explore those elements that are at once transcendent and ineffable.

Combining the Latin prefix *in* (upon) with *vocare* (to call), the word invoke traces an etymology of the human impulse to implore, to beseech understanding and some form of 'being with' or presence, which is deeply needed in the desolate geography of the inexplicable nature of violence. To invoke, to call upon—it is the cry of those who have experienced violence and who seek justice and peace-as-healing. A cry remains even when numbed, silent, and deeply interior. It calls for response and aid in the struggle to find the door or source of light that can in some way illuminate the overwhelming darkness. It calls upon the ineffable and transcendent, it seeks for a way to somehow remain *visible* and *heard*, and it seeks the capacity to feel our way into meaning. To invoke is also to implore or seek action, or some kind of transformative presence. Similarly, to invoke can involve re-membering—as when a memory brings a person or place into the present moment—and through that, can transform the present. Here precisely we find the mysterious, penetrative and whole-cell experience of music writ large.

As we enter the complexity of human healing, particularly in the aftermath of violence, we must note the place of music in the search for meaning. The search for meaning and healing requires us to navigate the rough seas of our past, present and future. These are equally important categories in peacebuilding. Truth commissions attend to how societies will collectively remember. Reparations attempt to restore in the present the harms caused in the past. Documents on "shared futures" and appeals to the horizons of reconciliation require a capacity to imagine the formation of our relationships in ways that do not now exist.

The Repetitive Power of Music

A significant view of therapeutic accompaniment that responds to deep harm suggests approaches for healing that engage in recalling and re-telling past experiences. Subconsciously submerged or actively present events from the past that have damaged and violated life occupy a place of prestige and power in the landscape of a person's and/or a group's narrative. These events, and memories of these events, provide markers that form and sustain identity and meaning. Embedded in personal and collective memory, these markers can become what Volkan called "chosen traumas," or conversely "chosen glories."[10] The memories can play out symptomatically through indirect, and at times dysfunctional and self-destructive, expressions. At the personal level, the therapeutic process orients itself toward the process of identifying these key markers and events. The retrospective telling and re-telling of the event or events, a creative act that simultaneously links perception, memory and inventiveness—for none of us can re-create past events without some dose of storytelling creativity—provides the opportunity to reframe, that is, to rename the experience, and by so doing create new or at least nuanced variations of meaning that no longer have the power to unilaterally and negatively define a person's existence, significance, and life. From this perspective, therapeutic repetition suggests that in the re-telling the experienced traumatic event becomes more commonplace in a person's life story. Repetition, if you will, flattens the significance of a particular event removing the sharpness of the trauma as *the defining* event and lens that gives meaning or, as the case may be, takes constructive life-giving meaning away from one's life story past, present and future. In so doing, repetition creates the platform from which a new kind of understanding and agency emerges that helps a person rediscover, redefine and rename their life story.[11]

Music also has this extraordinary repetitive power. We can listen over and over to the same melody or song without reflecting on the repetitive nature of what we are doing as redundant, because the music enters and attends to a sense of being, location, and purpose. Boyce-Tillman explains this as a natural aspect of music:

> The acceptance of the more hidden aspects of the personality, leads to a 're-membering' of the personality. The newly accessed areas are now reintegrated to form new patterns, more reflective of the re-formed person…music has certain characteristics that enable it to play a real part in the processes of integration and de-integration.[12]

Therapeutic explanations, based more on the spoken word, seem to place emphasis on the process of lifting out the event, talking about it so that we can then set it aside and release its power over us. We must take note that within this view "repetition" focuses on the *past* primarily as a landscape filled with harm to be released. A common phrase we may hear suggests we must "let go of the past in order to move in a healthier fashion into future." Though perhaps not expressed explicitly, this represents the purpose *sine qua non* of "repetition" in therapy and captures its metaphoric purpose: repeat to release in order to attain growth and wellbeing.

This linear explanation of repetition may however miss the deeper musical metaphor of what happens in the process. Understood as the presence of the muse that invokes creativity, repetition creates an inner sense of being an "author," a "poet," a "composer." Music represents the doorway into the ineffable, the touching of the "being" human again—recreating life, and providing a sense of place and location. The notion that repetition facilitates the entry into a space pregnant with the potential to locate and author, more closely approximates the possibility that the key transformation underway in music is one that permits people who carry trauma to transcend the weight of being an object of events and to enter the *essential space* of becoming artists. That is, music offers people the chance to experience creative agency, which is the root of being human, but it also offers a chance to be heard and acknowledged by others.

Music with its extensive use of incantation-like lyrics and repetition, circling over again with a melodic, rhythmic, or lyrical phrasing, seeks and touches something deep within us. For some listeners it invokes a sense of mystery. The repetition seems to re-create an opening into feeling wonder. Judy Atkinson found this in her work with aboriginal trans-generational trauma. She called it a "primary humanness." She wrote, "healing was shown to be transformational as people entered an evolutionary process of reclaiming the natural creativity of childhood."[13] Rather than attempting to put the past behind us, this view of repetition embraces the feeling that something sacred exists in the innocence and trust that was at one point experienced and needs to be found again, brought back if you will into the present so overwhelmed with cynicism and fear. Music has the potential to touch a place within us that remembers wonder and in the remembering, we re-member—that is, we recreate capacity for a deeper sense of awe and curiosity.

The incantations serve as a gateway, an opening that feels like a meditative space to touch something positive that once earlier in life was experienced but has been lost and is now again desired. The invocation and incantation of music is magical in the sense of changing how we see the world; it re-members or re-creates it. Whole-cell intake, circling and repetition create avenues that open and give way to healing because they touch and rise from a deeper place within the soul, a comfort and acceptance of oneself. Music has an innate capacity to create place—a feeling of being rooted, of being located that in some ineffable way places us in touch with our sense of self and a sensation that we are close to "home." In a word, music can open us toward the experience of feeling surrounded by unconditional acceptance and love. Boyce-Tillman suggests that music by its very nature:

> allows for juxtaposition and simultaneous combination; it therefore can accommodate difference and differing degrees of unity. It allows for things to stay separate or to be recombined into new ideas. It allows for the existence of chaos in certain sections and more ordered sections at other times. As such it provides a mirror of a mature person happy with order and acknowledging the presence of chaos.[14]

Circling and repetition in music do not flatten the trauma, or chaos, in order to control the overwhelming pain that produced the trauma. Rather these dynamics create a gateway permitting one to touch a deeper sense of self, voice and the recuperation of the sacred nature of life so damaged in the violations experienced. Indeed, music allows for the existence of chaos in life and places this chaos within a broader perspective, so that it becomes not the defining whole, but part can be understood as part of wider experience and potential for change.

In the programmatically oriented world of peacebuilding we are more accustomed to metaphoric language that we "produce" things, that project activities "take us somewhere," and can be conceptualized as having a "beginning and an end" in which we "intervene" and see our "impacts." These modalities of organizing activity are heavily influenced by, and dependent on, metaphors of linearity and control. Sound and music create the metaphoric shift wherein circularity, repetition and simultaneity become phenomena worth pursuing on their own merits precisely because of their innate capacities to deepen and touch aspects of personhood, and to recuperate and reconnect with a sense of being human that requires constant nurture and exploration.

These directional metaphors of repetition, circularity and deepening evoked and invoked by music have precedent in other aspects of ritual experience, though we tend not to connect these to the challenges of social healing and reconciliation. The Holy Sacrament or Communion within Christianity, the place of ceremony and prayers with chant and movement in Judaism, the daily prayers and annual fasting within Islam, or the mantras, sound and meditation as practiced daily by Buddhists, all point to deepening through repetition and circling behaviors. Only truly possible to understand within a soundscape context, these rituals are never understood as one-time events that propose a finality of outcome. They represent activities which are deeply embodied and embedded within shared soundscapes require the creation and re-creation of moment-spaces that touch the deeper journey of human experience, provide meaningful location, and offer the presence of the transcendent—all of which represent qualities that nurture personal and collective healing. Moreover, these rituals are deeply experiential and purposely create times that shift practitioners world of meaning, disrupt the numbing routine you will, out from the linear flow of life. That is, the rituals connect practitioners in the here and now with various there and thens, often significantly linking the individual with a sense of 'being with' broader communities—whether with Christ at the

Last Supper, or with the worldwide Umma of Islam, or in the spiraling pasts/presents of chant. The idea that song creates a sense of meaningful location and place is not entirely new, though perhaps not fully explored in terms of what takes place through the phenomenon of healing.

Musical Journeys Through Past, Present and Future Spaces

Music can invite listeners not only into familiar and new spaces, but also into painful pasts, complex present conflicts and hoped for peaceful futures. In his classic ethnography *The Songlines*, Chatwin attempts to follow and understand the Australian aboriginal notion that meaningful location in their harsh desert environment happened through song.[15] Wanderers by their very nature, the landscape, trails, and locations were known by the people through singing the feel and even smell that marked the places they walked. A person knew where they were by singing the song that identified the locations as they walked, a sonic pathway called a *songline*.

The songline creates a map, but not one that is visually oriented like those that we would read in an atlas. For the aboriginals, physical geography emerges through song whereby locations are experienced and recognized through the intoned vibration of sound, wherein "finding oneself" emerges through sonic connections to elements and spaces. This has a similarity to the way migrating birds use sound to locate their place and find direction, or the way dolphins bounce sound off features in their underwater world to orient themselves. "Aboriginal Creation myths tell of the legendary totemic beings," Chatwin wrote, "who had wandered over the continent in the Dreamtime, singing out the name of everything that crossed their path—birds, animals, plants, rocks, waterholes—and so singing the world into existence."[16]

In one exchange Chatwin records a question he posed to his aborigine colleague Arkady:

> "So a musical phrase," I said, "is a map reference?"
>
> "Music", said Arkady, "is a memory bank for finding one's way about the world."[17]

I am saying two things in relating what Chatwin learned from the aborigines. First, sound helps to orient ourselves in the world, but second sound can also evoke in the listener unexpected, even mysterious, ways of looking at the world differently. Sound can constitute place, and with it perhaps community and a sense of self or identity. It evokes sensations, memory and experiences from the past as if they were present in the here and the now. At times this can be deeply disabling, as in a sound evoking the harm once experienced that now vividly is re-experienced and can be paralyzing, like the sounds of bombs or guns. This quality to induce temporal sensations, particularly the past, is called *anamnesis* by those who study the impact of sound on the human experience. Augoyard and Torgue define this term as "an effect of reminiscence in which a past situation or atmosphere is brought back to the listener's consciousness, provoked by a particular signal or sonic context. Anamnesis, a semiotic effect, is the often involuntary revival of memory caused by listening and the evocative power of sounds."[18] Song and sound create transportability, that is, we have moments when the past, present and future merge, where we are capable of holding at the same time a sensation of being in more than one spatial and temporal sphere, as in the rituals discussed above.

Buddhist understanding of mindfulness posits a primary discipline of meditation that brings a person's awareness to fully focus on the present moment. Thich Nhat Hanh in his book *Being Peace* (1987) connects several themes. He notes that sounds, a use of a bell in particular, signal a calling to mindfulness. He in fact refers to it as the "bell of mindfulness" that functions like the voice "calling us back to ourselves."[19] The purpose of the sound, he suggests, requires us to "stop" and through the stopping, to concentrate on the moment and notice what is there. Walking meditation, a practice he has evolved, ironically has the same goal. He describes this as "walking not in order to arrive, just for the walking. The purpose is to be in the present moment and enjoy each step you make. Therefore you have to shake off all worries and anxieties, not thinking of the future, not thinking of the past, just enjoying the present moment." He adds that taking the "hand of a child" enhances this kind of walking. "You walk, you make steps as if you are the happiest person on Earth."[20]

With Christian contemplative movements the same concerns and disciplines pertain. "Listen" is the first of the disciplines provided in St. Benedict's guidelines for monks wherein he suggests they learn to "listen with the ear of the heart."[21] In the preface to Thomas Merton's collection of poems, Kathleen Norris writes that "the poet who is a monk lives in a way that intensifies this process, as a life pared down to its essentials encourages close attention to resonant tones of scripture and lighter notes of wind and birdsong."[22]

Both reconciliation and healing require a capacity to link and hold together the experience of the past which is still available in the present with the search for mechanisms to move in a healthy way toward a yet to be lived future. Linear approaches to this challenge tend to see the *past* as holding the difficulties that must be laid to rest, the *present* as somehow needing to free itself from this grip of the past, and the future as something that calls to us and that we are to shape or more narrowly find ways to control. Time falls on a line.

Music writ large offers the experience of simultaneous temporality. Simultaneity of temporal experience approximates the theory of neural Darwinism as put forward by Nobel Laureate Gerald Edelman. In several of his recent books he suggests how studies of the brain describe the processes by which humans handle and make sense of time from the perspective of a biological theory of the brain. With the provocative title *The Remembered Present,* he provides an in-depth exploration of how the brain creates consciousness. To paraphrase here in layman's terms the technical neurology I recognize I may not adequately handle, he posits that the "remembered present" constitutes a fleeting moment that takes in immediate circumstances through a series of rapidly moving scenarios that are perceived, held momentarily, captured, sorted and interpreted. For animals the remembered present is their exclusive temporal experience. In this moment a process of selective association happens in which an extraordinary amount of variables about their immediate environment are perceived, sorted, associations created, and meaning derived. This remembered present functions as a "first nature," the near instantaneous assessment of a moment.[23]

In his subsequent book *Second Nature,* Edelman suggests that the capacity to be conscious of this first nature, that is the ability to reflect on it, distinguishes the human brain from most animals in that we are capable of simultaneously holding in the moment of lived experience a longer term memory that retains past experience, the capacity to plan into the future, and a concept of who we are in our context.[24] In his words: "an animal with primary consciousness lacks an explicit narrative concept of the past, cannot extensively plan a scenario for a distant future, and has no nameable social self."[25] We notice again the human act of sensing as locating and naming require the artistic acts of evoking and invoking, which is suggested here as what defines consciousness and us as human beings.

Edelman argues that while most of us tend to have a "Heraclitean" view of time, we view and talk about time as a river-like movement from past to present to future, this represents an "illusion." He writes: "in a physical sense, only the present exists. The integration of core states leading to conscious states takes a finite time of two hundred to five hundred milliseconds. This time period is the lower limit of the remembered present."[26] Higher order consciousness of the kind we experience as humans adds the capacity to notice, experience, and reflect on the duration of time and to create meaning around that experience in far more expansive temporal frames of reference. This we construct as falling into past, present and future. However, curiously, the three temporal phenomena co-exist literally in the present. As part of making sense of things we are constantly engaged in creativity by the very mechanisms through which we see patterns, make associations, and attach meaning. In Edelman's perspective from the biology of the brain, "every act of perception is to some degree an act of creation, and every act of memory is to some degree an act of imagination."[27] In other words, history requires a creative act and imagination a memory.

This can perhaps be illustrated through an extreme case offered by Oliver Sacks in his recent book *Musicophilia*. Sacks describes the story of Clive Wearing who, following a devastating brain infection, was left with a form of amnesia that only permitted him a memory span of a few seconds. His wife Deborah writing of the experience noted that nearly every blink of his eye meant the loss of memory of what had just happened, leaving him "deprived of consciousness and life itself."[28] In one entry after another, Clive jots in his journal that he has just woken up, a minute later he writes the same thing with no recollection of what he had only moments earlier written or experienced. He cannot create new memories--except in music. A musician all his life, even after the infection he retained an extraordinary ability to play music, and when he plays the piano he becomes fully present. Sacks writes,

> It may be that Clive, incapable of remembering or anticipating events because of his amnesia, is able to sing and play and conduct music because remembering music is not, in the usual sense, remembering at all. Remembering music, listening to it, or playing it, is entirely in the present.[29]

"He has," Sack concludes, "dropped out of space and time altogether. He no longer has any inner narrative...yet one has only to see him at the keyboard or with Deborah to feel that, at such times, he is himself again and wholly alive."[30] Sacks ends the story with an excerpt from a letter Deborah had recently written:

> Clive's at-homeness in music and his love for me are where he transcends amnesia and finds continuum – not the linear fusion of moment after moment, nor based on any framework of autobiographical information, but where Clive, and any of us, *are* finally, where we are who we are.[31]

Music writ large invokes this mysterious journey of finding our way home to re-member who we truly are.

Conclusions: Music Writ Large

To explore music writ large requires a shift of perspective that reinforces spatial and circular aspects of personal and social change, the soundscape that fluidly moves between the inner and social worlds. The aural nature of human experience suggests that music writ large has the capacity to evoke, provoke, and invoke processes of making meaning and creating action that arise from the dissonance and consonance at the very core of conflict and peacebuilding. These observations and the claims that follow will be indirectly teased out, interrogated and developed in the three chapters on music that follow. The optimism of this current chapter and Chapter 7 on the value of songs in Northern Uganda, will be qualified by the critical account of the imposition and uses of Western music by a 'mixed orchestra' in the Palestinian territories in the subsequent Chapter 8. Nevertheless, several key points emerge as this section of the book explores both the place and understanding of music.

Music writ large evokes. Based on vibration, soundscapes holistically surround and penetrate the human experience, touching and putting us "in touch" with aspects of our lived experience not easily expressed in words. Sound has evocative capacity, at times in reference to painful experience, and as a mechanism to open and release constructive dynamics that help us "feel" the transcendent elements of human experience. Music writ large evokes creative perception. Music helps us feel and notice aspects of human experience and places us in touch with ways of knowing not exclusively tied to rational explanation.

Music writ large moves in and between the human process of sense making and taking action. Music provokes—a process that simultaneously permits us to place or locate ourselves and respond to events and experiences that surround our lives. This provocative element of music, like songlines, creates the spaces to feel that we know where we are, who we are, and how we might find our way toward purpose and response. Violence, the ultimate expression of destructive conflict, creates the numbness, what we might describe as a vibrationless state, that catalyzes a deep sense of feeling lost, displaced, in both the inner and outer worlds. Peacebuilding and the journey toward healing requires first and foremost a capacity to re-locate our bearings. Music writ large has this innate capacity to touch us in ways where, not unlike the aboriginal notion of invisible but sonically perceived maps of our surroundings, we can perceive in new and old ways our lived social landscape and find our place. Music writ large creates a soundscape that provokes the capacity to locate, name, and act.

Music writ large, the soundscape of our lives, invokes and transports us. Music incites the experience of feeling transported through temporal dimensions. Through music we notice the simultaneous availability of past and future narratives within our reach in the present. Music writ large suggests a view of temporal simultaneity that nurtures a continuous and creative engagement of this uniquely human capacity in any given moment with fuller appreciation of the past and the future.

Music writ large invokes a transcendent quality. The soundscape provides a portal that opens toward reflective spaces that engage with the human need for recuperating a sense of wider meaning that metaphorically reaches for *depth of understanding* and *nurturing of personal and collective purpose*. In the face of dehumanizing conflict, sonic experience can create the spaces to feel beauty within and around us, a process of re-humanization ultimately necessary in processes of rebuilding flourishing communities.

Notes

1. Throughout this chapter, I draw upon my earlier writing, paraphrased and at times more directly cited from the chapter titled "Following the Healing Muse" in John Paul Lederach and Angela Jill Lederach. *When Blood and Bones Cry Out: Journeys Through the Soundscape of Healing and Reconciliation* (Oxford, UK: Oxford University Press, 2010).
2. Wole Soyinka, *The Burden of Memory: The Muse of Forgiveness* (Oxford, UK: Oxford University Press, 1999).
3. Oliver Sacks, *Musicophilia* (revised) (New York, NY: Vintage, 2008); Gerald Edelman, *The Remembered Present: A Biological Theory of Consciousness* (New York, NY: Basic Books, 1989); Daniel Levitin, *This Is Your Brain on Music* (New York, NY: Penguin, 2007); and Anthony Storr, *Music and the Mind* (New York, NY: Ballantine Books, 1992).
4. Mitchell L. Gaynor, *Sounds of Healing* (New York, NY: Broadway Books, 1999), 85.

5. Gaynor, *Sounds*, 17.
6. Alan Watts, *Cloud-Hidden, Whereabouts Unknown: A Mountain Journal* (New York, NY: Pantheon Books, 1968), ix, italics mine.
7. June Boyce-Tillman, *Constructing Musical Healing: The Wounds That Sing* (London, UK: Jessica Kingsley, 2000), 54.
8. A.Y. Farah, *The Roots of Reconciliation* (London, UK: Action Aid, 1993).
9. John Paul Lederach and Angela J. Lederach, *When Blood and Bones Cry Out* (London, UK and New York, NY: Oxford University Press, 2012). Several parts in this current section draw directly upon this text.
10. V. Volkan, *Bloodlines: From Ethnic Pride to Ethnic Terrorism* (Boulder, CO: Westview Press, 1977).
11. See Ketty Anyeko and Tamara Shaya, "Storytelling and Peacebuilding: Lessons from Northern Uganda," Chapter 11 in this volume and Juliane Okot Bitek, "What Choice between Nightmares?: Intersecting Local, Global and Intimate Stories of Pain in Peacebuilding", Chapter 12 in this volume, for case studies of the use of storytelling in peacebuilding initiatives.
12. Boyce-Tillman, *Constructing Musical Healing*, 50.
13. Judy Atkinson, *Trauma Trails, Recreating Song Lines* (Melbourne, AU: Spinifex Press, 2002), 250.
14. Boyce-Tillman, *Constructing Musical Healing*, 51.
15. Bruce Chatwin, *The Songlines* (New York, NY: Penguin Books, 1987).
16. Chatwin, *Songlines*, 2.
17. Chatwin, *Songlines*, 108.
18. Jean-François, Augoyard and Henry Torgue, *Sonic Experience: A Guide to Everyday Sounds*, trans. Andra McCartney and David Paquette (Montreal and Kingston: McGill-Queen's University Press, 2006), 21.
19. T. Nhat Hanh, *Being Peace* (Berkeley, CA: Parallax Press, 1987), 145.
20. Hanh, *Being Peace*, 148–149.
21. L.R. Szabo, ed., *In the Dark Before Dawn: New Selected Poems of Thomas Merton* (New York, NY: New Directions Books, 2005), xv.
22. Szabo, *Dark Before Dawn*, xv.
23. Edelman, *Remembered Present*.
24. Edelman, *Second Nature: Brain Science and Human Knowledge* (New Haven, CT: Yale University Press, 2006), 100.
25. Edelman, *Second Nature*, 38.
26. Edelman, *Second Nature*, 93.
27. Edelman, *Second Nature*, 100.
28. Sacks, *Musicophilia*, 188.
29. Sacks, *Musicophilia*, 212.
30. Sacks, *Musicophilia*, 213.
31. Sacks, *Musicophilia*, 213.

CHAPTER 7

Engaging the "Other": Contemporary Music as Perspective-Shifting in Post-conflict Northern Uganda

Lindsay McClain Opiyo

Introduction

For more than two decades, northern Uganda was the site of protracted, open violence between the Government of Uganda and various rebel groups, most notoriously the Lord's Resistance Army (LRA). This essay explores the relationship between music and peacebuilding in developing constructive, compassionate relationships in the setting. Traced through the examples of three popular, secular conflict-era songs, this essay suggests that a great potential for transformative peacebuilding occurs when music strategically engages with groups labeled by society as the "other," in this context perpetrators of mass human rights violations, and also when music nurtures perspective-shifting within and between groups of polarized conflict actors.

L. M. Opiyo (✉)
Generations for Peace, Washington, DC, USA

J. Mitchell et al. (eds.), *Peacebuilding and the Arts*,
Rethinking Peace and Conflict Studies,
https://doi.org/10.1007/978-3-030-17875-8_7

Musical Engagement with the "Other": The Songs of Jeff Korondo and Jahria Okwera

Since independence, the people of greater northern Uganda have suffered from a series of conflicts that have taken a severe toll on civilians and combatants, especially during the most recent period from 1986 to 2006.[1] This has included severe persecution and marginalization at the hands of government forces and nearly two dozen rebel insurgencies, most notoriously the LRA. In addition to widespread incidents of sexual violence, torture, and murder, millions were forcibly displaced in squalid internally displaced persons (IDP) camps for more than ten years, and an estimated 60,000 people were abducted by rebels and forced to join their ranks.[2] Furthermore, northern Uganda has some of the highest levels of Post-Traumatic Stress Disorder (PTSD) recorded anywhere, with an estimated 54% of the population suffering from PTSD.[3]

In the midst of these conflicts, a plethora of contemporary and indigenous genres of music have been created by local artists and shared widely among communities.[4] Ranging from lamentations on the death and destruction caused by the war, to prayers for a peaceful resolution to the violence, local artists have captured popular sentiments and were listened to by all parties to the conflict, including IDP, rebels in the bush, and government forces.[5] When inquiring into this conflict-related music, two names are inevitably mentioned: Jeff Korondo (aka Jeffrey Opiyo, my husband) and Jahria Okwera (aka Charles Okwera). As friends and local artists, Korondo and Okwera have been involved in the development of the contemporary music industry in the Acholi sub-region of northern Uganda since the late 1990s and early 2000s, respectively. Both have released more than a dozen songs, many that directly address social issues facing conflict-affected communities, and have become known for their music activism initiatives, especially the founding of Music for Peace (MfP), to be discussed later in this essay. Specifically, many of Korondo and Okwera's songs have engaged the "other," primarily by appealing to the rebels to end the violence and to the communities to consider the dual victim-perpetrator identity of many combatants.

Song has been called the "most popular and important genre of Acholi orality."[6] Like the many artists who emerged during the conflict's peak (other well-known names include Lucky Bosmic Otim, Justin Obol Simpleman, and Lady Grace Atim), Korondo and Okwera's music blends indigenous rhythms with contemporary digital instrumentality. This hybridization of musical styles appeals to young and old alike in the society, especially when accompanied by emotionally-charged lyrics that relate to the human condition. Due to the close association many Acholi have with music—most people engage with it on a daily basis through radio, but it also features prominently in homes and social settings—enhances its peacebuilding potential, as it appeals to the common Acholi identity held by a wide spectrum of conflict actors.

The following introduces three of Okwera and Korondo's songs that exemplify the role of their music in facilitating engagement with the "other."

"Dwog Paco (Come Home)"

"Dwog Paco," meaning "come home," was composed by Okwera in 2003 in an inviting afrobeat style and was adopted as the theme song for a popular radio program by the same name on radio station Mega Fm shortly thereafter. The song and program aimed to appeal to LRA rebels still in the bush to abandon violence and return home. At the time, the Government was offering a controversial blanket amnesty to all combatants who denounced rebellion, however, there was considerable mistrust and misinformation within the LRA regarding the sincerity and willingness of the government and communities to forgive and accept perpetrators back in their midst. The radio program, which began airing in 2003 (three years after the amnesty was enacted following extensive lobbying from local cultural, political and faith-based leaders from the Acholi sub-region), featured testimonies from recently-returned persons regarding the defection process and their reception by the community, and appealed to those still in the rebel ranks to also come back home. Mirroring this call, in verse one, Okwera sings in the local Luo dialect:

> Hear the people pleading. They are calling for you all in the bush (to return home).
> Acholi and Lango elders are all calling you back (home).
> There is no problem. Hear us cry. Change your heart and return home.
> Everyone is calling for you, welcoming you. Please don't delay.[7]

In verse two, he urges combatants to, "Hear my words and think about it," because the combatants are his "brothers" and "sisters" and he still loves them. He reassures the LRA that they are not "wrongdoers" and have been forgiven. In the chorus, he emphasizes:

> There is no problem. Come back home please.
> People are pleading. We call you back.
> There is no problem, come back home please
> People are crying, crying for peace.

This song, whose primary audience was both rebels still at large, and those who held the power to influence their defection (such as collaborators), captures the objectives of the radio program to build confidence in the amnesty process, thus reducing the numbers of combatants participating in the conflict and bringing the war to an end. Although the radio station itself was government owned at the time, and much of the population, including the rebels, distrusted the government's actions for peace, the program's integration of a theme song by a much-loved artist, as well as its hosting by trusted and respected radio personalities from the region, broke down barriers and fostered communication across the conflict divide.

"Okwera Nono (You Reject Me for Nothing)"

Offering an inverse perspective to "Dwog Paco," which was composed from the perspective of the Acholi civilians, both Okwera and Korondo have popularized accounts of the conflict from the perspective of ex-combatants who have returned home. In "Okwera Nono," meaning, "You reject me for nothing," Jeff Korondo highlights the societal stigmatization experienced by many ex-combatants despite the government's supposed exoneration of their past through the Amnesty Act of 2000. In an afrobeat-reggae fusion and sung in the Luo dialect spoken by the Acholi, the song was released in 2008, in the declining days of the Juba peace process, in which the LRA and Government of Uganda attempted to negotiate a six-point peace deal mediated by the Government of South Sudan, but ultimately failed when the LRA leader Joseph Kony refused to sign the final peace agreement. In verse two, Korondo sings:

> Our little children are returning from the bush with different kinds of problems.

> Look! They are returning from the bush after immense suffering.
> Carrying heavy loads, witnessing horrific murders, and trekking long distances!
> The most painful is forcing them to murder against their wish. If it were you, what would you do?[8]

In this example, Korondo refers to the dual victim-perpetrator identity held by many ex-combatants who had already returned, and the unknown more who were expected to return had the peace process reach a settlement. Often abducted as children and forced to participate in initiation rituals to test their allegiance to the rebels and make returning to their home communities difficult, such as murdering one's parents or neighbors, a vast majority of LRA combatants are both perpetrators of atrocities and vulnerable victims of the conflict. Despite the reality of this joint identity and that nearly every family has had one of its members abducted, many people have been reluctant to accept this complex duality, and often blame returned persons for their experiences regardless of the circumstances that led former-LRA fighters to participate in the rebellion. In the chorus, Korondo aims to elicit deeper reflection in the community, asserting:

> My people, you reject me for nothing. Where do I go?
> Maybe it was meant to be like that. What if it were you? What would you do?

Furthermore, he highlights specific problems facing returned persons, such as "enmity, quarrels, and land wrangles" in the villages. By taking on the perspective of a returned person, the song humanizes ex-combatants and forces society to reflect on the indiscriminate violence of the conflict and how easily one could have suffered the same fate of the abducted.

"Ka in Kono? (What If It Were You?)"

Similarly, in "Ka in Kono?" meaning, "What if it were you?" Okwera channels the perspective of formerly-abducted persons who have returned from LRA captivity. This song, such in an afrobeat style, was released in 2006 at the onset of the Juba peace process and commissioned by World Vision as part of a campaign to end stigma against returnees. One year after the cessation of hostilities between the LRA and Government of Uganda was signed and with high expectations that the peace would hold and conflict would be ended through the peace talks, many international organizations were anticipating the closure of the IDP camps and the return of civilians to their original homesteads. Whilst life in the camps and in urban centers could afford one relative anonymity, they anticipated that resettlement on ancestral lands would exacerbate tensions between ex-combatants and their families and communities over limited resources and assistance. Further, the ceasefire, as well as growing attention on matters of peace versus justice sparked by the 2005 International Criminal Court indictments of the LRA leadership and subsequent backlash on the court by northern Ugandan civil society, resulted in an influx of research and documentation by national and international scholars and practitioners on the prevalence of rejection and stigmatization of former combatants. In the opening verse of "Ka In Kono?" Okwera sings:

> My people, why make me cry like that?
> I feel deep pain in my heart all the time.
> Whenever I try to sleep, I still feel afraid.
> Especially when people pinpoint at me all the time.
> People make mistakes. I ask you to forgive me.
> It wasn't my intention to enter the bush
> All was because of intimidation.
> I was taken forcefully to go and fight.
> There are many poor people. They force you to arrest others.
> They force you to loot.
> They force you to kill.
> You all, at least welcome me as your child.
> Please don't pinpoint at me.[9]

Like Korondo, Okwera captures the involuntarily actions of many LRA fighters, who were faced with a choice: kill or be killed. In the chorus, he asks:

> What if it were you?
> Why pinpoint at me?
> Yet I never intended to go and fight.
> What if it were you?
> Why do you talk bad about me?
> Take me as a living person also.

Like in "Okwera Nono," this song takes a risk of backlash by the local community in acknowledging the reintegration challenges of former combatants by speaking from their perspective and asking communities to forgive them and end their ostracization from society. However, both songs demonstrate how artists can serve as mediating channels through which controversial narratives can be communicated, creating opportunities for engagement across conflict divides and for new knowledge about oneself and the perceived "other" to be generated.

Music and Peacebuilding: Intersections to Engage the Other and Compassionate Dimensions of Humanity

This section will explore the significance of the above mentioned songs in fostering compassionate and creative spiritual dimensions of humanity in the wake of conflict, specifically by engaging with the "other" by rehumanizing the rebels and promoting empathy, as well as building "mediative capacity" by communicating among and between the rebels and the communities. This facilitates both the *perspective-taking* ("process of trying to engage with another community's perspective") and *perspective-making* ("process whereby [a community] develops and strengthens its own knowledge and practices") needed for building peace and transforming conflicts.[10]

Rehumanizing the Rebels

As the three earlier discussed songs suggest, in the context of northern Uganda, the rebel LRA initially took up arms in defense of the Acholi people, but quickly turned their anger and frustration against them and committed thousands of gruesome atrocities on unarmed civilians. Although originally members of that society, as Okwera notes the rebels are his "brothers" and "sisters," former and current members of the LRA have become the "other," outcasts and outsiders to be avoided and socially punished for their actions during the conflict.

According to Pumla Gobodo-Madikizela, the dialogue process of South Africa's TRC was imbued with:

> …a concept of human community that extended to others—even those responsible for gross human rights violations in the past. This inclusive concept of humanity recognizes that as an expression of being human, remorse transcends the evil deed of the perpetrator. The capacity to recognize the transcendence becomes an important bridge for the victim or surviving families of victims to reach out to the perpetrator.[11]

Songs such as "Okwera Nono" and "Ka in Kono?" create such bridges to transcend the evil deeds and reach out to the perpetrators in the context of northern Uganda.

According to Jodi Halpern and Harvey M. Weinstein, who look at these issues from a public health perspective, "interpersonal ruins, rather than ruined buildings and institutions… pose the greatest challenge for rebuilding [post-conflict societies]."[12] As such, a process of "rehumanization" must occur, in which "one becomes interested in another's distinct subjective perspective," causing a "perceptual shift."[13] More so, because "violence is frequently intimate and relational, repair also must function on that level."[14] Key to this process of rehumanization is empathy, or the "process in which one person imagines the particular perspective of another person."[15]

Building upon these concepts, I argue that songs which explore the perspectives and challenges of the rebels are an important step in rebuilding compassionate relationships in northern Uganda because they promote empathetic reflection among victims of the conflict by offering stories of suffering of the perceived "other," the returned LRA fighters. More so, by breaking the silence on the challenges facing ex-combatants, the songs may encourage returnees to further develop this narrative of stigmatization and adopt it into their own discourse, creating future opportunities for their communities to hear about their challenges and extend empathy.

Opening Avenues for Communication

Beyond encouraging empathy for the "other," music in northern Uganda has facilitated communication between conflict parties during and after the violence. For example, when there were limited avenues for reaching the rebels during the height of the conflict in the early 2000s, "Dwog Paco," was a conduit for messages from the community and returnees to reach the rebels in the bush. Despite bans on radios within the rebel camp, some commanders circumvented orders and listened to the song and broadcasts.

According to John Paul Lederach, the key to creating change is not a critical mass of opposition, but "getting a small set of the right people involved at the right places,"[16] or identifying the "critical yeast" that will allow the whole process to rise. When artists are viewed as the critical yeast and their audience the critical mass, music becomes the platform "that makes exponential growth strong and possible."[17] In particular, a critical role of the artists was facilitating communication between parties. They were:

> ...masters of web making for social change, spiderlike in their capacity to imagine the contours of the space and to imagine themselves in a relationship with challenging sets of people who were not like-minded and –situated and were extremely dangerous and antithetical to their desires for change... They were simultaneously advocates and conciliators.[18]

We traditionally think of mediation as a "socially narrow process of action carried out by a person (or small team) who moves or facilitates direct dialogue between well-defined actors representing particular interests and groups."[19] Rather than acting as mediators in this traditional sense, Okwera and Korondo exercise what Lederach terms "mediative capacity," by "focusing attention on introducing a quality of interaction into a strategic set of social spaces within the web of systemic relationships in order to promote constructive change processes in the conflict-affected setting as a whole."[20] While they never traveled to the bush to meet directly with the rebels, nor did they participate directly in the formal peace process in Juba, they facilitated communication between conflict parties in less overt ways, representing diverse views and interests creatively in their songs and arguably creating bridges for further interactions. In the end of his book, also cited in the previous essay, *The Burden of Memory, the Music of Forgiveness,* African philosopher Wole Soyinka narrates the story of the balafon, a xylophone-styled instrument that has represented (and fueled) more than eight centuries of conflict in West Africa. However, in a rare public performance of the instrument, he comes to understand that the balafon offers something more: "glimpses and echoes of the possibilities of harmonization... and can open up horizons for a humanized vision."[21] This is the legacy, power, and potential of music carried in the sound waves in northern Uganda.

Opportunities and Challenges for Peacebuilding Through Music

The intersection between the arts and peacebuilding is still a largely unexplored and untapped area of scholarship and practice, and the conflict resolution and peace studies fields have largely failed to acknowledge the contribution of music in building compassionate relationships in the wake of conflict.[22] In fact, expressive arts have been called the "missing link in the field of conflict resolution and peacemaking."[23] Within the Peace Studies field, John Paul Lederach and Lisa Schirch have been at the forefront of the arts in peacebuilding,[24] and Olivier Urbain's anthology *Music and Conflict Transformation* arguably provides the most comprehensive analysis to date on music and conflict.[25] There is budding interest in the arts and transformation in the Psychology (Art Therapy) and Ethnomusicology fields, as well.[26] As an under-researched and under-facilitated avenue for peacebuilding and rebuilding broken relationships, the following two short sections explore the opportunities and challenges for music and engaging the "other" in the context of northern Uganda.

Opportunities

The efforts of artists such as Korondo and Okwera have opened spaces for respectful dialogue, a vital perquisite for building compassionate, creative relationships. Whether serving as the opening song for a radio program encouraging rebels to come back home, or producing perspective-shifting songs that take on the struggles and challenges of the stigmatized and rejected, artists in northern Uganda have created platforms for community-level discussions with victims and perpetrators on pressing issues facing this post-conflict society.

Second, music has promoted an understanding of ethnic, political, religious, social and personal differences fueling conflict. Local artists have demonstrated in their songs and their engagement with other artists in the competitive music industry in northern Uganda that peacebuilding does not require that everyone agrees, but rather that we employ perspective-taking and listen to one another respectfully. More so, by taking this one step further, by not only listening but building empathy of the "other," whether LRA commanders still in the bush or those who have returned home, the war-affected community in northern Uganda can begin to rebuild broken relationships caused by the conflict.

Third, the local artists have exhibited the capacity for solidarity with the war-affected communities (i.e. victims), without offending or disengaging the alleged perpetrators of the violence (i.e. the government and the rebels). The ability to manage relationships with these parties simultaneously demonstrates their capacity to act as bridges and links between seemingly opposing perspectives. However, it must be emphasized that the artists are not third party neutrals. They all have been affected by war in various ways, some ex-combatants themselves, but their roles as allies and coaches offer promise for others to manage complex identities and roles, whilst maintaining ties with "others."

Lastly, the local artists serve as role models in the community and are viewed as public figures. Their activities and operations occur in the public sphere, and the wider community is always observing their actions and forming opinions based on their influence. The respect and reverence for these figures, most of whom were youth in their late teens and early 20s when their peace-related songs were released, create unique opportunities for them to serve as examples for others and deliberately model behaviors that they would like to see replicated, such as tolerance and respect for others.

Challenges

Despite the abovementioned opportunities, the artists face and have faced challenges that may significantly affect their ability to promote the building of compassionate relationships in northern Uganda.

First, the artist community as a whole in northern Uganda is less organized and unified than other peacebuilding constituencies, such as the religious leaders and some networks of civil society organizations. Although there are at least two associations for northern Ugandan artists, infighting and industry politics have largely prevented the artists from sustaining collaborative relationships with each other. Instead, smaller sub-groups of artists usually work together when there is an NGO campaign or short-term initiative. One possible exception is MfP, an initiative previously-mentioned as co-founded by Okwera, Korondo, and myself. In 2009, we formed MfP to promote music for peacebuilding and build a network of artists from conflict and post-conflict zones in Africa. Admittedly, since 2010, MfP has not been active due to a variety of factors, including a lack of funding and our pursuit of other academic and professional interests. However, during the months that MfP was fundraising and raising awareness of an exchange of northern Ugandan artists to Sierra Leone, we held a series of concerts and radio programs in northern Uganda that were well attended and well received by local artists. In 2014, we commenced efforts to revive and reorganize MfP by registering as a community-based organization (CBO) and opening a recording studio in the town of Gulu.

In contrast, religious leaders—under the auspices of the Acholi Religious Leaders Peace Initiative (ARLPI), an interfaith-based peacebuilding organization—have been organized into an integrated entity since the late 1990s. Throughout this period, they have adapted to the changing needs of their constituencies, but remained united as an interfaith voice for peace. My contention is that the artists could benefit from similar organization and cohesion if they are to scale up their peacebuilding activities.

Secondly, the artists have lacked recognition as peacebuilders. Not only do few of them recognize their own role in music-making as peacebuilding, but the wider society often dismisses their efforts as mere entertainment. For example, in 2011 Gulu district in northern Uganda hosted the national celebrations for International Day of Peace. The organizers, mainly expatriates or Ugandans from other regions posted to UN agencies in Gulu, invited headline performers from Kampala, who did not experience the war nor write songs about it, rather than prominently featuring local artists. Instead, northern artists were invited to open for these headliners or take their performances to amateur tents on the periphery. Dissatisfied with this arrangement, a handful of artists, including those involved in MfP, took to the radio, complaining about the perceived sidelining of northern artists and the lack of recognition of their music in promoting peace in the region, but this created discord amongst other artists who were interested in playing their set and collecting their paycheck. Had the organizers of the event viewed music as contributing to peace in northern Uganda, rather than a filler for the speeches to be made during the Peace Day celebrations, then the northern artists would have played a more central role in this program. As a result of this and other incidents, much of MfP's advocacy has focused on raising awareness of the role of music in peacebuilding in post-conflict northern Uganda and promoting further support of the arts in peacebuilding.

In contrast, a number of religious leaders and civil society groups self-identify as peacebuilders and have received numerous international awards and accolades for their efforts to reduce the violence and seek a peaceful end to the war. For example, in 2012, Archbishop John Baptist Odama of ARLPI was awarded the World Vision Peace Prize, and a series of celebrations were held in Gulu in his honor. In 2004, ARLPI was awarded the Niwano Peace Award and award monies were used to found their Interfaith Centre for Peace, a center that is dedicated to peace education training, and research and advocacy for non-violent conflict resolution. If northern Ugandan artists were to add intentionality to their work, explicitly emphasizing that they are contributing to peace as peacebuilders, they could greater strengthen their efforts for social change and receive greater support and recognition from the local and international community which could allow them to do even more.

Conclusion

In conclusion, music in northern Uganda has contributed to the building of compassionate, creative relationships between and among community members, many of whom were combatants during the region's longstanding conflict. Notably, the artists have encouraged empathy for the "other," former LRA combatants and those still at large, and created platforms for open, honest dialogue, communication and perspective-shifting on the difficulties facing this society recovering from more than two decades of violent conflict. By better understanding the contributions of local artists, such as Jeff Korondo and Jahria Okwera, it is possible to see the value of supporting music to do even more to rebuild relationships across economic, social, religious, and political boundaries in Uganda and elsewhere.

Notes

1. Sverker Finnström, *Living with Bad Surroundings: War, History, and Everyday Moments in Northern Uganda* (Durham, NC: Duke University Press, 2008); Chris Dolan, *Social Torture: The Case of Northern Uganda, 1986–2006* (New York, NY: Berghahn Books, 2011).
2. Phuong Pham, Patrick Vinck, and Eric Stover, *Abducted: The Lord's Resistance Army and Forced Conscription in Northern Uganda* (Berkeley: Berkeley-Tulane Initiative on Vulnerable Populations, June 2007), 3.
3. Bayard Roberts et al., "Factors Associated with Post-Traumatic Stress Disorder and Depression Amongst Internally Displaced Persons in Northern Uganda", *BMC Psychiatry* 8:1 (2008): 4.
4. Lindsay McClain, "Artistic Suggestions for Peaceful Transition in Northern Uganda: What Youth Are Saying", *African Conflict and Peacebuilding Review* 2:1 (April 2012): 152–163.

5. Lindsay McClain Opiyo, "Music as Education, Voice, Memory and Healing: Community Views on the Roles of Music in Conflict Transformation in Northern Uganda", *African Conflict and Peacebuilding Review* 5:1 (Spring 2015): 41–65.
6. Charles Okumu, "Acholi Orality", in *Uganda: The Cultural Landscape*, ed. Eckhard Breitinger (Bayreuth, Germany: Bayreuth University, 1999), 88.
7. Jahria Okwera, *Dwog Paco (Come Home)*, MP3 (Gulu, Uganda: Independent, 2003).
8. Jeff Korondo, *Okwera Nono (You Reject Me for Nothing)*, MP3 (Gulu, Uganda: Independent, 2008).
9. Jahria Okwera, *Ka in Kono? (What If It Were You?)*, MP3 (Gulu, Uganda: World Vision, 2006).
10. R.J.J. Boland and R.V. Tenkasi, "Perspective Making and Perspective Taking in Communities of Knowing", *Organization Science* 6:4 (1995): 350–372.
11. Pumla Gobodo-Madikizela, "Intersubjectivity and Embodiment: Exploring the Role of the Maternal in the Language of Forgiveness and Reconciliation", *Signs* 36:3 (March 1, 2011): 543.
12. Jodi Halpern and Harvey M. Weinstein, "Rehumanizing the Other: Empathy and Reconciliation", *Human Rights Quarterly* 26:3 (August 1, 2004): 563.
13. Halpern and Weinstein, "Rehumanizing", 565.
14. Halpern and Weinstein, "Rehumanizing", 566.
15. Halpern and Weinstein, "Rehumanizing", 568.
16. Lederach, *The Moral Imagination. The Art and Soul of Building Peace* (Oxford, UK and New York, NY: Oxford University Press, 2010), 91.
17. Lederach, *Moral Imagination*, 93.
18. Lederach, *Moral Imagination*, 94.
19. Lederach, *Moral Imagination*, 96.
20. Lederach, *Moral Imagination*, 97.
21. Wole Soyinka, *The Burden of Memory, the Muse of Forgiveness* (New York: Oxford University Press, 1999), 194.
22. Arild Bergh and John Slobada, "Music and Art in Conflict Transformation: A Review", *Music and Arts in Action* 2:2 (2010).
23. Michelle LeBaron, "Foreword: Eureka! Discovering Gold in a Leaden World", in *Art in Action: Expressive Arts Therapy and Social Change,* eds. Ellen and Stephen K. Levine (Philadelphia: Jessica Kingsley Publishers, 2011), 10.
24. Lederach, *Moral Imagination*; John Paul Lederach and Angela Jill Lederach, *When Blood and Bones Cry Out: Journeys through the Soundscape of Healing and Reconciliation* (New York: Oxford University Press, 2010); and Lisa Schirch, *The Little Book of Strategic Peacebuilding* (Intercourse, PA: Good Books, 2004).

25. Olivier Urbain, *Music and Conflict Transformation: Harmonies and Dissonances in Geopolitics* (London, UK: I.B. Tauris, 2008).
26. Stephen Levine, *Poiesis: The Language of Psychology and the Speech of the Soul* (London, UK: Jessica Kingsley Publishers, 1997); Shaun McNiff, *Art Heals: How Creativity Cures the Soul* (New York, NY: Shambhala, 2004).

Appendix 1: "Dwog Paco" Lyrics

*"Dwog Paco (Come Home)" by Jahria Okwera**

*Used with permission; translated from Acholi (Luo)

Chorus

There is no problem. Come back home, please.
People are pleading. We call you back.
There is no problem. Come back home, please.
People are crying, crying for peace.

Verse One

Hear the people pleading. They are calling for you all in the bush.
Acholi elders, Lango elders are all calling you back.
There is no problem. Hear us cry. Change your heart and return home.
Everyone is calling for you, welcoming you., and don't delay, please.

Chorus x2

Verse Two

Hear everyone call for you. My brother, please change your heart.
My sister, change your heart, please. People want peace. People cry.
Hear my words, and you think about it.
I'm your brother who will never differentiate you from others.
Hear your home people calling for you truly.
Meaning, people still love you.
People cry. Everyone. People want you to come back
People cry. Everyone. People want you to come back

Chorus x2

Verse Three

Our boys, think about the Acholi people, please.

At least think about the Lango.
Our boys, you come back now.
The world at large is calling for you.
Never think you are wrongdoers.
We have now forgiven you.
Come back and organize your clan
So that peace returns to the North.
Listen to us. Return home.
Listen to us. Return home.

Chorus x6

Appendix 2: "Okwera Nono" Lyrics

*"Okwera Nono (You Reject Me for Nothing)" by Jeff Korondo**
*Used with permission; translated from Acholi (Luo)
Chorus

My people, you reject me for nothing. Where do I go?
Maybe it was meant to be like that. What if it were you? What would you do?
Maybe it was meant to be like that. What if it were you? Where would you go?

Verse One

My people, if you look carefully, no one invites the sufferings of this world.
Trouble follows you. People bring troubles to you no matter how much you try to avoid them.
If you are in this world and still want to be afraid of poverty, then it is up to you
Because poverty is part of man, part of man!
And poverty is part of wealth, part of wealth!
Wealth has no relation, no relation!
Wealth shall leave you!

Chorus x2
Verse Two

Our little children are returning from the bush with different kinds of problems.
Look! They are returning from the bush after immense suffering.

Carrying heavy loads, witnessing horrific murders and trekking long distances.
Most painful is forcing them to murder against their wish. If it were you, what would you do?

Chorus x2
Verse Three

There is this issue of returning home. Even so, it has its problems.
Go to the villages, there is enmity. There are quarrels. There are land wrangles.
There are murders, and there is bloodshed.
There are landmines and even deaths.
Our cultural leaders, please arbitrate us. Political leaders, please arbitrate us.
We grew-up in camps and do not know our land boundaries.
Even towns are camps. We do not know our land boundaries.

Appendix 3: "Kano in Kono?" Lyrics

*"Kano in Kano? (What If It Were You?)" by Jahria Okwera**
*Used with permission; translated from Acholi (Luo)
Verse One

My people, why make me cry like that?
I feel deep pain in my heart all the time.
Whenever I try to sleep, I still feel afraid.
Especially when people pinpoint at me all the time.
People make mistakes. I ask you
To forgive me.
It wasn't my intention to enter the bush.
It was all because of force.
I was taken forcefully to go and fight.
There are many poor people. They force you to arrest others.
They force you to loot.
They force you to kill.
You all, at least welcome me as your child.
You, please don't pinpoint at my back.
Don't talk bad about me all the time, my dear.
Since there is no problem now, you help me
Like the public and NGOs.

I appreciate your words of encouragement.
My mind has settled finally.
And I have the love for everyone.

Chorus

What if it were you?
Why pinpoint at me?
Yet, I never intended to go and fight?
What if it were you?
Why do you talk bad about me?
Take me as a living person also.

Verse Two

The devil's in you. Keep looking for God's people.
You relieved us, and even you motivated us.
Sharing ideas is something meaningful.
My heart is finally settling.
I'm getting back to my senses.
Now one thing, please. Don't pinpoint at us.
It leaves me with anger.
It leaves me with more pain in my heart.
People should accept God's words.
You leave every issue with our leaders at home.

Chorus x2
Verse Three

We beg our people to welcome us all.
NGOs welcomed us.
World Vision welcomed us.
Even GUSCO welcomed us.
Even KICWA welcomed us.
Watelo Rehabilitation Center
We thank the government for introducing amnesty for us.
Religious leaders, we thank for encouraging us as you were preparing us for the right life.
Show us love so that we remain confident.
Give us your words of advice that encourage us for a better and future life.

Chorus x2

Verse Four

A child who returns, please welcome him or her.
An elder who returns, welcome him or her the same way.
People should stop pinpointing at the returnees.
At this moment, we would like to express our gratitude to NGOs like:
World Vision
GUSCO
KICWA
Watelo Rehabilitation Center
CCF
Caritas
War Child

CHAPTER 8

Music's Limits: The Early Years of the Barenboim–Said Foundation (2003–2009)

Rachel Beckles Willson

Introduction

Although music has long been regarded as dangerous enough to require censorship, it has also been welcomed and idealized as a vehicle of civilizing power. In late nineteenth-century Europe, the latter attitude became particularly influential. Music entered schools as a curricular subject associated with sobriety and model citizenship; authorities from governments and churches to social welfare organizations have held up music as an ideal medium for positive transformation; peacebuilding groups have joined the movement more recently. Yet the complexities and potential contradictions of music have not been eradicated. In this chapter I work through some of these in order to illuminate some of the multiple levels on which musical peacebuilding may be understood.

R. Beckles Willson (✉)
University of London, London, UK

J. Mitchell et al. (eds.), *Peacebuilding and the Arts*,
Rethinking Peace and Conflict Studies,
https://doi.org/10.1007/978-3-030-17875-8_8

Central to my thinking is a duality of representation and embodiment. On the one hand, music-making is almost always considered as a representation of something else, something that can be grasped symbolically, metaphorically, discursively (hence orchestras such as the "World Orchestra of Peace", but also the "English Chamber Orchestra"). On the other hand, musicians themselves have immediate sensory demands and experiences that are rather different from what the public takes as the music's "message"; similarly, listeners have embodied emotional responses to music that grow out of their individual past experiences. This duality is of course a simplification of complex processes, but it serves at least to highlight that there can be wide gaps between the impact of music on musicians and other individual listeners, and the function of the music in a range of broader spheres. The potential of music to influence conflict and peace may exist in all these spaces, but it is crucial to separate them out as a preliminary step toward recognizing music's multiplicity.

In my case study these and other complexities are particularly cogent. The Barenboim–Said Foundation is best known for its highly-publicized West-Eastern Divan Orchestra, which is an ensemble of young Arabs, Jews and Europeans that congregates in Spain each summer to prepare for an international concert tour under the baton of Daniel Barenboim. The Foundation's other projects are directly related to music education: an Academy for Orchestral Studies (in Seville), an Early Childhood Education Project in other parts of Andalusia, and a Scholarship Fund for West-Eastern Divan musicians studying outside the Middle East region. Finally, there is a Musical Education Project in Palestine and Israel. My discussion here, drawing on fieldwork inside and outside the Palestinian region between 2005 and 2009, will focus on aspects of this last project, as well as the West-Eastern Divan Orchestra.[1]

Peacebuilding i: Mediterranean Co-operation and European Lobbying

The broader political context for the Barenboim–Said Foundation is not widely known. It was established at the wish of Manuel Chaves, President of the *Junta de Andalucía* (Autonomous Regional Government of Andalusia) as a descendent of an organization called the Three Cultures Foundation that was formed in Spain in 1999 to promote dialogue between Morocco, Spain, and other Mediterranean regions. The Barenboim–Said Foundation emerged from that in 2005 with a different (and musical) emphasis, but the key ideas of "peace, dialogue and reconciliation" were sustained. One of the Foundation's original objectives was to "promote the spirit of peace, dialogue and reconciliation, primarily through music", understanding "the history of the peaceful coexistence of different cultures over the centuries in Andalusia [as] a central feature", striving to promote "an integral humanistic education" within music education, and to collaborate regionally in "Andalusia, Palestine and other Middle-Eastern countries".[2]

In the Spanish context, the West-Eastern Divan Orchestra thus constituted a celebration of Andalusia's most-celebrated historical moment: it represented a sort of a revitalization of Muslim Spain, and symbolic reparation for Spain's anti-Semitism in the early fifteenth century, offering collaboration between citizens of Christian, Jewish and Muslim communities as an expression of a better, peaceful world. In the context of the Spanish political field, it was also recognizable as a manifestation of the controversial and much critiqued *Andalucismo*, or Andalusian nationalism, elaborating what historian Khalid Duran has termed "Andalusia's nostalgia for progress".[3]

In Europe more broadly, the West-Eastern Divan Orchestra is understood as a peaceful vision for, and cultural intervention in, the region encompassing the Palestinian Territories and the State of Israel. Commentators respond to its version of utopia in a variety of ways, some arguing that it is bold and important to offer such visions of peace for the Middle East, others questioning the organization's use of public funds and its capacity to confront violence on a meaningful level. Others read it more globally, one Spanish commentator suggesting in 2006 that it should be taken to "countries which still need to be convinced about the importance of peace, such as the United States, Israel or England".[4] This was plainly a reference to twentieth- and twenty-first century interventions in the Middle East—one of the most recent being the disastrous intervention in Iraq from which Spain withdrew its support in 2004.

For a sense of the political potential of the orchestra to generate change, we can consider one of Barenboim's attempts to use it as a forum for political debate, and even as a lobbying mechanism. In the early years the orchestra involved Edward W. Said, who socialized with players and facilitated discussion between them. Said's untimely death in 2003 left something of an intellectual vacuum, which Barenboim strove to ameliorate by inviting a panel of intellectuals to the orchestra's rehearsal period in the following year for a Symposium.[5] Whereas during Said's life this workshop was an occasion for musical encounter between a mix of players as much as a concertizing venture, Barenboim gradually turned it into a vehicle of diplomacy. For example, he engaged the Symposium participants to co-author a Declaration calling upon the German and Spanish governments to intervene in the "political deadlock" between Israelis and Palestinians and to rescue them from their "inferno of mutual and self-destruction".[6] Subsequently, drawing on a briefing paper he had requested from one of the Symposium participants, Barenboim met with German Chancellor Schroeder and Havea Solana (High Representative for the Common and Foreign Security Policy of the European Union) to put forward some policy proposals, and two Symposium participants published related articles in the Spanish daily *El Pais*.[7] Each one of these texts presented the West-Eastern Divan Orchestra as its point of inspiration.

Ultimately there has been no indication that European governments were able to respond positively to the model offered by the West-Eastern Divan Orchestra, and change their policies in ways that could contribute to peace in the Palestine Israel region. On the other hand, the public display of musical collaboration provided by the West-Eastern Divan Orchestra has contributed to discussions that are still ongoing.

One of the challenges of peacebuilding is that it needs to be a continuous process on several levels.[8] Barenboim's actions mobilize one in particular, in that they suggest that musical activity could inspire new international political maneuvres. His work has certainly illustrated that a leading conductor of western classical music may gain access to highly elevated political circles. But this is a very specific social situation, a valuing of music professionals that is a product of a particular European history. And its impact is very limited: once the West-Eastern Divan Orchestra and its vision travel elsewhere, its politically-representational function is understood differently, and this is particularly pressing in the case of the regions to which the orchestra ostensibly refers—Israel and Palestine—where it has traveled on only one occasion. That sole visit of 2005 forms the centerpiece of the orchestra's promotional double DVD entitled *The Ramallah Concert*.[9] To this I turn next.

Peacebuilding 2: Importing Simulation, Fuelling Hostility

We learn from the film that orchestra members first heard about the idea of playing in Ramallah at their workshop in 2004 and reacted with consternation. Going to Ramallah was a frightening prospect for Israelis, who associated the West Bank with danger, and some of the Spanish players thought similarly. Barenboim enlisted the support of the Spanish government for the project in the following year, and attained thereby diplomatic passports for all players. This circumvented the problem that those traveling as citizens of Israel, Syria or Lebanon would otherwise have been present on the West Bank illegally.

Although the film provides this information, it is the symbolic role of music, and its place at the heart of the project, that dominates the tale, fleshed out by selected narratives of participants. Every one of these is highly emotional, whether excited by adventure, moved by the possibility of reaching a forbidden territory, overwhelmed by the musical experience, or stirred in another meaningful way.[10] In other words, it is the affective role of music that shapes the DVD presentation, implying that western concert music has the capacity to transcend the political situation. The entire performance itself is part of the DVD, and appears to be both warmly welcomed by the audience and hugely enjoyed by participants.

Enthusiastic viewers of the film rarely observe that it allows no sense of the orchestra's impact on the ground in Ramallah, except for some brief footage of Arab members of the orchestra enjoying a little shopping and meeting locals. Rather, the landscape is present as an unhappy backdrop (and the use of plaintive Arab music as an uncredited soundscape reinforces the Orientalized ambience). Moreover, beyond comments from the officials involved—a short logistical tale from the coordinator of the Barenboim–Said Foundation in Ramallah; and official celebratory greetings from the Deputy Prime Minister Nabil Shaath and politician Mustafa Barghouti introducing the concert—there is no footage showing Palestinian residents' responses. The film does reveal in passing that a number of the orchestral players from neighboring Arab nations were from Palestinian families exiled from the region in 1949, and also that there was at least one Palestinian participant from Israel. Yet at no point is the question even posed as to whether there was any participation by Palestinians from the Occupied Territories.

However, a review of local press articles helps to give a sense of the local impact and participation. Maureen Clare Murphy wrote in the Lebanon-based newspaper *The Daily Star*, that the concert "was unadvertised, and only at the last minute were local photographers allowed to document the event for Palestinian papers. The concert was invitation-only...."[11] She went on to observe that "[f]oreigners were disproportionately represented in the auditorium". Several of my own interviewees cited a recent rift between the Barenboim–Said Foundation and a Palestinian music school (of this more below) as a reason for low Palestinian attendance; at the time, there was also growing sympathy for a group promoting cultural boycotts. A substantial number of invited guests did not to attend, presumably for this reason.

Two Palestinian testimonies help to round out the picture. One offers a broad context, taking the form of a speech by a musician from Israel that he made while attending a conference in Japan. Nizar Rohana's summing up reveals a tension between international representation and local experience. He understood the image of the orchestra in the following way:

> What is the meaning of the Divan Orchestra for Palestinians? Is it significant for various Palestinian institutions, and for Palestinian society? It may be a very beautiful world, but it is far from the reality in Palestine, something like a "show". Palestinian people see this project like this. Palestine is still under the Israeli occupation, and the situation in Palestine, especially these days in the Gaza strip, is so hard and terrible, that we cannot accept the Divan project, because it serves more the interests of Israel. It announces Israel's look of peace to the people in the world, while the occupation still continues. Palestinian society is dependent on foreign donations, especially European, American, and even Japanese. But these foreign donors prefer to donate their money to projects like the Divan Orchestra that shows [sic] co-operation between Israel and Palestine.[12]

Rohana indicates that the European notion that a symphony orchestra of Jews, Arabs and Spaniards playing Tchaikovsky represents "peace" is unavailable on the West Bank. Rohana also questioned the appropriateness of western classical music education in Palestine where it was in conflict with music more traditional to the region:

> Palestinian people feel now that they should have a chance to build their own identity, before doing this kind of project. I think it is very important for Palestinian people to study and practice their own musical heritage.

Another testimony comes from the single player from the Occupied Territories who played in the West-Eastern Divan Orchestra in 2005, violist Mohammed Amr. He wrote his comments below at my request that he expand on a passing critique he made about the orchestra via email in 2010, after I asked whether or not he was attending the Divan workshop that year. I told him in my email message that I had spotted him on the DVD about the Ramallah concert, and had wondered why he had not been interviewed for that production. He responded as follows:

> [V]ery carefully chosen people are interviewed every time by different media [...] Barenboim is literally playing a chess game. During the closed debates, he decides who speaks and when, he knows the position of each and every one during rehearsal, he decides where everyone should sit depending on the colour skin and the image and the impression that a certain combination gives the western collective subconscious, everything is studied (the teacher once asked me to move more...) to give the best impression, he decides who should appear on the camera or the DVD. This whole image looks more like a theatre piece than reality. I was banned from all interviews because I didn't have any of the accepted profiles, because I was not ready to make such a concession.[13]

Amr then reflected upon his own experiences of crossing borders in comparison with the Divan's freedom to move. He had already told me about his journey to Spain when we first met in 2006, but he contextualized this experience nearly four years later, in the email:

> The absurdity of participating at this orchestra became very obvious to me one day while leaving Ramallah to go to Jordan to take a plane to Spain to play with the Divan [in 2006]. That day I waited about 3 hours at the Qalandia checkpoint to be able to quit Ramallah, I spent those 3 hours observing the misery and the humiliation that me and my Westbankers go through. I saw the paradox, I tried to find a reason to justify myself, and I couldn't! Later, I understood that this orchestra is a big machine to generate money through manipulation, and it's insensitive to the complaints of one of its rare Palestinians who represents somehow the real Palestinian youth who lived through occupation. This was the end.

Amr understood the orchestra's appearance in Ramallah as a triumph of foreign intervention and local government action:

> This orchestra is like a creature that can only live in a laboratory, the goal of the Ramallah concert was to show how a coalition of powers (Israeli Palestinian and Spanish governments) can get united and transform Ramallah into a laboratory where this creature can survive, no exchange was made with Palestinian public [...], what mattered was the challenge, the risk, the symbol, a purely mediatic concert; at this level it was a big success, but nothing else.

Amr's notion of a "purely mediatic concert" captures how the event was skewed away from Palestinians' own experiences. Not only was it largely closed to the general public, but all official speeches introducing the concert were presented in English rather than Arabic (they were intended for the film cameras, not the audience). As we have seen, this is part of a strategy on an international lobbying level. But the DVD consciously presents Palestine in a particularly negative way, indeed the whole idea of a "Ramallah concert" is inseparable from a notion of Ramallah as a place of danger, and simultaneously as somewhere that is difficult (or risky) to reach. This apparent difficulty and danger is developed in the DVD presentation well beyond the issue with the passports already discussed. The DVD shows Arab players arriving in Ramallah from Jordan, while Israeli *and Spanish* players were brought from Israel. Similarly, the DVD shows that the Arabs were there in time to look around the town and meet local people, whereas the others were rushed into rehearse, perform the concert, and quickly depart. It conjoins Israelis and Europeans, while dividing them from Arabs; and it reinforces the message that Palestine is a dangerous place for non-Arabs.

The impact of this is worth considering from several perspectives. Neither the Israelis nor the Spanish had any experience of Ramallah other than the Cultural Center, and what they observed through the windows of their minibuses (in a military-surrounded convoy). The Cultural Center is a recent building on a hill outside the town that was on the occasion, according to Murphy, surrounded by "uniformed, armed guards".[14] The Israeli and Spanish players had no opportunity, then, to form an impression of the place that might go beyond the one that they had prior to making the trip, and there was no hope of communication processes that might contribute to the serious work of peace-building. All the affective experience framed by the film cameras was limited to a small number of people who were already predisposed to be moved by this particular type of music making and the symbolism of the event.

Ramallah resident, Swedish writer Peter Lagerquist, observed that "the way the orchestra was whisked out of Ramallah immediately afterwards was comical, and also dismaying".[15] Lagerquist countered the prevailing foreign perception of Ramallah, saying that there is no "security situation" in Ramallah that threatens outsiders. "No foreign visitor has ever come to harm or been accosted here. [...] The place fairly crawls with expats particularly in the summer and people are so used to seeing them around that no one notices". Lagerquist identified the event as following a historical trope: "what was interesting about the exit in that sense was that it fairly approximated a sort of colonial nervousness. Fear of the Kasbah/Jungle/Ghetto".

In his reading, then, the way that the border crossing was arranged constructed Palestine as a place of such violence that the non-Arab (even the Spaniard) required military protection.

In fact, the event's celebration in the western media is, to a large extent, dependent on a fearful image of Ramallah that is common in people who have not visited it. But this is not an image shared by the people who live there (or those who live elsewhere in the Occupied Territories). Palestinians living in the Occupied Territories experience the borders around them as obstacles to movement: they are routinely prevented from crossing them. Yet many of them are in regular contact with foreign aid workers who enjoy easy freedom of movement across those same borders. So the very framework of the West-Eastern Divan Orchestra's documentary film, based on a difficult and dangerous crossing into Ramallah, is incongruous for Palestinians in Ramallah and elsewhere on the West Bank. Thus the image-making reinforces the essentialization of their communities as "dangerous", and their sense that the situation on the ground is misrepresented in Europe and North America. The image is, in other words, profoundly counterproductive.

Peacebuilding 3: Music Education in the Meantime

The Barenboim–Said Foundation's Musical Education Project in Palestine is of a different nature, but faces a number of related challenges. Its first employees from Europe arrived in Ramallah in 2003 after the second *Intifada* (uprising) had commenced, and by which time foreign interventions were regarded with suspicious weariness for very specific reasons. One decade after the Oslo Accords that had been set to establish a Palestinian State within 5 years, Palestinians had been in receipt of a flood of "peace" initiatives, but these had not been accompanied by political change, military withdrawal or widespread material improvements. Rather, the building of Israeli settlements on the West Bank had continued as before; the Palestinian Authority had been ruined by elitism and corruption; and the political process had ground to a halt. Even while the discourses of "peace process" and "democracy" had apparently no reality, the international community maintained them while diverting their monies toward emergency aid. Sponsors had come thereby to cooperate with Israel's occupation, rather than supporting the development of civil society within an emergent autonomous political unit for Palestinians.[16] For example, they compensated for ongoing damage by military operations rather than either addressing the causes or developing the infrastructure invoked in their discursive rationales.[17]

Some years before the Barenboim–Said Foundation arrived on the scene, music education on the West Bank had drawn on the post-Oslo influx of foreign interest and finance. The small number of Palestinians trained in western classical music living in Ramallah had long felt isolated. Their situation was very unlike such musicians in neighboring Israel, where a strong institutionalization of European musical traditions had been led by and for Jews who arrived from Europe and Russia in the 1930s. But from the early 1990s onwards, such Palestinians founded and developed a range of organizations that sought to disseminate formal music training, with a view to being able to contribute regionally and internationally in the future. The most significant for the purposes of this study was the National Conservatory of Music (1993), which functioned initially under the auspices of the University at Birzeit (10 kilometers North of Ramallah) with teaching based in Ramallah, and in subsequent years expanded into several branches (Ramallah, Bethlehem, Jerusalem). Its aim was to provide music education in Arab and other traditions (including western classical music and jazz).[18]

The Conservatory's goals for Palestinian music education were, however, profoundly challenged by the gulf opening up between political realities and the cultural discourses of funders. The problem can be grasped from an article published in Israel's daily newspaper *Haaretz* in 2004, in which the Palestinian National Conservatory's flute teacher and academic director is quoted at some length:

> When the occupation is over and people can relate to one another as equals and talk as equals it will be possible to do things together, and that will be wonderful. We are all hoping for this. As individuals, and not officially, of course there is no problem with making contact, and in any case the intentions of those who want to initiate such contacts are very important. Putting a concert under the heading "Concert for Peace", for example, is impossible: How can there be "peace" inside an occupation?[19]

Musicians arriving to teach for the Barenboim–Said Foundation in 2003 were obliged to negotiate this situation, but found themselves in conflict with the local people whose lives they were ostensibly there to enhance.

Central to the work of the Barenboim–Said Foundation has been expressing regret about, and transcendence of, Europe's anti-Semitic policies and actions: it strives for reconciliation. It is, then, wrapped up in earlier phases of events that are closely connected to the foundation of the State of Israel and the troubles of Palestinians displaced by that event. But reconciliation work on the earlier era cannot be simply imported to the West Bank, where the violence of displacement continues. Regrettably, peacebuilders may well import their own reconciliation processes without acknowledging its dangers. We can trace this through a clash that occurred between the National Conservatory and the Barenboim–Said Foundation. My sources for the following account are 6 interviews with faculty and ex-faculty from the two institutions.

The occasion was an orchestral workshop in Jordan in the summer of 2005, which was run collaboratively by the two schools. It was intended for Palestinian children from the West Bank, Jordan, Lebanon and Syria, children who share a heritage in historical Palestine, but who normally would never meet one another. It was understood by participants as an opportunity for new inter-Palestinian collaboration, then, but was also a preserved zone in a sense: there would be no collaboration with Israelis (for that, Lebanese and Syrian participants would have needed special permits to take part).[20] Faculty members from both the Foundation and the Conservatory were involved, but one of them—working for the National Conservatory—had Israeli citizenship. When this fact emerged at the workshop in Jordan, some Lebanese and Syrian participants were angry and alarmed, not least because they were contravening their government policy. They thus demanded that she leave. Adding to the furore, a faculty member from the Conservatory refused to take her on the coach.

The significance of the crisis here is that the teacher whose unannounced second citizenship caused the conflict was working, on a personal level, at precisely the sort of reconciliation that the Barenboim–Said Foundation promotes. I refer to her as SU here. SU had been a German non-Jewish citizen who had moved to Israel from Germany in 1991, having got a job there specifically in the interest of developing a link with the country. She understood this as a confrontation with Germany's anti-Semitism. She converted to Judaism, first with a "reformed" program, and then with an Orthodox one. However, she found the latter "distasteful and anti-intellectual with a strong Arab hatred", and gradually disengaged, becoming non-observant. A consequence of the experience was that she commenced learning Arabic, and joined Machsom Watch, a group monitoring Israeli military practices with Palestinians trying to cross checkpoints. She began teaching for the Conservatory in 2005.

The problem was resolved for the period of the workshop (the young musicians became apologetic but the teacher withdrew from participation, did some sightseeing and then returned only to attend the final concert). Later, however, it played out as a division between the Conservatory and the Foundation, who took different and separate paths forward. The Conservatory continued to develop the youth orchestra with Palestinians from Egypt, Jordan, Lebanon, and Syria; the Foundation broke away, establishing a connection with a Palestinian organization in Israel, and founding an orchestra bringing together its students with those from the Nazareth school. The upshot of an import of personal European "reconciliation", then, was a structural mirroring of aspects of the geopolitical division of the Palestine region, rather than a transcendence or transformation of them.

In broad terms, the problem is one of imposing ideals, whether or not this is undertaken intentionally. Another German musician who I interviewed had taken to Palestine what she considered desirable aims, which she characterized in a 2007 interview with me as "vague ideas about peace projects". This, she observed with hindsight, had been a mistake, a product of having "had no idea how strong the anti-Israeli sentiment was". Moreover, having attempted—unsuccessfully—to draw Palestinians into working for musical "peace", which she wished to understand symbolically rather than politically, she found herself participating in a symbolic projection that she herself could not stomach. The occasion was a children's concert in which she was conductor, and for which the programs printed by the National Conservatory expressed hope that pupils would play in "the liberated city of Jerusalem" in the future.[21] The implication of this for the German musician was the expulsion of Israelis—which was extremely problematic. A further concert in which she was involved was dedicated to Arab prisoners in Israel. This, again, was for her "too political". In short, there was a competition about representation between European and Palestinian ideals.

Peacebuilding 4: Music's Limits, Music's Specificity

In the first section of this chapter I highlighted the representational function that western classical music bears within Europe, and the consequent access that its most admired practitioners may have to elevated political circles. Implicit in my discussion throughout the chapter has been the particular system of musical values that developed within and around western classical music during the formation of modern European nations.[22] This has led people all over the world to associate classical music making with civilization, democracy and modern prosperity, and make it seem a suitable vessel for developing or projecting such values. Put baldly, classical music education in Europe absorbed and projected the ideals and practices of imperialism, along with its attendant dominance and exclusory practices.

It is particularly instructive to examine how classical music's representational function can mask the peculiar demands it makes on its practitioners. These include many hours of solitary intensive practice, devotion to particular and proscribed styles of achievement and, often, subservience to domineering figures of authority both alive (conductors) and dead (composers). Instructors are steeped in a tradition rooted in nation-building (and its attendant modernist exclusivity), and tend to propagate rigorous attention to and reverence for the textual authority of the European past. One foreign teacher in Ramallah told me in an interview in 2009 that Western classical music was superior to Arab music as a vessel of learning, and that although his students "wanted to play their culture's music", as he put it, he "insisted that they also learned Western classical music". When I asked him why, he connected it to a notion of "honesty" that resided in being "precise" before being "free", and being true to what was on the page in terms of dynamics and phrasing. He had attempted to play some Arab music while in Ramallah, but found it difficult, while asserting that "the traditional [Arab] music [was] imprecise, very open to interpretation".[23] Such a perspective is in sharp contrast to that of Nizar Rohana encountered above.

Foreign teachers that I interviewed had encountered a range of disparities between what they expected to teach, and the needs they discovered on the ground. Their responses were varied. Some felt confounded by the social and political situation that was either outside their field of training (many students have been profoundly traumatized by violence in the area) or that seemed to hinder real progress with music making (the home situation was of too limited support). A very few learned some Arab songs and started to use them as a bridge within teaching. Some were astonished to find themselves teaching children belonging to the upper classes of Ramallah, whose parents were political emissaries, the owners of banks or the directors of private schools. These children were accustomed to foreign vacations and large birthday presents, and were generally "spoiled...used to being given everything", as one teacher put it. Yet others discovered that affective aspects of music making were not always welcome in the forms that they themselves regarded as beneficial and important to disseminate. They were startled to have to hold back from offering concert performances as a means toward processing grief, and were frustrated by concerns about bodily control, propriety, and appropriate gender behaviors.[24]

Can the values of western classical music institutions be compatible with the complex, subtle and necessarily fluid demands of conflict-survival or even peacebuilding as it takes place in diverse cultural systems on the ground? Thanks to the values inculcated with education, institutions of western classical music tend to be replicated as Appadurai's "hard cultural forms", i.e. as resistant to change because their associated "value, meaning, and embodied practice" is "difficult to break".[25] For Appadurai, the values of hard cultural forms are "at their heart, puritanical ones, in which rigid adherence to external codes is part of the discipline of internal moral development"; this may, I suggest, provide the very authentication of the cultural forms (hence the unbreakable quality of the values). Just as has been observed in other peacebuilding and development fields, there are obvious perils in introducing institutional practices from remote contexts as if they are appropriate in a universal sense. Yet to deny Palestinians the opportunity to develop skills enabling them to participate in Europe's musical practices could be seen as problematic in other ways.

The clearest lessons from this case study may remain the distinctions between representation and experience, and the potential clashes between imported practices and dialogues about reconciliation and peace. On a positive note, the learning curve on the side of the western instructors has plainly been a very steep one, and some Palestinians have been challenged in ways that may also be educationally and socially useful. But it is far from clear that this functions as effective "peacebuilding", and a pressing question does emerge. To what extent are such western instructors, and western institutions, prepared to allow their authority to be challenged and transformed in their development of peace initiatives?

Notes

1. For more detailed discussion, see Rachel Beckles Willson, *Orientalism and Musical Mission: Palestine and the West* (Cambridge, UK: Cambridge University Press, 2013), 28–29, 243–247, 273–274.

2. "Foundation", www.barenboim-said.org/index.php?id=119, accessed 9 June 2009 (in the current form of the text these concepts are no longer there: see http://www.barenboim-said.org/en/fundacion/) and "Objectives of the Foundation", www.barenboim-said.org/index.php?id=166, accessed 9 June 2009; this latter has also been altered somewhat.
3. Khalid Duran, "Andalusia's Nostalgia for Progress and Harmonious Heresy", *Middle East Report* 178 (September–October 1992), 20–23.
4. Pablo Meléndez Haddad, "Soñando con la paz" [Dreaming Peace], *ABC Cataluña*, 13 August, 2006. Thanks to Eva Moreda Rodriguez for her translation. I discuss the concert in more detail in Rachel Beckles Willson, "Whose Utopia? Perspectives on the West-Eastern Divan Orchestra", *Music and Politics* 3:2 (Summer 2009): 1–21.
5. Those selected were Mustafa Barghouti, leader of the newly-founded Palestinian National Initiative, which had just set itself up as a democratic political force in the region; Yaron Ezrahi, Professor of Political Science at the Hebrew University in Jerusalem; Felipe González Márquez, the Spanish ex-Prime Minister and socialist politician; Rashid Khalidi, the Edward Said Professor of Arab Studies at Columbia University; Wadie Said, son of Edward Said; Raja Shehadeh, Palestinian writer; and Avi Shlaim, Professor of International Relations at the University of Oxford.
6. To the best of my knowledge, this text was circulated on a flier at the concert in Seville but not published or circulated in any other forms.
7. Felipe González, "Palestine: un nuevo relato" [Palestine: a new story], *El Pais*, 3 September, 2004 and Avi Shlaim, "Cuatro días en Sevilla" [Four days in Sevilla], *El Pais*, 9 September, 2004.
8. See John Paul Lederach's Peacebuilding Pyramid which identifies three levels: at the top elite, the middle-range and the grassroots levels, *Building Peace: Sustainable Reconciliation in Divided Societies* (Washington, DC: United States Institute of Peace Press, 1997), 39.
9. Paul Smaczny, *The Ramallah Concert: Knowledge Is the Beginning* (EuroArts Music International and Warner Classics, 2005).
10. For a critical discussion of the internal dynamics of the orchestra, see Rachel Beckles Willson, "The Parallax Worlds of the West-Eastern Divan Orchestra", *Journal of the Royal Musical Association* 134:2 (November 2009): 319–347.
11. Maureen Clare Murphy, "Freedom for Palestine—But Only for Ticket-Holders?" *The Daily Star*, 2 September 2005, www.dailystar.com.lb/article.asp?edition_ID=10&article_ID=18144&categ_id=4#axzz0vzrMg9Dx, accessed 7 June 2009 but now available at https://electronicintifada.net/content/freedom-palestine-ticket-holders-only/5732, accessed 9 June 2019.
12. Nizar Rohana, Yoshimi Ohshima, Akira Usuki, and Kumiko Yamama, "Orchestra Education for Peace by E. Said and D. Barenboim", in *Kyoto*

International Conference 2006: "Art and Peace: The Shape of Peace Designed by Art" (2006), 124–125.

13. Email to author, 6 August 2010.
14. Murphy, "Freedom for Palestine".
15. Peter Lagerquist. Email to author, December 2005.
16. Anne Le More, "Killing with Kindness: Funding the Demise of a Palestinian State", *International Affairs* 81:5 (2005): 982, 991–993. See also Sari Hanafi and Linda Tabar, "The Intifada and the Aid Industry: The Impact of the New Liberal Agenda on the Palestinian NGOs", *Comparative Studies of South Asia, Africa and the Middle East* 23:1 and 2 (2003).
17. Anne Le More, "Killing with Kindness", 993–994.
18. Dalia Habash, "The National Conservatory of Music: Where Talents Are Discovered and Nurtured", *This Week in Palestine* 59 (March 2003), www.thisweekinpalestine.com/details.php?id=165&ed=24&edid=24, accessed 10 July, 2014. The Conservatory's current activities can be viewed at http://ncm.birzeit.edu/en, accessed 10 July 2014.
19. Noam Ben Ze'ev, "Distant Trumpets", *Haaretz*, 21 May 2004.
20. Political relations between the various Middle-Eastern states require players from Egypt, Syria and Lebanon to gain special government permission to play with Israelis.
21. Interview with the author, Nazareth, 3 January 2007.
22. For examples of research on this topic, see David Gramit, *Cultivating Music: The Aspirations, Interests, and Limits of German Musical Culture, 1770–1848* (Berkeley and Los Angeles, CA: University of California Press, 1998) and Pamela M. Potter, *Most German of the Arts: Musicology and Society from the Weimar Republic to the End of Hitler's Reich* (New Haven, NJ: Yale University Press, 1998).
23. A detailed discussion of such interviews can be read in my *Orientalism and Musical Mission*, 292–309.
24. It is worth noting that very few of the teachers arriving after about 2005 were there for any reason other than the opportunity of a job (the political situation and cultural novelty were seen as little more than a sideline adventure).
25. Arjun Appadurai, *Modernity at Large: Cultural Dimensions of Globalization* (Minneapolis, MN: University of Minnesota Press, 2006), 90.

CHAPTER 9

The Role of Music-Making in Peacebuilding: A Levinasian Perspective

Kathryn Jourdan

Introduction

How might we understand the role of music-making in peacebuilding? Have we at times expected too much from music-making in this context? Whose music is it appropriate to "use" in contexts of peacebuilding? This section of the book has presented two contrasting perspectives drawn from music-making in the context of peacebuilding. In one, music-making by local musicians has "contributed to the building of compassionate, creative relationships between and among community members" (p. 137) in the setting of Northern Uganda after two decades of violent conflict. In the other, the importation of music-making in the Western classical tradition into the West Bank Palestinian territories have been identified as problematic, incompatible perhaps, "with the complex, subtle and necessarily fluid demands of conflict-survival or even peacebuilding as it takes place

K. Jourdan (✉)
St Mary's Music School, Edinburgh, UK
e-mail: kathryn@jourdan.me

J. Mitchell et al. (eds.), *Peacebuilding and the Arts*,
Rethinking Peace and Conflict Studies,
https://doi.org/10.1007/978-3-030-17875-8_9

in diverse cultural systems on the ground" (p. 158), bringing with it dangers of "potential clashes between imported practices and dialogues about reconciliation and peace" (p. 158). In the first, music-making through songs from a shared local, popular style, whose lyrics carry exhortations to empathize with the "other", is seen as an effective vehicle for the rebuilding of relationships following conflict. Here, music-making appears to bring about positive encounters, while in the second example, a set of unhelpful structural relationships accompany what is perceived to be the continuation of a colonial quest to "civilize" through Western musical forms.

This chapter seeks to situate understandings of how music-making might function in the context of peacebuilding within a conceptualization of music-making as "ethical encounter" developed within the field of music education. Firstly, a brief exploration of different notions of what music-making might bring to processes of peacebuilding raises questions of whether a utopian space can be opened up, a peace imagined, or a reflection of a difficult social reality offered. A pragmatic approach is considered which makes much more modest claims for the "power" of music-making, adopting a notion of music-making as an enabling "interruption" during processes of peacebuilding.

The chapter goes on to suggest tools for conceptualizing music-making's role in processes of "ethical encounter" in such contexts. Tools drawn from the writing of French Jewish philosopher Emmanuel Levinas are helpful both in recognizing the limitations of music's role, and paradoxically, suggesting the "infinity" of music-making's potential contribution. Music may enable "putting a world in common" and "looking into the face of the Other", aiding the building of non-violent relationships and re-humanizing the Other in settings where constructive social change is actively being sought.

Returning to questions of "whose music" might be appropriate, Rachel Beckles Willson's critique of Western classical music is considered, and here I provide a counterpoint from my own perspective as a professional player within this tradition. The skills, sensitivities and attentiveness acquired through music-making within a large ensemble such as an orchestra, are considered in the light of notions of "looking into the face of the Other", or perhaps "listening to the voice of the Other". The inter-personal aspects of music-making and the benefits these can bring are illustrated through the experiences of young people from challenged communities in the El Sistema-inspired Big Noise programmes in Scotland, where making music together has become the way of relating in a programme aimed at social transformation.

Processes of Peacebuilding Through Music-Making: Aims and Orientation

Re-Humanizing the Other

In his 2005 book, John Paul Lederach poses the question, "How do we transcend the cycles of violence that bewitch our human community while still living in them?"[1] Lindsay Opiyo's chapter in this volume highlights the priorities in peacebuilding of "developing constructive, compassionate relationships", of strategically "engaging with groups labelled by society as the 'other'". The lyrics of the songs she discusses have "captured popular sentiments" and have been listened to by all sides in the Northern Ugandan conflict. Here, local musicians have used shared cultural forms to carry a message of reconciliation and acceptance through the lyrics of their songs. Processes of peacebuilding are concerned with the development of non-violent relationships, and at the heart of this aim, Opiyo suggests, is the need to re-humanize the Other.

"Saying It How It Is" or "Pointing to a Better Place"?

Opiyo writes, "Crucially, the songs take as their starting point the terrible realities and the brutalizing effects of years of conflict". In contrast, Rachel Beckles Willson writes of a "staged scene of utopia", which she sees as being constructed in the various instances she investigates of European cultural forms being brought into the Palestinian communities of the West Bank. Instead of acknowledging and engaging with the "material realities" on the ground, the discourse she perceives from within the European classical musical tradition is one of "pointing to a better place", one which takes its own tradition to be in some senses universal, tending to overlook local musical traditions as well as political injustices, in its global reach.[2]

Is there a role within music-making in processes of peacebuilding for encompassing both an acknowledgement of the immanence of harsh social realities and for offering a fresh perspective, for "imagining a peaceful future", as Mitchell writes in this volume, a transcendent, even "utopian vision"? Lederach writes of the need to be "rooted in the day-to-day challenges of violent settings", while "rising above destructive patterns and giving birth to that which does not yet exist",[3] situated in, yet transcending the material realities in situations of conflict.[4] Might music-making be understood to facilitate such a holding-in-tension of immanence and transcendence in practices of peacebuilding? Or, must only one or the other objective be addressed at any given time?

Cynthia Cohen sets out a list of processes of reconciliation, at least some of which, she suggests, may be undertaken by former adversaries in appropriate and diverse cultural contexts.[5] Each task involves communities learning about themselves and the other, often "unlearning" what they had believed to be true. "In this sense, reconciliation can be conceptualized in terms of education"[6] and music and peacebuilding projects shaped so as to facilitate the necessary learning, and to restore the capacities and nourish the sensibilities required for reconciliation.[7] How then might music-making be understood to function in terms of learning and un-learning in contexts of peacebuilding?

Music-Making as a Mode of Ethical Encounter

An emerging strand in recent thinking among leading voices within music education has been the developing notion of "music-making as ethical encounter". Christopher Small's influential work on "musicking"[8] suggests that it is from within the local, situated set of relationships, which come into being when people make music together, that musical meaning arises, where "ideal" relationships as understood by the particular community who are making music together are "modelled":

> The act of musicking establishes in the place where it is happening a set of relationships, and it is in those relationships that the meaning of the act lies. They are to be found not only between those organized sounds which are conventionally thought of as being the stuff of musical meaning but also between the people who are taking part, in whatever capacity, in the performance: and they model, or stand as metaphor for, ideal relationships as the participants in the performance imagine them to be: relationships between person and person, between individual and society, between humanity and the natural world and even perhaps the supernatural world.[9]

The focus of music educators by implication then is on *musicking* as in itself a communicative activity rather than mere transmission of musical information:

> Music educators should work as dynamos that help the community members to establish new relationships through which to explore, affirm and celebrate their relations, and this can be taken as the ultimate goal of musicking.[10]

Lee Higgins, drawing on Derrida, and working in the field of community music, conceptualizes these relationships in terms of the practice of hospitality, of welcoming in the stranger, "a preparation for the incoming of the other, generating a porous, permeable, open-ended affirmation".[11] Writing from within the discipline of the philosophy of music education, taking this strand of thinking further, Wayne Bowman suggests that music-making offers "ethical resources", "practices in and through which people wrestle with and seek to answer the vitally important educational question, 'What kind of person is it good to be?'".[12] Intertwined throughout these notions of music-making is the thread of tension which holds together the here-and-now of local relationship, where power structures must be unmasked, conflict acknowledged, and the transcendent ideals of "how we might be" in a better world.

This emerging conceptualization of music-making as a mode of ethical encounter is a useful step towards an ethically grounded understanding of how music might be useful in contexts of peacebuilding. Arild Bergh writes of the problem he encountered at the outset of his research in the field of music and conflict transformation, "the amount of hyperbole surrounding music in general, and music and conflict transformation more specifically",[13] finding a widespread "taking for granted of the 'magic' of music, and a reluctance to look critically at the issues surrounding this field".[14] It is important to recognize that "music is not inherently peaceful and groups and individuals who want to create or maintain conflicts have often made good use of music to further their agenda".[15] Similarly, we must acknowledge the role of music in preparing for or in stoking conflict.16

A Pragmatic View

Bergh proposes a pragmatic approach to understanding music's potential role in peacebuilding, and cautions against the temptation to view music as possessing universal attributes.[17] He writes:

> Conflict transformation is about doing very difficult emotional work related to out groups against which there exists strong antipathy, and the role of music has traditionally been seen as a quick working 'magic bullet', but more

> grounded works indicate that this is a false picture, that the long term effects are uncertain, and overall the field requires more investigation as well as an understanding of what music really provides.[18]

When Bergh considers what role music might have in conflict transformation, he suggests:

> In very basic terms we can say that engaging with music can affect you physically or mentally, and that these two realms are often linked ... Music may bring out a range of emotions, emotions that come out of being reminded of specific or general memories, which Sloboda (2005) refers to as episodic and iconic associations, are relatively easy to explain and understand ... More difficult to explain are emotions not obviously linked to memories... Emotions and attitudes are not generated automatically or unidirectionally by music, but by people engaging in a back-and-forth manner with music and within *the spaces afforded by music* and a network that includes other people, objects and situations as DeNora (2001) and Gomart and Hennion (1999) have suggested.[19]

Music-making allows a space for participants to exercise their agency in terms of freedom to project, interpret and engage in emotional work. Bergh takes this a step further and wonders whether music might be seen as a source of diversion, a "beneficial interruption", where it ceases to be the focal point, demanding all our attention, and instead offers a break from the hard work of cognitive processing and intense emotion. Bergh gives the example of computer programmers who work on problem-solving while listening to music, and explores how music invites "occasional attention" which stops us from being stuck in a single thought.[20]

Beyond Empathy: "Looking into the Face of the Other" and the Philosophy of Emmanuel Levinas

While music undoubtedly affords opportunities for emotional work, and for a beneficial interruption socially and personally in situations of peacebuilding, I would like to explore behind these functions, to probe further the underlying, ethical nature of music-making. Opiyo's chapter in this volume foregrounds the role of empathy in rebuilding relationships between communities and those perceived as "the other", in this case those who have perpetrated horrific acts of violence. This "rehumanizing of the other" is achieved through an "empathetic reflection" among victims of the conflict, facilitated through the songs she discusses. Here, the designation as "the other" results, Opiyo insists, from stigmatization. Empathy functions as the "process in which one person imagines the particular perspective of another person".[21]

Elsewhere, however, notions of the "Other" have come to suggest "that which is not us", whether it be the one we see face-to-face or the distant Other as radically different from our self, whose difference is crucial to the very formation of ourselves. These conceptualizations of the Other render empathic processes problematic. The philosophical writings of Emmanuel Levinas point to a reorientation in the way in which we understand our positioning in the world, by identifying our relation to the Other as the first concern of our existence, constitutive of our own subjectivity.

In his first major work, *Totality and Infinity*, Levinas draws out two contrasting orientations to the Other:

1. Totality: In the first, we seek to make the Other the "Same", categorizing in order to control, to dominate. This he sees as the flaw throughout the history of Western philosophy. It was in response to the dehumanizing processes of the Shoah that Levinas, sensing a "crisis of humanism", was motivated to find a path towards a "new humanism", seeing that the "totalising" orientation of our Western philosophical tradition has repeatedly led to colonization, oppression and destruction.[22]
2. Infinity: Levinas exhorts us to take on a fresh orientation, where we perceive Infinity in the face of the Other, where the Other is recognized as profoundly different from us, but for whom we are unendingly, ethically responsible.

Empathy becomes problematic within this outlook, fraught with dangers of "reducing the Other to a common ground with the self".[23] Taking on a Levinasian orientation, however, grounds empathy within an ethical underpinning where, always in danger of totalizing through its tendency to "make you the same as me" in "putting myself in your shoes", empathy must be put aside in favour of the self-giving quality of Levinas' subjectivity, rooted in unending obligation to the Other.

Sharon Todd explains:

> While we can have a shared reality with the Other, feelings such as sympathy require renouncing the irreducibility of self and Other. This means, then, that in everyday communication within social situations ... we of course do commiserate, sympathize, and pity ... For Levinas, it is not that these everyday feelings are unimportant, it is just that they have little to do with the necessary maintenance of alterity, an alterity that is revealed in the encounter with the face ... It is where the Other is not merely heard, seen or felt with, but where the self is receptive to the revelation of difference and is thereby moved to a level of responsibility.[24]

For Levinas, empathy is not a sufficient response to the Other. His thinking suggests that the relationships of those engaged in peacebuilding processes must be grounded in a level of ethical responsibility as the self encounters the infinity of the irreducible Other.

Todd elucidates how Levinas' thinking goes beyond common conceptualizations of empathy:

> Feeling with others cannot lead to transcendence, for it blurs the distinction between self and Other that Levinas is so adamant to maintain. What matters for empathy in this view is not whether it bridges the divide of difference ... but to what degree it maintains this divide through respecting the Other's alterity.[25]

Todd warns that processes which seek to bring about social change through empathetic engagement "cannot but mask ... the Other's radically different feelings, experiences, and needs as unique".[26] She highlights the "implicit struggle with the ethical aspects of encountering difference",[27] reflecting Levinas' suggestion that our unending ethical relation to the Other is a costly one.

Levinas takes a foundationalist ethical position: for him there is nothing more primary to human existence than the ethical. His conception of ethics is in "encounter" with the Other, where the Other calls the self into question. It is our openness to the Other as we look into their face which is the condition for processes of "knowing". Our very subjectivity is formed in our relation to the Other, which he describes as an asymmetric responsibility. Levinas describes the profound "ethical call" we experience as we "look into the face of the Other", a demand which is enormously costly to those who are prepared to answer it. We are responsible for the Other before any sort of understanding about the world comes into play—ethics before ontology—and our response is not conditional upon a reciprocation. There is no limit to our responsibility for the Other, and the more we respond, the more demanding the ethical call upon us will be.

Following Levinas, the discourse of peacebuilding is situated within the encounter with the face of the Other, the site of non-violent relationship. There are plenty of processes and practices which might "efface" the Other, of which Beckles Willson has identified one, where neo-colonialist musical practices from Western Europe are seen to efface the harsh reality of the Palestinian cause.

Language as Ethical: Putting a World in Common

Levinas reorients our outlook. As I turn my face, with humanity, towards those who are different from me, my own self is called into question: "The calling into question of the I, coextensive with the manifestation of the Other in the face, we call language".[28] He writes, "The beginning of all language is in the face".[29] Language is understood by Levinas as a reaching out to the Other, a primordially ethical act before it is a communication of any specific meaning. He writes: "To speak is to make the world common, to create commonplaces. Language does not refer to the generality of concepts but lays the foundation for a possession in common".[30] Just as discourse is situated within the "looking into the face of the Other", Levinas suggests that language is, at its first impetus, ethical. The very subjectivity of the self is produced through the revealing of myself to others in discourse.[31]

Music-Making Otherwise

What if we conceptualize music-making in this way, following Levinas? Conventional notions of music as a "universal language" are endlessly problematic, as Bergh has reminded us above, but what if music-making were understood as primarily an ethical act, a reaching out to the Other before any meaning were intended to be communicated, a "speaking the world to the Other"?[32] Levinas writes:

> Language does not exteriorize a representation pre-existing in me: it puts in common a world hitherto mine...it inserts us into the world, with the risks and hazards of all action. The analyses of language that tend to present it as one meaningful action among many others fail to recognize this offering of

> the world, this offering of contents which answers to the face of the Other or which questions him, and first opens the perspective of the meaningful.[33]

He describes here the act of putting ourselves into the world, which occurs when we speak; putting ourselves at risk in an act of generosity to open up a world "put in common". Making music is then a reaching out to others, in an act of becoming vulnerable which Levinas describes as "putting a world in common" as a response to looking into the face of the Other, or in the context of music-making perhaps, hearing the voice of the Other.

What would it mean for us to approach music-making as "language" in the light of Levinas' ethical situating of language? Levinas writes, "The relationship with the Other, transcendence, consists in speaking the world to the Other". This reorientation has profound implications for an understanding of the "aesthetic" of the Western art tradition, which would regain its ethical moorings,[34] as making music (and creating "art") would be understood primarily as a response to looking into the face of the Other, hearing the voice of the Other, and would seek to "put the world in common".[35] Aesthetic experience or aesthetic sensitivity might then be understood as agential, and ethical encounters take place in any context of music-making, even within the Western concert hall.

Small criticized the practices of the concert hall as "dehumanizing" in that the audience remains supposedly inert, practices he saw as preventing communication and relationship between the participants of the "music event". Odendaal et al. however suggest:

> In a more extensive sense, it should make no difference what musical–cultural genre is in question: there can be practices of musicking in any culture … While Small builds his argument against dehumanising musical practices on the empirical differences he finds between (certain) African or Afrodiasporic and European musical systems of agency, his more general argument seems to be that whatever music we are involved with, there is always a possibility to 'do' it in a way that promotes ethical relationships between people immersed in community life.[36]

In affirming that music-making is "much richer and more complex" than a Western outlook has often allowed for,[37] a Levinasian reorientation provides an ethical underpinning for Small's "musicking", where "practices of facing" bring about a looking into the face of the Other in music-making,[38] where performer and the listener move towards outward-turning and receptivity. A performance then becomes an "offering", a "making common what was hitherto mine". This lays an ethical imperative upon performers, but also upon composers (in traditions where these roles are distinct) to develop an outward-turned orientation, putting themselves at risk in an act of generosity. Performers and composers invite the audience to join them in their encounter with the infinity of a piece of music, where musical meaning takes shape through the ethical relating between performers and with the audience.

Whose Music?

Returning to the question of whose music it appropriate to use in processes of peacebuilding, Beckles Willson has powerfully unmasked oppressive and outdated values and structures in the practices of the East West Divan Orchestra's projects, which reflect unhealthy practices in European "classical" music educational institutions.[39]

At the close of her 2013 book, she invokes Levinas through the writings of Judith Butler (2004), and asks:

> Whether the delivery of Western classical music is compatible with close attention to the face of an 'other' … We might consider the face as something that we not only see, but to which we must 'listen'. Are the types of listening that are expected by practitioners of Western classical music compatible with listening to the face of the 'other'?[40]

In Opiyo's account of music-making in Northern Uganda, the songs used so effectively were in an idiom familiar to all sides of the conflict. Whose music to use in contexts of peacebuilding is a complex question and will depend, among other considerations, upon whether there are shared musical expressions common to the different parties in a post-conflict environment, and whether the priority at the time is to "bear witness", "remember grief and anger" or to "imagine a peace", as Mitchell enumerates in this volume. Bringing in musical expressions from a culture outside of that of the participants, particularly one implicated in oppression and colonial exploitation, might be harmful, as Beckles Willson outlines. Just as has been observed in other peacebuilding and development fields, there are obvious perils in introducing institutional practices from remote contexts as if they are appropriate in a universal sense.

Beckles Willson highlights the tension between imagining a peace and acknowledging the harsh day-to-day realities of people's lives, as the projects she reports upon raise questions which lie "on the line dividing 'peace' in the aesthetic realm and 'justice' in the legal and economic realms".[41] Yet the Western classical tradition of "musical works" holds rich resources still, which might be used in contexts of peacebuilding, as they might within educational settings, resources appropriate to both sides of the dichotomy Beckles Willsson presents above. From a quick survey of instrumental music from the last century, in Mitchell's terms processes of "bearing witness" are powerfully addressed in Schoenberg's "Survivor from Warsaw". Otto Dix's remark that "all art is exorcism" is movingly elucidated as Maxim Vergerov walks through the "Arbeit macht frei" gates and out of the Auschwitz concentration camp playing Bach's D minor Chaconne for solo violin in the BBC's *Holocaust: A Music Memorial Film from Auschwitz* (2005).[42] "Remembering grief and anger", and telling the harsh realities of conflict, is accomplished vividly in Shostakovich's 8th string quartet (1960), dedicated "To the victims of fascism and war". Schoenberg's *Verklärte Nacht* or Messiaen's Quartet for the End of Time (1941), composed and first performed in a prisoner of war camp, give voice to processes of "building and imagining peace".

At the close of her 2013 book, Beckles Willson draws upon Judith Butler's "need to build non-violent relationships to 'others'". In her essay "Violence, mourning, politics" Butler asks "What allows us to encounter each other?".[43] The question is posed through a feminist lens, and Beckles Willson emphasizes Butler's assertion that "It is not possible to impose a language of politics developed within First World contexts on women who are facing the threat of imperialist economic exploitation and cultural obliteration".[44] Beckles Willson goes on to use this lens to formulate her own question, "Is it useful to impose a musical practice developed within First World contexts on adult and child civilians who are facing colonization, economic exploitation and cultural obliteration?" She refers to the way Butler draws upon the notion of the "face" developed by Levinas, suggesting "In order to engage successfully with another, the key is to respond to the face, 'To be awake to what is precarious in another life or, rather, the precariousness of life itself'".[45]

Beckles Willson however fails to appreciate Butler's next assertion, that these First World/Third World identities have been confounded:

> These topographies have shifted, and what was once thought of as a border, that which limits and bounds, is a highly populated site, if not the very definition of the nation, confounding identity in what may well become a very

> auspicious direction. ... For if I am confounded by you, then you are already of me, and I am nowhere without you. I cannot muster the 'we' except by finding the way in which I am tied to 'you', by trying to translate but finding that my own language must break up and yield if I am to know you. You are what I gain through this disorientation and loss. This is how the human comes into being, again and again, as that we have yet to know.[46]

Butler's explorations here bring into sharp relief the underlying priority of peacebuilding emphasized in Opiyo's report, the rehumanizing of the other, with Butler's confession here, following Levinas, that there is no conceptualizing the self, other than through a relationship to the Other. Beckles Willson, in this volume, also acknowledges the contesting of boundaries as she observes: "Yet to deny Palestinians the opportunity to develop skills enabling them to participate in Europe's musical practices could be seen as problematic in other ways". Boundaries have become indistinct around different musical traditions and expressions, giving rise to questions of social justice concerning access to forms of music-making which are seen as bringing enhanced agency.

Seeking Social Transformation Through Music-Making in Other Settings

Topographies are shifting in other senses too, as fresh conceptualizations of music-making are beginning to take hold.[47] Where music-making is seen as relational, as putting a world in common, and where subjectivities are understood to be formed through encounters with others, possibilities for social change through music-making in a variety of settings have been recognized. Sistema Scotland's Big Noise programmes first established in 2008 in Raploch near Stirling, then Govanhill in Glasgow, Torry in Aberdeen and most recently Douglas in Dundee, seek to bring about social transformation in challenged communities through enabling children, young people and adults to make music in the context of the orchestra, playing music of all kinds of different styles and traditions. Originally inspired by the Venezuelan music education programme El Sistema, established over forty years ago, the Big Noise staff work through local schools to offer opportunities to the whole community to learn orchestral instruments and to relate together through music-making.

Pre-instrumental music-making in baby and toddler groups, then in curriculum sessions from nursery into the first two years of primary school, prepares children to learn string instruments from six or seven years old, then woodwind, brass and percussion instruments from the upper primary years, with sessions taking place afterschool for up to four days each week, and throughout much of the school holidays. Adult orchestras offer parents, carers, grandparents and other community members the opportunity to learn an instrument within the context of the orchestra too.

The 2015 evaluation of the Govanhill and Raploch Big Noise centres by the Glasgow Centre for Population Health has highlighted short and projected longer-term transformations among participant communities, encouraging educational engagement, enhancing well-being and encouraging the development of life-skills, while the learning and playing of music alongside others opens up new vistas, as described by a 14-year old Big Noise participant, quoted in the evaluation report:

> The music, how we hear music, how we get involved, build up your communication, build up your confidence. Coming to Big Noise, you've got music behind your back, pushing you. So it's like somebody pushing you to do something, but it's music, and it's pushing you to make good things like building your confidence. When I started Big Noise I was shy, look at me now. Anyone can achieve any goals they want.

The evaluation report highlights the organization's emphasis on the quality of relationships between Big Noise staff and participants. The evaluation report makes clear in its conclusions that, underpinning the "musical excellence" found within the programme, is the guiding principle that "people change lives" rather than services, programmes or even music.[48] It is the face-to-face encounter between staff and young people, the daily practice of taking responsibility for and looking into the face of the Other, through the shared experience of music-making, which is being recognized as bringing about change in children's lives and life trajectories.

The Orchestra as a Model for Social Learning

The orchestra affords a model which makes explicit music-making's nature firstly as a social activity where healthy relationships are formed musically and socially, and where the individual can thrive within a community; secondly as agential, whereby members of the community are empowered to bring about change in their own lives and to transform their community through participating in music-making together. Unlike other programmes based on sporting models, for instance, the orchestra allows a world-class professional to play to the best of their ability alongside a virtual beginner, as any piece of music lends itself to adaptation for a spectrum of simple to much more complex lines. This side-by-side model of rehearsal and performance is a central practice of Big Noise programmes, in partnership with professional orchestras in Scotland, such as the BBC Scottish Symphony Orchestra, and beyond, for instance the Simón Bolívar Symphony Orchestra of Venezuela.

The model of the orchestra is a useful one within a Sistema-inspired context partly because there are possibilities for all levels of player to join in, with specially-adapted parts for younger players to sit alongside those more experienced others who are playing the complete parts. This is why the "side-by-side" experience with professional orchestral "buddies" has become common practice in Sistema-inspired programmes. Sistema practitioners such as those in the Big Noise programmes work hard to be attentive to the needs of the young people they teach, establishing ethical musical and social practices in every area of their programme, from positive behaviour management and highly developed child-protection strategies to progressive pedagogies and the inclusion of all kinds of musical styles in arrangements for young players to enjoy learning together.

The notion of the orchestra as a model within music education and social pedagogy has its critics. Just as Willson makes an important structural critique of the West East Divan Orchestra, commentators such as Geoff Baker see El Sistema and Sistema-inspired programmes as perpetuating an outdated model for society, one still based upon nineteenth century, hierarchical practices. Baker insists that, "the pursuit of social justice requires the critique of oppressive structures and exclusive forces in conventional music education, not their perpetuation and expansion in new guises". The object of his critique, he writes, is "not classical music per se but institutions, pedagogies and practices that mediate it".[49]

There is no doubt that the orchestral music profession and, despite recent advances, the conservatoire culture which prepares young people for the profession, are ripe for re-envisaging, and record labels, influential festivals, arts management agencies and others hold onto an inordinate amount of power, and tend to shape practice in the profession without concern for a wider social benefit, sometimes without concern even for the longer term development and health of their own protégées. Yet Baker concedes:

> The ethical values fostered by music education institutions may be quite different from those informing the music itself. Classical music has emancipatory potential (Harper-Scott, 2013) and an important part to play in music education if taught ethically and educatively sound ways.[50]

This emancipatory potential became evident when conductor Gustavo Dudamel, himself a product of Venezuela's El Sistema programme, brought the players of the Simon Bolivar Orchestra to sit side-by-side with the young people of the Big Noise, Raploch for an outdoor concert broadcast live from Raploch in June 2012 at the opening of the Cultural Olympiad. For those of us watching the rehearsals there was something revolutionary in what Dudamel brought. His ability to inspire and gently lead young musicians was very apparent (Jourdan 2012). Players and conductor reached out to the younger musicians in a nurturing manner as they played, physically affirming them by leaning in towards the children to encourage their sound beyond what the young people had thought possible for them to produce, and to build a new level of confidence.

Within their overarching, structural critiques, commentators such as Baker have for example criticized the discipline required in orchestral rehearsals and performance as oppressive. For Amy, however, interviewed as one of the founder participants in the Big Noise, Raploch, the boundaries of the orchestral rehearsal provide a discipline which she finds liberating:

> Music relaxes me. Playing music – you're sitting there. You can't talk or scream or make noises, you can't fidget, and that's what I used to do. I used to bite my nails. And scratch my knees, but I always knew that if I was sitting there with my instrument I can't fidget, I can't scream or start greeting [crying]. And it would always give me that time to think about stuff.

Amy describes playing in the orchestra as "an escape place". Not only does it give her "headspace" in this unusual situation of sitting still, concentrating and listening to those around you, she makes an interesting observation:

> Because it's not pop music, I'm not sitting with the lyrics going round my head. With classical [instrumental] music you're listening to the actual music. It's quite relaxing.[51]

The abstract quality of the music on its own, without words and their immediacy of meaning to focus thoughts, makes for a relaxing of the mind, the emotions, the spirit, perhaps. This unexpected testimony from Amy illustrates the need to hold both structural and personal perspectives in tension. For Amy the orchestral rehearsal affords a space within which she can find a refuge, where important work takes place within her, an interruption in her everyday experience.

Playing within the context of the orchestra brings Big Noise participants a host of wider benefits not only in terms of increased agency and educational engagement, but also in the moment-by-moment experiences and skills developed within the orchestra, practices I am very familiar with as a viola player for the past thirty years, firstly with the City of Birmingham Symphony Orchestra with conductor Sir Simon Rattle, then as a freelance player with the Scottish Chamber Orchestra, in the last few years under Robin Ticciati's leadership. On the one hand a structural critique might characterize the professional string *tutti* player as disempowered and oppressed, experiences I have been familiar with in the past.[52] Yet on the other hand, the ability to yield to others, play within the sound of another, to lead gently, to contribute strongly while being sensitive and alert to players around you, these are agential aspects of our daily experience and acquired expertise which require intense sensitivity and a deep sense of teamwork, skills which the young musicians of the Big Noise programmes can take with them into other aspects of their lives, and which through a Levinasian perspective might be understood as learning to "look into the face" of each other.[53]

Conclusion

I introduce the Big Noise initiatives in Scotland in order to draw out common strands between music-making in processes of peacebuilding and in programmes which seek to bring about social transformation in other contexts. The thinking of Emmanuel Levinas has provided tools with which to explore further notions of music as ethical encounter, developed first within the context of music education, and offered here as a means of considering an ethical basis to ground experiences in peacebuilding through the arts. At the heart of Levinas' work is the exhortation not to do violence to the Other. Violence toward the Other is perpetrated through "totalizing" tendencies, which Levinas saw as at the very heart of the historical sweep of Western philosophy. Following Levinas, peace-builders must eschew these totalizing tendencies when conceptualizing encounters between those on opposing sides of conflict, grounding empathic processes in a robust ethical framework that acknowledges and is prepared to uphold radical difference, while taking unending responsibility for the Other.

Is this a reasonable demand? Is it not an impossibility for parties traumatized through unimaginable suffering at the hands of another to "look into the face of the Other" in this way? Higgins, drawing on Derrida, acknowledges the "passion for the impossible" with which community musicians work, presenting "daring ways to imagine the future",[54] while Paul Standish, working with Levinas' ideas in the field of the philosophy of education, highlights the kind of perfectionism in Levinas' thinking, "the sense of unattainable height and sense of mystery".[55] At the same time, Standish challenges us to recognize this very implausibility as itself a product of our being "steeped in those assumptions of modernity that are at issue here", that is, our tendency towards totalizing practices.[56] Just as Standish believes that "education must expose the limits of totality through its sense of infinite responsibility",[57] so too those committed to conflict transformation can welcome "the presence of infinity breaking the closed circle of totality",[58] so that we might embrace "the possibility of an otherness that does not stand on the same plane as me, does not contest me, but opens me and in so doing founds me".[59]

Notes

1. John Paul Lederach, *The Moral Imagination* (Oxford, UK: Oxford University Press, 2005).
2. R. Beckles Willson, *Orientalism and Musical Mission: Palestine and the West* (Cambridge, UK: Cambridge University Press, 2013), 287.
3. Lederach, *Moral Imagination*, 182.
4. Jolyon Mitchell, "Peace-Building Through the Visual Arts", *Peacebuilding and the Arts, Rethinking Peace and Conflict Studies* (2019, this volume).
5. Appreciating each other's humanity and respecting each other's culture; Telling our own and listening to each other's stories, and developing more complex narratives and nuanced understandings of identity; Acknowledging harms, telling truths, and mourning losses; Empathizing with each other's suffering; Acknowledging and redressing injustices; Expressing remorse, repenting, apologizing, letting go of bitterness, forgiving; Imagining and substantiating a new future, including agreements about how future conflicts will be engaged constructively, see Cynthia Cohen, "Creative Approaches to Reconciliation", in *The Psychology of Resolving Global Conflicts: From War to Peace*, eds. M. Fitzduff and C. Stout (Westport, CT: Greenwood Publishing, 2005).
6. Cohen, "Creative Approaches", 31.

7. Cohen, "Creative Approaches", 32.
8. "To music is to take part in any capacity, in a musical performance, whether by performing, by listening, by rehearsing or practicing, by providing material for performances (what is called composing), or by dancing". See C. Small, *Musicking: The Meanings of Performing and Listening* (Hanover, NH: Wesleyan University Press, 1998), 9.
9. Small, *Musicking*, 13.
10. A. Odendaal, O.T. Kankkene, H.M. Nikkanen, and L. Vakeya, "What's with the K? Exploring the Implications of Christopher Small's 'Musicking' for General Music Education", *Music Education Research* 16:2 (2014): 169–170.
11. Lee Higgins, "Acts of Hospitality: The Community in Community Music", *Journal of Music Education Research* 9:2 (2007): 284 following J. Derrida and A. Dufourmantelle, *Of Hospitality*, trans. R. Bowlby (Stanford, CA: Stanford University Press), 2000.
12. Wayne Bowman, "The Ethical Significance of Music-Making", *Music Mark Magazine* 3: (2014): 3.
13. Arild Bergh, "Emotions and Motion: Transforming Conflict and Music", in *Music and the Mind: Essays in Honour of John Sloboda*, eds. Irène Deliège and Jane Davidson (Oxford, UK: Oxford University Press, 2011), 364.
14. Bergh, "Emotions and Motion", 365.
15. John Sloboda and Arild Bergh, "Music and Art in Conflict Transformation: A Review", *Music and Arts in Action* 2:2 (2010): 4.
16. Sloboda and Bergh, "Music and Art", 3. See Sloboda and Bergh for a good overview of the way music has been used in conflict.
17. Bergh, "Emotions and Motion", cites Einarsen: 'It is … important not to assume that there is anything universal about music, neither in its appeal to people, nor in the way it is received and understood' (Einarsen, 1998), 370.
18. Bergh, "Emotions and Motion", 371.
19. Bergh, "Emotions and Motion", 371, my emphasis. Bergh cites: J. Sloboda, *Exploring the Musical Mind* (Oxford, UK: Oxford University Press, 2005); T. DeNora, "Aesthetic Agency and Musical Practice", in *Music and Emotion*, eds. P. Juslin and J. Sloboda (Oxford, UK: Oxford University Press, 2001); and E. Gomart and A. Hennion, "A Sociology of Attachment: Music Amateurs, Drug Users", *The Sociological Review* 47:S1 (May 1999).
20. Teresa Lesiuk, "The Effect of Music Listening on Work Performance", *Psychology of Music* 33:2 (2005).
21. J. Halpern and H.M. Weinstein, "Rehumanizing the Other: Empathy and Reconciliation", *Human Rights Quarterly* 26:3 (2004), 568.
22. C. Katz, *Levinas and the Crisis of Humanism* (Bloomington, IN: Indiana University Press, 2012a); C. Katz, "Turning Toward the Other", in *Totality and Infinity at 50*, eds. S. Davidson and D. Perpich (Pittsburgh, PA: Duquesne University Press, 2012b). Although his wife and child were kept

safe by a French monastic community, Levinas' wider family perished in the Holocaust.

23. Sharon Todd, *Learning from the Other: Levinas, Psychoanalysis and Ethical Possibilities in Education* (Albany, NY: State University of New York Press, 2003), 51.
24. Todd, *Learning*, 51.
25. Todd, *Learning*, 52.
26. Todd, *Learning*, 63.
27. Todd, *Learning*, 146.
28. Levinas, *Totality*, 171.
29. Levinas, *Ethics*, 169–170
30. Levinas, *Totality*, 76.
31. Anna Strhan, *Levinas, Subjectivity, Education: Towards an Ethics of Radical Responsibility* (Chichester, UK: Wiley-Blackwell, 2012), 19.
32. Levinas, *Totality*, 173–174.
33. Levinas, *Totality*, 173–174.
34. See Daniel Chua, *Absolute Music and the Construction of Meaning* (Cambridge, UK: Cambridge University Press, 1999) for a discussion of Kant's legacy, Western art music's 'loss of purpose' and D. Chua, "Beethoven's Other Humanism," *Journal of the American Musicological Society* 62:3 (2009) for an exploration of how a musical "work" might function as an Other.
35. Levinas challenges Kant's view of the self as morally autonomous, and encourages us to see the already-existing responsibility towards the Other which shapes our existence, so that our freedom flows from our responsive relation to the Other. Our sense of self is formed from the very outset by the presence of the Other. Rather than Schiller's conception of aesthetics as the development of a sensibility that augments reasoned principle to ethical effect, Levinas' work points towards the practice of aesthetic encounter as a training which enables us to look more fully into the face of the Other, to hear their voice and to respond. Our responsibility towards the Other is the underpinning of aesthetics. This vision unmasks alternative conceptions of autonomous aestheticization presented to us by Foucault or Baudrillard. A Levinsian reading breaks open a self-centred aesthetic as the infinite of the Other ruptures our autonomy.
36. Odendaal et al., "What's with the K?", 172.
37. Small, *Musicking*, 19.
38. K. Jourdan, *Through the Lens of Levinas: An Ethnographically-Informed Case Study of Pupils' "practices of facing" in Music-Making* (PhD diss., Cambridge, UK: University of Cambridge, 2015a).
39. Conservatoires and specialist schools in the UK have lately been confronted with the need for reform through a series of widespread historical abuse allegations, bringing into question their structures and teaching practices

as well as the values and structures of the wider profession, which tend to shape these educational institutions. See Rosie Burt-Perkins, "The Learning Cultures of Performance: Applying a Cultural Theory of Learning to Conservertoire Research", *Proceedings of the International Symposium on Performance Science*, eds. A. Williamson, S. Pretty, and R. Buck (Utrecht, Netherlands: European Association of Conservatoires, 2009), 249–254, on 'learning cultures' in the conservatory.

40. Beckles Willson, *Orientalism*, 317. See also Chua, *Absolute Music*, for a discussion of music functioning as an Other.
41. Beckles Willson, *Orientalism*, 288.
42. *Holocaust: A Music Memorial Film from Auschwitz*. Directed by James Kent (London, UK: British Broadcasting Corporation, 2005). Film.
43. Butler, *Precarious Life*, 49.
44. Beckles Willson, *Orientalism*, 316.
45. Beckles Willson, *Orientalism*, 316, citing Butler, *Precarious Life*, 134.
46. Butler, *Precarious Life*, 49.
47. See K. Jourdan, "Musicking Otherwise: Ethical Encounters in Music-Making", *National Association of Music Educators' Magazine* 1 (Spring 2013) for a discussion of experiences of ethical encounter as an orchestral viola player, in relation to the role of conductor, player and audience.
48. Glasgow Centre for Population Health and Education (GCPH), "Evaluating Sistema Scotland: Initial Findings Report" (Glasgow, UK: GCPH, June 2015), 14. Available at http://www.gcph.co.uk/assets/0000/5424/Sistema_findings_report.pdf.
49. G. Baker, *El Sistema: Orchestrating Venezuela's Youth* (Oxford: Oxford University Press), 12.
50. Baker, *El Sistema*, 12–13.
51. Name has been changed to protect participant's anonymity.
52. K. Jourdan, "Book Review", review of *El Sistema: Orchestrating Venezuela's youth* by G. Baker, *Scottish Journal of Performance* 2:2 (2015): viii.
53. Jourdan, "Book Review".
54. Higgins, "Acts of Hospitality", 171 and J. Derrida, *Of Grammatology* (Baltimore, MA: Johns Hopkins University Press, 1997 [1967]).
55. Paul Standish, "Data Return: The Sense of the Given in Educational Research", *Journal of Philosophy of Education* 35:3 (2001): 346.
56. Standish, "Data Return", 343.
57. Standish, "Data Return", 346.
58. Levinas, *Totality*, 171.
59. R. Gibbs, *Why Ethics? Signs of Responsibilities* (Princeton, NJ: Princeton University Press, 2000), 33.

PART III

Literature

CHAPTER 10

Literature and Peace Studies

Sandra M. Gustafson

Beyond Perpetual War

Let me begin this section on literature and peacebuilding with an exploration of contending narratives about the history of violent conflict. Stories structure our understanding of the world, and competing stories about the trajectory of violence present a sharp contradiction, with broad implications.

A major narrative emerging from the field of peace studies emphasizes positive change. Our era is one of the extraordinary achievements in international peacebuilding and a dramatic reduction in the rates of violent death. Since 1989 the "long peace" of the Cold War era has not only lengthened but deepened, extending to regions where proxy wars between the United States and the Soviet Union once took a heavy toll.[1] In 2005 the *Human Security Report* (HSR) documented marked improvements in human security following the end of the Cold War, which include dramatic declines in war and other forms of violence as well as in human rights violations.[2] This does not mean that war and violence have ended,

S. M. Gustafson (✉)
University of Notre Dame, Notre Dame, IN, USA
e-mail: sandra.m.gustafson.6@nd.edu

J. Mitchell et al. (eds.), *Peacebuilding and the Arts*,
Rethinking Peace and Conflict Studies,
https://doi.org/10.1007/978-3-030-17875-8_10

as the deadly conflicts in Congo, Syria, and Yemen sadly illustrate. The 2005 *HSR* identified two hundred and thirty-one armed conflicts since World War II that resulted in millions of deaths and displaced millions of more people. Subsequent versions of the *Report* note modest variations upward as well as downward and add nuance to the generally encouraging picture, while focusing attention on specific issues such as sexual violence or conflicts driven by environmental change.[3] The promise of the United Nations, whose effectiveness was diminished by the Cold War, has begun to be realized, but there remains work to do.[4]

There is substantial evidence that rates of violence have fallen dramatically over the long term of human history as well as in the near term documented by the Human Security Project, evidence that Steven Pinker surveys in *The Better Angels of Our Nature: Why Violence Has Declined*.[5] A Harvard-based psychologist and linguist, Pinker challenges an anti-modern narrative that understands history since World War I as a steady march into the abyss. Unlike Pinker's eight-hundred-page account, this dystopian historiography offers both a reaction against overly optimistic, "whiggish" theories of history from the previous century and a response to contemporary events. Writers including Walter Benjamin and Norman Mailer helped consolidate this story in the middle decades of the twentieth century, as the world struggled to come to terms with the Holocaust, nuclear weapons, and the Cold War. Benjamin's "angel of history" that sees "one single catastrophe which keeps piling wreckage and hurls it in front of his feet"[6] expresses the tragedy of the Nazi era, and his suicide in 1940 lends added poignancy to the narrative of civilization's decay. Mailer's apocalyptic vision in "The White Negro" of the possibility that "the fate of twentieth-century man is to live with death from adolescence to premature senescence"[7] captures an emerging sense of despair sparked by the Cold War era and the nuclear arms race.[8] By contrast, Pinker offers a longer, more hopeful narrative that attends to the rise of institutions and capacities that foster peace.

Pinker's narrative can seem counterintuitive, particularly in a media-saturated, militarized society such as the United States, which has gone to war more than seventeen times since 1945 (a greater number than any other country except for the United Kingdom and France), and has spent over thirty years of that period involved in military conflict. American popular culture and news media have long thrived on violence, and the intensified militarism following the September 11 attacks has affected countless aspects of life in the United States, including political rhetoric, narrative conventions, and everyday language.[9] The militarist elements in American society, including a powerful arms industry, promote force as a means of resolving international conflicts. By suggesting that these elements are on the wrong side of history, Pinker has helped to create a counter-narrative focused on prospects for a broader peace. This counter-narrative is my story as well.

Overwhelming and devastating as the events of the first half of the twentieth century were, they sparked a slow revolution in peacebuilding that has contributed to the achievements documented in the *Human Security Report*. One aspect of this transformation has been the post-World War II dismantling of empires and the rise of democracies in Europe, India, and elsewhere. The crisis that impelled Walter Benjamin to take his own life, led within a few years to the establishment of the United Nations, with the United States playing a central role—even as it skirted issues of civil rights within its borders, until the nonviolent movement led by Martin Luther King, Jr. forced changes.[10] The institutions of global governance established in the immediate post-war period, including the United Nations and the International Court of Justice, have matured and gained acceptance in many quarters, and on July 1, 2002 the International Criminal Court opened its doors at The Hague. Much of the credit for the growth of these organizations goes to humanitarian and human rights-focused non-governmental organizations (NGOs) and civil society organizations (CSOs) such as Amnesty International, which have expanded dramatically since the 1960s, achieving special prominence and effectiveness since the end of the Cold War.

Meanwhile peace studies has emerged as an academic field that blends research and practice, maturing into a multidisciplinary field focused on "the causes and conditions that generate and sustain violent conflict; the mechanisms and models for the resolution of violent conflict; and the norms, practices and institutions for building peace."[11] Though it overlaps with proximate fields such as international relations and war studies, peace research is distinguished by its focus on reducing war and violence and promoting alternative approaches to conflict. It is sometimes compared to the field of public health, which concentrates on the sources of illness with the goal of promoting wellbeing. Peace practitioners and researchers study the nature of violent conflict and the means to develop "capacities which are creative, responsive, constructive, and nonviolent," with the goal of building a global society where violence and war are less prevalent.[12]

In recent years the quantitative dimensions of peace research have been advanced through data collection projects including the Correlates of War project, the Peace Accords Matrix, and the Uppsala and PRIO databases.[13] Quantitative analyses, while subject to the usual concerns regarding the appropriateness of definitions and the accuracy of data, allow for greater clarity about trends and effectiveness than values-based or qualitative studies, which however contribute their own crucial dimensions to peacebuilding. Numbers are often necessary, but they are rarely sufficient for, as John Paul Lederach and R. Scott Appleby observe, "at its core, peacebuilding nurtures constructive human relationships."[14]

The humanities and fine arts have had a relatively small place in peace studies curricula, but they have not been entirely absent.[15] Literature courses on such topics as "The Literature of Peace and War" and "The Literature of Nonviolence" date back at least to the 1970s.[16] Moreover recent developments in the NGO world suggest an expanding place for arts-based peace work. As Hal Culbertson has recently observed, collaborations between performing arts groups and peacebuilders have proven to be fruitful ways to transform conflict.[17] Michael Shank and Lisa Schirch emphasize the importance of finding "strategic ways of incorporating the arts into the work of peacebuilding and to create a space where people in conflict can express themselves, heal themselves, and reconcile themselves through the arts."[18] Shank and Schirch focus on the what, when and how of the ways that community groups, NGOs, and other peacebuilders have employed the arts in conflict situations to reduce violence and transform relationships.

The Peacebuilder's Hermeneutic

John Paul Lederach's work on the moral imagination offers a formulation of the value of the arts to strategic peacebuilding that opens out to humanistic studies and other literature-based approaches. Lederach brings an unusual sensitivity to language and an interest in the constructive role that imagination can play in what he terms "conflict transformation." Unlike conflict resolution, which stresses an end to violence in and for itself, conflict transformation has a broader focus. Recognizing that "conflict is normal in human relationships, and conflict is a motor of change," Lederach emphasizes peace with justice and "the building of healthy relationships and communities, locally and globally."[19] "Peace" does not mean only the absence of violence and does not eliminate conflict over injustices. It is not a static condition. Rather as Lederach defines peace, it is "a continuously evolving and developing quality of relationships… characterized by intentional efforts to address the natural ebb and flow of human conflict through nonviolent approaches, which address issues and increase understanding, equality, and respect in relationships."[20]

The arts in general, and literature in particular, have much to contribute to the processes of conflict transformation that Lederach describes. As explored further in the fifth and final section of this book on "Theatre," Drama can often have an especially direct relationship to peacebuilding, since it can be adapted to local settings and actors, and so is well suited to fieldwork. It has close connections to narrative-based approaches to trauma therapy, such as those pioneered by James W. Pennebaker, which have been adapted in a number of post-conflict settings.[21] The study of fiction, and literary narrative generally, involves a different aspect of peace work—conflict analysis—that can be approached in a manner that contributes to conflict transformation. Often traced to Aristotle's discussion of tragedy in *The Poetics,* the analysis of conflict in literature is a traditional humanistic method. As H. Porter Abbott notes in *The Cambridge Introduction to Narrative,* "you might say that conflict structures narrative." Abbott reflects on the social purposes served by narrative conflicts, observing that "one very plausible possibility is that the representation of conflict in narrative provides a way for a culture to talk to itself about, and possibly resolve, conflicts that threaten to fracture it (or at least make living difficult)."[22] A narrative may present one side in a conflict, or negotiate competing claims, or help people live with an irresolvable conflict. This account of the social roles played by literary narrative resonates with the work of historian Lynn Hunt and philosopher Martha Nussbaum, who suggest that the modern novel can nurture latent capacities for identification and empathy, contributing to the invention of human rights and the historic declines in violence discussed by Steven Pinker.[23]

Yet as Abbott's formulation suggests, and as Pinker's emphasis on *cultivable* capacities for empathy implies as well, narrative also has the potential to reinforce or even escalate real-world conflicts. Psychologist Phillip Hammack describes this process in a study of identity formation in Palestinian and Israeli teenagers. Hammack relates how a Palestinian girl named Lubna began her life narrative by summarizing the plot of a work of Palestinian literature that portrays the radicalization of a Palestinian boy exposed to Israeli violence. Hammack quotes Lubna's reaction to this story: "All the stories are supposed to end, 'They lived happily ever after.' But the only answer I thought was that this was our life, and the suffering never ends in Palestine. Welcome to home."[24] Lubna had participated in youth groups aimed at building cross-cultural understanding, yet she identified more strongly with the literary narrative of violence and radicalization than with the peacebuilding project. Hammack's empirical research shows that narratives have complex, situation-dependent effects on individual experiences of identity and fellow feeling.

Narrative is a powerful means of communicating a sense of identity and relationship, and while a "chosen trauma" narrative can have the effect of perpetuating conflict, the opportunity to "restory," or transform the narrative, is always present. Restorying can sometimes be accomplished by truth-and-reconciliation tribunals and other restorative justice practices.[25] Lederach compares the dialectical nature of peacebuilding to the artistic process, which "arises from human experience and then shapes, gives expression and meaning to, that experience." While acts of violence are based on "a deep, implicit belief that desired change can be achieved independently of the web of relationships," peacebuilding "requires a vision of relationship" that is essentially creative and involves the recognition that "the quality of our life is dependent on the quality of life of others."[26] He employs the metaphor of the web to describe this interdependence, and he offers examples of how an appreciation for complexity, and a willingness to let go of artificial dualisms, can break historic cycles of violence. Transformative moments can involve "a haiku-like quality" when "out of complexity and historic difficulty, the clarity of great insight makes an unexpected appearance in the form of an image or a way of putting something that can only be described as artistic."[27] Lederach identifies five capacities that are central to conflict transformation: to look at immediate issues while seeing beyond them to context and relational patterns; to integrate multiple time frames; to think in terms of "both/and" rather than "either/or"; to embrace complexity; and to understand issues of identity and their relationship to both conflict and narrative.[28] All of these capacities, which I will call the "peacebuilder's hermeneutic," involve analytic skills that can be developed through the close reading of literary narratives.

Lederach draws some of his main themes, including the image of the web and the focus on story, from indigenous practices, and so it is not a coincidence that his work resonates powerfully with Leslie Marmon Silko's novel *Ceremony* (1977). Of mixed Laguna, Mexican, and European ancestry, Silko grew up at Laguna Pueblo in New Mexico, in the conflict-ridden borderlands region of the United States once claimed by Mexico and contained within Aztlán, the projected homeland of the Uto-Aztecan peoples. *Ceremony* offers an uncommonly clear example of a literary narrative that embodies and enacts the principles of peacebuilding. Published just two years after the end of the Vietnam War, *Ceremony* was greeted with immediate acclaim. Silko's message of reconciliation was compelling to war-weary readers, and her bold formal experiments weaving Laguna oral narratives into the western novel spoke to a burgeoning interest in multicultural literature. *Ceremony* emphasizes the theme of post-traumatic healing by way of an embrace of social and cultural hybridity coupled with a privileging of indigenous traditions.

Tayo, the novel's main character, is a World War II veteran suffering from complex trauma that is as much a result of prejudice due to his mixed race heritage, his abandonment by his mother, and his emotional abuse by the aunt who raised him as it is to his wartime suffering during the Bataan Death March and his internment by the Japanese. The novel opens with a series of temporal shifts and a layering of perspective that register the complexity of what is to come. The first page presents a version of the Laguna creation myth about Ts'its'tsi'nako, or Thought-Woman, which is followed by an unidentified male voice describing the power of stories, which in turn is followed by the words, "The only cure/ I know/ is a good ceremony,/ that's what she said." The reader eventually learns to associate the male voice with the Navajo medicine man Betonie and the female voice with Ts'eh, Tayo's lover and an avatar of Ts'its'tsi'nako. Each "voice" is presented on a separate page, broken up by varying amounts of blank space. The following page contains a single word, "Sunrise," at the top, and then, on the bottom of the next page, Tayo is introduced in the act of awakening from a bad night's sleep.[29] These mild violations of the reader's expectations for linear narrative draw attention to the formal properties of the novel, including its juxtaposition of narrative traditions and forms.

The reader's disorientation extends into the opening lines of the main narrative, when Silko describes Tayo's dreams as a dark flood of voices and languages from different times and places, suggesting that character and reader alike need to sort through the tangle in his mind. Tayo compares his memories to the "colored threads from old Grandma's wicker sewing basket" that "spilled out of his arms into the summer weeds and rolled away in all directions." The more urgently he tried to unravel them, the more they "snagged and tangled."[30] This image of tangled threads contrasts with an alternative vision of interconnectedness offered by old Ku'oosh, the medicine man who performs a traditional healing ceremony on Tayo. Ku'oosh uses a Laguna word for "fragile" to describe the world, which

Silko develops in a passage that resonates with Lederach's description of strategic peacebuilding:

> The word he chose to express 'fragile' was filled with the intricacies of a continuing process, and with a strength inherent in spider webs woven across paths through sand hills where early in the morning the sun becomes entangled in each filament of web. It took a long time to explain the fragility and intricacy because no word exists alone, and the reason for choosing each word had to be explained with a story about why it must be said this certain way. That was the responsibility that went with being human, old Ku'oosh said, the story behind each word must be told so there could be no mistake in the meaning of what had been said; and this demanded great patience and love.[31]

Silko contrasts this image of an interconnected world held together by an ethos of care manifested through scrupulous attention to language and story with the nuclear weapons and other ways of "killing across great distances" that have come to characterize "white warfare."[32] The small indigenous community at Laguna Pueblo has been transformed into the center of human existence by reason of its proximity to the uranium mines that powered the development of nuclear weapons at nearby Sandia Labs, and whose testing at White Sands is recalled in the novel. Tayo's recovery becomes synonymous with the recovery of humanity, made possible by the spiritual healing that unfolds within the pages of the novel, which doubles as a ceremony for the reading community beyond the pueblo.

Silko's mix of indigenous and European narrative techniques is mirrored in Tayo's hazel eyes, which mark him and several other spiritually potent characters whose power seems to derive from their racially mixed heritage. True indigeneity, the novel suggests in both form and content, welcomes a variety of influences. This theme is developed most clearly through the character of Betonie, the multiracial Navajo healer whom Tayo consults after Ku'oosh's traditional ceremony fails to heal him fully. Betonie's hogan is filled with old calendars and telephone books suggestive of the collapse of time and space, signaling a capacity for flexibility that Lederach associates with peacebuilding.[33] The ceremony that Betonie conducts unfolds into a quest narrative drawn from the stars. Tayo sets out on a search for his Uncle Josiah's stolen Mexican cattle that leads him to Ts'eh, the mountain woman with whom he shares a therapeutic intimacy that is also a healing of the relationship between humans and their environment.

Silko portrays the forces of witchery, or bloodlust, and shows them to exist in all cultures. The challenge is to create the conditions for their defeat, which Silko suggests must start with each individual's rejection of impulses toward violence, thus breaking down the narrative conventions favoring violent conflict. Tayo is finally able to accomplish this rejection when he resists the forces compelling him to attack his fellow Laguna veteran Emo, who embodies racial hatred and blood lust, though he does so at the cost of the lives of his friends Harley and Leroy. The witchery prompts him to come to the rescue of his friends and die violently himself, like a protagonist in a formulaic Hollywood action movie, but Tayo refuses this media-driven narrative. Instead, he quietly settles into family life at Laguna. The novel concludes with an invocation to be vigilant against the return of violence and an offering to the hope represented by sunrise.

Confronting Militarism: American Fiction About the Iraq War

In 2012, two novels about the Iraq war by writers from the United States—Ben Fountain's *Billy Lynn's Long Halftime Walk* and Kevin Powers's *Yellow Birds*—attracted critical favor and prestigious prizes.[34] Like *Ceremony*, these novels portray individuals and communities trapped in a cycle of war and desperate for a way to escape. The novels have a common theme, namely, the consequences and costs of American militarism for the citizens of the United States, but they approach their subject in strikingly different ways.

Billy Lynn's Long Halftime Walk is a satire on American society that takes its place in the tradition of *Catch-22* (1961) and *Slaughterhouse Five* (1969). Set at a Dallas Cowboys game on a rainy Thanksgiving Day, the novel follows the Bravo Company through its adventures at the Cowboys's stadium, where they have been brought as part of a Victory Tour designed to shore up domestic support for the war. One of Fountain's central themes is the pervasive overstimulation endemic to American society, represented by the football game. The Company is being celebrated and exploited for their valor in a firefight in Baghdad captured on video by embedded Fox News journalists that went viral on the Internet. Lynn, the son of a Rush Limbaugh-style Texas radio personality, has performed with special distinction. His reasons for enlisting were far from heroic, however. As an impulsive late adolescent, Billy destroyed the car of his sister's former fiancé and then chose to enlist rather than do time in prison. He views his heroic actions in Iraq as simply doing what he was trained to do while trying to save the life of his friend and mentor, a soldier nicknamed Shroom.

During Billy's military service he has matured and deepened, largely as a result of a course of reading and reflection pursued under Shroom's tutelage. This informal education draws out the latent nobility in his character and gives Billy perspective on the crazy spectacle of the football game and its real-world double, the war itself. Billy's double education as a warrior and as a reader and thinker has shaped him into a promising type of youthful America. For all his worldly experience, Billy is a virgin whose basic decency is captured in his budding romance with Faison, a cheerleader for the Cowboys who, like Billy, has a good heart and a longing for commitment. And yet it is Faison who effectively seals Billy's fated return to war. He rejects his sister's arrangements to help him escape from the Army after it becomes clear that Faison would refuse to join him in exile. She is attracted to his image as a war hero, not to his inner self. The novel closes on an ambiguous note, as Billy deliberately empties his mind and prepares to return to combat in Iraq, anticipating that he may not make it home. As this ending suggests, Fountain's novel has elements of allegory as well as satire, with Billy representing an America that cannot find a way out of perpetual war. The core values that he stands for have been so overpowered by a culture of spectacle and sensory overload that they no longer provide a moral compass to a nation at the mercy of its own militarism.

Billy Lynn's Long Halftime Walk is briskly paced, set mostly in the present moment of Bravo Company's U.S. tour, with occasional flashbacks and temporal cuts. Only a few of those flashbacks come from their time in Iraq, and those are indistinctly sketched. The dialogue is routinely profane and often funny, the motives of the characters mostly on the surface. The Bravo company soldiers crave booze and sex and money and fame, and they hope a film deal for their story will bring them more of these things. They don't want to return to the battlefield, but they don't see any way out, and they are not given to brooding. They know that they are being exploited and occasionally push back, but their efforts at establishing a space of autonomy are almost entirely unsuccessful. Sergeant Dime, one of the novel's few reflective characters, briefly disrupts the filming of a spot designed both to bolster support for the war and to market the Cowboys when he goes off script in an act of mild insubordination, sardonically wishing "our brother and sister soldiers out in the field…PEACE THROUGH SUPERIOR FIREPOWER!"[35] The media people filming the spot are not amused, and they eventually get what they want. Fountain has written a novel about the causes and consequences of war viewed from within the American society that produced it—in both the causal and media industry senses of "produced," which are shown to overlap in significant ways.

Kevin Powers's novel about the Iraq War comes from a very different place. Powers enlisted in the Army in the late 1990s, when he was seventeen, and he served as a machine gunner in Mosul and Tal Afar in 2004 and 2005. After his honorable discharge he attended university, where he studied literature and then creative writing, with a focus on poetry.[36] *The Yellow Birds* has a distinctive combination of rawness, authenticity, allusiveness, and imagistic prose that bear a family resemblance to works by Ernest Hemingway and Cormac McCarthy. Powers opens his novel with contrasting epigraphs. The first is a "traditional U.S. Army Marching Cadence" based on the nursery rhyme about a yellow bird on the windowsill, but with the variant ending "I smashed / His fucking head." This grisly image is paired with a passage on the blessings of forgetfulness taken from the writings of the melancholic Sir Thomas Browne. Together these epigraphs anticipate the three temporal frames of the novel: the weeks in late 2003 when the narrator, a young Virginian named Private John Bartle, undergoes basic training and is given responsibility for a slightly younger enlistee, a fellow Southerner named Private Daniel Murphy (nicknamed Murph); the extended battle against insurgents for control of the city of Al Tafar in Nineveh Province some nine months later; and the months from March to August 2005 when Bartle returns home and struggles to cope with his wartime experiences. Like *Ceremony*, the plot of *Yellow Birds* is structured to evoke post-traumatic stress disorder, with a repeated return to the war in alternating chapters. A final chapter, set in April 2009, takes a longer, more reflective view back on the battle of Al Tafar. The novel ends with a description of Murph's transfigured corpse floating down the Tigris River, while an American soldier on the riverbank calls "Peace out, motherfucker" (226). In an image inviting closure, Murph's body finally breaks apart and is swept out to sea.

The nonlinear plot is one major difference between *The Yellow Birds* and *Billy Lynn's Long Halftime Walk*. Another is the lyrical style of Powers's prose, which contrasts sharply with Fountain's vigorous and frequently profane satire. Powers's lyricism is often driven by allusions that situate the novel in an American literary tradition shaped by the King James Bible. The acclaimed opening, which begins "The war tried to kill us in the spring," juxtaposes biblical history with the history of the United States. Powers evokes both "the plains of Nineveh" and the "tall grass" of the Great

Plains traversed by "pioneers"[37] drawn from the pages of Willa Cather's fiction. Al Tafar, where the main events of the novel take place, is near the ruins of Nineveh, an ancient imperial city in the Fertile Crescent. Nineveh appears repeatedly in Hebrew scripture, most notably in the Book of Jonah, connecting *The Yellow Birds* to another American classic, *Moby-Dick*. The themes of monomaniacal bad judgment, religious conflict, and spiritual confusion run through both books.

In the novel's only overt scene of religious prejudice, Sargent Sterling is shown sprinkling salt over the earth as the unit decamps. He explains, "It's from Judges," and then, "It's just a thing I do."[38] Judges 9:45 refers to the salting of soil to prevent reoccupation. Up to this point Sterling has been portrayed as an exemplary soldier, professional and highly motivated, but this scene hints at an underlying instability, which leads Murph to worry that the Sargent is "losing his shit."[39] Moments later Murph watches in horror from a distance as Sterling mutilates an Iraqi corpse. This scene, as well as the brutal killing of an elderly Iraqi couple, exemplifies the inhumanities perpetrated by American forces.

Murph's own unraveling is catalyzed by the death of an attractive, compassionate female medic who tends a wounded soldier and is visibly moved by his death. Her sensitivity makes the medic's tent seem to Murph and Bartle like "the last habitat for gentleness and kindness that we'd ever know."[40] Murph is drawn to the medic because he desperately wants to choose for himself. His opportunities in life have been brutally constrained. Before enlisting, he worked long hours in a coal mine under miserable conditions, and the war seemed to offer an escape. Like the soldiers of Bravo Company in *Billy Lynn*, Murph desires a measure of autonomy, and watching the medic is the only way he can find to get it. Yet his sense of freedom is brought to a disastrous end when a mortar strikes the chapel where the medic has gone to pray. Distraught, Murph disappears. Bartle narrates his discovery of what happened next. After removing his uniform, Murph wandered dazed and naked into the city, his path marked by bloody footprints. Bartle and Sterling discover his body at the foot of the minaret where he was brutally tortured and dismembered. There are a few ways to read this scene and the novel as a whole. The destruction of the chapel, followed by the firing of the minaret, suggest the element of religious conflict in the war. At the same time, both sides have denied Murph's quest for autonomy. By stripping off his uniform and walking into the city he makes a plea to be recognized outside the categories of the conflict, American vs. Iraqi,

Christian vs. Muslim. Neither the U.S. Army nor its opponents in Iraq will allow Murph that freedom.

The novel closes on the theme that resignation and the passage of time will heal, but only partially, and that the transfiguration of suffering is an achievement of language and imagination. It is a less hopeful—and more passive—ending than the sunrise of *Ceremony*, which communicates a greater sense that while violence is always latent, readers have an opportunity to choose peace and to cultivate the means to achieve it. The difference can be traced, I believe, to the more active role of spiritual healing in Silko's novel. In Powers's novel, religious identities are fixed and religious symbols are implicated in the violence. For Silko, the flexibility, syncretism, and ceremonial embodiment of indigenous spiritual traditions make them an ideal vehicle for reconciling parties in conflict.[41]

Both *Billy Lynn's Long Halftime Walk* and *The Yellow Birds* reward consideration using the peacebuilder's hermeneutic drawn from John Paul Lederach's work. Both novels encourage readers to see a web of relationship and yield insight with a method based in the five capacities (looking at immediate issues while seeing beyond them to context and relational patterns; integrating multiple time frames; thinking in terms of "both/and" rather than "either/or"; embracing complexity; and understanding issues of identity and their relationship to both conflict and narrative). Both novels lend themselves to a critique of American militarism. Perhaps the most salient common ground between them is that both novels illustrate the consequences of war for vulnerable young men.[42] Billy Lynn, Bartle, and Murph grow up in difficult family circumstances with limited resources and few educational opportunities. Their wartime experiences make them more reflective, though their options remain sharply constrained. Wouldn't it be better if they could learn those lessons and improve their economic circumstances by reading and thinking instead of fighting? Fountain suggests as much through the relationship between Billy and his mentor Shroom. Bartle has the opportunity to reflect and mature in a military prison. Murph never gets that chance, though his desperate actions after the medic's death imply that he longs for an alternative to the war.

Writing for professional peacebuilders, Lederach describes a "School for the Moral Imagination," a kind of continuing education program for those who "direct the course of public and human affairs" where they can talk openly and honestly with one another in a safe environment, and engage in artistic expression. They would be led by Paulo Freire-type teachers who "would only be storytellers, mostly common folk chosen for their life stories of how they overcame what seemed insurmountable odds to break out of injustice and threat without resorting to violence."[43] As the essays in this section of our volume by Ketty Anyeko and Tamara Shaya, Julie Okot Bitek, and Alison Rice show, narrative can be an effective tool for post-conflict reconciliation and transformation. In more conventional schools, courses in literature and peace studies can have as their goal the cultivation of the moral imagination in a younger population that will be making future decisions about war and peace. Young people can learn to employ the peacebuilder's hermeneutic in settings that foster open and honest discussion, cultivate analytic and critical thinking, and develop effective communication skills. The overarching goal is to build a culture of peace by developing strategic approaches to conflict transformation and by encouraging imaginative engagement with peace as concept and practice. Lederach writes, "Violence is known; peace is the mystery. By its very nature, therefore, peacebuilding requires a journey guided by the imagination of risk."[44] The peacebuilder's hermeneutic offers an approach to literature that cultivates new forms of imagination and transforms the narrative of perpetual war to one focused on the possibilities for peace.

Notes

1. John Lewis Gaddis coined the phrase "the long peace" to describe the absence of great power conflicts after World War II in *The Long Peace: Inquiries Into the History of the Cold War* (New York, NY: Oxford University Press, 1989).
2. Andrew Mack, ed., *Human Security Report 2005: War and Peace in the 21st Century* (New York: Oxford University Press, 2005).
3. The Uppsala Conflict Data Program illustrates these shifts: http://ucdp.uu.se.
4. David Keen sums up the trends in *Useful Enemies: When Waging Wars Is More Important Than Winning Them* (New Haven, CT: Yale University Press, 2012), 169.
5. Steven Pinker, *The Better Angels of Our Nature: Why Violence Has Declined* (New York, NY: Viking, 2011). The most recent Human Security Report, from 2013, reviews Pinker's arguments and the challenges to them. Andrew Mack, ed., *Human Security Report 2013: The Decline in Global Violence—Evidence, Explanation, and Contestation* (Vancouver: Human Security Press, 2014). *Human Security Report Project* (https://reliefweb.int/sites/reliefweb.int/files/resources/HSRP_Report_2013_140226_Web.pdf), accessed 17 December 2018.

6. Walter Benjamin, *Illuminations: Essays and Reflections* (New York: Schocken, 1969 [1955]), 256–257.
7. Norman Mailer, "The White Negro", in *Advertisements for Myself*, ed. Norman Mailer (New York: G.P. Putnam's Sons, 1959 [1957]), 339.
8. This style of catastrophist historical thought remains very current and broadly informs a 2009 special issue of *PMLA* on war. In "Introduction: Perpetual War" (*PMLA* 124 [2009]: 1505–1514), Srinivas Aravamudan alludes to Benjamin and updates the style of thought that Mailer's essay represents when he writes that "war is an extreme case of the superfluous evils around us, evils that range from poverty, exploitation, and unfreedom to our unsustainable growth, fueled by capitalism and leading to species suicide through overpopulation and ecological devastation. The angel of history is now missing in action: war's detritus may be blown along to a devastated posthuman future" (1512).
9. Andrew J. Bacvich, *The New American Militarism: How Americans Are Seduced by War* (New York: Oxford University Press, 2005). Deborah Tannen discusses the prominence of conflict and violence in American public culture in *The Argument Culture: Stopping America's War of Words* (New York: Random House, 1998). The statistics on U.S. military engagements are from World Bank and Human Security Report Project, Simon Fraser University, *The Miniatlas of Human Security* (Brighton, UK: Myriad Editions, 2008).
10. Elizabeth Borgwardt, *A New Deal for the World: America's Vision for Human Rights* (Cambridge, MA: The Belknap Press, 2005); Ramachandra Guha, *India After Gandhi: The History of the World's Largest Democracy* (New York, NY: HarperCollins, 2007); and Tony Judt, *Postwar: A History of Europe Since 1945* (New York, NY: Penguin, 2005).
11. George A. Lopez, "Dynamics Affecting Conflict, Justice, and Peace", *Peace, Justice, and Security Studies: A Curriculum Guide*, eds. Timothy A. McElwee, B. Welling Hall, Joseph Liechty, and Julie Garber (Boulder: Lynne Rienner, 2009), 91–104; quotation on 94.
12. John Paul Lederach, *The Little Book of Conflict Transformation* (Intercourse, PA: Good Books, 2003), 70.
13. Correlates of War Project: http://www.correlatesofwar.org/; Peace Accords Matrix: https://peaceaccords.nd.edu/; Uppsala Conflict Data Program: http://ucdp.uu.se/; PRIO databases: https://www.prio.org/Data/, accessed 20 October 2016.
14. John Paul Lederach and R. Scott Appleby, "Strategic Peacebuilding: An Overview", in *Strategies of Peace: Transforming Conflict in a Violent World*, eds. Daniel Philpott and Gerard F. Powers (New York: Oxford University Press, 2010), 22.
15. See Introduction of this volume and Mitchell's discussion in Chapter 2 of the Visual Arts and Peacebuilding.

16. Burns H. Weston, Sherle R. Schwenninger, and Diane E. Shamis, "The Literature of Peace and War", in *Peace and World Order Studies: A Curriculum Guide* (New York, NY: Institute for World Order, 1978), 148–151; Barbara J. Wein, ed., "The Literature of Nonviolence", in *Peace and World Order Studies: A Curriculum Guide*, 4th edition (New York, NY: World Policy Institute, 1984), 109–114. Lederach includes literature on his syllabus for "The Vocation of Peacebuilding", in *Peace, Justice and Security Studies: A Curriculum Guide*, 7th edition, eds. Timothy A. McElwee, et al. (Boulder, CO: Lynne Rienner Publishers, 2009), 340–344.
17. Hal Culbertson, "Peacebuilding and the Performing Arts Through the Collaborative Lens", Chapter 18 in this volume.
18. Michael Shank and Lisa Schirch, "Strategic Arts-Based Peacebuilding", *Peace & Change* 33:2 (2008): 217.
19. Lederach, *Little Book*, 5.
20. Lederach, *Little Book*, 21.
21. Pennebaker is a social psychologist known for his work on the therapeutic effects of writing. He has published both academic studies and popular books on the topic, including *Writing to Heal: A Guided Journal for Recovering from Trauma and Emotional Upheaval* (Oakland, CA: New Harbinger, 2004).
22. H. Porter Abbott, *The Cambridge Introduction to Narrative* (Cambridge, UK: Cambridge University Press, 2008), 55.
23. Discussed in Pinker, *Better Angels*, 588–590.
24. Phillip L. Hammack, "Identity as Burden or Benefit? Youth, Historical Narrative, and the Legacy of Political Conflict", *Human Development* 53 (2010): 174.
25. John Paul Lederach, *The Moral Imagination: The Art and Soul of Building Peace* (New York, NY: Oxford University Press, 2005), 146.
26. Lederach, *Moral Imagination*, 34–35.
27. Lederach, *Moral Imagination*, 69.
28. Lederach, *Little Book*, Chapter 8.
29. Leslie Marmon Silko, *Ceremony* (New York, NY: Penguin Books, 2006 [1977]), 1–6.
30. Silko, *Ceremony*, 6–7.
31. Silko, *Ceremony*, 35–36.
32. Silko, *Ceremony*, 36.
33. Lederach, *Moral Imagination*, Chapter 12.
34. Ben Fountain, *Billy Lynn's Long Halftime Walk* (New York, NY: HarperCollins, 2012); Kevin Powers, *The Yellow Birds: A Novel* (New York, NY: Little, Brown, 2012). At the time of writing, two prize-nominated Iraqi–authored novels about the war have been translated into English: Ali Bader's *The Tobacco Keeper* which was longlisted for the International Prize for Arabic fiction in 2009; and Inaam Kachachi's *The American Granddaughter*,

which was shortlisted for the prize in the same year. Several more Iraqi-authored works on the war have been considered for the prize and may soon become available in English.

35. Fountain, *Billy Lynn*, 167.
36. Creative writing has recently emerged as a form of post-conflict therapy in the United States, with numerous programs aimed at helping veterans of the wars in Iraq and Afghanistan heal from trauma by writing about their experiences of those conflicts.
37. Powers, *Yellow Birds*, 3.
38. Powers, *Yellow Birds*, 94.
39. Powers, *Yellow Birds*, 94.
40. Powers, *Yellow Birds*, 164–165.
41. Appleby discusses the ways that religion both contributes to violence and offers possibilities for transcending conflict in *The Ambivalence of the Sacred: Religion, Violence, and Reconciliation* (Lanham, MD: Rowman & Littlefield, 1999).
42. Karl Marlantes offers a personal account of the psychological functions that the Vietnam War fulfilled for him in *What It Is Like to Go to War* (New York, NY: Atlantic Monthly Press, 2011). Keen analyzes related issues of shame and the psychological functions of violence in *Useful Enemies*, Chapter 9; on masculinity, see esp. 207 and 210.
43. Lederach, *Moral Imagination*, 177.
44. Lederach, *Moral Imagination*, 39.

CHAPTER 11

Storytelling and Peacebuilding: Lessons from Northern Uganda

Ketty Anyeko and Tamara Shaya Hoffmann

Introduction

> To say that storytelling moves us, transports us, carries us away, or helps us escape the oppressiveness of our real lives, is to recognize that stories change our experience of the way things are. But stories are not only journeys because of the effects they have upon us: stories are so commonly and conspicuously *about* journeys… that one may see in journeying one of the preconditions of the possibility of narrative itself.[1]

The opinions expressed in this article are the authors' own and do not reflect the view or official policy of the Department of State or the United States government.

K. Anyeko (✉)
University of British Columbia, Vancouver, BC, Canada

T. Shaya Hoffmann
U.S. Department of State, Washington, DC, USA

J. Mitchell et al. (eds.), *Peacebuilding and the Arts*,
Rethinking Peace and Conflict Studies,
https://doi.org/10.1007/978-3-030-17875-8_11

Stories and storytelling have the power to move us. In telling and retelling our stories, we reevaluate our circumstances, see ourselves in relation to others, and garner feedback and insights from our audiences. Storytelling helps us to make sense of events, using voice and bodily gestures to articulate the meaning of our experiences. As we listen to stories, we 'affirm the unique character and voice of each teller as the story is brought to life by a living tongue and breath.'[2] Storytelling is a process that engages both narrator and listener, allowing them to connect in an intimate setting. In this chapter, we explore how these interpretive, creative, interactive, and personal qualities of storytelling make it a valuable resource for strategic peacebuilding and conflict transformation. Strategic peacebuilding emphasizes the importance of working over the long term to address the roots and ongoing effects of violent conflict, and the importance of working with grassroots and mid-level actors as well as with political and military elites.[3] Strategic peacebuilders draw attention to the way that:

> violent conflict creates deep disruption in relationships that then need radical healing–the kind of healing that restores the soul, the psyche and the moral imagination. Such healing…draws on profound rational, psychological, and transrational resources, especially the spiritual dimension of humanity.[4]

Conflict transformation approaches emphasize the need to 'identify experiences and issues that have caused a sense of harm, trauma, and injustice, build relationships between people in conflict, develop creative solutions that meet everyone's needs, [and] empower all people involved to transform their own conflict.'[5] In what follows, we argue that storytelling parallels these key principles of strategic peacebuilding and conflict transformation, and that it can be an important ally in their central task of healing broken humanity.[6] Our argument in this chapter makes these general claims by telling a particular story: the story of the Justice and Reconciliation Project (JRP) in Northern Uganda, and the personal stories of the formerly abducted women who took part in it. We argue that storytelling has been a powerful peacebuilding tool in that context, allowing the women to make sense of their experiences, to journey from being victims to being advocates, and to promote their unique justice needs. We begin by discussing the background of the conflict in Northern Uganda, the particular challenges faced by women in this context, and the origins of the storytelling project for formerly abducted women. We then move on to explore the connection between storytelling and peacebuilding, with a particular focus on storytelling as a means of pursuing justice.

Conflict in Northern Uganda

The two decades' war in Northern Uganda between the Ugandan government army—the Ugandan People's Defense Force (UPDF)—and Joseph Kony's Lord's Resistance Army (LRA) has inflicted unspeakable pain on civilians in northern Uganda. As a result of the conflict, over 1.8 million people were displaced in internally displaced persons (IDP) camps for more than 10 years, and over 75,000 Acholi people from Northern Uganda were abducted and forced to fight against their own communities.[7] Civilians were massacred, maimed, and tortured, and their property was destroyed. Young girls abducted into the LRA were forced to become 'wives' to top rebel leaders, fight civilians, serve as porters, and bear children with men the age of their fathers. As a result of forced marriage and sexual violence, many women who escaped or were released from captivity returned to their communities with unwanted children. They then struggled to meet their basic needs and those of their children, including school and medical fees. Returning women also often lacked sustainable sources of livelihood, as their education was hampered due to the long period of time spent in captivity. The following quote by a former forced wife of brutal LRA leader Joseph Kony depicts some of the reintegration challenges faced by such mothers and their children: '[My son] is called "Kony" even from our own home. They do not call him any other name…They say that his mind is like Kony, that he acts like Kony in every way, and people should just wait and see, because the boy will be a General like his father.'[8] Contrastingly, male LRA commanders returned under blanket amnesties and the government has provided them with attractive reinsertion packages, such as jobs in the national army. Despite this, many male commanders have neglected their children and refused to offer apologies to women they abused while serving the LRA. Since some LRA commanders concealed their identities in the bush, some women do not know the clans of their children, thus limiting their children's access to land, as land in the region is accessed through paternal lineages.[9] As well as facing practical difficulties in returning to their communities, women were also affected by significant psychosocial trauma, causing many of them to feel ashamed about the sexual violence they faced.

As a result, women felt silenced, and sometimes used silence as a way to protect themselves from harm, particularly when their memories contradicted metanarratives of victimhood or when they were stigmatized.[10]

In recent years, a moderate level of peace has returned to the region, following the peace negotiations that took place between the LRA and the Ugandan government from 2006 to 2008. Unfortunately, the final peace agreement was not signed, and the LRA still remains at large in neighboring countries like Southern Sudan, the Democratic Republic of the Congo, and the Central African Republic. Nevertheless, the prevailing level of calm has allowed the war-affected communities of Northern Uganda to begin rebuilding their lives. For some women in Gulu, taking part in a storytelling project with a non-governmental organization, the JRP, has been a major part of this process of moving past violence.

Origins of Storytelling at JRP

Aware of the various challenges faced by formerly abducted women and the impact of trauma on their lives, Erin Baines—a co-founder of JRP—proposed a research project to pilot storytelling methods among women once abducted by the LRA. Baines observed that, despite the women's silences, they longed to speak about their experience and wanted safe spaces in which to do so.[11] She settled upon storytelling as a method because of the Acholi oral practice of *wang-o*, in which families gather together around a fire with elders to narrate stories, as a way of passing down family histories, allegories, and life lessons. These *ododo* (folk tales) have 'moral endings that instruct [Acholis] how to relate to people…as *dano adana*, human persons…and which determined how the individual viewed self, and how the individual was treated by others within the community.'[12] Storytelling was thus a culturally appropriate and familiar practice for the women, and Baines saw that it might allow them to process their time in the LRA and express their hopes and fears about reintegrating back into society. *Ododo* was an especially helpful form, as it gave women the opportunity to articulate injustices and 'provide[d] important insight into human agency and the struggle to remake one's life after so much pain.'[13]

With this knowledge, Erin Baines, together with her research assistant Ketty Anyeko, launched the first storytelling group, consisting of twenty-seven formerly abducted women.[14] The informal settings of the storytelling sessions, under a mango tree or in an open field, for example, helped to reduce women's fear and intimidation with regard to their sharing experiences. Additionally, storytelling allowed women to provide advice, encouragement, and peer support to each other—an essential element for women who did not have strong ties to other family or friends due to stigma. As the pilot project came to an end, the team facilitated six new storytelling groups, and the research project eventually became known as 'Ododo Wa,' or 'Our Stories' in Acholi. As the project developed and the women involved recognized their collective needs, they created a platform for all the storytelling groups to communicate their message to community and government leaders, leading to the creation of the Women's Advocacy Network (WAN) in May 2011.[15]

Storytelling and Justice

Following the near-conclusion of the peace negotiations between the Ugandan government and the Lord's Resistance Army, violence in Northern Uganda has decreased. Peacebuilding, however, involves more than just the reduction and management of violence, and the end it seeks:

> is perhaps best expressed by the idea of a justpeace, a dynamic state of affairs in which the reduction and management of violence and the achievement of social and economic justice are undertaken as mutual, reinforcing dimensions of constructive change.[16]

The pursuit of peace necessarily involves the pursuit of justice—a dimension particularly important in Northern Uganda following widespread human rights violations during the war. As well as facing distinctive challenges during the conflict itself, as we have already explored, women returning from abduction also face significant barriers in their pursuit of justice. Because Ugandan traditional justice processes exclude women, and there are no formal justice mechanisms to address war crimes—for example, through a truth and reconciliation commission or through pursuing trials at the International Criminal Court—there are limited options for women to seek justice.[17] In this context, storytelling can become a way for women to pursue 'a form of justice making that restores the imbalances of individual value necessary for returned women to successfully reintegrate into their communities.'[18] Storytelling contributes to restorative and procedural justice,[19] and also promotes grassroots peacebuilding initiatives by helping women to articulate their experiences and advocate for their justice needs.[20]

Defining justice is not an easy task, and the difficulty of finding an adequate definition of what justice means is amplified in a post-conflict setting, where different understandings of justice and differing views of how it should be pursued can be the source of renewed conflict. In this chapter, we follow Bastiaan Wielenga's definition of justice, which he defines as 'the unwavering and enduring will to give to each their right'—a definition that emerges from the way that the women involved in the storytelling project spoke of the need for fairness, equality, and entitlement after war.[21] We also include the transitional justice framework in our analysis, since Ugandans and local peace practitioners regard transitional justice as the model for Uganda's current state. The International Center for Transitional Justice (ICTJ) defines transitional justice as 'a response to systematic or widespread violations of human rights. It seeks recognition for victims and promotion of possibilities for peace, reconciliation, and democracy.'[22] Transitional justice measures include criminal prosecution, truth commissions, reparations programs, institutional reforms, and gender justice. A major purpose of transitional justice is to mark a bridge from a lawless past of no accountability, toward greater levels of societal justice and peace.[23] In what follows, we explore how storytelling became a means of promoting justice by and for Acholi women, through three key characteristics: empowerment, voice, and healing.

Experiencing Empowerment

As it relates to peacebuilding, in its simplest terms, empowerment is 'the restoration to individuals of a sense of their own value and strength and their own capacity to handle life's problems.'[24] Most striking in this context is the way storytelling empowered the participants in the project to communicate their experiences, and helped them develop strategies to deal with the past and move forward with their lives. This is especially important in the context of the sexual violence experienced by many of the participants, as most women who experience sexual trauma feel shame, anger, and despair, which often inhibit their ability to express themselves, and thus limit their capacity to move past the experience.[25]

Research on group narrative therapy with sexually abused adolescents reveals that storytelling helps PTSD victims realize their sense of self worth, recognize they are not defined by their abuse, and realize they are not to blame for what occurred.[26] These effects were reflected in the experience of participants in the storytelling project. Although initially unable to articulate their experience, participants expressed that sharing stories with other formerly abducted women promoted a sense of empowerment and support, especially in moments of despair. Lema, a rape survivor, said that the trauma she experienced resulted in anger, distress, and depression, causing her to consider suicide, partially as a result of not being able to share her story. Lema said, 'when I first returned from the bush, I didn't talk to anyone, but when I met others who also [returned from] the bush, I knew they would understand me. After telling my story, I became strong.'[27] The experience of telling her own story allowed her to acknowledge the traumatic events of her past, and develop better ways to cope with her experience. Being able to tell her story in a supportive group setting also helped her to feel empowered, and to decide against harming herself.

As well as helping women to tell their own stories and acknowledge the pain of their pasts, storytelling also helped the women to speak with their families about their war experience. This is particularly vital in Uganda, where family ties are profoundly important. Ajok expresses her experience in this way:

> At first when I returned...I could not tell my family members that I was taken by force, given to a man, and raped, but as a result of being in a storytelling group, now I have the courage to share with my family members, because if I can share with these others, why not my family?...at first I didn't want to tell my children that they were born in captivity, but storytelling has helped me to get the courage to tell my own children: 'I bore you in captivity. This is your father and this is where he came from.'[28]

Ajok's new-found ability to communicate her experiences, and her willingness to share her story with her children is significant for numerous reasons. Ajok knew that by revealing the father's identity, her children could potentially seek out their father's clan. If the children pursued this relationship, they would potentially interact with the same LRA commander who raped and mistreated her. Although Ajok may want to break ties with the commander's clan, her willingness to tell the truth about her children's father opens up a potential avenue for reconciliation. Furthermore, Ajok told her children they were born while in the bush, a brave act considering the possible stigma her children may face if they reveal this to others. Through the storytelling process, Ajok shared that she has become courageous in declaring the nature of her children's birth and identity, and is willing to take strides in the future to help her children cope with their circumstances.

In addition to sharing stories with family members, storytelling has empowered women to respond appropriately to community stigma and interact with those who were not abducted. Gladys said storytelling reduced her feelings of insecurity and increased her confidence when relating to those who were not abducted, and were thus able to complete their studies. She said, 'storytelling has taken my fear away. I find that I am so strong that I can compose myself very well and say something even better than someone who was educated or those who I used to be afraid of.'[29] In this sense, Gladys' story helped move her toward more equal participation with the community, helping her engage with others whose judgment she once feared.

Participation in the storytelling project has helped the women involved to see themselves as agents of change and not solely as victims. Storytelling as a tool elicited women's grassroots social activism and gave them confidence to speak out about various forms of injustices that they suffered during the war. Rather than turning to the JRP or other organizations to speak for them, they have become their own agents of change. Through the formation of the Women's Advocacy Network (WAN), the women broke the silence on their experiences and are working to end marginalization of formerly abducted women, and promote reintegration for them and their children in their communities. As part of their activities, WAN participants have met with government and grassroots leaders to advocate for reparations and accountability, organized bi-weekly radio talk shows, and developed community outreaches addressing social stigma and reconciliation. They also are creating an environment for reconciliation within the communities affected by the LRA. The following statement, made by Evelyn Amony, Chairperson of WAN, reveals how women are taking the lead in advocating for redress:

> We have realized that if we do not come together, speak out about our issues and seek solutions to our problems then no one will do it on our behalf. We have made a resolution to break our silence and become advocates of our own cause.[30]

The WAN recently petitioned the Uganda government parliament for reparations in 2014. The women's social activism that began with telling stories of the war under the trees has led the Ugandan Parliament to pass a resolution and commitment to provide reparations and redress to the war-affected in northern Uganda. Furthermore, women have engaged with a wider audience in northern Uganda to regain their dignity and question perpetrators. Through radio talk shows they host on a local radio station, they have spoken about the nature of violations they suffered and cited examples of abusers living with them in the same community who have not been held accountable and have refused to apologize for their actions. As a result, some of their abductors have approached them to ask them to stop embarrassing them on the radio. Instead of feeling intimidated, one of the WAN leaders told the former LRA commander that they are now free and can say whatever they want, which they will continue to do until they receive the acknowledgment and apologies they deserve.

Elevating Voice

Through telling their stories, the women participating in the storytelling project felt empowered to communicate their experiences to family, community, and government. Their ability to share their experiences during the war not only helped them to articulate how their rights had been violated, but to pursue reconciliation and justice in light of that knowledge. This leads to our second point: the ability of storytelling to elevate voice. John Paul Lederach and Angela Jill Lederach note that:

> many victims of violence experience a profound sense of powerlessness, an overwhelming and deeply rooted feeling that they do not have a voice in the processes of response and the decisions that affect their lives or in the events happening around them, though officially these processes are portrayed as being conducted *on their behalf*...When a person says, 'We do not have a voice' or 'We want a voice', the guiding metaphor suggests they seek spaces of inclusion and power that take the shape of acknowledgement, respectful exchange, meaningful conversation, and which affect actual decisions that affect their lives.[31]

Procedural justice theory holds that, when people have an opportunity to voice their concerns, share their opinions, or express their views before important decisions are made, they feel decision-making processes are fair.[32] Studies consistently reveal that in procedural justice processes, people value being taken seriously and heard over having a particular outcome. In the same way, women in the storytelling project wanted to express their concerns and have their voices heard but, most importantly, they wanted some kind of process in which they felt heard, and were treated with respect and fairness.

Three of the women spoke about how storytelling helped them to gain a voice and feel heard in this sense. Danay said:

> storytelling is an opportunity for our voices to be heard, because if what we share is disseminated in other avenues, other people will know what we think. So we look at storytelling as an avenue for our voices to be heard elsewhere, including what we went through and what we want to be done, in regards to justice and reconciliation.[33]

Aber explained how storytelling helps her feel respected and listened to: 'storytelling is good because there were things we used to fear about sharing, but now people can hear our thoughts. Coming to discuss has given us a platform to speak about our issues and what we think, without fear.'[34] In a similar vein, Grace said, 'it's easier to attain justice [with storytelling], because other people hear what we think. We are encouraged because we realized that we are now free to express ourselves in any way.'[35]

These examples reveal the women's need to tell their side of the story and feel respected during the process of seeking justice.[36] Interestingly, the concept of restorative justice, defined as 'an approach to criminal justice that emphasizes restoring the victim and the community rather than punishing the offender,'[37] draws upon the twin ideals of voice and respect to develop processes that bring offenders and victims together.[38] Framed in this way, procedural justice can lead to restorative justice and contribute to peacebuilding. Through articulating their thoughts, women in the storytelling group express their opinions about procedures like truth telling, but also their perspectives on justice frameworks. Women's voices thus serve as a tool for contributing to new structures in Uganda and provide insight into women's agency.

The WAN has played an important role in making the storytelling groups' voices heard by local community and local government leaders. The WAN illustrates a model of social change championed by the war-affected women themselves.

Healing

In addition to empowering women as agents of change and giving them a voice in seeking justice, participants in the storytelling project also shared how the experience of storytelling had brought them healing on a personal level, and helped them to cope with the traumatic experiences of their past. Here, the group setting was again important, and participants valued the opportunity to share their stories in a setting where others speaking and listening had suffered similar experiences. As one woman put it, 'just sitting together to share stories brings healing. You can meet someone who has a lot of problems, even more than yours. When you share, you feel that your experience is a little bit better and you get encouraged...if we continue storytelling, we will not have a lot of problems.'[39] Where storytelling can provide a safe space for people to share their experience, it can be an important source of healing. Some of the participants explained how simply being able to speak about their experience brought them relief, as they began to process the experience. Julianne said:

> This storytelling group has helped me so much. Before, there were people who had pain from what happened to them. Our heads were aching and we didn't know who to tell these stories to, but it is through this storytelling that we are free... Storytelling has given me a chance to talk about what happened to me, which was so hard, because I was thinking about whom to tell the story to, but now I am free and relieved.[40]

Julianne's statement reveals the potential of storytelling to reduce some of the symptoms of trauma, including flashbacks and nightmares, and suggests that women who articulate their stories of violence may experience relief as a result of doing so. The relief that Julianne reported from her participation in the storytelling project is illuminated by research on similar psychological therapies used with people affected by Post Traumatic Stress Disorder. Studies show that female American veterans recovered more quickly from PTSD when participating in cognitive behavioral therapy (CBT), in which they 'repeatedly and vividly "re-experience" traumatic events rather than simply discussing current difficulties with a therapist.'[41] This type of therapy can lead to feelings of liberation, reduce stress, and help victims to move toward psychological control.[42] Other desensitization therapy techniques used with PTSD victims include imaginal exposure, where clients discuss their experience with a counselor. Although certain memories may be difficult to articulate, clients are encouraged to speak about the memory, relating their level of discomfort using a scale of 1–100 during different points of sharing. A counselor encourages clients to retell their story to him or her, until the client feels comfortable sharing and experiences limited stress during the process. While some critics may cite the possibility of retraumatization as a reason not to discuss traumatic memories, studies prove that this type of therapy helps clients to differentiate between remembering and processing the trauma, and reliving the trauma again. As a result, clients report feeling relief from flashbacks, anxiety, stress, and other traumatic consequences.[43] While the storytelling project in Uganda does not use the same techniques outlined above, the process of sharing has similarities to CBT and imaginal exposure, which may explain why participants report relief from symptoms of trauma. Like CBT and imaginal exposure, storytelling provides opportunities to share difficult experiences and directly engage with trauma, eventually leading to less mental stress and fewer symptoms. For some participants, relief from shame and fear even extended to the experience of relief from physical pain.[44] Otek, a woman in the group who suffered burns to her hand during the war, claimed that storytelling gave her physical relief, saying, 'I feel as if my hand has been cured because of storytelling. I don't worry so much about it anymore.'[45] Although it is important not to overstate the case for the healing capacity of storytelling, it is worth noting that its psychological and emotional impact may also help those whose physical pain is experienced as inseparable from their mental pain and memory of traumatic events.

The process of telling their stories, and sharing them with others who had undergone similar experiences, helped some of the women to address their feelings of guilt and shame arising from forced participation in LRA battles. Women like Simone said, 'storytelling has taken away the guilt of feeling I was a perpetrator and made me realize that I was a victim and that I was forced to do certain things like kill people.'[46] Simone later shared that a large part of her decision to no longer blame herself was a result of multiple women sharing their experiences in combat and recognizing they were forced to participate. This realization helped women understand that their journey toward healing would involve forgiving themselves, as well as seeking justice from and reconciliation with others.

Conclusion

Throughout this chapter, we have argued that storytelling can be a powerful tool for peacebuilding. The voices of the participants in the storytelling project speak for themselves about the capacity of storytelling to influence positively the lives of formerly abducted women, allowing them to make sense of their experiences, moving them from victims to advocates, and helping them to voice their unique justice needs. We have explored how storytelling allowed the women to reflect on their own particular experience of violent conflict, and to articulate their own sense of what justice and reconciliation meant for them in light of that. On a very practical level, we saw how storytelling helped the women to develop a sense of agency, and developed skills and capacities that enabled them to engage with the challenge of reintegration in their local communities, and the challenge of seeking justice from the Ugandan government. This has been particularly important given the lack of other mechanisms for women to seek justice in northern Uganda: the storytelling project, and the WAN emerging from it, has become the primary means for women to call for their rights and pursue justice. In other conflict settings where lack of accountability and past or current human rights violations pose a major challenge, similar storytelling initiatives may prove an important resource for peacebuilding, and the establishment of transitional forms of justice.

As well as showing how storytelling can be a means for advocacy and pursuing justice, we have also argued that it provides a unique way for women survivors of war to begin healing the wounds inflicted by violent conflict. The opportunity to tell their stories and listen to others' experiences was something the participants in the project valued, both as a way of addressing the continuing effects of their traumatic past, and as a constructive way of moving toward a more hopeful future. Storytelling helped the women to process their own traumatic memories, alleviating their feelings of isolation, shame or guilt, and gave them the confidence and freedom to participate in their local communities, moving them toward greater levels of justice and reconciliation.

To conclude, we refer again to Michael Jackson. He writes:

> storytelling gives us a sense that though we do not exactly determine the course of our lives, we at least have a hand in defining their meaning...stories enable us to regain some purchase over the events that confound us, humble us, and leave us helpless, salvaging a sense that we have some say in the way our lives unfold.[47]

Storytelling participant Lokoko would agree. She says, 'I stopped being heartbroken, thanks to storytelling...through sharing, we have learned so much and now storytelling has spread to other groups; it is good that this is happening. We have come very far.'[48]

Notes

1. Michael Jackson, *The Politics of Storytelling: Violence, Transgression and Intersubjectivity* (Copenhagen, DK: Museum Tusculanum Press, 2002), 30.
2. Jeff Gere, Beth-Ann Kozlovich, and Daniel Kelin II, *By Word of Mouth: A Storytelling Guide for the Classroom* (Honolulu, HI: Pacific Resources for Education and Learning, 2002). Available at https://eric.ed.gov/?id=ED467521.
3. John Paul Lederach, *Building Peace: Sustainable Reconciliation in Divided Societies* (Washington, DC: United States Institute of Peace, 2010), 37–55. See also Lisa Schirch, *The Little Book of Strategic Peacebuilding* (Intercourse, PA: Good Books, 2004). Strategic peacebuilding seeks to respond to the particular challenges posed by contemporary conflict, which Lederach summarizes in *Building Peace*, 3–10.
4. John Paul Lederach and R. Scott Appleby, "Strategic Peacebuilding: An Overview", in *Strategies of Peace*, eds. D. Philpott and G. Powers (Oxford, UK: Oxford University Press), 27.
5. Lederach and Appleby, "Strategic Peacebuilding", 19–44.
6. Lederach and Appleby State, 'The Framing Question for Strategic Peacebuilding Seems to Be: How Do We Heal Broken Humanity?' See Appleby and Lederach, "Strategic Peacebuilding", 27.
7. Michael Otim and Marieke Wierda, *Uganda: Impact of the Rome Statute and the International Criminal Court.* Briefing (New York, NY: International Center for Transitional Justice [ICTJ], 2010), 2
8. Storytelling Session, Uganda 2009.
9. In Uganda, the paternal clan is responsible for providing financial and psychological care for the child and providing land for male children. Some children may seek out their father for relational reasons, while others do so for economic reasons.
10. Pilar Riaño-Alcalá and Erin Baines, "The Archive in the Witness: Documentation in Settings of Chronic Insecurity", *International Journal of Transitional Justice* (2011): 18.
11. Erin Baines, "Gender, Responsibility, and the Grey Zone: Considerations for Transitional Justice", *Journal of Human Rights* 10:4 (2009).
12. Erin Baines and Beth Stewart, "I Cannot Accept What I Have Not Done: Storytelling, Gender and Transitional Justice", *Journal of Human Rights Practice* 3:3 (2011).
13. Baines and Stewart, "I Cannot Accept What I Have Not Done".
14. Baines and Stewart, "I Cannot Accept What I Have Not Done".

15. The WAN is "a forum where war-affected women come together to advocate for justice, acknowledgment and accountability for gender-based violations inflicted upon them during war in northern Uganda. It was formed with the aim of empowering women survivors to participate in post-conflict policy debates and to engage grassroots communities in gendered discussions on reintegration and reconciliation...[and] created with the goal of bridging the existing gaps in gender justice." The WAN provides opportunities for women to engage in peer-support and storytelling, advocacy and lobbying to the community and government, and capacity building and leadership training. For more information, visit http://justiceandreconciliation.com/2012/05/introducing-the-womens-advocacy-network-wan-at-jrp/, accessed 4 September 2014.
16. Lederach and Appleby, "Strategic Peacebuilding," 23; see also Michael Shank and Lisa Schirch, "Strategic Arts-Based Peacebuilding", *Peace & Change* 33:2 (2008).
17. See Iris Marchand, "Legal Cultures, Blurred Boundaries: The Case of Traditional Justice in Uganda" (2007), for more details on the difficulties of formal justice seeking in the aftermath of the war in Uganda: paper published online, accessed 4 September 2014, http://www.academia.edu/591406/Legal_Cultures_Blurred_Boundaries_the_Case_of_Transitional_Justice_in_Uganda.
18. Baines and Stewart, "I Cannot Accept What I Have Not Done".
19. Here we follow the definition for restorative justice as found in Liebmann: "an approach to criminal justice that emphasizes restoring the victim and the community rather than punishing the offender." See Marian Liebmann, *Restorative Justice: How It Works* (London, UK and Philadelphia, PA: Jessica Kingsley Publishers, 2007), 25. We describe restorative justice in more detail later in this chapter. Procedural justice theory says that when people have an opportunity to voice their concerns, share their opinion, or express their views before important decisions, they feel the decision making processes are fair. See E. Allan Lind and Tom R. Tyler, *The Social Psychology of Procedural Justice* (New York, NY: Plenum Press, 1988), 170.
20. Clare Coburn (2012), "Storytelling As a Peacebuilding Method", in *The Encyclopedia of Peace Psychology*, ed. Daniel J. Christie (Malden, MA and Oxford, UK: Wiley-Blackwell, 2011). Published Online http://onlinelibrary.wiley.com/doi/10.1002/9780470672532.wbepp268/abstract.
21. B. Wielenga, H. Klenner, and S. Lettow, "Justice", *Historical Materialism* 13:3 (2005).
22. International Center for Transitional Justice, "What Is Transitional Justice?" Factsheet. International Center for Transitional Justice (2009), accessed 29 March 2013, http://ictj.org/publication/what-transitional-justice.

23. Dan Snodderley, ed., *Peace Terms: A Glossary of Terms for Conflict Management and Peacebuilding* (Washington, DC: Academy for International Conflict Management and Peacebuilding, US Institute of Peace 2011), 1–64, accessed 16 February 2013, http://www.usip.org/sites/default/files/files/peaceterms.pdf.
24. Robert A. Baruch Bush and Joseph P. Folger, *The Promise of Mediation: The Transformative Approach to Conflict* (San Francisco, CA: Jossey-Bass, 1994), 2.
25. Edna B. Foa and Barbara Olasov Rothbaum, *Treating the Trauma of Rape* (New York, NY: The Guilford Press, 1998), 119.
26. Janet Adams-Westcott and Cheryl Dobbins, "Listening with Your 'Heart Ears' and Other Ways Young People Can Escape the Effects of Sexual Abuse", in *Narrative Therapies with Children and Adolescents*, eds. Craig Smith and David K. Nylund (New York: Guilford Press, 1997), 196.
27. Storytelling Session, Uganda, 28 July 2012.
28. Storytelling Session, Uganda, 1 September 2012.
29. Storytelling Session, Uganda, 18 August 2012.
30. Evelyn Amony, 28 September 2012, 'Women's Advocacy Network (WAN)—Our Journey", *The Justice and Reconciliation Blog*, accessed 4 September 2014, http://justiceandreconciliation.com/2012/09/wan-our-journey/2012.
31. John Paul Lederach and Angela Jill Lederach, *When Blood and Bones Cry Out: Journeys Through the Soundscape of Healing and Reconciliation* (Oxford, UK: Oxford University Press, 2010), 65–66.
32. Lind and Tyler, *The Social Psychology of Procedural Justice*, 170.
33. Storytelling Session, Uganda, 22 September 2012.
34. Storytelling Session, Uganda, 22 September 2012.
35. Storytelling Session, Uganda, 22 September 2012.
36. Robert MacCoun, "Voice, Control, and Belonging: The Double-Edged Sword of Procedural Fairness", *Annual Review of Law and Social Science* 1: (2005): 172.
37. Liebmann, *Restorative Justice*, 25.
38. MacCoun, "Voice, Control, and Belonging", 178.
39. Storytelling Session, Uganda, 1 September 2012.
40. Storytelling Session, Uganda, 18 August 2012.
41. Samson Kurt, "Cognitive Behavioral Therapy: 'Revisiting' Traumatic Events Speeds PTSD Recovery in Women Veterans", *Neurology Today* 7:7 (2007): 34–37.
42. Kurt, "Cognitive Behavioral Therapy", 36.
43. Foa and Rothbaum, *Treating the Trauma of Rape*, 159–161.
44. Gershen Kaufman, *The Psychology of Shame: Theory and Treatment of Shame-Based Syndromes* (New York, NY: Springer Publishing, 1989), 113.
45. Storytelling Session, Uganda, 28 July 2012.

46. Storytelling Session, Uganda, 22 September 2012.
47. Jackson, *Politics of Storytelling*, 16–17.
48. Storytelling Session, Uganda, 28 July 2012.

CHAPTER 12

What Choice Between Nightmares?: Intersecting Local, Global and Intimate Stories of Pain in Peacebuilding

Juliane Okot Bitek

Introduction

This chapter focuses on the responsibility of the reader or listener in the presence of difficult stories in the aftermath of violence. I draw upon a single story to illustrate the ethics of storytelling: what to do with stories that are difficult, traumatic and yet necessary in the peace and recovery process after mass violence. I recognize the need to give voice, visibility and agency to women whose voices are often contextualized and rooted in victimhood along with an author's responsibility to honor their experiences, and yet not do further harm in the representation of these stories. This chapter outlines the challenges of and a possible way through to peacebuilding by a focused responsibility of the listener and writer in alliance with survivors of trauma.

This essay provides a complementary argument to the previous chapter, though it focuses on both the reader and writer, and offers an original

J. Okot Bitek (✉)
University of British Columbia, Vancouver, BC, Canada

J. Mitchell et al. (eds.), *Peacebuilding and the Arts*,
Rethinking Peace and Conflict Studies,
https://doi.org/10.1007/978-3-030-17875-8_12

short story to embody the theories discussed. The woman whose story informs this chapter is part of a larger group of women who were abducted by the Lord's Resistance Army, a guerilla group (now largely defunct) that waged war against the government of Uganda (1987–2007). When the National Resistance Movement/Army overthrew the government of Uganda in January 1986, several rebel organizations were formed from the ranks of the overthrown former government and later, civilians that joined them in resisting what they claimed was the ill-treatment of the new government. The Pece Peace Accord (1988) that was signed in Gulu between the Ugandan government and the Uganda People's Democratic Movement signalled the dissipation of major resistance toward the government and the emergence of the LRA which was formed on the heels of the defeat of the Holy Spirit Movement (1986–1987). Originally made up of a small group of volunteer members, the LRA began to kidnap civilians when it was apparent that people were not willing to join them. Tens of thousands of people from northern Uganda—children, women and men—were forcefully taken from their homes, off the street, from school, or while at work in their gardens. These abductees were often kept in captivity for years. Some escaped, many died, some returned home to northern Uganda and many have never been seen again.

The history of the war in northern Uganda between the government of Uganda and the LRA provides the context for the story on which this chapter is based (also see Chapter 11) but as we saw in the previous chapter the culture of storytelling harks back to a cultural tradition of storytelling among the Acholi people on whose lands this story is located. Wang'oo, storytelling around the evening fire, was traditionally the time and place for education, dissemination of information and entertainment in a homestead after dinner. Wang'oo was co-opted by the formerly abducted women who worked with Erin Baines and Ketty Anyeko at the Justice and Reconciliation Project (hereafter JRP) in Gulu to work through and make sense of their experiences by speaking the truth and articulating their stories to each other. I worked with Baines and Anyeko, in my capacity as a writer and storyteller, to document the stories[1] of these women's narratives in poetic and prose form[2] for a wider audience. I came to this project as a woman who hails from northern Uganda and wanted to show solidarity by listening/reading and writing/compiling their stories.

The stories of the women in JRP were often laden with pain, but were also coded with moments of resistance, memories of better days and sometimes, a more beautiful past. Too often, stories of formerly abducted people are couched in the suffering they encountered in captivity and the only identity ascribed to them is as survivors. In the presence of the stories, my responsibility was to listen and/or to read, but as a writer I had to balance the respect I have for the experiences that were narrated and the need to document them within the goal of imagining and creating a future without harm. This meant that I had to deal with what seemed, sounded and felt like impossibly difficult narratives to work with, and at the same time seek out and highlight spaces of agency, support[3] and solidarity within these narratives. I felt the need and responsibility to allow space between these stories of suffering and a new beginning from which we can remember[4] or re-memory[5]and re-story. In this chapter, I focus on one story from a woman in the JRP group, I outline the challenges of retelling this especially difficult story and then offer a story written in response to what I heard and had to record. This in turn provides a practical method for dealing with and representing stories that are laden with painful experiences.

Sara[6]

Sara is a formerly abducted woman who lives in Gulu, my hometown. She, along with tens of thousands of young people in northern Uganda, was abducted by the rebel Lord's Resistance Army who had been fighting the government of Uganda since 1987. Sara is a member of a storytelling group who later organized themselves into the Women's Advocacy Network, a women's advocacy network (WAN).[7] WAN has as its mandate, the need for women's stories to be taken seriously in post-conflict policy debates in the post-war recovery in northern Uganda. Her stories, like many of the women survivors, are full of horrific details. Anyeko and Shaya and colleagues (see Chapter 11) have worked with women who share their experiences both of during the conflict and after their return. However, Sara's remarkable recall and detailed telling mark her stories from the others.

Sara recounted an event in the forest in which she came across a body in a shallow grave and made concession[8] as she must, for disturbing the rest of the dead. I must be clear here, that Sara's story of this event is not in itself remarkable. Sadly, such stories are all too ordinary as many bodies of people who lost their lives in the war have never been recovered and it is not uncommon to come across such a grave in the forest. Sara's story affected me at a profound level. So much so, that I was quite prepared to let it remain unwritten. But the story stayed in my mind and body. For months, I experienced insomnia, irritability, headaches and had nightmares when I did sleep. Sometimes my then husband would wake me up, telling me that I'd been crying in my sleep. Although other things may also have been affecting me, the experience was deeply haunting.

What stands out is the way Sara's account of that event dripped with pain. The excruciating and harrowing details she provided will not be repeated here but suffice to say, it hurt to read, as much as I'm certain, it must have rent the hearts of those who heard her tell it aloud. Sara, in her telling, locates herself as a person who couldn't have been responsible for the death, but knows that there must be serious repercussions for disturbing the dead. She appeals to the dead to forgive her for being in this space and prays that her ritual act of placing a leafed branch on the body will signify her remorse for its death and lack of proper burial. If, by itself, this was not a remarkable story—many people have spoken about coming across unburied bodies, then what business of mine was it to retell this story? Bound by the exquisite refrain from the women of WAN—our stories must be told—and Sara's powerful telling, I knew that my work as a storyteller would entail the responsibility of both documenting and seeking ways toward a possible future without the weight of this painful encounter from the past.

Stories bind us; in the telling or reading, we're caught in the narration or events that suspend the world and afterwards the world is changed because it has been imbued by the experience of the story. I had to reproduce Sara's account. Like her, and in the tradition of Toni Morrison, I felt a responsibility to both the story and the dead. But "since why is difficult, one must take refuge in how."[9] I went about thinking *how* to tell this story without distancing the reader through a direct recounting of the tale while respecting fully the ways in which the teller and the listener are connected by the tale. I needed to connect with an unknowable reader, to make this story universal and yet have it *remain* a particular, intimate and localized story. The story I eventually wrote emerged out of months of working itself out. I had to find a way to reach a reader who would have limited access to, but still be able to relate to an untold horror. I needed to access the senses, evoke hearing, feeling and memory of the inaccessible—to speak/write the unspeakable.

A Groan, a Wailing

It was a clearing in the forest on the way to the well, or to collect firewood. It was a clearing in the forest that claimed silence, even with everything alive, around it – birds, crickets, mute worms that inched along on their bellies, ants carrying and passing on, stories and luggage, luggage and stories. It was a clearing with fallen leaves, half composted, soft underbrush, some grass, thin branched trees, bushes, really.

It was an afternoon. It could have been late morning, perfectly warm, still, not yet hot. It could have been high noon.

It was definitely a clearing.

It was a clearing in the forest on the way to fetch water, or was that fire wood or an errand to run? It doesn't matter. It was a clearing in time, a moment that yesterday and today and yesterday before it and before it stretched back, much like this moment right now. It was a silence that spoke without saying anything.

Look!

Fallen leaves half composting, their siblings still on the tree waiting for a gust in the wind, waiting for the bang at the door in the middle of the night – get out! Get out right now or we will kill you if we have to come inside. Get out or we will burn the house down! Get out or we will come in and shoot you all.

Get out!

Leaves on the tree, not yet broken off, hanging on, hanging on.

Oh, grant me peace in these thy tender mercies. Prayers remained stuck in the moment.

What's going on? What's going on?

A moment like that followed another and another in those days. It was everywhere – going to the forest to get firewood, run an errand or was that to fetch water? It doesn't matter now. It didn't then.

In this moment, yesterday and today collapses and nothing speaks. Nothing says a word. Nothing whispers that this, too, is a haunted space. This too, like everywhere else we step on, in all the days of our lives are haunted spaces. Here, where everywhere is now and never was, we know to pick up a branch and lay it on the ground and say, I'm sorry, I didn't kill you.

The shame is mine and it is not mine. I'm ashamed. I'm ashamed to be here. I'm ashamed. The shame is mine. The shame is not mine. Still, I'm ashamed to be here and I'm sorry. I'm sorry. I'm ashamed. All I know is to pick up a branch, lay it on the ground and say, I'm sorry. I didn't kill you. It was not my wish to desecrate your resting place. I'm sorry. I'm sorry. I'm sorry. I'm so sorry.

> A murmuring, a muted conversation. Others walk by.
>
> A spot of sunlight overhead, or is the sun already thinking of setting out in the horizon? A quiet heart, a moment unlike any we've ever had, and yet this is the moment. This is the moment that is yesterday and right now and yesterday before it, and before that.
>
> We return and look to fit in an existence without this story. We wish to fit as if nothing happened. We need to fit back. It never happened, I tell myself, so that I can forget. But the shame remains, trailing a story I wish I never told or never had to tell. But after all this, we're nothing without our stories. I'm ashamed of this story and yet I am of it. It was not my shame and it is my shame. But here I am. I knew to place a branch on the body. I knew to say sorry.
>
> We return to nothing and the leaves won't even acknowledge that we were ever here. And so we pass on these stories and whisper to the bark of trees that still stand against the wind.

In writing "A Groan, a Wail," I was cognizant of the need to present nature as a witness, one that would not testify and yet remain in solidarity with Sara. I needed to evoke an insistence on that memory and allow it to be in the realm of the unforgotten and yet not be completely remembered. It had to be a recollection that could not be pinpointed to a specific day or time—something that is familiar to readers—something almost lost, but not quite. I use allegory, repetition, anthropomorphy, prayer chant and absence to indicate Sara's utter aloneness along with evidence of Sara's prior knowledge to save herself, to clear a path forward. Rather than focus on the horror, this retelling should also remind us that there is hope to be found in what we already know. In so doing I hope to touch a reader who has felt alone; who has wondered about fate; who has lost faith in prayer but continued to pray anyway; and for whom the moment seemed to signify everything. I felt that there was no need to focus on the graphic detail of death that would hijack Sara's experience. Instead, I aim to focus on an empathetic connection, one that can carry forward in a way that does not re-create but alludes to the horror and to the unspeakable.

The Unspeakable

Many post-colonial writers have reflected on what to do and to write in face of the unspeakable. For Kenyan writer, Ngugi wa Thiongo, remembering is part of the process of decolonialization. The aim being that formerly colonized people can re-history and reclaim their own country and being.

Similarly, Toni Morrison's concept of "re-memory" is a way of re-creating the past that lives within individuals, peoples and nations. I suggest that this process of remembering or re-memorying and re-storying is part of healing—whether from colonization or other trauma, but more than this, it is part of taking charge of one's story both in the past and in the future. Further, there is a responsibility to do this that extends from individuals, to nations, to all those who hear or listen to stories. Canadian First Nations writer, Thomas King[10] and African American scholar, Saidiya Hartman,[11] both believe in the transformative power of the ability to construct a new, competing and subversive, history narrative in the face of the dominant and violent version of history of their people.[12] Hartman is explicit that retelling stories of violence must have an end-goal of subversion of that violence in a process of "reconstruction of society". She asks, "To what end does one conjure the ghosts of slavery if not to incite the hopes of transforming the present?" (171). To speak these stories is to speak a different truth.

However, in many ways, the violence of these stories is "unspeakable." That is, the violence of slavery, colonization, or other forms of violent domination, represents "violations of the social contract that are too terrible to utter aloud."[13] And yet, as above, post-colonial authors and others, insist upon the importance of speaking the unspeakable. These unspeakable stories, these unspeakable histories, are a condition of the present, and, as both King and Hartman argue, a precondition for imagining and creating a new future. Indeed, Leanne Simpson suggests that storytelling and the writing of stories can be a *method* that helps create a just reality.[14] This is a bold claim and is obviously not always the case, as writing can sometimes contribute to unjust realities.

Several writers have reflected on how trauma can initially prevent expression. Judith Herman's work on the effects of silencing and silenced stories in her book *Trauma and Recovery* is remarkable in the parallels that she draws between war veterans and victims of rape, both of whom are stymied by the way the world seems to present as a place that is unwilling, unready and unable to bear the stories of their experiences. According to Herman, survivors of trauma exhibit the same symptoms of post-traumatic stress syndrome (PTSD), implying that the effects of the battlefield may also be found in the domestic space, a terrifying collapse of insight.[15] Survivors of rape and war veterans remain vulnerable because their experiences shatter the way the world reveals itself. She quotes Leo Eitinger, a psychiatrist who worked with Nazi concentration camp survivors: "War and victims are something the community wants to forget; a wall of oblivion is drawn over everything painful and unpleasant [...] on one side victims who perhaps wish to forget but cannot, and on the other those [...] who very intensely both wish to forget and often succeed in doing so."[16] And yet, as Herman maintains, "atrocities refuse to be buried."[17] For Herman, it is not so much a responsibility to express the inexpressible, as it is an imperative impulse—there's no escape from the telling, even though the intention might be to relegate the accounts into wordless formations, like an opacity that prevents sight and access to understanding.

Other writers highlight how silence, not speaking or not writing, can be a form of expressive communication. Veena Das, in her work with women victims of violence in India, shows that along with the inexpressible burden of difficult knowledge, silence may also be a *tactic* used by victims to underscore the weight of horror of their experiences.[18] Das shows how some women in India decided to keep silent about their stories of trauma, refusing to pollute the world through words that might create the possibility of reoccurrence. They chose instead, to let their stories remain inside their bodies, like unbirthed babies.[19] Some chose to sit in silence, leaving their hair to grow, refusing to wash their bodies, being vessels of and embodying, but not verbalizing the tales they carry inside.[20]

It is important to recognize that these women were not simply passive. The silence of these women can be seen as gatekeeping, holding in anything that might interfere with the establishment of peace after mass violence.[21] Das explains their need to hold on to these stories, arguing that:

> there is a deep moral energy in the refusal to represent some violations of the human body, for these violations are seen as being against nature, as defining the limits of life itself... The intuition that some violations cannot be verbalized in everyday life is to recognize that work cannot be performed on these within the burned and numbed everyday. (90)

These women thus take on the responsibility of their individual and societal stories by refusing to continue the shattering of the moral order which their experiences represent. However, these women also mark their bodies out as polluted, speaking the trauma of their experiences visually in an embodied way. In other words, they both speak and do not speak the pollution of their stories; they are a constant reminder to society of past events and their visible pollution challenges society to take responsibility for the brutal past. But at the same time, in their silence, they do not continue the violation of the moral order.

Conversely, Toni Morrison insists that writers have a moral responsibility to "to rip off the veil drawn over proceedings 'too terrible to narrate'"[22] and that we must use the tools we have, even reinvent traditional tools, to tell them. For Morrison, it is the things that happened long ago that hold sway over us. The work of the writer, she asserts, is to alleviate this hold and mould it to help us ascertain who we are today. In her 1992 collection of essays, *Whiteness in the Literary Imagination*, Morrison observes the relegation of Black Americans to the edges of representation in literature, encased as sexualized and racialized beings who are also immutably powerless and voiceless in the American canon. Being only marginally represented, and then usually by white others, Black Americans remain only partially (or racially hyphenated) American.[23] That these representations are to be found in the literary canon of [white] American fiction must give us pause to think about what it means to claim a cultural identity that is founded on "a fiction of nationhood that is steeped in a toxin of [the] past."[24] Morrison is interested in implicating both white male writers and the *reader*,[25] a daring and necessary step in taking responsibility for the stories we acquire and read. She challenges storytellers to take responsibility to tell difficult stories, but, like the Indian women which Das discusses, Morrison places a responsibility on *all* members of a community for its stories.

Earlier writers have explored these themes in different ways. In Conrad's *Heart of Darkness* (1899), the responsibility of the storyteller is bound to the teller as an arbiter of, or an editor of pain. In the novel, the unnamed narrator positions the character Marlow as the person who carries the legacy of Kurtz back to Europe, representing a recreation of an image of the European in colonial Africa that we still see in the papers today. Kurtz is the savior, the entrepreneur, the brave and selfless man who dies in the Congo among the locals who mourn his death. Marlow knows, as does the reader, and the unnamed narrator and all three men sitting in a boat, that the telling of the story in the end will be defined by the measure of the audience's ability and capacity to receive the details. Kurtz' Intended, presented as the first audience of Marlowe's tale, is fragile in her beauty and innocence—a rendering of Europeans as unable and incapable of redress for the reality of European damage in colonial (and contemporary) Africa. Marlowe wants to protect the intended from the truth and so he tells her what she wants to hear—a protective fiction, even though Kurtz's last words were actually, "*the horror! The horror!*" Both the narrator and the reader recognize that he is guilty of painting over truth with something more palatable and representing this as the truth. More than this, the narrator comes to associate the horror with the intended and she thus comes to represent her own lack of awareness as well as the ignorance and inability of Europe to deal with the truth of its colonial interests and horrific activities in the Congo. Indeed, we're all implicated in the horror, especially after we have resolved it, as Marlow does, as the realization of the loss of preciousness. In this instance, the *not* telling, while still an act of gatekeeping represents a replacement of truth with a lie. Marlow makes, and must live with, his "choice of nightmares."[26]

Thus the challenges for Conrad, as indeed for the other researchers and writers above, *and* their readers is: what do you do with difficult knowledge? How much do you let it burden you? What is your responsibility to a terrible tale? What kind of world do you create with what you have heard or read? By the end of Conrad's tale, the Thames is still and dark and nature remains the ultimate witness, as I explore below. But after the telling is done, the responsibility for the tale remains with the audience.

Conclusion

The method of storytelling I used above is thus an attempt to recreate a world in which the personal and the global collapses through the experience of the story, bypassing the local and yet including, by the very act of creating a reading/writing (or telling/listening), the community of story production. Like Herman, I internalized the trauma of Sara's story and came to feel that it was a story that must be told in order to move beyond the unspeakable, both for myself and for the society from which this story arises. As Morrison advocates, it is the responsibility of the reader/listener to take the story forward in co-creation with the teller. The "choice of nightmares," as Marlow would have it, remains a difficult aspect of social repair among artists who need to document the horror without replicating it. Morrison's goal to claim a canon worthy of its culture is an important one for we who claim a heritage as rich as the Acholi one in northern Uganda. As King and Hartman advocate, who we become beyond a broken citizenry may yet be the result of the worlds we create through (re)membering and (re)storying ourselves.

In this chapter I have combined practice and theory to explore how writing can cut through the unspeakable. Memories drenched in pain are difficult to touch, to listen to and to engage with. Nevertheless, by focusing on a single story and then offering an imaginative response, my intention has been to highlight the difficulties of re-narrating painful stories. This obviously may not always be the best way to express the unspeakable, but it does provide an example of a practical way of dealing with and representing stories that are laden with traumatic experiences. This in turn can be a good way for laying the foundations for a sustainable peace:

> So we pass on stories and whisper to the bark of trees that still stand against the wind.

Notes

1. Each woman in the project had the opportunity to create a personal life history book as a keepsake for themselves. I was not involved in that part of the process.
2. Selected pieces from *Stories from the Dry Season* have been published in various publications but not yet as a unified manuscript.
3. This is in specific reference to cultural knowledge that seemed a useful resource for many women as the familiar in their lives fell away.
4. Ngũgi wa Thiong'o, *Re-membering Africa* (Nairobi, Kenya: East African Educational Publishers, 2009), 12.
5. Toni Morrison, *Beloved* (New York, NY: Alfred A. Knopf, 1987).
6. Not her real name.
7. The Women's Advocacy Network (WAN) is an offshoot of the Justice and Reconciliation Project, which was founded in 2012 in Gulu, Uganda.
8. It is customary among the Acholi people, in encountering a dead body, to place a branch or some leaves over it and apologize for disturbing its resting place. This encounter illustrates how Acholi custom allowed Sara to offer an act of placation to avoid vengeance from the dead. In a horrific moment, Sara's background and identity as an Acholi person allows her a space for conciliation and forgiveness.
9. Toni Morrison, *The Bluest Eye* (New York, NY: Vintage International, 2007 [1970]), 6.
10. Thomas King, *The Truth About Stories: A Native Narrative* (Toronto, CA: Anansi Press, 2003), 10.
11. Saidiya Hartman, *Lose Your Mother: A Journey Along the Atlantic Slave Trade Route* (New York, NY: Straus & Giroux, 2007), 171.
12. I am indebted to African American and African Canadian writers along with Canadian First Nations and Native American writers who continue to challenge the dominant histories of the Americas that have not fully appreciated the impact of genocide and slavery on the descendants of the peoples who experienced them.
13. Judith Herman, *Trauma and Recovery: The Aftermath of Violence—From Domestic Abuse to Political Terror* (New York: Basic Books, 1992). The 'unspeakable' also recognizes the terror and experience of atrocity for which language sometimes has no place as I develop in this chapter.

14. Leanne Simpson, *Dancing on Our Turtle's Back: Stories of NIshnaabeg Re-creation, Resurgence and a New Emergence* (Winnipeg, CA: ARP Books, 2011), 32–33.
15. Judith Herman, *Trauma*, 32.
16. Herman, *Trauma*, 1 and 8.
17. Herman, *Trauma*, 1.
18. Veena Das, *Life and Words: Exploring Violence and the Descent Into the Ordinary* (Berkeley, CA: University of California Press, 2007). Das is concerned with the expression of violence in stories as it intersects with the national narrative. She asks, "What is it to lose one's world?" (2). Das is interested in the effect of violent memories on people (8). For further reading on silence as a strategy that doesn't rule out the showing of the devastation, see Chapter 11, 'Revisiting Trauma Testimony and Political Community.'
19. Das, *Life and Words*, see Chapter 10, "Three Portraits on Grief and Mourning", 184–204.
20. Das, *Life and Words.*
21. Das, *Life and Words.*
22. Toni Morrison, "The Site of Memory", in *What Moves at the Margin: Selected Nonfiction*, ed. Carolyn C. Denard (Jackson, MI: University Press of Mississippi, 2008), 65–82. Toni Morrison describes the job of the writer as having the responsibility "to rip off the veil drawn over proceedings 'too terrible to narrate'" (70) as part of her insistence on giving voice to marginalized people who have not been able to take part in the discourse on their own lives.
23. Toni Morrison, "Black Matters", in *Playing in the Dark: Whiteness and the Literary Imagination* (New York, NY: Vintage, 1992), 1–28. In this lecture, Morrison focuses on her journey from reading as a reader to reading as a writer. As a writer who is also a Black woman and an American, Morrison provides an analogy of recognizing the fishbowl when all along she'd not missed the details inside it (17). The literary imagination is required in order to 'become' (4); it is a process of creation.
24. Toni Morrison, "The Nobel Lecture in Literature", in *What Moves at the Margins*, 198–208.
25. Toni Morrison, "Afterword", in *The Bluest Eye* (New York, NY: Plume, 1970), 214.
26. Conrad, *Heart of Darkness (A Norton Critical Edition)*, ed. Robert Kimbrough (New York: Norton, 1970), 63, 69. I co-opt this phrase for the title of the chapter to focus on the tension between telling and not telling; this is something that Marlow knows well. "It seemed to me that the house would collapse before I could escape, that the heavens would fall upon my head. The heavens do not fall for such a trifle. Would they have fallen, I wonder, if I had rendered Kurtz that justice which was his due? Hadn't he said he wanted only justice? But I couldn't. I could not tell her. It would have been too dark altogether…" (79).

CHAPTER 13

Literary Strains: The Challenges of Making Meaning and Promoting Peace Through Written Works

Alison Rice

Introduction

Four years after the 1994 genocide in Rwanda, ten African writers came together to contribute to a collaborative project dedicated to the memory of those who perished in the massacres. These writers hailed from different countries, cultures, and linguistic traditions, but they were united in their purpose to visit this troubled land in the aftermath of unimaginable violence and create written works that bore witness to what they learned during their travels. The texts that emerged from their trip belonged to different genres; some consisted of poems, others were travel narratives, and a number were novels. One of the most provocative publications inspired by this collectively conceived mission was written by a francophone author from Djibouti, Abdourahman Waberi. Waberi's *Harvest of Skulls* is a hybrid text that is part essay and part testimony, with bits of fiction intermingled

A. Rice (✉)
University of Notre Dame, Notre Dame, IN, USA
e-mail: arice1@nd.edu

J. Mitchell et al. (eds.), *Peacebuilding and the Arts*,
Rethinking Peace and Conflict Studies,
https://doi.org/10.1007/978-3-030-17875-8_13

throughout. There is no doubt that Waberi struggled with the writing of this unusual literary creation, as the very first sentence of his preface attests: "This work almost apologizes for existing."[1] He goes on to admit that his personal itinerary had consisted of no activism up to this point, and that this "human experience" in Rwanda has proven to be so "demanding," so "urgent," and so "grueling" that his natural response is to want to curl up and play dead. But his commitment to the project has prevailed nonetheless, and his perceived duty to respect the memory of the events of the genocide has led the accomplished author to reproduce some of them in textual form, all while placing an emphasis on the limitations of this written work: "This book does not have the pretention of explaining anything at all."[2]

It is clear that Waberi does not intend for his account of some of the atrocities of the Rwandan genocide to be an authoritarian text. He is faced with the anguish of writing about something that lies beyond representation, and he is quick to hark back to the probing, painful inquiry that he attributes to Romanian-born German-language poet Paul Celan: "How can one write after Auschwitz?"[3] Faced with the inadequacy of words to truly capture the "world and its turpitudes,"[4] confronted with the arduous task of writing in the wake of a tragic war, Waberi creates a text that is innovative in structure as well as potentially problematic, for it gives voice to those from both sides of the conflict. What is perhaps most mystifying in *Harvest of Skulls* is that the individuals who express themselves are not described or defined in any conventional way, so readers often do not know who is speaking. In addition, their words are not contained within quotation marks; so little or no distinction is made between opinions from individuals from opposite sides of the struggle, and any or all of these expressions could be mistaken for the narrator's. The result is that readers must attempt to figure out for themselves who various speakers might be, and discern the reasons behind such speech. When the perpetrators of the violence are allowed to provide some of the rationale for their horrific deeds, when bystanders are permitted to explain their inaction as mass murder took place around them, and when survivors are given a chance to recount anecdotes about the many family members they lost, the text may inspire readers to put away preconceived notions as they approach this work. Such a text might motivate them to realize that, rather than hastily assigning blame, it can be worthwhile to open up our ears to a variety of strains that make us aware of the complexity of this particular conflict. For many readers who find the genocide difficult to understand, the literary text provides a point of entry into comprehending such appalling actions without giving any definitive reasons for them. Even though the written endeavor isn't easy, Waberi effectively revives a series of episodes from the recent past in ways that will preserve this past in human memory. He does so not in order to reproduce the feelings of hatred and desire for vengeance that ultimately motivated such widespread killings, but in the hope that such emotions can be identified as potentially dangerous and thereby can be addressed and expressed, so that we may move forward.

Waberi's literary venture in *Harvest of Skulls* involves the transposition of oral accounts into the text. Taking the spoken words of others and placing them into a written work is a complicated gesture that often weighs heavily upon authors who are aware of the responsibility involved in such an undertaking. This is the challenge that Juliane Okot Bitek articulates with tremendous subtlety earlier in this volume in her essay "What Choice between Nightmares?". According to her analysis, the writer must respect the inimitability of each story, as well as the unique perspective of the person who tells it, all while rendering the story comprehensible to readers who may come from a very different background. Preserving the local and appealing to the universal values in each experience is the difficult textual enterprise that Bitek engages in when she feels compelled to tell another woman's story in poetic language. Like Waberi, Bitek grapples with the "inexpressibility of traumatic stories" and, like him, she opts for a literary creation that is concerned less with providing dates and facts than it is with "access[ing] the senses, evok[ing the] hearing, feeling and memory of the inaccessible," as Bitek so eloquently puts it. Bitek is aware of the danger of reinforcing negative sentiments through written accounts of misdeeds, and that is why she insists upon the importance of telling stories in a manner that will not perpetuate the hurt forward, but that will "vaccinate" instead. This is a powerful metaphor for literature's potential to prevent further harm and suffering from the social diseases that plague us. While Waberi addresses a similar possibility that today's pen can "heal" yesterday's wounds,[5] Bitek's emphasis on a changed future that is communicated through the verb "vaccinate" is especially encouraging because of its implications for an improved life for many in the years to come. While we certainly hope to come to terms with the events of faulty pasts through literature, it is an even nobler goal to prevent such events from recurring, and this is the promise of Bitek's conception of literary work.

In their complementary reflections on storytelling among women in Northern Uganda in this volume, Ketty Anyeko and Tamara Shaya also evoke the "possibility of retraumatization" inherent in the revisiting of painful events. As Sandra Gustafson astutely pinpoints in her introductory chapter to this section on literature "narrative also has the potential to reinforce or even escalate real-world conflicts." Works of literature come up against a great challenge when their authors seek to do justice to the past without creating texts that remain entrenched in a discourse of anger or retribution and that might stir up deeply negative feelings among their readers. While written texts possess the capacity to reveal wrongs, their movement should inevitably be in the direction of reconciliation. When Gustafson underscores the potential to "restory" a narrative, taking up John Paul Lederach's concept from *Moral Imagination*, she hints that various versions of stories are possible, that alternative understandings of these stories are feasible, and that learning to engage in close readings of texts is an invaluable tool when it comes to the study of literature.

Literature is a unique discipline because of its focus on the interpretation of words and their multiple meanings, and while precise study of its structure is often indispensable to determining the sense of a particular passage, what makes certain works of literature especially rich is that they do not contain a single meaning, but instead lend themselves to a variety of possible valid understandings. What is crucial to the work of literature is that it cannot be paraphrased. In other words, the text cannot be rendered "in other words," because its form is indispensable to its message. *How* something is communicated is just as important as *what* is communicated. Meaning is inextricably connected to the form that meaning takes on. What makes a text truly literary is that it *couldn't be said otherwise*, and this is what Bitek is pointing toward as she seeks to explain in detail the intimately creative process in her contribution to this volume. What makes this task so deeply difficult in her case is that this is not her own story to tell. This is the conundrum that celebrated Algerian-born francophone author Assia Djebar's struggles in both her novels and essays. Djebar highlights the challenges of adequately representing the stories and struggles of the women from her homeland in her work. She wants to valorize the storytelling tradition that reigns among the Berber women of her mother's tribe by putting their words in written form. She aspires to testify to the suffering of these women at different points in her country's history, including victimization at the hands of the French colonizers dating back to the conquest of Algeria in 1830, as well as struggles during the war for independence between 1954 and 1962, and more recent difficulties in the decade of civil war in the 1990s. But the author feels that she cannot properly tell the stories of these women she holds dear, that her literary efforts will fall short and inevitably betray the truths of their lived experience. Perhaps the greatest source of anguish for Djebar is that she is obliged to translate her countrywomen's oral accounts from her mother's tongue, Berber, into French, the language of the former colonizer. Translating a voice from one language to another is a difficult enterprise, no matter what the circumstances, and Djebar is certain that her efforts have not reached their goal: "I have captured your voice; disguised it with my French without clothing it. I barely brush the shadow of your footsteps."[6] The task of translating is rendered unspeakably painful for this author, for the only language in which she is capable of writing is a tongue with a history of rape and murder in her land, as she states in stark terms: "This language was formerly used to entomb my people."[7] Even though the context complicates her work, Djebar does not renounce her objective of bringing to light the experiences of women from her homeland. At the same time, she denies the role of spokesperson, insisting that she does not wish to be seen as someone who represents others who hail from her birthplace. An awareness of the colossal responsibility placed on someone who plays that role is what makes her speak out against its assignation. In a particularly poignant passage, she explains what she attempts to do through literary composition: "I do not claim to 'speak for' or worse, 'speak about,' but to gently speak *close to* and, if possible, *right up against*."[8] Djebar attempts to be as near as possible, to be physically and emotionally next to the women whose stories she tells. The idea of proximity that is communicated in this quotation comes through in a turn of phrase that is similar in English and in French, in which the potentially negative word "against" becomes positive when it is part of the larger expression "right up against," indicating that close, careful listening is an integral part of Djebar's written rendering of the stories recounted by others.

Listening "heartfully" is at the center of Juliane Okot Bitek's quest to meaningfully relate the story of another woman, as she expresses it in a neologism in this volume. This emphasis on listening, on listening in specific ways, is of great importance to an understanding of the possibilities of literature for promoting peace. The French feminist theorist Luce Irigaray has argued in favor of listening "with another ear," in order to perceive significations that may lie outside typical means of communication, "as if hearing *an 'other meaning' always in the process of weaving itself, of embracing itself with words, but also of getting rid of words in order not to become fixed, congealed in them.*"[9] As Ketty Anyeko and Tamara Shaya reveal earlier in this section on Literature, victimized women occasionally shy away from words; they sometimes deliberately "use silence … to protect themselves from harm, particularly when their memories contradict metanarratives of victimhood." These silences are not devoid of import. In fact, rather than failing to signify, moments of silence are often pregnant with meaning. Allowing various forms of silence to come through in the literary text is something Algerian writer Assia Djebar does in innovative ways, ranging from the use of ellipses to inserting blank spaces on the page. Just as a rest in music serves as an indispensable part of the score, so these indications of silence in Djebar's novels play a crucial role in creating significance. Scholars of literature learn to study texts with an ear tuned to possible exclusions, paying attention to what is omitted alongside what is made explicit.

In a very intimate narrative composed in French by an Algerian-born woman writer named Zahia Rahmani, the first-person narrator describes the silence that characterizes her adopted country's treatment of her. Though she has lived in France since the age of five when she and her family fled their native country to save their lives, she has never felt accepted in her new place of residence. This is because she and others like her suffer from their status as the offspring of *harki*, Algerian soldiers who fought on behalf of France during the Algerian War. As Rahmani explains it, the children of traitors carry within them their fathers' "betrayal" of their countrymen, and they lead their lives as "banished" figures devoid of a homeland.[10] What is striking in Rahmani's autobiographical text is that she finds solace in literary works that come from what may appear to be an unexpected location. She maintains that she cannot connect with French literature, since this tradition is concerned with a certain class and a social situation that are far removed from the immigrant's humble existence in the countryside. The literary texts that touch her, that provide her with a sense of belonging, depict characters and landscapes from a great distance. It is American literature that reaches out to her, that speaks to her. It is with the characters in the books written by Hemingway, Fitzgerald, Steinbeck, Caldwell, Melville, Faulkner, and Williams that Rahmani takes refuge from a society that condemns her.[11] Richard Wright's *Black Boy* serves as a special revelation to her, for the title character is "a stranger in his country," and she vows "a filial respect and a faithfulness" to literary creations like this one because they are "devoted" to those who are "uprooted, to humans who have been torn, and to their steps" in positive directions, to their desires to hold onto hope and realize their dreams.[12] It is thanks to this "empathic identification" with individuals who possess very different backgrounds but encounter problems that resonate with her own that Rahmani finds the inspiration to achieve her goals in the academic setting and beyond.[13]

In 2010, an article came out in a Turkish newspaper that compellingly lauded the capacities of literature to inspire empathic identification.[14] Composed of interviews with a variety of authors, the article was written following a deadly Israeli raid on the Mavi Marmara aid ship, an action that attracted such vehement responses on an international scale that the blockade of the Gaza Strip was scaled down. The article's author, Kitap Zamani, was not interested in taking sides in this terrible conflict. On the contrary, he was eager to examine a new alternative that he argued would be particularly effective in promoting peace in the Middle East: "The attack, which cannot be justified by any means, was a reminder once again that violence cannot be a solution. The critical topic has been addressed by political, economic, military, social and religious circles, but what it needs most is another look from a literary perspective." Zamani was convinced that literature can lead to the much-needed understanding of others that is indispensable to conflict resolution: "Literature and the artisans of literature aren't decision makers when it comes to a solution. Yet it is undeniable that the sway of authors when it comes to getting people to understand one another is unparalleled." Among the renowned writers who responded to Zamani's inquiries figured Amos Oz, who thoughtfully affirmed that literature plays an indispensable role in peace processes: "What an author can do is to tell the people's story and ensure that people on the other side listen to it. Only in this way can we be saved from stereotypical thoughts." It is noteworthy that Oz should speak in terms of storytelling and listening, for these words underscore the type of meaning-making that figures so prominently in this literary section of the present volume. Allowing women to tell their stories, and making these stories heard, is what resonates throughout the contributions of Juliane Okot Bitek, Ketty Anyeko and Tamara Shaya. What is absolutely crucial is that the right type of reading—a close reading akin to attentive listening—accompany literary storytelling that combats negative stereotypes. In her discussion of Joseph Conrad's novel *Heart of Darkness*, Bitek maintains that listeners must be open to receiving the message of any story, otherwise the storytelling will be ineffective: "the telling of the story in the end will be defined by the measure of the audience's ability and capacity to receive the details." Coming to the literary work with the right attitude is indispensable to reading it with ears that are open to what it has the capacity to impart.

Listening Up: Testimony, Truth, and Taking Action

In her book devoted to texts written by individuals who have undergone torture, Kate Millett has recourse to the French term "*témoignage*" to refer to the particular type of writing under study, "the literature of the witness."[15] She insists on the fluidity of this genre that "crosses" typical boundaries and "can be autobiography, reportage, even narrative fiction." While it may contain elements of fiction, this writing is nonetheless based in "fact passionately lived and put into writing by a moral imperative rooted like a flower amid carnage with an imperishable optimism, a hope that those who hear will care, will even take action."[16] If the testimonial genre is especially apt to inspire positive transformations that take place beyond the printed page, then there can be no question as to its relevance for peace studies. The optimism that Millett highlights in her analyses of texts written by survivors is an outlook that is worthy of embrace. The critic's assertions underscore the fact that testimonial writing possesses the power to move people to effect real change in the world. Indeed, if some readers are likely to take action in response to the sobering revelations of the written work since it has made them sensitive to another's plight, then this form of literary creativity should be valorized for its positive potential.

But it is necessary to mention that those who wish to promote peace around the world through the writing or reading of works of literature must exercise wisdom in their interpretations, as well as in their resulting actions. In their elaboration of the concept of "strategic peacebuilding," John Paul Lederach and Scott Appleby recognize that effective approaches "must take cognizance of their 'echo effect' in related areas of the conflict," for "practices that seek to forge solutions or end disputes" have potential "implications for other official and unofficial mediation practices."[17] Given the ongoing emphases on "listening" and "hearing" in literature that we find in the comments of writers and theorists alike, the term "echo effect" has particular resonance for the domain of literature. While it carries positive connotations for literary texts that play a role in bringing peace to lands that have been plagued by violent conflict, this expression is wisely employed in a cautionary tone in the above quotation. Writing, in various forms, can sustain hope in the midst of war and restore a sense of unity to those who are bereaved and helpless in its wake. But we must be wary of the possibly negative ripples of written works that take up violence and loss as their topics. We must also be aware of the difficulty and complexity of adequately responding to certain texts, particularly when their content is not always simple to discern.

The testimonial texts that Millett touts for their indecipherability, as their authors move among genres in an effort to appropriately represent in writing the difficult moments of lived experience, are sometimes challenging precisely because they are so hard to decipher. Since they depend heavily on the reliability of the memories of individuals who have been through tremendous ordeals, who have often undergone enormous suffering, these written works might also incorporate dreams, or even nightmares, as Juliane Okot Bitek illustrates so well in this volume. The line between what was imagined and what was actually endured might be blurred in these literary creations, and the memories evoked might not be entirely lucid. In their jointly authored study, *Testimony: Crises of Witnessing in Literature, Psychoanalysis, and History*, Shoshana Felman and Dori Laub make explicit the possibly tenuous relationship between memory and testimony. In the introduction to this work, they assert: "As a relation to events, testimony seems to be composed of bits and pieces of a memory that has been overwhelmed by occurrences that have not settled into understanding or remembrance, acts that cannot be constructed as knowledge nor assimilated into full cognition, events in excess of our frames of reference."[18] What literature helps readers to understand is precisely that sometimes we are unable to fully understand, that sometimes we must come to terms with how "not to know," as French author and critic Hélène Cixous explains: "One of the first lessons about living is the one that consists of *knowing how not to know*, which does not mean not knowing, but knowing how to not know, knowing how to avoid getting closed in by knowledge, knowing more and less that what one knows, knowing how not to understand, while never being on the side of ignorance."[19] As the closing phrase of this quotation reveals, Cixous is not advocating lack of knowledge. Rather, she is decidedly in favor of seeking truth through careful considerations of the text, and she is pointing out the importance of understanding that sometimes we will not emerge from the reading experience with a clear comprehension of what we have learned from it. In this view, it is essential to remain open to later revelations about any given text, as well as to revised readings that may shed additional light on the work and its many possible meanings. This stance is crucial to a reading process that is ongoing and always fresh.[20]

As Felman and Laub specify in their conception of the term, "In its most traditional, routine use [...] testimony is provided, and is called for, when the facts upon which justice must pronounce its verdict are not clear, when historical accuracy is in doubt and when both the truth and its supporting elements of evidence are called into question."[21] The legal implications of testimony are weighty, for when witnesses are called to provide testimony in a courtroom setting, what they say can influence a judgment. Their words have the power of determining whether a decision of innocence or guilt is made in the judicial system. When we transpose testimony to a different setting and insert it into creative written work, it is important to ask questions about the specificity of this method of human communication and its import. When we approach a literary text containing testimony, we cannot help but ask ourselves the following questions. What is the role of fictional works in bearing witness? To what extent do they recreate the past, revive individual memory, contribute to collective and historical memory, and participate in a movement toward "justice"? How do they evoke the possible shortcomings of memory and the uncertainties of fully knowing that might threaten the truth of testimony in the aftermath of traumatic events?

Abdourahman Waberi cannot help but pose questions about the effectiveness of literature when he sets out to write a text devoted to the genocide in Rwanda. He finds himself obliged to express his doubts, taking up his personal questionings in an incantatory style: "You say to yourself that literature, this factory of illusions, with its suspension of disbelief, remains derisory. You say to yourself that fiction can hardly remedy such a situation."[22] Though he may not be sure of the written text's outcome, Waberi indicates that he is nonetheless moved to write because of an understanding he gleaned from Wole Soyinka's *The Open Sore of the Continent: A Personal Narrative of the Nigerian Crisis.* Waberi attributes to the Nigerian poet the idea that "One death is a tragedy, but a million deaths are a simple statistic."[23] In response, Waberi asserts that "Our humanity demands that we give, even for just a few moments, a face, a name, a voice, and a living memory to the hundreds of thousands of victims, so that they will not simply be synonymous with figures, or worse, precipitated into the vaults of forgetting."[24] He wants to strengthen our collective consciousness by preserving what would otherwise quickly be lost forever. The sentence that follows the aforementioned moments of questioning in Waberi's preface indicates that, if literature is not the ideal way to touch people, there is no perfect way to reach a potential public: "You say to yourself that journalistic testimony is not any more efficacious in this globalized world racked with indifference, for it may be well informed, but it is little inclined to react promptly and efficiently."[25]

In order to react appropriately to literary texts, we must be open not only to learning about others and engaging in "*empathic identification*," according to Adolf, but we must also be cognizant of the fact that "peace literature can facilitate *empathic ascription*, by which writers and readers become able to examine their intellectual and affective preconceptions with regard to content, contexts, and correlates."[26] Literature can contribute to our self-awareness. It can help us discover what prejudices lie within us that taint our approach to the written work. Both the experience of writing and that of reading participate in this coming to terms with what we may have previously ignored about our own presuppositions and stereotypes. And this will change not only how we read and accept the truths of a text, but also what we do with those truths. When we write and read in subtle and informed ways, then we move outside preconceived ideas about right and wrong, good and bad, and we begin to perceive things differently, outside of binaries, of opposites, that fail to take into account the complexity that is restored through the literary text. When Sandra Gustafson calls for a "literary critique-as-*more*" in her introduction to this section, when she lauds the possibility of reading in terms of "both/and" rather than "either/or," she is pointing toward an understanding of literature that moves outside of reductive reasoning and that is thereby ready to embrace multiple meanings and varying solutions. She is also describing an attitude that can lead to appropriate responses to literary revelations.

While Waberi is right to shed doubt on the efficacy of literature in the early stages of his text, one might counter his hesitancies with an argument that written works are the response *par excellence* to the question of how to touch readers with truths that are not as effectively communicated through other means. Stories, with their rhythms and flows, with their intimacies and idiosyncrasies, move people in ways that differ from factual accounts and statistical lists. Fiction is not synonymous with falsehood. To the contrary, creative literary works often possess the capacity to communicate truths with great effect, as Zahia Rahmani realizes with respect to her mother's transmission of her family's history. This illiterate parent who has been transplanted to France insists on the importance of giving her children a sense of inheritance, a sentiment of pride in their past. She instills in them a feeling of belonging that transcends the prejudice that surrounds them by relating their "familial saga" through "tales" and "fables."[27] Her creative words give her offspring something that helps them stand up to the denial of the past that marks this postcolonial, postwar environment: "Colonialism annihilated these inheritors so that this memory would not subsist."[28] But this memory lives on, thanks to the stories of a persistent mother, stories telling the "epic song" of a people, of their "history" and "vocation," and these stories, narrated aloud, are decidedly literary; we just have to learn how to listen.[29]

Rahmani describes the men and women in her small French town as content to remain in the "coma of their lives," unaware of the foreigners who live among them, oblivious to the violent history between Algeria and France that is not included in the textbooks of their schools.[30] They are not interested in learning, and they are even less interested in culture: "In my village, those whom I know do not possess any books. None of them go to the theater. Nobody listens to music. The cinema doesn't exist. Art, history, literature — all that can nourish thought — is foreign to these inhabitants."[31] These people are not ill intentioned; they are simply ignorant. As Rahmani explains, "They cannot conceive that I do not wish to resemble them."[32] They do not want to hear the person who lives in their midst who has another story to tell, one that diverges from their narrow set of experiences and resulting mindset. They cannot even begin to comprehend her difference, in part because they have never engaged in experiences that would bring them to see another perspective, such as reading a work of literature, examining a piece of art, attending a theatrical production, or watching a film. Exposure to the arts might rid them of their complacency and inspire them to feel in new ways. If they came to literary works with open minds, for instance, the reading experience would elicit what Adolf identifies as "ethical and affective reader responses."[33] These would not be prescriptive reactions to texts. Instead, these responses would remain open to Waberi's understanding of literature as containing the possibility of healing, if we learn to listen with our hearts. Listening in this way does not preclude the use of our critical faculties. If we hear Waberi's use of the French word "*panser*," meaning "to heal," as intricately tied to, even inseparable from its homophone "*penser*," which signifies "to think," then we might be heading in the right direction.[34] This aural connection should move us to consider the *healing* that can come through writing and reading works of literature as inextricable from the *thinking* that goes into these literary processes of making meaning and seeking appropriate responses to the truths of these texts. Engaging with literary texts is not easy, since the efforts required of those who read and write works that grapple with painful pasts and contentious contemporary issues are considerable. This is one of the meanings of "literary strains." Such efforts will test the limits of our understanding and push us outside of our comfort zones, forcing us to face preconceptions, prejudices, and insecurities. But these efforts can also be deeply rewarding, for the expression "literary strains" also refers to the melodic, polyphonic outcomes of written compositions that sing, forever differently and in combinations that are ever new, of the possibilities of peace.

Notes

1. Abdourahman A. Waberi, *Moisson de crânes* [*Harvest of Skulls*] (Paris, France: Le Rocher, 2004), 13.
2. Waberi, *Harvest*, 14.
3. Waberi, *Harvest*, 14.
4. Waberi, *Harvest*, 15.
5. Waberi, *Harvest*, 17.
6. Assia Djebar, *Fantasia: An Algerian Cavalcade*, trans. Dorothy S. Blair (Portsmouth, NH: Heinemann, 1993), 202.
7. Djebar, *Fantasia*, 215.
8. Djebar, *Femmes d'Alger dans leur appartement [Women of Algiers in Their Apartment]* (Paris, France: Des femmes, 1980), 8.
9. Luce Irigaray, *This Sex Which Is Not One*, trans. Catherine Porter (Ithaca, NY: Cornell University Press, 1985), 29, emphasis in the original.
10. Zahia Rahmani, *France, récit d'une enfance* [*France, Story of a Childhood*] (Paris, France: Sabine Wespieser, 2006), 101.
11. Rahmani, *France*, 58.
12. Rahmani, *France*, 59–60.
13. Antony Adolf asserts that peace literature "elicits an *empathic identification* between readers, writers, contents and contexts beyond identitarianism, because it can and does happen across identities." Antony Adolf, "What Does Peace Literature Do? An Introduction to the Genre and Its Criticism", *The Canadian Journal of Peace and Conflict Studies* 42:1–2 (2010): 13. In this volume, Sandra Gustafson mentions the fact that scholars from various academic disciplines, such as historian Lynn Hunt and philosopher Martha Nussbaum, "suggest that the modern novel can nurture latent capacities for identification and empathy."
14. Kitap Zamani, "Israeli Writers Reflect on Literature's Role in Peacemaking", *Today's Zaman*, 6 July 2010. http://www.todayszaman.com/tz-web/news-215226-101-israeli-writers-reflect-on-literatures-role-in-peacemaking.html. Accessed 20 February 2014.
15. Kate Millett, *The Politics of Cruelty: An Essay on the Literature of Political Imprisonment* (New York, NY: Norton, 1994), 15.

16. Millet, *The Politics of Cruelty*, 15.
17. John Paul Lederach and R. Scott Appleby, "Strategic Peacebuilding: An Overview", in *Strategies of Peace: Transforming Conflict in a Violent World*, eds. Daniel Philpott and Gerard F. Powers (Oxford, UK and New York, NY: Oxford University Press, 2010), 38.
18. Shoshana Felman and Dori Laub, *Testimony: Crises of Witnessing in Literature, Psychoanalysis, and History* (New York, NY: Routledge, 1992), 5.
19. Hélène Cixous, *"Coming to Writing" and Other Essays*, ed. Deborah Jenson (Cambridge, MA: Harvard University Press, 1991), 161.
20. Rereading works of the past in new ways is a deeply pertinent exercise, as critic Edward Said has argued: "Each cultural work is a vision of a moment, and we must juxtapose that vision with the various revisions it later provoked." Edward Said, *Culture and Imperialism* (New York, NY: Knopf, 1994), 67. Some perspectives on peace studies as a literary discipline have focused on rereading great canonical works through a new lens. Laurence Lerner has advocated for examining texts by prominent authors such as Shakespeare and Milton with attention to the ways in which "organized conflict and its dangers can lead to [...] insights when studying literature." Laurence Lerner, "Peace Studies: A Proposal", *New Literary History* 26:3 (1995): 643.
21. Felman and Laub, *Testimony*, 6.
22. Waberi, *Harvest*, 16.
23. Waberi, *Harvest*, 17.
24. Waberi, *Harvest*, 17.
25. Waberi, *Harvest*, 16.
26. Adolf, "Peace Literature", 13.
27. Rahmani, *France*, 116.
28. Rahmani, *France*, 116.
29. Rahmani, *France*, 115.
30. Rahmani, *France*, 126.
31. Rahmani, *France*, 119.
32. Rahmani, *France*, 119.
33. Adolf, "Peace Literature", 12.
34. Waberi, *Harvest*, 17.

PART IV

Film

CHAPTER 14

Catalyzing Peace: Re-humanizing Through Embodied Experience of Cinema

Joseph G. Kickasola

Introduction: Cautionary Tales

The romantic comedy *Miss Congeniality* (2000) turns on the amusing idea that Gracie, an undercover cop, must root out crime and corruption within the vain and insular world of an American beauty pageant.[1] Annoyed at her assignment, Gracie finds herself on a television stage, jammed into an evening gown, waiting to be asked "What is the most important thing our society needs?" Contestant after plastic contestant flashes a smile and responds: "World peace," and each time, the crowd roars with enthusiasm. When Gracie's turn comes, she strikes the obligatory pose and answers: "Harsher punishment for parole violators, Stan…" Silence. Crickets chirp. Gracie hastily adds: "… and… world peace." The audience cheers and jumps to its feet.

J. G. Kickasola (✉)
Baylor University, Waco, TX, USA
e-mail: joe_kickasola@baylor.edu

J. Mitchell et al. (eds.), *Peacebuilding and the Arts*,
Rethinking Peace and Conflict Studies,
https://doi.org/10.1007/978-3-030-17875-8_14

Has "world peace" become the generic answer because no one seriously expects anyone to attempt it? Turning this important ideal into a catch-phrase remains significantly easier than, say, implementing justice, constraining violent evil, or resisting the urge to vengeance after one's family has been slaughtered. *Miss Congeniality* winkingly critiques the vacuity of de-humanizing, mediatized spectacle, but also poses an implicit challenge for us: can film do anything positive for the cause of peace without lapsing into meaningless commodification?[2] If it can, we must first get beyond pat phrases and oversimplified stories that fail to reflect the hard, long-suffering work peacebuilding requires.

In this same vein, another question should be considered first: how might *false* conceptions of peace be "sold" in the screening of them? Consider how the following example did so, and paved the way for war.[3] A trumpet sounds, and intensifies, as the opening shot fades up to a close up of the instrument and a camera moves in upon its bell. This is followed by pounding, insistent drums, played by children. We then see expanding shots of children, row after row, standing at attention, intercut with others, overcome with enthusiasm and anticipation. Suddenly, arms rise in salute in a canted composition, amplifying the power of allegiance by sheer gravitational means (Fig. 14.1).

Adolph Hitler salutes, and gradually ascends *above* the "eye level" of the camera (where he will remain). In crystal focus, he rises over the sea of humanity he commands. His power appears irresistible. The band shifts to a military anthem, and the scale of the shots becomes more intimate. *Der Führer*'s watchful close-up edits tightly against numerous faces of German youths in various poses of adoration. Only Hitler's gaze is fully visible, nearly on-line with the camera axis, commanding power (Fig. 14.2).

When he steps to the microphone, the camera begins to move, and will continue so in nearly every shot from this point forward. He announces "a German movement," as the camera tracks past face after youthful face. Those shots alternate Hitler's visage, suggesting he is the dynamic force that will unite them all. The camera surveys him as if he were a monument, moving from side to side with an upward gaze of admiration. This visual-motoric trope ties him to a long history of strong, exalted leaders, and renders him imposing and powerful (Fig. 14.3).

> And what does Hitler have to say to the future of Germany?
> "We want a society with neither caste nor ranks…"

Fig. 14.1 *The Triumph of the Will*. Dir. Leni Riefenstahl (Berlin, Germany: Reichsparteitag-Film, 1935). Film stills, used by permission of Das Bundesarchiv, Berlin, Germany

> "We want this people to be obedient, and you must practice obedience in yourselves."
>
> "We want this people to be peace-loving, but at the same time to be courageous. And you must, for that reason, be both peace-loving..."
>
> The crowd erupts with thunderous applause and outstretched arms. His face radiates satisfaction.
>
> "You must be both peace-loving... and strong."

What made *Triumph of the Will* (1936) feel so utterly *right* to its initial viewers? No doubt, there were many factors, but we cannot ignore the basic irony here: Hitler sold the coming war with the language of peace, and cinematic power helped him do it. We see, here, a cautionary tale for cinematic peacebuilding.

Two central lessons have emerged that will serve as background for this exploration of cinema and peacebuilding. The first is obvious from our examples: cinema is an ethically nuanced and complicated affair, culturally contextualized in numerous ways, and should not be viewed simplistically or in isolation. "World peace" as a theme is not enough. Merely flooding

Fig. 14.2 *The Triumph of the Will*. Dir. Leni Riefenstahl (Berlin, Germany: Reichsparteitag-Film, 1935). Film stills, used by permission of Das Bundesarchiv, Berlin, Germany

the market with hastily conceived, simplistic "peace-themed" movies will likely lead to disappointing results and the commodification of our most cherished ideals. *Miss Congeniality* demonstrates that we can commodify and de-humanize peace through overuse and de-contextualization. More nefariously, *Triumph of the Will* instructs us in the manipulation of "humanizing" rhetoric (verbal and cinematic) toward a fascist (and, ultimately, warmongering) end. The second lesson lies more implicitly in the cinematic technique of that film, and so requires more elaboration: cinema is every bit an embodied experience as it is a cognitive one, and its persuasive powers—for true or false peace—hinge upon that dynamic. Once we understand this better, we may begin to see some ways that peacebuilding and the cinema can find an effective partnering.

In this essay I hope to promote that understanding, while exploring how the cinema can play a role in re-humanizing conflict situations, avoiding the pitfalls discussed above. I do so through extended discussion of what "re-humanization" might mean and outlines some fundamental "target zones" for re-humanizing cinema. This is not a "recipe" for peace through

Fig. 14.3 *The Triumph of the Will*. Dir. Leni Riefenstahl (Berlin, Germany: Reichsparteitag-Film, 1935). Film stills, used by permission of Das Bundesarchiv, Berlin, Germany

cinema, as if such a thing were possible, but, a re-imagination of the cinema as a tool in multivalent, multidisciplinary peacebuilding efforts.

The Cinema, the Human, and Re-humanization

Cinema generates significant experiences at numerous levels; it is not the same as "real life," of course (and it is problematic to assume too much correspondence), but it does emulate our general experience of perception of the real in a number of significant ways.[4] Attention to this "simulative" power of cinema, and particularly its affectual/sensual/embodied dimension, harmonizes with the general turn toward embodied approaches in the humanities, film studies, and cognitive theory.[5] "Experience," in this context, refers to the way all our faculties—sensory, affectual, emotional, cognitive, rational, perceptual, and so on—work in concert to apprehend and engage the world before us. Cinema presents us with an experientially charged "world" in which to engage those faculties without the normal consequences of doing so; to "run our emotions off-line," as the philosopher Gregory Currie argued some time ago.[6] It can be a type of rehearsal or practice of those faculties; the cognitive film theorist Torben Grodal has even called the cinema a type of "cognitive fitness center."[7] It is incumbent upon us to use that "practice" wisely and discriminately.[8] For instance, the cinema can be used to simulate situations that may encourage humane feelings when they are sorely lacking.

But what do we mean by "humane feeling?" These are feelings that support not just human rights and fellow feeling for other humans, but help to shore up essential human qualities, so often damaged in conflict situations. In *Moral, Believing Animals: Human Personhood and Culture* Christian Smith says contemporary sociological theory has overlooked two truths about humanity that remain essential for human persons: we are inherently "moral" (that is, morality of some kind guides our choices), and we are inherently "believing," in the sense that we very often act on presuppositions (i.e., unprovable starting points, acts of faith, for everyone, religious and nonreligious alike).[9] For example, one such presupposition is that the world is real, and we are a part of it.

The philosopher Matthew Ratcliffe argues that even the "believing" part of Smith's formula is affectually and somatically foundationalized. That is to say, belief is *felt*, resting on foundational pre-cognitive assumptions, so the act is not wholly rational.[10] The cinema, as one of the great mediums of human feeling, contributes not just to momentary experiences but to beliefs about the way the world is. The goal of peacebuilding through cinema is often to help others feel that peace is possible, when it previously felt impossible. In a sense, we strive to expand the experiential parameters of reality for those who struggle to see peace as a real and desirable ideal.

At the end of his book Smith adds one more "human essential" to his formula: "we are moral, believing, *narrating* animals."[11] Stories are one of the primary ways humans make sense of the world, and cinema is one of the great narrativizing mediums… but we have already perceived a challenge here. Cinema always functions with multiple levels of "story" in operation and the largest narratives are often the ones most fraught with the danger of being propagandistic or counterproductive, such as the implicit narrative in *Triumph of the Will*: "Germany is destined to be the greatest nation in history."

The overarching "cultural" narratives that define politics—and wars, and the peoples that fight them—are what emerge from years and years of smaller narratives clashing and convulsing in the culture. Often, the most effective stories that the narrative arts offer us are experiential, best used to help us *feel* (and, so, understand in a *felt* way) all the "clashing and convulsing" that created the conditions for the larger, political narrative conflict.[12] If we are to discover how aesthetic forms prime us for peace (psychologically, culturally, and spiritually) we may do well to shift down a level from the larger political or cultural narrative, to the personal story that eventually interacted with, and *gave rise* to, the larger narratives. For example, a larger narrative may be "a disaffected group becomes a militant organization," but the smaller narrative focuses on how this came to be on the human level: an individual's need for social identity, the breakdown of basic social structures for varying reasons, and the comforts of "solidarity" found in joining a group with common interests, challenges, and goals.

This is not to suggest that one can clinically extract and completely separate these levels of narrative, but only to recommend a new focus, in keeping with the practice of successful mediators like Giandomenico Picco.[13] Picco argues that the larger narratives often function as a fortress, a bulwark against fear, whereas the smaller narrative formulation offers more access to what might be universally human in any given situation: "It was only later when I had real encounters with people who had suffered as a result of war that I was obliged to think about how we all inhabit a similar emotional world of pain and pleasure, hopes and fears."[14] In telling the stories at this level, we might be able to identify the conditions whereby this "comfort seeking," so often misdirected in conflict situations, can be redirected.

Having established the embodied, experiential, and narrative dimensions of cinema, and their overlaps with some critical elements of "the human" we are prepared to more specifically define what re-humanization might be, as a response to the de-humanizing forces of conflict. I'm using the notion of "de-humanizing" as it is commonly used to describe contemporary, overly commodified society (which reduces individuals to numbers and marketing targets), but also in the way that conflict naturally encourages adversaries to be seen in simplistic, objectifying terms, so as to justify committing violence against them, treat them as less than human, or deny them basic human rights.[15] The notion of "re-humanization" is more complicated, as it seeks to repair that which has been horribly broken, and each scenario will require a different amalgam of efforts and strategies depending on the needs.[16] And yet, some basic principles can be gleaned and addressed here. John Paul Lederach, a leading scholar in Peace Studies and a contributor to the section in this book on Music, broaches this notion in his essay "The Long

Journey Back to Humanity," wherein he declares that "reclaiming human dignity" is a critical part of the way "back to humanity" (a synonymous phrase for re-humanization).[17] For a practical application of this principle, he quotes Latin American peacemaker Father Rafael Cárdenas Ortiz: "I always remind myself that behind that pointed gun is a person, a human being, somebody's son or daughter."[18]

Picco echoes this idea, from his own peacemaking efforts: "Behind every face there was a human story, indeed more than one, there was a life and there were hopes and aspirations, fears and anger, hatred and pain."[19] It is true that such re-humanization poses a risk (i.e., walks "a fine line between empathy and advocacy"[20]), but no serious peacebuilder argues that we "merely" or "simply" empathize. Reckoning with the truth of history—that is, knowing it and facing it *as* truth, to which we are all accountable—is also a fundamentally "human" act. Ethics are fundamentally human, as are the virtues that surround them (justice, love, forgiveness, guilt, morality). However, we should also note that there are dimensions of the creative and the imaginative that are also uniquely human, and part of "re-humanization" is combining these capacities to bring about a society wherein they can flourish.

So, "re-humanization" here refers to the ways in which cinema (and arguably all the arts) may provide critical support to classic and essential dimensions of human personhood through experiential, empathetic and embodied means. Indeed, a closer look at specific cinematic target zones for re-humanization shows there are unique resources here, providing we understand and carefully deploy them. In the space remaining, we will explore these resources in more detail.

Fundamental Target Zones for Re-humanization in Cinema

Of course, film (and other media) can reinforce a radicalized mentality, as examples from *Triumph of the Will* to contemporary extremist videos demonstrate, but it can it also "open up" a space for alternate narratives we need to hear and humane experiences we need to have. Here we explore three broad trajectories toward peace that the cinema offers: empathy, truth and possibility, and shared aesthetic investment.

Empathy Through Cinema

In the popular use of the term, empathy means a general ability to emotionally feel what others are feeling; feeling "with" someone as opposed to feeling "for" someone (popularly designated as sympathy). Empathy is also what is most often jettisoned when one is threatened.[21] Likewise, self-expression is often hamstrung by emotional turmoil.[22] When peacebuilding, a simultaneous, double work of empathy for others and self-expression is required. Both these concerns can be addressed by the arts, which marshal both those capacities in the project of "world-building," wherein the self is transformed and the world that emerges is an imaginative future not limited to the self.[23]

The making of a film can function in the role of therapeutic self-expression, as it was for the former child soldiers of Colombia in the making of their film *Life's Roulette* (*Ruleta de la Vida*, 2008).[24] Here, young victims of socio-political upheaval and violence were given an opportunity to create, and through their own, semi-autobiographical story, were able to voice truths about their experience they could not otherwise easily say.

Indeed, pain demands a medium that gets us closer to the experience than words can, as Elaine Scarry asserts that pain not only defies language but "breaks" the *describable* world:

> Whatever pain achieves, it achieves in part through its unsharability, and it ensures this unsharability through its resistance to language.... Physical pain does not simply resist language but actively destroys it, bringing about an immediate reversion to a state anterior to language, to the sound and cries a human being makes before language is learned.[25]

So, mere mention of pain or descriptions of it will not do, but if we are attuning our own experience of pain to someone else's, we are generating solidarity. This is why it is critical to understand empathy not as a "taking on" someone's feelings. We are not "using" them or "appropriating" them when we are truly empathetic. Rather, true empathy is a *harmonizing* of one's own feelings with that of another. Pain is not "shareable," but individualized experiences of pain can be productively aligned, and out of this alignment we may begin to build a new, reconstituted language, different from the original but still, nevertheless, functioning. This is why Scarry describes Ingmar Bergman's film *Cries and Whispers* (1972) as "a sustained attempt to lift the interior facts of bodily sentience out of the inarticulate pre-language of 'cries and whispers' into the realm of shared objectification."[26]

Indeed, the viewing of such films can help to promote empathy through this "shared realm." Within this expression/empathy binary, the film becomes an act of "worldmaking" as Stephen K. Levine (channeling Paolo Knill) has described, where the past can be *experientially* acknowledged, the stories can be told, and a joint future can be imaginatively *felt*.[27]

Indeed, Murray Smith argues that empathy in film viewing does not function as an abandonment of one's identity for the sake of "thinking the thoughts of another," but a type of investment of the self in the other's situation, through their eyes. It is a negotiation of one's perspective with another, amid an affectual catalyst. A complex of factors operate in creating "character engagement," as Smith terms it, and both voluntary and involuntary processes contribute to cinematic empathy.[28] In this arena, we tune *our own* emotional experience, as much as possible, with that person, particularly around the experiences of grievance and suffering.

Some contemporary neurological research suggests this alignment is even more powerful and extensive than we have previously imagined. The discovery of the mirror neuron system (MNS) has been much discussed, and some attempts to apply these findings have overblown or overdetermined their function (even in the estimation of one of its discoverers, Vittorio Gallese[29]). Yet, the foundational discovery remains immensely powerful and provides strong support for the assertion of Maurice Merleau-Ponty that the fundamental ground from which all human meaning works is not "I think" but "I can."[30] MNS researchers found that we don't merely perceive the movements of others, but engage parts of our *motor* system, the aspect of our brains dedicated to *personal movement* and agency (as opposed to the perception of movements outside the self). That is to say, at some level, when we perceive movement we are "moving" (in the broadest sense of engaging the motor system), not merely "imagining movement" in some abstract way. In sum, perception is more *action-oriented* than many scientists have historically believed. This opens up enormous questions about the nature of memory, action, perception, and empathy, and all of these dimensions are being actively rethought today.[31]

On top of this mirrored response, alignment with others' experiences can be supported through our own past experiences, even if they are not identical. The philosopher Mark Johnson argues that structures of experiential knowledge (called "image schemata") exist in all humans, and function as "trans-modal" (i.e. intersensory) gestalts, allowing us to take our basic experiences and deploy them as experiential knowledge in new situations.[32] Through image schemata, a movement situation—such as constricted movements of refugees in an intolerably cramped refugee camp—can resonate with us without recourse to language or concept. We may have never experienced such a camp, but we have felt tight spaces, intense heat, claustrophobia, and the mix of emotions these experiences generate, and so perception of such a camp can cinematically *resonate* with us, through a combination of mirrored action and the deployment of personal image schemata. We cannot fully "take on" the refugee camp experience, but we can align ourselves with it at the corporeal level, and, so, imaginatively feel the experience as our own. This is where cinema begins to lend some of its unique powers to the empathic effort. Whereas empathy through literature is certainly possible and even powerful, cinema has the unique ability to present faces, movement, and other generators of empathic response in more vivid detail, and in ways that more fully engage motor and image schematic response.

And, so, this helps explain the critical role that cinema can play in bridging historical divides in conflict. It does not simply present the "expressions" of a wounded party, for the intellectual consideration of the adversary. Rather, it allows for the sort of embodied empathy and corporeal simulation that art therapists have argued is so critical for the work of healing and peace. Indeed, several active peacebuilders have so used the cinema.[33]

Truth-Telling and Imagining Alternative Futures

Randall Butler is one such peacebuilder. He was a successful trial lawyer in Texas before he felt a call—driven by his Christian faith—to focus his skills on peacemaking, and so the Institute for Sustainable Peace (ISP) was born.[34] ISP travels around the world helping people find peace in conflict.

Butler agrees with Jolyon Mitchell that "bearing witness" is a crucial role for film in the peacebuilding process,[35] enabling the truth to be told so that forgiveness and reconciliation can be built on a meaningful foundation. Likewise, such truth-telling can function as therapeutic self-expression for the wounded, who have not been permitted to tell their stories, and help the guilty parties clearly see the humanity of their victims. Very often "no one's hands are completely clean" in conflict situations, and so, film can function as a moral leveler as well as a catalyst for reconciliation.

At the same time, Butler forcefully urges caution about such applications, as they run the risk of re-traumatizing the victims in a conflict.[36] This has led him to explore other dimensions of cinematic truth-telling. He tells a story of trying to promote conflict resolution in the Sudan, and being confronted with a room of incredulous Sudanese participants. "Our government has secret police who can enter my home any time, day or night, and make me disappear if [dictator Omar al-] Bashir wishes it," they told him. To suggest "conflict resolution" in such a situation, without any discussion of justice, was simply unimaginable, Butler decided, and this got Butler thinking about peacebuilding as something more than simple conflict resolution. If *sustainable* peace is to be effected, the discussion needs to revolve around justice, and the legitimate, nonviolent means of attaining it, and what sort of just, stable form of government might replace a dictator once he falls. In this manner, truth-telling is inescapably tied to the human capacity to imagine other possibilities.

Bringing Down a Dictator (2002) is a documentary about a student nonviolent movement to bring down the Milosevic government in Serbia, and Butler has used it many times in his own efforts.[37] It chronicles Gene Sharp's work with nonviolent resistance to dictatorships, and when Butler shows this to young leaders, it helps them imagine a pathway to changing the future other than violent revolution. Future resisters use it as a type of training manual for resistance, as well as a playbook for building a lasting, sustainable peace.

Cinema can also frame the truth in such a way that personal transformations appear possible, in both fictional (or semi-fictional) film as well as documentary. Butler often motivates his participants to honest conversation through "the audition" scene from James Mangold's *Walk the Line* (2005), the story of country singer/songwriter Johnny Cash.[38] The scene depicts a young Cash auditioning for legendary producer Sam Phillips. After a saccharine gospel song, Phillips declines: "I don't believe you." Cash takes offense, and then asks for another chance to "bring it on home." Phillips poses him a thought experiment: if he were hit by a passing truck and he was lying in a ditch, dying, and he had time to sing one song that would sum up his feelings toward the world and God in that moment, what would it be? "Because that's the sort of song that truly saves people," he says. Cash pauses, then, impromptu, plays him "Folsom Prison Blues":

I hear the train a comin'
It's rolling round the bend
And I ain't seen the sunshine since I don't know when,
I'm stuck in Folsom prison, and time keeps draggin' on,

But that train keeps a rollin' on down to San Antone.
When I was just a baby my mama told me, Son,
Always be a good boy, don't ever play with guns.
But I shot a man in Reno just to watch him die.
When I hear that whistle blowing, I hang my head and cry.

The success of this new song is immediately evident, even though it suggests that Cash callously killed a man for no reason at all. Of course, he never did such a thing, but used this American mythic form—a trope from the American Western—to "bear witness" to human nature, evil, and the capacity for violence amid inequality. The fact that this film is (loosely) based on a true story is not the point. Rather, we see here *human* truths that require "witnessing."

Butler has shown the scene to men and women who very well may have committed such violence, or supported those who have. Yet, for him, the power of the scene is less about "the facts" and more about "dropping the social façade" in a peacebuilding context and witnessing a transformation. What sort of transformation is possible, once honesty is engaged? The slow reveal of Cash's authentic inner world through his moving performance is crucial to understanding that authenticity is a process, charged with affect, power, and a certain type of self-donation.[39] The aesthetic zone in which this plays out, according Butler, enables a shared *felt understanding* of the power and potential of authenticity within a peacebuilding context.

The Power of Mutual Aesthetic Investment

We have seen how aesthetic experience can be a de-militarized zone for shared experiences and conversation, even among those in conflict. Since most aesthetic experiences can be interpreted in various ways, yet still create a shared intensity of feeling, this can be fertile ground for mutual emotional investment. In addition, G. Gabrielle Starr's study of aesthetic experience yields some additional discoveries that hold great promise for peacebuilding applications.[40]

The first is "mattering." The more scientists look at emotion, feelings, and sensation, the more they see that these functions are about *relevance to us* for our happiness, survival, well-being, etc. Starr summarizes: "Ultimately, all aesthetic experience is the result not so much of perceiving the outside world as becoming aware of our own judgment of what matters to us."[41] Art addresses and reveals the mattering *structure*, which we could not easily articulate, and gives experiential weight to thoughts that we could not really evaluate or place in a hierarchy with other experiences. Starr believes that art doesn't typically give us "new facts," but rather new configurations of the facts, which create the structure for them mattering to us.[42] Art can help us care about things we've never cared about, or make us care anew about things we have forgotten.

The second value is "restructuring and expanding" the structure of mattering.[43] Works of art produce paradigm shifts in how we see, hear or think, a shift in the hierarchies of value that motivate and map daily life. It is not just that new links between ideas and perceptions are formed in aesthetic experience, but that the "hedonic value" assigned to these perceptions and ideas at a neural level "enables powerful connections that had not existed before." Indeed:

> Aesthetic experience thus makes possible the unexpected valuation of objects, ideas, and perceptions and enables new configurations of what is known, new frameworks for interpretation, and perhaps even a new willingness to entertain what is unfamiliar or strange.... We may then acquire new knowledge, which enters into our lives differently – by showing us undiscovered similarities or contrasts, and opening new room for comparison and evaluation.[44]

The "mattering structure" is clearly a key component of our mental architecture in any peacebuilding application, as we seek to make "peace" matter more intensely to those who have not prioritized it. And, so, artworks (and, presumably, films), are most helpful in altering these things productively. Starr found these two ideas most powerfully confirmed in her study of aesthetic experiences. In addition, during "peak" aesthetic experiences—that is, exceptionally strong emotional experiences above the casual artistic encounter—she found even more, surprising benefits for peacebuilding.

The "Default Mode Network" (DMN) is a concert of particular brain processes that runs when we are not focused on the external world. It is operational in activities like daydreaming, envisioning future possibilities, thinking intently about one's self, and working out identity markers (such as, "I like Matisse, I like opera, I hate pop music"). It is also operational when we imagine other worlds, other people, and other people's thoughts, and this is the critical ground for the empathy we've established as critical for peacebuilding. The DMN doesn't normally run when we are working on something specific or attending to a task or generally operating in the world, nor when we are simply looking at art, Starr confirms.[45] However, to her surprise, in the most "transcendent" artistic encounters it *does* run.

As a relatively new discovery, this finding needs some discussion and additional research to clarify all its ramifications, but Starr maintains that peak aesthetic experiences bring the internal and external worlds uniquely into contact. This is not just "you" as yourself, and not just the world "out there," but the *relation* of both worlds, internal and external. This is not just "who we are" but being *aware* of who we are.[46]

When building peace, do we not wish to help actors attend to concrete situations less insularly, and provide them with emotional and personal investment in the cause of peace? Are we not asking people to "imagine" a different world, and bring that vision into a concrete situation that may seem utterly incompatible with that world? It may take a miracle to bring those worlds together, but peak aesthetic experiences could be a powerful tool in doing just that.

Assuming that Julian Hanich is correct when he argues that film spectatorship should normally be seen as "joint action," we have a foundational ground for peace, bringing parties around and having them *act together* at a minimal level, if only to agree to watch the same thing attentively.[47] As argued, however, spectators are not merely watching, but experiencing the film in all sorts of ways: multisensory, corporeal, internal and emotional. In the case of "peak aesthetic experiences," if given truly remarkable films, we may have an opportunity for all parties to restructure their categories of value, and re-envision their entire relation to the world.

In addition, the cinema gives us a unique tool for corporeal understanding of the dynamics of human life and value. That understanding is not merely one of interpersonal empathy, but a bodily engagement with the aesthetic form that can help us to feel the dynamics of transformation, change, and possibility we wish to see realized in our concrete peacebuilding situations. This unique form of empathy was described by nineteenth century German aestheticians as *Einfühling*, which literally means "feeling into."[48] It captures the notion that we perceive, affectually engage, and, to some degree, conform to aesthetic forms before us. Within those aesthetic forms, we can *partially live* concepts like peace, transformation, and reconciliation even as we experience something like them manifest in an aesthetic experience. This can predispose one toward actualizing those experiences beyond the cinema.

And, perhaps this is where we can start to make some peace with Leni Riefenstahl. Most fortunately, *Triumph of the Will* was not her only film.

Olympia (1938),[49] her documentary of the 1936 Berlin Olympiad, is not without propagandistic elements, but her best moments in this film rise well above them. The famous diving sequence illuminates the sorts of peace-building tools shared aesthetic investment can yield.

The beginning of the sequence looks more like a standard documentary montage, assembling *reportage* of the diving event. International divers walk the board, jump, spin, and enter the water, accompanied by reaction shots of the crowd. We note some adventurous camera angles, but, beyond that, it seems rather conventional. Yet, even here, in the most ordinary part of the sequence, there is an important difference from *Triumph of the Will*. The structure of the situation is not nationalistic but global, and some care is given to representing divers from different nations.

Bit by bit, the editing pace increases, and, if we are attentive, we notice the walks to the end of the dive gradually disappear, as do the splashes into the water. The climax of the sequence features a thrilling and transformative emphasis on the human male body as a singular, universal form (an amalgam of divers), spinning and rolling in mid-air. Combine this increasingly truncated editing pattern with silhouetted photography and unusual, expressive techniques like reverse motion, underwater photography, slow motion, and inverted camerawork, and the effect is a marvelous *loss* of individual (diver) identity within a homogenous realm of abstract form in movement. Through visual abstraction and *Einfühling*, human bodies become something utterly different, folding and unfolding in stunning transformations that bleed one into another. Many people become one, transcending corporeal, physical, and geopolitical limits to soar like birds in the sky (Fig. 14.4).

And so, gradually, the sequence becomes less about what this or that diver did for this or that country and fuses them into an image of one humanity, in silhouette against the heavens. There may be no better image for the soaring and transcendent benefits of peace.

Conclusion: The Soft, but Essential, Value of Cinema and the Arts

This all seems inspiring, but we soberly recall that *Olympia* did not forestall *Kristallnacht*. For every example of peacemaking here, there are counterexamples where a filmmaker used the same techniques to promote strife, war, xenophobia, and division. So what can be said?

Fig. 14.4 *Olympia*. Dir. Leni Riefenstahl (Berlin, Germany: Olympia Film, 1938). Publicity still. *Photo credit* IOC/USOC

At the end of the day, we still need strong moral visions from our filmmakers. *Triumph of the Will* situated its powers within a nationalistic context, to the *exclusion* of those outside the circle, and genocide was just around the corner. This is why we must stress that film—and all its attendant powers—is most useful for peace when it is deployed by peacebuilders in a carefully designed context, with structural emphasis on those both inside and outside the circle. That context often involves willing (or semi-willing) participants, and various other extra-cinematic dimensions (such as face-to-face contact and bodily movement of the sort psychologist Sara Savage [2013] and Randy Butler utilize). Such a context can positively redirect the cinema's powers for the cause of peace.

In addition to moral courage, we need cinematic artists who have understood the powers of cinema to generate particular experiences, and so *utilize* those experiences to help us see and feel differently. The filmmaker Wim Wenders and the philosopher Mary Zournazi argue:

> To imagine peace – and its worldly qualities – involves a renewal of stories, values and beliefs. In some instances, it is images that 'shock' us out of habitual ways of looking that can offer the alternative visions of hope and peace.... [T]his involves a creative 'revolt' to change perceptual habits rather than continuing historical trauma and grief .... Imagination can lead to a re-enchantment with the world and our usual ways of looking at it.[50]

Wenders and Zournazi see particular value in artists who *at once* help us imagine possible worlds and see the *current* world anew through manipulation of time, space, form, and detail:

> The films of [Michelangelo] Antonioni, [Yasujiro] Ozu and [Robert] Bresson ask us to wait in different ways, to be with a different reality, its rhythms and responsibilities .... And the paintings of [Edward] Hopper and [Andrew] Wyeth invite us to look at the radiance and eeriness of this world with a certain responsibility, wonder and care.[51]

Indeed, the filmmakers and painters they admire do not encourage consumerism of sight—a torrent of images for superficial effects—but in patient and carefully crafted images that require reflection:

> [The painter Andrew] Wyeth teaches us the second and third sight. He says: "Look at all the responsibility that is involved in the art of seeing. Look at the pleasures of digging deeper. Look at the rewards of putting yourself into the very 'presence' of a person, or a thing, or a landscape. Let the glance out of the corner of your eye lead you to really look and recognize and see each other, the world and its radiance, with more durability, with more sincerity, with more pleasure, and with more communion happening."[52]

Re-humanization is, at least partially, to see again and anew, before conflict became the all-demanding overlay atop reality. As Viktor Shklovsky famously observed: "Habitualization devours work, clothes, furniture, one's wife, *and the fear of war*.... And art exists that one may recover the sensation of life; it exists to make one feel things, to make the stone stony."[53]

And, so, the battleground for peace is not simply in the realm of ideas, but in the realm of feeling, practice, and perception. For this reason, we must not become jaded to the virtues of the arts and their usefulness. We must also be mindful of their essential nature: that they are inherently hard to measure, unsuitable to metrics because they are "soft." That is to say, their social impact is not typically immediate but, as a zone of emotional negotiation, calibrators of value ("mattering"), expression, discussion, and a repository of feelings. In this way, they serve as the foundation for cultural trends and ideas for years to come. Those who fund peace efforts often need numbers to justify their investment, but the arts are like the soft tissue of the body, holding the hard, skeletal parts together; they don't show up in the most obvious way in X-rays, but the anatomy would be impossible without them. It might take 40 years for the arts to do their work, building character in their respective audiences, and it might take double that time to realize the damage we've done by ignoring them.

Everyone has aesthetic experiences—and depends on them—all the time. It's not likely that a conflict will end because we showed all the parties *Olympia*, but showing them *Olympia* may be a way for them to feel critical sensations together, re-discover their common humanity, and marvel as they witness a form of transformation and miracle. This aesthetic moment is not a plan for peace, nor is it simply a hopeful idea. It is a bodily simulation, and hence, the first rehearsals of unity and peace in people who need to believe such transformation is still possible.

Notes

1. *Miss Congeniality*. Directed by Donald Petrie (Hollywood, CA: Warner Brothers Pictures, 2000).
2. Of course, the challenges posed here are not the only ones; there is the media and violence debate, and the "military-industrial-entertainment complex" that runs on (and quite literally profits from) the combination of nationalistic mythology and ethos of military-technological might in entertainment. These issues require extensive, separate discussion, and have been addressed

elsewhere: see Stephen Prince, ed., *Screening Violence* (New Brunswick, NJ: Rutgers University Press, 2000); James Kendrick, *Film Violence: History, Ideology, Genre* (New York: Wallflower Press, 2009); and James Der Derian, *Virtuous War: Mapping the Military-Industrial-Media-Entertainment Network*, 2nd edition (New York: Routledge, 2009).

3. *The Triumph of the Will.* Directed by Leni Riefenstahl (Berlin, Germany: Reichsparteitag-Film, 1935).
4. The key here is not the classic "ontological" question (whether cinema conveys the real, or whether we are "fooled" into something) but the ways in which our apprehension of both the real and the cinema align, because it is here that the cinema may teach us something about ourselves.
5. In film studies, Gilles Deleuze initiated a huge interest in cinema as a flow of sensations, within the context of continental theory and aesthetics. See Gilles Deleuze, *Cinema 1: The Movement Image* (Minneapolis, MN: University of Minnesota Press, 1986) and Gilles Deleuze, *Cinema 2: The Time Image* (Minneapolis, MN: University of Minnesota Press, 1989). Recent phenomenological film theory sees perception in terms of an embodied dynamic between self and world. See Vivian Sobchack, *The Address of the Eye: A Phenomenology of the Film Experience* (Princeton: Princeton University Press, 1992); Laura U. Marks, *The Skin of the Film: Intercultural Cinema, Embodiment and the Senses* (Durham, NC: Duke University Press, 2000); and Jennifer Barker, *The Tactile Eye: Touch and Cinematic Experience* (Berkeley, CA: University of California Press, 2009). In cognitive theory, various thinkers have creatively thought through the compatibility of phenomenological theory with embodied theories of perception in cognitive linguistics as well as the larger notion of embodied simulation theory. See Mark Johnson, *The Body in the Mind: The Bodily Basis of Meaning, Imagination and Reason* (Chicago, IL: University of Chicago Press, 1987); Vittorio Gallese, "Mirror Neurons and Art", in *Art and the Senses*, ed. Francesca Baci and David Melcher (Oxford, UK: Oxford University Press, 2013).
6. Gregory Currie, *Image in Mind: Film, Philosophy and Cognitive Science* (Cambridge, UK: Cambridge University Press, 2008).
7. Torben Grodal, "Concluding Address" (paper presented at the Festsymposium: Torben Grodal 70th Birthday, Institute for Media, Cognition and Communication, Copenhagen, Denmark, 25 January 2013). In a similar vein, the psychologist Ed S. Tan calls cinema "an emotion machine." See Ed S. Tan, *Emotion and the Structure of Narrative Film: Film as an Emotion Machine* (New York, NY: Routledge, 1995). Simulation theory in film studies gained traction with Currie's *Image in Mind*, 2008.
8. That distance from reality in the simulation—to feel without real immediate consequence—is not without dangers, however. Jean Baudrillard famously made the hyperbolic suggestion that the copy has replaced the real. See Jean Baudrillard, *Simulcra and Simulation* (Ann Arbor, MI: University of

Michigan Press, 1994). We see a bit of that critiqued in the scene from *Miss Congeniality.*

9. Christian Smith, *Moral Believing Animals: Human Personhood and Culture* (Oxford, UK: Oxford University Press, 2003). Smith's later book *What is a Person?: Rethinking Humanity, Social Life and the Moral Good from the Person Up* (Chicago, IL: University of Chicago Press, 2010) is a more extensive discussion of the topic, arguing for a robust, fully humanistic (anti-reductionistic) social theory of persons.
10. Matthew Ratcliffe, *Feelings of Being: Phenomenology, Psychiatry, and the Sense of Reality* (Oxford, UK: Oxford University Press, 2008). In fact, he argues, these assumptions are bodily feelings that, when they go awry, result in various psychoses like schizophrenia.
11. Smith, *Moral Believing Animals*, 145, emphasis mine.
12. It's often true that the arts don't serve as good instruments for presenting all sides of an issue. That is not to say that artists are exempt from responsibility to *basic* fairness, but that is different from an obligation to present a comprehensive view of an issue.
13. Picco is one of the most admired negotiators of modern times. See http://www.giandomenicopicco.com/about.html.
14. Gabrielle Rifkind and Giandomenico Picco, *The Fog of Peace: The Human Face of Conflict Resolution* (London, UK: I.B. Tauris, 2014), xix.
15. See the International Online Training Program on Intractable Conflict (University of Colorado, Boulder) definition of "De-humanization",http://www.colorado.edu/conflict/peace/problem/dehuman1.html, accessed 16 March 2015. See also: P. Holtz and W. Wagner, "Dehumanization, Infrahumanization, and Naturalization", in *Encyclopedia of Peace Psychology*, ed. D.J. Christie (Malden, MA: Wiley-Blackwell, 2012).
16. See Roberto Rodriguez, "Forgiveness as Part of the Rehumanization Process", *Peace Review: A Journal of Social Justice* 12:2 (2000): 325–328. For another example, see Rianna Oelofsen, "De- and Rehumanization in the Wake of Atrocities", *South African Journal of Philosophy* 28:2 (2009): 178–188.
17. John Paul Lederach, "The Long Journey Back to Humanity", in *Peacebuilding: Catholic Theology, Ethics, and Praxis*, ed. Robert J. Schreiter, R. Scott Appleby, Gerard F. Powers (Maryknoll, NY: Orbis Books, 2010).
18. Lederach, "The Long Journey", 44–45.
19. Rifkind and Picco, *The Fog of Peace*, xv.
20. Rifkind and Picco, *The Fog of Peace*, 46.
21. Rifkind and Picco, *The Fog of Peace*, 7.
22. Stephen K. Levine, "Art Opens to the World: Expressive Arts and Social Action", in *Art in Action: Expressive Arts Therapy and Social Change*, ed. Ellen G. Levine and Stephen K. Levine (London, UK: Jessica Kingsley Publishers, 2011), 21.

23. Levine, "Art Opens to the World", 24, 26.
24. *Ruleta de la Vida* [Life's Roulette]. Directed by the Empanada Rellena Film Collective (Bogotá, Colombia: Shine a Light, 2008).
25. Elain Scarry, *The Body in Pain: The Making and Unmaking of the World* (Oxford, UK: Oxford University Press, 1985), 4. When Scarry wrote this, it was more common to assume that the brain structured thought entirely through language, and so her thesis was much more radical. Today most cognitive scientists agree there are many domains that precede or otherwise work around language, and language often flows *from* physical experience, rather than the opposite (see Johnson, *The Body in Mind*, 1987).
26. Scarry, *The Body in Pain*, 10, 11.
27. Stephen K. Levine, "Art Opens to the World." Levine (following Knill) argues for "intermodality" in arts therapy, which does not limit itself to one medium, but deploys any and all mediums that might be helpful in engaging the various sensory and emotional registers necessary for such worldmaking (21–22). The cinema's capacity here to combine and engage multiple modalities makes it an ideal candidate for such work.
28. Murray Smith, *Engaging Characters: Fiction, Emotion and the Cinema* (Oxford, UK: Oxford University Press, 1995), 102. Smith lists some voluntary responses such as sympathy and certain forms of mimicry, as well as involuntary responses, such as affective mimicry, motor mimicry and autonomic responses (like the startle response). We might also consider that "facial feedback" (the theory that mimicry actually triggers the same emotions in us as those on the faces we perceive) may play a role in cinematic empathy. See Carl R. Plantinga, "The Scene of Empathy and the Human Face on Film", in *Passionate Views: Film, Cognition, and Emotion*, ed. Carl R. Platinga and Greg M. Smith (Baltimore, MD: Johns Hopkins University Press, 1999).
29. Gallese, "Mirror Neurons and Art", 461.
30. Maurice Merleau Ponty, *The Phenomenology of Perception*, trans. Colin Smith (London: Routledge & Kegan Paul, 1962 [1945]), 137.
31. Gallese, "Mirror Neurons and Art", 456.
32. Johnson, *The Body in the Mind*, 44–75. Johnson describes image schemata in ways that demonstrate their fittingness with the notions of embodiment and prelinguistic knowledge articulated in this essay. He states that perceptions are structured and given "connectedness" (75) to our concepts by them. They are also pre-conceptual and non-propositional (14, 23), of a continuous, analog nature (i.e., they are not concrete images, representations or concepts), and are not subject to verification (i.e., non-propositional) (23). Likewise, they "operate in our bodily movements, perceptual acts, and orientational awareness" (75) and are used by the brain to structure and comprehend phenomena in those domains. Johnson considers this schematic

level of brain/nervous system operations the genesis of "meaning" in experience, despite its non-propositional and non-concrete (non-imagistic) nature, because the schemata have "sufficient internal structure to generate entailments and constrain inferences" (22) and are "experientially basic meaningful patterns in our experience and understanding" (61).

33. For example, Cambridge University researcher Sara Savage, in her work with families and groups concerned with religious radicalization, pairs the cinema with movement therapy and other embodied activities to help people engage other perspectives (personal interview with Sara Savage, 2 March 2013, and her essay "Head and Heart in Preventing Religious Radicalization", in *Head and Heart: Perspectives from Religion and Psychology*, eds. Fraser Watts and Geoff Dumbreck [West Conshohocken, PA: Templeton Press, 2013]), 157–194. Other entities, such as the Manhattan International Film Festival (http://www.wya.net/programs/miff/) and the "Film for Peace" festival (http://www.unfilmperlapace.it/paceeng.html) deploy film for the promotion of human dignity and peacebuilding.
34. I.S.P.'s strategy and presuppositions are listed here: http://www.sustainablepeace.org/index.php/page/c/vision-and-principles/.
35. Mitchell, Jolyon. *Promoting Peace, Inciting Violence: The Role of Religion and Media* (London: Routledge, 2013), chapter four.
36. Personal interview with Randall Butler, 17 March 2015.
37. *Bringing Down a Dictator.* Directed by Steve York (Washington, DC: York Zimmerman, 2002).
38. *Walk the Line.* Directed by James Mangold (Hollywood, CA: 20th Century Fox, 2005).
39. See Miroslav Volf, *Exclusion and Embrace* (Nashville, TN: Abingdon Press, 1996). Volf considers self-donation to be crucial in the reconciliation process, though he generally considers that to be a quality of the person *in need of* forgiveness (23–27, 188–189). Here, we see all parties needing forgiveness and self-donating.
40. G. Gabrielle Starr, *Feeling Beauty: The Neuroscience of Aesthetic Experience* (Cambridge, MA: MIT Press, 2013).
41. Starr, *Feeling Beauty*, 16.
42. Starr, *Feeling Beauty*, 15, 36.
43. Starr, *Feeling Beauty*, 15, 20.
44. Starr, *Feeling Beauty*, 20.
45. Starr, *Feeling Beauty*, 59.
46. Starr, *Feeling Beauty*, 60.
47. Julian Hanich, "Watching a Film with Others: Toward a Theory of Collective Spectatorship", *Screen* 55:3 (2014): 338–359.
48. For a succinct history of this term, see the introduction (specifically pp. 17–18) in *Empathy, Form and Space: Problems in German Aesthetics, 1873–1893*, eds. Robert Vischer, Harry Francis Mallgreave, and Eleftherios

Ikonomou (Los Angeles, CA: Getty Center for the History of Art and the Humanities, 1994).
49. *Olympia*. Dir. Leni Riefenstahl (Berlin, Germany: Olympia Film, 1938). Film.
50. Wim Wenders and Mary Zournazi, *Inventing Peace: A Dialogue on Perception* (London, UK: I.B. Tauris), 107.
51. Wenders and Zournazi, *Inventing Peace*, 161.
52. Wenders and Zournazi, *Inventing Peace*, 156.
53. Viktor Shklovsky, "Art as Technique", in *Russian Formalist Criticism: Four Essays*, eds. Lee T. Lemon and Marion J. Reis (Lincoln, NB: University of Nebraska Press, 1917 [1965]), 11,12, emphasis added.

CHAPTER 15

Peacebuilding and Reconciliation in and Through Film: The Case Study of Rwanda

Robert K. Johnston

Introduction

Over a period of one hundred days in Rwanda in the spring of 1994, many Hutus (who made up some 85% of the population) killed around 800,000 Rwandan Tutsis (12%) and their sympathizers in a government-sponsored genocide. Some of the roots of this atrocity go back to colonial days, when Germans and then Belgians favored the supposedly "lighter-skinned" and "finer-featured" Tutsis, giving them better education and jobs, and introducing separate ID cards for the two groups. When the battle for national independence broke out in the late 50s, it naturally also became a war for Hutu control as well. Coming to power in 1962, the Hutus sporadically persecuted the Tutsi, their former "rulers." The continuing tension was not helped by the mass killings of Hutu in neighboring Burundi in 1972 by their Tutsi-controlled government army.

R. K. Johnston (✉)
Fuller Theological Seminary, Pasadena, CA, USA
e-mail: johnston@fuller.edu

J. Mitchell et al. (eds.), *Peacebuilding and the Arts*,
Rethinking Peace and Conflict Studies,
https://doi.org/10.1007/978-3-030-17875-8_15

After several thousand Tutsi rebels invaded Rwanda in 1990, animosity increased exponentially. Hutu Power (with its slogan, "The Hutu should stop having mercy on the Tutsi") was called for and over the next three years, several thousand Tutsi people were murdered. Even more ominously, armed militia, or killing groups (*Interahamwe*—"those who fight/kill together") were formed, genocide was openly discussed in governmental cabinet meetings and organized by leaders of the military, and over 500,000 machetes were imported by businessmen close to President Habyarimana. The news media—both radio and print—emphasized falsely gained Tutsi wealth and power, Tutsi women as sex objects who were weakening Hutu men, past horrors under Tutsi rule, and present atrocities by the Tutsi that were often fabricated or greatly exaggerated. Tensions simply escalated.

When President Habyarimana's plane was shot down on April 6, 1994 as it was landing in Kigali, Rwanda's capital, what semblance of peace that was left evaporated as a highly organized genocide took place. The *Interahamwe* set out to kill all the Tutsis they could find. Age or gender did not matter. Neighbors killed neighbors and fellow villagers. The machete was the weapon of choice. When Tutsis tried to flee, roadblocks were set up; when Hutu citizens were reticent to act, the Presidential Guard came in and did it for them, often killing the unwilling Hutus as well. Over the next one hundred days, Rwanda experienced somewhere between 200 and 400 killings an hour. About 400,000 children were left orphaned, and thousands upon thousands of women were raped and mutilated, many also later finding themselves HIV-positive.

It is difficult even now to comprehend the speed, scope, and brutality of this human slaughter. At the time, it was even more incomprehensible, particularly to the larger international community. The UN's only response to the violence was to reduce their "peacekeeping" force to 270 men. It was considered too dangerous to keep the rest in Rwanda. The United States was similarly reluctant to get involved, choosing to call the genocide a "local conflict," something then-President Bill Clinton later deeply regretted. Clinton came to believe that if he had been willing to send in even 5000 US peacekeepers, perhaps 500,000 lives could have been saved. But hindsight is always, and in this case tragically, better.

Responses of Peace and Reconciliation

Given the speed and scope of this atrocity, it seems impossible to imagine what steps could have happened in its aftermath that would have promoted peace and reconciliation. Yet there have been several hopeful signs, with Rwanda's National Unity and Reconciliation Commission being the most significant. It is the concern of this chapter, however, to focus elsewhere, in particular on the possible contribution of one art form—film—to the ongoing peace and reconciliation process. And here, one notes two quite different approaches, given the need to address two quite different audiences. The genocide that occurred in Rwanda in 1994 produced the need for movements toward peace and reconciliation both (1) by those outside Rwanda who had tragically remained silent and inactive while the carnage was going on, either by ignorance or neglect; and (2) by those within Rwanda, both Hutu and Tutsi, who needed to rebuild relationships and trust in a torn and divided country. Filmmakers responded by producing movies intended for both audiences.

The Need for Confession and Peacebuilding by Those Outside Rwanda

Certainly former President Clinton's confession was an important early step in the peace and reconciliation process, a step toward building a new beginning for relationships between the West and Rwanda. But also important has been the use of film to both raise consciousness of the genocide outside Rwanda and to encourage action. In the first decade after the genocide took place, several smaller movies were produced, including: *Shooting Dogs* (A.K.A *Beyond the Gates,* d. Caton-Jones, 2005), HBO's *Sometimes in April* (d. Peck, 2005), *100 Days* (d. Hughes, 2001), and the documentary *The Last Just Man* (d. Silver, 2002). These and other films according to Jolyon Mitchell "bear witness" to the realities of genocide in Rwanda.[1] Two more recent movies in particular stand out. They are both adaptations for the screen of books written by key participants in the war who tried to help rescue Rwandans from sure death.

Shake Hands with the Devil (d. Spottiswoode, 2007) is a Canadian film that tells the frustrating story of Lieutenant General Romeo Dallaire (Roy Dupuis), a Canadian who headed the UN peacekeeping mission in Rwanda. Dallaire tried to stop the madness of the genocide, despite an ever-increasing shortage of both soldiers and supplies. But given the growing disinterest by the UN and the refusal of those in Europe and North America to intervene (partly due to the opposition of the United States in the Security Council), Dallaire's efforts proved a failure. Seen in the movie often talking to his therapist, Dallaire's memories of all he could not do almost pushed him to suicide. The movie is somber and a little wordy, even if in its own way, it is quietly moving. The book's subtitle perhaps best captures its theme: "The Failure of Humanity in Rwanda."

With inadequate funding and a limited release, it is not surprising that *Shake Hands with the Devil's* impact was slight, though it did win some smaller awards and perhaps helped raise the consciousness of some in the West. Not so, however, for the second film intended to address those outside Rwanda who had contributed to the genocide by failing to intervene, *Hotel Rwanda* (d. George, 2004). Though the screenplay was initially a difficult sell to Hollywood studios and the financing a modest $16 million, the movie, nonetheless, received three Oscar nominations and more than doubled its investor's money, earning $34 million at the box office. Sometimes compared with Steven Spielberg's *Schindler's List* (d. Spielberg, 1993), the film challenged its audience to rethink what it means to be part of the human community. Writer and director Terry George was quoted as saying, "The goal of the film is not only to engage audiences in this story of genocide, but also to inspire them to help redress the terrible devastation."[2] And because many viewers appear to have sympathized with the film's main characters, they ended up being moved by the film to want to do something lest the tragedy be repeated, as the viewer response on IMDB (the Internet Movie Database) illustrates.

In the months following its release, 584 viewers chose to go on IMDB and post their reactions to the film. Rosalind Chick from the United States (8 February 2005) wrote: "Everyone must see this movie and know we are all human beings and it is our responsibility to be there for each other. Jesus Christ… this cannot happen." Surecare from Canada (9 November 2004) said, "It is gripping, heart-wrenching, and opens your eyes to so many things." Bob the moo from the United Kingdom (31 March 2005) responded: "… the film is devastatingly effective and is impossible to watch without feeling lost, helpless, and utterly ashamed for our inaction." Released during the time when the poor in the Darfur region of Sudan were again being slaughtered while the West did nothing and with the backdrop of previous brutalities in Congo, Uganda, Nigeria, and Somalia, *Hotel Rwanda* urged its viewers "not only to look back at history and have a reaction, but to look at today and forward into the future and to seek out the injustices that occur now so that perhaps those in need will not become abandoned again" (druss44121-1 from the United States).[3]

Based on the autobiography of Paul Rusesabagina, the movie narrates an Oscar Schindler like story of the Rwandan manager of the Mille Collines, a four star hotel in Kigali. This unlikely hero, the movie tells us as it closes, ended up saving 1268 Tutsis and Hutu supporters. He did so by housing them in his hotel compound and keeping them safe despite bribe attempts, bluff, and blackmail from the Hutus who wanted to murder them. Trained in Belgium and a person of culture, though also self-centered and a master of the art of accommodation, Rusesabagina (skillfully underplayed by Don Cheadle) is no saint. He has learned how to keep his mainly American and European guests happy through flattery and apology, and to supply them with the luxuries they desire by dealing with the black market. Even when the genocide comes to his front door, he is slow to act. But confronted first by the pleas of his wife (Sophie Okonedo) and then by others who are at risk, this hotel manager slowly learns to assume responsibility for the humanity of others. And the result is both harrowing and inspiring.

As portrayed in the movie, the genocide was not so much an irresistible challenge to Rusesabagina's "morality," as it was to his "amorality." Confronted by Hutu militants who wanted to exterminate all the "cockroaches" (the Hutu name for the Tutsi people), Rusesabagina was forced to take his family and some neighbors to the relative safety of his hotel. But the situation simply escalated. Whether experiencing the horror of unknowingly driving over a dark, bumpy road that turns out to be "paved" with thousands of dead bodies or confronting the pleas of others fleeing from machete-wielding Hutus, Paul finds himself slowly pulled into the world around him. And so are the film's viewers. Watching the movie, viewers may find themselves asking, how is it that those in the West could have been so disengaged from this tragedy, so "amoral" you might say? Did the West even know it was going on?

The memorable opening scene portrays a television journalist (Joaquin Phoenix) showing the hotel manager footage of a massacre he has just shot blocks from the hotel. While Rusesabagina is certain that when shown abroad, such images will force the West to become involved, the journalist proves right with his cynical reply. He says, "If people see this footage, they'll say, 'Oh my God, that's terrible,' and they'll go on eating their dinners."[4] Here is the real intention of the movie: to challenge the amorality of those outside Rwanda who remained indifferent to the carnage, a challenge that was in fact realized for many who saw the film if the sample of IMBD user comments is representative. *Hotel Rwanda* pulls its viewers into the world around them. In this way, confession for their sin of omission is invited. The film's story might even become the occasion for some to seek reconciliation with their African brothers and sisters whom they have ignored.

The Need for Reconciliation and Peacebuilding by Rwandans

But though such a process of contrition and concrete action is key to the expression of our full humanity by those in the West, there is also a parallel and perhaps more difficult rebuilding process that involves Rwandans addressing fellow Rwandans. How are those who lived through these atrocities to deal with the horror they witnessed and participated in? How are they to begin a process of peacebuilding—of contrition, forgiveness, and reconciliation—related to their neighbors? And what might that future look like? Again, filmmaking has attempted to play a small but important role in helping the country in its post-genocide period move beyond its deep divisions as it seeks a fragile unity. Consider, for example, two movies made in Rwanda for Rwandans.

Kinyarwanda (d. Brown, 2011).

This small, independent film was written in two weeks, prepped in one week, and shot in Rwanda in 16 days using both professional and amateur actors. Produced and conceived by a young Rwandan, Ishmael Ntihabose, who had limited film experience, and shot with a mainly Rwandan crew consisting of heads of departments who had previously been assistants to assistants on other movies, many might assume the movie had little hope of being coherent, let alone significant. But they would be wrong. Winner of the "World Cinema Audience Award" at the Sundance Film Festival in 2011, as well as similar awards at the AFI Fest in Los Angeles and the Starz Film Festival in Denver, though the movie has a certain unevenness, it has proven to be deeply moving for those who have seen it.

The movie benefits from several factors. Firstly, with a budget of $250,000, given support from the European Union and assistance both from the Association of Muslims of Rwanda and the Rwandan government, the movie had more resources to draw upon than most independent films made in Africa. Secondly, with a Rwandan location and a largely Rwandan company, the sense of authenticity conveyed in the film comes naturally. It is both intense and personal. Viewers sense while watching the film that here is a movie made in Africa for Africans. Reading the director's comments that as the movie was shot, cast and crew were struggling personally with their own memories and demons, viewers are not surprised.

Thirdly, the three previous movies that executive producer Ishmael Ntihabose had worked on as an assistant were Rwandan genocide films that focused on the atrocity. Given the chance to produce his own film, Ntihabose decided early on not to emphasize the horror of the past (though that is everywhere present as the backdrop), but instead to hold up images of human possibility that emerged during and after the genocide's death and violence. He wanted, through the process, to show the importance of forgiveness and faith. "His goal, he said, was to portray the reality of Rwanda's remarkable efforts at unity and reconciliation".[5] His director, Alrick Brown, wrote in the press kit, "Because forgiveness, truth and reconciliation are such a huge part of Rwanda's journey, it is also an important part of this film. We hope that audiences can bring some of that 'power of forgiveness' into their own journey."[6]

Key, as well, to the success of the film was Ntihabose's decision to go outside the Rwandan pool of talent and hire Alrick Brown, a young Jamaican graduate of NYU's film school, as screenwriter and director. Working with an intense schedule, Brown listened to the extensive collection of stories Ntihabose had gathered from survivors, as well as to individuals represented in Kigali's Genocide Museum. Taking these, he mixed fiction and history to create the shell of six different story lines, interweaving them together into one larger narrative, in the style, as he has said, of Paul Haggis' *Crash* and Alejandro González Iñárritu's *Babel.* Brown then trusted cast and crew to fill in the story lines with a nuance and dialogue that was true to their own experiences.

The chief protagonist in the film is Jeanne (Hadidja Zaninka). As the movie opens, she has gone on a date and is seen dancing, singing, and laughing with friends. But reality swiftly changes as she comes home to discover that her parents have been butchered by a killing unit who are attacking Tutsis. As she attempts to cope with this tragedy, she must eventually confront another of the central characters, Emmanuel, the man who murdered them (Edouard Bamporiki). Other story lines involve a Catholic priest, Father Pierre (Mazimpaka Kennedy) who learns the importance of forgiving one's self; the Muslim Mufti of Rwanda (Mutsari Jean) who tells his people to protect all Tutsi for this is what Allah wants; Lt. Rose (Cassandra Freeman) who heads a Hutu military unit that seeks peace, not bloodshed, even rescuing Tutsis from certain death and who later works as a leader in the truth and reconciliation process in Rwanda; and finally, the small boy Ishmael (Hassan Kabera), who innocently, after he hears soldiers saying they are searching for guns and "cockroaches," almost gives away the hiding place of the Tutsis his father is hiding. His quick thinking, however, brings not only a sense of relief to the viewer, but redemption to the situation.

Three themes stand out in the movie: first, the importance of Rwandan unity. As one of the characters says in the movie, "There are no Hutu, Tutsi and Twa [hunting peoples often termed "pygmies"] anymore…there are only Rwandans." Though the movie mentions the Belgian colonizers as seeking to divide the Rwandan people by tribe, demanding that they always carry and show their tribal ID cards, the filmmakers see for Rwanda a different future, a country where unity and reconciliation are possible. In an interview for the Sundance Film Festival, Ntihabose said, "Rwanda is now a peaceful country. A country with one identity, one language and with good governance. We're moving on from grief to a brilliant future – other countries which experienced internal conflicts should learn from our experience."[7] Whether this is an overly optimistic picture of Rwandan reality or not, it is a fact that no one in Rwanda today is permitted to identify themselves by their tribal ancestry—they are simply Rwandans. And there is no question that this is the theme of the movie. The film's title, *Kinyarwanda*, is the name of Rwanda's common language, something its two major tribes have always shared. Here is a concrete expression of that greater unity and reconciliation Rwanda is learning to live into.

A second theme is forgiveness. With some villages estimated to have had 60–70% of their population clinically depressed following the genocide, Rwandans realized that they could not as a country afford to be mired down in sorting out and exacting the precise dimensions of justice.[8] Too many were implicated, the lines of responsibility were often too messy, and it was impossible to imagine another bloodletting as thousands upon thousands of perpetrators were punished. Instead, what was needed was widespread repentance and forgiveness, both with regard to others and with regard to one's self. In the posters that were produced for the movie, the juxtaposed words "Love"/"Hate," "Forgiveness"/"Vengeance," and "Life"/"Death" are superimposed over the images of the main characters and the tag line is added, "There is always a choice." Here is the movie's challenge to all who have seen it. As *Kinyarwanda* draws to a close, Emmanuel is asking through the reconciliation process for Jeanne to forgive him. And Jeanne responds with her pardon. She says he will be her friend, as once he was a friend to her father and mother. And then she adds, "And I will respect you."[9] The movie closes with Jeanne about to be married, sharing a drink with the now older Ishmael, and there is again dancing. She has found peace.

And thirdly, the movie portrays the power of inter-religious cooperation—in particular, the role of the Islamic people in Rwanda in protecting

Christians who were threatened with death. During the genocide, the Mufti of Rwanda, the most respected Muslim leader in the country, issued a fatwa forbidding Muslims from participating in any way in the killing of Tutsi. As the slaughter raged, it was the mosque that became a place of refuge for not only Muslims but Christians, not only Tutsi but those Hutu who also wanted peace. *Kinyarwanda* brings to life this historical reality, showing the Grand Mosque of Kigali as a place of sanctuary with the Imams cooperating with Catholic priests in working for peace. The fact that the movie has not exaggerated the positive role that Muslims played during and after the conflict in Rwanda is supported by the marked increase of Muslim adherents in Rwanda after the cessation of violence—from 8 to 14% of the population by one estimate.[10]

Kinyarwanda is a movie that shows Rwanda in a positive light, even during its darkest days. With life under siege, we see people making tough choices against all odds—to love and not to hate, to offer forgiveness rather than seek vengeance, to choose life and not death. Mixing historical events with eschatological hope, the film presents a "truth and reconciliation" process as powerful as that in South Africa. What has "not yet" fully been realized has also "already" happened.

Munyurangabo (d. Chung, 2009).

A second semi-local Rwandan movie also deserves consideration. It is the movie *Munyurangabo*, directed, cowritten, filmed, and self-financed by a young Korean- American graduate of Yale, Lee Isaac Chung. He worked closely with local Rwandans on this project. Again, though it was an even smaller movie that *Kinyarwanda*—eleven days shooting, a crew with no experience except what Chung taught them, nonactors in all the leading roles (speaking in Kinyarwanda, which Chung did not speak), and a micro-budget—it also was a surprise winner on the festival circuit, being accepted to the Cannes Film Festival in 2007 in the Un Certain Regard section and later playing in Berlin, Toronto, and the AFI Film Festival in Los Angeles where it won the Grand Jury Prize.

Chung, who grew up on a farm in rural Arkansas, went to Kigali in the summer of 2006 on a Christian mission sponsored by the organization, Youth with a Mission. His wife, Valerie, was returning with that group to Rwanda to help those affected by the genocide by offering art therapy, and Chung agreed to come along to teach youth in the slums of Kigali how to make movies. As he prepared for the assignment with Samuel Anderson, a screenwriting friend, he decided the only way to effectively teach these youth filmmaking was actually to make a film with them. *Munyurangabo* was the result, a movie that used Chung's Rwandan students as crew, friends of students and locals as actors, and a class assignment on poetry inserted as the climatic heart of the movie.

To make it all work, in the six months prior to his nine week class, Chung and his writing partner developed a 9–10 page outline of a story about two teenage boys from Kigali who set out on the road with a stolen machete to confront the killer of the father of one of the boys during the genocide. But Chung also decided early on about several key parameters to the movie that would shape its storytelling and deepen its impact. First, he decided the movie would be made by, for and about Rwandans. Chung commented, "I tried to make *Munyurangabo* a cinema of listening rather than self-expression."[11] He said he wanted the movie to almost have the feel of a documentary, though it would be a fictional narrative. To facilitate this, Chung refused to story board or even to write a complete script, for both, he believed, would impose his judgments on the project. Instead, like Brown had done with *Kinyarwanda*, he chose to trust crew and actors both to flesh out the narrative skeleton and to add to it, using their own intuition and experiences as guides.[12]

Particularly important in rooting his movie in Rwandan soil was Chung's decision to cast two teenagers from the Kigali slums in the lead roles. Discovered in a soccer league run by one of the students in Chung's class, they were best friends, though one was a Hutu and the other a Tutsi. In the movie, Jeff Rutagengwa plays Ngabo (short for Munyurangabo), the Tutsi whose father has been butchered; and Eric Ndorunkundiye plays Sangwa, his Hutu friend, who agrees to go with Ngabo to find his father's killer if they will first stop off briefly at his family farm along the way. Both young men had come to Kigali after losing their fathers, and neither had acted before. The friendship and yet strain in relationship that is portrayed on the screen mirrors their real lives together. Here, art matches life, or is it life matching art?

Compelling, as well, in anchoring the movie in Rwandan soil (understood in this case quite literally) is a scene where Sangwa's estranged father tries to reconnect with his long-absent son by teaching him the rhythm of hoeing the soil. With Ndorunkundiye being a city orphan unused to working the field and the actor playing his father a poor, rural farmer who in real life prepares his soil by hand, the scene has a natural authenticity. Hoeing comes easily for the father, but for Sangwa, his efforts lack grace. Rooted in contemporary Rwandan life, the event is both believable and poignant.

Secondly, having seen other Rwandan films about the genocide, Chung noted, like Ntihabose who would follow with his own film two years later, that most of the other movies were centered in past atrocity, not focusing upon how Rwandans might find peace and reconciliation today. These other movies seemed colonial in their orientation, focusing politically on the guilt of the West for its nonaction and usually having an outside observer/participant in the story to help make the connection to the West clear. What became lost in the process, however, was anything memorable for the Rwandan people themselves. Chung, instead, wanted to focus personally on the present, on what A. O. Scott labeled "the bruised tranquility of ordinary life" following the slaughter.[13] Thus the movie follows the teen boys on their long trek across Rwanda to Sangwa's parents' rural farm, where his family has continued to work the soil after Sangwa ran away to the city, and then on to the film's final confrontation with the killer of Ngabo's father. Will he choose to be like his ancient namesake, Munyurangabo, a mighty warrior, even at the expense of his friendship with Sangwa? Viewers of this movie come to care both about Sangwa and Ngabo. Their lives matter.

Thirdly, in Rwanda today, as was observed in the discussion above of *Kinyarwanda*, there is on the public level a strong, government imposed impetus toward reconciliation, such that one encounters almost the automatic response, "Oh yes, there's no more racism." As Chung observes, "you're no longer allowed to say 'Hutu' or 'Tutsi' in Rwanda. It's a big taboo."[14] You are instead to only say that you are a Rwandan. Yet, on the personal level, racism lingers. So Chung decided that this too must be shown in the movie. Aware that one of the girls working at the Reconciliation Center in Rwanda had to deal with angry parents because she as a Tutsi would be helping Hutus, Chung included in the movie the painful banishment of Sangwa from his father's house for befriending Ngabo. And then of course, the overarching story line is Ngabo seeking vengeance upon his father's Hutu butcher, a feeling that is so seared into his young conscience that it even creates a rupture in his relationship with his best friend Sangwa. Just as in *Kinyarwanda*, reconciliation remains a future hope, even as it partially becomes present reality. Here the movie's final, powerful images in particular leave the viewer with as many questions as answers.

Lastly, Chung chooses quite consciously to make an "art" film. Chung's aesthetic, by his own reflection, has been influenced by both Terence Malick and the Dardennes brothers from Belgium. Chung rarely "tells"; instead, he lovingly shows, allowing scenes to play out slowly and naturally, but never with a sense that they have lingered too long. The images of poor rural life allow for a certain dignity to emerge, even among broken plastic jugs and mud huts. Chung's art, as one reviewer comments, is intelligent about life. In the opening scene, for example, we see Ngabo stealing a machete from an open market and then sitting down to reflect on what lies ahead. As he sits to consider what he is to do, we see the machete's blade with dried blood on the end of it. Yet a short time later, the blade is clean, with no blood showing. Is this meant to suggest a possible trajectory for Ngabo as well? And what of Rwanda itself? Nothing is said; viewers are left to interpret for themselves what such magical realism is meant to convey.

The movie also uses Rwandan music and poetry to strong effect. Particularly compelling is a poem read to Ngabo at a roadside café as he comes near to his father's killer's house.[15] It is read by the young poet himself (the same Edouard Bamporiki who two years later would play Emmanuel in *Kinyarwanda*) who tells Ngabo he needs to practice his recitation for a public gathering where he is to read his poem. In one single long close-up as the camera follows the movement of the artist, the movie's informing vision is given voice. We hear the poet passionately call for a new Rwanda, one where peace and reconciliation is projected to go beyond simply a cessation of violence and the end of poverty to embrace a land of unity, freedom, and equality.

The poem, together with Ngabo ending his journey by going alone into the Hutu murderer's hut, only to find him dying of AIDS and asking for a drink of water, produce the context for the movie's surprising ending. With no dialogue, but rather with two powerful images of reconciliation, the movie leaves it to the viewer to decide how realistically the scene is meant to be taken. Chung has said he did not want the movie to end with a "message" of reconciliation; an "image" of reconciliation was better. And as in *Kinyarwanda*, this ending is perhaps more an eschatological hope than a present reality. But it is also one that the film's whole journey has prepared the viewer to think at least possible. Certainly the movie does not presume to give answers to how reconciliation can happen, but it does offer hope.

In an interview, Chung comments, "we wanted to highlight the desire for reconciliation and offer a scenario for it that could even be regarded as a fantasy. Perhaps faith is a lot like this, requiring the act of imagination.... Part of me understands the impossibility of this reconciliation on earth, but the other part believes and hopes that it will [happen]. In the meantime, the work is important. I think that's what the creation of art can embody –

the act of memorializing, mourning, preparing – the act of waiting, which I think isn't very far from the act of questioning."[16]

A Concluding Reflection

Can these four movies actually make a difference? While it is important not to over claim the power or significance of the films considered above, nevertheless, it is useful to ask this and other related questions: Can aesthetics actually alter ethics, or at least influence them? What is the role of the imagination in reconciliation and peacebuilding? In cases of extremity as in Rwanda, where peace and reconciliation were so radically denied, can images of eschatological hope (or depictions of their radical absence) contribute to the enhancement of peoples' lives? Can filmic acts of memorializing, mourning, preparing, and envisioning become transformative, and if so, how? As one effort to engage such questions, eight years after *Munyurangabo* came out, I asked its filmmakers, Sam Anderson and Lee Isaac Chung, as well as Eugene Suen who produced their next film in Rwanda, to comment on the effect they believed their filmmaking had had on the Rwandan people. Their several observations provide the beginning of what must be an ongoing evaluation of the power of film in the peacebuilding process in Rwanda.[17]

Although according to these filmmakers the initial project was propelled by a strong idealism, it proved difficult to discern the impact this movie had on the Rwandan community at large. The one exception was the direct feedback given by expatriate Rwandans who saw the movie at festivals. To see a Rwandan story onscreen told in Kinyarwanda, suggested the team, seemed to bring some expatriates closer to home. But truth be told, these filmmakers also realized that though they attempted to avoid crafting *Munyurangabo* according to Western taste and style, "we were still influenced artistically by a tradition that came from outside Rwanda, and [we] imposed a particular form on this story." (Recall Chung's comment above that his aesthetic was influenced by Terence Malick and the Dardennes brothers.) Chung's team came to realize that "even though we had in mind making a film specifically for a Rwandan audience, we still shaped the reality that we encountered through an international convention that tends – for good and bad – to appeal to a specific community of film-lovers spread all over the world, rather than to a broad audience in a single nation." The result? Any direct impact in aiding the dialogue toward peacemaking and reconciliation in Rwanda became quite limited.

But this is not to say that the film was without influence. *Munyurangabo* has arguably had a continuing influence in the field of film production in Rwanda. With relatively little local film production in 2006 when the movie was shot, Rwanda now has a growing and extensive professional film industry. Hillywood, Rwanda's international film festival, is becoming increasingly well known. The 2013 documentary *Finding Hillywood* tells the story of the early days of local Rwandan cinema, while also celebrating film's ability to heal the wounds of past individual and national trauma. The festival itself, which travels around the country using an inflatable screen, reflects a growing national film industry driven by pioneering local directors and producers such as Eric Kabera, as well as visiting filmmakers.[18] Chung has returned multiple times to Rwanda to teach and to train both new students and those he worked with on the initial film. Three short films that were subsequently shot by Rwandans dealing with life in contemporary Rwanda were shown at the 2011 Tribeca Film Festival in New York City as a showcase entitled "Perspective: Rwanda" and several of those Rwandans involved in the project subsequently received outside grants and assistance. In part, because of the training that the initial filming of films such as *Munyurangabo* provided, the team reported that "an entire community of filmmakers has grown in Kigali over the intervening years, working in both documentary and fiction, and largely shooting in Kinyarwanda."[19] Although there were many other influences in the development of a Rwandan film industry, *Munyurangabo* was one of a number of cinematic productions that played a catalytic role in inspiring some young filmmakers.

When the movie was originally planned there was no specific idea about how the film could contribute to the peacemaking and reconciliation process in Rwanda, only a general hope based in the decision that the filmmakers would be providing a Rwandan audience authentic representations of their experience. But as both local independent and other kinds of collaborative filmmaking has continued, there has developed a more specific hope—that Rwanda might become "a place for a new movement in cinema – thinking of the ways in which great movements like Italian Neo-Realism, the French New Wave, and the German New Cinema emerged in countries facing recent or ongoing crises of national identity."[20] According to the team of filmmakers, "These movements did not necessarily succeed in bringing healing to their respective nations, but they did provide a model for ways in which cinema can be more deeply involved in contemporary reality and speak from within a very specific national context to the wider world."[21]

Of course, Rwandan cinema as it has continued to develop has not focused exclusively on the peace and reconciliation process. Increasingly, locally produced films have played both in Rwanda and around the world, especially in film festivals and art house cinemas.[22] The local mobile film-festival, Hillywood, recently had several years where films related to the genocide were intentionally excluded. Over a million immigrants have moved into Rwanda over the last two decades. Post-genocide Rwanda has become a rapidly developing country with modernization and economic growth, and while the genocide continues to cast a long shadow, the long reach of the entertainment industries of Nigeria and Hollywood has also been felt. Films are increasingly reflecting this reality. Thus, just as in India or the United States, movies that invite reflection have needed to find their place alongside movies that are created chiefly for leisure. But Rwanda is now a place where filmmakers have the opportunity to create art which speaks to the dilemmas of their own context. And as they do, their films offer the wider world images that challenge and refresh the senses of those in other societies where peacemaking and reconciliation are also important issues.

Finally, believing that they helped the Rwandans they worked with on *Munyurangabo* to develop a new means of cultural reflection, Chung, Anderson, and Suen returned to Rwanda in January of 2014 to begin work on a new film project, *I Have Seen My Last Born* (2015).[23] A hybrid of documentary and fiction, the movie tells the story of one man, Jean Kwezi, who survived the wars in Eastern Congo and Rwanda in the 1980s and 1990s. The filmmaking process was again collaborative, drawing on storytelling elements rooted in Rwanda itself, with the goal of creating a cinematic form that did justice to where the country is today. The team wrote, "I think we are driven in this by the idea that a work of art, and especially one that emerges through a collaborative practice like cinema, speaks most effectively about reconciliation not by doing so directly, but by drawing people together into an ongoing project; first in the process of making, but having the potential to then extend to the audience, if the aesthetic form does justice to the intention behind the work."[24] Theirs is a collaborative model for peacebuilding and reconciliation through the arts, one that begins with the artistic community and extends out to include those who actively engage with it. It is a model that reaches back into the past for its roots while finding its focus in the present, even while it envisions a hope for a future that is "already," but remains "not yet."

Notes

1. For an extensive and comprehensive discussion of both feature and documentary films about the genocide in Rwanda, see Jolyon Mitchell, *Promoting Peace, Inciting Violence: The Role of Religion and Media* (London and New York: Routledge, 2012), especially Chapter 4 'Bearing Witness through film', 109–147. See also *Shooting Dogs* [Beyond the Gate]. Directed by Michael Caton-Jones (London, UK: BBC Films, 2005); *Sometimes in April.* Directed by Raoul Peck (New York, NY: HBO Films, 2005); *100 Days.* Directed by Nick Hughes (Nairobi, Kenya: Vivid Features); and *The Last Just Man*. Directed by Steven Silver (Toronto, CA: Entertainment One Television [Barna-Alper Productions], 2001).
2. Terry George, quoted by the United Nations Foundation, "The UN Foundation and Hotel Rwanda partner to create 'The International Fund for Rwanda'", http://www.unfoundation.org/news-and-media/press-releases/2005-1997/2005/unf-hotel-rwanda-international-fund.html, accessed 18 November 2012.
3. See Internet Movie Database, www.imdb.com/title/tt0395169/reviews?start=0to584, accessed 4 June 2014.
4. *Shooting Dogs*, 2005 has a similar discussion, this time between a TV journalist and a young teacher.
5. Ishmael Ntihabose, referenced in Linda Mbabazi, "'Kinyarwanda' to premiere at Sundance Film Festival", *The New Times*, 21 January 2011, www.newtimes.co.rw/section/article/2011-01-21/27800/, accessed 27 September 2016.
6. Alrick Brown, Press kit for *Kinyarwanda* (d. Brown, 2011), http://www.kinyarwandamovie.com/2011/kinyarwanda-huffington-post.html, accessed 10 January 2018.
7. Ishmael Ntihabose, in Mbabazi, "Rwanda: 'Kinyarwanda'".
8. Byrant Myers, a former vice-president at World Vision International, one of the major relief groups that sought to help Rwanda in the aftermath of the Genocide, panelist at Reel Spirituality screening of *Kinyarwanda*, Fuller Theological Seminary, 2 March 2012.
9. Tellingly, when an earlier draft of this paper was given at a conference in Jerusalem in December 2012, one participant from Israel responded immediately and viscerally by saying such forgiveness was impossible to conceive as occurring so quickly. It simply couldn't happen like that. And perhaps that is tragically true in Israel. But the "miracle" of Rwanda is that it is happening, even while much remains to be done.

10. Geoff Wisner, "The Mosques of Rwanda", 20 December 2011, www.warscapes.com/reviews/mosques-rwanda, accessed 27 September 2016.
11. Lee Isaac Chung in Jeffrey Overstreet, "A Cinema of Listening and Looking: A Filmwell Conversation with Lee Isaac Chung, Part Two", 9 June 2009, http://theotherjournal.com/filmwell/2009/06/09/a-cinema-of-listening-and-looking-at-film, accessed 27 March 2012.
12. A more radical example of the same process is that of the award-winning, English film writer and director, Mike Leigh (cf., *Naked*, 1993; *Secrets & Lies*, 1996; *Vera Drake*, 2004) who begins each film project with no script, but only a basic premise. This is then developed into a screenplay by gathering the actors together for an extended period of improvisation.
13. A. O. Scott, "15 Years Later, A Quiet Film About a Still-Traumatized Rwanda", *New York Times*, 28 May 2009, www.nytimes.com/2009/05/29/movies/29muny.html, accessed 27 September 2016.
14. Lee Isaac Chung, quoted in Michael Guillen, "TIFF Report: MUNYURANGABO—Interview with Director Lee Isaac Chung and Scriptwriter Samuel Anderson", 22 September 2007, Twitchfilm.com/2007/09/tiff-report-munyurangabointerview-with-director-leeisaac-chung-and-scriptw.html, accessed 18 November 2012.
15. The poet was a member of Chung's film making class and his poem was added to the movie only after he read it for a class assignment.
16. Lee Isaac Chung in Overstreet, "A Cinema of Listening and Looking".
17. Private correspondence with Sam Anderson, Eugene Suen, and Lee Isaac Chung, 28 May 2014. Cf., Christopher Vourlias, "US Shingle Grows Rwanda Film Biz", an article on Lee Isaac Chung's influence and work in Rwanda in *Variety*, 4 February 2012, http://variety.com/2012/film/news/u-s-shingle-grows-rwanda-film-biz-1118049700/, accessed 28 September 2016.
18. Eric Kabera is often described as one of the founding fathers of the Rwandan film industry, with films such as *Keepers of Memory* (Director, 2004) and *Africa United* (Producer, 2010) to his name. He is also the founding director of the Rwandan Cinema Center.
19. Anderson, Chung and Suen, private correspondence, 2014.
20. Anderson, Chung and Suen, private correspondence, 2014.
21. Anderson, Chung and Suen, private correspondence, 2014.
22. For a wide range of examples of films, see Jolyon Mitchell, *Promoting Peace, Inciting Violence: The Role of Religion and Media* (London & New York: Routledge, 2012), 109–147.
23. *I Have Seen My Last Born*. Directed by Lee Isaac Chung and Samuel Gray Anderson (New York, NY and Kigili, Rwanda: Almond Tree Films, 2015).
24. Anderson, Chung and Suen, private correspondence, 2014.

CHAPTER 16

The Power of Film: Grassroots Activism in Ousmane Sembène's *Moolaadé*

Lizelle Bisschoff

Introduction

Listen to the words of the Ivorian actress Naky Sy Savane, who has acted in many francophone West African films. Her words provide a good starting point for this discussion:

> ...the fight against excision, we cannot talk about it, we must each fight in our own way, and as best we can. For many years, I have been fighting against this practice for my daughter, because she risks being excised. [...] The fact is that I fight each year for my daughter because it is a continuous battle. You are vulnerable to this practice right up until marriage. However, most people are not ready to listen to this opposition, it is still part of our tradition. I think the best solution is that each woman in her own work, in her own society, fights to protect her daughter.[1]

L. Bisschoff (✉)
University of Glasgow, Glasgow, Scotland, UK
e-mail: lizelle.bisschoff@glasgow.ac.uk

J. Mitchell et al. (eds.), *Peacebuilding and the Arts*,
Rethinking Peace and Conflict Studies,
https://doi.org/10.1007/978-3-030-17875-8_16

Naky Sy Savane also plays a role in pioneering Senegalese director Ousmane Sembène's *Moolaadé*,[2] the topic of this chapter. I saw this film when it had its African premiere at the 2005 FESPACO film festival, the biennial African film festival, held in Ouagadougou, Burkina Faso, with a packed audience comprised predominantly of locals. As the powerful narrative, a carefully constructed, culturally sensitive call for the eradication of the harmful tradition of female genital mutilation (FGM), unfolded on the big screen in front of me, the audience response was rapturous and emphatic. When *Moolaadé*'s heroine, Collé, played by another well-known and beloved West African actress, Fatoumata Coulibaly, finally succeeds in persuading a small village in West Africa to denounce the tradition in their local community, the audience burst into spontaneous applause and ovation. As with most of Sembène's films, its local appeal was also reinforced by international recognition, with the film awarded the *Prix Un Certain Regard* at the 2004 Cannes Film Festival.

Moolaadé, which translates as "sanctuary" or "magical protection", is the last film by Sembène, made when he was already 81 years old. The film was the second in a planned trilogy on what he called "everyday heroism". The first film in the trilogy is *Faat Kiné*,[3] about a tough and uncompromising single mother and successful business owner in Dakar; Sembène passed away before the final film in the trilogy was made. Sembène's entire corpus of films deals with deeply African stories, themes, characters, situations and locations. Sembène was resolutely committed to the educational and awareness-raising power of film and was outspoken about the fact that he made his films first and foremost for African audiences. While they often entail social realist representations of African societies, traditions and cultures, they are also often visionary and progressive, showing a way forward and presenting possible resolutions to Africa's challenges. *Moolaadé* is such a film; it represents the reality of FGM in a truthful way, interspersed with pathos and humour, and offers a compelling argument for the ending of the tradition and ways in which this could be achieved. As with his previous work, Sembène once again had his finger closely on the pulse of contemporary African society, knowing exactly when the time was right to present his alternative vision for social change.

Sembène was born in 1923 in Senegal and is widely regarded, by theorists, critics and film practitioners alike, as the "Father of African cinema", being credited as the first black African to direct a film on the continent. However, Sembène was as much a writer as he was a filmmaker—he often converted his written work into films or the other way around. Through his remarkably long career, still an active filmmaker and writer until shortly before his death in 2007, Sembène established a corpus of work that has a continuing influence on African (and international) writers, filmmakers and audiences. Sembène was essentially a self-taught intellectual who left school at the age of 14 to become a fisherman like his father. He was drafted into the French army at the outbreak of World War II, and after a brief stay in Senegal, he moved to France in 1949. He joined the French Communist Party and became a union organizer and leader while working as a docker in Marseilles. After the international success of his novel *God's Bits of Wood*,[4] Sembène turned to filmmaking: "What books can do is limited by purchasing power. I go into schools, colleges and cinemas and meet people and I find that the image affects them directly, which a book cannot do".[5] This statement is indicative of Sembène's vision of cinema as an educational tool, a way to reach people at the grassroots of African society and convey social messages to them via film. His political consciousness, shaped through his experiences in Africa and Europe, and the templates for sociopolitical and socio-economic change that he offered through his films and writing are prevalent through all his work in which he overtly addresses social, cultural and political themes and issues. Sembène also spoke out against the paternalistic relationship between the West and Africa and condemned neo-colonialism both from France, as ex-colonizer of much of West Africa, and from within the post-colonial African elite. He understood the importance of tackling change from within and of taking on this task with patience and perseverance, but also with anger and urgency when needed. His work often gives a voice to the resistance of those on the margins of society. Amongst his depictions of various shifting and modified social roles, he attempted to present alternatives for positive change through his representations of gender, as in *Moolaadé*. Sembène believed in particular that African women could play a vital role in bringing about change and progress in Africa.

Given Sembène's preoccupation with female roles and positions in African societies, it is perhaps unsurprising that he chose to tackle the controversial subject of FGM in his final film. FGM is still widely practiced in parts of Africa, the Middle East and Indonesia, and, while statistics vary, according to UNICEF it affects more than 125 million girls and women globally in at least 29 countries. It is an issue that has often been taken up as a cause by NGOs and charities in Europe and America, while it is of course also fought against by activists within the countries where it occurs. Given the often uneven and problematic relationship between developed and developing countries, frequently smacking of neo-colonialist and paternalistic approaches, such attempts by foreign NGOs to intervene in the practices of local communities are fraught with problems. The cultural issues surrounding FGM are particularly complex and contentious, with African feminists, activists and cultural practitioners often criticizing the approach of Western activists to the issue, who have taken it up as a major cause of feminist struggle in a way that resembles earlier attempts of Western feminism to universalize womanhood. This approach runs the risk of reinforcing the conception that Western women are much more "liberated" than African women, and that African women need the assistance of their Western "sisters" to overcome this form of oppression. Rather than attempting to impose change from the outside, it is widely understood within activism that change is most successful when it originates from within, and *Moolaadé* is exactly that: a remarkable and powerful call to action from a local filmmaker, an activist film through which Sembène is speaking from the heart to the local community at a grassroots level.

Within the overall framework of this volume on peacebuilding and the arts, I am interested in exploring how a film such as *Moolaadé* could change perceptions and attitudes, how it could help communities reassess harmful traditions and uneven power relationships and ultimately how it could contribute to bringing about change in order to alleviate oppression, pain, trauma and suffering. The next section will give a brief background of some of the pragmatic and theoretical issues around FGM—in particular in relation to its occurrence in Africa, and specifically from an African feminist viewpoint—and an overview of some of the ways it has been dealt with in film. This will be followed by an in-depth analysis of *Moolaadé* as anti-FGM campaigning film, in order to consider its success as an example of grassroots activism.

Female Genital Mutilation, Feminism and Film

The World Health Organization defines FGM as a surgical procedure "involving partial or total removal of the female external genitalia or other injury to the female genital organs for cultural or other non-therapeutic reasons".[6] The terminology used to describe the practice is indicative of the complexity around the subject. Umbrella terms used to describe the various forms and types of the practice are as follows: FGM, excision, genital cutting, genital surgeries, genital operations and even female genital torture. The term female circumcision has been criticized because it seems to equate the practices performed on women with the much less invasive and severe practice of male circumcision. FGM is likewise a controversial term because of the negative connotation of the word "mutilation", which does not allow for a nuanced interpretation of the practice and its many dimensions, such as it being a rite of passage for young girls. In order to follow the dominant view on the practice, which is that it is harmful and causes unnecessary suffering to young girls and women, I will generally refer to FGM in this piece, though it should be noted that this term is not used in *Moolaadé*. The spoken language in the film is mostly Bambara, and some French, and the English subtitles translate spoken references to the practice in the film's dialogue as "purification" or "cutting", which is indicative of the ways it is viewed by the proponents of the practice in the village represented. As with the terminology, the different practices and methods used are also culturally specific and vary in degree and severity across different regions.

While the statistics of women and girls who have been subjected to some form of the practice vary according to how and by whom these were obtained, all researchers on the subject agree that it affects the lives of millions of African women and girls. FGM is mostly carried out on young girls between infancy and the age of 15, and, within the African continent, it is still widely performed in West Africa, North Africa (in particular in Egypt), the horn of Africa and some parts of East Africa. It also affects communities from these regions living in the diaspora. FGM is widely regarded as a practice to control women's sexuality.[7] The operations are often carried out without anaesthetic, especially where medical professionals are not involved. According to information on the End FGM European Network's website, immediate consequences of FGM can include severe pain and bleeding, shock, difficulty in passing urine, infections, injury to nearby genital tissue and sometimes death.[8] The event itself is traumatic as girls are held down during the procedure. Risk and complications increase with the type of FGM and are more severe and prevalent with infibulations. In addition to the severe pain during and in the weeks following the cutting, women who have undergone FGM experience various long-term effects—physical, sexual and psychological. Women may experience chronic pain, chronic pelvic infections, development of cysts, abscesses and genital ulcers, excessive scar tissue formation, infection of the reproductive system, decreased sexual enjoyment and psychological consequences, such as post-traumatic stress disorder.[9] A multi-country study by the World Health Organization in six African countries found that women who had undergone FGM had significantly increased risks for adverse events during childbirth and that FGM in mothers put newborn babies at risk.[10]

The first major female African voice to emerge against FGM was that of Senegalese sociologist Awa Thiam, who published *Black Sisters, Speak Out: Feminism and Oppression in Black Africa* in 1978.[11] Thiam dispels the myth that the practice of excision originated with Islam and emphasizes that there is no allusion to this in the Quran, which can be verified by referring to the Arabic text or to the translations into different foreign languages.[12] Indeed, many contemporary activists and Islamic leaders continue to condemn the practice in an effort to delink it from religion. They argue that the practice takes its roots primarily in tribal culture, and not in religion, while religious scholars who contest otherwise are misguided. Thiam points out that, at the time of the prophet, excision was already a current practice which was neither forbidden, nor advocated by him. According to Thiam, infibulation (the most invasive and severe form of FGM) constitutes the most eloquent expression of the control exercised by the phallocratic system over female sexuality. Her book contains interviews with various African women, some who are outraged by the practice, some who want to stop it and some who support it. From the interviews, she gained the insight that women have a manifest desire to absolve their elders on the grounds of their ignorance of scientific information about practices such as clitoridectomy, but "[t]his is to underestimate them" she states.[13] The motive for the practice most frequently invoked by respondents in Thiam's book is the control and influence it has on the sexual life of girls, based on a notion that a woman must be made solely into an instrument of reproduction. What should not be underestimated, Thiam states, is that excision and circumcision in many African countries is a purification ceremony, a rite of passage and a coming of age for the young, male and female, of African societies such as the Dogon in Mali. Excision, where the clitoris is removed, is viewed as the purification of the feminine element, whereas the primary function of infibulation is to curb the sexuality of women. This specific form of FGM is intended to make a girl into a desirable bride and to ensure that she will be chaste and virginal until marriage and faithful after marriage. Infibulation is also associated with beauty, fertility and health.[14]

As Thiam outlines, female circumcision operations can form part of initiation ceremonies and an entry into adulthood and integration into the community, and critiques of the practice should not lose sight of this or underestimate the cultural value of these practices. African American social scientist and feminism writer Stanlie M. James[15] describes how Jomo Kenyatta, Kenya's first postcolonial leader, regarded Kikuyu circumcision for girls and boys as a critical aspect of sacred rites of passage. It is regarded as a ritual embedded in a series of activities that symbolize the rebirth of a child as part of the entire tribe, which culminates in the acceptance of the child as an adult member of the society. Kenyatta argued that the tradition was critical to the identity of the Kikuyu and ultimately to the survival of the society. Most communities who practise clitoridectomy in the context of puberty rites also practice male circumcision.[16] Excising the clitoris is seen as removing the male principle from females, whereas male circumcision is regarded as removing the female principle from males. Elders deem these rites necessary to establish gender identity and induct the youth into adulthood.

Nigerian feminist scholar Obioma Nnaemeka is one of the strongest female African voices on FGM to emerge in contemporary critical theory. As an African feminist, Nnaemeka's work often positions itself in opposition to certain tenets of Western feminism, and her work on FGM critiques the ways in which Western feminists have dealt with the issue. In the introduction to the collection of writings *Female Circumcision and the Politics of Knowledge*, edited by Nnaemeka, she states that the contributors to the volume engage from "'the other side' the hot-button issue of female circumcision".[17] Nnaemeka's purpose with the collection is to engage with the issue from an African perspective (all contributors were African and most were female) and in the process expose and assess the long lineage of imperialist and colonial discourses on the subject. She maintains that there is a relationship between knowledge, politics and history—the politics of knowledge and the history of gender, race and class in shaping imperialism. Since racism, ethnocentrism and ignorance about other cultures often colour feminist and human rights struggles, Nnaemeka argues that the feminist-led insurgency against female circumcision in Africa has more to do with what is happening to Western feminists and to their countries and less to do with the African women themselves, resulting in objectifying and inferiorizing African women. Nnaemeka's volume ultimately creates an important space for Africans to participate in the debate as active agents and producers of knowledge. Women from outside of Africa who write about female circumcision and make films about the subject are often mimicking the imperial arrogance of white explorers, imperialist and colonizers, and it is the complex and multi-layered hierarchy on which the imperialist project rests which is exposed and assessed in Nnaemeka's volume. In its interrogation of foreign and Western modus operandi and interventions in the so-called Third World, the volume shows how the resistance that these projects from the outside often generates can impede development work and undermine true collaboration and partnership. Nnaemeka states further that the contested terrain of female circumcision is not a disagreement about the urgent need to put an end to a harmful practice: it is against the strategies and methods, and in particular their imperialistic underpinnings, used to pursue this goal.[18] The resistance of African women against enforced outside activism is not against the campaigns to end the practice, but against their dehumanization and the lack of respect and dignity shown to African women in the process. Ultimately, foreign debates around female circumcision become part of constructing the African woman as “Other”.

While not solely a feminist and anti-patriarchal issue, patriarchal traditions within African societies certainly contribute to the perpetuation of FGM, since, in cultures where it is still practised widely, a man would often not consider marital relations with a woman who has not undergone the ritual. However, a simplistic approach to the subject as another example of male domination over women becomes problematic when one considers the fact that it is also African women who sustain the tradition, since the operations are usually carried out by older women. The issue of older women maintaining traditions which are oppressive to other women, as well as the issue of women-on-women violence is a phenomenon which needs much deeper exploration by cultural theorists. Turshen and Twagiramariya state that it is difficult to understand why women sometimes collude in their oppression and are even complicit in the oppression of other women, beyond the fact that many are politically or economically unable to resist.[19] Nnaemeka writes of the “pain and betrayal of woman-on-woman abuse” and states that the oppression of women is not simply a masculinist flaw as some feminist analyses claim but that it also entails woman-on-woman violence that is often the outcome of institutionalized, hierarchical female spaces that make women victims and collaborators in societal violence.[20] The older African women who carry out and contribute to maintaining the tradition of FGM are often tied to this position out of economic need and a reluctance to relinquish the societal status that the position brings, as they simply have no access to other roles to replace their role as circumciser. Societal violence should indeed not be regarded as solely patriarchal.

A plethora of films, mostly documentaries, have dealt with FGM, predominantly as campaigning films to raise awareness of the issue, although they have mostly been produced by outsiders and non-Africans.[21] One of the best-known examples of a flawed and problematic Western-made film on the subject is Alice Walker and Pratima Parmar's *Warrior Marks* (1993), which has been praised and criticized in equal measure. The film is a poetic and political deliberation of FGM constructed through interviews with women from Senegal, Gambia, Burkina Faso, the US and the UK, intercut with Walker's own personal reflections on the subject. Stanlie M. James states that Walker interviewed the circumcisers in a manner that fails to articulate or even recognize that such practices have provided women with opportunities to attain status, respect and income in societies where there are often very few such avenues available to women.[22] James further claims that the film is marred by a not-very-subtle form of cultural imperialism, which is jarring given Walker's feminist and womanist writings that are typically characterized by sophisticated analyses of patriarchy and oppression.[23] Nnaemeka states that Walker and Parmar came in search of Africa and had their documentary already made in an ideological sense before they even set foot on African soil.[24] African women see and live their lives in ways that are much more complex than the obsessive one-dimensional and one-issue-oriented depictions that appear in books and films about FGM made by outsiders.[25]

Significantly, relatively few female African directors have made films addressing FGM, indicative perhaps of the reluctance of African women to take up subject matters in their films that might fulfil outside expectations of the kind of themes female African directors should address. Female African directors are also aware of the dangers of voyeurism and sensationalism, which such films could fall victim to, as well as the ethical implications in making films on this subject. In addition to *Moolaadé*, another prominent West African male director has made a fiction feature film on the subject, Malian director Cheick Oumar Sissoko's *Finzan*[26] (1989). Both these films deal with the subject in much more complexity and depth than most campaigning documentaries succeed in, while both films condemn the practice through an elaborate fictional narrative negotiation with agency from an exclusively African point of view.

A Call to Action: An Analysis of *Moolaadé* as Activist Filmmaking

Moolaadé's fictional narrative reiterates and elucidates many of the realities and complexities around FGM as described in the previous section. Set in an Islamic village in an unidentified West African country, it tells the story of Collé, herself a victim of FGM who has previously publicly refused to allow her daughter to undergo it, who sets up a sanctuary (the "moolaadé" of the film's title) in her compound for four young girls who turn to her for refuge. The magical protection of the "moolaadé" is represented by a piece of wool strung across the entrance of the compound, which no one can cross. Collé invokes an ancient spell which means that punishment will befall anyone trying to harm the girls while they are in her care. Collé keeps the young girls inside the compound and refuses to surrender them to the "salindana", the older woman who performs the ritual, her defiance creating a conflict that affects everyone in the village and threatens to destroy the village's social stability. The social hierarchies—between men and women, the first and second wives within a polygamous marriage, the salindana and the other women in the village—are clear, but the traditional hegemonic and patriarchal structures are being jeopardized by various influences. One is the battery-operated radios that the women have purchased from Mercenary, a travelling salesman and an outsider in the village. His shop brings many modern items into the village, including radios, batteries, modern clothes and shoes and candy for the children. At one point, the women discuss a news piece they heard on the radio in which an Imam has said that FGM is not required by Islam, and consequently, one of the male village elders insists that all the radios should be confiscated and destroyed, in order to protect the village from outside ideas. Another outside influence is Mercenary himself, who it is revealed, was once a UN peacekeeper dismissed from a UN mission for exposing corruption. A third outside influence is the son of the village chief, who returns home from Paris to claim his bride, Collé's uncircumcised daughter Amasatou. The village chief declares that his son cannot marry Amasatou, as she is a "bilakoro", a derogatory term to refer to an uncircumcised girl or woman. Amasatou is even forbidden to welcome the wealthy returning son back with the traditional calabash drink offering.

The pressure mounts gradually on Collé to release the four girls and allow Amasatou to be circumcised. It is revealed that her resistance to the practice stems from her own experiences as a circumcised woman: she lost her first two daughters during childbirth due to FGM-related complications, and she still bears disfiguring scars from the emergency caesarean that was needed to save her only surviving child, Amasatou. Collé is also shown to bite her finger until it bleeds during sexual intercourse with her husband, in an attempt to displace the pain of sexual intercourse due to having undergone FGM. Collé's unwavering resistance gradually galvanizes the women of the village to support her, spurred on by further tragic events: it is discovered that two young girls committed suicide by jumping into the village well in order to escape the ritual, and when the mother of one of the four girls Collé is protecting forcefully takes her to the salindana to be circumcised, her daughter dies in her arms after the operation. These events finally mobilize the women to support Collé in her quest to end the practice, and she then approaches the village men to announce the collective decision of the women. In a dramatic scene that is very difficult to watch, Collé's husband whips her viciously in front of the entire village in order to force her to submit and end the "moolaadé" with a spell-breaking word, but she is unyielding, supported by the outcries of the women urging her not to say a word. In the end, Collé and the village women are triumphant and the practice is abolished in the village. Where it was previously the radios that the men burned in a pile, it is now the knives of the salindana that they are forced to relinquish and that are set ablaze. The film is bookended by two parallel shots—at the beginning of the film we see the village mosque, a Sudanese style mud structure, with an ostrich egg on top; at the end, we see the mosque again but this time with a television antenna on top. Change and modernity have come to the village and are unstoppable.

Amy Borden states that Sembène provides a blueprint for grassroots human rights activism in *Moolaadé*, because the film animates universal human rights conventions within a local context.[27] As such, the film provides a template of how localized social activism may strengthen women's rights within traditionally patriarchal communities. The film demonstrates a critique of the practice tied to the overall status of women within the community's public institutions. The ways in which change is negotiated in the film and whether it comes from the inside or the outside are carefully interwoven within the narrative and reinforce the strength of the film as a work of social activism. Collé is initially a lone agent for change, but her allies gradually increase—first she persuades her two co-wives to join her protest, then the village women join, and eventually, she convinces the male elders and the salindana too. Indeed, Sembène has said about the film:

> It is not about whether one is for or against the eradication of excision. It is that women in the village refuse. And this refusal is an act of courage. To stand against a group is sheer madness. But to mobilize the others, that is

> courage. Daily struggles, one step, then another, then another. This is what brings about the evolution of attitudes.[28]

While Collé is an insider, Mercenary is an outsider to the village, and his influence is thus limited. When he intervenes and tries to stop Collé's humiliating public lashing, he has disappeared by the next morning and it is assumed that he pays with his life for this inadmissible intervention. While Mercenary's fate might be a broader critique of unwelcome foreign intervention, outside influences are nonetheless also seen as irrepressible and indeed positive—the presence of radios and television symbolizes that globalization and modernity have reached this remote rural village in West Africa. The role of the media, and in this instance, the radio, is positive insofar as it provides information to the women of the village, informing them that "purification" practices are not required by Islam. Outside influences could of course also be seen as negative, and Sembène was outspoken about his criticism of neo-colonialism, cultural imperialism and the "Westernization" of African cultures. It is important not to set up simplistic binary oppositions and oppositional value judgements between Africa and "the West", local and global and tradition and modernity. While *Moolaadé* critiques the harmful tradition of FGM, Sembène also recognizes that traditional beliefs can play a constructive and positive role in African societies: it is the magical spell, the "moolaadé" of the film's title, which provides protection from FGM to the young girls and sets into motion the events that would lead to the eradication of the practice. Sembène seems to say that positive African traditions should be retained, but negative and oppressive traditions and cultural practices should be re-evaluated and abolished if necessary. The challenge for African societies is to find the balance between celebrating and retaining the positive aspects of their traditions, often suppressed and diminished by colonialism, while simultaneously being fully part of the modern, globalized world. The productive consolidation of the oft-cited tradition versus modernity "conflict" within Africa is an important step towards the continent's progress and future.

As is evident from the quote at the beginning of the chapter, Naky Sy Savane, who plays the role of Sanata, the griot, in *Moolaadé*, has in her private life advocated for the eradication of FGM and so has Fatoumata Coulibaly, who plays the role of Collé. In fact, Sembène has stated that all the women who acted in the film, including the "salindana", have undergone the practice themselves. Aware that the practice continues in France amongst the immigrant population, as director of *Groupe femmes pour l'abolition des mutilations sexuelles* in Marseilles, Naky Sy Savane continues the fight that she started in her country of origin, Ivory Coast. She has stated that FGM and forced marriage often go hand in hand and are cultural issues and should thus be fought with cultural tools. For Fatoumata Coulibaly, the film is a reflection of her own life. Having undergone FGM herself, she has been actively involved in a women's association that fights FGM, and similar to the narrative of *Moolaadé*, she attempts to raise awareness of the harmfulness of the practice on the ground amongst village chiefs and excisers.[29]

Moolaadé has, of course, also been used widely as a campaigning tool by NGOs advocating against FGM. Foundation for Women's Health Research and Development (FORWARD) received a grant in 2006 from the Sigrid Rausing Trust to use the film as an advocacy tool with which to tackle FGM and campaign for the advancement of the reproductive and sexual rights of girls and women in Africa. The programme, entitled "Advancing the Human Rights of African Girls", took place initially in Sudan, Ethiopia and Tanzania. FORWARD launched the UK premiere of the film in London in May 2005, in the presence of Sembène, followed by a panel discussion led by FGM and development experts including representatives from FORWARD, the World Health Organization Regional Office for Africa (WHO AFRO) and the Inter-African Committee on Harmful Traditional Practices (IAC).[30] A real-life example of the story of *Moolaadé* can be found in the work of the Senegalese charity Tostan. The organization played a pivotal role in banning FGM in Senegal in 1998 through educating rural women. After the women of one village made their case to the village council, the practice was banned, and the news quickly spread to other villages, eventually leading to a law against the practice.[31]

Conclusion

One important question that *Moolaadé* brings to the fore is whether it is possible to oppose the harmful practice of FGM without perpetuating stereotyped oppositions between Africa and the West, such as developing versus developed and traditional versus modern. Western media is inundated with negative and clichéd stories and imagery of Africa as a corrupt, war-torn, poor and underdeveloped continent, and African scholars and cultural practitioners alike constantly need to strive against reinforcing these stereotypes in their work. I would argue that Sembène succeeds in creating a nuanced, multi-dimensional and complex narrative around the issue of FGM in *Moolaadé*, one that avoids a one-sided or simplistic view of African societies. Despite all the problems around outside intervention in Africa as outlined above, cultural relativism should also not be used as a defence to ignore the practice. Cultural relativism can be used as a critical device and should not be conflated with moral relativism. It is possible to take a moral standpoint against a harmful practice such as FGM, like Sembène does in *Moolaadé*, without taking a moral relativist position, and while maintaining a sense of cultural relativism and difference. It is particularly significant, in this regard, that campaigns for the eradication of harmful traditional practices should first and foremost be created from within. Nnaemeka argues that those who fight against FGM have often blamed it on "tradition" and "culture" and, consequently, have attempted to eradicate Africa's traditional and Islamic past.[32] But, she states, tradition is not about a reified past, but about a dynamic present: a present into which the past is projected and to which other traditions are linked. Sembène's erudite handling of traditional practices and belief systems in *Moolaadé* exemplifies Nnaemeka's suggested approach.

Nnaemeka further states that much of the credit for what has been achieved against the practice must go to African women and men and Africa-based NGOs that work at the grassroots level.[33] African activists may often lack the material and structural conditions necessary for the accomplishment of their goals, but they do not lack agency. Africa-based NGOs often place culture and cultural expressions as a positive force at the centre of their work: the importance of visual and performing arts in development work cannot be underestimated. Sembène understood this, and my experience of watching *Moolaadé* with an African audience invoked at the beginning of this chapter could perhaps be seen as an indication of the potential success of such an approach. A film such as *Moolaadé* is situated at the intersection of advocacy, activism and cultural production, and its main significance lies in the fact that it is a cry from the heart, a voice from the inside that speaks with cultural knowledge and sensitivity, arguing for the eradication of unnecessary suffering in order to promote a peaceful, just and equal society.

Notes

1. Naky Sy Savane quoted in Beti Ellerson, *Sisters of the Screen: Women of Africa on Film, Video and Television* (Trenton and Asmara: Africa World Press, 2000), 293.
2. *Moolaadé*. Directed by Ousmane Sembène (Senegal: Filmi Doomireew, 2004). Film.
3. *Faat Kiné*. Directed by Ousmane Sembène (Senegal: Filmi Doomireew, 2000). Film.
4. Ousmane Sembène, *God's Bits of Wood* [*Les Bouts de Bois de Dieu*], trans. Francis Price (London, UK: Heinemann, 1962).
5. Sembène quoted in Olivier Bartlet, *African Cinema: Decolonizing the Gaze* (London and New York: Zed Books Ltd., 1996).
6. World Health Organization. "Fact Sheet: Female Genital Mutilation", http://www.who.int/mediacentre/factsheets/fs241/en/index.html, accessed 1 July 2015.
7. Awa Thiam, *Black Sisters, Speak Out: Feminism and Oppression in Black Africa* (London, UK: Pluto Press, 1978), 68.
8. End FGM, European Network. "Female Genital Mutilation: What Is FGM?" http://www.endfgm.eu/en/female-genital-mutilation/what-is-fgm/effects-of-fgm/, accessed 1 July 2015.
9. End FGM, "Female Genital Mutilation".
10. End FGM, "Female Genital Mutilation". The study showed that an additional one to two babies per 100 deliveries die as a result of FGM.
11. Awa Thiam, *Black Sisters.*
12. Thiam, *Black Sisters*, 58.
13. Thiam, *Black Sisters*, 68.
14. Thiam, *Black Sisters*, 68.
15. Stanlie M. James, "Listening to Other(ed) Voices: Reflections Around Female Genital Cutting", in *Genital Cutting and Transnational Sisterhood: Disputing U.S. Polemics*, eds. Stanlie M. James and Claire C. Robertson (Urbana and Chicago: University of Illinois Press, 2005), 91.
16. James, "Listening to Other(ed) Voices", 91.
17. Obioma Nnaemeka, "Introduction", in *Female Circumcision and the Politics of Knowledge*, ed. Obioma Nnaemeka (Westport, CT and London, UK: Praeger, 2005), 3.
18. Nnaemeka, "Introduction", *Female Circumcision*, 29.
19. Meredeth Turshen and Clotilde Twagiramariya, "Introduction", *What Women Do in Wartime: Gender and Conflict in Africa* (London, UK and New York, NY: Zed Books, 1998), 10.
20. Obioma Nnaemeka, "Introduction", in *The Politics of (M)Othering: Womanhood, Identity, and Resistance in African Literature* (London, UK and New York, NY: Routledge, 1997), 19.

21. It would be a significant project to compile an exhaustive list of films on FGM. Some examples include: *FGM: A Cruel Ritual* (1991), *Another Form of Abuse* (1992), *Fire Eyes* (1994), *FGM in Egypt* (1994), *Reham's Story* (2001), *The Day I Will Never Forget* (2002), *Dabla! Excision* (2003), *A Handful of Ash* (2007), *Desert Flower* (2009), *Africa Rising: The Grassroots Movement to End Female Genital Mutilation* (2009), *The Cutting Tradition* (2010), *Female Genital Mutilation and Pregnancy* (2010), *Abandon the Knife* (2011), *Silent Scream* (2011), *Cut That Thing* (2012), *A Pinch of Skin* (2012), *Sara's Story* (2014), *True Story* (2012), *I Will Never Be Cut* (2012), *The Cruel Cut* (2013), *A Change Has Begun* (2014), *The Imam's Daughter* (2015), *Calm* (2015), and *Jaha's Promise* (2017).
22. James, "Listening to Other(ed) Voices", 88.
23. James, "Listening to Other(ed) Voices", 92.
24. Nnaemeka, "Introduction", *Female Circumcision*, 36.
25. Nnaemeka, "Introduction", *Female Circumcision*, 36.
26. *Finzan* [A Dance for Heroes]. Directed by Cheick Oumar Sissoko (Mali: Centre National de Production Cinématographique [CNPC], Kora Films, ZDF [Zweites Deutsches Fernsehen], 1989). Film.
27. Borden, Amy. "At the Global Market: Ousmane Sembène's *Mooladé* and the Economics of Women's Rights", *Jumpstart*, http://www.ejumpcut.org/archive/jc53.2011/bordenMoolade/index.html, accessed 1 July 2015.
28. Sembene quoted in the documentary *Référence Sembène*. Directed by Yacouba Traoré (Paris, FR: Médiathèque des Trois Mondes, 2002). Film.
29. In Ellerson, "African Women in Cinema Confront FGM".
30. FORWARD UK, "Using *Moolaadé* to Advance the Rights of African Girls", 22 February 2006, http://www.forwarduk.org.uk/new-forward-programme-in-africa-using-moolaade-to-advance-the-rights-of-african-girls/, accessed 1 July 2015.
31. Gannon Gillespie, "Ending Female Genital Mutilation, One Household at a Time", *The Guardian*, 22 August 2013, http://www.theguardian.com/global-development-professionals-network/2013/aug/22/social-network-fmg-senegal, accessed 1 July 2015.
32. Nnaemeka, "Introduction", *Female Circumcision*, 37.
33. Nnaemeka, "Introduction", *Female Circumcision*, 4041.

CHAPTER 17

Towards a Disarmed Cinema

Olivier Morel

Disarming Thoughts

In his renowned essay on the rise of cinema as an industrial art of the masses, Gilles Deleuze asserts that despite the oft-held hope that cinema would provoke thought while "communicating the shock"[1] in order to invent a better world ("changer le monde"), the art of what he calls "movement-image" instead became quickly characterized by "experimental abstraction", "formalist antics [*pitreries formalistes*]" and other "commercial configurations [*figurations commerciales*]"[2] of sex and blood. According to this definition of "bad" cinema, shock is a part of the apparatus that enables violence. A prime example of this can be found in propaganda films. He concludes that "the art of masses was already showing a disquieting face",[3] that of the totalitarian use of cinema as a tool for manipulation of masses, and of political *mise-en-scènes*:

For Vincent Emanuele.

O. Morel (✉)
University of Notre Dame, Notre Dame, IN, USA
e-mail: omorel@nd.edu

J. Mitchell et al. (eds.), *Peacebuilding and the Arts*,
Rethinking Peace and Conflict Studies,
https://doi.org/10.1007/978-3-030-17875-8_17

> Everyone knows that, if an art necessarily imposed the shock or vibration, the world would have changed long ago, and humans would have been thinking for a long time. So this pretention of the cinema, at least among the greatest pioneers, raises a smile today.[4]

Deleuze's sarcastic or disillusioned tone about cinema's pretention to positively change the world is echoed by a recent statement from the legendary German film-maker born in 1945, Wim Wenders, in a radio conversation with the Australian philosopher Mary Zournazi who co-authored their book titled *Inventing Peace: A Dialogue on Perception*.[5] Considering the missed opportunity for peace that the worldwide compassion for the victims of 9/11 made possible, Wenders says, "Talking about peace has bad press".[6] Wenders here follows some of the most powerful developments of the book, in which the authors state baldly that "peace is largely invisible" while "war always demands centre stage".[7] The wording, here, is essential, especially for a film-maker like Wenders: war occurs on *stage*, and peace is largely *invisible*. If war takes place on the stage of the world's theatre in a highly visible way, how are we to understand or put peace into the picture if it is "invisible"? Wenders implies that even if peace is [working] backstage or offstage, its "invisibility" still depends on what happens *within the theatrical sphere*. Wenders is arguing that *conceiving of*, or as we say in French, *thinking peace [penser la paix]* today requires a capacity to envision what he calls generically the "stage" that is peace's theatrical dimension, the spectacle. For Wenders that performative space includes, of course, cinema. However, "Wings of Desire", in which "Homer" asks, "Why is there no epic peace?"[8] raises questions about how far peace is *thinkable* without falling into the same performance space of war or using conceptual categories such as "image", "performance" or "spectacle" in the same ways.

Wenders's reflection and his cinema suggest that in order to think the *possibility of peace*, we have to be able to engage in a deconstruction of theatre, of spectacle, of cinema understood as a centre part of the production of the "theatre of war". That is, we must deconstruct the "stage", on which war takes place. The "theatre of war" has long led the world of imaginary and iconographic representation (since Homer at least, as Wenders has indicated) raises questions about the *essence of cinema*. For the nature of war is spectacular and the short time of destruction dominates the field of cinematic vision in a way that forces the longer time of peacebuilding out of the frame. In Wenders' terms, the very "visibility" of war renders peace "invisible". Conceiving of peace thus requires us to conceive a certain cinematic invisibility, and Wenders (in his cinema and elsewhere) belongs to those film-makers who wrestle with this conceptualization.

The preceding case study chapters in this section on Film have reflected on how film can help to bear witness, thereby making both genocide (Robert Johnston, Chapter 15) and FGM violence against young women (Lizelle Bisschoff, Chapter 16) more visible. Film can make violence more visible, though not necessarily always in shocking or spectacular ways. These examples highlight the potential for films to build peace, even if this process can be both gradual and largely invisible. In this way, cinema can contribute to what Joseph Kickasola describes as "re-humanizing", by being a catalyst for empathy, imaginative world-making, creative truth-telling and imagining alternative futures. My aim in this chapter is to contribute to the discussions found in these earlier essays, but offer a complementary argument, exploring both theoretical and practical moves towards a "disarmed cinema".

In his 1985 essay titled *War and Cinema*,[9] the French philosopher Paul Virilio extends Deleuze's thought in a radical way. For Virilio, it is not that cinema was distorted or alienated as a mediocre industrial art of the masses dedicated to propaganda, to the organizing of war and ordinary fascism. It is rather that the logistics of weapons is *essentially not separable* from that of images and sounds. The Gulf War (1990–1991) gave Virilio a perfect illustration of this theory. Virilio argued that the viewer of the images of the "surgical bombings", which were widely used by newscasters and other "information" networks, was implicated in the violence shown. That is, there is no discontinuity between the violence recorded and perpetrated by the killing machine and the appearance of these recorded images on screens. Not only was Virilio saying that this "theatre" dissolved time and distance, he was saying that the eye that killed was not substantially different from the eye that watched the war on TV as if it were a football game.[10] With others, he has pointed out that at the end of the twentieth century, war was still dramatically served by complacent audiences within a system where cinematic and media apparatuses do not distinguish between observing, attacking and "communicating".

Cinema and the Performance of Violence

Without explicitly referencing Deleuze and Virilio, Joram Ten Brink & Joshua Oppenheimer's edited volume *Killer Images, Documentary Film,*

Memory and the Performance of Violence comes from the same standpoint, arguing that historically:

> Cinema has long shaped not only how political violence, from torture to warfare to genocide, is perceived, but also how it is performed. Today, when media coverage is central to terror campaigns, and newscasters serve as embedded journalists in the "war on terror's" televisual front, understanding how the moving image is implicated in the imagination and actions of perpetrators and survivors of mass violence is all the more urgent. The cinematic image and mass violence on huge scales are two defining features of modernity.[11]

Brink and Oppenheimer here focus on the *performance* of violence stating that not only is cinema a prolongation of the war machine (Deleuze, Virilio) but that it also *shapes* how war is conducted by social actors. In other words, the cinema industry understood in a broad sense ("tele-technologies" as Derrida puts it) is not just a passive element in a gigantic prosthetics of perception devoted to the killing of people in war, it is also a powerfully *active* system that produces a dramaturgy and shapes a worldview with no exteriority. That is, today's totally cinematic representation of the world takes a crucial part in the *performance* of violence.

The philosopher Bernard Stiegler goes even further when he argues that if language has always been writing, today, *life* is always, already, *cinema*. Godard called the twentieth century the century of cinema, and it coincided with the apogee of the industrial age in which our perception and production of the world—as well as our imagination—was entirely cinematic. Stiegler argues that in what he calls "cinematic time",[12] cinema would always be an *armed cinema*.[13] The enormous cinematic industry has become the key industry of industrial development where cinematic technologies (cameras, microphones, broadcasting technologies, etc.) are *constitutive of desire*. That is, they have taken control of our libido (our impulses or drives), to the point where cinema becomes a substitute for individuals' desires—understood as commodified psyches—allowing the cinematic scheme to control consumers' pulses. Cinema is no longer understood as a *prosthetics* of conscience, but as conscience *itself* (what Stiegler calls the "archi-cinematography of the psyche").[14] The consequence is that the ongoing war takes place in our conscience and the distinction between perception and imagination, between reality and fiction, has faded. This is probably the most important stake of our [cinematic] time, the fact that it is not that cinema serves the war, but that our cinematic conscience is at war—at war with itself. This might be the original "shock" by which Deleuze defines cinematic power. This shocking movement-image I call an essential traumatopoietic and traumatophile apparatus.

Deleuze argues that cinema's power is to generate a shock that enables *thought*: "It is as if cinema were telling us: with me, with the movement-image, you can't escape the shock which arouses [éveille] the thinker in you. A subjective and collective automaton for an automatic movement: the art of the 'masses'".[15] This central moment prompts Deleuze to [re-] reflect on how Hitler's instrumentalized cinema was used as a war machine. He comments on the German film-maker Hans-Jürgen Syberberg's analysis: "This is what compels Syberberg to say that the end-product of the movement-image is Leni Riefenstahl, and if Hitler is to be put on trial by cinema, it must be *inside cinema*, against Hitler the film-maker, in order to 'defeat him cinematographically, turning his weapons against him' [Serge Daney]".[16] (This claim provides additional insights to Kickasola's critical engagement, in Chapter 14 of this book, with Riefenstahl's cinematic work.) What Deleuze observes in the history of thought "from Heidegger to Artaud" is that the *powerlessness of thought* is what forces thought.[17] He asks: "By what means does cinema approach this question of thought, its fundamental powerlessness [impuissance essentielle] and the consequences of this?"[18] Deleuze's ideas on cinema are driven by a refusal to concede that if cinema has to be intrinsically dominated by warfare, it does not mean that cinema is unable to have the *force* (power) to change the world and to build and ensure peace. His argument is that cinema is paradoxically both armed and powered by a disarmed, powerless capacity to "shock" people. Deleuze asks if a "powerless" and "disarmed cinema" is possible and under what conditions would a cinema be possible that reverses the course of its dominant history? In other words, is a cinema possible that would not fall into the trap of being used as a war machine?

Filming the Invisibility of Peace

Thinking a "disarmed cinema" as a condition of thinking the cinematic machineries of war begins with discussing what Wenders calls the "invisibility" of peace. If we follow Deleuze's footprints, thought consists of enduring the power of thinking the cinema's essential powerlessness, that is in thinking something that resists thought. One might say that the possibility of a cinema of peace would begin with the capacity to film the invisible. Filming, recording, showing, struggling with the invisible and letting it occur on the screen is what film-makers like Errol Morris, Rithy Panh and Joshua Oppenheimer have attempted to do with gut-wrenching, powerful and disarmed non-fiction films during the past decade.

Errol Morris: Revealing the Frame

Morris's notorious film *Standard Operating Procedure* was produced in 2008 in the USA and presents a meticulous investigation of how the infamous pictures known as the "Abu Ghraib Pictures" were taken and became the iconic worldwide representation of torture perpetrated in the post-9/11 era. In a sense, this is not a film about the Abu Ghraib scandal itself. Morris's point is that these pictures are only the *small visible part* of what happened and that the victim's voice and suffering were kept silent. Essentially, what Morris makes visible is what the pictures *reveal*, that is, for him, *what they do not show*, their "out-of-frame". Morris elaborates,

> [...] there are all kinds of hidden assumptions in photographs—and in the process of looking at photographs. I'm sure that you've read about so-called "selection effects", where we think that having seen a part of the whole, that we're seeing everything. And the Abu Ghraib photographs are a perfect example of that sort of thing. Because *we think we've seen Abu Ghraib*, and *we think that we've seen the crimes that were committed at Abu Ghraib*, when in fact what we've seen is a couple hundred images which were taken in a very restricted period of time on Tier 1A of the prison during the fall of 2003. And *the real story of Abu Ghraib is in no way contained in those images. Nor do those images contain the worst of the violence*.[19]

The power of Morris's film is to give visibility to the gigantic invisible continent in which the couple hundred images taken at Abu Ghraib constitute an epiphenomenon. The film is about the "worst violence" that was performed in the post-9/11 conflicts, and the worst is out-of-frame. In the introduction to her book *Frames of War*, Judith Butler writes:

> The frame does not simply exhibit reality, but actively participates in a strategy of containment, selectively producing and enforcing what will count as reality. ... [Framing] remains structured by the aim of instrumentalizing certain versions of reality. This means that the frame is always throwing something away, always keeping something out, always de-realizing and de-legitimating alternative versions of reality, discarded negatives of the official version.[20]

The "out-of-frame" revealed in Morris's film allows the viewer to *envision* the systemic torture that was planned and performed. Morris's film deconstructs the official version provided by the Bush administration alleging that those pictures had been taken by a "few bad apples", as the military claimed. The film shows how a seeming disaster—a public relations disaster—for the Bush administration was manipulated to its advantage. In this case, as in other similar situations, forgetting, erasing, minimizing violence *is part of the apparatus of violence* and *Standard Operating Procedure* finds itself precisely where the machinery of erasure functions. This blind spot, this frame that excludes other realities, is what makes Morris's cinema a powerful, armed cinema, as a practical deconstruction of what was widely presented as the "real story of Abu Ghraib". This is a conjuration of the effacement of the violence that the "infamous pictures" do not show.

Rithy Panh: When Cinema Writes the History of the Victims

"Genocide is the unnamable: parents felt that their greatest challenge was to speak. It is the role of art, of cinema, like that of any other artistic form, to help us name things. If art cannot do this, then, we risk confusing everything and rewriting history".[21] So declares the film-maker Rithy Panh in an interview with the journalist Anne Chaon about *The Missing Picture* (2013).[22] This masterpiece is the Cambodian-French director's third major film featuring the performance of violence that allowed the Khmer Rouge's genocide. *S21: The Khmer Rouge Killing Machine* (2003) and *Duch Master of the Forges of Hell* (2012) focus on the Khmer killing machine, specifically on the S21 prison in which 17,000 persons were tortured and executed. "Duch", Kaing Guek Eav, who directed this prison, was formally charged with war crimes and crimes against humanity on 31 July 2007, and found guilty on 26 July 2010. Panh explains how he conceives of his filmmaking:

> When making the film I thought a great deal of the dead, of course. In making the film *the dead were with me always*... the very fact that I am here, to a certain degree, suggests that somebody left a place for me. So my job is to transmit to the following generation what happened, but also not for them to feel guilty for what happened.[23]

The invisible victims are who drive Panh and shape his cinematic space; this is the picture outside the frame. Filming with the spectral presence of the dead, of the genocide's victims, means that Panh's camera is always placed somewhere on the thin border that divides the visible and the invisible. The invisible people, victims of the Khmer Rouges, are not just the subject of Panh's films, they are also a *power.* The invisible dead drive a powerful *act of filming*. This act is intrinsically correlated to Panh's attempt to *write history.*

In the Cambodian context, the perpetrators of the violence of the Khmer Rouge are still not perceived as such. In such a case, relatives of the victims may both voiceless and carry a sense of guilt, while at the same time, feel confused about what caused their relative's arrests and punishments. In this sense, they fit Derrida's definition of being haunted: "Being haunted by a ghost is to remember something you've never lived through, for memory is the past that has never taken the form of the present".[24] As Panh explains, the younger generations "go around thinking that their grandparents committed a crime, and that's why they were killed. They go around feeling guilty themselves for that".[25] He adds: "There was a young woman that I met who said she'd seen the film, which had made her suffer a lot, but at the same time *it returned her dignity to her*".[26] Here, the social presence of the crime is so obvious that the perpetrators are not trialed and convicted, so the violence perpetrated continues to live under the surface and have emotional and moral consequences. Peace remains invisible, as Wenders suggests. This is where the missing picture finds itself, and this is the place where the dead are still voiceless and cannot proclaim their innocence. This is the space claimed by Panh and where he aims his camera. Or to be more precise, this space is created by Panh as a ghostly, spectral location, in the making of the film. Panh shoots his film in the space of the dead. Cinema speaks from this side of death, and it produces a liberation and an invention of location which could be understood as cinema's radical out-of-frame, the invisible space of peace. This space allows what Panh calls "dignity" to come into the frame, instead of the war that occupied "centre stage" (Wenders). According to Panh, it fulfils a function that is similar to the judicial process:

> I think justice cannot resolve the problem, only a small part of the problem. People have waited a long time for this tribunal to bring them a solution. But they will be disappointed. Because a tribunal cannot bring a solution to their questions. But we need it because a tribunal can recognize who is the victim and who is the perpetrator, like the film does. [...] If people who killed millions do not face justice, how can you put a guy who steals a bicycle to jail?[27]

Panh was born in Phnom Penh in 1964 and saw his family, his parents, siblings and other relatives die of overwork and malnutrition under the Khmer Rouge regime. Cinema is the language that he has tried to find while attempting to express his tremendous unspoken suffering through painting, singing and writing:

> Cinema came by chance. Something that cinema can do which literature can't do, in the same way for example, is when you have somebody in the film, as he does, say, 'I killed', and then there's a long silence before he says, 'and I take responsibility'. This is something you cannot do as easily, as powerfully with literature. [...] And how do you, for example, describe in literature the scene where he goes through the gestures of his day, or his nights' work as a guard?[28]

For Pahn, cinema engages a process of writing history in the sense that *it names the unnamable*, it makes the invisibility of the victims visible, it empowers powerless individuals, and it gives a face to the faceless crime that was perpetrated and still dominates/poisons social interaction. Panh's cinema is thus a *performance of peace.*

In *S21*, the social invisibility of the victims and their need for peace is fulfilled through re-enactment of the violence perpetrated by the guards in the prison. This is the "missing picture:" the *impossibility of naming* is not just a derivation of the traumatic event, it is trauma itself, for bound up in trauma is the destruction of the experience. Panh films this traumatic destruction: when the guard returns to the prison to re-enact the tortures, none of the victims are seen on the screen; they are physically absent. But their invisible presence stops the cinematographer from entering in the empty room where the former guard re-enacts the violent gestures of assaulting and beating the prisoners. This "repeated" destruction of the prisoners is deeply lived, recorded, marked by Panh and *marking* as a *lack* (the absence of the victims). It touches on the destruction of the conscience, not just of the viewer and of Cambodian society, but potentially of the perpetrator also. What is recorded in the cinematic process engaged in by Panh is the lack, the missing experience of the victims and their powerlessness.[29] Filming this powerlessness, giving it a [cinematic] creative space, is what cinema can do as a peacebuilding apparatus.

For the very few survivors of the tortures like Nath, this experience is haunting. Being haunted implies being subjected to involuntary repetitions, to the compulsive iteration of reliving the traumatic event. As Freud wrote about victims of accidents in his *Beyond the Principle of Pleasure*: "Dreams occurring in traumatic neuroses have the characteristic of repeatedly bringing the patient back into the situation of this accident".[30] The return, or emergence of the repressed, or here the re-activation of the dead is *a process of virtualization*. To me, this process is *cinematic in essence*; it is cinematography of the psyche: repetition and virtualization. It also means that this repetition figures the *war of phantoms*, of spirits, of images. The choreographic-like reiteration of the performance of violence inaugurates a sort of *ceremony* which operates for the victims as a re-actualization of the trauma.

However, one of Panh's most powerful moves consists of engaging the *perpetrators* in the process of repetition when he asks them to re-enact the gestures of the crime. If a forgiveness is possible, this repetition is necessary—to include the perpetrator in this process of haunting, allows for the possibility of the return of conscience.[31] To me, the mere fact that the guards are willing to repeat gestures indicates that a [cinematic] possibility of reconciliation may be already in progress. The repetition is also ritualistic and reveals the complex relationships that the perpetrators have to the crime as shown in *S21*. The wound is ritually and symbolically re-opened by the guards, as it is also physically embodied in the guards' "bodily memory"[32] as a ghostly presence.

Joshua Oppenheimer: Rehearsing the Crimes, Reversing the Logics of War

The killer plays his own role in *S21*; acting turns him into a ghost. Acting means that the person who moves and talks is always, already, a phantom. When Joshua Oppenheimer asks Anwar Congo to re-enact the gestures of the killings in the Indonesian massacres of 1965 in *The Act of Killing*, he films a perpetrator who is already a ghost, fighting, as he has been throughout his life, with the ghosts of the mass killing in which he played "the killer". The perpetrators used American gangster-killer films for their inspiration, drives, motivation and excitement before they went out to kill. Oppenheimer's masterpiece shows how in this they were social "actors". Thus in a sense, *The Act of Killing* is a film about cinema. The making of this film occurred in an Indonesian public space precisely where the spectral power is insidiously operating in a society where the visibility of the killers is widespread since they are perceived and shown as heroes in Indonesian society today. In a sense, Oppenheimer is not showing how individuals are behind the war crime and crime against humanity perpetrated in Indonesia. Instead, he depicts a cinematic landscape in which, as Oppenheimer puts it, the killers are "instruments of a system rather than its masters—they show themselves to be culpable functionaries".[33] The very fact that the perpetrators perceive themselves as actors on stage during and after the perpetration of the crime reveals how intricately intertwined are the crime, the performance of the crime and its comprehension in society. The crime is profoundly buried in Indonesia's cinematic psyche. Here, war continues to take centre stage to the point where the "stage" has ceased to be thought of as such and has become normalized. The first act in Oppenheimer's film consists of making the viewers aware of *the existence of this stage* while filming the perpetrators as if they were actors rehearsing the crime perpetrated in 1965. Oppenheimer writes that "the route to the historical scene through fiction, no matter how transparently direct, remained open".[34]

Oppenheimer's cinematic intervention reverses the logic of cinematic war while pushing the crime's theatrical and cinematic spectacle to the extreme. This is what re-enactment is all about in his film. With the full consent of the killers, Oppenheimer pushes re-enactment to its most surrealistic obscene extremity (visibility). The "actors", Anwar Congo and his squad, play the role, until their representation falls apart:

> These displays of excessive visibility, by eclipsing with their generic gore the terrible singularity of each murder, make visible the relationship between obscenity (in the everyday sense) and its own obscene—the historical real itself. And in this evocation of the historical real, what is made real is the *absence of the victims*—that is, their death.[35]

There is a mysterious turning point in *The Act of Killing* that occurs while Anwar Congo re-enacts the tortures he perpetrated in a scene when he is "playing" an American gangster on a film set. During this scene, it becomes very clear that Anwar Congo's ghosts are terrifying him. Throughout the film, he has been bragging with his co-perpetrators when suddenly he asks the other "actors" to stop the acting. Oppenheimer's camera is still rolling while the killer gives up on acting. This is the moment when he reaches what Panh defines as: "I killed and I take responsibility". At this moment, the perpetrator's "fake" gestures become excruciatingly painful and unbearable for Congo. This moment of re-enactment has all the appearance of fiction, and yet it reveals the "real" in the documentary film: "Narrative has the power to conjure terror, and somehow, as with ghost stories, this power is attractive".[36] This is the moment when the missing people, Congo's invisible victims, become present. Perhaps, as Oppenheimer argues, "the spectacle of filmmaking functions like a fetish, a substantive metonym for the *missing audience*, as well as a concrete metaphor for the abstract apparatus of television and media as a system of images".[37]

Conclusion

Stiegler argues that we can never establish a strict distinction between what Husserl calls primary and secondary retention—that is between perception and imagination, between reality and fiction.[38] Here, he potentially opens what I see as a possibility of *reconciliation*. Forgiving implies a subtle possibility of imagining, or what I also call a sublimation or cult. This can be likened to what Oppenheimer calls a "fetish", or what Panh calls a "ceremony". These are all operations that are required in a process of reconciliation understood as projection in the future, the conjuration of the ghosts of violence, of the invisible and non-recognized victimhood. As long as the return of the ghosts is not *cinematically constructed*, victims live in a limbo, their suffering proliferates in a blurry sense of illegitimacy, they feel guilty, and their unnamed pain never ends. Cinema is a *materia medica* [pharmacopée] in this context; its potentially toxic power is here used as a healing power. Among its powers (fetishization, ceremony, etc.), it helps locate and qualify the wound while making its virtual occurrences concrete (ghostly repetition, trauma). It realizes the war of phantoms and opens up a chance to reverse the destructive progression of the war in societies long after the ceasefire took place. Aside from *Standard Operating Procedure*, *S21*, *Duch* and *The Act of Killing*, there are many other of examples of how films have deeply transformed the way crimes are perceived in the societies where they were committed.[39]

What this disarmed cinema does with such conviction is take the out-of-frame's invisible powerlessness of the victims and make it visible. Filming is therefore an act that dignifies. If peacebuilding is possible through cinema, it occurs when this out-of-frame is opened and becomes the *invention of space, a phantom-space* that allows the wounds to be sublimated (or fetishized) through cinematic performance (acting) and the repetition that occurs on screen. There is no peace until this wound is cinematically located, until cinema allows the victims to reveal their space where this space has been kept sociologically nonexistent, politically blocked, censored, forgotten or forbidden. This process creates the opportunity to cinematically *interrupt* what the cinematic war has created: the war of phantoms. This affects not only the "actors" of the film (victims, perpetrators) but also the viewers (ceremony). As the philosopher Eyal Peretz writes about Brian de Palma's subtle use of the sound and of the out-of-frame in his cinema:

> Not being located, not finding a place, inside the cinematic frame nor locatable in any identifiable, actual (spatial or temporal) realm outside the frame, these sounds continue to haunt the visual image and to undermine any separate position the viewers might attempt to adopt in relation to it. The viewers therefore remain implicated and addressed by this dimension of non-place and cannot cancel their dependence on, their passivity to, or their passion of, the image, their subjection to that which calls them despite themselves. The visual image itself, then, seems to be missing something, to have a 'hole' punctured in it, *as a result of its disjunction from the soundtrack*, and becomes an enigmatic fragment [...]. But more than the breathing and the beating sustain this haunting of the image, for the unseen moving camera itself, as yet lacking motivation for its selection of the visual field [...], marks a *disturbance* that operates as a phantom introducing a haunting enigma, a non-identifiable Otherness at the heart of the image.[40]

Cinema as understood in this chapter has the ability to isolate, to decontextualize and to interrupt violent continuities. It is this that Wenders describes as the ongoing war that has centre stage and it allows us to include the Other in the frame. What cinema opens up is a disarmed space for otherness, without which there is no peace imaginable. This conception of cinema allows a profound change in the way societies legitimate themselves while lying to themselves, while keeping the victims' voices and faces out of view. This is why films like the ones discussed here have the social power described by Joshua Oppenheimer below, who can no longer set foot on the Indonesian soil because of his film, but whose work is currently and irreversibly changing Indonesian society today:

> There was a screening in a village in central Java, students of a religious organization that participated in the killings in 1965, and they held a screening at a mass grave with survivors. Now I would never suggest holding a screening of this film at a mass grave, but they wanted to. Every year survivors would want to go to this particular grave during Ramadan to pay their respects to their dead, and the Pancasila Youth [a right-wing paramilitary Indonesian group] would physically stop and sometimes attack them.
>
> But they held this screening at the grave, and ever since, both survivors and the children of perpetrators have gone to pay respects to the dead, together.

It's that kind of opening of a space for reconciliation—we don't want our country to be like this, like what you see in the film—that has been the most wonderful response.[41]

Notes

1. Gilles Deleuze, *The Time-Image 2*, trans. Hugh Tomlinson and Robert Caleta (Minneapolis, MN: University of Minnesota Press, 1989), 166. "It is this capacity, this power, and not the simple logical possibility, that cinema claims to give us in communicating the shock".
2. Deleuze, *Time-Image 2*, 167.
3. Deleuze, *Time-Image 2*, 167.
4. Deleuze, *Time-Image 2*, 167. Translation modified.
5. Wim Wenders and Mary Zournazi, *Inventing Peace: A Dialogue on Perception* (London, UK: I.B. Tauris, 2013).
6. "The philosopher and the Filmmaker".
7. Wenders and Zournazi, *Inventing Peace*, 147. "War must have been utterly successful! It has formed into a solid notion, the sum of all its images, the BIG PICTURE OF WAR! 'Peace', however, somehow doesn't amount to a sum! 'There's no BIG PICTURE OF PEACE'", 64.
8. *Wings of Desire*. Directed by Wim Wenders (Berlin, Germany: Road Movies Filmproduktion, 1987).
9. Paul Virilio, *War and Cinema: The Logistics of Perception*, trans. Patrick Camiller (London, UK and Brooklyn, NY: Verso, 2009). Born in 1932, Virilio often defined himself as a "war baby" and certainly war has shaped his thought since at least the age of eleven when he saw the French city of Nantes being destroyed by bombs in 1943 and 1944.
10. In my 1996 interview with Paul Virilio, he states: "What is being set up today is a war of information, an 'info-war:' the location of war—if we want to locate it because it is precisely de-territorialized and de-realized—is the NSA (National Security Agency), which is way more powerful than the CIA" ["Ce qui se met en place est une guerre de l'information, une info-war: le lieu de la guerre aujourd'hui — si on voulait lui donner un lieu puisque justement elle est déterritorialisée et déréalisée — c'est la NSA (National Security Agency), qui est bien plus puissante que la CIA".], Olivier Morel, "Interview de Paul Virilio" [Interview with Paul Virilio], *Journal de la République des Lettres*, Wednesday, 1 March 1995, http://www.republique-des-lettres.fr/190-paul-virilio.php, accessed 30 May 2014. My translation.
11. Joram Ten Brink and Joshua Oppenheimer, "Introduction" in *Killer Images, Documentary Film, Memory and the Performance of Violence*, ed. Joram Ten Brink and Joshua Oppenheimer (London, UK and New York, NY: Wallflower Press, 2012), 1.

12. Bernard Stiegler, *Technics and Time 3: Cinematic Time and the Question of Malaise*, trans. Stephen Barker (Stanford: Stanford University Press, 2010). See also Mary Ann Doane, *The Emergence of Cinematic Time: Modernity, Contingency, the Archive* (Cambridge: Harvard University Press, 2003).
13. In her short essay titled "Shooting with Intent: Framing Conflict", Alissa Lebow recalls that one of the very first prototypes for the motion picture camera, Etienne Marey, "Fusil Photographique" was fashioned out of and modelled upon the revolving rifle able to "shoot" twelve photographs per second in rapid succession. She adds: "Here, at the origins of cinema, we find an inspiration less innocent than implicated, where the sightlines of a camera mimic and will come to eventually support the sightlines of a weapon". Alissa Lebow in Ten Brink & Oppenheimer, *Killer Images*, 41.
14. Steigler, *Technics.*
15. Deleuze, *Time-Image 2*, 166.
16. Deleuze, *Time-Image 2*, 264. Here, Deleuze is reflecting upon reading Benjamin and Kracauer's famous essays ("The Work of Art in the Age of Mechanical Reproduction", 1936, *From Caligari to Hitler*, 1947).
17. Deleuze, *Time-Image 2*, 168, following Maurice Blanchot's observation of Artaud's work.
18. Deleuze, *Time-Image 2*, 168.
19. "Misunderstanding Images: *Standard Operating Procedure*, Errol Morris" Interview with Errol Morris conducted by Joshua Oppenheimer, in Ten Brink & Oppenheimer, *Killer Images*, 311–312. My emphasis.
20. Judith Butler, *Frames of War* (London, UK and Brooklyn, NY: Verso, 2010 [2009]), xiii.
21. Rithy Panh, quoted by Anne Chaon, "Rithy Panh, la mémoire endeuillée", *Lettre de la SCAM* (Paris, FR: SCAM, April 2014), 7. My translation. ["Le génocide, c'est l'innomable: les parents l'ont senti, le défi à relever c'était de dire. Et c'est aussi le rôle de l'art, du cinéma comme de toute forme d'art, d'aider à nommer les choses. Faute d'y parvenir, on confond tout et on réécrit l'histoire".]
22. The film was nominated for an Academy award and won the 2013 Cannes Film Festival top prize of "Un Certain Regard".
23. Rithy Panh, quoted in an interview with Joshua Oppenheimer, "Perpetrators' Testimony and the Restoration of Humanity: S21, Rithy Panh" in *Killer Images*, 250. My emphasis.
24. Jacques Derrida in Ken McMullen's film *Ghost Dance*. Directed by Ken McMullen (London, UK: Channel 4 Films, 1983).
25. Rithy Panh, in Ten Brink & Oppenheimer, *Killer Images*, 250.
26. Rithy Panh, in Ten Brink & Oppenheimer, *Killer Images*, 250. My emphasis.
27. Rithy Panh, in Ten Brink & Oppenheimer, *Killer Images*, 254–255.
28. Rithy Panh, in Ten Brink & Oppenheimer, *Killer Images*, 248.

29. "The shock of the mind's relation to the threat of death is thus not the direct experience of the threat, but precisely the missing of this experience [...]" writes Cathy Caruth in *Unclaimed Experience, Trauma, Narrative, and History* (Baltimore and London, Johns Hopkins University Press, 1996), 62
30. Sigmund Freud, *Beyond the Principle of Pleasure, the Standard Edition of the Complete Psychological Works of Sigmund Freud*, trans James Strachey, Anna Freud, Alix Strachey, and Alan Tyson (London: Hogarth, 1953–1974), Vol. 18, 13.
31. Of course, this repetition cannot be "pure". There is a profound deformation and transformation in any repetitive process.
32. "Sometimes the violence is so strong that words don't suffice to describe it. And also that violence may be so strong that the words become inaudible" says Panh in Ten Brink & Oppenheimer, *Killer Images*, 244.
33. Ten Brink & Oppenheimer, *Killer Images*, 303.
34. Ten Brink & Oppenheimer, *Killer Images*, 303.
35. Ten Brink & Oppenheimer, *Killer Images*, 300–301. My emphasis.
36. Ten Brink & Oppenheimer, *Killer Images*, 300.
37. Ten Brink & Oppenheimer, *Killer Images*, 302. My emphasis.
38. Steigler, *Technics.*
39. One remarkable recent example is Ari Folman's film *Waltz with Bashir*, about which Asher Kaufman writes: "Now, in January 2009, Israel is engaged in another bloody round of its hundred-year war with the Palestinians, this time in the Gaza strip. As Israeli commentator wrote [about] *Waltz with Bashir* [...], 'the Israeli animated and anti-war movie by Ari Folman continues to bring honor [to Israel], helping to raise the national morale of a people who need now more than ever.' Here is another, though by no means the last, twist in the evolution of the 1982 invasion of Lebanon", Asher Kaufman, *Shadows of War: A Social History of Silence in the Twentieth Century*, eds. Efrat Ben-Ze'ev, Ruth Ginio, and Jay Winter (Cambridge: Cambridge University Press, 2010), 216.
40. Eyal Peretz, *Becoming Visionary* (Stanford, CA: Stanford University Press, 2008), 88–89.
41. Janet Kinosian, "Joshua Oppenheimer on 'The Act of Killing,' reconciliation", *LA Times*, 18 February 2014, http://www.latimes.com/entertainment/envelope/moviesnow/la-et-mn-joshua-oppenheimer-act-of-killing-20140218,0,6446847.story#ixzz2vi1ieTOU; http://www.latimes.com/entertainment/envelope/moviesnow/la-et-mn-joshua-oppenheimer-act-of-killing-20140218,0,6446847.story#ixzz2vi1eRL1G, accessed 30 May 2014.

PART V

Theatre and Dance

CHAPTER 18

Peacebuilding and the Performing Arts Through the Collaborative Lens

Hal Culbertson

The Collaborative Lens

The interaction of peacebuilding and the performing arts can be fruitfully viewed through the lens of collaboration. For present purposes, collaboration is understood as an interaction between different organizations, initiatives or communities of practice designed to further some positive end.[1] Collaborations extend from the simple partnership between two organizations to highly complex coalitions of nonprofit, commercial and governmental agencies. The entities involved might be quite similar, as when two humanitarian aid organizations agree to jointly run a refugee camp, or very different, as when those same humanitarian organizations collaborate with UN peacekeeping forces to provide security at the camp.

The collaborative lens is useful for several reasons. First, this approach treats both peacebuilding and the performing arts as distinct fields of practice with their own goals, historical trajectories, and organizational cultures

H. Culbertson (✉)
University of Notre Dame, Notre Dame, IN, USA
e-mail: culbertson.1@nd.edu

J. Mitchell et al. (eds.), *Peacebuilding and the Arts*,
Rethinking Peace and Conflict Studies,
https://doi.org/10.1007/978-3-030-17875-8_18

and practices, as well as their own weaknesses, blind spots, and idiosyncrasies. Yet it maintains a degree of critical distance from both. The collaborative lens thus provides a way of looking at how these distinct fields work together, focusing on how the unique assets and resources each bring to the relationship complement each other, while also not ignoring the potential challenges they may face in their interactions.

In this regard, the collaborative lens captures the interaction of peacebuilding and the performing arts from a different perspective than approaches drawing on peacebuilding or applied theatre frameworks. For example, Shank and Schirch formulate their inquiry as follows: "the task for peacebuilding practitioners is to find ways of incorporating the arts into the work of peacebuilding and to create a space where people in conflict can express themselves, heal, and reconcile themselves through the arts."[2] They describe the arts as a "tool" for peacebuilding and explore its capacity and limitations. This approach assumes a certain kind of collaboration between the arts and peacebuilding in which the goals of peacebuilding largely define the goals of the collaborative relationship. References to the arts as a "methodology" or "vehicle" for peacebuilding tend to make this kind of assumption about the nature of the collaborative relationship. Approaches to the relationship rooted in Applied Theatre which analyze theatre as a tactic for achieving social change make similar assumptions.[3] As will be discussed further below, this approach is too narrowly focused on peacebuilding objectives to capture the full range of collaborative interactions. This chapter examines the relationship between these fields through the collaborative lens in order to avoid some of the pitfalls of these approaches, and to attain a more nuanced picture of the interaction.

Second, the field of peacebuilding makes extensive use of cross-sector collaboration in pursuing its goals. This stems in part from the historical development of the field. Many fields of international practice have emerged through the founding of Non-Governmental Organizations (NGOs) committed to the field, which in turn shape the practice within that field. A prominent example of this is the field of human rights, which has been significantly shaped by the work of Amnesty International, founded in 1961, and Human Rights Watch, founded in 1978. The work of these organizations has generated both a working methodology for the human rights field and a set of norms and expectations for what a "human rights NGO" is and does. However, this mode of emergence also seems to have generated a degree of insularity for the field. As Nelson and Dorsey argue, the human rights field had virtually no interaction with development efforts during the first 40 years of its existence, and only recently have the development and human rights fields begun significant interactions, with the emergence of rights-based approaches to development in development organizations and the defense of economic and social rights by human rights organizations.[4]

While the peace movement and peace organizations have a long history stretching back to the nineteenth century, peacebuilding did not emerge as a field of practice until the mid-1990s within relief and development organizations. Peacebuilding responded to the growing number of internal conflicts that erupted after the end of the Cold War, which could quickly erase years of development efforts. In addition, the faith-based character of several relief and development NGOs, including World Vision, Catholic Relief Services, and Mennonite Central Committee, provided an internal impetus for them to develop peacebuilding programs and initiatives alongside existing programs.[5] While organizations with a peacebuilding or conflict transformation mission, such as Search for Common Ground and International Alert, have gained prominence as peacebuilding actors, they have not played the same role in shaping the field as Amnesty International or Human Rights Watch.

From the beginning, the field strongly emphasized the need for integration with other fields of practice, and resisted formulaic approaches or replicative methods. As a result, it has sought to be a crosscutting theme across a wide range of NGOs and other institutions rather than developing specific working methodologies or forms of organizational practice. The strategic peacebuilding approach, as articulated by the University of Notre Dame's Kroc Institute, particularly emphasizes the need for relationship building across a diverse range of societal sectors, organizations, and institutions, as well as between local, national, and global actors.[6]

As the recently published volume *Integrated Peacebuilding* documents, peacebuilders frequently have worked across organizational divides, developing integrated initiatives with development, humanitarian aid, human rights, business, gender, religion, security, health, and other fields.[7] The volume on *Integrated Peacebuilding* includes a chapter on peacebuilding and the media, but only a brief discussion directly addressing the role of visual or performing arts in a chapter on peacebuilding and religion.[8] Likewise, a recent survey by the Alliance for Peacebuilding of US organizations involved in peacebuilding touted the diverse range of partnerships that peacebuilders have formed with other sectors, but did not include the arts or arts organizations as a partner, or arts-based initiatives as a strategy.[9]

Given that peacebuilding and performing arts initiatives have been undertaken by several major US NGOs—including some that were part of the Alliance for Peacebuilding survey—one wonders why these initiatives have been neglected in studies focusing on cross-sector collaboration. One factor may be the "softness" of the arts in comparison to other partners.[10] Peacebuilding is still struggling to be taken seriously by donors and the public more widely as a field which can foster genuine, sustainable change in personal, social, political, and cultural behaviors and practices. As a result, partnerships with entities such as the military, businesses, or the healthcare industry are often put forward to enhance the credibility of the field, or its capacity to achieve concrete results, whereas partnerships with the arts are seen as reinforcing stereotypes that peacebuilders are only about lofty ideas and not real change. Another factor may be the fact that the arts are not seen by some in the peacebuilding field as a separate field of activity as much as a unique methodology or tool for pursuing its objectives. Whatever the reason, the present chapter seeks to understand the interactions between peacebuilding and performing arts within a framework comparable to other peacebuilding collaborations.

Third, theatre is a highly collaborative endeavor. As Snyder-Young observes, one of the unique characteristics of theatre as an art form is the live, in the moment, interaction between actors, and between actors and their audience.[11] Behind the scenes lies another layer of collaboration, as the theatre company works with donors, publicists, set-designers, and sometimes a host of other specialists to produce a theatrical performance. Applied Theatre—understood as a wide range of dramaturgical practices, and particularly participatory elements, that are used to address social and political issues—expands the theatrical repertoire by making this collaborative dimension central to the performance itself.[12] Many of the dramaturgical techniques employed in Applied Theatre seek to engage the community in the development of a performance event, engage the audience in co-creating the performance, and stimulate all involved to participate in social change activities beyond the performance.

It is thus no surprise that the Applied Theatre community has found kindred spirits in the peacebuilding community, both in terms of their orientation toward social change and their interest in collaborating to bring about that change. In practice, interactions between peacebuilding and the performing arts are often enacted through collaborative endeavors between organizations and institutions of various kinds. These include initiatives such as NGO partnerships with local performing artists, government commissions of theatrical works, or UN engagement with national theatre companies. The collaborative lens focuses on a key point where these fields intersect.

Of course, the two fields also intersect in other, more subtle ways that may not involve a joint organizational or institutional endeavor. For example, in reflecting on how haiku has affected his approach to peacebuilding, John Paul Lederach observes that:

> Whenever I find myself in the middle of a tense conversation, working with or between groups involved in a serious conflict, and the situation seems endlessly complex, I ask myself a simple question: If you were to capture the heart of this thing in a sentence of fewer than eight words, what would you say: This is the haiku attitude and moment.[13]

In similar ways, a playwright might draw on peacebuilding principles or practices in resolving a dramatic conflict, for example, by personifying an internal struggle as a negotiation between characters.

Conceptual or metaphorical borrowings such as these are not the primary focus of this chapter, which examines collaborative efforts involving organizations and communities. However, they are important in at least one respect: it is often a hope, or even an expectation, that a collaborative endeavor between two different fields of practice will generate new insights such as these through the interaction of the various participants. These may not be the primary objectives of the collaboration as envisioned by the organizations involved or its sponsors; the primary objectives of performing arts and peacebuilding collaborations often focus on social changes in the local community, attitudinal or behavioral changes in the participants in the project or the members of the audience, or the development of new models of theatre. However, the generation of insights such as these is often understood, perhaps without being explicitly identified, as an additional benefit that will naturally emerge from collaborating.

Forms of Collaborative Relationship

The impetus for organizations or communities of practice to collaborate can come from a wide variety of sources. In the nonprofit sector, which includes many peacebuilding and performing arts organizations, organizations may collaborate in response to external demands or requirements, such as jointly seeking funding from a potential donor. Indeed, many donors have come to see collaboration between different organizations and even different sectors as a desired outcome of their support, and thus often require collaboration as a condition for receiving a grant. This has become common in the international development sector, where collaboration between international NGOs and local partners is regularly required by international donor agencies.

Collaboration can also emerge from internal factors in the organizations involved in the partnership. For example, a peacebuilding organization working in a conflict environment may learn that media reporting on violent incidents have been biased in the past and have inflamed tensions between conflicting groups in a community. Journalists in the region may be interested in how reporting can contribute to conflict reduction or transformation. This might lead the peacebuilding organization to work with a journalists' association to build awareness and generate resources that can reduce the biased reporting. The common interest between the organizations thus leads to a collaborative endeavor.

Organizations pursue collaborative initiatives for complex reasons. As Huxham and Vangen observe, the goals of a collaboration operate on 3 levels.[14] The individuals involved in a collaboration have goals they hope to achieve through the collaboration, such as strengthening their network or learning new ways of working or thinking. The organizations involved also have goals they hope to achieve, such as developing a new capacity, gaining access to a new community, or generating new revenues or resources. At the highest level is the goal for the collaboration itself, which often is articulated as going beyond the benefits to the organizations involved to creating unique new value, or as Huxham and Vangen call it, "collaborative advantage." These levels interact in complicated ways, and success on one level can sometimes mask failure on another.

One of the challenges in discussing collaboration is the diverse array of interactions that are often referred to under the umbrella of "collaboration." Austin developed a useful framework for distinguishing different types of collaborative relationships between businesses and NGOs.[15] Austin argued that collaborative relationships between businesses and NGOs fall into 3 broad categories. On the lowest level, relationships are largely *philanthropic*. The business provides monetary or human resources to the NGO, largely as a charitable contribution to its work. On the next level, relationships are more *transactional* in character, with specific, ongoing resource exchanges aimed at a common goal. An example of this kind of collaboration would be McDonald's longstanding partnership with the Environmental Defense Fund to increase recycling of waste products.[16] At the highest level, Austin posited a form of interaction which he termed *integrative*. In this type of collaboration, the missions, personnel and identities of the two entities become significantly intertwined as they pursue joint ventures and initiatives.

Austin's characterization of the highest level of collaborative relationship as "integrative" is only applicable in some contexts. When a nonprofit is engaged in policy advocacy, for example, its credibility is often rooted in its autonomy from other organizations and its freedom from external influences. In such a context, integration with a collaborative partner could in fact undermine the very purposes of the partnership.

This dynamic is often at work in partnerships with peacebuilding organizations. For example, in a study of business-NGO partnerships in war-ravaged Congo, Kolk and Lenfant use a framework rooted in Austin's approach, but view the highest type of engagement as "transformative," largely based on the intent of the collaboration to transform conflict in society through new forms of organizational interaction.[17] In these relationships, there is no intent to merge the commercial and nonprofit organizations involved. On the contrary, the independence of the organizations, and particularly the need for the NGOs to maintain their independence from the businesses, was often critical to their capacity to offer advice to businesses operating in conflict areas. In relationships with advocacy NGOs, Kolk and Lenfant observe that several collaborations did not involve financial support for the NGO, as the NGOs involved did not want to appear biased or co-opted by the business partners.[18]

Vangen and Huxham take this point further, observing that at the heart of collaboration is a paradox. This paradox arises not only from the practical difficulty of defining and agreeing on collaborative goals, but from the nature of collaboration itself.[19] If the entities involved are too similar, it may be difficult to generate unique, new value by working together, as they already have similar capabilities and may even be competitors in the same marketplace, complicating the collaborative relationship. Entities in a collaboration often need a certain degree of difference or distance in order to justify or support the collaboration as creating something new and different. Yet the greater this difference is, the more difficult it is for the entities to understand each other and work together toward a common goal.

For example, NGOs involved in the Kimberley Process to certify diamonds as conflict free collaborated closely with the diamond industry to design and implement the process, even as they sought to maintain their status as industry watchdogs on the process. When the process became plagued with problems in recent years, and needed changes were not implemented, Global Witness, an NGO which had stimulated the process, decided to withdraw.[20] As this suggests, high level, strategic collaborations which go beyond mere transactional interactions may not involve integrative behavior. For situations such as these, Huxham's emphasis on the paradoxical character of collaborative relationships is probably a more apt analytical tool.

Collaboration Between Peacebuilding and the Performing Arts

Austin's framework can be integrated with Huxham's analytical tools to suggest an overall approach to analyzing collaboration patterns between peacebuilding and performing arts (Fig. 18.1).

The chart[21] builds on Austin's three-tier approach. However, since neither peacebuilding, nor the performing arts are primarily sources of funds

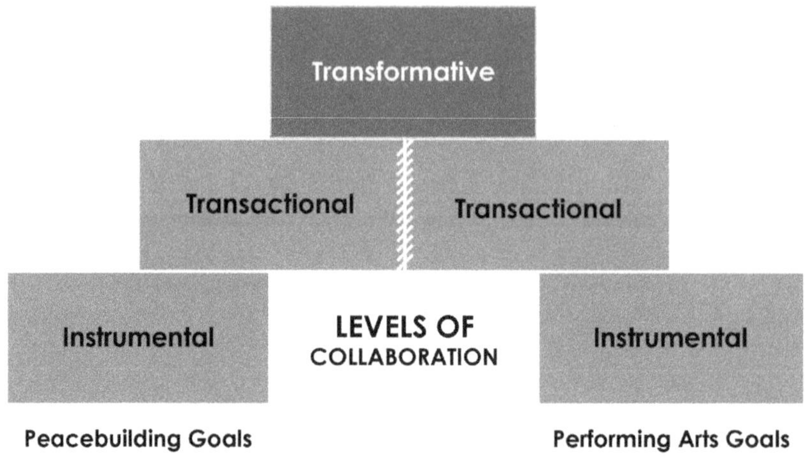

Fig. 18.1 *Levels of collaboration* between peacebuilding and performing arts organizations

(although, funds often do change hands between them), the chart treats the lowest level of interaction as involving an "instrumental" relationship with the other, rather than a "philanthropic" relationship.

Drawing on Huxham's distinction between organizational and collaborative goals, the figure above treats the goals of peacebuilders and performing artists separately, at least at the two lower levels, in order to better articulate the relationship between them. However, if the two entities develop a more transformative relationship, their goals tend to converge, as represented by the shared transformative goal. The chart adopts the term "transformative" as the highest level of interaction, following Kolk and Lenfant,[22] and understands this to involve a mutual transformation of peacebuilding and the performing arts, which results in a new way of practice that neither could have achieved alone. The use of the term "transformative" also signals an approach which is open to the kind of collaborative paradox that Huxham describes.

It is not the intent of this discussion to treat "transformative" relationships as somehow normatively superior to other forms of relationship, although they are sometimes perceived as such. As will be argued, each kind of relationship has its role, and depending on many surrounding circumstances, it may be best to form instrumental or transactional relationships to achieve certain goals, even as a transformative relationship may be needed for others.

Also, it is not assumed that relationships progress from one level to the next. One does not have to have an instrumental collaboration before moving on to a transactional and then a transformative relationship. On the contrary, forming one kind of collaboration may inhibit the development of a different kind of relationship between the same partners, as this might involve significantly changing the patterns of interacting. For example, if a theatre organization receives funding from the UN peacebuilding agency, this may weaken its credibility in presenting performances that put UN peacebuilding in a positive light. Of course, collaborations can and often do operate on multiple levels at the same time, and may move fluidly back and forth as the relationship unfolds. This creates some of the more difficult challenges for managing collaborative relationships, as the different levels imply different modes of communication, decision-making, action, and assessment. Thus, presenting each level separately may distort the reality of actual collaborations to a degree, but it does so in order to generate insights into the complexities of collaboration between these fields.

Instrumental Collaboration

Instrumental collaboration tends to focus on particular goals of one of the entities involved. The collaborative relationship that is formed often takes on a contractual character with one side requesting services of the other in order to advance specific goals of the primary partner. In the nonprofit context, these partnerships sometimes form in order to support fundraising or awareness-raising efforts of an organization, as when Comic Relief uses performances by comedians and other public figures to raise funds for international relief efforts.[23]

These kinds of relationships can also be used to deliver services in the field. For example, the peacebuilding organization Search for Common Ground has worked with local theatre troupes in the Democratic Republic of the Congo to provide information and strategies for conflict resolution to returning refugees and local residents.[24] The information and strategies to be conveyed were defined by Search for Common Ground and the funding agency for the project, the US Department of State's Bureau of Population, Refugees, and Migration. The role of the theatre troupes was to communicate about these matters in engaging and compelling ways. The instrumental character of the relationship is often reflected in the scope and focus of the evaluation of the project. In the case of the Search for Common Ground project in Congo, the evaluation focused on whether the participatory theatre initiative provided a space for open, collaborative dialogue about conflicts and whether theatre spectators had increased knowledge about conflict transformation.[25]

On the performing arts side, one also sees instrumental goals for collaborating with peacebuilding for both financial and strategic reasons. A survey of Kenyan performing artists involved in Theatre for Development revealed that over 90% pursued this form of theatre primarily because they felt that international resources were available for addressing social issues like peace and conflict.[26] The International Labor Office at the UN has explored the performing arts as an area of potential employment growth in the southern African region.[27] While performing artists face significant financial obstacles, especially in resource-poor regions, the labor-intensive character of the field, together with the fairly low capital needs and cultural significance, give it some potential as a way of fostering economic development in fragile environments. In addition, theatre groups in conflicted societies might choose peacebuilding as a theme because it will generate the biggest audience for their production, or because it is a topic of concern to their audience members.

Of course, international NGOs, including peacebuilding NGOs, are often criticized for treating local organizations as merely implementing agencies, instead of as equal partners. This becomes especially problematic when the relationship is characterized as a partnership, when in fact the funding and decision-making about the theatre production are effectively in the hands of the peacebuilding organization. Since the peacebuilding organization is typically the international actor which brings financial resources to the relationship with local theatre groups, the nature of a peacebuilding organization's goals for the relationship will play a significant role in determining what sort of collaborative relationship is most appropriate.

If the peacebuilding NGO seeks to foster the growth of a local performing arts culture in a conflicted society, or to encourage local performing artists to integrate peacebuilding themes into their ongoing work, an instrumental relationship with a local theatre organization will likely not be appropriate or effective. In such a case, the local performing arts organization will have relatively little power over the broader goals and direction of the production, the artistic goals of the production will likely be treated as of secondary importance, and the performing arts organization may struggle to develop a local, sustainable funding base. A transactional relationship, discussed below, may prove more fruitful in such cases. However, where the peacebuilding goals are the primary objective, as in the case of Search for Common Ground's work with Congolese returning refugees and local communities, an instrumental collaboration between a peacebuilding organization and local performing artists may be the most appropriate structure for the relationship.

Transactional Collaboration

In a transactional collaboration, the organizations involved seek to develop an endeavor which meets some of their own goals, and some goals articulated by the partner organization. Transactional relationships typically involve more regular, ongoing interaction between the collaborators, and a deeper level of engagement. Since the organizations are committed to achieving their own goals as well as the goals of the collaborator, they pay more attention to how their own actions affect the other, and may restrain their own actions when these might inhibit the other from reaching their goals. As this suggests, a fundamental dynamic in transactional collaborations is a compromise.

In interactions between peacebuilding and the performing arts, this often occurs between an international peacebuilding NGO, or other international agency with a peacebuilding agenda, and a local NGO or theatre group involved in creating theatre productions. The local organization may be a local affiliate of the international NGO, as in the case of Centre Lokole in the Democratic Republic of Congo, the local branch of Search for Common Ground in the country.[28] Alternatively, the local partner may be a local NGO or theatre group, as in the case of Tehrik e Niswan, a Pakistani theatre group that received support from the British Council, in conjunction with a grant to a local human rights organization.[29] In both cases, the funding ultimately comes from international donor agencies, such as the UN, USAID, or DFID, which seek to achieve certain ends, such as greater awareness of women's rights, through the theatre project. The local organization then seeks to achieve its own objectives, such as learning new approaches to theatre or building its reputation for theatre that addresses social justice, through the collaboration.

This pattern, which is common across a wide range of programmatic areas, raises difficult issues of global and local interactions. International NGOs are sometimes seen as hypocritical for touting their support for local participation and ownership, while at the same time making sure that key aspects of a project are consistent with donor agency goals. International peacebuilding organizations have sometimes been criticized for promoting the "liberal peacebuilding" agenda of the international community, which typically involves support for economic liberalization, democratic institutions (often equated with elections), and an active civil society sector (often equated with local NGOs), all of which may or may not be appropriate in the local situation. Some peacebuilding NGOs have resisted being associated with this agenda by developing their own approach to peacebuilding activities. For example, some have built their approach to peacebuilding on their religious identity, and with funding from religious individuals and groups, which provides both a counterweight to external pressure to adhere to the liberal peacebuilding agenda and a grounded basis for respecting the dignity of local people and their role in peace processes.[30]

Likewise, local theatre groups in areas of conflict face difficult dilemmas over whether to give up some of their artistic independence by accepting international, or even local, funds, and engage with the complex and often politically charged agenda that accompanies them. On the one hand, the international community brings financial resources that can provide the needed support that may be unavailable elsewhere, as well as opportunities to develop new approaches to the performing arts. Joining a collaboration like this may provide access to international experts in the field, as well as connections to groups in other countries using similar approaches.

However, such relationships also present risks. They may undermine indigenous or local practices and perspectives. Local groups also risk losing their identity as a source of political criticism as their political edge may be gradually softened by requests from international donors, or their artistic independence is questioned.[31] In the case of Eoan, a local opera company founded in 1933 to serve as a cultural organization of the "colored" community in Cape Town, South Africa, the group decided to accept funding from the Coloured Affairs Department of the South African government after other sources of financing became insufficient for the organization to continue. Accepting these funds meant the group had to perform to segregated audiences. This in turn led to a boycott by colored audiences, which ultimately ended its opera productions.[32]

Donor influence on theatrical productions can also play out in more subtle ways. In reflecting on the practice of Theatre for Development in Bangladesh, Ahmed notes how NGO staff working with local theatre groups shaped the theatre productions through influence over the issue selection process. Despite their commitment to empowering local groups to develop their own voice and capacities, the issues addressed in the plays frequently aligned closely with international donor agendas.[33]

As this suggests, transactional collaborations in peacebuilding contexts often involve taking calculated risks involving complicated tradeoffs. Mundrawala's comparative analysis of divergent strategies taken by Pakistani theatre companies toward international funding agencies provides a glimpse of the choices involved.[34] She observes how one theatre group, Katha, undertook theatre projects with support from the United Nations Development Program (UNDP) and other NGOs, but was not able to leverage these relationships into further grants. While the NGOs did not put significant restrictions on the work of Katha, the director felt the need to stay close to their agenda, and that this was compromising his values. After Katha disassociated itself from NGO funding, it initially found financial support for productions from corporations and individual donors, but eventually had to make commercial television productions to sustain itself, effectively leaving behind its ideological identity.

In contrast, Tehrik e Niswan (The Women's Movement) has received a number of grants from international donors over the years, yet has maintained a significant degree of artistic independence in developing theatrical works, including critical portrayals of public figures, and used these to develop a strong local reputation. Mundrawala's analysis suggests several factors that have allowed Tehrik e Niswan to flourish, including the structure of the funding relationship as a commissioning of a theatrical work, Tehrik e Niswan's effective use of its dual identity as both a theatre company and an NGO, and a willingness of both the organization and its funding partners to compromise.

Transformational Collaboration

Transformational collaboration involves an interaction which combines the mission and values of those involved to pursue a distinctive collaborative goal. Unlike transactional relationships, the focus is not on achieving the goals of each collaborator, but rather creating a collaborative goal that transcends their individual goals. Thus, the collaboration transforms those involved, giving new purpose or approaches to their endeavors.

It is difficult to identify examples of this kind of collaboration, particularly between organizational entities. While transformational interactions occasionally arise in the midst of other forms of collaboration, extended interactions of this sort are unusual, in part because international funding dynamics favor project-based, instrumental or transactional initiatives, where the roles of the participants are predefined, rather than exploratory, joint endeavors. Recent research on peacebuilding and the performing arts documents and analyzes a wide range of examples of initiatives from around the world.[35] Those cases where peacebuilding or other NGOs are involved as collaborators typically involve instrumental or transactional relationships. One indication of this is that most research initiatives document changes in the performing arts organization, but few document significant changes in peacebuilding organizations or NGOs involved, which would be expected in a transformative collaboration.

An intriguing exception to this is the case of the Mashirika Creative and Performing Arts Group and the government of Rwanda.[36] The theatre company, led by Hope Azeda, a Rwandan artist who returned to Rwanda after the genocide, entered partnerships with the Rwandan government to produce plays raising awareness about the Gacaca court system and the importance of reconciliation. While the government had specific strategic objectives for the plays, Azeda also had some degree of artistic control over the project. At one point in the process, the Ministry of Justice, which had reviewed a draft text of a play, requested that one of the characters pursue forgiveness and reconciliation. Azeda resisted, in part because she had not experienced forgiveness and therefore felt uncomfortable portraying it dramatically, but also because she questioned the ubiquitous political use of the language of reconciliation in its governing strategy. Azeda resolved the tension through a creative, dramaturgical solution, by ending the play on a point where reconciliation was clearly needed, and even requested, but not enacted.

The interaction between Azeda and the government became a space where both peacebuilding and artistic goals intermingled, contributing to a unique outcome. This is apparent not only in the exchanges between the Ministry and Azeda, but also in the internal conflict Azeda faced between the government's approach to peacebuilding and her own, and the artistic dilemmas this posed. As a result, the content of the play was not just determined by the government, and not just by Azeda, but rather jointly arrived at through complicated negotiations about the nature and reality of peacebuilding in Rwanda. The intriguing parallel between this creative ending to the play, and the experience of ordinary Rwandans, probably would not have occurred without the tensions between the collaborators.

The case illustrates the sometimes paradoxical character of collaborative goals, as each entity involved seeks to remain true to its sense of mission and purpose, even as it rubs against, and adapts to, the mission of the other. The government commissioned the play by Azeda presumably because it wanted a high-quality product from a respected artist. However, Azeda's sense of artistic quality prevented her from producing a play that did not reflect her understanding of peacebuilding. In this case, the performing arts functioned less like a tool for peacebuilding, and more like a mirror on both the conflict in society and the efforts to build peace. The transformation happened not from simply adopting the peacebuilding agenda of the collaborative partner, but from critically engaging with it.

As this suggests, transformative collaboration requires practitioners in both fields who seek to critically engage with the other. It requires performing artists who recognize that peacebuilding agendas, whether they are official agendas of government bodies or seemingly benign individual agendas of peacebuilding NGOs, have political dimensions which may need to be confronted or addressed in performance. Likewise, it requires peacebuilding practitioners who recognize the performing arts are not just a vehicle for conveying messages or changing behaviors, but a space for creative reflection by performers and their audiences. A growing cadre of practitioners with experience and training in both fields, as well as new academic programs focusing on the interaction between peacebuilding and the performing arts, create significant opportunities for this kind of cross-fertilization.

Conclusion

When examined through the collaborative lens, relationships between peacebuilding and performing arts organizations can take a variety of distinct forms, each with its own strengths and weaknesses. Potential collaborators should be explicit about the form of their relationship, as misunderstandings and tension that can undermine the success of the endeavor often arise from differing assumptions about the nature of the relationship.

A mutual understanding of the kind of collaboration being formed is an essential ingredient for a successful collaboration. If a theatre group views a joint endeavor as transactional, and thus hopes to develop new acting methods for doing theatre as an outcome of the collaboration, the group may be disappointed or disillusioned if the peacebuilding partner understands the collaboration as instrumental. Likewise, if an international NGO uses language suggesting it is co-creating a theatre work with a local group, this may create difficulties in the relationship if the NGO in fact is operating within specified donor guidelines.

The performing arts certainly can function as a tool for peacebuilding, but the performing arts have much more to bring to the peacebuilding endeavor. Theatre can function as a mirror on society, as commentary, as an escape or diversion, as catharsis, as a reflective space, or in myriad other capacities. Unlocking the full potential of the performing arts for peacebuilding requires peacebuilders who recognize the intrinsic power and capacity of the performing arts, and performing artists who engage the peacebuilding endeavor critically and creatively.

Notes

1. Chris Huxham and Siv Vangen, *Managing to Collaborate: The Theory and Practice of Collaborative Advantage* (London, UK: Routledge, 2005), 4.
2. Michael Shank and Lisa Schirch, "Strategic Arts-Based Peacebuilding", *Peace & Change* 33:2 (2008): 218.

3. Dani Snyder-Young, *Theatre of Good Intentions: Challenges and Hopes for Theatre and Social Change* (Basingstoke, UK: Palgrave Macmillan, 2013), 3.
4. Paul E. Nelson and Ellen Dorsey, *New Rights Advocacy: Changing Strategies of Development and Human Rights NGOs* (Washington, DC: Georgetown University Press, 2008).
5. L.C. Gerstbauer, "The Whole Story of NGO Mandate Change: The Peacebuilding Work of World Vision, Catholic Relief Services, and Mennonite Central Committee", *Nonprofit and Voluntary Sector Quarterly* 39 (2010): 5.
6. Daniel Philpott and Gerard Powers, eds., *Strategies of Peace: Transforming Conflict in a Violent World* (Oxford, UK: Oxford University Press, 2010).
7. Craig Zelizer, ed., *Integrated Peacebuilding: Innovative Approaches to Transforming Conflict* (Boulder, CO: Westview Press, 2013).
8. Zelizer, *Integrated Peacebuilding*, 161.
9. Alliance for Peacebuilding, *Peacebuilding 2.0: Mapping the Boundaries of an Expanding Field* (Washington, DC: Alliance for Peacebuilding, 2012).
10. Shank and Schirch, *Strategic Arts-Based Peacebuilding*, 217–218.
11. Snyder-Young, *Theatre of Good Intentions*, 4.
12. Snyder-Young, *Theatre of Good Intentions*, 4.
13. John Paul Lederach, *The Moral Imagination: The Art and Soul of Building Peace* (New York: Oxford University Press, 2005), 71.
14. Huxham and Vangen, *Managing to Collaborate*, 83.
15. James E. Austin, "Strategic Collaboration Between Nonprofits and Businesses", *Nonprofit and Voluntary Sector Quarterly* 29:1 (2000): 69.
16. Environmental Defense Fund (EDF). "McDonald's Reduces Waste—and Saves Money", https://www.edf.org/partnerships/mcdonalds, accessed 12 November 2016.
17. A. Kolk and F. Lenfant, "Business-NGO Collaboration in a Conflict Setting: Partnership Activities in the Democratic Republic of Congo", *Business & Society* 51:3 (2012): 478.
18. Kolk and Lenfant, "Business-NGO Collaboration", 504.
19. Siv Vangen and Chris Huxham, "The Tangled Web: Unraveling the Principle of Common Goals in Collaborations", *Journal of Public Administration Research and Theory: J-PART* 22:4 (October 2012): 731–760.
20. Theo Leggett, "NGO Global Witness Leaves Diamond Vetting Scheme", *BBC News*, 5 December 2011, http://www.bbc.com/news/business-16027011, accessed 14 November 2016.
21. This illustration was designed by Naomi Culbertson.
22. Kolk and Lenfant, "Business-NGO Collaboration", 478.
23. "Comic Relief", www.comicrelief.com, accessed 10 November 2016.
24. Search for Common Ground, *Mass Information in Support of Peaceful Congolese and Burundian Refugee Repatriation*, Final Study A: DR

Congo, Search for Common Ground (2008), https://www.sfcg.org/wp-content/uploads/2014/08/DRCPRMFINALEvaluationAppendices1.pdf, accessed 11 January 2017.

25. Search for Common Ground, *Mass Information in Support of Peaceful Congolese and Burundian Refugee Repatriation.*
26. Christopher Odhiambo Joseph, "Theatre for Development in Kenya: Interrogating the Ethics of Practice", *Research in Drama Education* 10:2 (2005): 192.
27. Annabell Lebethe, *Promoting the Culture Sector Through Job Creation and Small Enterprise Development in SADC Countries: The Performing Arts and Dance* (Geneva, Switzerland: International Labor Office, 2003).
28. James Thompson, Jenny Hughes, and Michael Balfour, *Performance in Place of War* (London: Seagull, 2009), 167.
29. Asma Mundrawala, "Fitting the Bill: Commissioned Theatre Projects on Human Rights in Pakistan: The Work of Karachi-Based Theatre Group Tehrik E Niswan", *Research in Drama Education* 12:2 (2007): 149.
30. Gerstbauer, *The Whole Story of NGO Mandate Change*, 859–860.
31. Mundrawala, "Fitting the Bill", 149.
32. Wayne Muller and Hilde Roos, *Eoan: Our Story* (Johannesburg: Fourthwall Books, 2013), 23–26.
33. Syed Jamil Ahmed, "Wishing for a World Without 'Theatre for Development': Demystifying the Case of Bangladesh", *Research in Drama Education* 7:2 (2002): 207–219.
34. Mundrawala, "Fitting the Bill", 149.
35. Cynthia Cohen, Roberto Gutierrez Varea, and Polly Walker, *Acting Together: Performance and the Creative Transformation of Conflict* (Oakland, CA: New Village Press, 2011).
36. Thompson, Hughes, and Balfour, *Performance in Place of War*, 219.

CHAPTER 19

Peacebuilding and the Theatre Arts

Paul Burbridge and Geoffrey Stevenson

> The artistic five minutes, I have found rather consistently, when it's given space and acknowledged as something far beyond entertainment, accomplishes what most of politics has been unable to attain: It helps us return to our humanity, a transcendent journey that, like the moral imagination, can build a sense that we are, after all, a human community.[1] (John Paul Lederach)

Introduction

This chapter approaches the conjunction of art and peacebuilding by examining a work of live theatre in the context of the present conflict in Israel/Palestine. In it we will present the genesis and production of *Salaam*

P. Burbridge (✉)
Riding Lights Theatre Company, York, UK

G. Stevenson
University of Edinburgh, Edinburgh, Scotland, UK
e-mail: G.Stevenson@ed.ac.uk

J. Mitchell et al. (eds.), *Peacebuilding and the Arts*,
Rethinking Peace and Conflict Studies,
https://doi.org/10.1007/978-3-030-17875-8_19

Bethlehem, a play commissioned by Riding Lights Theatre Company and performed in the UK in 2007.[2] We also consider the collaborative processes in the working partnership between the York-based company and contacts and partners in Israel and the Palestinian Occupied Territories. We will argue that the work stands within a long and honourable tradition of theatre that carries a message, while it seeks to avoid the extremes of polemical, propagandist or "agitprop" theatre.[3] While recognizing moreover that art is seldom if ever susceptible to analysis using the tools of the social scientist, we nevertheless argue that there are vital and dynamic connections between live theatre and processes of peacebuilding and the transformation of conflicts.

Can theatre ever "accomplish what most of politics has been unable to attain" as Lederach put it in our opening quotation? The question seems to belong to another era, before the arrival of mass mediated conduits and then more recently digital social media that, while extending drama's reach, subsume its best efforts into the insatiable maw of a globalized entertainment industry. The framing of a work limits and delimits its interactions and effect (which is a reminder that no work should be considered apart from its context and reception). But from Plato's suspicion of art that stirs the emotions and has unpredictable effects on society, to the many politically and religiously grounded attempts to censor or suppress theatre that would corrupt or defile, it is clear that theatre has not been without power.

Thus Aristotle in his *Poetics* sought to refine the concept of catharsis, and rescue theatre from Plato's negative view of the effect of artistic *mimesis* on the audience.[4] In the west, we might note examples from late eighteenth century France, when theatre became something of a cultural weapon leading up to the French Revolution.[5] The Moscow State Jewish Theatre, from its founding in 1919 to its closing in 1948, specialized in polemic theatre.[6] Also in post-revolutionary Russia, there was a stream of unabashedly propagandist touring theatre productions that gave rise to the term *agitprop* and most notably influenced Bertolt Brecht.[7] In South America, Brazilian theatre director Augusto Boal, inspired by educator and writer Paulo Freire, developed popular pedagogical theatre forms.[8] In a rich anthology of case studies from across the globe, Cynthia Cohen, Roberto Varea and Polly Walker have explored contemporary peacebuilding and socially engaged theatre in two volumes that provide a wealth of theoretical insights and practical wisdom.[9]

The English stage has long presented intentionally polemical theatre, stretching back to Elizabethan drama and finding twentieth century expression in the work of playwrights such as John Osborne and David Hare; in Scotland, John McGrath founded the Scottish popular theatre company 7:84, touring his most famous play, *The Cheviot, The Stag and the Black, Black Oil* (1974).[10] By intentionally polemical, we mean works that are concerned to produce change in their audiences, whether improvement through educational spurs to political action, or solidarity enabling resistance to oppression. And yet it was John McGrath who argued that theatre can never "cause" social change. He wrote "It can articulate pressure towards one, help people celebrate their strengths and maybe build their self-confidence... Above all, it can be the way people find their voice, their solidarity and their collective determination".[11] In what follows we suggest three areas in and through which theatre can interact with the "real world" in ways useful or stimulating to peacebuilders.

Collaborative Models, Safe Places and Ambiguity

Theatre is an intensely collaborative art form. Directors, writers, actors, costume, set and lighting designers, technicians and administrators work together for months on perhaps 120 minutes of finished performance. But even after all their creative interactions and production negotiations, the work will depend utterly on a "collaboration" with audience members who are prepared to "suspend disbelief" and imagine together a new narrative world. By the end of this multistranded process, there will be unpredictable outcomes and changes in the lives of many of the participants. Theatre makes one of its strongest contributions to peacebuilding through enabling and modelling uniquely fluid and open-ended collaborative processes.[12] Cynthia Cohen writes:

> ...because of the collaborative nature of the creative processes that lead to productions, these performances can reflect, embody and juxtapose a range of perspectives and sensibilities. And because of the variety of symbols used, and the multiple levels on which any symbol communicates, performances can be crafted to bring together people of different cultural backgrounds, generations and political beliefs.[13]

Secondly, theatre, in common with so many of the creative arts, simultaneously seeks danger and safety. The danger comes in the form of challenges to prevailing political conservatism or moral myopia or wilful aesthetic blindness, the questioning of what is socially taken for granted, the testing of alternative ethical hypotheses and the exploring of metaphysical explanations. Almost by definition it cannot be popular within entrenched power structures nor flourish within the market for narcoleptic, bread-and-circuses "divertissements". Creativity and pushing boundaries go together. But such challenges require a safe arena wherein to articulate difficult things: thus theatre's traditions of welcome and hospitality. Dangerous challenges also benefit from a solid framing device—the play—in which to see human beings behaving in newly imagined ways. Theatrical forms such as "Forum" and "Verbatim" theatre can enable protected social dialogue that is attempting to find solutions to intractable problems.[14] Parallels with peacebuilding and conflict transformation are not difficult to find. During processes of dialogue and negotiation, significantly unstable points between warring parties occur where each party's own historical narrative admits no room for softening or self-questioning, where forgiveness and humility are notably absent, and where a future without conflict and retribution cannot be imagined. By creating a safe place, theatre issues a gracious invitation to watch characters learn the means of gracefull interaction and reimagine together a more peaceful future.

Finally, we note the importance of ambiguity and lack of closure in theatrical works like *Salaam Bethlehem*. Riding Lights principally seeks to inspire, enlighten and educate, rather than have influence at the ballot box or barricade, and a key concept in this respect is ambiguity. This approach has a psychological as well as an aesthetic rationale: an audience being told what to think is less likely to change its mind (or heart or will) than an audience given the freedom and respect to make up its own mind. The free play of the imagination is at the heart of the reception as well as the creation of a work of art, and such imagination rarely flourishes without ambiguity and allusiveness. Similarly, Lederach argues that one of the key components of the moral imagination necessary for peacebuilding is the embrace of paradox and complexity.[15]

In our consideration of the *Salaam Bethlehem* project we will seek to sharpen and develop these three concepts—collaboration, safe places and ambiguity—and their relationship to building peace. In order to do this, some background to the theatre company is helpful, along with an outline of way the project developed, and a brief synopsis of the play itself.[16]

Peaceable Values

Through comedy, new writing and classic drama, Riding Lights' work has been shaped by the peaceable values seen in Jesus's "manifesto", proclaimed publicly in Nazareth (Luke 4.18ff): declaring good news, offering insight, bringing freedom, giving liberation, and revealing the loving favour of God. This "transformational agenda" has helped to create an aspirational agenda for Riding Lights' work, delivered through theatre performances and educational projects across both secular and faith-based communities as well as in the more familiar spaces of public communication and entertainment.

Germane to this study, the company presented *Wrestling with Angels,* the story of the warring biblical brothers Jacob and Esau, at the opening session of the worldwide Anglican bishops' Lambeth Conference in 1998. It was intended to help defuse a potentially fractious atmosphere between delegates with sharply differing views on a number of issues, and to lay a platform for peacebuilding in the ensuing discussions. This play also inadvertently provided the catalyst for a significant meeting with Bishop Riah of Jerusalem, who used the play (in a way the company had not anticipated) to highlight the suffering of the Palestinian Christian community. As a result, seven years later, Riding Lights embarked on a long-running theatre project interacting with people living in this part of the Middle East.

Pray for us, Visit us, Tell our story was the memorable call by Bishop Riah for worldwide support on behalf of the Palestinian Christian community. His threefold appeal (made shortly after our first meeting with him in the Press Room of the Lambeth Conference) gave an overarching structure to a theatre project which grappled with one of the most ingrained conflicts of our time, marked by ancient hostilities, scriptural trip-wires, persistent misunderstanding, outrageous suffering and international interference. As artists and theatre makers, Riding Lights has tried in a small way to contribute to peacebuilding, both in the impact and message of *Salaam Bethlehem* and also in the processes of creative development and collaboration with people living in Israel/Palestine (Fig. 19.1).

An Unfolding Artistic Project

Pray for Us

The project begins in 2005, as Riding Lights (RLTC) is invited by a friend who has worked extensively in the Middle East, to research, create and tour

Fig. 19.1 *Salaam Bethlehem* poster (York: Riding Lights, 2007)

a new play in the UK focusing on the current experience of the Palestinian church within the wider regional conflict and, in particular, the impact on the whole Palestinian community of the Israeli separation wall and the second Intifada. Among other accounts, Rev. Dr. Mitri Raheb's book *Bethlehem Beseiged*[17] becomes essential background reading.

In May 2006, a small group of RLTC personnel are given a guided tour, during which we visit Galilee, the West Bank and Jerusalem, storing up images and fitting in as many meetings as possible with theatre makers such as *Al-Harah*,[18] Christian leaders, political and community activists. This face-to-face contact is crucial to the start of the creative process as it highlights the reality of human life so full of hope and tears, of hospitality and alienation, clarity and confusion. The trip acts as a call to prayer, not only for peace but also for artistic inspiration in response to all that we have encountered.

Our playwright, Bridget Foreman, returns the following spring to do further research, staying this time with a local family in Bethlehem. Her husband meanwhile runs drama workshops for young Palestinians under the *Bright Stars* scheme at the International Centre in Bethlehem, headed up by Dr. Raheb.[19]

Tell Our Story

From April to September 2007, Bridget Foreman writes *Salaam Bethlehem*, though the other members of the creative team are closely involved as we all wrestle with the process of drafting and re-drafting the script to arrive at a play that will give space to all the different voices we have heard. Our publicity about the show begins to trigger some deeply critical emails from supporters and we are constantly reminded of how provocative this subject is for many people in the UK who seem to have already made up their minds about relationships between Palestine and Israel.

Between October and December 2007, RLTC tours *Salaam Bethlehem* in the UK. Over 5500 people attend 42 performances from Aberdeen to Plymouth. Although occasionally greeted with hostile protest, the play generally promotes constructive discussion and greater understanding of the lives of ordinary people deeply affected by the conflict. Each performance is followed by on-stage discussion between cast and audience over Palestinian mint tea.

Visit Us

In July 2008, the company raises funds to bring six Palestinian young people, linked to the Al-Harah Theatre Company, to our Summer Theatre

School. Later in the year RLTC entertains *Al-Harah* directors and actors in York when they bring their show *Born in Bethlehem* to the York Theatre Royal.

As a means of deepening the effect and reach of *Salaam Bethlehem*, the company gives the opportunity to people in the UK to accompany us on our *Living Stones* tours to Israel and the West Bank. These tours in 2008, 2011, 2013 and 2015 combine sight-seeing and pilgrimage with on-location performances and, most importantly, meeting members of the Palestinian community and listening to presentations from leaders on both sides of the conflict. On one visit, RLTC gives a joint performance in the International Centre in Bethlehem with *Al-Harah*. The cast includes one of the young actors who attended our Summer School. By May 2015 the theatre company has been able to give over 130 people a transformational insight into the conflict, equipping them to return to continue the work of peacebuilding in the UK by "telling the story" in their own way, among their own networks.

Salaam Bethlehem—A Brief Synopsis

The play in three Acts is set in a Palestinian home in Bethlehem at Easter, Summer and Christmas 2006, with three Interludes that act as a "framing device". Each Act is prefaced by a short scene, tightly framed by spotlights, giving the unfolding story of a young immigrant Polish/Jewish couple, Tobit and Yehuda, who arrive in Palestine in 1946, displaced from Europe after World War II. They arrive with nothing, inspired by a Zionist dream they hardly dare to believe, hoping for permanent safety and peace. They have a child, Moshe, and they end up living in an Israeli town close to the village of Abu Kishk. The grandparents of the play's central Palestinian family were driven from this same village by the Israelis in 1948 after the declaration of the State of Israel.

The Main Characters

The Palestinian family, Christians in the Orthodox tradition, are:

Ibrahim (45), a primary school teacher, who continues to teach even though the Palestinian Authority has not had money to pay him for several months.

Malaak (43) his wife and a community nurse working with limited resources at a Bethlehem clinic.
Alena (25) their daughter, a graduate law student, who was seriously wounded ten years previously in a suicide bombing in Jerusalem. The bomber, as the play reveals, was Imad, a Muslim friend of the family.
Hassan (18) their son, a labourer, who earns money building Israeli settlement homes outside Bethlehem.
Suhir (47) a Muslim widow and mother of Imad, also lives with the family, having been made homeless when her house was blown up by the Israelis in reprisal for her son's suicide bombing.

Act One

Immediately after the first Prelude scene with Tobit and Yehuda, the lighting comes up on a domestic interior in Bethlehem and the audience is presented with characters who have normal family concerns, jokes, parent/teenager disagreements, work to be getting on with and community commitments similar to their own. If the audience had some preconception that they were coming to witness an "issue-based" play in a strongly Brechtian style, the first Act is a disarming point of entry. The politics, the history, the international tragedies and the intensity of the conflict are clearly going to be understood through the lens of ordinary human life, albeit life increasingly squeezed by deprivation.

There is tension between father and son about Hassan's involvement in building illegal Israeli settlements that encircle Bethlehem. Hassan's pragmatic view is that it is the only paid work he can get, in contrast to his father who continues to work at the school without pay. Alena's response is to work hard to acquire the skills for a different kind of future. She is also regularly emailing a young male Israeli student in Jerusalem (we later discover this is Tobit and Yehuda's son Moshe) as part of a university program. The Act closes with the discovery of a requisition order for their land because the next section of the wall is to run between their home and their olive grove. Ibrahim will no longer be able to get to school to teach.

Act Two

Despite the imprisoning effect of the wall on their home, there is a sense of the family pulling together to make the best of it and also to celebrate

Alena's 25th birthday. Ibrahim is stoical about the future. Hassan is no longer building Israeli homes but now carves wooden souvenirs for the Bethlehem tourist industry. An ill-judged gift of her dead son Imad's watch from Suhir to Alena, leads to the details of Imad's suicide coming out into the open for the first time. Malaak and Ibrahim have lied to Hassan for years about this, telling him that Alena's leg was injured in a car crash, because they were so fearful of Hassan having any excuse to copy Imad and risk his life in violent resistance.

Hassan feels humiliated by the family and rushes out of the house. In the final scene of this Act, when Ibrahim brings him back, Hassan is bleeding from a bullet wound. In his rage, he was throwing stones at an Israeli observation tower and was fired upon. The family's worst nightmare has become a reality—although they have tried to prevent it, Hassan's frustrations have made him, like other young Palestinian men, extremely vulnerable to violence.

Act Three

Christmas in Bethlehem. There is an atmosphere of hopelessness typified by dwindling attendance at mass in the Church of the Nativity. Faith is somehow clinging on, in need of a miracle. For his own safety, Hassan is being sent out of the country to stay with Ibrahim's brother who has previously emigrated to the USA. Ibrahim is a shadow of the man he was eight months ago. There is an angry, heartfelt exchange between brother and sister about the nature of effective "resistance": whether throwing stones is outweighed by continuing to work with meagre resources at the clinic (Malaak), becoming a taxi driver (Ibrahim), caring for cuttings from a requisitioned olive grove (Suhir) or studying for the professional skills (Alena) necessary for any society that wishes one day to be self-governing. Hassan leaves home.

A broken Ibrahim is urged by Alena to consider applying for a job co-ordinating a project to bring Palestinian children into contact with Israeli children through their schools, but Ibrahim is reluctant. In response to Alena's accusation that he has never campaigned, protested or fought for Palestinian rights, he describes a lesson he learned from *his* father when, as a sixteen year old, he became intoxicated with the story of a Palestinian woman who bombed a bus in which several Israelis died. The lesson, learned graphically and physically as he carried firewood home on his shoulders, was that the young Ibrahim was welcome to hit back, to fight, as long as he never put down "the cross of Christ" in order to do so.

In the final phase of the play, Hassan unexpectedly returns to talk to his father, having felt unable to flee to the USA once he reached the checkpoint. Hassan wants to tell his father that to cling to the dream of returning one day to the house in Abu Kishk from which the previous generation were driven in 1948 is pointless, as the house has long since been demolished. Hassan discovered this on a school trip but never had the courage to tell his father the truth because he knew how tenaciously his father held onto the possibility of return to the family home. But Hassan also describes a curious circumstance at the checkpoint that has changed his mind about leaving the country: while Hassan is standing in the queue to cross, the soldier on duty is stung by a wasp and suffers a potentially fatal allergic reaction. Hassan runs to fetch the doctor from his mother's clinic, who injects an antidote as Hassan holds the soldier in his arms. While the doctor asks him to pray for the soldier, Hassan realizes it is the same soldier who fired on him four months ago.

Part 2—Aims and Evaluation

The Style of the Play

It is difficult in this brief synopsis to convey the tone of warmth, love and familial good humour which was a strong part of the play's naturalistic atmosphere—the accuracy of which was praised by some Palestinian Muslim students who came to see the production in Leeds. The play was staged in traverse (where the action is central and the audience sit on either side), a style of staging in which the actor does not directly address the audience. Instead the audience are intimate observers of a truthful reality created by the actors, and they themselves form the backdrop to the other half of the audience's view of the action. In traverse, the audience becomes an important visual part of the scene, increasing their sense of involvement in the debate raised by the story.

This debate was also emphasized by the set of *Salaam Bethlehem*, which placed the carefully observed details of a Palestinian home onto a stage floor decorated with a map of Bethlehem. So, in the continuing, and at times violent dispute about ownership of the land, the family were clearly living in the middle of the inescapable political problem. It was important that the setting of the play conveyed both sides of the same coin: that the abstract issues of "the conflict" were deeply rooted in day-to-day realities and conversely that everyday human life was inextricably bound up with the ideological arguments. Having said that, the acting style of the play remained firmly in the naturalistic, family-centred theatrical worlds of O'Casey or O'Neill rather than engaging in the alienating and politically didactic modes of Brecht or McGrath.

An important question is: Can the experiences a member of an audience might have in the imagined world of theatre be transformative for their life in the real world? The empathy the characters in *Salaam Bethlehem* created with British audiences was powerful—allowing the audience to experience emotional turmoil by identifying with those in the play whose best intentions with regard to peace are tested to breaking point. These genuine emotional experiences within the imagined world of theatre are perhaps too ambiguous to give an audience any conclusive ideological answers, but emotional experience through art is obviously affecting and can therefore be transformative. Such experience, carried away in the heart after the performance, may be re-applied elsewhere. It may also be capable of softening ingrained or prejudiced attitudes. In this way, by focusing on the microcosm, by inviting an audience to imagine standing in another's shoes, theatre speaks to the wider issues and appeals to a commonly understood humanity.

Aims Behind the Creative Process

Knowing that the Israel/Palestine conflict is waged as vehemently in western religious and political arenas as it is in the country itself, the primary purpose of *Salaam Bethlehem* was clear: to educate and to influence the influencers looking in from the outside. Our job was twofold: to "tell the story" as we had come to understand it, and to build peace. We attempted to build peace in a number of ways: by giving attention to the different voices within the conflict and acknowledging that there is pain on all sides; by raising informed debate about the causes and nature of the Middle East conflict; by exploring ideas of peaceful resistance to injustice; by reflecting back to the audience the hopes and difficulties of peacebuilding initiatives already in place in the country; by resisting the powerful pressure both within and beyond some churches and other religious communities to interpret the current political disaster in terms of over-simplistic and inappropriate citation of Old Testament scripture.

Along the way we hoped to shine a light onto a significant but threatened part of the worldwide church by expressing support for the spiritual descendants of those who formed the community at the birthplace of Christianity. We also hoped that our theatre would create in others a desire to forge relationships by visiting people and businesses within this diminishing Christian community. In other words, that our play would be a springboard for cross-cultural enrichment.

Ultimately, we hoped that our theatre would create an accessible space for imaginative engagement with present events and a potential future, however uncertain; a space where assumptions and prejudice about the mess and tragedy of the Middle East could be set aside for a couple of hours; where difficult things could be articulated without immediate rebuttal and where it might be possible to observe characters like ourselves, learning the "grace" that can lead to peace. This may well be the primary gift that theatre has to offer to the peacebuilding process. And this process of "journeying with characters", watching them grow in response to hardship, learning from mistakes and becoming wiser through failure is one reason why theatre is so absorbing. For example, anyone who has travelled with King Leontes in Shakespeare's *The Winter's Tale* through his monstrous jealousy, family chaos and yet subsequent penitence arrives with him at an extraordinary place of grace and redemption in the play's final scene.

An Evaluation

It would have been relatively easy to respond to the impact of the Israeli separation wall on the Palestinian community, corralled in the West Bank and the Gaza Strip, with a piece of agitprop theatre that created an emotional connection for the audience with the suffering of the people on the "other" side of the wall. However, a loud, polarized piece of theatre was not really going to add anything new to a problem that is such an intractable web of overlapping historical, religious and political fortunes, and shouted claims and counter-claims over this piece of land. Our play had to attempt to extend the hand of peace to all parties in the conflict and to encourage that same generosity of spirit in anyone in the UK who was prepared to listen.

Early drafts of the play framed the contemporary events with the story of the suffering of the Arab grandparents, dispossessed by the new State of Israel in 1948. Eventually, we realized that we needed to replace this with a different framing story, lightly sketched, of a young Jewish couple arriving in Palestine in 1946 from Poland. This not only created a better equilibrium in acknowledging the pain of the Jewish side of the story, but it also provided one seed of hope in the play's final act as Moshe, the son of the Jewish couple, and Alena find each other via the internet and begin an email conversation across the wall; the young generation finding ways to leave behind the pain of their parents and start something new.

Salaam Bethlehem reflects a society that is hemmed in, deeply affected by the terrorism which arises from despair, and fearful of the future. It fears in particular for the thwarted aspirations of youth and the recklessness this causes, especially in young men. It would have been untruthful and illogical to have avoided this, but we also discovered that the play itself needed to reflect a peace process and become a kind of "negotiation" between three stories woven together—Muslim, Jewish and Christian. It needed to show a re-imagined, more generous future where representatives from each of those groups move beyond their suffering and reach out to one another in love, rather than react to one another out of bigotry. Of course this is not just in the future but thankfully is already occurring here and there between individuals and groups.

In line with the peaceable values that undergird the inspiration for the play, we also felt we had to include the renunciation of violence, whether nation on nation or person to person, whether through suicide bombing or by driving a concrete wall through communities. The sad and bloody history of Jerusalem shows that for centuries, each act of violence has been "justified" by a previous one. We thus included some imagined reversals to this cycle: the painful lesson Ibrahim was taught by his father about refusing to put down the cross of Christ in order to free his fists to fight—a lesson taught by a man who had been driven out of his home in 1948. It was followed by Hassan's "lesson" at the checkpoint, when he finds himself caught up in a profound Good Samaritan experience and discovers that his deepest instinct is to help another human being, even an enemy.

Just as the point of entry into the imagined world of the play for the audience has to be carefully created (when and how does the play start, for example), so of course does the exit. If the audience have come with you on a journey, where and how do you want to leave them? With a warm, fuzzy feeling, relieved that everything has been resolved? Or with the exit door, as it were, opening onto an ambiguous re-connection with the real world through which the audience can leave inspired, and perhaps with a number of new determinations and emotional experiences to process.

Salaam Bethlehem ended with many things unresolved. For instance, the Palestinian protagonists have arguably renounced violence naively, without procuring any structural change. However, a few pieces of a mosaic of hope that would take millions of people to complete have been filled in. Each character of this representative but imaginary community within the play was doing something to rebuild relationships: Ibrahim by overcoming by his pride and offering his services to the Israeli/Palestinian school interaction project; Malaak by promoting the blood exchange at her clinic; Alena by studying hard to be in a position to contribute to a re-envisioned society and building a real relationship out of a virtual one with an Israeli boy across the wall; Suhir by continuing to grow olives from "cuttings snatched from under a soldier's boot"; Hassan by refusing to emigrate, but also refusing to cling onto to the fantasy of returning to a pre-1948 lifestyle, choosing instead to wrestle with the current reality in Israel/Palestine.

Conclusion

Collaboration

The creation and devising, touring and performing of *Salaam Bethlehem* were marked by a multi-stranded and indeed cross-border collaborative process in which the ends were not predictable at the beginning. Collaboration took many forms. Some of these were structured, as between RLTC and Al-Harah Theatre Company, and between RLTC and the host theatres of the UK tour. Some were more implicit and embedded in the nature of the artistic medium, from the writer/director/actor transactional relationships to the less analysable but no less important (indeed vital) moments when audience and performer experience together the *punctum* of theatrical truth.

We have suggested that modelling and engaging in fluid and open-ended collaborative processes may provide one of theatre's distinctive contributions to peacebuilding. The collaborative nature of theatrical creation is instructive in this context.

It is very seldom the case that theatre is created by just one deviser with a completely free hand. Much more often theatre is the work of a larger group, a group committed to a common goal, the production of the play, but with messiness and much unpredictability. Contributions may be made that are vital ingredients and yet indistinguishable in the final outcome and when the credits are printed. Without wishing to force a parallel, theatre is marked by participants who are continually and sometimes painfully letting their contributions be part of a process with uncertain outcomes. If and when theatre makers are brought into a conflict transformation, it is good to be aware that they have "been there before". So one question we pose to peacebuilders is: "Can the administration and planning of conflict transformation processes embrace the dynamic yet unpredictable and sometimes messy models of theatrical collaboration?"

Safe Spaces

The theatrical goals of creating a safe space, while simultaneously exploring dangerous ideas, have clear parallels with community-level processes of conflict transformation. In *Salaam Bethlehem*, characters not only experience the hope and the means of grace, of forgiveness, of the beginnings of the possibility of reconciliation, but are seen to step over the threshold and move towards peacebuilding action. It is of course not the theatre or the cinema that is a safe place in a geographic sense, but the works of art and their relationship with their audiences that temporarily create safe places where dangerous ideas can be explored. Such dangerous ideas include the dialectical process of placing narratives of identity of one group in ambiguous tension with the narratives of another group. Watching such dramatic action has cathartic potential, from a play like *Salaam Bethlehem* to the stories from South Africa's Truth and Reconciliation Commission told so movingly in the documentary *Long Night's Journey into Day*, or in Debbie Tucker Green's *Truth and Reconciliation*, an edgy, painful and powerful play, drawing on several intractable conflicts worldwide.[20] Danger, risk, pain and catharsis—these are only possible in a work of art when a safe place has been created where imagination can freely roam, but the creation of safe places will always take time. They may need more than the "artistic five minutes" in the quotation at the beginning of this chapter. So the second question we pose to peacebuilders is: "Where are the safe places in peacebuilding processes that art can help create, in order to entertain dangerous ideas and to foster re-imaginings of past, present and future?"

Ambiguity

Evaluation of a work of theatre, as mentioned at the beginning of this chapter, is hindered by the open-ended nature of a work of theatre such as

Salaam Bethlehem, where the intention is to provide a stimulus to entertain dangerous possibilities and a springboard to imagine the outlines of an as-yet-undreamt-of peace. As mentioned above, the free play of the imagination is at the heart of the reception of a work of art. Ambiguity and allusion rather than direct statements are at the core of affective and thought-provoking theatrical dynamics.

There is a tightrope to walk—as any peacebuilder knows. On the one side, there is seldom anything ambiguous about the oppression and injustice experienced by many groups who have turned to armed struggle seeking survival and cultural identity, let alone justice. The oppressed have stories to tell. Theatre and the narrative and figurative arts have played a part in telling these stories, in giving a voice to the voiceless, in empowering peoples to gather around shared narratives of oppression and of hope.

On the other side of the tightrope, such mythic narratives have a tendency to ossify. They can assume a status of universal truth and so shut out the voice and identity and stories of the Other. It is understandable that the pain of past injustice and the ineradicable quality of grief at the loss of family, of home, of homelands should fuel the wailing, keening demand for retributive justice that fixes on revenge and cannot see the shared humanity of the Other. But when they shut out dialogue and negotiation, creativity and the embrace of ambiguity and paradox can sometimes allow light to come in around the sides of drawn curtains, and provide a moment of relative quiet in a safe space to hear the stories of the other side. The final question we raise for peacebuilders in this paper is, "Can peacebuilders learn from the artistic world a 'language of ambiguity' that may be trusted in the scientific world of evaluating social and economic programs intended to promote peace?"

In this chapter, we have presented the outlines of the *Salaam Bethlehem* theatre project in terms of the search for peaceful solutions to an intractable conflict. There are no illusions that theatre in this, or any other form, is a magic wand that can be waved to transform bitterness, the lust for vengeance and the grievances of centuries of injustice. However, by understanding that the theatre arts can seldom be neatly slotted into processes of peacebuilding or conflict resolution, peacebuilders can avoid the attitudes of instrumentalism that can devalue the work of artists and damage relationships between artists and peacebuilders. By recognizing both the limitations and the unique values and methods of the theatre arts, peacebuilders can work with artists to go further in creating safe places in which to explore dangerous but potentially transformative ideas. And by using art forms marked by multiple layers of meaning and by the use of ambiguous symbols rich in allusion, peacebuilding artists can encourage and develop experiences of shared humanity and the imaginative development of peaceable virtues.

Salaam and Shalom.

Notes

1. John Paul Lederach, *The Moral Imagination* (New York and Oxford: Oxford University Press, 2010), 153.
2. Riding Lights Theatre Company has been based in York, England since 1977 and at its own Friargate Theatre since 2000. Its origins owed much to the practical support of a local Anglican church, St Michael-le-Belfrey. Since then, the company has developed into one of the UK's most productive and enduring independent theatre companies, working at all levels of theatre, from grassroots community engagement to mainstream theatre production. See also, http://rltc.org.
3. A combination of agitation and propaganda that aimed to combine emotional appeal with rational argument. In our view such extremes often seem, at present and in our culture, to diminish the perceived aesthetic values of a work of art, and to weaken its impact.
4. D.W. Lucas, ed., *Aristotle: Poetics* (Oxford, UK: Clarendon Press, 1968).
5. E.g. Voltaire's 1760 play *Le Café, ou L'Ecossaise*. See Logan J. Connors, *Dramatic Battles in Eighteenth-Century France: Philosophes, Anti-philosophes and Polemical Theatre* (Oxford, UK: Voltaire Foundation, 2012).
6. Jeffrey Veidlinger, *The Moscow State Yiddish Theatre: Jewish Culture on the Soviet Stage* (Bloomington, IN: Indiana University Press, 2000).
7. Richard Bodek, *Proletarian Performance in Weimar Berlin: Agitprop, Chorus, and Brecht* (Columbia, SC: Camden House, 1997).
8. Augusto Boal, *Theatre of the Oppressed*, trans. Charles A. McBride, et al. (London, UK: Pluto, 2000).
9. Cynthia E. Cohen, Roberto Gutierrez Varea, and Polly O. Walker, eds., *Acting Together: Performance and the Creative Transformation of Conflict* (Oakland, CA: New Village Press, 2011).
10. John McGrath, *The Cheviot, the Stag, and the Black, Black Oil* (London, UK: Eyre Methuen, 1981 [1974]).
11. McGrath, *The Cheviot*, xxvii.
12. See 'Partnering Patterns' by Hal Culbertson in this volume for a full description of the collaborative dimensions in the relationship between artists and funding bodies.
13. Cohen et al., *Acting Together*, 170.

14. Forum theatre, developed by South American practitioner Augusto Boal, seeks to explore socially difficult issues utilizing audience interaction and intervention. Verbatim theatre refers to plays that have their origins in extensive interviews with conflict participants.
15. Lederach, *Moral Imagination*, 5.
16. The play script of *Salaam Bethlehem* is available from Riding Lights Theatre Company, Friargate Theatre, Lower Friargate, York, YO1 9SL.
17. Mitri Raheb, *Bethlehem Besieged: Stories of Hope in Times of Trouble* (Minneapolis, MN: Fortress Press, 2004).
18. Al-Harah Theatre Company was founded in 2005. It seeks to produce, develop and promote the theatre arts throughout Palestine. For more information, see http://alharah.org/en/.
19. Bright Stars of Bethlehem is a charitable organization based in Bethlehem and connected to Christmas Lutheran Church, headed by Rev. Dr. Raheb. In partnership with other local and Palestinian partners, it provides various programs in Palestine (including a theatre arts program) aimed at enriching the lives of Palestinian children, young people, families and seniors: http://www.brightstarsbethlehem.org/.
20. The processes described were a defining feature of the powerful documentary of the TRC proceedings in *Long Night's Journey into Day* (2000), directed by Deborah Hoffmann and Frances Reid.

CHAPTER 20

Peacebuilding and Dance in Afro-Colombian Funerary Ritual

Sandra Milena Rios Oyola and Thania Acarón Rios

Introduction

Dance as an art form has an unwavering focus on and with the body. Dance draws upon social meaning; constituting its own movement vocabulary, which each sociocultural context decodes in a multiplicity of ways. Dance represents a conglomeration of movements functionalized to express the interrelation between body, space, place, culture and history.[1] Dance may include the presence and influence of sounds, songs, silence, words or images, yet it is this primary focus on the body's expression that distinguishes the processes of dance from those of other art genres and provides a useful vector for the understanding of non-verbal relational aspects in

S. M. Rios Oyola (✉)
Institut de sciences politiques Louvain-Europe, Université Catholique de Louvain, Louvain-la-Neuve, Belgium

T. Acarón Rios
Faculty of Creative Industries, Dance Department, University of South Wales, Cardiff, Wales

J. Mitchell et al. (eds.), *Peacebuilding and the Arts*, Rethinking Peace and Conflict Studies,
https://doi.org/10.1007/978-3-030-17875-8_20

peacebuilding. Scholars within the fields of anthropology, dance ethnography and sociology of dance emphasize the ways in which the various activities and practices of dance, including choreography, performance, improvisation and tradition, serve to both reflect societies, and to produce them.[2] Dance is therefore both constructive and constructing, a feature Taylor notes in drawing attention to the tension between conceptualizations of arts performances as artifice, and as providing a version of truth to a society.[3] This tension can allow the performing arts to function as subversive communication enabling artists, as community members, to convey messages of transformation or advocacy, to address injustices, or to unearth voices that are then put forth symbolically and literally at a community's forefront.

In this chapter, we argue that the activities and practices of dance mediate social transformation and can support peacebuilding and memorialization processes in settings where atrocities have recently occurred and where threats of violence are still present. We also present arguments for the importance of focusing on dance in conflict and in moving towards peace, which at times remains "unseen" in peacebuilding literature. These claims are brought forward through a case study that explores how dance performances, in the form of funerary rituals performed in the annual commemoration of the massacre of Bojayá, Colombia, affect both those that perform as well as those who witness them. These rituals represent a "cultural and historical specificity"[4] manifested through bodily practices, and they aim to mediate the memory of the grievances that have been committed and continue to occur within this community. In this context, the body in both material and symbolic form serves as a vehicle of resistance, expression and visibility of the potential for transformation.

This chapter is interdisciplinary in its outlook and its authorship: its analysis of the peacebuilding functions of dance draws on Acarón's research[5] into the role of dance/movement in peacebuilding, while the case study draws upon Rios' fieldwork in Bojayá,[6] including excerpts from Rios' fieldwork interviews and analysis of videos of the performances of the funerary ritual known as *Gualí*. We begin the chapter by setting out some functions of dance as a vehicle for social change, and its particular application to arts-based peacebuilding. We then move on to introduce the conflict in the Pacific region of Colombia and the massacre of Bojayá, and describe the dance performed by local victims during the re-enactment of the *Gualí*, during the ten-year commemoration of the massacre. Finally, the chapter concludes with a critical analysis of the social functions of dance in the context of peacebuilding and the challenges presented by this case study.

Functions of Dance in Social Change and Protest

Dance anthropology literature offers multiple examples of specific cultural contexts in which dance has been able to mediate, change or translate social processes. The capacity of dance to mediate social change in this way has been particularly evident in contexts and traditions in which ritual and dance are closely enmeshed into cultural practices. This kind of enmeshment is more prevalent in sociocentric (community-focused) cultures than in individual-focused cultures.[7] Hence, there has been particular emphasis in dance anthropology on ethnographic research in African, Latin American and South-East Asian traditions where dance, through ritual practices, has remained deeply connected to social and political life.[8]

The role of dance in peacebuilding can be observed in the sphere of social peace processes, wherein people at the grassroots level and in civil society find means to express and resist what has been otherwise repressed by mechanisms of terror, and contribute towards the restoration of broken bonds of solidarity. The idea of a "peace process" can be understood in negative terms as the reduction of violence as a product of political agreements, or it can be understood in positive terms as the transformation of the social causes that allowed the conflict to happen in the first place.[9] For these reasons, Brewer has addressed the distinction between political and social peace processes. Brewer argues that "the social peace process is about the repair and rebuilding of social relationships, interpersonal and intergroup reconciliation, the restoration of community and the social bond, and social and personal healing".[10] Similar claims have been attributed to the role of dance in societies which are explored in the section below. We list seven functions of dance, and comment briefly on their significance for social change in general, and as a resource for peacebuilding in particular.[11]

a. *Release* or "*security valve*".[12] Dance allows a way to release mounting tensions and emotions and can thereby serve as the "pulse" of situations, experiences and sentiments. This idea of dance as a form of release is grounded in neurophysiological functions of movement and activity, which secrete endorphins, dopamine and affect cortisol levels.[13] Dance can therefore provide a physiological outlet that may help to regulate and manage stress and aggression, which may in turn be associated with violence prevention.[14] Spencer argues, however, that this function has been attributed to dance in a simplistic and reductionist way and needs to be expanded.[15]

b. *Stimulant.* Dance can provide impetus and momentum to a specific issue by awarding its visibility among the community, or may act as a way to enable, or a marker of life transitions (i.e. marriage, adulthood, death).[16]
c. *Mediator.* Dance can provide ways in which positive and negative occurrences that affect the community can be negotiated. Community members engage in exposing and discussing their positions through dance.
d. *Controller.* Not all functions of dance may serve a positive purpose. It may serve to inculcate codes of conduct, preserve the status quo, instil competition for survival and defend territories and boundaries, which can also perpetuate oppressive power structures.
e. *Shield.* Through its use of metaphor, image and symbol, dance can provide a "prophylactic"[17] space in which issues can be voiced under certain degrees of artistic "protection". Much recent literature alludes to these "safe spaces" that dance provides due to its non-verbal nature in places where speaking about the atrocities could have life-threatening consequences.[18]
f. *Diversion.* This function portrays a duality in which, as well as serving a covert purpose, dance can be devalued in its capacity for change, disregarding the possibility for transformation by its ascription as a "mere aesthetic distraction". Dance as a "diversion" refers to the ability of the art form to deflect from a current state of being, or its capacity to redirect attention from a specific issue. Dance may provoke a momentary forgetting of a current state of being, allowing people to lose themselves in the performance. This power to distract, however, can be very strategic in extreme cases of oppression. Hanna states that "pleasant forms of distraction can often increase the effectiveness of persuasive appeal".[19]
g. *Transmitter.* Dance ethnography has previously presented examples from across history and cultures where dance has been used for the purpose of cultural transmission.[20] This transmission has been used in political projects to bring awareness of diverse cultural traditions, especially in the case of refugees' and asylum seekers' identities that hold an oppressed and hidden visibility in the cultures they inhabit.

> Taylor refers to performance as an "act of transfer" in which embodied knowledge is transmitted and preserved by cultures.[21]

These functions ascribed to dance may be applied to a variety of contexts of social change and peacebuilding, and in varying combinations. In what follows, we argue that they are particularly useful for analysing the performance of the funerary ritual (Gualí), which involves a particular articulation of ritual dance, in the case of the Bojayá massacre commemoration. Before moving on to the description and analysis of the commemoration and the place of the funerary ritual within it, we offer a general background on the Colombian conflict and specifically the massacre in Bojayá, in order to establish the context in which these functions of dance are deployed.

The Colombian Conflict

The conflict in Colombia was one of the longest contemporary conflicts in the Western hemisphere. The confrontation between extreme right-wing paramilitaries, leftist guerrillas and the army lasted for over fifty years. The most intense period of the conflict was between 1995 and 2005, marked by the establishment of the paramilitary project that culminated in the alleged reintegration of paramilitaries in 2005. During this period, mechanisms of terror such as massacres, selective killings, body disappearances, and extra-judiciary killings increased. The massacre of Bojayá is one of 2505 massacres in Colombia registered between 1982 and 2007.[22] In 2016, the Colombian government and the FARC guerrillas reached an agreement for peace, which has been implemented through the establishment of a special domestic tribunal, a truth commission and an intricate network of support to victims in the local territories. Nevertheless, there is an ongoing violence in the regions due to the actions of armed actors such as FARC dissident groups, other guerrillas, criminal bands and ex-paramilitary networks.

In this chapter, we focus on a massacre that occurred during one of the highest points in the conflict and its commemoration before the peace agreement was signed. This case allows us to understand the role of dance and memory rituals in peacebuilding amid conflict. The massacre of Bojayá occurred in 2002 during a confrontation between extreme right-wing paramilitaries and leftist guerrillas, with the complicity of some of the members of the official army. In the massacre, which took place in a Catholic church, where close to a hundred people died, half of whom were children. The paramilitaries used the church of San Pablo Apostol as a shield, in which 300 civilians had sought refuge. The guerrillas launched three explosives in stray cooking gas cylinders filled with shrapnel, thereby creating a primitive and extremely inaccurate gas bomb. These rudimentary weapons are prohibited under international humanitarian law. One of these gas cylinder bombs hit the church, killing or seriously maiming the civilians taking refuge.[23] Despite the carnage during the day, the shootings did not stop, and in the aftermath there was even machine-gunning from the air by the Colombian army.[24] This region of Chocó has been part of the territory dominated by the FARC, which means that perpetrators continue to live in the area and also some of the FARC members had relatives there.[25]

Rosa Chaverra and her family were victims of the massacre of Bojayá. Her testimony, presented in an exhibit at the National Museum of Colombia to commemorate the massacre ten years after it took place, reflects the multiple ways in which victims were affected. Her case provides an insight into the consequences of the massacre, since this woman lost her parents, nephews, cousins, uncles, aunts and brothers. In addition, six of her eight brothers have been displaced to Quibdó with their families, and one of her sisters was permanently injured in the massacre. She says:

> I have seen my dad and my mom in my dreams, and I ask them what they wanted because I saw them upset. And they answered to me, 'oh darling, I am very hungry', and that was because she [my mother] did not eat since the armed groups entered. She did not eat anymore, so she left very hungry. I ask her about my dad, and she points over there, he is working, and then I wake up, and then I can sleep no more. The next day I tell my dream to one of my neighbours, and he tells me that I should pray for them, because they are people that were gone without praying [funerary rituals]. I did not see where my parents were when they killed them. The truth is that my brother went to search for them to bury them. He did not find them, the grave was open and they had to close it again empty. The truth is that I don't know where my parents are because my brother did not find them… because my parents were like minced meat. And that makes me very sad; not being able to bury my parents is too much pain for me.[26].

Rosa's pain at the loss of her family is increased by the lack of funerary rituals for her relatives, especially her parents to whom she feels she had a particular obligation. She and her brother made a grave that had to be closed empty because they could not find the bodies to bury. In this case, the victims' grief is enhanced by the particular conditions of the deaths of their relatives, particularly of the children, and the lack of funerary rituals. There are strong emotional and moral consequences for the surviving victims due to the lack of funerary rituals, and it is in this context that dance has become a vehicle to cope with the cultural and psychological damages caused by the conflict.

One of the damaging factors affecting local communities is the fear and terror that creates silence. In this context, dance provides a *shield* that allows people to speak about violence and injustice in a non-confrontational manner, therefore reducing the risk for those who find symbolic tools of resistance through dance. In addition, even beyond the conflict, poor mechanisms of reparation have created conditions that affect solidarity in the communities and promote division. In response to this situation, dance also fulfils a function of *mediation*, as explained below. Further, the cultural, therapeutic and religious resources mobilized through dance help people to cope with the absence of funerary rituals for those who died in the massacre.

The Afro-Colombian Funerary Ritual

Dance in this context takes the form of the re-enactment of a traditional Afro-Colombian funerary ritual for children, known as Gualí or Chigualo. There is a strong connection between the world of life and the world of death in Afro-Colombian religious representations. This connection is enacted through elaborated funerary rituals that permit a "good death", which allows the deceased relative to become an ancestor who can protect the community. These funerary rituals are expressed through dances to a specific repertoire of songs. It is reported that this tradition has slowly decayed, particularly in those communities that have been displaced to the cities because of the ongoing conflict. In addition, the Gualí is also less common because the average number of deaths of children under five years of age has decreased in the last twenty years. However, this tradition continues in some of the rural areas of this region, as in some of the communities in Bojayá.

The funerary rituals for adults consist of songs and prayers over nine days. The funerary songs used in the ritual for adult burials are known as Alabaos, in which profuse sorrow and tears are displayed. In contrast to adult funerals, less sorrow is displayed in child funerals, because it is believed that children become *angelitos*, "little angels", who protect their families and their godparents. It is said that tears should not be displayed during the rite because it runs the risk that the child's soul will drown in those tears. In the Gualí, the corpse of the child is dressed in white and thrown from person to person, passed around the neighbours and the family through rhythmic patterns and dance. While people are dancing around the child, the *cantadoras* sing traditional funerary songs and people play musical instruments.[27] Once the Gualí is finished, there is a procession led by the older children to the cemetery where the child's corpse is buried.[28]

The inclusion of dance and song in a funerary ritual may seem an unorthodox notion to some, but not within cultures where movement is central to their values and serves as cultural signifiers for life transitions such as marriage, death, birth and transitions into adulthood. Serrano[29] argues that funerary rituals within a Latin American historical context were not only ways of expressing grief, but also ways of subverting colonial power. Further, in Amerindian and communities influenced by African traditions, most of their dances are collective dances that aim to construct their communities as collective bodies.[30] These are public demonstrations of collective grief that have political power by demonstrating that these deaths deserve to be grieved and commemorated because they are unjust deaths and they also expose our shared vulnerability in society.[31] The body, through dance and song, transmits deep sorrow and grief; it expresses a simultaneous duality between the individual experience, and its impact on collective identity and memory.

Restrepo claims that the roots of this tradition are located in the slave history of Colombian black communities, and the "celebration" of death in a funerary rite of a child would mean the celebration of his/her escape from a life of slavery.[32] However, the Gualí can also be interpreted as the celebration of death of a pure soul that does not need to be saved. According to the beliefs of Afro-Colombian communities, children's souls only need guidance to go to heaven, not mediation. Tobon describes Alabaos as praying in dialogue within the structure of a song, following the style of "romance de pasión" with religious motives.[33] The songs in the Gualí have historical themes, picaresque humour and satire. They are playful and joyfully emotive songs. The Gualí, as most death rituals, helps individuals and communities to cope with and work through the emotions associated with the loss of a loved one.[34]

In the context of the Colombian conflict, the Afro-Colombian communities often find that their death rituals are prohibited or profaned, which is considered to be an ethnocidal practice oriented toward the weakening of the community's networks of solidarity and mechanisms of transmission of cultural memory.[35] The interruption of funerary rituals could be considered as a practice of cultural annihilation that, far from being collateral damage from situations of war, is a premeditated act oriented towards the spiritual destruction of social groups, particularly of ethnic groups with bonds socially constructed through rituals. It aims to strip away "effective cultural resources for resistance; not the killing of bodies but the spirit".[36] Similar situations were present in other cases of conflict, such as in Peru, where the Senderistas burned Catholic churches, and peasants had trouble celebrating holidays or death rituals due to lack of safety.[37] The Historical Memory Group[38] described some of the lived consequences of the massacre aftermath in the community of Bojayá, where funerary rituals could not be carried out due to the continuation of combat and the destruction of bodies by the explosion. The absence of rituals has permanently affected the identity of the community and their feelings of solidarity. The Historical Memory Group claim the survivors felt that the absence of rituals and neglect of the deceased victims have "broken the spiritual and social order and eliminated any possibility to create meaning".[39] However, survivors are far from being passive spectators of their cultural annihilation; they have developed several grassroots initiatives that have contributed to their resistance in their territory and their mobilization for the recognition of their rights as victims.[40] Initiatives of construction of cultural memory through dance, songs, and performances are paths towards denunciation of past and current violence and increasing feelings of solidarity in a context of fear and distrust.

A Gualí was re-enacted during the tenth commemoration of the massacre of Bojayá in 2012, a three-day event including political, social, cultural and religious acts. On one side there were local leaders discussing mechanisms of negotiation for the unfulfilled reparation from the national government. On the other, there were religious leaders trying to carry out religious ceremonies. There were also local groups of singers, actors and dancers. At the local stadium, after the initial speeches during the first night, a group of women from Pogué, a village from Bojayá, performed a Gualí.

As in a traditional setting of a child funeral in rural Chocó, a group of traditional *cantadoras*, from Pogue were in a circle singing very emotive and satirical songs, voice and body collaborating in an integrated fashion.[41] The songs had a call-response format, in which a main singer starts and a choir answers. There is both a repertoire of songs but also an improvisational element in song, as in the dance. As Tobon noted from his fieldwork in San Miguel, the *cantadoras* claimed that they would not sing romances, because even though they are "happy songs, they are very sad… it is very sad to sing them, and they can bring death to children here".[42] Thus, it is relevant that this was not an everyday, but an extraordinary situation that allowed the *cantadoras* to perform these songs outside the traditional context. The dance consisted of a circle of women moving their hips and feet rhythmically, while a woman at the centre of the circle performed gestures symbolizing the rocking of a baby in her arms. They then proceeded to throw the figure of the baby, usually represented by a doll, or a piece of cloth or a bag, to other women in the circle. The women were at the centre of the arena while a couple of hundred people watched from the chairs of the local stadium. Religious missionary women also accompanied them in the dance.

The performance evokes both an emotive and joyful response but knowing the background and context, is tragic in its own way. In later conversations with these women, some of them manifested enthusiasm for performing these rituals even in a context different from the traditional; others claimed that initially they felt very tired and did not want to continue performing the Gualí at the commemoration of the massacre every year. These women claimed that they had been convinced by some of the missionary women, who had also joined them during the Gualí. The singers were persuaded when it was suggested that if the women of Pogué stopped singing their songs and performing their Gualí, the violent actors would win.

The Gualí, as performed during the commemorative events, presents an extreme involvement of the body with high-intensity vocalization, and the physical passing of the symbolic body of the child, which is rocked and soothed. The bodies of both performers and witnesses are involved in active engagement through dance or keeping the rhythm through bodily percussion. The circle serves as a holding space for the experience, in which each of the community members, as well as relatives of the disappeared children, come in one by one while they dance. Rhythm, as a universal organizer, serves to maintain cohesion in performers and spectators, as well as it serves as a mode of connection into the ritual through synchronicity.[43] The disappearance of the physical bodies that were damaged in the massacre disable the community's ability to perform funerary rituals, which constitutes a cultural trauma.[44] The community reconfigures this absence through the public manifestation of the danced ritual, where the disappeared body is re-presented through the symbolic passing of the child's body in the Gualí. The ritual serves to create a path of transformation from the "mala muerte" (bad death) to their consecration as "angelitos" in the community. In the performance of the Gualí in the public commemoration of the massacre, there is significance held in the object passed as a symbolic body, as a figure of the disappeared bodies and as a symbol of collective grief. The body as object, as performer, as survivor of the massacre, is thus understood, as MacLeod claims, as a focal site for experiences of violence.[45] The dance expressed through the funerary rituals becomes a mechanism "to heal, cope with, combat and ameliorate destructive experiences of violence" that pose a threat to individual and collective ways of coping and preserving cultural memory.[46] As this chapter discusses, however, this comes at a cost to the bodies of the people re-enacting the rituals, which is held in tension against the greater communal benefit perceived of preserving the memory of the massacre.

The re-enactment of the Gualí, with its duality and complexity, is a liminal expression of grief and transformation within the community performed through a combination of dramatization and ritual. These rituals have contributed to the communities' ability to cope with the strong emotions associated with the experience of the atrocity and to socially construct a memory of the massacre. Dance is inherently an organic mechanism in which community members relate to each other, as most Colombian gatherings involve dancing as a quotidian way of coexistence and social interaction.[47] Dance remains connected to the social fibre of Latin American culture, not regarded as a separate genre accessible only to some, but as "an integral part of the lives of bodies in the communities that have produced dance traditions".[48] "The diasporic dancing body becomes the vehicle for the articulation of a culture under siege. This suggests that dance within the Colombian context contributes to an understanding of these performance practices as mechanisms of grassroots peacebuilding. Dance literally remembers cultural practices repressed over centuries of conflict".[49]

Functions of Dance in Peacebuilding

As a mix of indigenous, African and European heritages, and as a result of imperialist and oppressive slavery practices, rituals underwent change through assimilation and transformation, and the battle to preserve them continues in modern times in Colombia. As Highwater stresses, "ritual is never successfully imposed on the people. When such missionary efforts are made, the imposed ideology is thoroughly assimilated into pre-existing ritual forms".[50] This was the case in the transformation that took place in the

Americas after African religious traditions met Christian missionary pressure. However, the local Church in Chocó, influenced by liberation theology, has supported the continuation of Afro-Colombian and indigenous rituals, in contrast to other cases in which missionaries have discouraged such ritual practices.[51]

In the context of the Bojayá massacre commemorations, the functions of dance for social change create a transient space for those who grieve, providing a spiritual, historical, communal and traditional connection to the deceased. The visibility of dance creates an impact on not only the performers, but also on the Bojayá audience as witnesses of the experience, which also includes the perpetrators still living in the community. The processes of transformation, connection and transition are essential to processes of grief and mourning.[52] Grief is embodied in these rituals in a way that connects and speaks to the other members of the community, and which provides a voice and a symbolic cultural mechanism for the disappeared bodies of the massacre victims to become publically present-in-time and remembered within the community. The bodies of the dancers become a channel for expression, and provide a cathartic emotional release. Dance helps to *mediate* the atrocity of the events that continue to plague this community. The performative aspects of dance, music and song also provide a *shield* that enables community members to express what has transpired, as jokes and humour are also used as diffusive techniques that provide a release. The shielding function of dance provides a platform for social commentary and the search for justice and enables a type of haven from consequences usually applicable to overt verbal expression[53]: "In these realms the 'unsafe' can be explored without the consequences of such a thrust in the 'real world'".[54]

The symbolic object used instead of the *angelito* is passed and sometimes thrown from hand to hand, providing a shared focus for individual and collective experience. In the field of dance movement psychotherapy, the metaphorical utilization of objects that hold heavy emotional content is held as an invaluable tool towards healing, but the significance of the *angelito* extends beyond the individual and therapeutic, and becomes a metaphor for the shared responsibility of bearing the pain and duty of re-enacting these rituals every year.[55] The continual embodiment of the victims of the massacre becomes a ritualistic remembrance of the disappeared. LeBaron, MacLeod and Acland, echoing Lederach's *The Moral Imagination*, argue that metaphor in movement is important for peacebuilding because it allows the building of multilayered perspectives that can enable complex, embodied narratives to shift.[56] Metaphor in the Gualí serves as a vehicle for meaning that projects the participants' action into a liminal space, and Harris suggests that the use of metaphor and liminality in this way can provide a space for advocacy, restoration and reconstruction in the aftermath of war.[57]

The re-capturing of a traditional ritual linked to Afro-Colombian tradition also serves as a *transmitter* of the historical legacy of the community. These rituals, as revived for new generations, have also inspired contemporary dances that incorporate these rituals in a renewed form. For instance, a piece by the Colombian dance company Zajana, entitled *Alabaos*, integrates these rituals into contemporary dance choreography.[58] As a transmitter of a cultural heritage, the performative aspects of this ritual also have activated influences from grassroots religious organizations. The missionaries who insist that the *cantadoras* should continue performing the Gualí during the commemorations of the massacres argue that these commemorative dances will serve as a *stimulant* towards visibility, reparation and continued construction of the cultural memory in the community. Dance in this context may be also functioning as a form of *control*. Some missionaries follow the principle that building cultural memory from victims' perspectives is a form of accompaniment that can contribute to denouncing present and past violence while vindicating victims' rights. However, this poses some challenges and consequences to the bodies of both performers, survivors and witnesses, which we explore below.

Challenges of the Performance of the Gualí

Much research on the biopsychosocial basis of trauma indicates that traumatic memories are inherently non-verbal and stored in the body as images, perceptions and sensations that do not necessarily carry a correlating verbal narrative.[59] The direct involvement of the body of performers, survivors and witnesses in such an intense manner has a positive impact of making an embodied social protest. This positive outcome has been recognized in Colombia, where several official and grassroots initiatives integrate dance as a tool for peacebuilding. Some examples of these initiatives are the Danza por la Paz lab, which brings over thirty artists together from all over the country[60] or music and dance workshops with demobilized youth organized by the reintegration office.[61]

An issue rarely mentioned in the literature of arts and peacebuilding is the risks adverse consequences of the embodied memorialization of atrocity, as images and memories evoked may not be able to be re-integrated or transformed. The focus here is on the impact of trauma on the dancing body, and the importance of understanding the challenging position these performances offer its performers given the cultural weight placed on re-enacting this grief in a public arena. This can be an ambiguous practice as perpetuated repetition can evoke grief through the embodied re-experiencing of traumatic memories, which may also cause harm and perpetuate violence from the perpetrators who still cohabitate the Bojayá community. Thus, there is an impact on the body–mind of individuals who feel pressured to preserve the memory of this atrocity, and at the same time have to go through a repeated individual bereavement of their lost loved ones. Yet, as the repetitive nature is conducive to the construction of cultural memory, the tension remains between individual sacrifice and claims for social justice. At a macro-level, as detailed before, the ritual serves a "higher purpose" as a tool for peacebuilding, yet, for some, the re-creation of the ritual every year has a major impact at a personal level. As Valentine states: "urgent social issues may take precedence over individual grief".[62] The notion of individual sacrifice, duty and the ongoing battle for remembrance, recognition and justice put these two effects on a very tentative scale. The struggle between the experience of grief of individual and collective bodies' and the pressure and hope for societal change still persists.

Conclusion

The inability to perform the Gualí after the massacre of Bojayá has impacted the Afro-Colombian community severely, in a manner that constitutes a form of cultural annihilation on behalf of the perpetrators. Nevertheless, the re-enactment of the Gualí and other traditional rituals during the commemoration of the massacre has also served to encourage cultural memorialization of the massacre through artistic and non-verbal means and resist the imposition of cultural annihilation. The ultimate goal of the Gualí in the commemoration is to present mourning and grief in a public manner, evoking shame in perpetrators, empathy in witnesses and solidarity among the victims. It also serves the purpose of continuing to transmit Afro-Colombian traditions that were interrupted during the conflict. Dance, as an inherent part of the Colombian communities' historical heritage, remains present as an important medium in celebrations, transitions and mourning. It provides an instrumental link to peacebuilding practices by ritualistically engaging with an embodied expression of communal mourning and remembrance. This chapter considers that the danced performances of the Gualí in the commemoration have helped victims to embody their social protest in the context of peacebuilding, which is the recognition of their rights to truth, justice, reparation and guarantees of non-repetition of violence. In that sense, dance is a mechanism that has been used to challenge impunity and contribute to a process of peacebuilding in the region.

Notes

1. Maxine Sheets-Johnstone, "On Movement and Objects in Motion: The Phenomenology of the Visible in Dance", *Journal of Aesthetic Education* 13:2 (1978): 33–46.
2. Judith Lynne Hanna, "To Dance Is Human: Some Psychobiological Bases of an Expressive Form", in *The Anthropology of the Body*, ed. John Blacking (London and New York: Academic Press, 1977), 211–232; Judith Lynne Hanna et al., "Movements Toward Understanding Humans Through the Anthropological Study of Dance", *Current Anthropology* 20:2 (1979): 313–339; Anya Peterson Royce, *The Anthropology of Dance*, 2nd edition (Hampshire, UK: Dance Books, 2002); and Drid Williams, *Anthropology and the Dance: Ten Lectures*, 2nd edition (Urbana, IL: University of Illinois Press, 2004.
3. Diana Taylor, *The Archive and the Repertoire: Performing Cultural Memory in the Americas* (Durham: Duke University Press, 2003), 3.
4. Taylor, *The Archive and the Repertoire*, 13.
5. Thania Acarón, *The Practitioner's Body of Knowledge: Dance/Movement in Training Programmes that Address Violence, Conflict and Peace* (PhD thesis, University of Aberdeen, 2015).
6. Sandra Milena Rios Oyola, *Religion, Social Memory, and Conflict: The Massacre of Bojayá in Colombia* (Hampshire, UK: Palgrave Macmillan, 2015).
7. David Harris, "Pathways to Embodied Empathy and Reconciliation After Atrocity: Former Boy Soldiers in a Dance/Movement Therapy Group in Sierra Leone", *Intervention* 5:3 (2007): 203–231.
8. Hanna, *To Dance Is Human*, 128–178; Hanna et al., *Movements Towards Understanding Humans*, 313–339; Royce, *The Anthropology of Dance*; and Williams, *Anthropology and the Dance*.
9. John D. Brewer, *Peace Processes: A Sociological Approach* (Cambridge, UK: Polity, 2010).
10. Brewer, *Peace Processes*, 200.
11. In our analysis we build on Paul Spencer's (*Society and the Dance: The Social Anthropology of Process and Performance* [Cambridge, UK and New York: Cambridge University Press, 1985]) and Judith Hanna's (1979) work on the

functions of dance in sociocultural change and protest according to recent research, particularly from an anthropological perspective. Acarón (2015) focuses her research on how these functions frame unique contributions that dance/movement offers to peace practices.

12. Spencer, *Society and the Dance.*
13. Jeremy West et al., “Effects of Hatha Yoga and African Dance on Perceived Stress, Affect, and Salivary Cortisol”, *Annals of Behavioral Medicine* 28:2 (2004): 114–118.
14. Rena Kornblum, *Disarming the Playground: Violence Prevention Through Movement and Pro-Social Skills, Activity Book* (Oklahoma City: Wood’N’Barnes Publishing, 2002); Lynn Koshland and Jean La Sarre Gardner, *Peace Through Dance/Movement Therapy: A Violence Prevention Program for Elementary School Children* (United States: Self-Published, 2003).
15. Spencer, *Society and the Dance*, 4–8.
16. Amber Elizabeth Lynn Gray, “Dancing in Our Blood: Dance/Movement Therapy with Street Children and Victims of Organized Violence in Haiti”, in *Dance, Human Rights and Social Justice: Dignity in Motion*, ed. Naomi Jackson and Toni Shapiro-Phim (Lanham, MD: Scarecrow Press, 2008), 222–236; Alcinda Manuel Honwana, “Healing for Peace: Traditional Healers and Post-War Reconstruction in Southern Mozambique” 3:3 (1997): 293–305; Harris, “Pathways to Embodied Empathy and Reconciliation”; David Harris, “Dance and Child Soldiers—FPIF”, *Foreign Policy in Focus*, 2009, http://fpif.org/dance_and_child_soldiers/; and David Harris, “The Paradox of Expressing Speechless Terror: Ritual Liminality in the Creative Arts Therapies’ Treatment of Posttraumatic Distress”, *The Arts in Psychotherapy* 36:2 (2009): 94–104.
17. Hanna, *To Dance Is Human*, 107, 110.
18. Gray, “Dancing in Our Blood”; Harris, “The Paradox of Expressing Speechless Terror”; Honwana, “Healing for Peace”; Pilar Riaño-Alcalá and Erin Baines, “The Archive in the Witness: Documentation in Settings of Chronic Insecurity”, *International Journal of Transitional Justice* 5:3 (November 1, 2011): 412–433, https://doi.org/10.1093/ijtj/ijr025.
19. Hanna, *To Dance Is Human*, 90.
20. Helen Thomas, *The Body, Dance, and Cultural Theory* (New York, NY: Palgrave Macmillan, 2003).
21. Taylor, *The Archive and the Repertoire*, 2–53.
22. GMH-CNRR, *Trujillo. Una Tragedia Que No Cesa* [Trujillo: A Tragedy That Never Ceases] (Bogotá, Colombia: CNRR, Planeta, 2008).
23. GMH-CNRR, *Bojayá: La Guerra Sin Limites* [Bojayá: The War Without Limits] (Bogotá, Colombia: Ediciones Semana, Taurus, 2010), 59.
24. Paco Gomez, *Los Muertos No Hablan. Edición Bojayá Una Década (2002–2012)* (España: Otramerica, 2012).

25. The events described in this chapter took place before the FARC offered a public apology to the community of Bojayá in December 2015.
26. Rosa Chaverra in the public forum "Bojayá una década después", National Museum of Colombia, Bogotá, 27 April 2012.
27. The cantadoras hold a great symbolical position in the country; they have been present in several important events such as the signature of the peace agreement between the FARC and the government and the FARC public apology event in Bojayá in 2016.
28. Anne Marie Losonczy, "El Luto de Sí Mismo. Cuerpo, Sombra Y Muerte Entre Los Negros Colombianos Del Chocó" [Mourning Itself: Body, Shadow and Death Between the Black Colombians of Chocó], *América Negra* [Black America] 1:1 (1991): 43–61; Eduardo Restrepo, *Identidad, Poder Y Cultura Entre Los Grupos Negros de Los Ríos Satinga Y Sanquianga, Pacífico Sur Colombiano* [Identity, Power and Culture Between the Black Groups of the Rivers Satinga and Sanquianga, Colombian South Pacific] (Medellín, Colombia: Universidad Nacional de Colombia, 1995); Jose Serrano, "Cuando Canta El Guaco: La Muerte Y El Morir En Poblaciones Afrocolombianas Del Río Baudó, Chocó" [When the Guaco Sings: Death and Dying Amongst the Afrocolombian Populations of the River Baudó, Chocó] (Medillín, Colombia: Universidad Nacional de Colombia, 1994).
29. Serrano, "Cuando Canta El Guaco".
30. Ana Carolina Avila. "Danza Como Instrumento de Paz y Construcción de Identidad", in *Pensar El Arte Hoy: El Cuerpo*, eds. Carlos Eduardo Sanabria and Alvaro Corral Cuartas (Bogotá: Universidad Jorge Tadeo Lozano, 2015), 158–174, 169.
31. Judith Butler, *Precarious Life: The Powers of Mourning and Violence* (London: Verso, 2004).
32. Eduardo Restrepo, *Memories, Identities, and Ethnicity: Making the Black Community in Colombia* (Chapel Hill, NC: University of North Carolina at Chapel Hill, 2002).
33. Alejandro Tobon, "La Cultura de La 'Gente Sin Cultura'. Clasificación de Los Géneros Musicales Tradicionales: El Caso de Los Romances En La Cuenca Del Río Atrato (Colombia)", *Revista Acontratiempo* 14 (December 2009), http://acontratiempo.bibliotecanacional.gov.co/?ediciones/revista-14/artculos/la-cultura-de-la-gente-sin-cultura-clasificacin-de-los-generos-musicales-tradicionales-el-caso-de-lo.html.
34. Douglas James Davies, *Death, Ritual, and Belief: The Rhetoric of Funerary Rites* (London, UK: Cassell, 1997), 15.
35. Jaime Arocha and F. Gonzalez, "Museos, Etnografía Contemporánea Y Representación de Los Afrodescendientes", *Antipoda* 9: (July–December 2009): 140.
36. Brewer, *Peace Processes*, 22.

37. Kimberly Susan Theidon, *Intimate Enemies: Violence and Reconciliation in Peru* (Philadelphia, PN: University of Pennsylvania Press, 2013).
38. This was an autonomous research group in charge of building the historical memory of the conflict in Colombia, part of the National Commission of Reparation and Reconciliation; the GMH-CNRR.
39. GMH-CNRR, *Bojayá: La Guerra Sin Límites*, 103.
40. Riaño-Alcalá and Baines, "The Archive in the Witness".
41. *Cantaoras or Cantadoras* are women who know the traditional songs of the rituals. In the last years the Group of Cantadoras de Bojayá have participated in many national and regional events related to the peace process. See: *Las Musas de Pogue*. Directed by German Rendon Arango, 2016. https://www.youtube.com/watch?v=PEQ3LW9a3KU, accessed 26 October 2016. Film.
42. "La Cultura de La 'Gente Sin Cultura'."
43. Claire Schmais, "Healing Processes in Group Dance Therapy", *American Journal of Dance Therapy* 8:1 (December 1985): 17–36, https://doi.org/10.1007/bf02251439.
44. It was only in 2017 that an official exhumation of the victims' remains was conducted.
45. Carrie MacLeod, "Choreography of Conflict", in *The Choreography of Resolution*, ed. Michelle Lebaron, Carrie MacLeod, and Andrew Floyer Acland (Chicago, IL: American Bar Association, Section of Dispute Resolution, 2013), 45–57.
46. Acarón, *The Practitioner's Body.*
47. Peter Wade, *Music, Race, and Nation* (Chicago: University of Chicago Press, 2000).
48. Barbara Browning, *Samba: Resistance in Motion* (Bloomington, IN: Indiana University Press, 1995).
49. Celeste Fraser Delgado and Jose Esteban Muñoz, *Everynight Life: Culture and Dance in Latin/o America* (Durham, NC: Duke University Press, 2004), 17.
50. Jamake Highwater, *Dance: Rituals of Experience* (New York, NY: A & W Publishers, 1978), 28.
51. Nancy Scheper-Hughes, *Death Without Weeping: The Violence of Everyday Life in Brazil* (Oakland, CA: University of California Press, 1993), 529.
52. Bronna D. Romanoff and Marion Terenzio, "Rituals and the Grieving Process", *Death Studies* 22:8 (November 1998): 697–711, https://doi.org/10.1080/074811898201227.
53. Riaño-Alcalá and Baines, "The Archive in the Witness."
54. Hanna, *To Dance Is Human*, 134.
55. Robin Ellis, "Movement Metaphor as Mediator: A Model for the Dance/Movement Therapy Process", *The Arts in Psychotherapy* 28:3 (August 2001): 181–190, https://doi.org/10.1016/s0197-4556(01)00098-3.

56. LeBaron, MacLeod, and Acland, *The Choreography of Resolution*; Carrie MacLeod, "Choreography of Conflict".
57. Harris, "The Paradox of Expressing Speechless Terror"; Harris, "Dance and Child Soldiers—FPIF."
58. Compañía Zajana, http://www.zajanadanza.com/web/.
59. Babette Rothschild, *The Body Remembers: The Psychophysiology of Trauma and Trauma Treatment* (New York, NY: Norton, 2000); Bessel van der Kolk, "The Body Keeps the Score: Memory and the Evolving Psychobiology of Posttraumatic Stress", *Harvard Review of Psychiatry* 1:5 (1994): 253–265; and Peter Levine, *In an Unspoken Voice: How the Body Releases Trauma and Restores Goodness* (Berkeley, CA: North Atlantic Books, 2010).
60. Danza por la Paz en Bogota, http://centrodememoriahistorica.gov.co/de/noticias/noticias-cmh/danza-por-la-paz-se-toma-la-ciudad, accessed 4 December 2018.
61. Proyecto Piloto de Educación Artística para Jóvenes en Proceso de Reintegración, carried out by the Alta Consejería para la Reintegración de la Presidencia de la República; Avila, *Danza como instrumento de paz*, 163.
62. Christine Valentine, "Academic Constructions of Bereavement", *Mortality* 11:2 (2006): 63.

CHAPTER 21

Doing Justice to the Past: Time, Drama and Peacebuilding

Frances Clemson

Introduction

A large and growing body of work in the field of peacebuilding attests to the significance of history, memory and a sense of intergenerational responsibility in efforts to create an enduring peace.[1] Parallel to this concern is an increasing recognition that peacebuilders need to consider the timing and duration of peacebuilding efforts.[2]

In this chapter, I propose that *time* is a fruitful thematic point of contact between peacebuilding and dramatic performance. I test this proposal by offering a case study of a particular dramatic work, written and performed against a background of conflict: Dorothy L. Sayers' *The Just Vengeance* (1946).[3] This play was commissioned as part of a festival at Lichfield Cathedral marking the 750th anniversary of the commencement of the building of the Cathedral. The play was a collaborative work, as in the examples presented by Culbertson above (in Chapter 18), with Sayers working closely

F. Clemson (✉)
Durham University, Durham, UK
e-mail: frances.clemson@durham.ac.uk

J. Mitchell et al. (eds.), *Peacebuilding and the Arts*,
Rethinking Peace and Conflict Studies,
https://doi.org/10.1007/978-3-030-17875-8_21

with the Cathedral's Dean and Chapter. The anniversary actually fell in 1945 but the festival was delayed by a year because of the Second World War. The context for Sayers' play was thus one of celebration, marking both the long history of the Cathedral and a more recent history of survival and ultimate victory. Sayers' play, however, is darker and more discomforting than one might expect in this context. It depicts the death of an airman, shot down during the recent conflict. The Airman finds himself in his home city of Lichfield and encounters generations of citizens from across the city's past, themselves perpetrators and victims of violence. As in the case examined by Oyala and Acarón (in Chapter 20), this production took place in the wake of terrible losses. As one of the actors in the original production commented: '... we had come through the war, but many of our friends had not ... we were bewildered'.[4]

Sayers was a Christian thinker and her play is explicitly religious. With the 'secularist paradigm' coming under ever-greater scrutiny, peacebuilders are increasingly seeking to draw upon the richness of thought and practice within religious communities to resource their work.[5] The reader may nonetheless wonder precisely what a play structured around Christian concepts can offer to peacebuilders operating in a diversity of contexts. To address this concern, I want to begin by framing my approach in this chapter in terms of *challenging hospitality*.

This framing is informed by my experience of Scriptural Reasoning (SR) with faith groups, through my work with the Cambridge Inter-faith Programme in the UK. SR gathers members of religious groups in what Peter Ochs has characterised as a 'hearth-to-hearth dialogue', centred on reading and interpreting together their respective sacred texts.[6] SR contests the notion that the best way forward for peaceable inter-religious dialogue is to try to minimise religious difference. Instead, SR suggests that it is precisely those places of deeply specific commitment that offer 'the best resources for long-lasting conflict transformation'.[7] The intention of an SR group is to provide a context in which participants can be both 'host' and 'guest' to one another. The believer invites someone of another faith to be a guest in their religious 'home' by reading their scriptures, and is hosted in return.[8] The aim of this interaction is not consensus. Rather the goal is that such disagreement as exists between the members of the SR group might be practised in ways that are generative rather than destructive.[9] In his assessment of the potential of SR as a peacebuilding initiative, Ochs acknowledges that it is, in some respects, a 'dangerous' practice. To invite others to gather with you around your own 'hearth' is also to draw attention to those places where the fires of conflict often spring up.[10] Thus SR involves a challenging hospitality.

In this chapter, I want to create a hospitable space in which the reader can join me in attending to an artwork that has been profoundly shaped by Christian commitment. My aim is not that all readers should accept the Christian beliefs in evidence here but rather that they might come to see these beliefs as generative of new possibilities for thinking about peacebuilding. I also want to suggest that the content of Sayers' play itself opens up further for us the idea of a challenging hospitality. Burbridge and Stevenson note in their essay in this volume (Chapter 19) that theatrical performance can provide a welcoming space in which to explore dangerous issues. I will argue that this is the case in *The Just Vengeance*.

In the sections that follow I will take time over the play, closely following the action as it unfolds. Reflection on this dramatic action will be set against the background of John Paul Lederach's recent account of the importance of time for peacebuilding efforts. It is with Lederach's discussion of this issue that I begin.

Peacebuilding and Time

Time is a recurring motif in John Paul Lederach's work *The Moral Imagination: The Art and Soul of Building Peace.*[11] Lederach's account of his own experiences suggests that the significance of time is frequently misunderstood by peacebuilders. It is possible to identify from Lederach's study two notable loci for this mishandling of time: the first is found in the role of the 'turning point' in peace processes; the second, in the treatment of the past.

For peace to become possible there must be turning points: 'moments pregnant with new life, which arise from what appear to be the barren grounds of destructive violence'.[12] Where extreme violence is a daily reality there is naturally 'a deep sense of urgency' about the need to reach a turning point, however small.[13] Lederach writes of his own desire in crisis situations to 'control time', seeing it as a 'commodity' which must be expended efficiently and rapidly so as to make progress, a 'fleeting moment that somehow must be taken advantage of and shaped'.[14]

The paradox that Lederach uncovers, however, is that such an intense, controlling approach to time can work against the possibility of arriving at and building on a true turning point. This sense of urgency is fed by and further encourages a 'narrow view of time'.[15] Not only does this narrow perspective make it easier to miss potential turning points in the rush to respond, it actually leads to a misapprehension of the nature of such moments. Turning points are fertile spots for the flourishing of something new, surprising, creative and nourishing. They are not in and of themselves moments of resolution or wholesale change: they are starting points as much as they are turning points. To be generative in this way, Lederach suggests, such moments need to be both perceived and developed through a time-taking process, akin to the 'artistic process' or indeed to the process of attending to and reflecting on a performance.[16]

The second aspect of peacebuilders' mishandling of time is, like the first, rooted in a readily comprehensible assumption. Just as it is understandable that one might associate 'turning points' with an urgent desire to make use of the 'commodity' of time, so it also seems self-evident that in contexts dominated by long-lasting patterns of violence, a complete break with the past is essential. Lederach highlights how the quest for peace is often understood in terms of moving forward, motivated by 'the vision and belief that the future is not the slave of the past'.[17] Whilst the most recent events in a conflict might be considered important to the discussion of immediate issues, any attempt to include the more extensive past in negotiations can be thought of as an irrelevance or a hindrance.[18]

Yet Lederach attests once again that this belief may be linked to a 'narrow' approach to time that can actually impede the building of peace. He suggests that peacebuilders risk mistaking the status and significance of the past for many of those involved in conflict. Lederach gives a range of examples—from the Philippines, Ireland, Kenya—in which individuals and groups made clear to him that for them the long past was 'alive' and thus deeply relevant to their present actions and hopes for the future.[19] This liveliness of what might be assumed to be dead and gone can take a number of forms. It is the 'lively' presence of the graves of the long lost which act as markers by which the present community orients itself; it is the strong sense of intergenerational responsibility which includes within it awareness of and contact with the past as much as it does thought of the future; it is the identity-shaping narrative of a community stretching back over centuries. Lederach insists that the 'imagination' which peacebuilding needs must include a refusal to see the past as 'something to be laid aside, overcome or forgotten in order to move into a better future'.[20] Peacebuilders must avoid the 'narrow' view and develop instead a more 'expansive' conception of time.[21]

In the remainder of this chapter I want to suggest that Sayers' play offers us an understanding of time which speaks to and takes further Lederach's argument for this 'expansive' approach.

Doing Justice to the Past? Time, Violence and Suffering in *The Just Vengeance*

Sayers' play was written for a specific performance context, as part of a celebration of local history in the year after the conclusion of the Second World War. We might assume this context to be free of the pressures involved in peacebuilding, as described by Lederach; after all, the war was over, victory secured. The prologue to the play, delivered by a character who identifies himself as Lichfield's 'Recorder', certainly seems to support this idea of recovered stability. The Recorder refers to the Cathedral's anniversary and expresses the hope that the building may stand:

> To tell her story in this English land
> Until the fingers of slow time come round
> To their last moment, and the trumpets sound![22]

The Recorder further reassures the audience that the scenes they are about to watch are 'but as pictures painted in a book', quite detached from reality.[23]

Then the dramatic action begins with what one spectator at the original performance recollected as the 'screams' of an aeroplane crashing, followed by a 'tirade' in which a man steps forward and cries out[24]: 'Woe to the bloody city of Lichfield!'[25] This startling opening to the play is the beginning of a portrayal of Lichfield's past which would have been deeply challenging for the original audience seated in the Cathedral. The speaker of this line, it transpires, is the seventeenth-century figure George Fox, founder of the Religious Society of Friends, or Quakers. Fox's journal recounts that upon entering Lichfield he received a vision of 'a channel of blood running down the streets' and was commanded by God to make his disturbing proclamation.[26] This action begins the play's depiction of the city's darker past, of events and persons whose connections with the city were unlikely to be memorialised and celebrated.

Fox repeats his cry several times before the entrance of the play's protagonist, the Airman. Core to the Airman's character is his sense of being trapped within seemingly inextricable patterns of violence, and his fervent desire for these patterns to be broken. In his opening dialogue with Fox he speaks of being caught up in a 'damnable' situation, with 'no choice except between bloody alternatives'[27]:

> We try to do right
> And someone is hurt – very likely the wrong person;
> And if we do wrong, or even if we do nothing,
> It comes to the same in the end. We drop a bomb
> And condemn a thousand to sudden death,
> The guiltless along with the guilty. Or we refuse
> To drop a bomb, and condemn a thousand people
> To a lingering death in a concentration camp[28]

The Airman expresses to Fox a wish to meet others who are 'fellow victims/And fellow criminals', similarly entangled in relations of culpability and victimhood.[29] As a result, he is confronted by a 'Chorus' of past generations of citizens of Lichfield. These include martyrs and their executioners, a labourer hanged for theft, a potter poisoned in his work, an unemployed man for whom the 'city had no use', a prostitute, a widow, a lunatic.[30]

After meeting the citizens, the Airman is asked by the Recorder about his own life. He responds that, though he had mapped out the contribution to society he intended to make, ultimately he 'had no time,/Except to be killed – and kill'.[31] The Airman protests against the suffering which he and the citizens have undergone and demands 'justice'.[32]

As the play continues it becomes clear that the Airman's desire for justice is bound up with a particular approach to *time*. It is possible to see in the Airman something like the urgency which Lederach identifies as a shaping force in the outlook of those who seek to end violence. For the Airman this urgency goes along with considerable *certainty* about what must be achieved.

When the Recorder asks him about his beliefs, the Airman announces: 'I believe in man [sic], and in the hope of the future,/The steady growth of knowledge and power over things, .../And a just world where everyone will be happy'. The Recorder asks who this vision applies to, who will receive justice. The Airman's frank answer appears to expose the redundant nature of the question: 'Everybody', he replies.[33] Justice and equality are, by definition, not partial. Yet, when the Recorder asks whether the Airman's vision includes the citizens of Lichfield's bloody past, the Airman is clear that this cannot be so. On the contrary, he says: 'The past is dead. We must turn our backs on it,/Forget it, bury it. I denounce the past'.[34] It is worth quoting at some length the dialogue which follows this pronouncement:

RECORDER:	*You* are the dead and the past. Must *you* be forgotten?
CHORUS:	Must you be forgotten with us?
RECORDER:	Must *you* be denounced?
CHORUS:	Denounced with us and the city?
AIRMAN:	No! that's not justice! I believed in the future— I fought and died for the future.
CHORUS:	Did we not die? You were our future; did we not die for you? ...
AIRMAN:	But what could I do? I had no time; I was killed; It was not my fault, but the fault of the old people.
CHORUS (*generation after generation, from the most recent to the earliest*):	It was not our fault, but the fault of the old people.[35]

The Airman continues to resist the citizens, telling them he has no connection with them. The citizens then begin to drift away with the words: 'You have no part in us - /No part in the dead, no part in the living city'.[36]

It is appropriate at this point to draw together some of the different threads of the play's handling of time in these early scenes. The first point to note is the way in which the play acutely represents, in more than one sense, the difficulty of 'doing justice' to the past. On an occasion intended to celebrate the history of the Cathedral, the play lays bare a past which it seems better to forget. The Airman's belief that justice can never be done to these wronged generations is understandable. Yet the play also indicates that any future 'just world', such as the Airman envisions, will be compromised if it cannot take account of the past. Indeed, the final line quoted above, directed to the Airman, underscores the link between the 'dead' and 'living' community.

Secondly, the play points us towards the paradoxical attitudes to time inherent in a certain kind of belief in progress. It will be helpful here to borrow a line of thought from theologian Ben Quash. Using the dramatic example of *Macbeth*, Quash reflects on the 'ethical loss' which occurs when one is utterly clear about one's future. Macbeth's knowledge of his destiny from the first moments of the play precipitates for him:

> the collapse of the sphere of ethical responsibility – as the play bloodily reveals. For if your future is already assured, then your relationship with all that stands between you and it can be made to seem of very little (or no) consequence. … You can feel free to treat intermediate things (and, perhaps more important, intermediate *people*) as the mere epiphenomena of your destiny.[37]

Clearly, unlike Macbeth, the Airman is not in a position of having an assurance of his own personal destiny. However, Quash suggests that such thinking likewise underlies broader 'myths of progress'.[38] The belief in progress towards a just world which the Airman articulates is a vision which claims to understand the 'shape and direction of temporal events'.[39] In this vision, the meantime before the goal of justice is realised has no inherent worth in and of itself. Time becomes a waste and the dead, overtaken by time, are wastage on an all-too-slow journey to a known future. So it is that, though the Airman talks of 'steady growth' over time, he is in fact quick to dismiss the past generations of Lichfield as having no connection to the future for which he is so impatient. The problem here is not the Airman's strong desire for radical change for the better but rather an approach to such change which renders valueless both the meantime before the arrival of the foreseen resolution and, crucially, the persons who inhabit this meantime. It is only in becoming part of the past himself, and being confronted with interconnections of guilt and suffering stretching across generations, that the Airman is forced to reconsider his vision, as the play presses once more the question of whether it is ever possible to do justice to the past.

Before turning to the alternative, theologically-shaped, understanding of time which the play offers, I want to pause for a brief interlude to examine Dorothy L. Sayers' response to the handling of time in another dramatic work: J. B. Priestley's 1937 play *Time and the Conways*.

The 'Long View' in J. B. Priestley's *Time and the Conways*

In Priestley's three-act play the first and third acts show the Conway family enjoying a party in 1919. The central act 'interrupts' the party, depicting the family's future in 1937 (the original audience's present). It is a future horribly discordant with the optimistic expectations of the characters in 1919. The audience is shown the broken relationships, frustrated ambitions, financial crises, loss and grief which will afflict the young Conways in later life.

Time and the Conways makes a similar connection between attitudes to time and the perpetration of violence to that found in Sayers' *The Just Vengeance*. In the play's central act the characters of Kay and Alan Conway discuss this directly. Kay finds it 'hideous and unbearable' that the 'happy young Conways' of 1919 are gone: 'Every step we've taken – every tick of the clock – making everything worse'.[40] Alan's response is to diagnose a link between the belief that time is running out, the urgency with which people try to make things right, and acts which actually devalue or even harm others. As Alan says: 'we think Time's ticking our lives away. That's why we snatch and grab and hurt each other'. The solution he offers Kay is that she should 'take a long view'.[41] Alan urges Kay to step back from the immediacy of the linear movement of time and to see the past as just as real as the present. The 'happy young Conways' can be understood, Alan suggests, as 'real and existing, just as we two, here and now are real and existing. We're seeing another bit of the view – a bad bit, if you like – but the whole landscape's still there'.[42]

This view of time might be considered as fitting in some respects with Lederach's advocacy of a more 'expansive' conception of time which treats the past as living and relevant. It is important for our purposes, therefore, to note that Sayers strongly criticized the handling of time in Priestley's play in a short essay written in 1939.

In the essay Sayers agrees that an attitude of resentment and despair in the face of the passage of time can be dangerous. It can lead, Sayers writes, to 'the vicious and desperate fury of a trapped beast'.[43] The problem with the 'long view' proposed within Priestley's play, however, is two-fold. Firstly, this view implicitly accepts that linear time must be understood negatively; secondly, it seeks to respond to this conclusion by trying to take a step back from life in time and its tragedies.

On the contrary, Sayers insists, in the face of irrevocable acts of wrong-doing and experiences of loss, our response should not be to seek to 'escape either *from* the bad past or *into* the good past' but to follow an approach which takes seriously 'the *whole* past'.[44] This approach does not deny the nature of life in time; rather it looks for a way to treat life in time with deep seriousness, 'grappling' closely with the horror it can bring.[45] Sayers writes that this perspective will offer 'release' from the hostility towards time exhibited by Kay Conway—and by the Airman—yet it will be a 'release, not from, but *into* Reality'.[46] This approach to time is rooted for Sayers in her understanding of Christ's death and resurrection and it is to the depiction of these events in *The Just Vengeance* that we now turn.

Taking Time, Transforming Time

The Airman's attitude to time brings him to something of an *impasse* in the first part of Sayers' play. In his urgent desire to see a just resolution, he attempts to turn his back on his city's past and, in so doing, cuts himself off from the community of both the dead and the living. The remainder of the play offers three insights into an alternative account of time.

Taking Time to Attend to Dramatic Performance

First, in a meta-theatrical move, the play signals the importance of attending to drama as a way of entering into this theological understanding of time. When his own approach breaks down the Airman presses once more for an answer to his difficulties. He wants to know, he says, 'why there is no justice,/And why it is that everything we do,/Turns to a horror we never contemplated'.[47] Asking for a solution, the Airman instead receives a performance.

The Recorder summons the citizens to 'play your chosen parts'.[48] The remainder of the dramatic action takes the form of two plays-within-the-play: one depicting the story of Cain and Abel and another playing out the Gospel narrative of Christ's life, death and resurrection. The play's own protagonist is thus drawn into a time-taking process of watching and listening to drama.

In this way, the play suggests that the task of making sense of the connections between time, loss and violence, exposed in the first part of the dramatic action, is less a matter of arriving at an explanation or resolution and more a case of attending to enacted stories. This raises questions for the audience about their own experience of attending to performance. At the beginning of the play the audience were reassured by the Recorder that the scenes they were about to see would be as inconsequential as 'pictures painted in a book'.[49] The Airman's experience as audience of the plays-within-the-play challenges this conviction, since it is in witnessing the citizens' playing of their roles that his understanding of time, and of his own life and death, is remade.

Taking Time to Wait with Suffering and Complicity

The second insight the play offers is linked to the first. Just as the *form* of the remainder of the dramatic action involves the Airman in a time-taking practice of attending to performance, so also the *content* of the plays-within-the-play encourages both Airman and audience to wait with, and go deeper into, instances of suffering and complicity.[50]

The first play enacted involves Cain and Abel. The depiction of these characters continues the move begun by the Airman when he blamed the problems of the present on 'the old people', with this handing on of blame rippling back through the citizens '*generation after generation*'.[51] The story of Cain and Abel has frequently been understood as representing an archetypal or originary instance of human beings' violence towards one another. One might assume that here, if anywhere, justice may be achieved through a straightforward allocation of blame. Instead, this play-within-a-play poses still more acutely the often-embroiled nature of suffering and wrongdoing.

Cain murders Abel with an axe, fashioned as a means of 'progress' for humanity.[52] His motivation for the act is a desire for justice which he believes has been contravened by God's favouring his brother. The play-within-the-play goes on to show that a desire for swift retributive violence *against* Cain, avenging his brother, is both comprehensible, according to certain conceptions of justice, and in itself an action which may be likened to Cain's crime. The play culminates with small groups of the citizen-players speaking alternately: 'Our name is Abel; you have murdered us – Are you not Cain and shall we not have justice?'; 'If you take vengeance on us, we are Abel/And you Cain, and shall we not have justice?' These strands of speech interweave until all the players are confessing themselves to be both 'Cain and Abel'.[53]

In the second play-within-the-play the citizens take up roles in the Gospel narrative, as those forgiven or healed by Christ and as those who condemn him. Towards the climax of this play, all the citizens join together performing as a crowd calling for Jesus to be crucified. Even the Airman is caught up in the crowd's fervour, continuing this cry as the rest of the citizens fall silent: 'Crucify! crucify! ... What on earth am I doing?/That is not in the least what I meant to say'.[54] Emphasis is here placed on the culpability of the community, as well as on the pain and loss borne by many.

Significantly, some citizens 'chosen parts' in this play—those of Pilate, Herod, Caiaphas and Judas—lead them to exit before the final scene showing the Resurrection. Lest we assume that here at last the play enacts a form of justice centred on the abrupt and punitive exclusion of those who have done wrong, there are two points worth noting. First, this exit comes after the call for Jesus to be crucified, a moment in which all the citizens are implicated. The exit is then prompted by these characters' rejection of Jesus' invitation to them to continue as part of the community of citizens, bringing to him the culpability in which they all share. The characters exclude themselves from the remainder of the action in a series of speeches which express their unwillingness to engage with the history of wrongdoing and victimhood of which they have been part. Each character rejects any response to this history as either futile or unnecessary. This evokes what Rowan Williams has described as the inaudibility of the 'authentic word of forgiveness, newness and resurrection... for the one who has not "turned" to his or her past', who will not own the memory of actions which have diminished the selfhood of the perpetrator as well as that of the victim.[55]

Second, in the original production those playing these roles were costumed as representatives of respected authorities, recognisable to the contemporary audience; most notably, Caiaphas was dressed as a bishop in vestments provided by the Cathedral.[56] Sayers, in a letter written around the time of the production, underlined her intention here to push back against any assumption that 'the Church [is]... trying her best and doing her bit ... and there, outside, are all the sins, betrayals, denials and crucifixions'.[57] In this way, the play complicates once more any attempt the audience might make to distance themselves from the entanglement of suffering and sin depicted on stage. There can be no easy dismissal of the characters who exit before the Resurrection, as these characters in themselves frustrate efforts to locate responsibility for Lichfield's bloody history 'outside' the contemporary community.

For the remaining players, there is yet one more move deeper into the city's tragic past. As Jesus is led around the Cathedral, bearing the cross, each of the remaining citizens joins him and names the pain that they will 'carry', taking upon themselves once more the injustice which each protested against in their first encounter with the Airman. The play depicts the crucifixion as God's entering fully into the horror of life in time which the Airman and the citizens have experienced. This suffering entry into time does not provide a means to circumvent the long history of suffering set out in the play. Rather it leads still further into the acute 'wrongness' of this history, waiting with it. Here the boundary between the play-within-the-play and the wider dramatic action dissolves. Witnessing the Crucifixion, the Airman enters again into the darkness and helplessness of his own unjust death at another's hand: 'This is it. ... Let go. It is no use now clinging to the controls'.[58]

So it is that the majority of the dramatic action of *The Just Vengeance* is constituted by taking time over a history of violence and oppression. The final step in this time-taking process just described should not be thought of as one in which victims are encouraged simply to passively bear their suffering. Up to this point the play has insisted repeatedly that such suffering *is* truly unjust. It is not the Airman's protestations against the horror of the world which the play seeks to challenge. Rather, it is his belief that such tragedies must either be forgotten through turning our back on the past, or may somehow be rapidly resolved or otherwise made manageable, so that justice may be achieved. The second play-within-a-play by contrast suggests that there can be no way through this horror that does not take seriously, and does not take time over, the full force of the acts which human beings are capable of and the impossibility of detaching ourselves from the long histories of culpability and victimhood which undergird present-day communities.

Transforming Time—Resurrection and Eschaton

In the final scene of the play the dead citizens and the dead Christ are raised to new life. It might be assumed that here the play's approach is reducible to the claim that justice for those who suffer cannot be achieved in this world. On the one hand, it is certainly true that Sayers' play makes manifest her belief that 'God is a God of the living and the dead'[59] and that the play offers a striking depiction of the limits of human capacity to achieve a lasting and just peace. Yet, I also suggest that the play offers us something more clearly defined than a general hope for ultimate redress. Once again, the key here is *time*.

As described above, *The Just Vengeance* calls both Airman and audience to take time to attend to instances of suffering and of complicity, persistently refusing to offer a swift resolution which would cut through the complexities of violence and victimhood. The final scene of the play likewise does not offer a complete break with those past events. Instead, the final moments of the play recall for us once more parts of the earlier dramatic action, whilst also casting these earlier moments in a new light. This final scene offers recapitulations which are also transformations, 'doing justice' to the past in the sense of remaining seriously attentive to it, but also making it possible for the past to be opened up, to be the ground for the flourishing of something new.[60]

So, for example, we recall the startling early line from George Fox: 'Woe to bloody city of Lichfield!' In this early scene, Fox's repetition of this line was interspersed with a choir, proclaiming (growing in volume): 'Lichfield! Lichfield! Whisper the name of the city ... speak the name of the city ... cry the name of the city!'[61] At the end of the play this choir return with the line 'Speak, speak, speak the name of the city' but this time they call for 'The new name, the true name' and ask that Christ might 'Call us by name'.[62] Christ addresses the resurrected citizens, inviting them to 'take again' their 'sweet will' made 'more sweet' and 'receive again' their 'lost loves', 'lovelier than you knew', their city 'nobler than you planned'.[63] Recalling the hope expressed in the Recorder's prologue that the Cathedral might 'stand [...] Until the fingers of slow time come round to their last moment, and the trumpets sound!', the audience see before them 'time come round' and hear, as the stage directions stipulate, a '*trumpet-echo*'.[64] The Choir pronounce that the city: '...is set on a rock; she cannot be moved ... there is joy in her houses'.[65] This is not merely a repetition of the evocation of security with which the play opened. Any perception of Lichfield as straightforwardly victorious, peaceful, and safely distanced from past violence, has been thoroughly disrupted by the action of the play. If the city stands, if it is joyful, it has only become so through a time-taking process of grappling with the whole of its past.

To use Lederach's term, these final scenes can be viewed as offering a more 'expansive' account of time in two ways. First, the dangerous urgency exhibited by the character of the Airman in the early part of the play is countered here by an understanding of time in which, as theologian Stanley Hauerwas states, 'we are no longer driven by the assumption that we must be in control of history, that it is up to us to make things come out right'.[66] Instead, the play enacts a practice of bringing to God that which 'you can do nothing with', allowing these events to be taken up into the Resurrection movement, an action which brings life out of death. This is an eschatological, rather than merely a teleological, understanding of time. That is, it is an understanding in which the agent of the transformation and the consummation of time is God, freeing human beings to 'bear witness, peaceably and patiently' to that fulfilment.[67]

Yet the 'expansiveness' of this eschatological understanding and of the Resurrection movement does not entail stepping back from life in time. It is in this sense that the play offers more than a promise of vindication or restitution beyond time. The persistent, often discomfortingly close attention to the history of Lichfield across the play, is carried through into the final scene, where the recapitulations described above require the audience to remember these earlier parts of the drama. The risen citizens find their damaged selfhood, shaped by their history, 'replenished' but not overturned.[68] This work of resurrection and the ultimate healing looked for in the eschaton is not, in other words, work that happens *beyond* time, if we take this to mean remote from time.

The second way that the final scene is 'expansive' then, is that it expands the significance of the 'coming out right' of history (in God) such that this process is not remote from life in time but runs through that life, here and now. In the final moments of the play, in an echo of the liturgy of the Eucharist, the audience are sent out to witness to what they have seen, taking the transformation set out before them into their own lives. The Choir tells them: 'The City is yours… Proclaim the City!'[69] From the 'bloody city' of the play's opening, Lichfield has been renewed, yet without ever allowing its audience to turn their backs on their community's past.

Conclusion

First performed in the immediate aftermath of a world-shattering conflict that claimed over 50 million lives, *The Just Vengeance* takes further our understanding of the importance of avoiding the mishandlings of time diagnosed by peacebuilder John Paul Lederach. Through its depiction of the Airman, the play exposes the consequences of approaching the present as 'an urgent fleeting moment' that must be grasped and controlled to rapidly bring about definitive progress.[70] The dramatic action reveals that any conception of justice which fails to take account of the past (including past persons and events that the present community would rather forget) is likely to be at best partial, at worst an excuse to devalue lives lost as wastage incurred in moving towards a 'just' society. Together with Sayers' response to Priestley's drama, the play points to the potential dangers inherent in an approach which steps back from life in time so as to render life's tragedies out of focus. By contrast, *The Just Vengeance* insists on the need for close attentiveness to time's linear movement—most acutely manifest in death—as crucial in any effort to do justice to the past.

I return at this point to my framing of this chapter in terms of challenging hospitality. As we have seen, Sayers' play begins and ends with an invitation. In the play's prologue the Recorder welcomes the audience, inviting them into the dramatic action as a place of safety, underlining the performance's unreal nature. This welcome is disrupted by the action of the play as the audience are confronted with an exceptionally challenging depiction of their 'bloody city'. Yet the note of hospitality is not lost altogether. Just as the Airman finds himself drawn into the dramatic action, the audience too continue to be invited into a process of reflection on time, suffering and responsibility. In the play's final scene there is another invitation, this time from the character of Christ and from the Choir. The audience are invited to 'Come' and 'take' what is theirs, to see the city once more as belonging to them.[71] The Christian imagery of the heavenly city and the play's grappling with earthly events in Lichfield come together here to pose to the audience the question of how the heavenly vision of a world 'replenished' may be lived out in the here and now.

I suggest that this play offers peacebuilders too a challenging invitation to deeper reflection. The play suggests that it is only by taking time seriously that the transformation of long-standing patterns of violence, perpetrated and suffered, may be achieved. It does not simply point to an ultimate consolation but insists that such transformation begins within time. The case study presented here should encourage peacebuilders to take time over both the performance arts, and over distinctively religious material, as potential resources for their work. It is in taking time, in all these ways, that possibilities open up for the flourishing in the present of something new.

Notes

1. For an introduction, see Marc Howard Ross, "The Politics of Memory and Peacebuilding" and Anthony Oberschall, "History and Peacebuilding", in *The Routledge Handbook of Peacebuilding*, ed. Roger MacGinty (Abingdon, UK: Routledge, 2013), 91–102 and 171–182 respectively; Barbara Tint,

"History, Memory and Intractable Conflict", *Conflict Resolution Quarterly* 27:3 (2010), 239–256.

2. See, for example, I. William Zartmann's argument for the importance of "ripe moments" in conflict resolution and John Paul Lederach's responding critique of "ripeness" in favour of metaphors such as "cultivation" and "accompaniment", which evoke a greater sense of peacebuilding as a practice involving time-taking constancy: Zartmann, "The Timing of Peace Initiatives: Hurting Stalemates and Ripe Moments" and Lederach, "Cultivating Peace: A Practitioner's View of Deadly Conflict and Negotiation", in *Contemporary Peacemaking: Conflict, Violence and Peace Processes*, ed. John Darby and Roger MacGinty (Basingstoke, UK: Palgrave Macmillan, 2003), 19–29 and 30–37 respectively.
3. Dorothy L. Sayers, *The Just Vengeance* (London, UK: Victor Gollancz, 1946; Eugene, OR: Wipf and Stock, 2011). Hereafter *JV*. The play script is not divided into acts and scenes; references will be to page numbers in the first published edition.
4. Personal communication from Marcus Whichelow, quoted in Barbara Reynolds, *The Passionate Intellect: Dorothy L. Sayers' Encounter with Dante* (Eugene, OR: Wipf and Stock, 2005), 92.
5. Gerard F. Powers, "Religion and Peacebuilding", in *Strategies of Peace: Transforming Conflict in a Violent World*, ed. Daniel Philpott and Gerard F. Powers (New York, NY: Oxford University Press, 2010), 317–322; Peter Ochs, "The Possibilities and Limits of Inter-Religious Dialogue", in *The Oxford Handbook of Religion, Conflict, and Peacebuilding*, ed. Atalia Omer, R. Scott Appleby, and David Little (Oxford, UK: Oxford University Press, 2015), 491–492.
6. Ochs, "The Possibilities and Limits of Inter-Religious Dialogue", 488. On Scriptural Reasoning, see: http://www.scripturalreasoning.org, accessed 14 December 2018; David F. Ford and C.C. Pecknold, eds., *The Promise of Scriptural Reasoning* (Malden, MA: Blackwell, 2006); David F. Ford and Frances Clemson, eds., *Interreligious Reading After Vatican II: Scriptural Reasoning, Comparative Theology and Receptive Ecumenism* (Malden, MA: Wiley-Blackwell, 2013).
7. Ochs, "The Possibilities and Limits of Inter-Religious Dialogue", 505.
8. David F. Ford, "An Interfaith Wisdom: Scriptural Reasoning Between Jews, Christians and Muslims", in *The Promise of Scriptural Reasoning*, 5.
9. Ochs, "The Possibilities and Limits of Inter-Religious Dialogue", 494.
10. Ochs, "The Possibilities and Limits of Inter-Religious Dialogue", 505.
11. John Paul Lederach, *The Moral Imagination: The Art and Soul of Building Peace* (Oxford, UK: Oxford University Press, 2005).
12. Lederach, *Moral Imagination*, 29.
13. Lederach, *Moral Imagination*, 132.
14. Lederach, *Moral Imagination*, 132.

15. Lederach, *Moral Imagination*, 22.
16. Lederach, *Moral Imagination*, 29 and 105.
17. Lederach, *Moral Imagination*, 39.
18. Lederach, *Moral Imagination*, 133.
19. Lederach, *Moral Imagination*, Chapter 12.
20. Lederach, *Moral Imagination*, 148.
21. Lederach, *Moral Imagination*, 22, 132–133.
22. *JV*, 11.
23. *JV*, 11.
24. Personal communication from Stewart Lack, quoted in Reynolds, *The Passionate Intellect*, 95.
25. *JV*, 12.
26. George Fox, *The Journal*, ed. Nigel Smith (London, UK: Penguin, 1998), 57–58.
27. *JV*, 18.
28. *JV*, 17–18.
29. *JV*, 18.
30. *JV*, 19–22.
31. *JV*, 24.
32. *JV*, 25.
33. *JV*, 26.
34. *JV*, 27.
35. *JV*, 27.
36. *JV*, 28.
37. Ben Quash, "Making the Most of the Time: Liturgy, Ethics and Time", *Studies in Christian Ethics* 15:1 (2002), 97.
38. Quash, "Making the Most of Time", 99.
39. Quash, "Making the Most of Time", 99.
40. J.B. Priestley, *Time and the Conways*, in Priestley, *An Inspector Calls and Other Plays* (London, UK: Penguin, 1969), Act II, 59 and 60.
41. Priestly, *Time and the Conways*, Act II, 61.
42. Priestley, *Time and the Conways*, Act II, 60.
43. Dorothy L. Sayers, "Strong Meat", in Sayers, *Strong Meat* (London, UK: Hodder and Stoughton, 1939), 12.
44. Sayers, "Strong Meat", 22–23.
45. Sayers, "Strong Meat", 22.
46. Sayers, "Strong Meat", 25, my italics.
47. *JV*, 28.
48. *JV*, 29.
49. *JV*, 11.
50. For a discussion of the theme of complicity as it appears across a number of Sayers' dramatic works, see Suzanne Bray, "Guilt and Glory: The Message of Charles Williams' and Dorothy L. Sayers' Festival Plays", *Proceedings of the*

Joint Meeting of the Dorothy L. Sayers Society and the Charles Williams Society at the Michaelhouse Centre, Cambridge, 17 October 2009 (Hurstpierpoint, UK: The Dorothy L. Sayers Society, 2010), 13–33.

51. *JV*, 27.
52. *JV*, 34. 'Progress' is defined here (in line with my suggestions above about the Airman's understanding) as a matter of becoming 'Quicker and quicker, so as to get more/Of everything at once'.
53. *JV*, 43.
54. *JV*, 66.
55. Rowan Williams, *Resurrection: Interpreting the Easter Gospel*, 2nd edition (London, UK: Darton, Longmann & Todd, 2002), 14–15.
56. Dorothy L. Sayers to Dr. James Welch, 25 July 1946 in *The Letters of Dorothy L. Sayers*, III: *1944–1950: A Noble Daring*, ed. Barbara Reynolds (Cambridge: The Dorothy L. Sayers Society, 1998), 249.
57. Sayers to Welch, *Letters*, III, 249.
58. *JV*, 76.
59. Johann Baptist Metz, *Faith in History and Society: Towards a Practical Fundamental Theology*, trans. David Smith (London, UK: Burns & Oates, 1980), 74.
60. Williams, *Resurrection*, 29; Lederach, *Moral Imagination*, 29.
61. *JV*, 12.
62. *JV*, 77–78.
63. *JV*, 79.
64. *JV*, 11 and 79.
65. *JV*, 80.
66. Stanley Hauerwas, *The Peaceable Kingdom: A Primer in Christian Ethics* (Notre Dame, IN: University of Notre Dame Press, 1983), 87.
67. Stanley Hauerwas with James Fodor, "Performing Faith: The Peaceable Rhetoric of God's Church" in Hauerwas, *Performing the Faith: Bonhoeffer and the Practice of Nonviolence* (London, UK: SPCK, 2004), 97.
68. *JV*, 78.
69. *JV*, 80.
70. Lederach, *Moral Imagination*, 132.
71. *JV*, 79.

PART VI

Afterword

CHAPTER 22

Evoking the Yarragh

R. Scott Appleby

As I sat waiting on the upper level of a restaurant in West Belfast, Northern Ireland in late January of 2014, I realized that, with the possible exception of the birth of children and grandchildren, I had seldom felt so nervous, apprehensive—and almost giddy—at the same time. Unimaginably, I was about to meet Van Morrison, a musician whose vast canon of songs, records and performances dating back to the 1960s had held me in thrall for decades. One of my companions that day was my friend and colleague John Paul Lederach, who has written with his typical perceptiveness and insight about the restorative power of music and its deep resonance with conflict and the coming out of conflict toward a state of peace. (A concise expression of this Lederachian theme is found in Chapter 6 of this volume.) In one of his recent books, John Paul explores Morrison's "continual effort to link spirituality and music, to link the inner and outer journey, and … the understanding we may glean from one artist's lifelong struggle to reach into those difficult spaces of healing in the human experience."[1]

Even as I waited for Van the Man to arrive for our lunch date, I reflected, not for the first time, on the puzzling incongruity between the breathtaking

R. S. Appleby (✉)
Keough School of Global Affairs, University of Notre Dame, Notre Dame, IN, USA

J. Mitchell et al. (eds.), *Peacebuilding and the Arts*, Rethinking Peace and Conflict Studies,
https://doi.org/10.1007/978-3-030-17875-8_22

beauty and emotional, psychological and spiritual depth of the music he has created—evoked—from the very core of his being, and his widely reported confrontations with biographers and reporters.

The rock critic Greil Marcus typifies the observer's mixture of respect (for Morrison's profound musical gifts) and disdain (for his boorish behavior). Recalling Morrison's presence on stage during the days of his initial breakout in the mid-60s, Marcus describes him as "... small and gloomy, a burly man with more black energy than he knew what to do with, the wrong guy to meet in a dark alley, or backstage on the wrong night."[2] Tracking the manifestations of this persona over Morrison's career, Marcus concludes that "Van Morrison, then, is a bad-tempered, self-contradictory individual whose work is about freedom."[3] What an intriguing puzzle! The sublime poet who leads listeners "into the mystic" and seems immersed in a rapturous "sense of wonder," is also something of a curmudgeon, perhaps even a tad misanthropic. Morrison has complained, in song lyrics and interviews, about his sense of being "in exile"—certainly from the music industry, but also, he sometimes seems to imply, from his truest self. And yet, Marcus is correct: his voice soars! What, then, accounts for this resonant portrait of the dour artist as a radically free man?

Bearing Witness to the Ecstatic Freedom of the Artist

The question frames my reflections in this essay on the paradoxical mystery of the gift and its bearer— a mystery that dances at the edges of virtually every essay in this volume. Van Morrison is hardly the only artist, and certainly not the most disagreeable, to inspire such reflections. Indeed, the moral distance between the artist and his or her art has been a matter of comment as far back as Plutarch (c. 45–127 CE), who pithily observed: "It does not follow that because a particular work of art succeeds in charming us, its creator also deserves our admiration."[4] Leafing through the 294 biographical sketches in John Sutherland's massive tome, *Lives of the Novelists*, reinforces the point repeatedly: artists are very much like everyone else, perhaps even more so, in their vulnerability to the seven deadly sins and the terrors of addiction, alienation and violence. The young Graham Greene, according to one unsympathetic biographer, "drank to excess, chased prostitutes, flirted with suicide, investigated whipping establishments, and volunteered to spy against his own country."[5] J. D. Salinger, whose compassionate, generous and spiritually uplifting novel, novellas and short stories enchanted the generation of postwar American readers, lived as a recluse for forty years, during which time he apparently thwarted all efforts to end his self-imposed isolation, while also fending off accusations of inappropriate and abusive relationships with young women.[6] Alienation from her parents, sibling and son, along with bouts of serious illness, marred the life and strained the composure of Muriel Spark, who nonetheless dealt in her novels, David Lodge notes, with "solemn subjects like, like guilt, religious faith and death ... in a bright and sparkling epigrammatic style."[7]

The authors of the present volume provide us examples of artists evoking and representing a deeper dimension or perception of reality, made accessible to them, if only momentarily, by the liminal experience of deadly conflict. In his introductory chapter on the visual arts (Chapter 2), Jolyon Mitchell suggests that these moments are akin to epiphanies or sudden revelations of a previously opaque or cloaked dimension of the real. In this sense, he writes, the art and the artist are "bearing witness" to the meaning, or seeming absence thereof, of the horrible personal and collective suffering brought on by deadly violence. The gruesome sketches, drawn by the German artist Otto Dix and the British artist Paul Nash, of the devastations of the First World War are a case in point. But Mitchell also highlights the remarkable transformation of personal and collective wartime suffering into "seeds of hope," as in the aftermath of the sixteen-year civil war in Mozambique (1976–1992), when local artists creatively depicted the "beating of swords into ploughshares" by reshaping the bits and pieces of decommissioned weapons into art works such as the *Tree of Lif*e and a *Throne of Weapons*, as well metallic birds, crocodiles and musicians.[8]

It should be clear that the term "artist" encompasses not just painters, sketch artists and sculptors profiled in the Visual Arts section, but also the musicians, writers, storytellers, dramatists, dancers and filmmakers, working on local as well as national and global platforms, whose transformational artistry is on display throughout this volume. The stories told by women victimized by war in Gulu, Northern Uganda—recounted in these pages by Ketty Anyeko and Tamara Shaya (Chapter 11), and reflected in the theoretically informed imaginative story composed by Juliana Okot Bitek (Chapter 12)—were therapeutic and emancipatory for the subjects of the violence as they coped with feelings of isolation, shame and guilt. So, too, on a different time scale and for a different audience, Dorothy Sayer's play, *The Just Vengeance*, kindles imagination, memory and hopes for a nonviolent future by placing a fictional airman, killed in World War II, in dialogue with generations of deceased former citizens of "the bloody town of Lichfield," England (Chapter 21). Unlike other cinematic depictions of the genocide in Rwanda, Robert K. Johnston explains, the award-winning small independent Rwandan film, *Kinyarwanda*, "a movie made in Africa for Africans," focuses not on the atrocity itself but rather on the post-genocide efforts of Rwandans to forge bonds of unity through communal as well as individual practices of forgiveness and reconciliation. Johnston praises the filmmakers' compelling blend of secular history and eschatological hope (Chapter 15).

All of these artists, and others depicted in these pages, offer a vision, simultaneously harrowing and hopeful, of a way forward through pain and, frequently, unspeakable suffering. Arguably, then, one can read this volume on peacebuilding and the arts, first, as a coherent statement documenting and analyzing the ecstatic—self-displacing, self-transcending—encounter of the artist with an "extraordinary" realm of perception and reality underlying, encompassing and infusing one's "ordinary," quotidian sensibilities.[9]

The epiphanic encounter with a "depth dimension" of life is available to every person.[10] Mystics as well as neurologists, trauma survivors as well as artists have attempted to articulate an experience that initially leaves one inarticulate. If an "encounter" it is, whatever is encountered is *ineffable*, literally beyond the capacity of denotative language to comprehend; eventually, in the telling, one reaches for connotative, allusive, symbolic expression. As for interpreting the aesthetic and moral character of the encounter, one is potentially paralyzed by *ambivalence*. Is this the realm of meaning or no meaning, a glimpse of the abyss or a portal to transcendent new life?[11]

Ultimately, then, the artist, in the courageous act of representing, is hoping against hope by uttering a word or a wordless sound or image—into a void, perhaps, but also awaiting an echo, if only in the utterances of other artists. In this solitary sense, each painter, writer, musician, dramatist, or filmmaker struggles, first and foremost, not with the exterior landscape, but with the presenting symptoms, as it were, of his or her own partially disabled but still sentient interior self. Each subject strives, in his or her distinctive way, to break free of the paralyzing existential state of suspension between the contingency and fragility of the body and brain, on the one hand, and the exhilarating freedom of the unbounded spirit imbuing them, on the other. This spirit, which is the spirit of creation, seeks to soar past contingency toward a horizon of possibility that seems, uncannily, to beckon particularly urgently across the bleak physical and psychological landscape of social conflict, violence and war, as well as one's personal flaws and weaknesses. The artist senses this possibility of bridging the gap, and may hold herself in contempt if she judges her art as inadequate to the (herculean) task of breaking the impasse and freeing the spirit.

For the musician, working in a medium oriented to escaping the confinements of language, given that "the brain's music system appears to operate with functional independence from the language system," the frustration of falling short can be palpable.[12] Thus it is telling that Marcus, describing the young Van Morrison, notes that the singer evinced "a distrust of the audience" and came out, on any given night, "in anger, insult, drunkenness, disdain directed *at the singer's own songs* as much as toward whatever crowd might be present."[13]

Evocation is the artist's act of radical freedom. Unbidden, the muse rises and the artist evokes—summons to surface awareness—the formless, wordless depths of being. The artist beckons us to share the freedom of this "beautiful vision," however harsh its manifestation. After listening to Morrison roar, Marcus asks of his power: "How do you get it? What do you do with it? How do you find it when it disappears—and what is it?"[14]

Caught up in any "answer" to these questions, he suggests, is the role of the yarragh. The term, associated with the Irish poet William Butler Yeats, refers to "a cry of the heart, a haunting and haunted sound that could be found in Celtic (and particularly Irish) song and poetry. It was sorrow and lamentation for what had been lost, and for centuries of foreign oppression. It was anger and self-righteousness, a loud and belligerent cry that insisted on the inherent dignity and worth of a people."[15] To "get" the yarragh, Marcus suggests, citing Morrison, "you may need a sense of the song as a thing in itself, with its own brain, heart, lungs, tongue and ears. Its own desires, fears, will, and even ideas: 'The question might really be,' as [Morrison] once said, 'Is the song singing *you*?'"

Like other artists, *mutatis mutandis*, Morrison's music, Marcus continues, "can be heard as an attempt to surrender to the yarragh, or to make it surrender to him; to find the music it wants; to bury it; to dig it out of the ground … to strike a note so exalted you can't believe a mere human being is responsible for it, a note so unfinished and unsatisfied you can understand why the eternal seems to be riding on its back."[16]

Our conversation with the Man himself on that exciting afternoon in West Belfast seemed to confirm the notion that the artist as an historical actor, as a typically flawed and obtuse human being, somehow melts away in the crucible of inspiration—or is displaced by an inner voice both her own and other. After expressing our awe at a performance he had given the previous evening in a small, intimate venue, we asked Van, who was remarkably open, intense and focused: what *is* it? Acknowledging "this thing" he has or has been given, the extraordinary ability to channel something of the soul of things (my words, not his), he admitted that this power had been hard for him to control and understand in the past. It has been a lifelong struggle to master it, or at least his expression of it in composing, recording and performing songs.

But, we pressed, what, exactly *is* it? "Who knows or can know?" was our consensus response. Morrison referred, as he often does, to the mystical poets, to Blake and Donne and Eliot, but also, on this occasion, to the literature on archetypes, specifically the work of Carl G. Jung, the twentieth-century Swiss psychiatrist and psychoanalyst who founded the field of analytical psychology.[17] Does the yarragh, when the artist can evoke it, give expression to some primordial structure of knowledge or perception common to the species Homo Sapiens or, to use religious language, to the children of the living God?

Jungian archetypes are not to be conflated, of course, with other concepts of the transcendent or immanent, nonmaterial realms of consciousness or existence, such as the soul, mind, psyche, "the authentic self" of Christian mysticism or the Buddhist concept of Sunyata (Emptiness). Indeed, none of these concepts or traditions stand in for another. Yet our conversation that afternoon, echoing so many others over the centuries by ordinary people, sages and experts of all stripes, directed itself inexorably to the nagging, intriguing, destabilizing invitation to ponder the possibility of a "*there* there," a horizon of possibility—the poetic, allusive exploration of which is the artist's stock in trade.

Here I refer to our recurrent expectation and intimations of "fullness," to use the philosopher Charles Taylor's expression—that is, a "place (activity or condition) [wherein] life is fuller, richer, deeper, more worthwhile, more admirable, more what it should be." The sense of fullness may come "in an experience which unsettles and breaks through our ordinary sense of being in the world, with its familiar objects, activities and points of reference." In such cases "ordinary reality is abolished and something terrifyingly other shines through." It is a state of consciousness, Taylor writes, which the Austrian philosopher and modernist Robert Musil describes as "*der andere Zustand* (the other condition)."[18]

Assuming that this place or condition of fullness is not mere delusion, then the yarragh, whether as the cry of the soul or a rapturous exclamation of hope, possibility and healing, could be said to describe the art, or the source of the art, not only of Van Morrison but also of Otto Dix and Paul Nash, of the postwar sculptors of Mozambique, the women storytellers of Gulu, the playwright and novelist Dorothy Sayers, and of the director and producers of the film, *Kinyarwanda*.

Thus we come to the second overarching question of this volume: what has the yarragh—the cry of the heart and soul evoked by the artist—to do with the building of peace?

Unlocking the Capacity for Peace

Peacebuilding is a heroic practice, whether conducted by experienced senior diplomats, humanitarian aid workers, therapists and trauma healers, persistent local council members who keep or restore the peace in a fractured city or town, or mediators who accompany victims and support them in seeking reconciliation with enemies. Exacting and wearying, it is a dreadful business most of the time, straining the patience of even the most gracious practitioner. Cynicism and burnout, not to mention suffering torture or death, can be occupational hazards.

Victims of war and other forms of deadly or debilitating, dehumanizing physical violence or structural violence face uphill battles in their struggle against depression or in their—again, heroic—efforts to forgive and enact the mercies of peace. Every peacebuilder worth her salt is recovering from deep wounds of some kind.[19]

Heroism is not uncommon but it requires courage, persistence, a deep reserve of grace and a new way of seeing things—all elements of what Lederach has called a "moral imagination."[20] Key to the moral imagination of the peacebuilder is the ability to hold disparate gifts in creative tension: the capacity for *empathy*; the capacity for *lament*, over the irretrievable and incalculable losses exacted by violence and injustice; and, not least, the capacity for *hope*, the affirmation of possibility beyond what seems apparent to the eyes the world.[21]

But how are these attributes of the moral imagination cultivated in a person or a people? A theme threading through this volume is the empathy of the peacebuilder and of the artist—and the evocation of empathy in the hearts of those who are drawn into the artist's compassionate vision. The cry of the soul rising up in the yarragh finds resonance in those victims and peacebuilders alike, whose suffering endures but whose hope may be stimulated to soar.

The truth of that claim can be verified in innumerable accounts of the impact of artists, such as Carole Kane, whose artistry helps unlock the human capacity for transcendence and renewal. On August 15, 1998, in the waning days of open hostilities in Northern Ireland, the Real IRA planted a bomb in Omagh. The explosion killed 31 people, including unborn twins. This brutal act of spoiler violence was intended to inflame the very cross-cultural tensions which the peace process was attempting to quell. Working with the children of the town, Kane gathered the flowers placed by mourners at the bombsite and transformed them into Petals of Hope, a vivid memorial to the victims and a symbol of enduring compassion and courage in the face of senseless violence. Years later she canvassed the resident of Omagh, who now spoke of "feeling the bomb" rather than merely "hearing about the bomb." Kane noted how widely the impact of the Petals of Hope funerary ritual had stretched. "The vibration of the destruction [had] resounded far beyond the devastatingly physical impact on the immediate victims, right to the listener or the stranger who lived miles away. The immeasurable shock and pain stretched beyond those in this land. Their echo returned to Omagh in heartfelt sympathy and love, demonstrated in the sending of flowers, gentle words, prayers spoken."[22] In such quotidian ways is the moral imagination cultivated and communities inspired to risk reconciliation.

What, finally, is the relationship between the "it" with which the artist struggles—the yarragh, to which he or she gives voice, word, image—and the "it" which serves peace?

Art must not be instrumentalized, several authors in this volume caution, and there is no process—no linear process, anyway—leading directly from art to politics, from aesthetics to conflict resolution. Yet the ecstatic epiphany of the artist invites us to sense and "touch" the ineffable and, no small irony, it is that encounter with what some describe as "the eternal" that sets us on the long journey back to our full humanity.

Enduring peace among longtime enemies cannot be built through a formal process alone; a change of heart and a renewal of hope is necessary. Such interior transformations can only unfold in the depths of the soul. And such depths are plumbed most creatively and thus most powerfully in and through the arts.

Notes

1. John Paul Lederach and Angela Jill Lederach, *When Blood and Bones Cry Out: Journeys Through the Soundscape of Healing and Reconciliation* (Queensland, Australia: University of Queensland Press, 2010), 115.
2. Greil Marcus, *When That Rough God Goes Riding: Listening to Van Morrison* (New York: Public Affairs, 2010), 5.
3. Marcus, *When That Rough God Goes Riding*, 10.
4. Plutarch, *Life of Pericles*, translated by Peter Jones, public domain.
5. Michael Shelden, quoted in John Sutherland, *Lives of the Novelists: A History of Fiction in 294 Lives* (London: Profiles Books Ltd., 2011), 450.
6. Sutherland, *Lives of the Novelists*, 559.
7. David Lodge, *Lives in Writing* (London: Harvill Secker, 2014), 51.
8. For an extended discussion of this phenomenon and the practice of turning 'Swords into Ploughshares,' see Jolyon Mitchell, *Promoting Peace, Inciting Violence: The Role of Religion and Media* (London and New York: Routledge, 2012). On the practice of "bearing witness" in peacebuilding, see Bernie Glassman, *Bearing Witness: A Zen Master's Lessons in Making Peace* (Google Books, 1998).
9. Catherine L. Albanese makes the distinction between "extraordinary" and "ordinary" experience in her *America Religion and Religions*, 5th edition (Wadsworth, 1999), 12.
10. In this general formulation, this claim has been articulated and nuanced by aesthetes, philosophers, scientists, historians, cultural anthropologists, theologians, psychologists, therapists and anthropologists. Even in our so-called "secular age," the debate centers not on the recurring phenomena of "displacement," but in their etiology and significance.
11. On the concept of ambivalence in this context, see R. Scott Appleby, *The Ambivalence of the Sacred: Religion, Violence, and Reconciliation* (Lanham, MD: Rowman & Littlefield, 2000), 28–29.
12. Daniel J. Levitin, *This Is Your Brain on Music: The Science of a Human Obsession* (New York: Penguin Publishing Group, 2007), 127.
13. Marcus, *When That Rough God Goes Riding*, 10. Italics added.
14. Marcus, *When That Rough God Goes Riding*, 10.
15. https://www.pastemagazine.com/blogs/whitman/2008/03/searching-for-the-yarragh.html, accessed 28 January 2019.
16. Marcus, *When That Rough God Goes Riding*, 8.
17. In *Man and His Symbols*, Jung defines an archetype as the psychological tendency to form conscious representations of mythological images or motifs (e.g., the hostile brethren, shattered glass, the Janus face). These motifs operate on an unconscious level as well, according to Jung; also known as "archaic remnants" (Freud) or "primordial images," they are often manifest in dreams whose content cannot be derived from the dreamer's personal

experiences but rather seem to be "aboriginal, innate and inherited shapes of the human mind." Carl G. Jung, *Man and His Symbols* (Dell/Random House, 1968), 57.

18. Charles Taylor, *A Secular Age* (Cambridge, MA: Belknap/Harvard University Press, 2007), 5–6.
19. On the wounds inflicted by systemic injustices, see Daniel Philpott, *Just and Unjust Peace: An Ethic of Political Reconciliation* (New York: Oxford University Press, 2012), Ch. 3.
20. John Paul Lederach, *The Moral Imagination: The Art and Soul of Building Peace* (New York: Oxford University Press, 2005).
21. The African theologian Emmanuel Katongole has written compellingly of lament and hope as inextricably intertwined in the lives of moral exemplars within the African Christian community. See Emmanuel Katongole, *Born from Lament: The Theology and Politics of Hope in Africa* (Grand Rapids, MI: Eerdmans, 2017).
22. http://omaghpetals.blogspot.com/p/i-have-explained-my-involvement-in.html, accessed 28 January 2019.

Bibliography

Abbot, H. Porter. *The Cambridge Introduction to Narrative*. Cambridge, UK: Cambridge University Press, 2008.

Acarón, Thania. *The Practitioner's Body of Knowledge: Dance/Movement in Training Programmes That Address Violence, Conflict and Peace*. PhD thesis, University of Aberdeen, 2015.

Achebe, Chinua. "An Image of Africa: Racism in Conrad's Heart of Darkness." *Massachusetts Review* 18 (1977): 782–784.

Adam, James, ed. *The Republic of Plato*. Cambridge, UK: Cambridge University Press, 2010 [1902].

Adams-Westcott, Janet and Cheryl Dobbins. "Listening with Your 'Heart Ears' and Other Ways Young People Can Escape the Effects of Sexual Abuse." In *Narrative Therapies with Children and Adolescents*, edited by Craig Smith and David K. Nylund, 195–220. New York, NY: Guilford Press, 1997.

Adolf, Antony. "What Does Peace Literature Do? An Introduction to the Genre and Its Criticism." *The Canadian Journal of Peace and Conflict Studies* 42: 1–2 (2010): 9–21.

Ahmed, Syed Jamil. "Wishing for a World Without 'Theatre for Development': Demystifying the Case of Bangladesh." *Research in Drama Education* 7: 2 (2002): 207–219.

Ahn, Byung-mu. *Christ in the Midst of Minjung Event*. Seoul, Korea: Theological Study Institute, 1989.

Akkoc, Raziye. "Banksy in Gaza: Street Artist Goes Undercover in the Strip." *The Telegraph*, February 26, 2015.

J. Mitchell et al. (eds.), *Peacebuilding and the Arts*, Rethinking Peace and Conflict Studies, https://doi.org/10.1007/978-3-030-17875-8

Albanese, Catherine L. *America Religion and Religions*, 5th ed. Belmont, CA: Wadsworth, 1999.

Alliance for Peacebuilding. *Peacebuilding 2.0: Mapping the Boundaries of an Expanding Field*. Washington, DC: Alliance for Peacebuilding, 2011.

Amony, Evelyn. "Women's Advocacy Network (WAN)—Our Journey." *The Justice and Reconciliation Blog*. http://justiceandreconciliation.com/2012/09/wan-our-journey/2012.

Appadurai, Arjun. *Modernity at Large: Cultural Dimensions of Globalization*. Minneapolis, MN: University of Minnesota Press, 2006.

Appleby, R. Scott. *The Ambivalence of the Sacred: Religion, Violence, and Reconciliation*. Lanham, MD: Rowman & Littlefield, 1999.

Appleyard, Bryan. *The Pleasures of Peace: Art and Imagination in Post-war Britain*. London, UK: Faber & Faber, 1989.

Aravamudan, Srinivas. "Introduction: Perpetual War." *PMLA* 124 (2009): 1505–1514.

Arocha, Jaime and F. Gonzalez. "Museos, Etnografía Contemporánea Y Representación de Los Afrodescendientes" [Museums, Contemporary Ethnography and Representation of Afrodescenants]. *Antipoda* 9 (July–December 2009): 155–163.

Artaud, Antonin. *The Theater and Its Double*. Translated by Mary Caroline Richards. New York, NY: Grove Press, 1958.

Ashworth, Pat. "Where Their Art Is Housed." *The Church Times*, July 15, 2015. www.churchtimes.co.uk/articles/2015/17-july/features/features/where-their-art-is-housed.

Atkinson, Judy. *Trauma Trails, Recreating Song Lines*. Melbourne, VIC: Spinifex Press, 2002.

Auerbach, Erich. *Mimesis: The Representation of Reality in Western Literature*. Princeton, NJ: Princeton University Press, 2003.

Austin, James E. "Strategic Collaboration Between Nonprofits and Businesses." *Nonprofit and Voluntary Sector Quarterly* 29: 1 (2000): 69–97.

Australian Broadcasting Corporation (ABC). "The Philosopher and the Filmmaker: Wim Wenders and Mary Zournazi Talk About War, Peace and Filmmaking." December 15, 2013. http://www.abc.net.au/radionational/programs/philosopherszone/the-philosopher-and-the-filmmaker/5143988.

Ayindo, Babu. "Arts Approaches to Peace: Playing Our Way to Transcendence?" In *Peacebuilding in Traumatized Societies*, edited by Barry Hart, 185–203. Lanham, MD: University Press of America, 2008.

Bacvich, Andrew J. *The New American Militarism: How Americans Are Seduced by War*. New York, NY: Oxford University Press, 2005.

Bader, Ali. *The Tobacco Keeper*. New York, NY: Bloomsbury, 2011.

Baines, Erin. "Gender, Responsibility, and the Grey Zone: Considerations for Transitional Justice." *Journal of Human Rights* 10 (2009): 477–493.

Baines, Erin and Beth Stewart. "I Cannot Accept What I Have Not Done: Storytelling, Gender and Transitional Justice." *Journal of Human Rights Practice* 3: 3 (2011): 245–263.

Barenboim-Said Foundation. "Foundation" and "Objectives of the Foundation." www.barenboim-said.org. Accessed June 9, 2009.

Barker, Jennifer. *The Tactile Eye: Touch and Cinematic Experience*. Berkeley, CA: University of California Press, 2009.

Barron, Stephanie, ed. *"Degenerate Art": The Fate of the Avant-Garde in Nazi Germany*. New York, NY: Harry N. Abrams, 1991.

Bartlet, Olivier. *African Cinema: Decolonizing the Gaze*. London, UK and New York, NY: Zed Books Ltd., 1996.

Baruch Bush, Robert A. and Joseph P. Folger. *The Promise of Mediation: The Transformative Approach to Conflict*. San Francisco, CA: Jossey-Bass, 1994.

Baudrillard, Jean. *Simulation and Simulacra*. Ann Arbor, MI: University of Michigan Press, 1994.

BBC News. "Bloody Sunday: Key Soldiers Involved." *BBC*, June 15, 2010. http://www.bbc.co.uk/news/10322583.

BBC News. "Derry Teenager Manus Deery 'Totally Innocent', Says Coroner." *BBC*, April 10, 2017. http://www.bbc.co.uk/news/uk-northern-ireland-foyle-west-39551974.

BBC Northern Ireland. "NI Talks Issues Explained: Flags, Parades, the Past and Welfare Reform." *BBC*, December 12, 2014. http://www.bbc.co.uk/news/uk-northern-ireland-25429676.

BBC Radio 4. *Käthe Kollwitz: Suffering Witness*, Part of a Series *Germany: Memories of a Nation*, October 29, 2014.

Beckles Willson, Rachel. "Whose Utopia? Perspectives on the West-Eastern Divan Orchestra." *Music and Politics* 3: 2 (Summer 2009a): 1–21.

Beckles Willson, Rachel. "The Parallax Worlds of the West-Eastern Divan Orchestra." *Journal of the Royal Musical Association* 134: 2 (November 2009b): 319–347.

Beckles Willson, Rachel. *Orientalism and Musical Mission: Palestine and the West*. Cambridge, UK: Cambridge University Press, 2013.

Begbie, Jeremy S. *Theology, Music and Time*. Cambridge, UK: Cambridge University Press, 2000.

Benjamin, Walter. *Illuminations: Essays and Reflections*. New York, NY: Schocken, 1969 [1955].

Ben Ze'ev, Noam. "Distant Trumpets." *Haaretz*, May 21, 2004.

Bennett, Arnold. *"Prefatory Note" to "Void of War": An Exhibition of Pictures by Lieut. Paul Nash*. London, UK: Ernest Brown and Phillips, 1918.

Bergh, Arild. "Emotions and Motion: Transforming Conflict and Music." In *Music and the Mind: Essays in Honour of John Sloboda*, edited by Irène Deliège and Jane Davidson, 363–378. Oxford, UK: Oxford University Press, 2011.

Bergh, Arild and John Slobada, "Music and Art in Conflict Transformation: A Review." *Music and Arts in Action* 2: 2 (2010): 1–16.

Biggar, Nigel. "Forgiving Enemies in Ireland." *Journal of Religious Ethics* 36: 4 (2008): 559–579.

Bingham, Hettie. *Banksy: Art Breaks the Rules.* London, UK: Wayland, 2016.

Bleiker, Roland. *Aesthetics and World Politics.* Basingstoke, Hampshire and New York: Palgrave Macmillan, 2009.

Bleiker, Roland, ed. *Visual Global Politics.* New York and London: Routledge, 2018.

Bodek, Richard. *Proletarian Performance in Weimar Berlin: Agitprop, Chorus, and Brecht.* Columbia, SC: Camden House, 1997.

Boal, Augusto. *Theatre of the Oppressed.* Translated by Charles A. McBride, Maria-Odilia Leal McBride, and Emily Fryer. London, UK: Pluto, 2000.

Boland, R.J.J. and R.V. Tenkasi. "Perspective Making and Perspective Taking in Communities of Knowing." *Organization Science* 6: 4 (1995): 350–372.

Borden, Amy E. "At the Global Market: Ousmane Sembène's *Moolaadé* and the Economics of Women's Rights." *Jump Cut: A Review of Contemporary Media*, No. 53, summer 2011. http://www.ejumpcut.org/archive/jc53.2011/bordenMoolade/index.html.

Borgwardt, Elizabeth. *A New Deal for the World: America's Vision for Human Rights.* Cambridge, MA: The Belknap Press, 2005.

Borthwick, Stuart. *The Writing on the Wall: A Visual History of Northern Ireland's Troubles.* Liverpool, UK: Bluecoat Press, 2015.

Bouvier, Paul. "'Yo Lo Vi.' Goya Witnessing the Disasters of War: An Appeal to the Sentiments of Humanity." *International Review of the Red Cross* 93: 884 (2011): 1107–1133.

Bowman, Wayne. "The Ethical Significance of Music-Making." *Music Mark Magazine* 3 (2014). www.musicmark.org.uk.

Boyce-Tillman, June. *Constructing Musical Healing: The Wounds That Sing.* London, UK: Jessica Kingsley, 2000.

Bray, Suzanne. "Guilt and Glory: The Message of Charles Williams' and Dorothy L Sayers' Festival Plays." *Proceedings of the Joint Meeting of the Dorothy L. Sayers Society and the Charles Williams Society at the Michaelhouse Centre, Cambridge*, October 17, 2009, 13–33. Hurstpierpoint, UK: The Dorothy L. Sayers Society, 2010.

Brewer, John D. *Peace Processes: A Sociological Approach.* Cambridge, UK: Polity, 2010.

Bringing Down a Dictator. Directed by Steve York. Washington, DC: York Zimmerman, 2002. Film.

Brook, Peter. *The Empty Space.* New York, NY: Penguin Books, 1968.

Brown, Alrick. "Press Kit for *Kinyarwanda.*" Directed by A. Brown, 2011. http://www.kinyarwandamovie.com/2011/kinyarwanda-huffington-post.html.

Browning, Barbara. *Samba: Resistance in Motion*. Bloomington, IN: Indiana University Press, 1995.

Bruckner, D.J.R. Seymour Chwast, and Steven Heller. *Art Against War: 400 Years of Protest in Art*. New York, NY: Abbeville Press, 1984.

Burt-Perkins, Rosie. "The Learning Cultures of Performance." In *Proceedings of the International Symposium on Performance Science*, edited by A. Williamson, S. Pretty, and R. Buck, 249–254. Utrecht, The Netherlands: European Association of Conservatoires, 2009.

Butler, Judith. *Precarious Life: The Powers of Mourning and Violence*. London, UK: Verso, 2004.

Butler, Judith. *Frames of War*. London, UK and Brooklyn, NY: Verso, 2010 [2009].

Buttner, Nils, ed. *Otto Dix and the New Objectivity*. Stuttgart, Germany: Hatje Cantz, 2013.

Cameron, Dan. "Survey: A Procession of the Dispossessed." In *William Kentridge*, edited by Dan Cameron, C. Christov-Bakargiev, J.M. Coetzee, and Italo Svevo, 38–81. London, UK: Phaidon, 1999.

Caruth, Cathy. "Unclaimed Experience: Trauma and the Possibility of History." *Yale French Studies* 79 (1991): 181–92.

Caruth, Cathy. *Unclaimed Experience: Trauma and the Possibility of History*. Baltimore, MA and London, UK: Johns Hopkins University Press, 1996.

Casciani, Dominic. "Painting Politics in Northern Ireland." *BBC News Online*. May 31, 2000. http://news.bbc.co.uk/1/hi/northern_ireland/771314.stm.

Causey, Andrew. *Paul Nash Landscape and the Life of Objects*. Farnham, UK: Ashgate, 2013.

Certain Doubts of William Kentridge. Directed by Alex Gabassi. São Paulo, Brazil: Associação Cultural Videobrasil, 2000. Film.

Chaon, Anne. "Rithy Panh, la mémoire endeuillée." *Lettre de la SCAM*. Paris, France: SCAM, April 2014.

Chatwin, Bruce. *The Songlines*. New York, NY: Penguin Books, 1987.

"Chinua Achebe, Africa's Greatest Storyteller Died on March 21, Aged 82." *The Economist*. March 30, 2013. http://www.economist.com/news/obituary/21574453-chinua-achebe-africas-greatest-storyteller-died-march-21st-aged-82-chinua-achebe.

Christov-Bakargiev, Carolyn. *William Kentridge*. Brussels, Belgium: Société des Expositions du Palais des Beaux-Arts de Bruxelles, 1998.

Christov-Bakargiev, Carolyn. "Interview with William Kentridge." In *William Kentridge*, edited by Dan Cameron, C. Christov-Barkargiev, J.M. Coetzee, and Italo Svevo, 6–35. London, UK: Phaidon, 1999.

Chua, Daniel. *Absolute Music and the Construction of Meaning*. Cambridge, UK: Cambridge University Press, 1999.

Chua, Daniel. "Beethoven's Other Humanism." *Journal of the American Musicological Society* 62: 3 (2009): 571–645.

Cixous, Hélène. *"Coming to Writing" and Other Essays*. Edited by Deborah Jenson. Cambridge, MA: Harvard University Press, 1991.

Coburn, Clare. "Storytelling as a Peacebuilding Method." In *The Encyclopedia of Peace Psychology*, edited by Daniel J. Christie. Malden, MA and Oxford, UK: Wiley-Blackwell, 2011. Published Online https://doi.org/10.1002/9780470672532.wbepp268/abstract.

Cohen, Cynthia. "Creative Approaches to Reconciliation." In *The Psychology of Resolving Global Conflicts: From War to Peace*, edited by M. Fitzduff and C. Stout. Westport, CT: Greenwood Publishing, 2005.

Cohen, Cynthia E., Roberto Gutierrez Varea, and Polly O. Walker, eds. *Acting Together: Performance and the Creative Transformation of Conflict*. Oakland, CA: New Village Press, 2011.

Colton, Adrian (Justice). *In the Matter of an Inquest Into the Death of Manus Deery*. Befast, Northern Ireland: Lord Chief Justice's Office and the Office of the Judiciary, April 10, 2017. https://www.judiciary-ni.gov.uk/sites/judiciary-ni.gov.uk/files/decisions/In%20the%20matter%20of%20an%20inquest%20into%20the%20death%20of%20Manus%20Deery.pdf.

"Comic Relief". www.comicrelief.com. Accessed July 17, 2019.

Conflict Archive on the Internet (CAIN). http://cain.ulst.ac.uk/. Accessed July 17, 2019.

Connors, Logan J. *Dramatic Battles in Eighteenth-Century France: Philosophes, Anti-Philosophes and Polemical Theatre*. Oxford, UK: Voltaire Foundation, 2012.

Conrad, Joseph. *Heart of Darkness*, edited by Robert Kimbrough. New York, NY: W. W. Norton, 1970.

Cork, Richard. *A Bitter Truth: Avant Garde Art and the Great War*. New Haven, CT: Yale University Press and The Barbican Art Gallery, 1994.

Cullingford, Allison. *100 Objects Blog*. www.100objectsbradford.wordpress.com.

Cummings, Bruce. *Korea's Place in the Sun: A Modern History*. New York, NY: W. W. Norton, 2005.

Currie, Gregory. *Image in Mind: Film, Philosophy, and Cognitive Science*. Cambridge, UK: Cambridge University Press, 2008.

Das, Veena. *Life and Words: Exploring Violence and the Descent Into the Ordinary*. Berkeley, CA: University of California Press, 2007.

Davies, Douglas James. *Death, Ritual, and Belief: The Rhetoric of Funerary Rites*. London, UK: Cassell, 1997.

Debby, Nirit Ben-Aryeh. "War and Peace: The Description of Abrogio Lorenzetti's Frescoes in Saint Berdardino's 1425 Siena Sermons." *Renaissance Studies* 15: 3 (September 2001): 272–286.

Deleuze, Gilles. *Cinema 1: The Movement Image*. Minneapolis, MN: University of Minnesota Press, 1986.

Deleuze, Gilles. *Cinema 2: The Time Image*. Minneapolis, MN: University of Minnesota Press, 1989.

DeNora, Tia. "Aesthetic Agency and Musical Practice." In *Music and Emotion*, edited by Patrick Juslin and John Sloboda, 161–180. Oxford, UK: Oxford University Press.

Der Derian, James. *Virtuous War: Mapping the Military-Industrial-Media-Entertainment Network*, 2nd ed. New York, NY: Routledge, 2009.

Derrida, Jacques. *Of Grammatology*. Baltimore, MD: Johns Hopkins University Press, 1997 [1967].

Derrida, Jacques and A. Dufourmantelle. *Of Hospitality*. Translated by R. Bowlby. Stanford, CA: Stanford University Press, 2000.

Derry Journal. "'Sunday' Families Support Search for Truth About Annette McGavigan." *Derry Journal*. September 8, 2006. http://www.derryjournal.com/news/local-news/friday-september-8-sunday-families-support-search-for-truth-about-annette-mcgavigan-1-2109114.

Derry Journal. "Hume and Cooper Honoured in Bogside Artists' Restored Mural." October 19, 2015. http://www.derryjournal.com/what-s-on/arts-culture/hume-and-cooper-honoured-in-bogside-artists-restored-mural-1-7019100.

Derry Journal. "The Bogside Artists: 20 Years on and Still Standing Strong." *Derry Journal*. September 7, 2014. http://www.derryjournal.com/what-s-on/arts-culture/the-bogside-artists-20-years-on-and-still-standing-strong-1-6283526.

Dix, Otto. *Otto Dix: 1891–1996, Exhibition Catalog*. London, UK: Tate Gallery, 1992.

Dixon, Andrew Graham. *Paul Nash: The Ghosts of War*. BBC Radio 4, September 17, 2014.

Djebar, Assia. *Femmes d'Alger dans leur appartement* [Women of Algier in Their Apartment]. Paris, France: Des femmes, 1980.

Djebar, Assia. *Fantasia: An Algerian Cavalcade*. Translated by Dorothy S. Blair. Portsmouth, NH: Heinemann, 1993.

Doane, Mary Ann. *The Emergence of Cinematic Time: Modernity, Contingency, the Archive*. Cambridge: Harvard University Press, 2003.

Dolan, Chris. *Social Torture : The Case of Northern Uganda, 1986–2006*. New York, NY: Berghahn Books, 2011.

Dower, John W. and John Junkerman, eds. *The Hiroshima Murals: The Art of Iri Maruki and Toshi Maruki*. Tokyo, Japan: Kodansha International, 1985.

Duran, Khalid. "Andalusia's Nostalgia for Progress and Harmonious Heresy." *Middle East Report* 178 (September–October 1992): 20–23.

Edelman, Gerald. *The Remembered Present: A Biological Theory of Consciousness*. New York, NY: Basic Books, 1989.

Ellerson, Beti. *Sisters of the Screen: Women of Africa on Film, Video and Television*. Trenton, NJ and Asmara, Eritrea: Africa World Press, 2000.

Ellerson, Beti. 2011. "African Women in Cinema Confront FGM." *African Women in Cinema Blog*. http://africanwomenincinema.blogspot.co.uk/2011/02/african-women-in-cinema-confront-fgm.html.

Ellis, Robin. "Movement Metaphor as Mediator: A Model for the Dance/Movement Therapy Process." *The Arts in Psychotherapy* 28: 3 (August 2001): 181–190. https://doi.org/10.1016/s0197-4556(01)00098-3.

End FGM, European Network. "Female Genital Mutilation: What Is FGM?" http://www.endfgm.eu/en/female-genital-mutilation/what-is-fgm/effects-of-fgm/. Accessed July 17, 2019.

Environmental Defense Fund (EDF), 2017. "McDonald's Reduces Waste—And Saves Money." https://www.edf.org/partnerships/mcdonalds, and "McDonald's saves Billions Cutting Waste." https://www.edf.org/partnerships/mcdonalds. Accessed July 17, 2019.

Escalona, Alejandro. "75 Years of Picasso's Guernica: An Inconvenient Masterpiece." *The Huffington Post*, May 23, 2012.

Esslin, Martin. *An Anatomy of Drama*. London, UK: Temple Smith, 1976.

Executive Office for Northern Ireland. *Together: Building a United Community Strategy*. Belfast, Northern Ireland: Executive Office for Northern Ireland, 2013.

Faat Kiné. Directed by Ousmane Sembène. Senegal: Filmi Doomireew, 2000. Film.

Farah, A.Y. *The Roots of Reconciliation*. London, UK: Action Aid, 1993.

Felman, Shoshana and Dori Laub. *Testimony: Crises of Witnessing in Literature, Psychoanalysis, and History*. New York, NY: Routledge, 1992.

Finnström, Sverker. *Living with Bad Surroundings: War, History, and Everyday Moments in Northern Uganda*. Durham, NC: Duke University Press, 2008.

Finzan [A Dance for Heroes]. Directed by Cheick Oumar Sissoka. Mali: Centre National de Production Cinematographique (CNPC), Kora Films, ZDF (Zweites Deutsches Fernsehen), 1989. Film.

Foa, Edna B. and Barbara Olasov Rothbaum, *Treating the Trauma of Rape*. New York, NY: The Guildford Press, 1998.

FORWARD UK. "Using *Moolaadé* to Advance the Rights of African Girls." February 22, 2006. http://www.forwarduk.org.uk/new-forward-programme-in-africa-using-moolaade-to-advance-the-rights-of-african-girls/.

Fountain, Ben. *Billy Lynn's Long Halftime Walk*. New York, NY: HarperCollins, 2012.

Fox, George. *The Journal*. Edited by Nigel Smith. London, UK: Penguin, 1998.

Fraser Delgado, Celeste and Jose Esteban Muñoz. *Everynight Life: Culture and Dance in Latin/o America*. Durham, NC: Duke University Press, 2004.

Freire, Paulo. *Pedagogy of the Oppressed*. Translated by Myra Ramos. London, UK: Continuum, 2000 [1970].

Freud, Sigmund. *Beyond the Principle of Pleasure, the Standard Edition of the Complete Psychological Works of Sigmund Freud.* Translated by James Strachey, Anna Freud, Alix Strachey, and Alan Tyson, Vol. 18. London, UK: Hogarth, 1953–1974.

Gaddis, John Lewis. *The Long Peace: Inquiries Into the History of the Cold War.* New York, NY: Oxford University Press, 1989.

Gallese, Vittorio. "Mirror Neurons and Art." In *Art and the Senses*, edited by Francesca Baci and David Melcher, 441–449. Oxford, UK: Oxford University Press, 2013.

Gaynor, Mitchell L. *Sounds of Healing.* New York, NY: Broadway Books, 1999.

Geertz, Clifford. *The Interpretation of Cultures.* New York, NY: Basic Books, 1973.

Gerstbauer, L.C. "The Whole Story of NGO Mandate Change: The Peacebuilding Work of World Vision, Catholic Relief Services, and Mennonite Central Committee." *Nonprofit and Voluntary Sector Quarterly* 39: 5 (2010): 844–865.

Ghost Dance. Directed by Ken McMullen. London, UK: Channel 4 Films. Film.

Gibbs, R. *Why Ethics? Signs of Responsibilities.* Princeton, NJ: Princeton University Press, 2000.

Gillespie, Gannon. "Ending Female Genital Mutilation, One Household at a Time." *The Guardian*, August 22, 2013. http://www.theguardian.com/global-development-professionals-network/2013/aug/22/social-network-fmg-senegal.

Gittings, John. "Icons of War and Peace." In *The Oxford International Encyclopedia of Peace*, edited by Nigel Young. Oxford, UK: Oxford University Press, 2010.

Gittings, John. *The Glorious Art of Peace: From Iliad to Iraq.* Oxford, UK: Oxford University Press, 2012.

Glasgow Centre for Population Health and Education (GCPH). *Evaluating Sistema Scotland: Initial Findings Report.* Glasgow, UK: GCPH, June 2015. http://www.gcph.co.uk/assets/0000/5424/Sistema_findings_report.pdf.

Glassman, Bernie. *Bearing Witness: A Zen Master's Lessons in Making Peace.* Google Books, 1998.

Glover, Margaret. *Images of Peace in Britain: From the Late Nineteenth Century to the Second World War.* PhD thesis, University of Reading, 2002.

GMH-CNRR [Historical Memory Group-National Commission of Reparation and Reconciliation]. *Trujillo. Una Tragedia Que No Cesa* [Trujillo. A Tragedy That Never Ceases]. Bogotá, Colombia: CNRR, Planeta, 2008.

GMH-CNRR (Grupo Memoria Histórica-Centro Nacional de Memoria Histórica). *Bojayá: La Guerra Sin Limites* [Bojayá: The War Without Limits]. Bogotá, Colombia: Ediciones Semana, Taurus, 2010.

Gobodo-Madikizela, Pumla. "Intersubjectivity and Embodiment: Exploring the Role of the Maternal in the Language of Forgiveness and Reconciliation." *Signs* 36: 3 (March 1, 2011): 541–551.

Goerig-Hergott, Frédérique. 'Otto Dix: Painting to Exorcise War,' at Arts and Societies Seminar 'Conjuring Away: War', March 3, 2013. http://www.artsetsocietes.org/a/a-goerig.html.

Gomart, Emilie and Antoine Hennion. "A Sociology of Attachment: Music Amateurs, Drug Users." *The Sociological Review* 47: S1 (1999): 220–241.

Gomez, Paco. *Los Muertos No Hablan. Edición Bojayá Una Década (2002–2012)* [The Dead Don't Speak. Edition Bojayá a Decade]. España: Otramerica, 2012.

González, Felipe. "Palestine: un nuevo relato" [Palestine: A New Story]. *El Pais*, September 3, 2004.

Gramit, David. *Cultivating Music: The Aspirations, Interests, and Limits of German Musical Culture, 1770–1848*. Berkeley and Los Angeles, CA: University of California Press, 1998.

Gray, Amber E.L. "Dancing in Our Blood: Dance/Movement Therapy with Street Children and Victims of Organized Violence in Haiti." In *Dance, Human Rights and Social Justice: Dignity in Motion*, edited by Naomi Jackson and Toni Shapiro-Phim, 222–236. Lanham, MD: Scarecrow Press, 2008.

Grodal, Torben. "Concluding Address." Paper presented at the Festsymposium: Torben Grodal 70th Birthday, Institute for Media, Cognition and Communication. Copenhagen, DK, January 25, 2013.

Guha, Ramachandra. *India After Gandhi: The History of the World's Largest Democracy*. New York, NY: HarperCollins, 2007.

Guillen, Michael. "TIFF Report: MUNYURANGABO—Interview with Director Lee Isaac Chung and Scriptwriter Samuel Anderson." September 22, 2007. Twitchfilm.com/2007/09/tiff-report-munyurangabointerview-with-director-leeisaac-chung-and-scriptw.html.

Guttsman, W.L. *Art for the Workers: Ideology and the Visual Arts in Weimar Germany*. Manchester, UK: Manchester University Press, 1997.

Habash, Dalia. "The National Conservatory of Music. Where Talents Are Discovered and Nurtured." *This Week in Palestine* 59: (March 2003). www.thisweekinpalestine.com/details.php?id=165&ed=24&edid=24.

Haddad, Pablo Meléndez. "Soñando con la paz" [Dreaming Peace]. *ABC Cataluña*, August 13, 2006.

Halpern, Jodi and Harvey M. Weinstein. "Rehumanizing the Other: Empathy and Reconciliation." *Human Rights Quarterly* 26: 3 (August 1, 2004): 561–583.

Hammack, Phillip. "Identity as Burden or Benefit? Youth, Historical Narrative, and the Legacy of Political Conflict." *Human Development* 53 (2010): 173–201.

Hanafi, Sari and Linda Tabar. "The Intifada and the Aid Industry: The Impact of the New Liberal Agenda on the Palestinian NGOs." *Comparative Studies of South Asia, Africa and the Middle East* 23: 1 and 2 (2003): 205–214.

Hanich, Julian. "Watching a Film with Others: Toward a Theory of Collective Spectatorship." *Screen* 55: 3 (2014): 338–359.

Hanna, Judith Lynne. "To Dance Is Human : Some Psychobiological Bases of an Expressive Form." In *The Anthropology of the Body*, edited by John Blacking, 211–232. London, UK and New York, NY: Academic Press Inc., 1977.

Hanna, Judith Lynne. *To Dance Is Human : A Theory of Nonverbal Communication*. Austin: University of Texas Press, 1979.

Hanna, Judith Lynne, Roger D. Abrahams, N. Ross Crumrine, Robert Dirks, Von Gizycki, Paul Heyer, and Alan Shapiro. "Movements Toward Understanding Humans Through the Anthropological Study of Dance." *Current Anthropology* 20: 2 (1979): 313–339.

Hanson, Eric O. *Catholic Politics in China and Korea*. Maryknoll, NY: Orbis Books, 1980.

Harrington, Peter. *British Artists and War: The Face of Battle in Paintings and Prints, 1700–1914*. London, UK: Greenhill Books, 1993.

Harris, David. "Pathways to Embodied Empathy and Reconciliation After Atrocity: Former Boy Soldiers in a Dance/Movement Therapy Group in Sierra Leone." *Intervention* 5: 3 (2007): 203–231.

Harris, David. "Dance and Child Soldiers—FPIF." *Foreign Policy in Focus*, 2009a. http://fpif.org/dance_and_child_soldiers/.

Harris, David. "The Paradox of Expressing Speechless Terror: Ritual Liminality in the Creative Arts Therapies' Treatment of Posttraumatic Distress." *The Arts in Psychotherapy* 36: 2 (2009b): 94–104.

Harris, Merrion. *The War Artists*. London, UK: Michael Joseph, IWM and Tate, 1983.

Hartman, Saidiya. *Lose Your Mother: A Journey Along the Atlantic Slave Trade Route*. New York, NY: Straus & Giroux.

Haycock, David Boyd. *A Crisis of Brilliance: Five Young British Artists and the Great War*. London, UK: Old St. Paul Publishing, 2009.

Hellfire: A Journey from Hiroshima. Directed by John Junkerman. New York, NY: First Run Features, 1986. Film.

Herman, Judith H. *Trauma and Recovery: The Aftermath of Violence—From Domestic Abuse to Political Terror*. New York, NY: Basic Books, 1992.

Higgins, Lee. "Acts of Hospitality: The Community in Community Music." *Journal of Music Education Research* 9: 2 (2007: 281–292.

Highwater, Jamake. *Dance: Rituals of Experience*. New York, NY: A & W Publishers, 1978.

Hill, Andrew and Andrew White. "Painting Peace? Murals and the Northern Ireland Peace Process." *Irish Political Studies* 27: 1 (2011): 71–88.

Holtz, P. and W. Wagner. "Dehumanization, Infrahumanization, and Naturalization." In *Encyclopedia of Peace Psychology*, edited by D.J. Christie. Malden, MA: Wiley-Blackwell, 2011. https://doi.org/10.1002/9780470672532.wbepp079.

Hong, Sung-dam. *May Gwangju*. Gwangju, Korea: Institute of the Study of Jeonnam Social Issues, 1989.

Honwana, Alcinda Manuel. "Healing for Peace : Traditional Healers and Post-war Reconstruction in Southern Mozambique." *Peace and Conflict: Journal of Peace Psychology* 3: 3 (1997): 293–305.

Human Security Report Project. https://css.ethz.ch/en/services/css-partners/partner.html/13296. Accessed July 17, 2019.

Hume, John. "Interview." http://www.nobelprize.org/nobel_prizes/peace/laureates/1998/hume-interview-transcript.html. August 31, 2006.

Huxham, Chris and Siv Vangen. *Managing to Collaborate: The Theory and Practice of Collaborative Advantage*. London, UK: Routledge, 2005.

Hyman, Timothy. *Sienese Painting: The Art of a City Republic (1278–1477)*. London, UK: Thames & Hudson, 2003.

Hynes, Samuel. *A War Imagined: The First World War and English Culture*. London, UK: Pimlico, 1992.

I Have Seen My Last Born. Directed by Lee Isaac Chung and Samuel Gray Anderson. New York, NY and Kigili, Rwanda: Almond Tree Films, 2015. Film.

Institute for Sustainable Peace. "Vision and Guiding Principles." http://sustainablepeace.org/guiding-principles/. Accessed July 17, 2019.

International Center for Transitional Justice. "What Is Transitional Justice?" Factsheet. http://ictj.org/publication/what-transitional-justice. Published January 1, 2009.

International Online Training Program on Intractable Conflict. "Dehumanization." July 2003, University of Colorado, Bouder, CO. https://www.beyondintractability.org/essay/dehumanization

Internet Movie Database (IMDB). "*Hotel Rwanda*: User Reviews." https://www.imdb.com/title/tt0395169/reviews?ref_=tt_ov_rt. Accessed July 17, 2019.

Irigaray, Luce. *This Sex Which Is Not One*. Translated by Catherine Porter. Ithaca, NY: Cornell University Press, 1985.

Jackson, Michael. *The Politics of Storytelling: Violence, Transgression and Intersubjectivity*. Copenhagen, Denmark: Museum Tusculanum Press, 2002.

James, Stanlie M. "Listening to Other(ed) Voices: Reflections Around Female Genital Cutting." In *Genital Cutting and Transnational Sisterhood: Disputing U.S. Polemics*, edited by Stanlie M. James and Claire C. Robertson, 87–113. Urbana and Chicago, IL: University of Illinois Press, 2005.

Jarman, Neil. "The Ambiguities of Peace: Republican and Loyalist Ceasefire Murals." *Causeway* (Spring 1996): 23–27.

Jeon, Tae-il. "Letter to the President." In *Creeds and Confessions of the Korean Church* (in Korean), edited by Rhie Deok-joo and Cho Yee-jei. Seoul, Korea: Han Deul, 1997.

Johnson, Mark. *The Body in the Mind: The Bodily Basis of Meaning, Imagination and Reason*. Chicago, IL: University of Chicago Press, 1987.

Jorgensen, E.R. *Transforming Music Education*. Bloomington, IN: Indiana University Press, 2003.

Joseph, Anthony C. *The People's Gallery*. Derry, Northern Ireland: A Joint Production by the Bogside Artists, 2007.

Joseph, Christopher Odhiambo. "Theatre for Development in Kenya: Interrogating the Ethics of Practice." *Research in Drama Education* 10: 2 (2005): 189–199.

Jourdan, Kathryn. "Musicking Otherwise: Ethical Encounters in Music-Making." *National Association of Music Educators' Magazine* 1 (2013): 34–38.

Jourdan, Kathryn. *Through the Lens of Levinas: An Ethnographically-Informed Case Study of Pupils' "Practices of Facing" in Music-Making*. PhD thesis, University of Cambridge, 2015a.

Jourdan, Kathryn. "Book Review: Review of El Sistema—Orchestrating Venezuela's Youth by G. Baker." *Scottish Journal of Performance* 2: 2 (2015b): 105.

Judt, Tony. *Postwar: A History of Europe Since 1945*. New York, NY: Penguin, 2005.

Jung, Carl G. *Man and His Symbols*. Dell/Random House Publishing, 1968.

Kachachi, Inaam. *The American Granddaughter*. Doha, Qatar: Hamad bin Khalifa University Press, 2012.

Kane, Carole. "Petals of Hope Revisited." http://omaghpetals.blogspot.com/p/i-have-explained-my-involvement-in.html. Accessed January 28, 2019.

Katongole, Emmanuel. *Born from Lament: The Theology and Politics of Hope in Africa*. Grand Rapids, MI: Eerdmans, 2017.

Katz, C. *Levinas and the Crisis of Humanism*. Bloomington, IN: Indiana University Press, 2012a.

Katz, C. "Turning Toward the Other." In *Totality and Infinity at 50*, edited by S. Davidson and D. Perpich, 209–226. Pittsburgh, PA: Duquesne University Press, 2012b.

Kaufman, Asher. "Forgetting the Lebanon War? On Silence, Denial and Selective Remembrance of the 'First' Lebanon War." In *Shadows of War: A Social History of Silence in the Twentieth Century*, edited by Efrat Ben-Ze'ev, Ruth Ginio, and Jay Winter, 197–216. Cambridge, UK: Cambridge University Press, 2010.

Kaufman, Gershen. *The Psychology of Shame: Theory and Treatment of Shame-Based Syndromes*. New York, NY: Springer, 1989.

Keen, David. *Useful Enemies: When Waging Wars Is More Important Than Winning Them*. New Haven, CT: Yale University Press, 2012.

Kelly, Tom, Kelly William, and Kevin Hasson. "Who? What? Why?" http://www.bogsideartists.com/.

Kendrick, James. *Film Violence: History, Ideology, Genre*. New York, NY: Wallflower Press, 2009.

Kennan, George F. *The Decline of Bismarck's European Order: Franco-Russian Relations 1875–1890*. Princeton, NJ: Princeton University Press, 1981.

Kerr, Adrian, ed. *Murals of Derry*. Derry, Northern Ireland: Guildhall Press, 2016.

Kim, Chi Ha. *The Gold-Crowned Jesus and Other Writings*. Maryknoll, NY: Orbis Books, 1978.

Kim, Jun-tae. "Oh, Gwangju! The Cross of Our Nation!." Translated by Chae-Pyong Song and Melanie Steyn. https://jaypsong.wordpress.com/2012/05/06/oh-gwangju-the-cross-of-our-nation-by-kim-jun-tae/. Accessed February 11, 2017, no longer available.

Kim, Sebastian. "Minjung Theology: Whose Voice for Whom?" In *Moving Forms of Theology: Faith Talk's Changing Contexts*, edited by Israel Selvanayagam, 149–153. Delhi, India: ISPCK, 2003.

Kim, Sebastian, Pauline Kollontai, and Greg Hoyland, eds. *Peace and Reconciliation: In Search of Shared Identity*. Aldershot, UK: Ashgate, 2008.

Kim, Sebastian. *Theology in the Public Sphere*. London, UK: SCM Press, 2011.

Kim, Sun-jae. "Yesterday, Today and Tomorrow of Minjung Theology." *Sinhak Sasang* (Spring 1998): 8–9.

King, Thomas. *The Truth About Stories: A Native Narrative*. Toronto, CA: Anansi Press, 2003.

Kinosian, Janet. "Joshua Oppenheimer on 'The Act of Killing' Reconciliation." *LA Times*, February 18, 2014. http://www.latimes.com/entertainment/envelope/moviesnow/la-et-mn-joshua-oppenheimer-act-of-killing-20140218,0,6446847.story#ixzz2vi1ieTOU; http://www.latimes.com/entertainment/envelope/moviesnow/la-et-mn-joshua-oppenheimer-act-of-killing-20140218,0,6446847.story#ixzz2vi1eRL1G.

Kolk, A. and F. Lenfant. "Business-NGO Collaboration in a Conflict Setting: Partnership Activities in the Democratic Republic of Congo." *Business & Society* 51: 3 (2012): 478–511.

Kollwitz, Käthe. *The Diary and Letters of Kaethe Kollwitz*. Evanston, IL: Northwestern University Press, 1988[1955].

Koo, Ha-gen. "Emerging Civil Society: The Role of the Labor Movement." In *Korean Society: Civil Society, Democracy and the State*, edited by Charles K. Armstrong. London, UK: Routledge, 2007.

Korea Democracy Foundation. *A History of the Democracy Movement in Korea*. Seoul, Korea: Dolbegae, 2009.

Kornblum, Rena. *Disarming the Playground: Violence Prevention Through Movement and Pro-Social Skills, Activity Book*. Oklahoma City, OK: Wood'N'Barnes Publishing, 2002.

Korondo, Jeff. *Okwera Nono* [You Reject Me for Nothing], MP3. Gulu, Uganda: Independent, 2008.

Koshland, Lynn and Jean LaSarre Gardner. *Peace Through Dance/Movement Therapy: A Violence Prevention Program for Elementary School Children*. Salt Lake City, UT, USA: Self-Published, 2003.

Kurt, Samson. "Cognitive Behavioral Therapy: 'Revisiting' Traumatic Events Speeds PTSD Recovery in Women Veterans." *Neurology Today* 7: 7 (2007): 34–37.

Küster, Volker. "Minjung Theology and Minjung Art." *Mission Studies* 11: 1 (1994): 108–129.

Last Just Man, The. Directed by Steven Silver. Toronto, CA: Entertainment One Television [Barna-Alper Productions], 2001.

LeBaron, Michelle, "Foreword: Eureka! Discovering Gold in a Leaden World." In *Art in Action: Expressive Art Therapy and Social Change*, edited by Ellen and Stephen K. Levine, 9–18. Philadelphia, PA: Jessica Kingsley, 2011.

LeBaron, Michelle, Carrie MacLeod, and Andrew Floyer Acland. *The Choreography of Resolution: Conflict, Movement, and Neuroscience*. Chicago, IL: American Bar Association, Section of Dispute Resolution, 2013.

Lebethe, Annabell. *Promoting the Culture Sector Through Job Creation and Small Enterprise Development in SADC Countries: The Performing Arts and Dance*. Geneva, Switzerland: International Labour Office, 2003.

Lebow, Alissa. "Shooting with Intent: Framing Conflict." In *Killer Images, Documentary, Memory and the Performance of Violence*, edited by Joram Ten Brink and Joshua Oppenheimer, 41–62. London, UK and New York, NY: Wallflower Press, 2012.

Lederach, John Paul. "Cultivating Peace: A Practitioner's View of Deadly Conflict and Negotiation." In *Contemporary Peacemaking: Conflict, Violence and Peace Processes*, edited by John Darby and Roger Mac Ginty, 30–37. Basingstoke: Palgrave Macmillan, 2003a.

Lederach, John Paul. *The Little Book of Conflict Transformation*. Intercourse, PA: Good Books, 2003b.

Lederach, John Paul. "The Vocation of Peacebuilding." In *Peace, Justice and Security Studies: A Curriculum Guide*, 7th ed., edited by Timothy A. McElwee, B. Welling Hall, Joseph Liechty, and Julie Garber, 340–344. Boulder, CO: Lynne Rienner, 2009.

Lederach, John Paul. *Building Peace: Sustainable Reconciliation in Divided Societies*. Washington, DC: US Institute of Peace, 2010a.

Lederach, John Paul. *The Moral Imagination: The Art and Soul of Building Peace*. New York, NY and Oxford, UK: Oxford University Press, 2010b [2005].

Lederach, John Paul. "The Long Journey Back to Humanity." In *Peacebuilding: Catholic Theology, Ethics, and Praxis*, edited by Robert J. Schreiter, R. Scott Appleby, and Gerard F. Powers, 23–55. Maryknoll, NY: Orbis Books, 2010c.

Lederach, John Paul and R. Scott Appleby. "Strategic Peacebuilding: An Overview." In *Strategies of Peace: Transforming Conflict in a Violent World*, edited by Daniel Philpott and Gerard F. Powers, 19–44. Oxford, UK and New York, NY: Oxford University Press, 2010.

Lederach, John Paul and Angela Jill Lederach. *When Blood and Bones Cry Out: Journeys Through the Soundscape of Healing and Reconciliation*. Oxford, UK: Oxford University Press, 2010.

Lee, Chul-soo. *A Mind Carved in Wood: Selected Woodblock Prints, 1981–2011*. Seoul, Korea: Culture Books, 2011.

Leggett, Theo. "NGO Global Witness Leaves Diamond Vetting Scheme." *BBC News*, December 5, 2011. http://www.bbc.com/news/business-16027011.

Le More, Anne. "Killing with Kindness: Funding the Demise of a Palestinian State." *International Affairs* 81: 5 (2005): 981–999.

Lerner, Laurence. "Peace Studies: A Proposal." *New Literary History* 26: 3 (1995): 641–665.

Lesiuk, Teresa. "The Effect of Music Listening on Work Performance." *Psychology of Music* 33: 2 (2005): 173–191.

Levinas, Emmanuel. *Totality and Infinity: An Essay on Exteriority*. Translated by A. Lingis. Pittsburgh, PA: Duquesne University Press, 1969.

Levinas, Emmanuel. *Ethics and Infinity: Conversations with Phillipe Nemo*. Translated by R.A. Cohen. Pittsburgh, PA: Duquesne University Press, 1985.

Levinas, Emmanuel. "Philosophy and the Idea of Infinity." In *Collected Philosophical Papers*, Translated by A. Lingis, 47–59. Dordrecht, The Netherlands: Springer, 1987 [1957].

Levine, Peter A. *In an Unspoken Voice: How the Body Releases Trauma and Restores Goodness*. Berkeley, CA: North Atlantic Books, 2010.

Levine, Stephen. *Poiesis: The Language of Psychology and the Speech of the Soul*. London, UK: Jessica Kingsley, 1997.

Levine, Stephen K. "Art Opens to the World: Expressive Arts and Social Action." In *Art in Action: Expressive Arts Therapy and Social Change*, edited by Ellen G. Levine and Stephen K. Levine, 21–30. London, UK: Jessica Kingsley Publishers, 2011.

Levitin, Daniel. *This Is Your Brain on Music*. New York, NY: Penguin, 2007.

Liebmann, Marian. *Restorative Justice: How It Works*. London, UK and Philadelphia, PA: Jessica Kingsley Publishers, 2007.

Limpkin, Clive. *The Battle of the Bogside*. London, UK: Penguin, 1972.

Lind, E. Allan and Tom R. Tyler. *The Social Psychology of Procedural Justice*. New York, NY: Plenum Press, 1988.

Lodge, David. *Lives in Writing*. London: Harvill Secker, 2014.

Loffler, Fritz. *Otto Dix: Life and Work*. Translated by R.J. Hollingdale. New York, NY: Holmes and Meier, 1982.

Long Night's Journey Into Day. Directed by Deborah Hoffmann and Frances Reid. Berkeley, CA: Iris Films, 2000. Film.

Lopez, George A. "Dynamics Affecting Conflict, Justice and Peace." In *Peace, Justice, and Security Studies: A Curriculum Guide*, edited by Timothy A. McElwee,

B. Welling Hall, Joseph Liechty, and Julie Garber, 91–104. Boulder, CO: Lynne Rienner, 2009.

Losonczy, Anne Marie. "El Luto de Sí Mismo. Cuerpo, Sombra Y Muerte Entre Los Negros Colombianos Del Chocó" [Mourning Itself. Body, Shadow and Death Between the Black Colombians of Chocó]. *América Negra* [Black America] 1: 1 (1991): 43–61.

Lucas, D.W., ed. *Aristotle: Poetics*. Oxford, UK: Clarendon Press, 1968.

MacCoun, Robert. "Voice, Control, and Belonging: The Double-Edged Swort of Procedural Fairness." *Annual Review of Law and Social Science* 1 (2005): 171–201.

MacGregor, Neil. "Director's Foreword." In *Throne of Weapons: A British Museum Tour*, edited by J. Holden. London, UK: British Museum, 2006.

MacGregor, Neil. *A History of the World in 100 Objects*. London, UK: Penguin, 2010.

Mack, Andrew, ed. *Human Security Report 2005: War and Peace in the 21st Century*. New York, NY: Oxford University Press, 2005.

MacLeod, Carrie. "Choreography of Conflict." In *The Choreography of Resolution*, edited by Michelle Lebaron, Carrie MacLeod, and Andrew Acland, 45–57. Chicago, IL: American Bar Association, Section of Dispute Resolution, 2013.

Mailer, Norman. "The White Negro." In *Advertisements for Myself*, edited by Norman Mailer, 337–358. New York, NY: G.P. Putnam's Sons, 1959 [1957]).

Marchand, Iris and Barbara Oomen. "Legal Cultures, Blurred Boundaries: The Case of Traditional Justice in Uganda." In *Explorations in Legal Cultures*, edited by Fred Bruinsma and David Nelken, 161–182, Gravenhage: Reed Business, 2007. Also available online at: http://vsr.ruhosting.nl/page8/page36/files/RdW2007-3-ExplorationsinLegalCultures.pdf.

Marcus, Greil. *When That Rough God Goes Riding: Listening to Van Morrison*. New York: Public Affairs, 2010.

Marks, Laura U. *The Skin of the Film: Intercultural Cinema, Embodiment and the Senses*. Durham, NC: Duke University Press, 2000.

Marlantes, Karl. *What It Is Like to Go to War*. New York, NY: Atlantic Monthly Press, 2011.

Martin, Russell. *The Destruction of Guernica, and the Masterpiece that Changed the World*. London, UK: Plume, Penguin Books, 2003.

Maruki Gallery. "The Hiroshima Panels and the Truth of War." http://www.aya.or.jp/~marukimsn/english/indexE.htm. Accessed July 17, 2019.

Mbabazi, Linda. "Rwanda: 'Kinyarwanda' to Premiere at Sundance Film Festival." *The New York Times*, January 21, 2011. www.newtimes.co.rw/section/article/2011-01-21/27800/.

McCarthy, Patrick. "Peace and the Arts." In *Handbook of Peace and Conflict Studies*, edited by Charles Webel and Johan Galtung, 355–366. London, UK: Routledge, 2007.

McClain, Lindsay. "Artistic Suggestions for Peaceful Transition in Northern Uganda: What Youth Are Saying." *African Conflict and Peacebuilding Review* 2: 1 (April 2012): 152–163.

McCouat, Philip. "The Isenheim Altarpiece Pt2: Nationalism, Nazism and Degeneracy." *Journal of Art in Society*. www.artinsociety.com. Accessed July 17, 2019.

McGrath, John. *The Cheviot, the Stag, and the Black, Black Oil.* London, UK: Eyre Methuen Ltd, 1981.

McKay, Susan. *Bear in Mind These Dead.* London, UK: Faber & Faber, 2008.

McKechnie-Glover, Margaret. "Artists as Peace Activists." In *The Oxford International Encyclopedia of Peace*, edited by Nigel Young. Oxford, UK: Oxford University Press, 2010.

McNiff, Shaun. *Art Heals: How Creativity Cures the Soul.* New York, NY: Shambhala, 2004.

Merleau-Ponty, Maurice. *The Phenomenology of Perception.* Translated by Colin Smith. London, UK: Routledge, 1962.

Metz, Johann Baptist. *Faith in History and Society: Towards a Practical Fundamental Theology.* Translated by David Smith. London, UK: Burns & Oates, 1980.

Mihai, Mihaela. "Architectural Transitional Justice? Political Renewal within the Scars of a Violent Past." *International Journal of Transitional Justice* 12: 3 (November 2018): 515–536.

Millett, Kate. *The Politics of Cruelty: An Essay on the Literature of Political Imprisonment.* New York, NY: W. W. Norton, 1994.

Miss Congeniality. Directed by Donald Petrie. Hollywood, CA: Warner Brothers Pictures, 2000. Film.

Mitchell, Jolyon. *Promoting Peace, Inciting Violence: The Role of Religion and Media.* London, UK: Routledge, 2012.

Mitchell, Jolyon P. "Journalism." In *The Routledge Companion to Religion and Popular Culture*, edited by John C. Lyden and Eric Michael Mazur. London, UK: Routledge, 2015.

Möller, Frank. *Peace Photography.* Basingstoke, Hampshire and New York: Palgrave Macmillan, 2019.

Moltmann, Jürgen. *The Crucified God*, Revised edition. London, UK: SCM, 2001.

Moolaadé. Directed by Ousmane Sembène. Senegal: Filmi Doomireew, 2004. Film.

Moon, Ik-hwan. *How Can Unification Be Achieved?* Seoul, Korea: Hakminsa, 1984.

Morel, Olivier. "Interview de Paul Virilio." *Journal de la République des Lettres*, Wednesday, March 1, 1995. http://www.republique-des-lettres.fr/190-paul-virilio.php.

Morris, Allison. "Public Should Not Pay—Whether Murals Go or Stay." *The Irish News*, October 16, 2014. http://www.irishnews.com/opinion/2014/10/16/news/public-should-not-pay---whether-murals-go-or-stay-105214/.

Morrison, Toni. *The Bluest Eye.* New York, NY: Plume, 1970.

Morrison, Toni. *Beloved.* New York, NY: Alfred A. Knopf, 1987.

Morrison, Toni. *Playing in the Dark: Whiteness and the Literary Imagination.* New York, NY: Vintage, 1992.

Morrison, Toni. "The Site of Memory." In *What Moves at the Margin: Selected Nonfiction*, edited by Carolyn C. Denard. Jackson, MI: University Press of Mississippi, 2008a.

Morrison, Toni. "The Nobel Lecture in Literature." In *What Moves at the Margin: Selected Nonfiction*, edited by Carolyn C. Denard. Jackson, MI: University Press of Mississippi, 2008b.

Mundrawala, Asma. "Fitting the Bill: Commissioned Theatre Projects on Human Rights in Pakistan: The Work of Karachi-Based Theatre Group Tehrik E Niswan." *Research in Drama Education* 12: 2 (2007): 149–161.

Murphy, Maureen Clare. "Freedom for Palestine—But Only for Ticket-Holders?" *The Daily Star*, September 2, 2005. http://www.dailystar.com.lb/ArticlePrint.aspx?id=95992&mode=print.

Musas de Pogue, Las. Directed by German Rendon Arango. 2016. https://www.youtube.com/watch?v=PEQ3LW9a3KU. Accessed July 17, 2019. Film.

Myers, Bryant. "Panel Response." Reel Spirituality: Screening of *Kinyarwanda*, Fuller Theological Seminary, Pasadena, CA, March 2, 2012.

Nash, Paul. *Outline: An Autobiography and Other Writings.* London, UK: Faber & Faber, 1949.

Nelson, Paul E. and Ellen Dorsey. *New Rights Advocacy: Changing Strategies of Development and Human Rights NGOs.* Washington, DC: Georgetown University Press, 2008.

Nhat Hanh, T. *Being Peace.* Berkeley, CA: Parallax Press, 1987.

Nnaemeka, Obioma. "Introduction." In *The Politics of (M)othering: Womanhood, Identity, and Resistance in African Literature*, edited by Obioma Nnaemeka. London, UK and New York, NY: Routledge, 1997.

Nnaemeka, Obioma, ed. *Female Circumcision and the Politics of Knowledge: African Women in Imperialist Discourses.* Westport, CT and London, UK: Praeger, 2005.

Oberschall, Anthony. "History and Peacebuilding." In *The Routledge Handbook of Peacebuilding*, edited by Roger MacGinty, 171–182. Abingdon, UK: Routledge, 2013.

Odendaal, A., O.T. Kankkene, H.M. Nikkanen, and L. Vakeya. "What's with the K? Exploring the Implications of Christopher Small's 'Musicking' for General Musical Education." *Music Education Research* 16: 2 (2014): 162–175.

Oelofsen, Rianna. "De- and Rehumanization in the Wake of Atrocities." *South African Journal of Philosophy* 28: 2 (2009): 178–188.

Office of the First Minister and Deputy First Minister (OFMDFM). *A Shared Future: Policy and Strategic Framework for Good Relations in Northern Ireland.* Belfast, NI: Community Relations Unit and OFMDFM, 2005.

Ogle, George F. *Liberty to the Captives: The Struggle against Oppression in South Korea.* Atlanta, GA: John Knox Press, 1977.

Oh, Yoon. *Collected Works II: Dokkaebi Who Holds the Sword*. Seoul, Korea: Hyunshil Books, 2010.

Okot Bitek, Juliane and Grace Acan. *Stories from the Dry Season*. Forthcoming.

Okumu, Charles. "Acholi Orality." In *Uganda: The Cultural Landscape*, edited by Eckhard Breitinger, 65–95. Bayreuth, Germany: Bayreuth University, 1999.

Okwera, Jahria. *Dwog Paco* [Come Home], MP3. Gulu, Uganda: Independent, 2003.

Okwera, Jahria. *Ka in Kono?* [What If It Were You?] MP3. Gulu, Uganda: World Vision, 2006.

Omer, Atalia. "Religious Peacebuilding. The Exotic, the Good, and the Theatrical." *Practical Matters Journal* 5: 1 (2012). http://practicalmattersjournal.org/issue/5/centerpieces/religious-peacebuilding.

O'Neil, Michael. "Memorial." In *The Arts of Peace: An Anthology of Poetry*, edited by Adrian Blamires and Peter Robinson. Reading, UK: Two Rivers Press, 2014.

OpenCanada. "Rebuilding Lives in Uganda." *OpenCanada.org*, November 27, 2012. https://www.opencanada.org/features/ketty-anyeko-on-rebuilding-lives-in-uganda/. Accessed April 10, 2013.

Opiyo, Lindsay McClain. "Music as Education, Voice, Memory and Healing: Community Views on the Roles of Music in Conflict Transformation in Northern Uganda." *African Conflict and Peacebuilding Review* 5: 1 (Spring 2015): 41–65.

Oppenheimer, Joshua. "Misunderstanding Images: *Standard Operating Procedure*, Errol Morris." In *Killer Images*, edited by Joram Ten Brink and Joshua Oppenheimer, 311–324. London, UK and New York, NY: Wallflower Press, 2012a.

Oppenheimer, Joshua. "Perpetrators' Testimony and the Restoration of Humanity: S21, Rithy Panh." In *Killer Images*, edited by Joram Ten Brink and Joshua Oppenheimer, 243–255. London, UK and New York, NY: Wallflower Press, 2012b.

O'Rawe, Richard. *Blanketmen: An Untold Story of the H-Block Hunger Strike*. Dublin, Ireland: New Island Books, 2016.

Otim, Michael and Marieke Wierda. *Uganda: Impact of the Rome Statute and the International Criminal Court*. Briefing. New York, NY: International Center for Transitional Justice (ICTJ), 2010.

Overstreet, Jeffrey. "A Cinema of Listening and Looking: A Filmwell Conversation with Lee Isaac Chung, Part Two." June 9, 2009. http://theotherjournal.com/filmwell/2009/06/09/a-cinema-of-listening-and-looking-a-filmw.

Oyola, Sandra Milena Rios. *Religion, Social Memory, and Conflict: The Massacre of Bojayá in Colombia*. Hampshire, UK: Palgrave Macmillan, 2015.

Palmer, Kathleen. *Women War Artists*. London, UK: IWM, Tate Publishing, 2011.

Park, Chung-shin. *Protestantism and Politics in Korea*. Seattle, WA: University of Washington Press, 2003.

Park, No-hae. *Dawn of Labor*. Seoul, Korea: Geoleum, 2004.

Paul VI, Pope. "If You Want Peace, Work for Justice." January 1, 1972. http://www.vatican.va/holy_father/paul_vi/messages/peace/documents/hf_p-vi_mes_19711208_v-world-day-for-peace_en.html.

Peffer, John. *Art and the End of Apartheid.* Minneapolis, MN: University of Minnesota Press, 2009.

Pennebaker, James W. *Writing to Heal: A Guided Journal for Recovering from Trauma and Emotional Upheaval.* Oakland, CA: New Harbinger, 2004.

Peretz, Eyal. *Becoming Visionary.* Stanford, CA: Stanford University Press, 2008.

Philpott, Daniel. *Just and Unjust Peace: An Ethic of Political Reconciliation.* New York: Oxford University Press, 2012.

Philpott, Daniel and Gerard Powers, eds. *Strategies of Peace: Transforming Conflict in a Violent World.* Oxford, UK: Oxford University Press, 2010.

"The Philosopher and the Filmmaker: Wim Wenders & Mary Zournazi Talk About War, Peace and Filmmaking." ABC (Australian Broadcasting Corporation), December 15, 2013. http://www.abc.net.au/radionational/programs/philosopherszone/the-philosopher-and-the-filmmaker/5143988.

Phuong, Pham, Patrick Vinck, and Eric Stover. *Abducted: The Lord's Resistance Army and Forced Conscription in Northern Uganda.* Berkeley, CA: Berkeley-Tulane Initiative on Vulnerable Populations, June 2007.

Pickford, Henry W. *The Sense of Semblance: Philosophical Analyses of Holocaust Art.* New York, NY: Fordham University Press, 2003.

Pinker, Steven. *The Better Angels of Our Nature: Why Violence Has Declined.* New York, NY: Viking, 2011.

Plantinga, Carl R. "The Scene of Empathy and the Human Face on Film." In *Passionate Views: Film, Cognition, and Emotion*, edited by Carl R. Plantinga and Greg M. Smith, 239–255. Baltimore: Johns Hopkins University Press, 1999.

Plutarch. *Life of Pericles.* Translated by Peter Jones, Public domain.

Potter, Pamela M. *Most German of the Arts. Musicology and Society from the Weimar Republic to the End of Hitler's Reich.* New Haven, CT: Yale University Press, 1998.

Powers, Gerard F. "Religion and Peacebuilding." In *Strategies of Peace: Transforming Conflict in a Violent World*, edited by Daniel Philpott and Gerard F. Powers, 317–352. New York, NY: Oxford University Press, 2010.

Powers, Kevin. *The Yellow Birds: A Novel.* New York, NY: Little Brown, 2012.

Priestley, J.B. *Time and the Conways.* In *An Inspector Calls and Other Plays*, edited by J.B. Priestley, 7–82. London, UK: Penguin, 1969.

Prince, Stephen, ed. *Screening Violence.* New Brunswick, NJ: Rutgers University Press, 2000.

Quash, Ben. "Making the Most of the Time: Liturgy, Ethics and Time." *Studies in Christian Ethics* 15: 1 (2002): 97–114.

Quash, Ben. *Theology and the Drama of History* Cambridge, UK: Cambridge University Press, 2005.

Quesada-Palm, Dessa. "Rehearsal for Change: Reclaiming Senses Through Arts Approaches." Unpublished, 2006.

Raheb, Mitri. *Bethlehem Besieged: Stories of Hope in Times of Trouble.* Minneapolis, MN: Fortress Press, 2004.

Rahmani, Zahia. *France, récit d'une enfance* [France, the Narrative of a Childhood]. Paris, France: Sabine Wespieser, 2006.

Ratcliffe, Matthew. *Feelings of Being: Phenomenology, Psychiatry, and the Sense of Reality.* Oxford, UK: Oxford University Press, 2008.

Reference Sembène. Directed by Yacouba Traoré. Paris, France: Médiathèque des Trois Monde, 2002. Film.

Restrepo, Eduardo. *Identidad, Poder Y Cultura Entre Los Grupos Negros de Los Ríos Satinga Y Sanquianga, Pacífico Sur Colombiano* [Identity, Power and Culture Between the Black Groups of the Rivers Satinga and Sanquianga, Colombian South Pacific]. Medellín, Colombia: Universidad Nacional de Colombia, 1995.

Restrepo, Eduardo. "Memories, Identities, and Ethnicity: Making the Black Community in Colombia." Chapel Hill, NC: University of North Carolina at Chapel Hill, 2002.

Reynolds, Barbara. *The Passionate Intellect: Dorothy L. Sayers' Encounter with Dante.* Eugene, OR: Wipf & Stock, 2005.

Riaño-Alcalá, Pilar and Erin Baines. "Gender, Responsibility, and the Grey Zone: Considerations for Transitional Justice." *Journal of Human Rights* 10: 4 (2009): 477–493.

Riaño-Alcalá, Pilar and Erin Baines. "The Archive in the Witness: Documentation in Settings of Chronic Insecurity." *International Journal of Transitional Justice* 5: 3 (November 1, 2011): 412–433. https://doi.org/10.1093/ijtj/ijr025.

Richards, Amy and Jolyon Mitchell. "Journalists as Witnesses to Violence and Suffering." In *The Handbook of Global Communication and Media Ethics* (Volume II), edited by Robert S. Fortner and P. Mark Fackler, 752–773. Oxford, UK: Wiley-Blackwell, 2011.

Rifkind, Gabrielle and Giandomenico Picco. *The Fog of Peace: The Human Face of Conflict Resolution.* London, UK: I.B. Tauris, 2014.

Rhie, Deok-joo and Yee-jei Cho, eds. *Creeds and Confessions of the Korean Church* (in Korean). Seoul, Korea: Han Deul, 1997.

Roberts, Bayard, Kaducu Felix Ocaka, John Browne, Thomas Oyok, and Egbert Sondorp. "Factors Associated with Post-Traumatic Stress Disorder and Depression Amongst Internally Displaced Persons in Northern Uganda." *BMC Psychiatry* 8: 1 (2008). https://doi.org/10.1186/1471-244X-8-38. Accessed July 17, 2019.

Rodriguez, Roberto. "Forgiveness as Part of the Rehumanization Process." *Peace Review: A Journal of Social Justice* 12: 2 (2000): 325–328.

Rohana, Nizar, Yoshimi Ohshima, Akira Usuki, and Kumiko Yamama. "Orchestra Education for Peace by E. Said and D. Barenboim." *Kyoto International*

Conference 2006: "Art and Peace: The Shape of Peace Designed by Art", 2006: 123–125.

Rolston, Bill. "The War of the Walls: Political Murals in Northern Ireland." *Museum International* 56: 3 (2004): 38–54.

Rolston, Bill. "Re-Imaging: Mural Painting and the State in Northern Ireland." *International Journal of Cultural Studies* 15: 5 (2012): 447–466.

Rolston, Bill. *Drawing Support 4: Murals and Conflict Transformation in Northern Ireland*. Belfast, UK: Beyond the Pale Publications, 2013.

Romanoff, Bronna D. and Marion Terenzio. "Rituals and the Grieving Process." *Death Studies* 22: 8 (November 1998): 697–711. https://doi.org/10.1080/074811898201227.

Ross, Marc Howard. "The Politics of Memory and Peacebuilding." In *The Routledge Handbook of Peacebuilding*, ed. Roger MacGinty, 91–102. Abingdon, UK: Routledge, 2013.

Rothschild, Babette. *The Body Remembers: The Psychophysiology of Trauma and Trauma Treatment*. New York, NY: W. W. Norton, 2000.

Royce, Anya Peterson. *The Anthropology of Dance*, 2nd ed. Hampshire, UK: Dance Books Ltd., 2002.

Ruleta de la Vida [Life's Roulette]. Directed by the Empanada Rellena Film Collective. Bogotá, Colombia: Shine a Light. Film.

Ruskin, John. *The Crown of Wild Olive*. London, UK: George Allen, 1904.

Sacks, Oliver. *Musicophilia*. New York, NY: Vintage, 2008.

Said, Edward. *Culture and Imperialism*. New York, NY: Knopf, 1994.

Savage, Sara. "Head and Heart in Preventing Religious Radicalization." In *Head and Heart: Perspectives from Religion and Psychology*, edited by Fraser Watts and Geoff Dumbreck, 157–194. West Conshohocken, PA: Templeton Press, 2013.

Saville, Mark Oliver (Lord of Newdigate), William Hoyt, and John Toohey. *Report of the Bloody Sunday Inquiry (Vols. I–X)*. London, UK: HMSO (Her Majesty's Stationery Office), 2010.

Sayers, Dorothy L. "A Letter to Dr James Welch, 25 July 1946." In *The Letters of Dorothy L. Sayers, III: 1944–1950—A Noble Daring*, edited by Barbara Reynolds, 248–250. Cambridge, UK: The Dorothy L. Sayers Society, 1998.

Sayers, Dorothy L. 'Strong Meat.' In *Strong Meat*, edited by Dorothy L. Sayers, 9–27. London, UK: Hodder & Stoughton, 1939.

Sayers, Dorothy L. *The Just Vengeance*. London: Victor Gollancz, 1946 and Eugene, OR: Wipf & Stock, 2011.

Scarry, Elaine. *The Body in Pain: The Making and Unmaking of the World*. Oxford, UK: Oxford University Press, 1985.

Schechner, Richard. *Performance Studies: An Introduction*. London, UK: Routledge, 2002.

Scheper-Hughes, Nancy. *Death Without Weeping: The Violence of Everyday Life in Brazil*. Oakland, CA: University of California Press, 1993.

Schirch, Lisa. *The Little Book of Strategic Peacebuilding*. Intercourse, PA: Good Books, 2004.

Schmais, Claire. "Healing Processes in Group Dance Therapy." *American Journal of Dance Therapy* 8: 1 (December 1985): 17–36. https://doi.org/10.1007/bf02251439.

Scott, A.O. "15 Years Later, a Quiet Film About a Still-Traumatized Rwanda." *New York Times*, May 28, 2009. www.nytimes.com/2009/05/29/movies/29muny.html.

Search for Common Ground. *Mass Information in Support of Peaceful Congolese and Burundian Refugee Repatriation*, Final Study A: DR Congo, Search for Common Ground (2008). https://www.sfcg.org/wp-content/uploads/2014/08/DRCPRMFINALEvaluationAppendices1.pdf. Accessed January 11, 2017.

Sebold, Alice. *Lucky*. New York, NY: Little, Brown & Co. 1999.

Sembène, Ousmane. *God's Bits of Wood* [Les Bouts de Bois de Dieu]. Translated by Francis Price. London, UK: Heinemann, 1962.

Serrano, Jose. "Cuando Canta El Guaco: La Muerte Y El Morir En Poblaciones Afrocolombianas Del Río Baudó, Chocó" [When the Guaco Sings: Death and Dying Amongst the Afrocolombian Populations of the River Baudó, Chocó]. Medillín, Colombia: Universidad Nacional de Colombia, 1994.

Shank, Michael and Lisa Schirch. "Strategic Arts-Based Peacebuilding." *Peace and Change* 33: 2 (2008): 217–242.

Shklovsky, Viktor. "Art as Technique." In *Russian Formalist Criticism: Four Essays*, edited and translated by Lee T. Lemon and Marion J. Reis, 3–24. Lincoln, NB: University of Nebraska Press, 1965 [1917].

Shlaim, Avi. "Cuatro días en Sevilla" [Four Days in Sevilla], *El Pais*, September 9, 2004.

Shooting Dogs [Beyond the Gate]. Directed by Michael Caton-Jones. London, UK: BBC Films, 2005.

Silko, Leslie Marmon. *Ceremony*. New York, NY: Penguin, 2006 [1977].

Simpson, Kirk. *Truth Recovery in Northern Ireland: Critically Interpreting the Past*. Manchester, UK: Manchester University Press, 2009.

Simpson, Leanne. *Dancing on Our Turtle's Back: Stories of Nishnaabeg Re-creation, Resurgence and a New Emergence*. Winnipeg, CA: ARP Books, 2011.

Sloboda, John. *Exploring the Musical Mind*. Oxford, UK: Oxford University Press, 2005.

Smaczny, Paul. *The Ramallah Concert: Knowledge Is the Beginning*. EuroArts Music International and Warner Classics, 2005.

Small, C. *Musicking: The Meanings of Performing and Listening*. Hanover, NH: Wesleyan University Press, 1998.

Smith, Christian. *Moral Believing Animals: Human Personhood and Culture*. Oxford, UK: Oxford University Press, 2003.

Smith, Christian. *What Is a Person?: Rethinking Humanity, Social Life and the Moral Good from the Person Up*. Chicago, IL: University of Chicago Press, 2010.
Smith, Murray. *Engaging Characters: Fiction, Emotion, and the Cinema*. Oxford, UK: Oxford University Press, 1985.
Snodderley, Dan, ed. *Peace Terms: A Glossary of Terms for Conflict Management and Peacebuilding*. Washington, DC: Academy for International Conflict Management and Peacebuilding, United States Institute of Peace, 2011. http://www.usip.org/sites/default/files/files/peaceterms.pdf.
Snyder-Young, Dani. *Theatre of Good Intentions: Challenges and Hopes for Theatre and Social Change*. Basingstoke, UK: Palgrave Macmillan, 2013.
Sobchack, Vivian. *The Address of the Eye: A Phenomenology of the Film Experience*. Princeton, NJ: Princeton University Press, 1992.
Sohn, Hak-kyu. *Authoritarianism and Opposition in South Korea*. London, UK: Routledge, 1989.
Sontag, Susan. *Regarding the Pain of Others*. London, UK: Penguin, 2004.
Sou-hwan, Kim. *The Story of Cardinal Kim Sou-hwan* (in Korean). Seoul, Korea: Pyeonghwa Broadcasting, 2009.
Soyinka, Wole. *The Burden of Memory: The Muse of Forgiveness*. Oxford, UK: Oxford University Press, 1999.
Spencer, Paul. *Society and the Dance: The Social Anthropology of Process and Performance*. Cambridge, UK: Cambridge University Press, 1985.
Spiegleman, Art. *Maus: A Survivor's Tale My Father Bleeds History*. New York, NY: Pantheon Books, 1973.
Standish, Paul. "Data Return: the Sense of the Given in Educational Research." *Journal of Philosophy of Education* 35: 3 (2001): 497–518.
Standish, Paul. "Food for Thought: Resourcing Moral Education." *Ethics and Education* 4: 1 (2009): 31–42.
Stanley, Hauerwas. *The Peaceable Kingdom: A Primer in Christian Ethics*. Notre Dame, IN: University of Notre Dame Press, 1983.
Stanley, Hauerwas with James Fodor. "Performing Faith: the Peaceable Rhetoric of God's Church." In *Performing the Faith: Bonhoeffer and the Practice of Nonviolence*, edited by Stanley Hauerwas, 75–10. London, UK: SPCK, 2004.
Starr, G. Gabrielle. *Feeling Beauty: The Neuroscience of Aesthetic Experience*. Cambridge, MA: Massachusetts Institute of Technology Press, 2013.
Stiegler, Bernard. *Technics and Time 3: Cinematic Time and the Question of Malaise*. Translated by Stephen Barker. Stanford, CA: Stanford University Press, 2010.
Stieglitz, Ann. "The Reproduction of Agony: Toward a Reception-History of Grünewald's Isenheim Altar after the First World War." *Oxford Art Journal* (1989): 12 (2): 87–103.
Storr, Anthony. *Music and the Mind*. New York, NY: Ballantine Books, 1992.
Strhan, Anna. *Levinas, Subjectivity, Education: Towards an Ethics of Radical Responsibility*. Chichester, UK: Wiley-Blackwell, 2012.

Suh, Nam-dong. "Toward a Theology of Han." In *Minjung Theology: People as the Subjects of History*, edited by Kim Yong Bock. Maryknoll, NY: Orbis Books, 1983.

Sutherland, John. *Lives of the Novelists: A History of Fiction in 294 Lives*. London: Profiles Books Ltd, 2011.

Szabo, L.R., ed. *In the Dark before Dawn: New Selected Poems of Thomas Merton*. New York, NY: New Directions Books, 2005.

Tan, Ed S., *Emotion and the Structure of Narrative Film: Film as an Emotion Machine*. New York, NY: Routledge, 1995.

Taylor, Charles. *A Secular Age*. Cambridge, MA and Belknap: Harvard University Press, 2007.

Taylor, Diana. *The Archive and the Repertoire: Performing Cultural Memory in the Americas*. Durham, NC: Duke University Press, 2003.

Taylor, Peter. "Who Won the War? Revisiting Northern Ireland on the Twentieth Anniversary of Ceasefires." *BBC News Online*, September 26, 2014. http://www.bbc.co.uk/news/uk-northern-ireland-29369805.

Team America: World Police. Directed by Trey Parker. Hollywood, CA: Paramount Pictures, 2004. Film.

Ten Brink, Joram and Joshua Oppenheimer, "Introduction." In *Killer Images, Documentary Film, Memory and the Performance of Violence*, edited by Joram Ten Brink and Joshua Oppenheimer, 1–12. London, UK and New York, NY: Wallflower Press, 2012.

Thacker, Toby. *British Culture and the First World War: Experience, Representation and Memory*. London, UK: Bloomsbury, 2014.

Theidon, Kimberly Susan. *Intimate Enemies: Violence and Reconciliation in Peru*. Philadelphia, PA: University of Pennsylvania Press, 2013.

Thiam, Awa. *Black Sisters, Speak Out: Feminism and Oppression in Black Africa*. London, UK and Dover, NH: Pluto Press, 1978.

Thiong'o, Ngũgi wa. *Re-membering Africa*. Nairobi, Kenya: East African Educational Publishers, 2009.

Thomas, Helen. *The Body, Dance, and Cultural Theory*. New York, NY: Palgrave Macmillan, 2003.

Tint, Barbara. "History, Memory and Intractable Conflict." *Conflict Resolution Quarterly* 27: 3 (2010): 239–256.

Tobon, Alejandro. "La Cultura de La 'gente Sin Cultura'. Clasificación de Los Géneros Musicales Tradicionales: El Caso de Los Romances En La Cuenca Del Río Atrato (Colombia)" [The Culture of the 'People Without Culture']. *Revista Acontratiempo* 14 (December 2009). http://acontratiempo.bibliotecanacional.gov.co/?ediciones/revista-14/artculos/la-cultura-de-la-gente-sin-cultura-clasificacin-de-los-generos-musicales-tradicionales-el-caso-de-lo.html. Accessed December 14, 2017, no longer available.

Todd, Sharon. *Learning from the Other: Levinas, Psychoanalysis and Ethical Possibilities in Education*. Albany, NY: State University of New York Press, 2003.

Triumph of the Will. Directed by Leni Riefenstahl. Berlin, Germany: Reichsparteitag Film, 1935. Film.

Turshen, Meredeth & Clotilde Twagiramariya. "Introduction." In *What Women Do in Wartime: Gender and Conflict in Africa*, edited by M. Turshen and C. Twagiramariya. London, UK and New York, NY: Zed Books, 1998.

Tutu, Desmond. "Foreword." In *Speaking the Truth About Zionism and Israel*, edited by Michael Priory. London, UK: Melisende, 2004.

United Nations Foundation. "The UN Foundation and Hotel Rwanda Partner to Create 'The International Fund for Rwanda'." January 18, 2005. http://www.unfoundation.org/news and https://unfoundation.org/media/the-un-foundation-and-hotel-rwanda-partner-to-create-the-international-fund-for-rwanda/.

Urbain, Olivier. *Music and Conflict Transformation: Harmonies and Dissonances in Geopolitics*. London, UK: I.B. Tauris, 2008.

UTV. "Play Tackles Exile of Derry Protestants." February 6, 2013. http://www.u.tv/News/Play-tackles-exile-of-Derry-Protestants/14e32478-38a7-45af-9061-15897513498a. Accessed July 19, 2016, no longer available.

UTV. www.u.tv/News/2015/04/08/Philosopher-visits-Derry-murals-35053, and see James Adair. "Bogside Artists", April 7, 2015. http://www.jamesadair.co.uk/blog/2015/9/24/ph3atteu6fxaj32hrsb56jyr8r3ktb#. Accessed July 17, 2019.

Valentine, Christine. "Academic Constructions of Bereavement." *Mortality* 11: 2 (2006): 57–78.

van Bergan, Leo. *Before My Helpless Sight: Suffering, Dying and Military Medicine on the Western Front, 1914–1918*. Farnham, UK: Ashgate, 2009.

van der Kolk, Bessel. "The Body Keeps the Score: Memory and the Evolving Psychobiology of Posttraumatic Stress." *Harvard Review of Psychiatry* 1: 5 (1994): 253–265.

van der Kolk, Bessel. "The Complexity of Adaptation to Trauma: Self-Regulation, Stimulus Discrimination, and Characterological Development'." In *Traumatic Stress: The Effects of Overwhelming Experience on Mind, Body, and Society*, edited by Bessel van der Kolk, A. C. McFarlane, and L. Weisaeth, 182–221. New York, NY: Guildford, 1996.

Vangen, Siv and Chris Huxham. "The Tangled Web: Unraveling the Principle of Common Goals in Collaborations." *Journal of Public Administration Research and Theory: J-PART* 22: 4 (October, 2012): 731–760.

van Hensbergen, Gijs. *Guernica: The Biography of a Twentieth-Century Icon*. New York, NY and London, UK: Bloomsbury, 2004.

van Hensbergen, Gijs. "Piecing Together Guernica." *BBC News Magazine*, April 7, 2009. http://news.bbc.co.uk/1/hi/7986540.stm.

Veidlinger, Jeffrey. *The Moscow State Yiddish Theatre: Jewish Culture on the Soviet Stage*. Bloomington, IN: Indiana University Press, 2000.

Virilio, Paul. *Bunker Archéologie*. Paris, France: Galilée, 2008.

Virilio, Paul. *War and Cinema: The Logistics of Perception*. Translated by Patrick Camiller. London, UK and Brooklyn, NY: Verso, 2009.

Vischer, Robert, Henry Francis Mallgreave, and Eleftherios Ikonomou. *Empathy, Form, and Space: Problems in German Aesthetics, 1873–1893*. Santa Monica, CA: The Getty Center for the History of Art and the Humanities, 1994.

Volf, Miroslav. *Exclusion and Embrace*. Nashville, TN: Abingdon Press, 1996.

Volkan, V. *Bloodlines: From Ethnic Pride to Ethnic Terrorism*. Boulder, CO: Westview Press, 1977.

Vourlias, Christopher. "US Shingle Grows Rwanda Film Biz." *Variety*, February 4, 2012. http://variety.com/2012/film/news/u-s-shingle-grows-rwanda-film-biz-1118049700/.

Waberi, Abdourahman A. *Moisson de crânes: textes pour le Rwanda* [Harvest of Skulls: Texts for Rwanda]. Paris, France: Le Rocher, 2004.

Wade, Peter. *Music, Race, and Nation*. Chicago, IL: University of Chicago Press, 2000.

Walk the Line. Directed by James Mangold. Hollywood, CA: 20th Century Fox. Film.

Watson, Julian. "Brightening the Place Up?" *Circa* 8 (1983): 4–10.

Weekley, Carolyn J. *The Kingdom of Edward Hicks*. New York, NY: The Colonial Williamsburg Foundation, 1999.

Wenders, Wim and Mary Zournazi. *Inventing Peace: A Dialogue on Perception*. London, UK: I.B. Tauris, 2013.

West, Jeremy, Christian Otte, Geher Kathleen, Joe Johnson, and David Mohr. "Effects of Hatha Yoga and African Dance on Perceived Stress, Affect, and Salivary Cortisol." *Annals of Behavioral Medicine* 28: 2 (2004): 114–118.

Weston, Burns H., Sherle R. Schwenninger, and Diane E. Shamis, eds. "The Literature of Peace and War." In *Peace and World Order Studies: A Curriculum Guide*, edited by Barbara J. Wien. New York, NY: Institute for World Order, 1978.

Wielenga, B., H. Klenner, and S. Lettow. "Justice." *Historical Materialism* 13: 3 (2005): 333–357.

Willet, John. "Dix: War." In *Disasters of War: Callot, Goya and Dix*, edited by Susan Brades and Roger Malbert. Manchester, UK: Cornerhouse Publications, 1998.

William Kentridge on His Process. San Francisco, CA: San Francisco Museum of Modern Art, 2005. Film.

Williams, Drid. *Anthropology and the Dance : Ten Lectures*, 2nd ed. Urbana, IL: University of Illinois Press, 2004.

Williams, Raymond. *Drama from Ibsen to Brecht*. London, UK: Hogarth, 1993.

Williams, Rowan. *Resurrection: Interpreting the Easter Gospel*, 2nd ed. London, UK: Darton, Longman & Todd, 2002.

Williams, Stephen N. "Forgiveness, Compassion, and Northern Ireland: A Response to Nigel Biggar." *Journal of Religious Ethics* 36: 4 (2008): 581–593.

Wings of Desire. Directed by Wim Wenders. Berlin, Germany: Road Movies Filmproduktion, 1987. Film.

Winter, Jay. *Sites of Memory, Sites of Mourning: The Great War in European Cultural History*. Cambridge, UK: Cambridge University Press, 1995.

Wisner, Geoff. "The Mosques of Rwanda." December 10, 2011. www.warscapes.com/reviews/mosques-rwanda. Accessed September 27, 2016.

Whitman, Andy. "Searching for the Yarragh." March 18, 2008. https://www.pastemagazine.com/blogs/whitman/2008/03/searching-for-the-yarragh.html. Accessed January 28, 2019.

Women's Advocacy Network (WAN). Lindsay M. Opiyo "Introducing the Women's Advocacy Network." May 25, 2012. https://www.justiceandreconciliation.org/blog/2012/introducing-the-womens-advocacy-network-wan-at-jrp/.

Woodford, Paul. *Democracy and Music Education: Liberalism, Ethics and the Politics of Practice*. Bloomington, IN: Indiana University Press, 2005.

World Health Organization. "Fact Sheet: Female Genital Mutilation." January 31, 2018. https://www.who.int/en/news-room/fact-sheets/detail/female-genital-mutilation.

Yi, Mahn-Yol. *Korean Christianity and the National Unification Movement*. Seoul, Korea: Institute of the History of Christianity in Korea, 2001.

Yoo, Dong-sik. *The Mineral Vein of Korean Theology*. Seoul, Korea: Dasan Geulbang, 2000.

Young, Nigel, ed. *The Oxford International Encyclopedia of Peace*. Oxford, UK: Oxford University Press, 2010.

Zamani, Kitap. "Israeli Writer's Reflect on Literature's Role in Peacemaking." *Today's Zaman*, July 6, 2010. http://www.todayszaman.com/tz-web/news-215226-101-israeli-writers-reflect-on-literatures-role-in-peacemaking.html.

Zartmann, I. William. "The Timing of Peace Initiatives: Hurting Stalemates and Ripe Moments." In *Contemporary Peacemaking: Conflict, Violence and Peace Processes*, edited by John Darby and Roger MacGinty, 19–29. Basingstoke, UK: Palgrave Macmillan, 2003.

Zelizer, Craig, ed. *Integrated Peacebuilding: Innovative Approaches to Transforming Conflict*. Boulder, CO: Westview Press, 2013.

Index

J. Mitchell et al. (eds.), *Peacebuilding and the Arts*, Rethinking Peace and Conflict Studies, https://doi.org/10.1007/978-3-030-17875-8